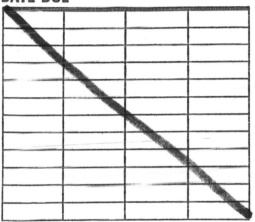

POPULISM

Kennikat Press
National University Publications
Series in American Studies

General Editor
James P. Shenton
Professor of History, Columbia University

JAMES M. YOUNGDALE

POPULISM

A Psychohistorical Perspective

National University Publications
KENNIKAT PRESS • 1975
Port Washington, N.Y. • London

TO THORSTEIN VEBLEN

Whom I have outgrown
Yet to whom I owe much

Manufactured in the United States of America

Published by
Kennikat Press Corp.
Port Washington, N.Y./London

Library of Congress Cataloging in Publication Data

Youngdale, James M
    Populism: a psychohistorical perspective.

    (National University publications) (Series in American studies)
    Bibliography: p.
    Includes index.
    1. Populism—United States. 2. United States—Politics and government. I. Title.
E183.Y7   322.4'4   75-30769
ISBN 0-8046-9102-9

CONTENTS

ACKNOWLEDGMENTS

I would like to mention and praise all of the "famous people" who have influenced by outlook and who have shared their experiences with me; however, it is possible to acknowledge only those who have played a more immediate role in the preparation of this manuscript.

I have enjoyed a profitable exchange of views with the American Studies faculty at the University of Minnesota, even with those who have not agreed with my unorthodoxies. I should like to express special gratitude to David Noble and Allan Spear, both of the History Department faculty, who have been generous both with time and suggestions.

Betty Ann Burch read the manuscript with an eye for editorial revisions. She was most helpful with suggestions for translating Veblenese into plain English.

My wife, Margaret, introduced me to Adlerianism, which she had found useful as a professional social worker. In studying the work of Alfred Adler, I have had useful conversations with Dr. William Pew, past president of the American Society of Adlerian Psychology; and it was from my talks with Dr. Pew that I came to use the concept of *offense mechanism* in contrast with the Freudian notion of *defense mechanism.*

This study has been enriched by interviews developed as a part of an educational television series, "Roots of Reform," with which I was involved as the research director and interviewer. For this series we interviewed more than thirty former leaders in populist and progressive reform movements, some of whom I quote with appropriate footnotes. I am grateful to Midwestern Educational Television, Inc., for permission to use material in written form from these interviews.

Last of all, I wish to acknowledge the patience of my children, who may has missed companionship because their father was too busy scribbling.

J.M.Y.

1

All things flow. One cannot step twice into the same river.

— Heraclitus

There is nothing so practical as a good theory.

— Kurt Lewin

INTRODUCTION

PERSPECTIVES ON POPULISM

One of the more heated and unresolved debates among historians and social scientists in recent decades has centered around something called "populism" in American history. Anyone who ventures into the debate soon finds that both the definition of a typical populist and the evaluation of populism as a force in American history vary widely with modes of historical interpretation. We find such disparate persons as Eugene V. Debs, George W. Norris, Lyndon Johnson, and George Wallace referred to as "populistic," both in popular and academic literature. Varying evaluations of the populists portray them either as the "good guys" or the "bad guys" in the unfolding drama of history. Some historians speak of populists as "irrational," while others suggest that the populists established a pattern for reform which was not only rational but deserving of emulation. It is clear that varying assumptions about historical analysis and about human nature are involved in these differing interpretations. Necessarily, then, a projection of a new perspective on populism will be concerned as much with explanation in history as with evidence supporting a new interpretation of this ambiguous "ism."

It is difficult to overemphasize the importance of laying out one's general philosophy of history and social science as a way of providing meaning for empirical data. The famous British physicist Arthur Eddington has warned: "Beware of facts not firmly embedded in theory," a warning which applies most cogently to social science analysis. "Facts" and "theory" make up the warp and woof of written history; any attempt to use one without the other can only result in a disintegration of any pattern or sense of process through time.

This study, then, is about populism, but it is more. Stimulated in part

5

by debates in American Studies circles over methodology, it explicates a theory of culture derived from several disciplines, using populism for illustrative evidence. While this study examines the gluing and ungluing of populist movements, one after another, as an integral part of the social process, the underlying theory of the integration and disintegration of social movements can by extension be applied to a wide range of historical phenomena. The effort here is to develop a broader theory for understanding culture in history, a theory grounded in a version of "history from below" in the form of populist movements.

Theories are never value-free. Each theory or subtheory is intimately bound up with some *weltanschauung,* with rejection or defense of some way of life. With numerous old theories already available and with new ones always being invented, historians at some point must make choices, choices which ultimately are rooted in their own subjective experiences and values. William Appleman Williams has stated the case neatly in a single sentence: "You commit yourself, and then—you see."

In my own case, I have lived much of my life among rural populists, among people who did not fit either the good guy or the bad guy stereotypes of populism. I have found these people to be warm human beings, with foibles and inconsistencies and always with some vision for reforming society. Thus, my own experiences and my own commitment to personal friends in populist movements has led me to question the existing interpretations of populism; and in turn, I have been propelled into a far-reaching examination of explanations of historical change in developing a counter-perspective.

It is, no doubt, already clear that I have a methodological quarrel with those who use static stereotypes as a basis for social analysis. The notion of the "ideal type" derived from Max Weber makes for good allegory, but it fails to portray internalized ambivalence and shifting attitudes between one way of life and another as people are caught in social transformation and are forced to make choices between different ways of viewing reality and different prescriptions for action which accompany each worldview. Furthermore, I quarrel with those social critics who overvalue the role of anxiety in the social process. To be certain, anxiety does prevail in human life; however, the specific response flowing from anxiety is shaped by both ideology and psychological mechanisms. Thus, diverse responses to a given type of anxiety might include joining a union, becoming violent, joining a cooperative organization, committing suicide, becoming religious, blaming a scapegoat, or becoming rigidly ascetic. This list does not exhaust the possibilities, but it serves to dramatize my contention that a mood of anxiety or a feeling of discontent alone cannot explain a particular form of behavior.

It is my thesis that populism was dynamic, with a shifting emphasis through time, and that it was pivotal in the larger social transformation from a petty capitalist mentality to progressivism. Populism has represented a tendency to break away from rugged individualism and toward a vision of society with cooperative profit sharing or socialist implications; yet, as a general movement, it has always stopped short of socialism and has always displayed ambivalence when faced with choices between socialist reforms and milder reforms less in conflict with the capitalistic system.

The series of movements known as populism has been subjected to many different interpretations, which have shaped the debate over the meaning of populism in American history. While it is not my intention in this study to engage in a prolonged analysis of these interpretations, it may be helpful to delineate three general views of populism as a basis for using these positions when appropriate as a counterpoint to my own thesis.

The first serious study of rural populism was John Hicks's *The Populist Revolt*, published in 1930. Friendly toward the agrarian rebels, Hicks surveys the rise and fall of the Farmers Alliance and the People's Party in the last two decades of the nineteenth century. He notes with sympathy those vicissitudes of rural life caused by such factors as bad weather, grasshoppers, falling farm prices, and mortgage foreclosures, which contributed to the rise of agrarian movements of protest. Hicks's study established a bias for seeing populism as a nineteenth century rural phenomenon closely associated with the People's Party movement of the 1890s, and thus it has obscured a broader view of reform stretching from the time of the Civil War well into the twentieth century, with urban as well as rural dimensions. Implicitly, Hicks is committed to the so-called Germanic school of historical writing, with its emphasis on accumulating "facts" to ascertain objective truth.

As with others in this tradition, Hicks failed to sense that competing conceptual frameworks make for conflicting definitions of "facts" and for relativity in the definition of "truth." Even though he was a pioneer in his empirical approach to populism, Hicks suffered from a severely limited analytical framework, so that a clear definition of populism does not emerge from his study. It may be inferred from Hicks's sympathetic response to the complaints of rural people, which had triggered the revolt, that he saw these reformers as the "good guys," as the standard-bearers for an equalitarian democracy in a world of petty capitalism. This view was more explicitly expounded by the famous literary critic, Vernon Louis Parrington, who described post-Civil War America as "the great barbecue," at which the railroads, the financiers and the rich ate the choice morsels while the farmers were left to gnaw on scraps and entrails.

"It was a fine spree in the name of the people," writes Parrington, expanding his metaphor. "They [the farmers] learned that they were no match at the barbecue for more voracious guests; and so they went home unsatisfied, a sullen anger burned in their hearts that was to express itself later in fierce agrarian revolts."[1] Here are the farmer heroes, standing at the ramparts, combatting the assaults of "un-American" forces of industrialism crushing "the man with the hoe," the symbolic hero of the idealized Jeffersonian economy. In the progressive autumn of the 1930s, Parrington used radical terminology as he movingly defended "the people" against "the capitalistic interests"; yet he failed to perceive that "the people," too, might be committed to a type of capitalistic ideology, and that "the interests" were not always monolithic in outlook, either, making his scheme of American history indeed simplistic in its allegorical splendor.

In presenting American history as a dramatic confrontation between "the people" and "the interests," Parrington stands in the Enlightenment tradition that assumed human nature to be inherently good until corrupted by institutions. The aphorism that "the voice of the people is the voice of God" is implicit in this outlook. Historians of this tradition further assume that "the people" do or can exist apart from an historically rooted cultural and social environment; and consequently, there is an idealization of "the people" which fails to account for actual people's motivations, behavior, and thought in the context of the larger social process.

With a built-in aversion to the baneful effects of institutions, it has been easy for many with Parrington's view to idealize the Jeffersonian dream and even to become social and political reactionaries celebrating rugged individualism. Hamlin Garland, John Dos Passos, and John Steinbeck come to mind as persons who have traversed the spectrum from apparent radicalism to right-wing conservatism because of a rigid commitment to this ideology. Much depends on definitions and terminology, but the question can be raised about whether or not these people, including Parrington, were ever really "radical," even though they have seemed to identify with popular causes.

It is well to digress for a moment to indicate the meaning of the term *radical*, which will be assumed in this study. This term will refer in all cases to movements or ideologies of a socialist or quasi-socialist character and implying an intent toward economic leveling. In this context, the term *radical right* is illogical, self-contradictory and not useful for social analysis. Likewise, it is inappropriate to conceive of nineteenth-century *liberals* in their various forms as *radicals*. It is confusion of these two terms that produces a grave defect in *The Age of Jackson* by Arthur Schlesinger, Jr., who lumps all people in the Jacksonian era together, including communitarians influenced by Robert Owen and the more normative types committed to petty capitalism and rugged individualism.

The Hicks-Parrington view of populism was sharply countered with the publication of Richard Hofstadter's *The Age of Reform*. In this book, the typical populist became the "bad guy." Hofstadter argues that the populists tended to look back to a lost Jeffersonian Eden, became frustrated in attempting to reach an illusory goal, and finally turned into hate-filled, cranky people, essentially conservative in their influence. In delving into the psychology of the petty capitalist mentality of the nineteenth century, Hofstadter finds, contrary to the Parrington scheme of things, that "the people" are not necessarily commendable.

The problem in Hofstadter's analysis lies with his definition of populism. He seems barely to be concerned with the specific reform movements or groups as such. Rather, he defines populism as a mood of revolt endemic to the middle class generally. This definition is noteworthy, for it permits him to avoid a detailed study of the various reform movements; instead, he deals with a stereotype of the populist apparently constructed by combining the personalities of William Jennings Bryan and Tom Watson, who seem to move from "left" to "right" through time. In projecting a populist type from the examples of Bryan and Watson, Hofstadter ignores the fact that Bryan was never a populist and that Watson, in his later racist and reactionary period, had left the populist movement. Later in this study I will utilize the term *bryanism* as the antithesis of populism; and I will argue that Hofstadter is mostly concerned with bryanism in *The Age of Reform*. He is quite explicit about his definition of populism as broadly representing the middle-class ethos of petty capitalism.

By Populism I do not mean only the People's or the Populist Party of the 1890's; for I consider the Populist Party to be merely a heightened expression, at a particular moment of time, of a kind of popular impulse that is endemic in American political culture. Long before the rebellion of the 1890's, one can observe a larger trend of thought, stemming from the time of Andrew Jackson, and crystallizing after the Civil War in the Greenback, Granger and anti-monopoly movements, that expressed the discontents of a great many farmers and businessmen with the economic changes of the late nineteenth century. The Populist spirit captured the Democratic Party in 1896, and continued to play an important part in the Progressive era. While its special association with agrarian reforms has now become attenuated, I believe that Populist thinking has survived in our own time, partly as an undercurrent of provincial resentments, popular and "democratic" rebelliousness and suspiciousness, and nativism.[2]

Hofstadter is quite right in suggesting that a mood of rebellion has existed among the petty capitalist middle class of America in times of disruptive change, and he is right in suggesting that this current also existed within overt populist movements. But to define populism itself in terms of an inherent impulse toward simplistic iconoclasm confuses matters. Hofstadter underplays the fact that the populist organizations projected, from time to time, various demands for institutional reform, such as the cotton and wheat warehousing plan, nationalization of railroads, banking reform and the progressive income tax. Some populists even called for a complete socialization of industry. All of these proposals move in the opposite direction from rugged individualism, from the Jeffersonian notion of minimal government, and from the individualistic denial of institutions in the petty capitalist paradigm.

There is a parallel between *The Age of Reform* and Erich Fromm's *Escape from Freedom.* Both books deal with the malaise of the alienated, isolated and anxiety-prone individual of industrial society. Fromm explains the gravitation to the authority of Hitler in Germany as arising out of this anxiety; Hofstadter likewise implies a proto-fascist tendency in populism stemming from the endemic discontents in American culture when he talks about nativism, a conspiracy theory of history, and provincial suspiciousness as earmarks of populism. This analysis is at best one-sided, in that it tends to place all of the blame for proto-fascist or authoritarian tendencies on the anxieties of the middle class, leaving the role of the various elites in society unexamined. Furthermore, in charging populists with nativism, he ignores the fact that northern populists, at least, were themselves mostly immigrants and at times victims of nativism. Certain empirical studies, such as Walter T.K. Nugent's *The Tolerant Populists* and Michael Rogin's *The Intellectuals and McCarthy,* have undermined the notion of populists as uniquely nativist or bigoted. These historians are to be commended for breaking the mold of the Hofstadter stereotype of the populist as a crank and a hater, even though they have not succeeded in creating a positive theory of populism.

At the opposite pole from Hofstadter, Norman Pollack has worked to define populist movements in a different perspective. In *The Populist Response to Industrial America,* he hails the populists as the conservers of the democratic covenant, as writing a "glorious chapter in the struggle for human rights,"[3] suggesting that populism was the prototype for modern socialism. It would appear, however, that Pollack has returned to the Parrington outlook as he sings the praises of the populist movements. He stresses the populists' commitment to participatory democracy and to the alleviation of human distress, but he barely examines the changing conceptual framework within which populists acted. As a matter of fact, Pollack has expressed sympathy with Max Weber's theory of the increasing bureaucratization of capitalist society, and he admires the populists for implicitly, at least, fighting for decentralization and for a destruction of top-heavy bureaucracies within the modern industrial infrastructure.[4] Pollack is most unclear about his definition of socialism, but his commitment to the Max Weber theory and to decentralization points logically to the Jeffersonian ideal of a social structure built around small landholders and petty capitalists as his version of "socialism."

Because of his failure to define socialism or proto-socialism clearly, Pollack seems to find socialism where it did not exist and to overlook the direct socialist influence where it did appear. He makes much of Governor Lewelling's "tramp circular" as evidence of populist tolerance in Kansas during the 1890s, but he fails to explore sufficiently the tendencies inherent in certain reform proposals, such as nationalizing railroads and utilities and the cotton warehousing plan, as steps toward a quasi-socialist platform. Thus, in Pollack, we fail to see the ambivalence among populists themselves as they are pulled between individualism and petty capitalism on one hand and institutional reform and socialism on the other; and we are not made aware of the various ways by which this ambivalence was resolved among populists at various times and places.

In finding the existing interpretations of populism inadequate, I am left with the alternative of projecting a new perspective for American populism. While this entire study is devoted to an explication of this new perspective, it may be helpful at this point to make certain preliminary assertions.

Populist movements cannot be understood simply in terms of the People's Party experience of the 1890s. Rather, a view of these movements from the time of the Civil War through the emergence of the Farmer-Labor Party of Minnesota in the twentieth century provides a perspective for seeing a shifting ideological response from Jacksonian individualism toward socialism, with radical neomercantilism as the predominant outlook. The populists were pivotal in creating the shift from the self-regulated market economy to the semi-regulated economy of the progressive and the New Deal periods. Yet, both the progressives and the New Dealers adhered to conservative neomercantilism, in contrast with the more radical populists, whose bias was toward economic leveling. More than any other person, Henry Demarest Lloyd stands as a symbolic representation of the populist position, moving away from rugged individualism and toward a cooperative commonwealth goal, yet incorporating cultural values from both poles in his outlook.

My general view of American history is consistent with that of William Appleman Williams's *Contours of American History,* which examines the American experience in the context of a shifting worldview from mercantilism to laissez-faire individualism and then to corporate capitalism. My views on populism fit into the Williams thesis in a general way. However, I differ with him on the specific issue of populism because he stands closer to Hofstadter's view that rural populists were primarily petty capitalists wearing only a thin veneer of radicalism. Yet Williams seems ambivalent. In his recent book, *The Roots of the Modern American Empire,* Williams hails those Republican farmers who became socialists after the 1890s for setting an example which should be emulated today.[5] I quarrel with him because he has no explanation of how and why these farmers became socialists or how this new social consciousness evolved from their earlier experiences. Also, Williams overstresses the identity between the working farmer struggling on 160 acres of land and business interests dealing in farm commodities who were directly engaged in expanding the market system on a worldwide basis. At times, working farmers and their spokesmen, including populists, supported expansionism and imperialism. Ignatius Donnelly, for example, dreamed of a Great Lakes Seaway to gain better and cheaper access to English markets for midwestern wheat. But, as we shall see, there were also important populist leaders, along with the peace progressives, who came to oppose expansionism, especially at times when international competition for trade and power resulted in war.

A typical populist, urban or rural, embraced petty capitalist ideology in the first place. Early reform demands were indeed aimed at destroying monopoly in order to restore a society of small entrepreneurs. However, as time passed, and as antimonopoly schemes for decentralization failed, new demands for social intervention were projected that had the effect of pushing populists in the direction of socialism, even though their initial intent may have been otherwise. Populism was not a static movement, nor can a typical populist be regarded as a static stereotype. People do not experience any social "fact," such as adversity, identically time after time. Rather, they learn; they adopt new outlooks and new psychological strategies in response to a repetition of some anxiety-provoking factor. Heraclitus was right in asserting that one cannot step in the same river twice, for both external reality and internalized ideology change by virtue of each experience. While those persons who became populists were often ambivalent in the tug of war between petty capitalism and socialism, the force of circumstances and their own choices tended to move toward a socialist or cooperative commonwealth vision of reform, even though the great majority gravitated toward a mentality that I choose to call radical neomercantilism as a resolution of the tension in which they found themselves.

The potential existed in populism for the kind of labor party socialism practiced in Great Britain and the Scandinavian countries, with an emphasis on welfare and economic equality. Generally, this labor party tendency failed to develop in the United States, especially where racism muddied ideological currents, where repression was especially violent, or where progressive co-optation was effective. The Minnesota Farmer-Labor Party is the outstanding exception in the United States of a populist third-party movement bearing a strong resemblance to the European labor party tradition. The Farmer-Labor Party deserves attention as the strongest manifestation of populism within any state in this country's history; yet, even with its powerful momentum in the 1930s, there was much ambivalence and vacillation within its ranks as emotions and values were strained by shifting conceptual tides.

My own frame of reference combines neo-Beardian and neo-Marxian elements, together with insights from Adlerian psychology and Leon Festinger's theory of cognitive dissonance. People do respond to social changes in terms of self-interest, as implied in the early Beardian approach; however, the definition of self-interest for a given person or group varies with the cognitive paradigm held by that person or group. There is never a simple behaviorist stimulus-response (S-R) mechanism at work without an intervening conceptual framework. And the social process gives birth to a number of conceptual frameworks, to a succession of paradigms for understanding reality, as in the model set forth by Thomas Kuhn in *The Structure of Scientific Revolutions.* Viewed in this context, people in the social world are constantly faced with the need for making choices between paradigms, in order to solve problems or to soften or eliminate dissonance or contradictions. Most often, people do not make a clear choice; rather, they develop an eclectic ideology with contradictory elements from different paradigms, which makes for ambivalence in human life.

In this study of populism, I will emphasize the ambivalence in the movements in terms of three internal, interacting intellectual currents. Laissez-faire or Tory populism[6] will be seen as one extreme pole, with socialism at the other extreme and with radical neomercantilism often as the central tendency in populism but with vacillation, too, between these three currents.

The choice-making process is often rendered obscure by many psychological strategies or personality complexes which come into play in human life as people attempt simultaneously to reach social and occupational goals while protecting the unique needs of their own egos. Out of a need for psychic homeostasis (sense of harmony) or cognitive consonance, in Leon Festinger's scheme, a person may rationalize away one side or the other of a contradictory mentality to avoid a debilitating schizophrenia; yet certain aspects of behavior may well emanate from his rejected views. Thus, there is a so-called unconscious or unadmitted side of mentality related to ideas and values inherent in a repressed paradigm, not to be confused with the Freudian concept of the unconscious rooted in the id. Alfred Adler has stressed the goal-directed and social quality of human life, including both conscious and unadmitted goals, as the foundation stones for social psychology. From this foundation, it is possible to view mental, emotional and social behaviors as strategies for reaching goals, leading to a variety of life styles and cognitive views of reality. At times when goals are unattainable, people tend to employ new strategies and to engage in reforming their outlook on reality. Populism is a case in point of a movement of people who were distressed and disillusioned with their failure to realize the "American Dream" and who responded finally by forming into mass movements and by choosing new theories about reality, theories which gravitated toward a socialist paradigm.

This study projects a notion of intellectual history as a series of paradigms arising through time as a part of the social process. This notion implies a debt to the Marxian model of social transformation in which revolution in ideology is seen as changing in stages from feudalism to capitalism and then to socialism as the economic mode of society evolves. Too often the Marxian model has been employed to suggest an automatic linear development through these stages, obscuring the choice making, the ambivalence, and the vacillation among people which mute or divert the course of revolutions in ideology. Populism has been one of many micro-transformations in outlook that have erupted within the social process, providing an excellent case study of social change in its more subtle and diverse manifestations.

Throughout this study, I shall speak of different levels of reality. It has become popular in academic circles to deal too exclusively with the life of the mind as the all-important level of reality, ignoring or failing to integrate social and economic factors or those aspects of human behavior which are rooted in biology. A macro-theory of social process requires that these three levels of reality be seen in interpenetration. In *American Historical Explanations,* Gene Wise moves in this direction with his notions of "grounded inquiry" and of "situation strategy" as concepts for suggesting that idea-patterns can be understood only in experience. However, Wise fails to develop the implications of his concepts as he lapses into a more typical discussion of ideas *qua* ideas in intellectual life. In speaking of contradictions as fault lines or strain, he argues, for example, that "the strain is not basically between the outer world and inner explanation, it's between competing behaviors inside the mind itself as it responds to the world."[7] This is an outlook which suggests that intellectual endeavor is simply a puzzle-solving activity in the abstract, without reference to the social and biological levels of reality. My own views differ from Wise on this point.

Initially, contradictions arise as an incongruity between *weltanschauung* and experience, between dream and reality, or between intent and result. It is these kinds of anomalies which provoke attempts to form new paradigms to better explain the dissonance experienced and to prescribe new modes of reform or new ways to resolve conflict. It is at this point, then, that there is a clash of ideas on an intellectual level, along with broader cultural conflict over ethical and artistic values. While intellectuals at times may become engrossed in the puzzle-solving aspects of life, somewhere in the background, as another level of reality, are social forces, such as the industrial revolution, urbanization, immigration, rapid capital formation, the rise of mass movements and more, just to note certain decisive factors in operation during the past one hundred years. We are made especially aware of these forces when certain events occur which are perceived as incongruities or strains on the dominant paradigm. For example, there was Coxey's Army of the unemployed in an age when economic theory preached that the economic system was self-regulating and that there should not be unemployment. Likewise, the great Midwest was pictured as the epitome of the American Dream, as a land of milk and honey; yet for vast numbers of farmers it was a nightmare during periods of economic crisis. More recently, the Watts rebellion drove home to Americans the vast gap between our egalitarian pretensions and the reality of life for minority Americans. In a study of populism, the experiential level of reality must always be in view, even though there may have been different interpretations of this experience among populists themselves and among historians who have studied populism subsequently.

As one delves into the field of social psychology, the problem of assumptions about the character of human nature continually rears its head. In this area I am much influenced by Alfred Adler, who rejected the instinctual explanations for behavior offered by Freud and Jung. Adler pioneered toward theories explaining behavior, thought and personality types as strategies in social situations for achieving goals; he regarded goals, moreover, as developed by persons and groups within a social context. Adler assumed that man does have certain inherited capabilities, or "instincts." However, he argued that these capabilities, such as the power to conceptualize in terms of myth and symbols, the ability to employ language, and the use of imagination to create a social environment for physical survival, are all prerequisites for understanding man as a social being. The particular ways in which these capabilities are utilized vary from culture to culture or from paradigm to paradigm. These arguments dealing with the use of psychology in history will be developed at greater length in a later chapter, in which an Adlerian version of psychohistory will be projected.

It is not my intention in this study to provide a detailed narrative account of the series of populist movements which have dotted the social landscape of America. Rather, I will develop my perspective on populism in terms of themes and ideological currents within the movements and the relationships of these currents to the larger paradigms in American history. Evidence in support of my perspective on populism will be drawn primarily from four upper Midwest states: Wisconsin, Minnesota, South Dakota and North

Dakota. There is already a substantial literature on the movements in these states, either in the form of case studies or in chapters within various state or regional histories. Certain of these studies will be cited directly as sources for empirical evidence at various points in this reevaluation of populism, and a larger listing of relevant material will be cited in the bibliography.

It may be helpful to catalogue the major populist movements which have emerged in the upper Midwest along with one or more of the prominent leaders associated with each movement. First, there was the Patrons of Husbandry (the Grangers), organized by Oliver Hudson Kelley in Minnesota in the 1870s to combat loneliness on farms; but other Grange leaders took aim at railroad abuses, such as free passes for political friends and special favorable rates for certain persons or locations. In the 1880s, the Farmers Alliance came into the area under Henry Loucks in Dakota Territory and with Ignatius Donnelly as a key figure in Minnesota. From the Alliance, the People's Party emerged in the 1890s, electing Eli Shortridge as governor of North Dakota in 1892, Andrew Lee as governor of South Dakota in 1896, but with less spectacular results in Minnesota, even though parts of the famous Omaha platform were drafted by Ignatius Donnelly.

The Robert LaFollette reform tradition emerged in Wisconsin in this decade in the midst of much urban and rural protest; it was a movement which was progressive in its inception but which shifted closer to a populist outlook with LaFollette's antiwar stand in 1917 and with his independent candidacy for the Presidency in 1924. Out of growing socialist sentiment in the 1890s, the Socialist Party was organized in 1901, primarily by Eugene V. Debs, Victor Berger, Morris Hillquit, and the Reverend George Herron of Grinnell College in Iowa. Milwaukee emerged as a socialist stronghold, sending Berger to Congress first in 1910 and again in the war years, when he was denied his seat because of his stand against the war. Also, Milwaukee became famous for its series of socialist mayors, ending with Frank Zeidler, who was defeated in 1960.

Farm cooperatives were organized during the first two decades of the new century under the auspices of the American Society of Equity, first established in Indianapolis in 1902. Along with organizing cooperative grain elevators for wheat farmers, the Equity engaged in political efforts to secure state-owned terminal elevators to which the local elevators might deliver wheat in preference to the private grain traders, efforts which were pushed by the colorful George Loftus in Minnesota and the Dakotas. It was during the agitation to win a terminal elevator in North Dakota that a conservative legislator allegedly told the farmers to "go home and slop your hogs." Out of this agitation, the Farmers Nonpartisan League was organized under A.C. Townley; and the League, spreading like political wildfire from a base of socialist clubs, captured the legislative house and governorship of

16

North Dakota in 1916 and the entire state government, including the State
Supreme Court, in 1918. Moving into other states, the Nonpartisan League
made political waves wherever it organized, especially in Minnesota, where
it spawned the Farmer-Labor Party in coalition with the labor movement.

In Wisconsin, the LaFollette sons left the Republican Party in 1934 to
form the Progressive Party, which suffered its demise in 1938 as Philip
LaFollette attempted to form a conservative and nationalistic third party.
Robert LaFollette, Jr., served in the United States Senate until 1946, at
which time he was defeated in a Republican Party primary contest by
Joseph McCarthy. Floyd Olson was elected Farmer-Labor governor in
Minnesota in 1930. After his death in 1936, he was succeeded by Elmer
Benson, who had already served two years in the United States Senate to
fill a vacancy. Governor Benson was defeated in 1938, and the Farmer-
Labor Party, with urging from Franklin Roosevelt, finally fused with the
Democrats in 1944.

The purpose of this thumbnail chronology of the movements in the four
upper Midwest states has been simply to provide an initial impression of the
persistence and variety of movements which have flourished in these states
in the nineteenth as well as the twentieth centuries. Hopefully, this brief
narrative is adequate to provide a framework in which thematic considerations will be meaningful.

The task now is one of clarifying my own commitment to a theory of
history, first to the notion of seeing history in terms of overlapping paradigms and then to a theory of social psychology to explain the resolution
of ambivalence as a person is torn between conflicting ways of viewing
reality.

NOTES

1. Vernon Louis Parrington, *Main Currents in American Thought,* vol. 3, *The Beginnings of Critical Realism in America* (New York: Harcourt Brace and Company, 1930), p. 23.
2. Richard Hofstadter, *The Age of Reform* (New York: Alfred Knopf, 1955), pp. 4-5.
3. Norman Pollack, *The Populist Response to Industrial America* (Cambridge: Harvard University Press, 1962), p. 143.
4. Pollack develops his commitment to Max Weber in the debate over populism carried in the April 1965 issue of *Agricultural History.* See Norman Pollack, "Fear of Man: Populism, Authoritarianism and the Historian," *Agricultural History,* 39:62-64, April 1965.
5. William Appleman Williams, *The Roots of the Modern American Empire* (New York: Random House [Vintage Books], 1970), p. 443.
6. I am indebted to Carl H. Chrislock for the term "Tory Populist" for describing the more conservative current within populism. Chrislock employs this term throughout his unpublished doctoral dissertation on reform movements in Minnesota in the 1890s. See: "The Politics of Protest in Minnesota 1890–1901: From Populism to Progressivism," University of Minnesota, 1955.
7. Gene Wise, *American Historical Explanations* (Homewood: The Dorsey Press, 1973), p. 180.

2

Bryan has never told any of the real truths of modern life because he does not know them. He has never made a fight on an issue of principle because he has no principle. He listens. He watches his audience. He gauges its intelligence and then makes his point. . . . Nothing in his public career, with the possible exception of his resignation as Secretary of State, has been based on hard-won or hard-fought principle. Rather he has yielded to the necessity of the moment, trusting that all would be well in the end, but without foreseeing the end or understanding its import.

Bryanism carries with it no taint of corruption—no suggestion of willful wrongdoing. It is the politics of an ignorant, unimaginative and rather vain mind that is quick in trifles and impotent before major issues. Reform politics has never existed on any other basis, and therefore reform politics has always proved an easy mark for the machinations of big business.

— *Richard Pettigrew, U.S. Senator*
from South Dakota, 1891-1901

POPULISM IN
AMERICAN HISTORY

Given: a meaningful definition of any phenomenon must be based on its relation to a contextual matrix. Then, one's perception and definition of a phenomenon, in this case populism, is guided in the first place by one's broader conceptual notions about "reality." Therefore, this chapter is concerned with the historical environment in which populism arose in order to understand the meaning of the protest movements which arose in the late nineteenth and early twentieth centuries in the upper Midwest. This undertaking necessitates an outline of a view of American history in order to understand, for example, the significance of the assertion here that the main thrust of populism was toward radical neomercantilism or the significance of the distinction postulated between bryanism and populism as modes of reform.

The history of any human society is manifested as a process in which a changing social reality is constantly being understood, interpreted, and acted upon in terms of changing paradigms. A paradigm can be defined variously as a conceptual framework, a cluster of ideas, a shared social consciousness, or a creedal commitment. All of these definitions can be blended together to make up a "way of life," including not only an intellectual component but also a valuative and emotional commitment around certain aspirations. Typical life aspirations and goals imply typical roles, life styles and short-range goals, all of which contribute to a definition of normative behavior for a given paradigm. While a paradigm thus implies the notion of cultural configuration, the stress in this chapter will lie with the intellectual dimensions of any given paradigm and with the tendency for any paradigm to project a special interpretation of reality from which behavior finally flows.

While the notion of a cluster of ideas, logically interlocked, can be traced to the concept of cultural configuration projected by anthropologists for understanding primitive societies, in recent years the views of Thomas Kuhn have become popular for his emphasis on the process of movement from one worldview to another with a focus on the process rather than simply on defining each paradigm as a static structural configuration. While Kuhn builds his theory of paradigm revolutions strictly around the process by which successive world views form in the field of physical sciences, his perspective is equally useful in regard to the evolution of successive social *weltanschauungs*. The general contours of the Kuhnian model are well summarized by Bruce Kuklick. A direct quotation from a recent article of his well serves the purpose of this study.

In a persuasive and now almost famous book, *The Structure of Scientific Revolution,* Thomas Kuhn has attempted to define and illustrate at length the manner in which changes occur in systems of scientific belief. Kuhn distinguishes between two kinds of change, that which is part of "normal" research and that which develops when a "scientific revolution" occurs. Normal scientific research progresses within what Kuhn called a "paradigm" or "disciplinary matrix." A paradigm is what makes a scientific community a scientific community and has three characteristic elements. The first is what Kuhn classes symbolic elements, generalizations—the laws, theories and definitions to which the scientists are committed. . . . The second element Kuhn terms models—large scale beliefs about the universe, analogies and heuristic maxims. . . . Lastly Kuhn speaks of exemplars, shared problem experiences or standard initiatory experiments. The best illustration of an exemplar that comes to mind is the high school experiment which tests for the presence of oxygen. . . . Its function is rather ritualistic: it socializes students to the correct procedures of science. . . .

In contradistinction to this type of change or "progress," Kuhn also analyzes what he terms a "scientific revolution." A revolution occurs when scientists perceive anomalies still unsolved by normal research . . . calling into question the justificability of the paradigm itself. . . . Out of this crisis a new paradigm may arise, one which defines radically different problems by a contrasting set of basic precepts. In fact, from his studies of actual scientific practices, Kuhn asserts that different paradigms quite literally imply different views of the world. He also insists that dramatic paradigm shifts—like the replacement of Newtonian physics by that of Einstein—involve a notion of "progress" which is not in any simple sense cumulative. A new theory displaces an old one: it does not simply build upon it. . . .[1]

In a study of populism, it is the problem of paradigm revolution in social sciences which commands attention. The anomalies or the falsifications of the laissez-faire model of economic individualism were perceived in the life experiences of people in many strata, especially among frontier farmers, as the "American Dream" of achieving a secure middle-class existence failed to square with the reality of insecurity, loneliness and anxiety. As normal prescriptions (such as hard work, abstinence and asceticism) for ending this anomaly under the paradigm of economic individualism failed to resolve the dissonance between life experience and the larger paradigm, a new world view formed which gravitated toward a socialist paradigm, a view which took shape within the various populist organizations.

As Kuhn observed about scientists, the transfer from one world view to another implies great emotional turmoil, both for those who make the leap in a "conversion experience" and for those whose commitment to the old paradigm makes for rigid resistance to change. The defense against a new social paradigm may take many forms, including intellectual defense, psychological defense and political defense; but it always involves emotional dimensions, leading at times to violence against the protagonists of a new paradigm.

Certain qualifications are necessary in order to apply Kuhn's view of intellectual revolutions to the social realm. Paradigm revolutions are not quite as clear-cut as Kuhn suggests, nor are they necessarily dualistic in form. Rather, there is a tendency for several world views to be generated at times when an existing predominant paradigm is found to be anomalous or defective in some way. One can perhaps generalize to suggest that new views have a tendency toward idealizing either a utopia of the past, as an exercise in nostalgia, or a utopia of the future, as a dream to be realized. There are always many variations within these two frames; and many of these variations (mini-paradigms) fall by the wayside as some new social consciousness emerges as a new predominant paradigm. Even the emerging predominant outlook incorporates elements from past paradigms and must itself, therefore, be seen as only a half-step shift in world view. Similar qualifications of the Kuhnian point of view have been offered by certain philosophers of science, several of whom discuss their differences with Kuhn in articles published in *Criticism and the Growth of Knowledge,* edited by Imre Lakatos and A.E. Musgrove; however, my own qualifications do not extend to endorse the views of Karl Popper, who argues that changes in theory are piecemeal undertakings, which denies the viability of the paradigm concept per se.

A central view throughout this study will be that paradigms overlap in time, which places any individual in a position of making choices throughout his life. In everyday life, a single person rarely chooses a single paradigm as a coherent whole, but rather he develops a special life view drawn from contradictory paradigms. This means that there is always a tendency for ambivalence and inconsistency even as a person strives for harmony. Even when life views are shared by a strata or a group, providing the potential for the formation of a mass movement, internal contradictions exist, as was indeed the case with the populists.

Ever present is the difficult question of which paradigm best describes and interprets changing reality at a given time. Thus we have the continual debate of "illusion" versus "truth," and linked with this debate is the moral tension between "good" versus "evil," which reflects people's varying commitments to the world views of an era. With a changing social reality and with new problems to be solved, yesterday's "truth" and "good" have a way of becoming today's "illusion" and "evil" as new conceptual ways of viewing the world emerge.

Let me reiterate that a commitment to seeing culture in terms of idea clusters should not be confused with a view of history as "the life of the mind." While there may be an apparent contradiction between an assumption of a three-level view of objective reality and the assertion that we know this reality only relatively in terms of some paradigm, this mind-reality dualism is mitigated by the view that "mind" is both a subjective and an objective force. Every viewpoint is simultaneously the basis for subjective perception and at the same time a part of the objective climate of opinion associated with some world view. Again the question arises as to truth versus illusion, rationality versus irrationality, or even sanity against madness. It is my contention here that these dichotomies can be best understood by regarding history in terms of overlapping paradigms, with individuals and collective movements making choices or developing strategies for resolving contradictions, leading at times to behavior which may seem deviant or revolutionary.

Because an explication of these observations falls under the rubric of social psychology, certain discussions will be reserved for the following chapter. That chapter and this present chapter, which deals with the main paradigms in American history, including populism, are yoked together to illuminate a theory of human behavior in history for which the term psychohistory is currently popular.

Certain outlooks and values in American history, especially those reflecting a view of society as a commonwealth and government as an intervenor and arbitrator, have roots in European mercantilism. With the exception of William Appleman Williams's *The Contours of American History* and Eli Heckscher's two-volume study *Mercantilism,* too few historians have stressed the importance of viewing the mercantilist epoch as a discrete era, insofar as any era can be seen as discrete, between feudalism and capitalism. The mercantilist period of the sixteenth and seventeenth centuries was a period of political consolidation under national monarchies in Europe and a period of expanding commerce and colonization. The notion of society as a cor-

porate community, in which individuals and classes lived in mutual interdependence, was retained from the feudal period. Prices and wages were
fixed, in theory at least, to prevent profiteering and to protect the lower
classes. In England, each parish was required to care for the destitute
through a system of poor laws. Professor Williams describes the English
Statute of Artificers of 1563 as follows:

The Legislation concerning artificers was an elaborate system to create and
sustain some order and balance in the process of economic development. . . .
Wage rates (and their relationship to prices), migration within the country,
terms and conditions of employment, and the principle of a seven year
apprenticeship were all written into the integrated system. . . . Poor laws
complemented this involved legislation prohibiting begging, placing pauper
children under apprenticeship, establishing a system of collecting and dis-
tributing alms for the aged and infirm, and putting the poor to work in
special enterprises.[2]

The reality of life may not have corresponded to the good intent of these
statutes; nevertheless, the notion of social responsibility is clearly inherent
in this legislation. Later, the Speenhamland regulations of the late seventeenth century in several counties in England provided a wage subsidy, really
an income supplement, for those in low income brackets. While these regulations may have served to subsidize rural landowners who paid a pittance
in wages, the point should not be ignored that this legislation did serve to
impede the formation of a detached working class in cities and did slow
down and soften the harshness of social change under the evolving factory
system.

During the mercantilist era, commerce, colonization and public works
were all subsidized by the crown or by the government at a city or local
level. The details of these subsidies make up the essential content of Heckscher's two volumes on mercantilism. Williams singles out Shaftesbury as a
much-neglected English ideologist of the seventeenth century, a man who
upheld the notion of commonwealth in contrast with the individualism of
Locke. In present-day parlance, mercantilism was a combination of the
welfare state and a subsidized economy, which has again been conceptualized with the Keynesian revolution of the 1930s but in the apparently new
context of solving industrial stagnation. The problem of stagnation, however, was not unique to the 1930s. Williams refers again and again to various
mercantilist theorists who noted the need for a "vent for their surplusses."
It was in securing such a "vent" that colonization and foreign investment
were undertaken.

Mercantilism gave way to laissez-faire capitalism with its theory of the
self-regulating marketplace. The theory of the "invisible hand" as the

social governor was more a myth than a model of reality. Karl Polanyi, in *The Great Transformation*,[3] argues persuasively that the marketplace was never self-regulating according to the model created by Adam Smith. The capitalists needed the strong arm of the state to subdue the landed gentry, who were still upholding feudal rights, as witness the Cromwellian and the Napoleonic revolutions. As soon as this process of shifting power from the landed to the industrial gentry was barely underway, the capitalists needed the power of the state, often with the aid of the landed gentry, to blunt various rural and working-class protest movements; and finally, they needed the power of the state to stabilize and expand markets through a process which has come to be known as political imperialism. Under these circumstances, the political institutions which arose under mercantilism, especially the national state, along with abstract theories for exercising political power, continued to be functional under later capitalism. Theories for exercising power, especially for neutralizing factionalism, are commonly transmitted from one generation to the next in colleges under the rubric of "political science," whereas populist techniques for protest and dissent are mostly untaught.

In summary, mercantilism can be viewed as a transitional system from manorialism to free enterprise capitalism. There are no sharp lines demarcating mercantilism in time. It had roots far back in feudalism and in the city-states, and it survives yet today in the neomercantilism of Keynesian economic theory and practice. In short, it was a system of political economy in which the state or central governments were formed and also involved in efforts toward economic planning and growth. It implied, therefore, a large government bureaucracy in contrast with the notions of minimal government under laissez-faire theory. It espoused subsidized and regulated trade as opposed to the free trade ideas of later capitalist economists. Mercantilism promoted nation formation and nationalism as a component of its ideology. As Eli Heckscher observes, it was a system that "unified social institutions, cities, provinces and corporations which had dominated medieval social activity.... Considered in this light, mercantilism is primarily an agent of unification."[4]

The value system of mercantilism found its primary expression in Calvinism, an outlook which implicitly assured salvation to the emerging commercial elite and which provided a rationalization for suppressing the aspirations of lower classes and American Indians, whose innate depravity denied them a place at the communion table and at the political councils of the saints. Nevertheless, the New England saints adhered to the notion of a holistic society, a notion which was expressed in the doctrine of covenant, for example, in John Winthrop's "Model for Christian Charity" and his phrase "all shall be one," symbolizing social commonwealth.

Mercantilism seemed barely established when signs of the impending rise of petty capitalism began to appear. These signs included tensions in such areas as political organization, religion, and of course in the "free" exercise of economic activity. In Puritan society, there was Anne Hutchinson, a forerunner of transcendentalism and a gadfly to Calvinism. There was a trend toward individual rather than communal agriculture, as noted by Samuel Chilton Powell in *Puritan Village*. The New England town meeting arose in conflict with saintly elitism. A significant factor for colonial independence lay in the emergence of a colonial mercantilist gentry with already well-developed interests in capitalist entrepreneurship. The publication of Adam Smith's *The Wealth of Nations* in 1776 provided ammunition for subduing the mercantilist theories of political economy, as Smith argued that the "true" wealth of nations rested upon production of goods rather than on accumulation of bullion. In the United States, only a short time elapsed until a paradigm shift occurred with the ascendancy of petty capitalism.

William Appleman Williams marks the shift from "gentleman's" mercantilism to *laissez-nous faire* with the ascent of Andrew Jackson in 1828. This date is as reasonable as any; however, we should bear in mind that paradigms overlap and that neomercantilism persisted as a subordinate outlook throughout the nineteenth century to reemerge differently as populism and progressivism.

A well-known cluster of ideas has come to be associated with the laissez-faire paradigm. There was the notion of autonomous man, the self-made man, often employed in artistic forms as Adamic man. The invisible hand of free competition was to act as an economic governor, allowing ideally for a withering away of government and practically for the notion that "government is best which governs least." Attached to this pattern was the celebration of the petty entrepreneur, the small businessman and the independent farmer, with an attendant high value on diffused property ownership. We have come to speak of this era as that of Jacksonian democracy, but a covert assumption prevailed that this was a democracy of petty capitalists, not of slaves, Indians or the dispossessed. Later, of course, the competitive system was idealized in William Graham Sumner's theory of social Darwinism as a deadly struggle for survival of the fittest without charity or succor to the losers, i.e., the poor.

The spiritual fountainhead of petty capitalism was transcendentalism, epitomized in the works of Ralph Waldo Emerson, who celebrated self-reliance, individualism, free will and a romantic stress upon feeling. Sons of the Enlightenment, the transcendentalists preferred to believe that man was innately good, in contrast with the Calvinistic assumption of innate depravity. The Achilles heel of this outlook was its intellectual denial of social

27

structure and group interaction by virtue of its affirmation of autonomous man. A social imagination based on the notion of unitary man precluded analysis of either class or group dynamics, even though these social interactions existed, as seen in retrospect through modern social theory. The gap between social reality and the laissez-faire paradigm was wide, as subsequently perceived.

The transcendental mind was in tune with the Kantian model for viewing reality as "two cultures" linked by an attempt to fuse scientific empiricism with the Platonic tradition based on a priori forms and moral truths, the latter becoming the "moral imperatives" of the Kantian system. The Platonic side of Kantian and transcendental thought produced a secularized version of Christian idealism, celebrating "nature" as a basis for symbolically unifying the two cultures in a pantheistic scheme. Kant's philosophy demanded a great leap from empirical knowledge to union with noumenal forms; likewise, transcendentalism required an intuitive leap from discrete experience to unity in abstract nature, which obscured the social character of man's existence. For example, Walt Whitman, as he alternately celebrates the individual and the soul, leaps from discrete experience to spiritual idealism, a leap which ignores social outlooks and organizations as factors in human life. For all of his fine portrayal of the "common people," Whitman stands as an exponent of nineteenth-century romantic individualism, lacking a theory of insight into the social process which lies at the root of the phenomenon known as "American innocence."

The transcendentalists were famous for their spiritual idealism, expressed in flowery rhetoric about such concepts as "freedom," "liberty," "democracy," "self-reliance" and "progress." This idealism as a commitment to certain abstract values pushed many of the transcendentalists into moral crusades aiming to reform the world by instilling individual perfection. Their crusades may have been worthy, but their denial of man's role in social institutions made them iconoclasts rather than reformers. This negative iconoclasm, whether attacking slavery, the Mexican war, or political corruption, aimed to liberate man from "bad" institutions and to achieve a good society through moral regeneration of individuals, not institutional transformation.

Following the election of 1884, the transcendental mentality came to be known as *mugwumpism,* in reference to certain Republican idealists who switched from Blaine to Cleveland, explicitly in protest against corruption but implicitly against the rise of corporate industrialism. Mugwumpism essentially characterized an attitude among educated and/or upper middle-class persons. Among less educated and lower middle-class people, a counterpart outlook emerged which can best be described by the generic term *bryanism,* after the example of William Jennings Bryan, the three-time presidential candidate who tried valiantly to hold back the tide of progressivism at the turn of the century. Bryan's personal commitments to money tinkering, to simple agrarianism, and finally to the crusade against teaching Darwin's theory of evolution provide initial clues for a definition of bryanism. Bryan usually displayed "isolationist" tendencies, even to the point of resigning as President Wilson's secretary of state in protest against involvement in the European conflict; yet, once the United States was committed to intervention on behalf of the Allied Powers, Bryan switched to become an ardent jingoist, finding in Germany the symbolic scapegoat, or snake in the Garden of the World. Richard Pettigrew's evaluation of Bryan, quoted as an epigraph on the title page of this chapter, provides further insight into bryanism as an impotent ideological outlook.[5] Since mugwumpism and bryanism are variations of liberalism, it is possible to use the terms almost interchangeably or as a pair in certain contexts, and again to make sharp distinctions between the two in other contexts, especially when class differences are stressed. Let me add that throughout this study the term liberalism will be used in reference to petty capitalist culture and progressivism will denote the reformism of the twentieth century.

In addition to the class differences between mugwumpism and bryanism, the former tended to be associated with liberal theology or transcendentalism while the latter was more likely to be connected with protestant revivalism. However, these two outlooks were opposite sides of the same coin of nineteenth-century liberalism, which was finally unable to deal with the depressions and urban evils that became overtly apparent in the late nineteenth and early twentieth centuries. In company with their transcendental peers, liberals lacked a theory of social process. Doctrines favoring individual regeneration, personal freedom and minimal government, along with belief in the efficacy of the invisible hand, all limited the imagination for reform and amounted to a version of conservative anarchism. At best, the liberal mind could celebrate the "common man," call for a return to free competition through antitrust action, and employ radical-sounding rhetoric inveighing against the concentration of wealth and power. This mind, both in its mugwump and bryanist facets, was quick to endorse money tinkering as a panacea, usually favoring "hard money" during periods of inflation and "soft money" or greenbackerism during panics, expedients which evaded an examination or alteration of the structure of the new industrial capitalism. The liberal mind romanticized the agrarian side of petty capitalism as the pastoral dream; and, in keeping with an idealized simple economy, this mind often disapproved of those foreign adventures that smelled of commercial imperialism on the part of corporate interests.

The liberal mind, whether embodied in a practical entrepreneur or in a person following intellectual pursuits, has had a penchant for turning to hatred and violence at times of crisis. The dream of the perfectability of man is mocked by the reality of grasping, greedy individuals whose individualism takes the form of arrogant conceit. This outlook at worst develops simplistic theories of social analysis with explanation in terms of a conspiracy of some minority group, giving vent to bigotry and scapegoatism as forms of emotional outlets. In striving for the simple petty capitalist economy, both the mugwumps and bryanists have offered little beyond money reform and antimonopolism; however, in recent periods, "law and order" and a revolt against taxes for "big government" have emerged as additional planks for negative reform. It is when these negative reforms prove to be inadequate or inappropriate that the laissez-faire liberal mentality can turn sour out of frustration.

The frustrated liberal, unable to understand social process, has often responded with total rejection of the status quo, with rhetoric about revolution as a total escape from history. Thus, we have witnessed millennial dreams of the second coming of Christ or a secular counterpart in the form of a search for a Wizard of Oz (mostly among bryanists) and the vision of nihilism and apocalypse (mostly among mugwumps). These kinds of "reform" find support in such diverse sources as the Book of Revelation and the anti-bourgeois writings of Nietzsche. These tendencies are reflected in such well-known intellectuals as Mark Twain and Henry Adams, both with a doomsday vision and both with a misanthropic view of mankind. In Adams we find, as well, anti-Semitism as a form of scapegoatism. Another variation on escape from history is to be found among those who pine for the days of a lost aristocracy, for example, Edgar Allan Poe, who detested both the commercial and the transcendental world and receded instead into his mental world of gothic mystery. There was also Orestes Brownson, who embraced Catholicism in his search for a sense of community; and there were numerous transcendentalists who gravitated toward religious communitarianism, which paradoxically gave impetus to socialism. Most often, the disillusioned liberal has displayed pessimism, apathy or a "disordered will" in response to his inability to cope with the disintegration of his paradigm when faced with new social forces.

An example of mugwump pessimism is found in a statement often attributed to Abraham Lincoln, in which he expresses concern for an approaching crisis that "unnerves me and causes me to tremble for the safety of my country." The statement continues: "As a result of the war, corporations have been enthroned and an era of corruption in high places will follow, and the money power of the country will endeavor to prolong its reign by working upon the prejudices of the people until wealth is aggregated into a few hands and the Republic is destroyed." Some scholars suggest that the quotation may be spurious. Be this as it may, the statement has been a popular one and has been reprinted often in populist and radical publications to "prove" that Lincoln was a radical even though we here can point to the sentiment only as one of mugwump disillusionment.

For purposes of this study, bryanism deserves more attention than mugwumpism, partly because Hofstadter and others so often confused bryanism with populism. The United States political landscape has been dotted with bryanistic reform movements with a lower middle-class constituency. Recall the Ku Klux Klan, Huey Long's "Every Man a King," and recent taxpayers' revolt movements. While bryanism evolved originally in connection with the tendency of protestant revivalism to single out Catholicism as an un-American scapegoat, bryanistic tendencies have developed within Catholic circles as well, as when Father Coughlin's movement of the 1930s selected communists as the scapegoat. For the past decade, Governor George Wallace of Alabama has been the leading practitioner of bryanism, with his demagogic promise to bring a message from the common man to the distant elite.

Bryanism is easily connected with "the West," or the frontier, partly, perhaps, because Bryan himself came from Nebraska and achieved fame as the Great Commoner of the West. It is essential, however, to understand "the West" as a point of view, not as a direction or a place in geography. In this sense, the aristocratic Jefferson from Virginia and the ascetic Thoreau from New England were as much men of "the West" as was Bryan, all committed to some form of petty capitalism. Furthermore, if "the West" is equated with Nature or with pantheistic doctrines, it is well to recall that pantheism was popularized in the East by the deists and later by the transcendentalists and that the theory of *natural* rights was a weapon of the petty capitalists against the mercantilists. In modern culture, the fantasy of the West as a symbol of individualism and freedom in the form of the cowboy on a horse has its greatest appeal to alienated urban man. Real cowboys know better.

Even though I submit that bryanism is the antithesis of populism, this is not to argue that some bryanists did not become populists. To the contrary, people do experience changes of mind and heart as they move from one paradigm to another. Just as I have suggested that a paradigm revolution is not as neat and complete as Kuhn implies, the transformation of an individual or a movement is never total; for there is continued ambivalence between the old and the new paradigm. In this context, we can understand the term *cultural lag,* referring to holdovers from an older world view; and if the holdovers into the populist and progressive era were forms of bigotry, we can expect to find unpleasant attributes in the new outlooks. There is the case of Ignatius Donnelly, always half-bryanist and half-populist, whose intellectual components were agrarianism, anti-Semitism and apocalypticism, along with support for the positive reforms outlined in the Omaha populist platform of 1892. The same kind of mixed transformation could occur as mugwumps became progressives. David Thelen has provided evidence of negativistic urban mugwump reformers in smaller Wisconsin cities in the 1890s who finally became supporters of Robert LaFollette, Sr., and his positive proposals for regulatory reforms.[6]

Examples of a more thorough transformation toward ideological radicalism are found among those who turned to socialism, some with a stopover in populism. There were those religious idealists who embraced the social gospel movement, a few of whom became socialists. Most notably, there was George Herron, professor of applied religion at Grinnell College in Iowa, who joined with Eugene Debs and Victor Berger to organize the Socialist Party in 1901. The most famous person of a transcendental mind who was moved by his moral sensibility to embrace socialism was Henry Demarest Lloyd. In making this leap, Lloyd came to reject autonomous individualism and to assert the primacy of community. Retaining the aphoristic literary style of the Emersonian tradition, Lloyd said:

"Regenerate the individual" is a half truth; the reorganization of society which he makes and which makes him is the other half. Man alone cannot be a Christian. Institutions are applied beliefs. The love of liberty became liberty in America by clothing itself in the complicated group of structures known as the government of the United States. . . . To love our neighbor is to submit to the discipline and arrangement which makes his life reach its best, and so do we best love ourselves.[7]

In this context, Lloyd's derision of the free silver issue as the cowbird of reform is seen as more than a pragmatic judgment on this single issue— indeed, as a rejection of the entire mugwump syndrome of reform.

A mugwump/bryanist reform of special interest in an analysis of populism is that of prohibition, which at times evolved into political movements and provided input into populist efforts. While this input will be considered later in depth, it is appropriate to stress here the origin of the prohibition impulse as an aspect of asceticism in the petty capitalist paradigm. This aspect is noted by James Timberlake in his study of the prohibition movement. "The Temperance movement fell squarely within the American tradition of self help and success. . . . Good character, it was believed, led to success, bad character to failure. . . ."[8] It was a short step, however, for many prohibitionists from fighting the "liquor monopoly" to fighting monopoly in general and then to embracing socialism in some cases; and thus, the asceticism associated with the prohibition movement and more generally with the "Protestant work ethic" was transferred into some sections of the populist culture as well.

Paradigm revolutions are never total. In the shift from mercantilism to petty capitalism, there was much carry-over, both in practice and ideology, from the mercantilist era. It is customary to view as neomercantilism the programs and practices for government intervention in the nineteenth century, including Hamiltonian subsidies to business, Henry Clay's American Plan, and railroad grants.[9] Neomercantilism and "fee" capitalism worked symbiotically in practice even though the two systems generated friction on political, cultural and religious levels. This friction often contributed to a consolidation of laissez-faire ideology as defeated interests in the political process would explode with charges of log-rolling, corruption, favoritism, and the demand for "equal rights for all; special privileges for none." The rhetoric could be iconoclastic and radical sounding, but it was essentially mugwump or bryanistic in its commitment to unfettered petty capitalism along with a reactionary imagination expressing nostalgia for a lost paradise.

The symbiotic relationship of neomercantilism and petty capitalism did operate to produce economic achievements and success stories for countless individuals. If there was not a take-off according to the model of W.W. Rostow in the nineteenth century, the United States did experience a tremendous surge of industrial growth. The growth process of the American economy has owed more to the frontier as an outlet for investment and as a consumer market among settlers than has commonly been admitted.

While current scholarship has properly rejected the thesis of Frederick Jackson Turner that the frontier served as a seedbed of democracy and as a safety valve for eastern laborers, it is still in order to suggest that the frontier did play a crucial role in sustaining economic growth in the nineteenth century. Even though the agricultural midcontinent, once established, developed needs for foreign markets as outlets for an overextended farm sector of the economy, the developing frontier in the first place served as a market outlet for the already established capitalistic enterprises. This argument has been somewhat developed by Ellen von Nardroff, who argued that agricultural exports helped to balance international payments and thus sustain eastern industrialization and that agriculture itself provided an investment outlet.[10] George Murphy and Arnold Zellner have contributed to this thesis, noting that the expanding frontier provided one-time-only investment stimuli as railroads, courthouses and towns were built as migration proceeded westward.[11] Consistent with these points of view is the additional observation that the private debts assumed by farmers and business enterprises also helped to fuel the economy and to stimulate economic growth.

An expanding market, in turn, meant that manufacturers could continually build new factories, utilizing the most advanced technological innovations, always with a sense of optimism that an increased flow of goods would clear the market. Thus, optimism, inventiveness and a sense of progress, often catalogued as character traits of Americans, were all functions of the expanding market; and the market, in turn, derived its sustenance from the millions of immigrants streaming into the frontier, immigrants who spent borrowed money, hoping in time to pay off their debts and to join the ranks of the comfortable middle class as a fulfillment of the American Dream.

Not only did the frontier provide an outlet for investment and a consumer market, but it also provided a basis for a replication of middle-class life for new generations of old-stock Americans. Sons of Yankee businessmen streamed to the West to become bankers, grocers, ministers, or land agents or to establish academies and colleges. Land speculation proved to be an especially effective avenue for social climbing, especially for those with the "right" political connections, i.e., politicians with knowledge of future railroad routes and town sites. European immigrants, too, soon entertained the romance of rags to riches through speculation, for example, by cashing in on inflated land values and then moving West again for cheaper land.

American economic growth was accomplished amid optimistic rhetoric about "freedom," "self-reliance," and "individual initiative." The myth of the Golden West, the land of milk and honey, spread far and wide, even into small European hamlets. The expanding market along with a replication of middle-class life on the moving frontier seemed to confirm the theory of free competition and the success story of Horatio Alger as reflecting a unique American "truth." Especially for those who succeeded, the ideology of Jacksonian democracy was flattering; and it seemed almost egalitarian to believe that unequal success was a function of individual initiative. Out of these circumstances arose the belief that the ladder of middle-class success was there to be climbed for anyone who would work hard, live frugally if necessary, and cultivate the "right" political connections if possible. The aim was to get rich eventually; however, smaller blessings might do with the hope that sons and daughters would catch the brass ring. Thus was born the American Dream in an era of optimistic rhetoric and self-righteous moralizing in an economy sustained by the impact of the frontier.

Even in the best of times, not everyone was able to cash in on the American Dream, even in a modest way; and in the worst of times, during a panic, for example, vast numbers could sense that the dream might be illusion. These were the marginal people of American society, the bankrupt farmer, the new industrial worker without job security or full-time employment, the sharecropper living a desperate existence, and at times the small businessman facing ruinous competition from larger competitors. All of these tried in some way to adopt strategies with which to counter their despair and disillusionment. In the mid-nineteenth century there were always certain options available to the "failures," such as joining a gold rush, going bac

East, escaping to live with Indians as mountain men and trappers, and always just going West again to try a new farm plot. However, by the end of the century, these strategies were no longer meaningful; and instead, some of the marginal people of America began to gravitate into movements for reform which have come to be known as populism.* The labor movement emerged, often engaging in strikes which seemed to threaten the hegemony and profits of the entrepreneurial elite. There were farm movements which threatened the political balance in state after state. There was the "army" led by Jacob Coxey, who demanded government spending for roads to provide employment, an early example of radical neomercantilism.

The role of the labor movement, especially the Knights of Labor and the Industrial Workers of the World, each with an anticapitalistic bias, has been underrated as an aspect of the general populist impulse of America, even though the IWW with its syndicalist tendencies refrained from joining political coalitions. The American Federation of Labor under Samuel Gompers was more progressive than populistic, as indicated by Gompers's active membership in the National Civic Federation.

Even though Gompers himself carried on a vendetta against socialism and other forms of political rebelliousness, nevertheless, the AFL in certain states joined with the populist forces. Chester McArthur Destler, in *American Radicalism, 1865-1901*, discusses the attempt to forge a labor-populist coalition in Illinois in the 1890s.[12] In Wisconsin, the Milwaukee socialists

*In viewing the social basis for populism as the various strata of marginal and insecure people who are victims of certain hardships inherent in the industrial system, it is helpful to define the various Indian rebellions as populistic in this sense as well. The Indians devolved into marginality with the demise of the fur trade, which had tied most tribes to the capitalistic trading economy (as both consumers and industrial producers for the European fur market) for at least a century before land settlers and depletion of fur-bearing animals ended a process of acculturation. If the Indians did not enunciate a reform program for the industrial system as did the populists, it was because they were cast out of the capitalistic orbit altogether, since they were not permitted to become settled farmers after fur gathering ended. Generally, the crisis for Indians developed as fur trading ceased, and their revolts appeared at intervals in step with the westward movement of the frontier. Indian revolts preceded populist rebellions by roughly half a century on the moving frontier; and thus, there was rarely a chance for common cause between settlers and Indians. Common cause would have been difficult in any event as long as the settlers seemed to be the cutting edge and the visible representatives of the industrial civilization which was bent upon expelling Indians and decimating their ranks. Both Indians and populists were concerned in an ultimate sense with the land question. For Indians, the symbolic enemy behind the white man's land grabbing were the "Boston men," corresponding with the "Wall Street bankers" who seemed to lie behind a mortgage system for the populists at a later time. If Indians did not espouse reforms with socialistic tendencies, they were nonetheless fighting in a fundamental sense to save their communally oriented culture at variance with the nineteenth-century paradigm associated with petty capitalism.

had deep roots in the labor movement after 1900. In North Dakota, labor collaborated with the Farmers Nonpartisan League to win advanced labor legislation in the 1917 legislative session; and in Minnesota, the state Federation of Labor spawned the Workingman's Nonpartisan Political League, which in turn played a dominant role in forming the Farmer-Labor Party from a coalition with the Farmers League. While the populist movements in the four states under consideration in this study were built primarily upon a rural constituency, the labor component in populism has been too much ignored. A later chapter dealing with the genesis of the Minnesota Farmer-Labor Party will serve to correct the view that populism has been simply a rural phenomenon.

As noted in the previous chapter, populism has not been monolithic in ideology but rather has contained currents which can be conceptualized as Tory populism, socialism and radical neomercantilism. Through time, there was a tendency for the socialist outlook to gain strength and thus to pull the ideology of populism leftward on the political spectrum, especially in Minnesota and North Dakota in the twentieth century. It is well to look more closely at these three currents for an appreciation of the dynamics within populism itself.

Especially in the late nineteenth century, Tory populists were little different from the bryanists, stressing antimonopolism and money reform linked with a commitment to petty capitalism. As the promise of these limited reforms faded, a more substantial catalogue of proposals was developed, including such items as nationalization of railroads and other utilities, the warehousing plan to insulate farm prices from the vagaries of the free market, regulation of hours and conditions for laboring men, the progressive income tax, and other proposals which were included in the Omaha Platform of 1892.[13] This kind of government intervention in the economy can be seen as an adaptation of the older mercantilist theories to provide for social responsibility and general welfare. However, populist interventionism was aimed chiefly at alleviating the distress of those threatened with marginality, whereas the Hamiltonian version of mercantilism was aimed chiefly at subsidizing manufacturing interests; hence the term *radical neomercantilism* seems most appropriate for describing this thrust of populism.

Too often, the socialist current in populism has been dismissed as a fringe with little organic connection with the major populist movements. Socialist sentiments growing out of Bellamy's nationalist clubs, Debs's labor leadership, the Owenite cooperative movement and other influences (catalogued by Howard Quint[14]) contributed to a vigorous socialist minority in the United States by the turn of the century. Destler points to the role of Henry Demarest Lloyd, who worked to radicalize the attempted populist-labor coalition in Illinois.[15] O. Gene Clanton, in *Kansas Populism,* notes that the Kansas populists began to study socialist doctrines, especially after they were accused of being "foreign" radicals by their opposition.[16] In South Dakota, Father Haire, a Catholic priest and former Knights of Labor organizer, helped found the Socialist Party in that state in 1901.[17] William Dobbyn, a Universalist minister, edited a socialist-prohibitionist periodical, *Progressive Age,* in Minneapolis while he was active in populist affairs.[18] In Milwaukee, the most important socialist center of the Midwest developed under the leadership of Victor Berger.

After the turn of the century and with the organization of the Social Democratic Party, primarily by Berger and Eugene Debs, the socialist current in the nation, and in the Midwest, flourished. Berger's influence remained primarily in the labor movement in Milwaukee; but in both Minnesota and North Dakota, persons of socialist persuasion helped organize and form the bureaucracy of the Farmers Nonpartisan League and of the Farmer-Labor Party. This is not to suggest that these movements were in fact socialistic; but the acceptance of socialist leadership speaks for further leftward movement on the part of rank-and-file populists and for a willingness to break more fully with the laissez-faire paradigm and its limited vision for reform.

Even with a general leftward tendency through time, populist reforms always displayed an ambivalence between bryanism and socialism. This ambivalence is evident in the famous Omaha Platform of 1892, which displayed typical bryanistic rhetoric about corrupt politicians and judges, along with a prophecy of impending calamity in the preamble written by Ignatius Donnelly; yet a more typical radical neomercantilist outlook appears in its positive planks for reform. Because the problem of ambivalence and vacillation will be examined throughout this study, it is sufficient here merely to mention this aspect of the populist movements.

We have seen that the shift from mercantilism to petty capitalism and from Calvinism to transcendentalism constituted America's first paradigm revolution. The second major turning point came with the emergence of the progressive *weltanschauung* at the turn of the twentieth century, partly as a response to populist agitation for reforms.

There were several elements within progressivism, including a pacifist movement at the time of World War I and the movement that led into the quasi-socialist League for Industrial Democracy in the 1920s and early 1930s, with spokesmen like John Dewey and Charles Beard. However, the main thrust of progressivism was one of conservatism and preservation of the capitalistic system, a view consistent with that of Gabriel Kolko in *The Triumph of Conservatism* and that of other revisionist historians who evaluate the progressive movement as being both elitist and conservative in its import.

The progressive leaders were generally from a solid, middle-class background. They espoused positive reforms, some reflecting populist concerns, which would eliminate social dissonance and smooth over disruptive tendencies in the economy. Their reformism barely went beyond eliminating political corruption exposed by muckrakers, attempting to control and soften the business cycle through money and banking reform, and establishing regulatory commissions over industries which were clearly monopolistic. Progressive reformism, whether pursued under the label of a Square Deal or a New Freedom, aimed to restore hope in a redefined American Dream and optimism for "the promise of America," as Herbert Croly suggested with his book title.

A central intellectual shift from the nineteenth-century laissez-faire world view to progressivism was the abandonment of an atomistic view of man in the social sciences. John Dewey formulated a pluralist model of social structure in which a great variety of group interests democratically interacted and in which any consensus on the part of a significant coalition was defined as the "public interest" and as a pragmatic political "truth" for the situation at hand.[19] There was a tendency among progressives to see a polarization between the "weak" people and "powerful" economic interests; and from this outlook, they advocated regulatory intervention in the economy on behalf of "the people" to redress the balance of power in the marketplace in favor of labor and farmers, an approach which was revived by John Kenneth Galbraith in his early writings as the theory of countervailing power. The progressive outlook gave impetus to studying groups or forces, such as the family, the labor movement, immigrants, and crime as matters of sociological interest. Progressive legalists, sparked by Brandeis, refused to honor the due process clause as a dictum for entrepreneurial laissez-faire; instead they began to interpret the constitution in conjunction with social and economic realities in support of regulatory reforms. While recognizing social institutions as forces, the progressives were often oblivious to larger structural dislocations as a source of problems. They took for granted an interest in expanding foreign markets, which they often clothed in rhetoric about "saving the world," and they failed to foresee crises arising from saturation of the world "frontier" just as the nineteenth-century individualists had been unable to cope with the closing of the United States' frontier. Progressivism was a new version of mercantilism, elitist to be sure, recapturing the social concerns for order and general welfare first expressed by Calvinist John Winthrop.*

With all paradigm revolutions, there is a cultural lag, a carry-over of old values and outlooks into a new setting; and progressivism was no exception.

The competitive idea was retained—with less emphasis on individual struggle in the style of the first Social Darwinists, but with a new emphasis on competition among groups and interests for claims in the marketplace and influence in political councils. This approach enabled well-organized groups in the political arena to get "a bigger piece of pie," but it did not lead either to a deeper examination of the plight of unorganized interests or to a look at the problem created by the ending of frontier expansionism. Mainstream progressivism continued to display nativism, bigotry, and the myth of Anglo-Saxon superiority (witness the racism of Woodrow Wilson). Progressives were biased against radicals, populists and immigrants, undoubtedly because these groups constituted a threat to their middle-class value system. And in the final analysis, much of their sentiment for reform and uplift revolved around a goal of acculturation, the melting-pot impulse to promote adherence to middle-class norms. Theodore Roosevelt was the epitome of this

---

*The following short portions from John Winthrop's "Model for Christian Charity," written at sea in 1630 before landing at Boston, illustrate both Winthrop's elitism and also his commitment to community as an organic concept.

"That every man might have need of other, and from hence they might be all knitt together in the Bond of brotherly affecction: from hence it appeares plainly that noe man is made more honourable than another or more wealthy etc., out of any perticuler and singuler respect to himselfe but for the glory of his Creator and the Common good of the Creature, man. . . . All men being thus (by divine providence) rancked into two sortes, riche and poore. . . . There are two rules whereby wee are to walke towards one another: JUSTICE and MERCY. . . . sometimes there may be occasion of shewing mercy to a rich man, in sudden danger of distress, and alsoe doeing of meere Justice to a poore man in regard to some perticuler contract. . .

". . . for the work wee have in hand, it is by mutuall consent through a speciall overruleing providence, and a more ordinary approbation of the Churches of Christ to seeke out a place of Cohabitation and Consortship under a due forme of Government, both civil and ecclesiasticall. In such cases as this, the care of the publique must oversway all private respects, by which not onely conscience, but meere Civil policy doth bind us; for it is a true rule that perticuler estates cannot subsist in the ruine of the publique. . .

"Now the onely way to avoyde shipwrack and to provide for posterity is to follow the Counsell of Micah, to doe Justly, to love Mercy, to walke humbly with our God; for this end, wee must be knitt together in this worke as one man, wee must entertain each other in brotherly Affeccion, we must be willing to abridge ourselves of our superfluities, for supply of others neccessities, wee must uphold a familiar Commerce together in all meekness, gentleness, patience and liberality, wee must delight in eache other, make others Conditions our own, rejoyce together, mourne together, labor and suffer together, alwayes haveing before our eyes our Commission and Community in the worke. . . soe shall wee keepe the unitie of the spirit in the bond of peace, the Lord will be our God and delight to dwell among us. . . . for wee must Consider that wee shall be as a Citty upon a Hill, the eies of all people are uppon us. . ."

kind of progressivism (he advocated shooting a dozen populists as a lesson to others). Indeed, this century may go down in history as "the Century of Theodore Roosevelt," because foreign adventures, reform rhetoric, and repression have been cleverly employed to shape social consciousness since the Spanish-American War. In final analysis, the main current of progressivism has been the intellectual and political counterpart of corporate capitalism.

Frequently there is confusion in distinguishing the populist from the progressive movements, often expressed by the old cliché that a progressive was simply a populist with the hayseed combed out of his hair. Such a serious study as Russel Nye's *Midwestern Progressive Politics* barely makes the distinction at all, tending to lump both kinds of reformers together as a common type. A more recent study, *The Search for Order* by Robert Wiebe, is open to the same criticism. Wiebe describes in detail the shift of the United States from a small-town society to a corporate/bureaucratic/ professionalized urban society; but he fails to project an adequate theory of social dynamics to explain this shift, and, in the process, fails to treat populism as a special force in history.

It has been observed that the progressives tended to steal planks from the populists and to win converts from the potential populist constituency; nevertheless, there have been significant differences between the two movements. First of all, populism tended to form around disillusioned and marginal groups, while progressivism formed around middle-class and even some upper-class elements. The difference was a case of underdogs versus upperdogs. Both groups might respond to the same social problems: railroad abuses, the business cycle, corruption in cities and autocracy over laboring men. But the underdogs, even while still adhering to the American Dream, would desperately want *some* reform to provide relief, whereas the upperdogs could bide their time, aiming for long-range economic stability rather than immediate relief from adversity.

If, at times, the populists and progressives have seemed to marry, there has always been an instability in the marriage, for the more marginal people in the lower middle-class have soon discovered the superficiality and fickle quality of progressive reformism. Thus, there has been an oscillating aspect to populism as new movements have arisen periodically to challenge progressive impotence in achieving structural social change. The populist uprising of the 1890s arose when the dream of "free men, free land and free labor" symbolized by Lincoln and the Republican Party proved illusory. By 1912 and throughout the second decade of the twentieth century, a vigorous socialist movement flourished, as the progressives could offer neither stability nor peace. Again, in the 1930s, various populist movements arose to influence New Deal progressivism; and the 1960s saw both ghetto uprisings and the youth rebellion in protest against the progressive conservatism and jingoism that had prevailed since World War II, clothed in a moral crusade against communism.

At those times when economic conditions were less pressing on marginal people, populism ebbed away and was coopted by the progressive movement, a pattern which was most evident in the Midwest during the first decade of the twentieth century. This was the period in which Robert "Fighting Bob" LaFollette was at the height of his popularity with his Wisconsin Plan of civil service, voting and regulatory reforms. In South Dakota, Coe Crawford was elected governor in 1906, using the Wisconsin Plan as his model.[20] After a period of decline, South Dakota progressives came to life again in 1916 with the election of Governor Peter Norbeck, who consciously used the program of the Farmers Nonpartisan League in order to undercut the League.[21]

In the first decade of the century, progressive reform found an outlet in the Democratic Party in Minnesota and North Dakota. Democrat John Burke was elected governor of North Dakota for three terms beginning in 1906; Burke assumed leadership to effect railroad reform and state-owned terminal elevator legislation that had first been advocated by populists in the 1890s.[22] Likewise, in 1902 Minnesota elected to the governorship John A. Johnson, a man who inspired audiences with his Emersonian aphorisms and who was considered to be a potential presidential candidate until his untimely death in 1909. Johnson also took progressive initiative by only mildly curbing "big business" malpractices and by adjusting taxes for the giant iron ore corporations of the state. That Johnson's reformism was not based on any ideological aversion to big business is clear from the fact that he was party to an "arrangement" with Frank Kellogg by which the governor bought mining stock at the low price of fifteen dollars a share and sold it five months later at thirty-five dollars for a profit greater than Johnson's annual salary as governor.[23] His death left the Democrats bereft of leadership, permitting the progressive impulse to find an outlet in the Republican Party, most notably in a progressive revolt in 1914.[24]

Out of the new progressivism in Minnesota Republican politics emerged Frank Kellogg, who later became famous as secretary of state under President Coolidge for helping to guide the Kellogg-Briand antiwar pact into fruition in 1927. Kellogg nicely fits the definition of a mainstream progressive type, having begun his career as chief counsel for the iron mining companies in Minnesota and then becoming counsel for the government in certain trust-busting cases at the behest of Teddy Roosevelt.

An uneasy marriage of populists with the peace progressives continued in the second decade among those who were alarmed by agitation and preparation for involvement in the war begun in Europe in 1914. Both groups were inclined to oppose "foreign entanglements" because of their residual commitment to the isolationism inherent in mugwumpism/bryanism. Over and above this consideration, some progressives with an eye for the baneful influence of "reactionary" interests came to suspect the call for war preparations as a boondoggle for certain "eastern" economic interests. LaFollette switched from expansionism to anti-imperialism in 1912, when he came to view the United States' growing dispute with Mexico as a veil for certain interested investors;[25] and George Norris announced after the declaration of war in 1917: "We have put the dollar sign on the American flag."[26] At the same time, many radicals were influenced by an economic interpretation of foreign policy as a capitalistic struggle for world markets and became committed to socialist internationalism. This propelled the Socialist Party into opposition to the World War in 1917 after war was declared.

Some of the peace progressives, such as United States Senator Porter McCumber of North Dakota and Frank Kellogg of Minnesota, switched to support the war in 1917. But others, including Wisconsin's Senator Robert LaFollette, Asle Gronna of North Dakota and George Norris of Nebraska, stood by their convictions and tended to become radicalized by virtue of their parallel stand with the socialists in opposition to the war. However, not all of the peace progressives were radicalized sufficiently to enjoy populist support. Senator Asle Gronna of North Dakota, who stood with LaFollette in 1917 in opposition to war, was defeated in 1920 by Professor Edwin Ladd, who was supported by the Nonpartisan League.

Two of the more famous progressives who became radicalized were George Norris of Nebraska and Richard Pettigrew of South Dakota. Both of these men had begun their careers as stalwart Republicans, intent upon destroying the populist "craze"; and both men became increasingly radical as time went on. Norris later won fame for his fight for the Tennessee Valley Authority and for government-owned electric power generation. Pettigrew, after supporting first Bryan and then, upon leaving the Republican Party, the Bull Moose movement, finally became a socialist and wrote a book called *Imperial Washington,* an exposé of his erstwhile stalwart and progressive friends. The examples of Norris and Pettigrew counter Richard Hofstadter's view that populists moved only to the right, as suggested by the life pattern of Tom Watson of Georgia.

Another famous progressive, Robert LaFollette, underwent a milder change than did Norris and Pettigrew. LaFollette emerged from World War I with a changed constituency and with tendencies toward more radical or populistic views; yet he was always ambivalent, oscillating between a populist outlook and traditional progressivism, a tendency which will be noted later in reference to his 1924 campaign. It is apparent that LaFollette was offended by the defection of Frank Kellogg from the peace bloc in the

Senate in 1917; for he campaigned for Kellogg's defeat by Shipstead in 1922, unleashing a petty tirade at one point in reference to Kellogg's physical deformity: "God Almighty, through men's nature writes men's characters on their faces and in their forms. Your Senator has bowed obsequiously to wealth and to corporations' orders and to his masters till God Almighty has given him a hump on his back—crouching, cringing, UnAmerican, unmanly."[27]

Even though a small minority of progressives veered into the peace camp and tended to become radicalized in ways which carried them toward a populist outlook, and even though some progressive urban reformers were not attuned to nativism and bigotry,[28] these tendencies should not be allowed to blur the differences between populism and progressivism in their mainstream aspects. While I have stressed here the tendency for certain midwestern progressives to become radicalized, the opposite tendency was also at work; for in a study of key progressives from the Theodore Roosevelt period, Otis Graham found that a majority of those still living had vacillated into anti-New Deal outlooks by the 1930s.[29]

While this study does not explore populism in the South as a source of evidence, a recent study by Sheldon Hackney of political currents in Alabama supports my general thesis on the distinction between populism and progressivism. Hackney observes that the populists were more responsive to material adversity while the progressives were troubled primarily by cultural dissonance.

The Populist experience suggests that when the gap between aspiration and achievement is caused by a deterioration of real conditions, the insurgents may reject traditional rulers but will find it difficult to substitute new values for old, to focus discontent on common goals, or to sustain motivation among the following. However, the Progressives are motivated by the dissonance between conflicting cultural commandments. For them the problem was to institutionalize the older ethical mandates while at the same time providing for stability and progress. The contradictory values of Christian brotherhood and American competitive success were thus rationalized, and the result was a powerful force that was restricted in its operation by the Progressives' sense of class loyalty and notions of a conflict-free society. In contrast to Populism, Progressivism's narrow commitment excluded any but the most traditional humanitarian concern for the working classes.[30]

Hackney goes on to suggest that the populists exhibited a static conception of social reality in their dedication to minimal government and low taxes.[31] His observation is undoubtedly valid for populism in Alabama and even in other states where Tory populism, with its close link to bryanism, predominated. In contrast to populists in the upper Midwest the Alabama populists, according to Hackney, scattered to the four winds after 1900 without leaving in their wake a more radical socialist minority to provide leadership for twentieth-century reform movements. Hackney mentions only one socialist who emerged from Alabama, W.H. Skaggs, who emigrated to Chicago and later published a scathing indictment of southern life in *The Southern Oligarchy*.[32]

Hackney's observations on the relation of populism to racism in Alabama are of more than passing interest. According to his view, the progressives organized a coalition different from that of the populists, a coalition including the white planters, who then "planted" racism in the progressive movement.

An analysis of the voting in the Constitutional Convention of 1901 shows there was a potential pool of support in the Black Belt for some Progressive measures, particularly railroad regulation. The Progressive urge there was inhibited by anti-Negro fixations among the Planters and by the fact that Negro suffrage was used by the machine to maintain itself in power. Disenfranchisement, therefore, was a prerequisite of Progressivism in Alabama. The melange of motives that made disenfranchisement a reality in Alabama, against the wishes of Populists and poor whites, included both the desire to make reform possible and the wish to make it impossible. . . . The disfranchisers thought they could cleanse their consciences, retain their power, and prevent a further recurrence of Populism all at the same time. They were wrong. Once the political aspect of the Negro problem had been solved by abolishing the Negro's political rights, and the rights of plenty of poor whites in the bargain, the way was open for the Progressives to assemble from the purged electorate a winning coalition, a coalition which owed little to Populist antecedents.[33]

We have described the populists on a status continuum as being lower middle-class with a tendency to become marginal or even outcasts in the industrial system. It is important to point out, however, that all political responses of lower middle-class people are not automatically populistic in the sense of moving toward radical neomercantilism or socialism; for, as will be explained in the chapter on social psychology, certain psychological complexes operate to repress intellectual change and to produce a kind of mugwump/bryanist rigidity as a pseudo-radicalism. Examples are abundant of lower-class people being "more royalist than the king" and of their identification with upper-class values and goals, in some cases with overt fascism. This observation, however, should not be taken as implying that populism and fascism are akin in some way. Rather, both movements, while deriving support in part from the same lower middle-class social stratum, represent an opposing ideological syndrome linked with opposing psychological responses.

The evidence presented in this chapter demonstrates that populism has been a distinct mode of social consciousness in American history and a pivotal force in the shift from Jacksonian individualism to Bull Moose and Wilsonian progressivism. The dynamic character of populism is evident not just in relation to the larger transformations in intellectual outlook but also within the populist movements themselves. The early populists were more inclined toward the Tory or laissez-faire outlook, still believing in the dream of success through hard work, piety and asceticism and bryanistic reforms. They differed from the bryanists mainly in associating with other marginal people, including laboring groups and socialists, to buttress demands for reform. While Tory populists may well have reacted to adversity at first with the moral indignation and even scapegoating so typical of the liberal mind, they could not ignore the realities which seemed to account for their troubles. Before long, they were assailing bankers and railroad magnates and developing an analysis of a society with a class structure. They read the Bible and rewrote old hymns to decry the plight of the poor and the oppressiveness of the rich. In effect, they began to reformulate Winthrop's "Model for Christian Charity," minus the elitism of Calvinist doctrine. In their concern with social realities, they passed beyond the stage of expressing moral indignation and reached toward specific reforms; this development shows implicitly that the populists conceived of society as an institutional structure amenable to reform. Even though their social analysis may have been simplistic, the populists—rural and urban—helped to force upon the emerging progressive outlook a recognition of institutions, partly by their own existence as an institutional factor in American life.

Populism was neither monolithic nor static. As the movements through time veered away from Tory populism toward quasi-socialism, there was internal dissonance and always ambivalence on the part of the individuals involved. The movements and individuals often stood in conflict with external society as well, which again was a source of tension and anxiety. Because problems dealing with relief of tension or reduction of dissonance have customarily fallen under the rubric of social psychology, it follows that some theory of social psychology is required to explain the emergence of that behavior we call populism, as a response to felt tensions and anxieties. The new perspective on populism being projected in this study is closely linked with a theory of social psychology based on the outlook of Alfred Adler, which makes up the substance of the chapter which follows.

NOTES

1. Bruce Kuklick, "History as a Way of Learning," *American Quarterly*, 22:609-610, Fall 1970.

2. William Appleman Williams, *Contours of American History* (Cleveland: World Publishing Company, 1961), p. 44.

3. Karl Polanyi, *The Great Transformation* (Boston: Beacon Press, 1967). See especially chapter 6, pp. 60-76, "The Self-Regulating Market and the Fictitious Commodities: Labor, Land and Money."

4. Eli Heckscher, *Mercantilism*, vol. 1 (London: Geo. Allen and Unwin, 1935), p. 22.

5. The epigraph describing Bryan is from R.F. Pettigrew's *Imperial Washington* (Chicago: Charles Kerr, 1922), p. 276.

6. David Thelen, "Prelude to Populism: A Study of Six Wisconsin Cities, 1891-1900" (Unpublished doctoral dissertation, University of Wisconsin, 1969).

7. Henry Demarest Lloyd, *Wealth Against Commonwealth* (Chicago: Harper and Bros., 1899), p. 522.

8. James H. Timberlake, *Prohibition and the Progressive Movement* (Cambridge: Harvard Press, 1963), p. 67.

9. For further discussion of the role of public enterprise in the nineteenth century, see Robert Lively, "The American System: A Review Article," *Business History Review*, 29:81-96, March 1955.

10. Ellen von Nardroff, "The American Frontier as a Safety Valve?: The Life, Death, Reincarnation and Justification of a Theory," *Agricultural History*, 36: 123-142, July 1962.

11. Arnold Zellner and George Murphy, "Sequential Growth, The Labor Safety-Valve Doctrine and the Development of American Unionism," *Journal of Economic History*, 19:402-421, 1959.

12. Chester McArthur Destler, *American Radicalism, 1865-1901* (Chicago: Quadrangle Paperbacks, 1966). See chapter 8: "The Labor-Populist Alliance of Illinois in the Election of 1894," pp. 162-174.

13. The full text of the People's Party Omaha platform of 1892 is reprinted in John D. Hicks's *The Populist Revolt* (Minneapolis: University of Minnesota, 1931), Appendix.

14. An excellent survey of many of the ideological currents which flowed into the socialist outlook is found in Howard Quint, *The Forging of American Socialism* (Indianapolis: Bobbs-Merrill Co. [The American Heritage Series], 1964).

15. Destler, pp. 162-174, with special attention to the role of Henry Demarest Lloyd.

16. O. Gene Clanton, *Kansas Populism* (Lawrence: University of Kansas Press, 1969), p. 147.

17. Herbert Schell, *History of South Dakota* (Lincoln: University of Nebraska Press, 1961), p. 241.

18. A file of *Progressive Age* is available at the Minnesota Historical Society. There is discussion of Dobbyn's role in the Minnesota populist movement in Carl Chrislock, "The Politics of Protest in Minnesota, 1890-1901: From Populism to Progressivism" (Unpublished doctoral dissertation, University of Minnesota, 1955).

19. John Dewey, *The Public and Its Problems* (Chicago: The Swallow Press, 1927). See especially chapter 1, "Search for the Public," in which Dewey defines the state or "the public" as consisting of lesser human associations.

20. Schell, pp. 264-265.

21. Ibid., pp. 266-269.

22. Elwyn Robinson, *History of North Dakota* (Lincoln: University of Nebraska Press, 1966), pp. 264-267.

23. Law firm records of Davis, Kellogg and Severance, cited in a manuscript in preparation by Gretchen and Kent Kreuter.

24. Carl H. Chrislock, *The Progressive Era in Minnesota, 1899-1918* (St. Paul: Minnesota Historical Society, 1971), pp. 18-21.

25. Padriac C. Kennedy, "LaFollette's Foreign Policy: From Imperialism to Anti-Imperialism," *Wisconsin Magazine of History*, 46:288-89, Summer 1963.

26. George Norris, *Fighting Liberal* (New York: Macmillan, 1945), p. 197.

27. Donald Young, ed., *Adventure in Politics: The Memoirs of Philip LaFollette* (New York: Holt, Rinehart and Winston, 1970), p. 77.

28. Irwin Yellowitz, *Labor and the Progressive Movement in New York State, 1897-1916* (Ithaca: Cornell University Press, 1965). See observations in opening pages in which Yellowitz notes that "unlike the socialists, the aims of the social progressives did not cross the theoretical boundaries of the capitalist system."

29. Otis L. Graham, *Encore for Reform* (New York: Oxford University Press, 1967), p. 24.

30. Sheldon Hackney, *From Populism to Progressivism in Alabama* (Princeton: Princeton University Press, 1969), pp. 327-328

31. Ibid., p. 328.

32. Ibid., p. 118.

33. Ibid., p. 326.

3

Alice felt she could not be denied, so she asked another question: "What sort of people live here?"

"In that direction," the Cat said, waving its right paw round, "lives a Hatter"; and in that direction, waving the other paw, "lives a March Hare. Visit either you like. They are both mad."

"But I don't want to go among mad people," Alice remarked.

"Oh you can't help that," said the Cat: "We're all mad here. I'm mad. You're mad."

"How do you know I'm mad?" said Alice.

"You must be," said the Cat, "or you wouldn't have come here."

Alice didn't think that proved it at all; however, she went on: "And how do you know that you're mad?"

"To begin with," said the Cat, "A dog's not mad. You grant that?"

"I suppose so," said Alice.

"Well, then," the Cat went on, "you see a dog growls when it's angry, and wags its tail when it's pleased. Now I growl when I'm pleased and wag my tail when I'm angry. Therefore I'm mad."

"I call it purring, not growling," said Alice.

"Call it what you like," said the Cat.

— Lewis Carroll

MADNESS
AND REALITY

WERE POPULISTS IRRATIONAL?

A study of populism quickly forces one into that area of cultural criticism known as psychohistory. In using such terms as "zany fringe," "much that was comic," and "sour, illiberal and ill tempered" in referring to populists, Richard Hofstadter, especially, focuses attention both on matters which fall under the rubric of psychology and on the problem of evaluating the gap between the subjective evaluation of reality by the actors in history and the objective paradigm imposed by the historian for understanding reality. The implied charge of irrationality in Hofstadter's analysis has drawn heavy fire from Norman Pollack, who suggests that the responsibility for discontent has been wrongly shifted from society to the populists.

The result has been that the extent of oppression has been increasingly minimized and finally glossed over. And because the basis for discontent has been almost totally denied, Populism became subject to the charge of double irrationality; not only was it regressive, but it also responded to non-existent grievances.[1]

The debate between Hofstadter and Pollack dramatizes the problem of evaluating myth versus reality as a central concern for the modern historian who wishes to transcend "factual," or narrative, history into the realm of motivation and interpretation, the "why" as well as the "who, what, where and when."

It is fitting to observe, however, that all historical writing, even the so-called scientific history, is value-laden and works with certain implied assumptions about human nature. For example, the filiopietistic historians of the nineteenth century, who often dealt with "great" events and "great" people as heroes, were in effect projecting role models with whom, it was assumed, ordinary people could feel a sense of identity; these historians also projected the "proper" normative values around mythic heroes as a response to such large moral questions as slavery or trustification. In heroes like Franklin and Jackson, one could find such qualities as honesty, industriousness and self-reliance, often with a touch of avariciousness, which molded the positive image of the nineteenth-century petty capitalist. In an earlier chapter, I have suggested that the later progressive historians, working with a dualism of "the people" versus "the interests," were committed to a view of inner human nature as inherently "good" but subject to corruption by "evil" social institutions, which at times led them paradoxically toward imagining an escape from institutions, like Huck Finn striking out for the territories.

Those matters which fall under the rubric of psychohistory, then, are not unique to the study of populism but, rather, pertain to all history writing. Having examined in the previous chapter the relation of ideology (understood as paradigm revolutions overlapping in time) to social reality (understood as a composite of forces in a state of evolution), in this chapter we shall deal with the relation of biological or instinctual reality to the other levels of reality and with culture generally. It will first be argued that the Freudian tradition, with its misplaced emphasis on instinctual forces, has seriously deformed and set back the cause of cultural criticism. Subsequently, a different perspective on psychohistory will be developed by integrating insights from Alfred Adler with the notion of history as overlapping paradigms.

Freud's influence has been so pervasive, both in his own right and in his influence on the so-called neo-Freudians, that much clarification is needed on the inadequacy of the Freudian point of view. First and foremost, Freud was a medical doctor, looking always for a physiological remedy for "mental illness." He attempted to reduce neurotic phenomena to a conflict between instincts and cultural prohibitions; but, of course, culture itself was a product of instinctual sublimation. Caught up in this circular logic, Freud overvalued the importance of instincts and by the same token ignored that middle level of reality which I am calling social reality. The overvaluation of biology is most apparent in Freud's analysis of female psychology. As evidence of his generalization that anatomy is destiny, he claimed that females are inherently uncreative because they do not suffer the guilt pangs of oedipal conflict as do males. There is barely a sense of history in Freud's outlook, only the notion of oedipal conflict repeated as generational conflict. At best, this is a highly truncated sense of history; and at worst, it is hopelessly irrelevant and misleading. Freudians who subscribe literally to this model ignore the realities of changing social systems and of conflicting world views as sources of internal individual and/or collective discord.

It is possible to discern within the Freudian scheme a highly elitist and conservative bias in a social sense, derived from identifying the superego as a necessary guardian of the status quo. The id in the model, with its animal-like aggressive drives, is analogous to Calvin's concept of human depravity as the inner nut of human nature. For both men, a highly ordered society was essential to control and channel the inner irrationality or depravity in man; and thus social elitism came easily to both Calvin and Freud. Calvinistic saints in New England usually turned out to be middle- and upper-class merchants and landowners; and Freud in turn identified with the norms of middle-class Vienna in opting for "civilization" as an ordering device for in-stinctual drives. The argument of this paragraph has been elaborated upon in an article, "The Prepared Heart," by Howard Feinstein, who comments on the ease with which a Calvinist America accepted the supposedly revolu-tionary doctrines of Freud.[2] Rollo May is perceptive in describing Freudi-anism as "Calvinism in Bermuda shorts."

Certain persons, known as left-Freudians, have used the Freudian model for advocating human liberation, freeing instinctual forces from the "prison" of civilization. For example, Herbert Marcuse, in *Eros and Civilization*, attempts to fuse Marx with Freud as an aid for viewing culture. The ten-dency among this group is to conceive of "natural" (instinctual) man outside of social institutions and in effect to ignore the institutional structure rather than transform it. Thus, this left-Freudian outlook places stress upon indi-vidual self-fulfillment in consonance with the nineteenth-century stress upon self-reliant individualism. Marcuse, however, has abandoned his earlier attempt to merge Freud with Marx.

Before turning to neo-Freudians, an observation about Carl Jung is in order. While Jung disagrees with Freud's alleged overemphasis upon the sex drive as a source of instinctual frustration, the basic model of the two men is very much alike. Jung expands the arena of genetic influence to include specific mental forms or myths residing in the collective unconscious, which somehow define the true inner self. Even if one accepts this highly ques-tionable role for genetics, the tendency in Jungian therapy is to find inner peace with the collective unconscious, ignoring the social reality which has presumably produced an unreal persona. The quest for inner liberation on an individualistic basis seems radical in its rejection of much in the status quo, as in the case of the left-Freudians, but it is extremely asocial in final analysis.

In conjunction with Jung, it is appropriate to digress further into those outlooks which come under the category of existentialism, again with ten-dencies to emphasize the search for inner freedom and authentic individual-ity and to seek liberation from the imperatives of culture. Carried to its logical extreme, this viewpoint also leads to a recognition of social reality only in the form of an iconoclastic rejection of this reality. While the existential viewpoint has antecedents far back in history, in Platonic idealism, in Christian mysticism and in many forms of romanticism, the prototype for this outlook within psychoanalytic circles is to be found in Jung (Sartre is an exception to this discussion), with Jung's prescription for man to abandon his worldly persona and to recapture, if possible, his inner self rooted in the collective unconscious. The existential point of view, akin to romanticism, is generally rudderless in the social world, unable to define a solution for the discontent which cries from the heart, often drifting either left or right on the cultural spectrum but responding anarchistically against imperatives for social organization and responsibility. Even though the varying moods (from joy to black despair) of romantics and existentialists serve as useful gauges for revealing and measuring cultural dissonance, their viewpoint has not been helpful for a deeper understanding of the social process in the field of psychohistory.

In much social science analysis, the neo-Freudians are more directly significant than Freud himself. The problem with this group is that they try to ride two horses at once; they retain some version of instinctualism while projecting theories of the ways in which social reality impinges on individual consciousness. Erich Fromm, for example, spoke of the internalization of external reality with his observation that "the social character internalizes external necessities and thus harnesses human energy for the task of a given economic and social system."[3] Even here, the emphasis is upon external reality as a deterministic force on the subjective personality without reference to the creative role of the individual in forming or choosing new paradigms for viewing reality. Not only does Fromm subscribe to a version of social determinism, but he retains from Freud the notion of instinctual determinism. This is evident when he digresses to excoriate Alfred Adler in *Escape from Freedom.*

And while we think of the wish for power as an irrational impulse to rule over others, Adler looked entirely at it from the rational side and speaks of the wish for power as an adequate reaction which has the function of protecting the person against dangers springing from his insecurity and inferiority. Adler, here, as always, cannot see beyond purposeful and rational human determinations of human behavior; and though he has contributed valuable insights into the intricacies of motivation, he remains always on the surface and never descends into the abyss of irrational impulses as Freud has done.[4]

More recently, in *The Crisis in Psychoanalysis,* Fromm criticizes Freud on several counts, especially for his social conservatism, yet he hails him for founding the "science of human irrationality" in developing psychoanalytic theory.[5] As will be more fully evident after we turn to Adler, it is less than helpful to speak as Fromm does of the "abyss of irrational impulses." For this point of view denies or obscures the social basis for ambivalence and tension caused by conflicting conceptual frameworks. Furthermore, Fromm grossly oversimplifies Adler's outlook in suggesting that his views can be subsumed under the "wish for power" as the controlling factor in human life.

Of special interest in this study are the views of Erik Erikson, who like other neo-Freudians combines a biological and a social environmental model. His biological scheme is more complex than Freud's in that he sees human growth taking place in essential developmental stages and thus avoids an overemphasis on childhood sexual trauma as the root of mental disorders. He is insightful in delineating the identity crisis in individuals as they suffer from role confusion in a social world, but he generally fails to relate role confusion to the larger paradigm revolutions experienced by individuals. Thus, Erikson's strength has lain in elucidating the development of an individual, not in explaining mass movements or in discerning the relation of an individual's identity crises to the social process. For practical purposes, the Erikson approach reduces to a "great man" interpretation of history, an approach consistent with nineteenth-century individualism.

My criticism of Erikson is sustained by a report from a 1971 meeting between him and forty leading historians gathered at the invitation of Arthur Schlesinger, Jr. A sampling of opinions reported in the *New York Times* suggests deep differences. Erikson himself stressed the need for studies such as his own of Luther and Gandhi, essentially the biographical approach. Columbia's Meyer Shapiro asked again and again for examples of how psychology contributes to an understanding of collective rather than individual behavior; and he apparently received no satisfactory answer. Professor Harold C. Syrett asked to be excused: "I'm an irrelevant man as far as this meeting is concerned. I came here as an empty vessel, and now it's overflowing with confusion."[6]

In addition to the psychoanalytic views on psychology, there is a range of outlooks which fall under the heading of social behaviorism. At one end of this spectrum is the Stimulus-Response point of view developed by J.B. Watson and later by B.F. Skinner. S-R psychology has been widely criticized for failing to include the human organism or ideology as an intervening factor between stimulus and response. This psychology is perhaps useful for studying habit formation and behavior reinforcement; however, this model cannot take into account the ambivalence in ideology as an element of complexity in the choice-making process and cannot explain the basis for a new choice in the first place. Certain neobehaviorists have developed more sophisticated theoretical outlooks in such areas as learning theory and group process; however, they too fail to relate to macro-processes in history in terms of overlapping paradigms.

In a certain fundamental way, Karl Marx reflects an adherence to S-R psychology in his dictum that social being determines social consciousness and in his view that exploitation and/or deprivation produces responses toward reform and revolution. There is a tendency in Marx to deprecate anomalies with such terms as "lumpen proletariat," for example, rather than to develop a more adequate explanation of the varieties of psychological strategies that people employ in striving to overcome dissonance and aliena-tion and to achieve a sense of harmony.

There is not an intent here to equate Marx with J.B. Watson; for the entire Marxian model is comprehensive, taking into account various levels of reality in a way that the Watsonian behaviorists do not. Actually, Marx-ists would be well armed to project a version of psychology which takes into account the ambiguity in myths and symbols arising from conflicting modes of social consciousness and ambivalence in individuals and movements. The noted English Marxist of the 1930s, Christopher Caudwell, notes the differ-ing meanings of "freedom" in different social systems.

The "free" market—the blind lawlessness by which laws of anarchy brutally assert themselves—has governed the bourgeois mind for four centuries. For four centuries, it has idealized one freedom, freedom from all social restric-tions except that by which the bourgeois class lives.[7]

Again, Caudwell observes: "Thus, a slave owning society sees freedom, not in absence of coercive relations but in a special coercive relation, that of will."[8] Caudwell is perceptive in seeing that meaning varies with paradigms. But in *Illusion and Reality,* he fails to develop a theory of the coexistence of conflicting symbolic meanings as an extension of a conflict theory of history, and he fails to note that the internalization of symbolic conflict creates a need for psychological mechanisms which will reduce internalized dissonance. (An exception to these observations regarding Marxist criticism is found in the work of Arnold Hauser, such as his *The Philosophy of Art History.*)

Another variant in behaviorist psychology comes from the progressives of the twentieth century, from such persons as George Herbert Mead and John Dewey, whose outlooks cast a long shadow on the present. Building upon William James's notion about the individual relativity of truth, these men developed systems involving situational psychology and morality. Necessarily, they came to view "human nature" as being highly elastic and variable in its potential for responding to widely differing socially defined situations; and thus, they have departed from the Freudian notion of an unchanging inner personality. Their difficulty arises with a tendency to define "social situation" in terms of small groups, for example, the family, the peer group or the immediate community, a view that has led to the development of transactional analysis. The result of this definition of "social" has been the exclusion of changing social systems and conflicting ideologies as facets of the social situation. Even though these progressives and their followers have developed new theories about the significance of symbolic and nonverbal forms of communication as forms of transactional interaction, they have tended to accept the larger status quo as a given and have failed to get at the root of ambivalence and ambiguity in paradigm conflict.

Often an instinctualist premise creeps into the progressive outlook, through the back door, so to speak. In the spirit of the rationalistic Enlightenment, these writers tend to assume that human nature is essentially "good" and "rational" or "born free" prior to the impact of social institutions; and thus, it becomes easy for progressives to hail "primitive simplicity" and "small group democracy" as techniques for resolving social conflicts. The assumption of primitivism among progressives has fed the romantic dream of unfettered individualism and escape from institutions, which easily was transformed into nostalgia for the political outlook of petty capitalism. This outlook was even present, for example, as an element in the Social Gospel outlook of Walter Rauschenbush, who deplored the church's departure from the primitivism of early Christians. Paradoxically, opposite assumptions of innate "goodness" and inherent "evil" as the instinctual essence of human nature have both contributed to conservatism, each in a different way; one through primitivism (romantic escape) and the other via elitism (authoritarian law and order) as American culture has tended to exhibit ambivalence between a "return to Eden" and Hamiltonian autocracy.

While progressives tended to let instinctualism in through the back door and to become involved in debates over the relative influence of instincts versus social environment, more recent social behaviorists have increasingly come to view genetic inheritance as a limiting factor in explaining behavior. At one extreme, there is a tendency to completely ignore the "instinctive" needs as factors in social variation. This point is succinctly stated in Don Martindale's *Social Life and Cultural Change:* "The core of social behaviorism is its theory of social interactionism which treats all social behavior as learned rather than instinctive."[9] Rudolph Dreikurs, a noted Adlerian psychiatrist, makes a similar observation while allowing for interplay between instincts and culture.

In themselves, hunger and sexuality are forces without direction. The individual personality alone sets a goal before the "instincts" and gives them special content. All the complications and conflicts involved in the "satisfaction of instincts" arise in this way.[10]

This outlook, as set forth by Dreikurs, serves as a starting point and as an introduction to the work of Alfred Adler. And Adler's outlook, when coupled with the notion of history as overlapping paradigms in a changing social reality, produces a special version of psychohistory.

Adler not only rejected the Freudian notion of internalized personality structure, but he also developed a positive theory emphasizing social environment as the factor which accounts for variations in personality types or life styles. In some ways, Adler is close to Mead, who viewed psychology in the context of social interaction; but Adler himself saw individuals interacting in a wider world of communities around work, love (sex), and friendships rather than the more narrow world of dyadic interaction stressed by Mead. It is noteworthy, too, that Adler is not easily open to the charge leveled against behavior modificationists that they would have the individual conform to existing norms; for Adler was consciously a socialist and saw various kinds of social reform as a precondition for successful individual therapy.

For Adler, all inherited capabilities, the physical as well as the so-called instinctual ones, are employed strategically by persons to accomplish certain goals they set before themselves. Critics of Adler point to his theory of organ inferiority as an idiosyncrasy; however, he is in effect arguing that a person with some physical deficiency is not bound by fate but can often overcome or manipulate the deficiency for success in social relations. The following observations of Adler describe his views on the social nature of man, views which are very much at odds with Freud's emphasis on the intrapsychic tensions between id, ego and super ego:

The psychic life is a complex of aggressive and security finding activities whose final purpose is to guarantee the continued existence on this earth of the human organism, and to enable him to securely accomplish this development. If we grant this premise, then further considerations grow out of it, which we deem necessary for a true conception of the soul. *We cannot imagine a psychic life which is isolated* [emphasis Adler's]. We can only imagine a psychic life bound up in its environment, which receives stimuli from the outside and somehow answers them, which disposes of capabilities and powers which are not fitted to secure the organism against the ravages of the outer world, or somehow bind it to these forces, in order to guarantee its life. The relationships which suggest themselves from this are many. They have to do with the organism itself, the peculiarities of human beings, their physical nature, their assets and their defects. These are entirely relative concepts, since it is entirely a relative matter whether a power or an organ shall be considered as asset or liability. These values can be given the situation in which the individual finds himself. It is very well known that the foot of man is, in a sense, a degenerate hand. In an animal which had to climb this would be a decided disadvantage; for man who must walk on the flat ground, it is of such advantage that no one would prefer a "normal" degenerate foot.[11]

Since Adler's time, new theories have been advanced dealing with relationships between inheritance and behavior. Generally, it has been observed that from any given genotype there is a wide range of phenotypes and that it is difficult to assign a fixed effect as flowing from a certain genotype; hence the improbable connection between skin color and intelligence or between sexual anatomy and creativity.

Recently, there has been a resurgence of interest in the instinctive or innate aspects of human life, most notably in the field of linguistics around Noam Chomsky and in anthropology around the structuralism of Levi-Strauss. Without passing judgment upon these newer theories in detail, we can agree in a general way that there are inherited capabilities which include the use of language and the power of abstract thought, involving such concepts as cause and effect, equivalence and similarity (hence metaphor). However, it is important not to fall into the logic that instincts are destiny and that man is fatalistically controlled by his "deep structures." Rather, various instinctive capabilities are employed variously in different cultures, and cultures and social change, in turn, are *social* phenomena to be understood in terms of history as overlapping paradigms. It has been too easy to evade a study of the social character of human existence by a preoccupation with the primal nature of man, expressed as primitivism in the arts or as instinctualism in psychology.

A central facet of Adler's model emphasizes the notion that human activities, thoughts and personality types can best be understood in the context of people carrying out general tasks and striving for specific goals. Adler speaks of three tasks—work, love and friendship—around which human activities are deployed. Later, I should like to add a fourth task, namely, a striving to achieve a coherent cognitive world view; however, let us persist for the present with defining more fully the Adlerian model before making qualifications. Around the general tasks of work, love and friendship, individuals develop specific goals in terms of occupation, marriage involving sexual gratification, and developing a circle of friends. Thus, a typical individual committed to the nineteenth-century petty capitalist paradigm might strive to become a successful independent farmer or businessman, to marry and live in a patriarchal family structure, and to enjoy friends primarily within a community defined by church membership; and such a typical person would adopt strategies for reaching these goals, strategies which become reflected in personality traits, which in turn define an individual's overt identity or life style.

For Adler, personality types emerge as kinds of strategies available for meeting the problems a person encounters in social reality, problems defined variously depending on a person's cognitive view of reality (which again is at variance with Freud's anal and oral types arising from instinctual repression). In one essay in his early writing, Adler catalogues a number of types, each in effect describing a tactical approach in social relations. He lists the following complexes: Inferiority (submissiveness, sense of failure); Superiority (will to power, domineering attitudes, egocentricity, godlike self-image); Oedipus (not universal as with Freud, but a part of the pampered-child syndrome); Redeemer (messianic); Proof (perfectionism); Predestination (chosen people); Polonius (the "as if" illusion); Exclusion (withdrawal, flight from community); Leader (king of the mountain); Spectator (passivity, apathy); and No (rebellion, negativism).[12] It should be noted that Adler later reduced this list to the two mechanisms involving superiority and inferiority and to the interplay of these complexes. Adler holds that every individual, by virtue of dependency as an infant, tends to have a feeling of inferiority and that the process of growing up involves a constant striving to overcome this inferiority. Depending on the total situation from which an individual emerges, his degree of success in overcoming inferiority will range from total failure to total egocentricity. In this view, a neurotic person can be defined as one who is insecure and overly bound to social norms, thus denying individual perceptivity; whereas, a psychotic person moves into a private world of egocentricity, operating with insufficient social feeling or consideration of social norms of any kind. Adler speaks of the superiority complex as overcompensation for inferiority, as a kind of masked inferiority which in men is often seen as masculine superiority. Adler's definition of democracy in interpersonal relations involves a fine balance between becoming meekly submissive or powerfully autocratic. The democratic individual is one who enjoys a feeling of community with fellow human beings, both drawing support from others and also playing a creative role in social relations, for which Adler uses the term, *gemeinschaftsgefühl,* as an ideal or normative value.

Adler's stress on the primacy of community in human life is central to his general outlook. His notion of gemeinschaftsgefühl can be translated variously as social feeling, social solidarity, sense of fellowship in the human community or as the emotional counterpart of movements.

What we call justice and righteousness, and consider most valuable in all human character, is essentially nothing more than the fulfillment of the conditions which arise in the social needs of mankind. These conditions give shape to the soul and direct its activity; responsibility, loyalty, frankness, love of truth, and the like virtues which have been set up and retained only by the universally valid principle of communal life. . . . In the course of our demonstrations it will become increasingly evident that no adequate man can grow up without cultivating a deep sense of his fellowship in humanity and practicing the art of being a human being.[13]

The need and feeling for community pervades all facets of society, according to Adler.

The compulsion toward the community and communal life exists in institutions whose forms we need not entirely understand, as in religion, where the sanctification of communal formula serves as a bond between members of the community. . . . The communal life of man antedates the individual life of man. In the history of human civilization no form of life whose foundations were not laid communally can be found. No human being ever appeared except in a community of human beings.[14]

The emphasis in Adler on the inseparability of the individual and the community runs counter to Freud's vision of the individual with internalized tensions which are discharged externally through sublimation. Rudolph Dreikurs has explicitly compared the two viewpoints:

For Freud, all human conflicts are intra-personal, caused by opposing conflicts within the personality structure. . . . For Adler, all problems are interpersonal. This implies a different emphasis on both the origin of conflicts and on therapeutic procedure. For Freud, the maladjustment with its consequent disturbance of human relationships originates in the inner-personal conflicts, while for Adler the inner conflicts express disturbed human relationships. Freud emphasized the inner needs, while Adler emphasized the significance of the attitude toward others.[15]

For the historian, the Adlerian point of view, with its emphasis on community as a central aspect of human experience, offers a special perspective on movements and associations; and at the same time, the relative sterility for historians of psychologies based on Freud or Erikson is evident in their tendency to turn inward into the internalized tension of individuals.

In projecting goals and aspirations as the cornerstone around which thought and behavior are organized, the Adlerians see much of the anxiety in our particular culture as derived from failure to fulfill aspirations, a failure which might appear as overambition on the part of individuals with regard to social goals. Whether this apparent overambition is due to unrealistic aspirations on the part of individuals or to niggardly possibilities within the social structure is always a matter for investigation; but regardless of one's judgment on this matter, individuals suffer from anxiety and frustration. Somewhat as Freud theorized that people develop defense mechanisms to allay tensions, Adler saw individuals adopting adaptive strategies (reflected as personality types) to blunt feelings of anxiety, but in Adler's view these measures are always related to the larger goals of the individual. The adaptive measures in the Adlerian model can better be seen as *offense mechanisms,* strategies either for realizing present goals or for achieving success (even as a successful criminal) within a new version of reality and a new sense of ego-identity.

According to Adler, an initial response to anxiety involves either choosing new personality traits or accentuating present traits, as the case may be. Adler preferred to view these traits as complexes. Terminology seems unimportant as long as the function of personality types is understood as an offense mechanism for confronting the world, including even "withdrawal" as a paradoxical tactic of confrontation. Furthermore, these complexes do not exist in the abstract, simply as psychic mechanisms; but rather, they filter through and attach themselves to social institutions and provide norms for life styles and personality patterns, often becoming attached to particular cognitive views of the world. Thus, such social organizations as the family, church, or political party tend in their concrete manifestations (1) to provide the individual with a commitment to a paradigm and (2) to institutionalize norms for life styles which reflect a deployment of one or more offense mechanisms or personality strategies.

It is of passing interest to note that Adler was influenced by Hans Vaihinger's *The Philosophy of As If* toward a view that each person's cognitive conception of the world is necessarily a fictive, mental abstraction about reality which is not identical with reality. This view made it possible for Adler to understand behavior, especially defiant behavior in an individual. as a product of the special fictive world view of each individual. He understood that a person chooses a world view which serves his strategic purposes, a point stressed by R.D. Laing in explaining schizophrenia. While this outlook is helpful for understanding the idiosyncratic behavior of any given individual, Adler generally failed to exploit the fact that "fictions" are shared (since people have shared experiences in social reality) and hence that common social outlooks develop, which we in this study call paradigms.

Earlier, we noted Adler's definition of the primary tasks in life as work, friendship and love, the essential human tasks around which specific goals are formed. To this list one must add the task of achieving an intellectual view of the world, a cognitive understanding of reality. In the case of inarticulate or uneducated people, the world view may be expressed in simple terms around prevailing symbols and myths; but a simple view (low culture) may be no different qualitatively than a sophisticated weltanschauung (high culture), in that both may express affinity for the same paradigm. To deny the groping for a world view as an essential task for every person is to be oblivious to the distinction between man and lower animals or between thinking man and man the idiot. The assumption that man understands "reality" in terms of intellectual constructs or paradigms is dramatized by Gene Wise in *American Historical Explanations,* in which he illustrates the meaning of idiocy with Benjy from Faulkner's *The Sound and the Fury.* Viktor Frankl implicitly makes the same argument for a "will to meaning" as the core assumption of logotherapy, although his approach is ahistorical and unrelated to larger paradigms.

Adler has described the social character of man's existence as an axiomatic assumption for psychology. An additional assumption, implicit in Adler but developed more fully by Leon Festinger, is helpful for a dynamic social psychology. This is the assumption that man strives for consonance in life, or that there exists in man a tropism for homeostasis. The concept of homeostasis is widely employed in such disparate fields as cell biology and economics; but it is especially useful in psychology to describe man's quest for psychic harmony. Using the situation of the cigarette smoker who knows that smoking causes cancer, Festinger notes that the alternatives facing such a person range from stopping smoking to developing various kinds of rationalizations that neutralize the knowledge about cancer and thereby permit continued smoking in harmony with new rationalizations. This situation illustrates the dynamics of paradigm revolutions. As discrepancies or contradictions appear in an existing paradigm, new strategies come into play, either as new forms of behavior or new theories about reality or both, to create a new sense of harmony. In developing a new theory about reality, a given person, for the sake of harmony, must repress or reject his previous belief structure or alter previous behavior patterns.

The notion of repression and/or rejection of a social outlook defines a new version of the unconscious (or barely conscious) that is at variance with the Freudian concept of instinctual drives as the core of the unconscious. In this view, based on Adlerianism, ambivalence can be understood; for often emotional ties exist with a repressed paradigm, and thus it is possible for a person to switch his commitment or "flip-flop" from one outlook to another as life experience changes. The striving for consonance at times produces an effect other than that of making a clear choice between paradigms and repressing the rejected outlook. This other alternative takes the form of rationalizing opposing views into some form of ambiguity to obscure conflict and to create a semblance of harmony; however, ambiguity is less a resolution of conflict than an intellectual obfuscation aimed at papering over anomalies in the social system.

While this study is concerned primarily with macro-movements in American history, we must be aware that larger anomalies and contradictions are reflected in minute ways as crises in an individual's life style or identity, as tensions in immediate relations with others, or as problems in finding meaning in work. While helpers (counselors, psychiatrists, et al.) may help people find practical expedients in these kinds of crises, the larger meaning of such crises can be fully understood only in terms of the state of paradigm conflict at a given time. Thus, a theory of social process which links the social structure and the individual in a symbiotic relationship makes it possible to move back and forth from macro- to micro-levels of human experience.

A typical person must live in both a micro- and a macro-society, striving for homeostasis and/or ego esteem* in personal relationships and yet being forced to alter personal life styles and strategies to deal with changing social reality and paradigm conflict. Thus, personality strategies adopted at one point in life may prove to be ill-suited at another stage. Obviously, the temper tantrum tactic employed by a child for attention and control over others usually fails for an adult. Likewise, a person who adopts an authoritarian personality in an occupation as a petty enterpriser may face a double crisis if his business goes bankrupt; for he may be forced to find a new occupation in which his personality does not "fit," and his difficulties in meeting these changes may evoke great emotional anguish. At times, of course, persons choose to adopt personality patterns which are judged to be neurotic or nonnormative, or behavior patterns which are antisocial or criminal in nature. Obviously, the range of human responses to defeat and frustration or to the need for change are various and finally unique with each individual. However, to the extent that social goals are shared and to the extent that personality traits are likewise similar for significant portions of a population, it is possible to understand the emergence and growth of mass movements in terms of shared experiences and shared offense mechanisms.

It is a central argument of this study that certain social goals tend to be apotheosized in any historical era, for example, the independent farmer or the small businessman under petty capitalism. It also is possible to suggest that predominant personality strategies emerge in each era as well. For example, the autocratic individualist of capitalist society was presented in exaggerated form in the fictional Captain Ahab in *Moby Dick*. If certain personality patterns emerge widely as reactions in a shared social crisis, it is possible then to assert the existence of a special character for a certain group; and it is possible to make assertions about "national character"— always with great risk, due to the variegated social structure of any given

---

*The concept of "ego esteem," implying a tendency for satisfaction based on a consistent and coherent life style, flows from Adler. He is often criticized by Freudians for being an "ego psychologist" and for ignoring the unconscious; however, both Freud and Anna Freud finally devoted more attention to the ego and the deployment of defense mechanisms somewhat in the Adlerian manner.

nation and due to the coexistence of competing cultural patterns at any given time. In any event, character formation flows from strategic responses to experiential problems. Thus it is inappropriate to treat "character" as an independent variable in the Max Weber style; rather, one should look to the interplay of cognitive framework with life experiences which generate a recognizable modal character under certain circumstances. I have already pointed to the much-celebrated American optimism, a nineteenth-century character trait, as a function of both the individualist paradigm and the social reality of an expanding market associated with the frontier and an influx of new immigrants. In the previous chapter, we noted the scapegoatism, millennialism and apocalypticism which emerged as social responses, especially among frustrated mugwumps and bryanists; and while these responses are not character traits as such, this attempted escape from history implies a withdrawal complex as a facet of a widely accepted life style.

On the larger scene, society is always changing and paradigms are continually emerging and overlapping in time, leaving a given person to make choices among major outlooks and social movements at any time in his life. Even though a person may consciously choose a certain view of the world, he may also unknowingly be influenced by past paradigms surviving in the present. For example, certain Christian values such as "brotherhood," surviving perhaps from primitive communal paradigms, are in contradiction to the every-man-for-himself value in a competitive world and may cause ambivalence in a person's value system. When there is a massive shift within a population from one paradigm to another, a revolution in social consciousness occurs, implying a massive reevaluation or transformation in the meaning of social and individual problems and in the meaning of received myths and symbols. This was the process at work as populism struggled to emerge as a new paradigm in America. Populists were pulled between a tendency to look back to a restoration of the laissez-faire world and to look ahead in the direction of a socialist restructuring of social life, causing ambivalence and "flip-flopping" as persons moved into and out of populist movements.

If we assume that ambivalence, ambiguity and dissonance are a rule of human life for people caught in conceptual revolutions, and if we assume at the same time that humans strive for harmony or relief of tension, it is clear that life in a general way devolves into an effort to produce concord out of discord, yet with new discord always being injected from the realm of the objective social process. The resolution of discord takes the form of a coupled process of meeting reality with psychological offense mechanisms and cognitive reorientation.

It is difficult to overstress the contention that the psychological strategies do not operate abstractly, but rather in a social context. For example, as Festinger's study *When Prophecy Fails* indicates, millennialism (the redeemer complex) was associated both with a social organization and with behavior which flowed logically from the expectation that the world would end. While Festinger in his small sample failed to uncover examples of millennialists who turned to populism or social radicalism when the second coming failed to materialize, the logic of his psychology would allow for such persons to easily embrace Social Gospel radicalism as their next step in cognitive reorientation. This hypothetical example illustrates the circuitous way in which people act and react in the process of arriving at social radicalism. A later chapter will deal with the impact of various cultural movements, especially religious and ethnic ones, which acted as factors either impeding or propelling the rise of populism in the upper midwestern states.

Once the view is embraced that community is prior to the individual but that the individual makes choices in response to the community in which he finds himself, the traditional dichotomy between the individual and the group fades into obscurity. Any social organization serves initially to provide gemeinschaftsgefuhl and strength for persons with shared outlooks and psychological strategies; but in the long run, organizations, like individuals, are caught in paradigm revolutions and perforce must deal with schismatic ("schizophrenic") tendencies within their ranks, even though such tendencies may be delayed by bureaucratic rigidities. Populism is a case in point; for as one prescription for reform failed to allay problems and anxiety, new reforms were advocated and justified ideologically in ways which made for conflict within the organized groups. The shifting currents and the persistent leftward tendencies in populism again and again made for schisms within the ranks of specific organizations, leading at times to bureaucratic realignments and at other times toward a dying movement and the need for forming a new organization.

While individuals tend to achieve harmony and consonance by rejection or repression of either the new or the old paradigm competing for attention at a given time, it is rare that a person can stabilize a state of harmony; for the social process continues and social problems, as defined by at least two conflicting paradigms, continue to protrude into life. Thus, the relevance of any particular world view is continually being tested, and this testing process is sensed most acutely by those who are somehow frustrated or failing in achieving life goals.

Persons who respond to failure and frustration by adopting a new personality strategy (in conjunction with a fictive world view) which leads to social dysfunction are ordinarily considered to be pathological cases; however, even such persons may be succeeding in manipulating others at a micro-level to assuage their egos and thus succeeding in certain short-range ways. The point must be stressed that the definition of pathological behavior varies from paradigm to paradigm as normative behavior and personality types vary, making for a social rather than a medical definition of "mental illness," in line with the argument of Thomas Szasz in *The Myth of Mental Illness.* While a person who imagines that he is Julius Caesar may be readily seen as living with a defective personal world view, the point must not be lost that all paradigms are fictive (in the sense of being conceptual constructs) and that collective judgments finally emerge as to the relevance and usefulness of a given world view for solving social problems. This view again raises the question as to who was "zany," the populists or Richard Hofstadter, if the question can be posed in an either-or form. In any event, the judgment here would hold that this question can only be resolved in terms of broader judgments as to the relevancy of competing paradigms.

If individuals tend to be "mixed up" and social movements "schizophrenic" in their confused relations to conflicting social paradigms, it is less than helpful to speak of this situation as "irrational." Erich Fromm speaks of a "pathology of normalcy" in the modern world as a part of a "chronic, low-grade schizophrenia which is generated in the cybernated, technological society of today and tomorrow."[16] In this same context, Fromm speaks of the "underworld of the unconscious" as the source of irrationality. It seems unnecessary to posit an "underworld of the unconscious" as a mystical explanation for the "low-grade schizophrenia" which exists; rather, it is possible to suggest that one or the other of conflicting world views becomes repressed and remains unexamined as a source of values and as a basis for aspirations and behavior, in contrast with the Freudian notion of the unconscious projected by Fromm. This is not to say that it is easy to discover the basis for behavior, thought, and emotions, for all these manifestations emerge partly from repressed or unadmitted world views and values, which stand in the way of insight. But the potential for insight is always present when the full range of social environment is taken into account, including the fact of paradigm revolutions. In any event, ferreting out the motivations of individuals and movements requires social analysis of culture, not a retreat into theories of an "underworld of the unconscious" such as Fromm makes with his Freudian baggage.

The implications for understanding populism by means of a social psychology based on insights from Adler and Festinger run counter to the implications suggested by Hofstadter and add a much needed corrective to the idealization of populists on the part of Norman Pollack. Once the notion of overlapping paradigms is introduced as part of a model for understanding history, it is possible to understand the ambivalence and vacillation of the populists along with the schismatic tendencies which appeared in the various mass movements.

Obviously, not all people who were disillusioned or anxious over their life circumstances in an emerging industrial America became populists, certainly not as the first step in the process of cognitive reorientation. Indeed, the American Dream was not given up easily, and initial reactions were generally to retain the hope in the Dream. The complexes listed by Adler describe almost without elaboration the strategies employed by middle-class Americans, strategies which imply formation of personality types as well as social movements. There was the "no," or negativistic reaction, often associated with mugwumpism and with bryanism. There was the "withdrawal" reaction into family and private concerns (kinder, küche and kirche) among persons hoping that social conflict would go away. Some, notably certain religious sects, adopted a "messianic" or "chosen people" attitude as a source of psychic support; and still others become rigidly perfectionist, a mechanism linked with a sense of superiority and a dogged determination to live with the Dream.*

In spite of the deployment of offense strategies to gain psychic harmony and to achieve goals, the world of objective reality continues to intrude into the lives of individuals and social movements. In other words, the industrial revolution continues, people are dislocated, they suffer from disappointments and unfulfilled aspirations. There is pressure to adopt a new weltanschauung as the frustration and anxiety recur, even though a person may have developed psychic mechanisms against changing his world view. Again referring to Heraclitus' observation about stepping into the river, it is not just the river (social reality) that changes but also the individual, who approaches a type of frustration differently the second (or tenth) time from the first time. Thus, an individual may finally abandon his psychic defenses against redefining reality and seek to achieve cognitive consonance with a more appropriate world view; and in this process, he becomes a part of the process of paradigm revolution.

*The perfectionist complex as a support for individual success in competitive striving is of special interest in American culture, especially as it relates to transcendentalism. The high moral idealism of the perfectionist is easily identified; however, the negative side of the complex has been too little noted. Dr. Rudolph Dreikurs, speaking as an Adlerian, has referred to the pathology of perfectionism in noting the paradox of morally upright persons becoming hateful and violent. The typical perfectionist stresses what he *is* rather than what he *does* in social relations, which brings about an attitude of aloofness toward others rather than an effort to be useful. Because he is committed to autonomous individualism and thus lacks a theory of social forces, such a typical person is prone to become a hater when social relations go sour or when social reality seems to diverge from idealized patterns. Witness the case of Roger Chillingworth in *The Scarlet Letter*. Recall that the sense of mission associated with Puritanism has led to the warning: "Beware a Calvinist just off his knees"; likewise, it can be observed of nineteenth century idealists: "Beware a transcendentalist just out of the woods." Dr. Dreikurs prescribed "the courage to be imperfect" as an antidote to perfectionism with its vanity and false sense of superiority.

As people make cognitive leaps from one paradigm to another, they do so incompletely. Old values and old personality traits persist and contribute to ambiguity as patterns of eclectic personality types emerge between old and new cultural configurations. For example, among the small sector of populists who made the leap from laissez-faire individualism to socialism, it was not unusual to find many who continued to exhibit messianic or ascetic personality traits, even though these traits may have been developed in their period of commitment to petty capitalism. As disputes arose among social-ists and as failures in organizing a new movement built up, frustrations mounted; and there were tendencies, even among socialists, to vacillate back to laissez-faire cultural patterns in a search for psychic harmony.

As populists organized into visible mass movements, they may have felt that their new world view was more relevant to their needs and problems; yet a new element of conflict and dissonance arose when a polarization de-veloped between themselves and their peers who chose not to become popu-lists. Indeed, there was conflict and sometimes violence between the radicals and the conformists wherever populist movements existed. To this day, a country road intersection in Goodhue County, Minnesota, is known as "shotgun corner"; it was there that a group of nonpopulists stood armed to prevent their neighbors from attending a Nonpartisan League meeting in 1918. Especially in communities where they were in a minority, populists felt a pressure to reduce tension by reverting to their old views, causing many persons to flip-flop out of the populist organizations.

Populist ambivalence about conflicting views of reality explains the ten-dency of some of them to vacillate. Examples are legion of those who re-verted to an old outlook, back to the mentality of economic individualism and Jacksonian petty capitalism. In reverting to an old view of reality, they repressed the new paradigm and often became the leading tormentors of their former comrades in deviance. A well-known example of this tendency is the case of Tom Watson of Georgia, a tolerant populist in the 1890s who turned savagely on Negroes, Catholics, and Jews in the twentieth century, especially in the pages of his monthly magazine, *The Jeffersonian.* Another example is that of Algie Simons of Milwaukee, who left the Socialist Party to join a Loyalty Committee in the official witch-hunt against socialists during World War I. Of course, ambivalence and vacillation are aspects of the larger social process, not just of populism. The phenomenon of vacilla-tion between paradigms is nicely illustrated by William Chace in "Ezra Pound and the Marxist Temptation," in which Pound's ambivalence between political radicalism and cultural elitism is outlined, concluding with Pound's final resolution of turning ideologically to Mussolini rather than Marx.[17]

The matter of flip-flopping because of ambivalence about competing world views raises a question in the evaluation of populism. Is a given person still a populist after he has reverted to bryanism? Was he only a populist as he was gravitating away from the laissez-faire outlook toward socialism? Did the "fascist" traits sometimes observed in populist organizations arise from the laissez-faire pole or the socialist pole within the spectrum of populist ideology? The version of psychohistory projected here makes it possible to answer these questions within a coherent frame of reference.

In a sense, any definition of populism is arbitrary, as with the cat's definition of purring in the excerpt from *Alice in Wonderland* quoted as the epigraph of this chapter. A distinction must be made between the "ism" and the multitude of people who have adhered to the "ism." Populism as a general movement, encompassing several discrete organizations, moved away from the simple iconoclastic bryanism of the laissez-faire syndrome toward the pole of socialist reform and values, coming to rest in the twentieth century mainly as a radical version of a Christian commonwealth ideology. The distinction between a bryanist and a Tory populist was often a narrow one, lying primarily in the willingness of the Tory populist to form a coalition with others in labor and farm circles with more positive proposals for reform; through such coalitions, even a populist with a laissez-faire mentality was inclined to be pulled leftward by his associations. In the upper Midwest in the twentieth century, the leftward direction was most observable in those organizations in which socialists emerged as leaders, a factor most pronounced in the Farmer-Labor Party in Minnesota. These tendencies will be examined in more detail in later chapters.

While the "ism" as a movement was one matter, the individuals who adhered to organizations within the movement were another. Out of tendencies to vacillate, certain individuals could be populists in one decade, Democrats or Republicans in another, and then populists again in the following decade. Indeed, in the upper Midwest states this precise pattern was probably followed by a host of populists, who drifted from the populism of the 1890s into accepting the promises of progressive reform after 1900, and then moved in large numbers into the Nonpartisan League after 1914. An exception to the pattern would be the narrow spectrum of socialists, who emerged after 1900 and expanded their influence far beyond their numbers.

This discussion illustrates the difficulty in defining this or that person as a populist, even though it is possible to define in a general way the meaning of the "ism." Defining historical populism as an ambivalence between conservative and radical poles, a researcher can provide empirical evidence to support any and all perspectives on the movement. It is possible to find examples of frustrated petty capitalists, as Hofstadter did, or of protosocialists, as did Pollack. It is possible to search out unattractive traits of persons within populist movements who turned sour and intolerant because continued commitment to their world view brought only frustration; and it is possible to find large numbers who worked with courage and tolerance toward reforms and who almost succeeded in achieving a paradigm revolution of their own before the progressives co-opted some of their specific reforms and deflected their revolutionary momentum.

The fact that a selective approach will yield empirical evidence which can be assembled to sustain any one of the various theories on populism does not vitiate, however, the larger hypothesis set forth in this study: that populists were breaking away from rugged individualism and petty capitalism and moving toward the pole of socialism, and that great individual ambivalence and vacillation existed within the overall movement.

If the vacillation of some individuals took them out of the realm of populist movements and back into "normal" channels of political expression, this vacillation can hardly be attributed to populism per se but rather stemmed from the cultural confusion coming from the state of paradigm transformation in the larger society. The case of Tom Watson is often used to "prove" that populism had its "dark" side. Certainly, Tom Watson showed his dark side as he switched to another side of his ambivalent self; however, this switch speaks not for an inherent tendency in populism but for the continued magnetism of the individualist syndrome in America as a source of cultural values, which still operated in the divided hearts and minds of persons such as Watson.

The main contention of this chapter is that ideological and cultural ambivalence is to be understood in terms of the larger process of paradigm transformation rather than in terms of the Freudian ego-id dichotomy or in terms of Erik Erikson's view of identity crises in a static world. In a world of overlapping paradigms, persons tend to repress one side or another of their ambivalent selves, so that a repressed identity operates as an unadmitted outlook. At times of vacillation or "conversion," people tend to switch these sides, bringing a previously unconscious attitude to the fore. In subsequent chapters we will take note of the many examples of individual vacillation in the populist movements of the upper midwest states. As we shall see, some populist leaders in these states became increasingly radicalized, moving from right to left; yet others, even prominent leaders, moved from left to right, with some coming to rest in the camp of frenetic, far-right conservatism, usually after leaving the populist organizations.

A final observation on the function of psychological mechanisms among populists is in order. While such "subjective" attributes as courage, love, hate, honesty, and dishonesty are rarely mentioned in "objective" analyses of social movements, these qualities deserve greater stress since they necessarily play a part among those involved in reform movements. Granting that such qualities can perhaps be sensed only as impressions, it is my view that courage has been one of the most important forces to sustain reform movements. The literature of populism along with my own observations suggest that populists generally tended to fight against the mechanism of "withdrawal" into a private world of apparent goallessness and apathy; and by this tendency they perforce became advocates of courage to face a new reality and to pursue a new course of behavior.

The story is told that A.C. Townley, president and charismatic leader of the Farmers Nonpartisan League, was asked by an irate farmer, "What good am I getting for the sixteen dollars dues I paid the League?" Townley's reply was sharp and incisive, "You got the courage to ask that question. You got your money's worth."

The IWW sympathizer and poet, Morris Chaflin, penned these lines deploring apathy and lack of courage in facing the evils of society.

> Mourn not the dead that in the cool earth lie
> But rather mourn the apathetic crowd
> The cowed and the meek
> Who see the world's great anguish and its wrong
> And dare not speak!

By preaching courage as a heuristic device and by showing courage themselves, many reform leaders acted out the social psychology described in this chapter. They sensed that certain psychological mechanisms stood in the way of anyone's adopting a new outlook on reality, and they implicitly understood that personality is plastic, that people can and do change.

NOTES

1. Norman Pollack, *The Populist Response to Industrial America* (Cambridge: Harvard Press, 1962), p. 7.

2. Howard M. Feinstein, "The Prepared Heart: Puritan Theology and Psychoanalysis," *American Quarterly,* 22: 116-117, Summer 1970.

3. Erich Fromm, *Escape from Freedom* (New York: Avon Books, 1967), p. 311.

4. Ibid., pp. 171-172.

5. Erich Fromm, *The Crisis in Psychoanalysis* (New York: Holt, Rinehart and Winston, 1970), p. 36.

6. *New York Times,* April 28, 1971, p. 31.

7. Christopher Caudwell, *Illusion and Reality* (New York: International, 1963), p. 272.

8. Ibid., p. 69.

9. Don Martindale, *Social Life and Cultural Change* (New York: Van Nostrand, 1968), p. 58.

10. Rudolph Dreikurs, *Fundamentals of Adlerian Psychology* (Chicago: Alfred Adler Institute, 1950), p. 35.

11. Alfred Adler, *Understanding Human Nature* (New York: Greenberg Publishers, 1925), pp. 18-19.

12. Heinz L. Ansbacher and Rowena R. Ansbacher, eds., *Superiority and Social Interest,* Collected later writings of Alfred Adler (London: Routledge and Kegan Paul Ltd., 1965), chapter 7, pp. 71-80, "Complex Compulsion as a Part of Personality and Neurosis."

13. Ibid., p. 32.

14. Ibid., pp. 27-28.

15. Dreikurs, p. 3.

16. Fromm, *The Crisis in Psychoanalysis,* p. 29.

17. William M. Chace, "Ezra Pound and the Marxist Temptation," *American Quarterly,* 22:714-725, Fall 1970.

4

With a little bit
With a little bit
With a little bit of luck
You'll never have to work.

— *"My Fair Lady"*

Here I am not yet twenty-six and on the verge of a
great fortune! How shall I be able to dispose of it?

— *Ignatius Donnelly*

We do not live, we only stay,
We are too poor to get away.

— *Folksong*

How happy I am on my government claim
For I've nothing to lose and nothing to gain
I've nothing to eat and nothing to wear
And nothing from nothing is honest and fair.

— *Folksong*

FROM ILLUSION
TO DISILLUSIONMENT

Thus far, a general theory of populism as a pivotal force in American history has been projected for understanding the watershed shift which happened to coincide with the turn of the century as a part of a larger view of American history. Until now, evidence has been introduced sparingly and only tangentially in an explication of the general theory. However, in the remainder of the study, an increasing emphasis will be placed on empirical manifestations supporting the larger perspective on populism. As previously mentioned, the documentary evidence for the new perspective will be drawn primarily from the states of Wisconsin, Minnesota, North Dakota and South Dakota, states in which there have been vigorous populist movements both in the nineteenth and twentieth centuries, although state-by-state differences there illustrate variations in populist experiences as well.

In general, the remainder of this study will trace the dynamics behind the rise of populist movements as a process of disillusionment with the American Dream, a groping for cognitive reorientation within the forms of established social movements, and finally the emergence of the new social organizations which we recognize as populist movements. Even within the populist organizations, the effort for cognitive reorientation can be divided into three currents, as has already been suggested: laissez-faire (Tory), socialist, and finally radical neomercantilism as the main thrust of the movements.

This chapter will review in cursory fashion the special version of the American Dream which emerged on the northern frontier, a version which stressed the aspirations of acquiring land and concomitant middle-class status as a property holder. Once land had lured the new settlers to the new frontier, the process of disillusionment began, as hard times, adverse weather or grasshoppers stalked the countryside. This chapter will treat the phenomena of illusion and disillusion with the American Dream by discussing the work of Hamlin Garland and Ole Rolvaag and by referring to appropriate folksongs which portray the moods of elation and despair and implied anxiety as sweet turned to sour. American literature and social studies are replete with treatments of the rural pioneer as a tragic or a sentimental hero, as a victim of fate; but he is rarely treated as a person becoming in some cases a political and social activist. This study aims to correct this omission.

John Hicks, in *The Populist Revolt,* and many who have published since his study appeared have discussed in some detail such objective factors as the falling price of wheat in the 1890s, the rate of mortgage foreclosures in certain areas, and the interest rates in the West as compared with interest rates generally. While there is disagreement among historians over what might be termed the objective reality for populist complaints, in final analysis the rise of populist movements was linked with the subjective interpretation of reality on the part of populists and potential populists. Feelings of despair ran much deeper than an objective measurement of mortgage foreclosures, for example, might indicate; for there were probably many farmers on the verge of bankruptcy at various times when a smaller number were actually forced off their farms. Those on the verge probably were as concerned and as ready to become populists as those who lost out completely, yet those who managed to retain their farms would appear statistically as "successful" farmers. This is not to argue that statistical information is pointless but rather that "facts" in history are only meaningful in some explanatory context.

It is not my intention in this study to delve into debates over the "objective" factors which lay behind the rise of populism; for example, whether or not wheat farmers were more subject to the vagaries of the marketplace than corn-hog farmers. It is sufficient to observe that there were variations of time, location and occupational group in the rise of populist movements (corn/hog farmers in Iowa in the 1930s, wheat farmers in the Dakotas, Kansas and Nebraska in the 1890s, and infusion of socialist strength into the labor movements in the 1910s). The objective of this study is to define the intellectual parameters of populism, with the assumption that objective factors existed in sufficient force to induce an intellectual reevaluation on the part of those who became populists.

There is no need to catalogue at length the existing literature revealing the poignancy of rural and urban people who were defeated in the striving for middle-class aspirations. A small sampling of this material serves to establish a rise of disillusionment with the American Dream as an initial link in the chain of events leading to populist movements.

Though the rural component of populism looms large in the four upper midwestern states, this fact should not be allowed to obscure the fact that people were threatened with marginality within the working class and among small businessmen in towns and cities. It is difficult to document illusions and expectations among working people, but it seems fair to assume that they expected at least a rising standard of living, rather than the wage cuts and unemployment which prevailed in times of crisis and which triggered support for the Knights of Labor, for Debs's American Railroad Union, and for Coxey's march on Washington. In rural towns, there was always a stratum of small shopkeepers, country editors, and lawyers who were pushed toward marginality or who sympathized with their marginal farm neighbors and who came to identify with populist movements as well. It will be evident in surveying the populist organizations of the upper midwest states that the leadership of these movements more often than not arose from among these small-town lawyers and editors. The tendency for small-town persons to assume populist leadership positions has been observed by Hofstadter, who describes them as a "ragged elite of professional men, rural editors, third party veterans and professional reformers—men who had much experience in agitation but little or no experience with responsibility or power."[1] Here again, Hofstadter's elitist bias against populists is evident in his sneering reference to these leaders, reflecting a contempt for marginal people matched only by that of such Social Darwinists as William Graham Sumner.

As I will note in more detail in later chapters, urban controversies over local corruption, prostitution, street railway service, and pure water supplies often touched off political expressions, more often in a progressive direction but at times feeding the populist impulse as well. Urban socialist movements in such cities as Milwaukee and Minot, North Dakota, were spin-offs of efforts toward urban reform. The evidence here points to expectations on the part of urban people, including working people, for job security, an orderly community, and a middle-class life style analogous to the expectations for security and status inherent in owning one's own farm on the rural countryside.

In order to appreciate the anxiety of settlers on the rural frontier, it is essential to recall the circumstances of their being uprooted either in Europe or in the eastern states as they settled the West in the nineteenth century. There was both a "push" and a "pull" that impelled them to move. While there were vigorous debates in European circles over emigrating, vast numbers of lower-class people were literally forced into emigration by famine, by the unemployment of younger sons and daughters under primogeniture, and by remnants of feudal customs, such as excessive labor obligations to landlords for the cotter class of peasants. At the same time, there

was a reluctance to emigrate; people were loath to leave their familiar surroundings, and an attitude existed that emigrating was somehow "traitor-
ous."[2] Even within the United States, there was mobility from East to
West, notably among sons and daughters of middle-class parents who faced
a lack of opportunity in middle-class pursuits in the East and who often
went West as potential entrepreneurs.

While European people were being "pushed" (with ambivalence) out of
their old environment, they were often "pulled" to America with glowing
reports of a land of "milk and honey" and even of gold after the California
discoveries. These reports were often exaggerated, derived from earlier
immigrants or from "America letters" circulated by railroads hoping to
attract a vast population to fill the American countryside. Especially for
the pietistically religious—for example, the Lasere adherents of Sweden,
who were persecuted for reading the Bible directly and giving sacraments in
homes—the United States beckoned as a land of religious freedom.[3] One
can speculate that the vision of the West came to assume the nature of a
millennial dream, as wishful thinking for a new utopia with associated psychological complexes for overcoming despair. If this was the case, the subsequent gap between the dream and reality could be all the more painful to
endure when reality proved to be harsh and disappointing.

While the simple aspiration of becoming a small farm owner may well
have initially motivated an immigrant to go West, it seems that this goal
often escalated into a larger dream involving a "pot of gold" at the end of
the western rainbow. This mood is represented in a folksong, which tells of
the "push" and "pull" on the part of a Norwegian living in Pennsylvania,
believing things were much better in Wisconsin.

On to Wisconsin

Since times are so hard, I've thought, my true heart,
Of leaving my oxen, my plough, and my cart
And away to Wisconsin, a journey we'd go
To double our fortune as other folks do
While here I must labor each day in the field
And the winter consumes all the summer doth yield.

Oh, husband, I've noticed with sorrowful heart
You've neglected your oxen, your plough and your cart,
Your sheep are disordered; at random they run
And your new Sunday suit is everyday on.
Oh, stay on the farm and you'll suffer no loss
For the stone that keeps rolling will gather no moss.

Oh, wife, let's go. Oh, don't let us wait
Oh, I long to be there. I long to be great!

While you some rich lady—and who knows but I
Some Governor may be before I die?
While here I must labor each day in the field
And the winter consumes all the summer doth yield.
(Three of several verses)[4]

For those addicted to the "pot of gold" version of the American Dream, the practical way to make a fortune in the West was speculation in land. While there was always some tendency for a hard pressed farmer in Wisconsin, for example, to sell out after an initial increase in land prices and then to move on to Dakota territory where land was cheaper, the primary and most lucrative method of aggrandizement lay in organizing townsites. Yankee immigrants from the East, sometimes with funds to invest and often with inside knowledge of future railroad development, were the most adept at cashing in on inflating land prices as towns sprang up on the frontier. If Yankees were the first to find success in land speculation, European immigrants and their sons soon caught townsite fever as well and made the best of any opportunity that presented itself.

To be certain, there were persons who did get rich as speculators and who have often been held up as models for emulation. One of the more famous midwestern land speculators who made his boodle was Alex McKenzie of North Dakota, known as "the Bismarck boomer," who won fame as the Republican Party boss of that state and as a political spokesman for railroad and milling interests. He suffered an eclipse after 1900 when it was learned that he had been sentenced to a year in prison in California (but pardoned by President McKinley) for misappropriating funds from an Alaska gold mine venture in which he had been involved. McKenzie's fall from grace helped open the way for the emergence of Democratic Party progressivism in North Dakota with the election of John Burke as governor in 1906.[5] But not all speculators cashed in as McKenzie did, and not many enjoyed presidential intervention when they overplayed their hand. There were those who failed, often from the start, being left destitute and with little more than their wits as resources for making a living. In a few cases, the "wit" of defeated land speculators was later employed in populist causes (most notably such persons as Oliver Hudson Kelley, Ignatius Donnelly, Richard Pettigrew, and William Lemke), each representing different tendencies within populism in later life.

One of the first of the townsite speculators on the scene in Minnesota was Oliver Hudson Kelley, later to found the Patrons of Husbandry (the Grange) as a rural equivalent of the Masonic organization with officers named after Roman gods and goddesses. Kelley had worked as a writer for the *Chicago Tribune* and apparently heeded the advice of Greeley to "go west, young man." He arrived in Minnesota in 1849 as an aide to Alexander Ramsey, who was a Republican governor and political "boss" of Minnesota following the Civil War.[6]

Kelley was soon a townsite promoter. First, he organized Itasca, near present-day Elk River, Minnesota, as a stopping place for the famous Red River carts to Pembina and as a trading center for the Winnebago Indians who had settled there after being expelled from Wisconsin. The town died when the Indians moved to more fertile land in southern Minnesota prior to their forced expulsion to Nebraska. Kelley next organized the town of Northwood in the same vicinity, but a drought in 1862 and 1863 left the town a failure and left him destitute.

With help from Governor Ramsey, he received a job in Washington and later was commissioned by President Johnson to survey the condition of agriculture in the defeated South. It was during this trip that he formulated the plan for the Grange, as a salve for loneliness and despair among southern people. The Grange never took root in the South. However, returning to Minnesota, Kelley organized the first Grange club in 1867, not with an intent of starting anything radical or populistic but rather of organizing social clubs to combat isolation. Once the Grange was organized, Ignatius Donnelly and other leaders unloosed the demand for regulation of railroads, a demand which bore fruit in several states and finally in federal legislation as well.

Another townsite speculator was Ignatius Donnelly, who came as a young Irish lawyer from Philadelphia hoping to make his fortune as the founder of Ninninger, Minnesota, downstream from present day Saint Paul on the Mississippi River. The site was poorly chosen and it failed, in spite of lavish promotion, projecting well over four million people by the year 2000. Turning protestant and Republican, no doubt better to identify with the emerging white-Anglo-Saxon-protestant middle class, Donnelly attached himself to Governor Ramsey, who represented milling and industrial interests in Minnesota politics. Donnelly was elected to Congress for three terms, but he lost his good standing with the Ramsey clique when his ambitions for a Senate seat collided with those of flour miller, W.D. Washburn. From this point onward, Donnelly gravitated to the Grange, the Farmers Alliance and finally to the Populist Party as a reformer. The Dream had not paid off.[7]

Richard Pettigrew, from a Vermont abolitionist family, arrived in Dakota territory in the early 1880s. Pettigrew saw the prospect for Sioux Falls becoming a major metropolis in the Midwest. He plunged into real estate speculation and politics at the same time. Because of his "fishy" dealings, he was soon known as "the pickerel." He helped organize the South Dakota state government in 1890, getting himself a seat in the United States Senate and outmaneuvering the populists in the process. Losing his fortune in the panic of 1893, Pettigrew saw the crisis as a result of monetary policy; and consequently, he shifted to support "soft" money and Bryan in 1896.[8] He served as Teddy Roosevelt's campaign manager for South Dakota in 1912, but finally he became a socialist radical, identifying with the Farmers Nonpartisan League. Always contentious, he was asked on the Senate floor on one occasion, "Do you spit lemon juice?" In his later radical phase, he became an agnostic as well as a critic of American materialism. There is a legend that Pettigrew recited the following parody on dominant values in lieu of a table prayer:

> Dollars and dimes, dollars and dimes
> To be without money is the greatest of crimes
> To get all you can and can all you get
> Is the first and the last and the sole duty of man.

Another populist who began his career not with "townsite fever" but with land speculation as his goal was William Lemke of North Dakota. An aspiring young lawyer, Lemke saw a shortcut to fame and riches in Mexican land. He was soon deeply involved with questionable land deeds trying to develop land sales to potential settlers on his "new frontier." For a time, he involved another North Dakota lawyer, William Langer, but the two men had a falling out during a visit to Mexico when their party came under attack by revolutionaries. This falling out colored North Dakota politics for the next thirty years. Lemke persisted with his dreams of enforcing his claims in Mexico, even attempting to secure the ambassadorship to Mexico under President Wilson to serve his private interests. Failing to secure satisfaction through establishment political movements, Lemke became an insurgent, first as an advisor to A.C. Townley and the Nonpartisan League, and later as a congressman and as a candidate for the Presidency on the anti-Roosevelt Union Party ticket in 1936 as a right-wing bryanist.[9]

These examples of populist leaders emerging from defeated land speculators should not be construed to imply that all immigrants came with larceny in their hearts and minds. On the contrary, the aspiration of the more typical settler from a European peasant background was the more modest one of becoming the owner of his own plot of land, free from rents and labor obligations to a landlord. One of the more realistic and poignant representations of this immigrant mentality is to be found in the characters of Ole Rolvaag's *Giants in the Earth*. Here we see Per Hansa, strong and stalwart, single-mindedly striving toward becoming an independent, self-sufficient farmer. For him the pastoral (American) dream, an organic relation to the land, was no myth; it was his vision of utopia to be realized.

Though Per Hansa's wife, Beret, breaks mentally as she rejects the American Dream, wishing deeply that she had remained in Norway in the security and community of her village, her husband plods optimistically through life toward his utopia, a tower of physical strength and personal dedication. If the dream was not realized before he lost his life in a blizzard, it was still a thing of hope for the next generation; for he symbolically named his son Peder Victorious.

If the illusion of the American Dream ran deep, the disillusionment in response to failure and frustration was at times equally profound. The response was rooted primarily in economic hard times, notably in mortgage foreclosures in rural areas. The Promised Land became the land of the promissory note; and a crabbed life style induced by such factors as weather, grasshoppers, isolation and poverty also contributed to the sense of disillusionment.[10]

A folksong entitled "Starving to Death on a Government Claim" describes the isolation and desperation of the subsistence farmer who staked out a piece of land under the homestead system. The locale might have been identical with that of the Per Hansa settlement described in *Giants in the Earth*, but the mood has veered from hope to despair:

Starving to Death on a Government Claim

Frank Baker's my name, and a bachelor I am
I'm keeping old batch on an elegant plan
You'll find me out west in the county of Lane
I'm starving to death on my government claim
My home is built of natural soil
The walls are erected according to Hoyle

The roof has no pitch, but it is level and plain
And I always get wet when it happens to rain
Hurrah for Lane County, the land of the free
The home of the grasshopper, bedbug and flea
I'll sing its praises and tell you its fame
While starving to death on a government claim.

Now don't get discouraged, you poor hungry men
For we are all here as free as a pig in a pen
Just stick to your homestead and battle the fleas
And look to your Maker to send you a breeze
Now, all you claimholders, I hope you will stay
And chew your hardtack till you are toothless and gray

But for me, I'll no longer remain
And starve like a dog on a government claim
Farewell to Lane County, farewell to the West

I'll travel back East to the girl I love best
I'll stop in Topeka and get me a wife
And there I'll stay the rest of my life

How happy I am on my government claim
For I've nothing to lose and nothing to gain
I've nothing to eat and nothing to wear
And nothing from nothing is honest and fair.[11]

Another folksong in the same vein tells the story of the American Dream as a nightmare for the immigrant settler.

Dakota Land

We've reached the land of desert sweet
Where nothing grows for man to eat
The wind it blows with feverish heat
Across the plains so hard to beat

Chorus

O Dakota Land, Sweet Dakota Land
We've reached the land of hills and stones
Where all is strewn with buffalo bones
O buffalo bones, bleached buffalo bones
I seem to hear your sighs and groans.

x x x

We have no wheat, we have no oats
We have no corn to feed our shoats
Our chickens are so very poor
They beg for crumbs outside the door

Chorus

Our horses are of bronco race
Starvation stares them in the face
We do not live, we only stay
We are too poor to get away.[12]

One of the first writers of national stature to give expression to the discontent of rural people was Hamlin Garland, whose father had migrated from Wisconsin to Iowa, and finally to South Dakota, always hoping to seize the brass ring. The father, in the process of disillusionment, joined the Grange and later the Populist Party as acts of protest. Still, at the end of his life, he hankered to move on to Montana, where he'd heard that irrigation took the risk out of raising wheat. For Hamlin Garland, disillusionment with the West came after a sojourn in Boston under the guiding eye of William Dean Howells. Visiting his parents back in the West, he came to see the bleak and limited culture of farmers living in isolation from one another. He was especially sensitive to the effect of this style of life on the women as he witnessed its effects on his mother and sister:

I got back home once again to the solid realities of farm life, and the majesty of the colorful sunsets could not conceal from me the starved lives and lonely days of my little sister and my aging mother.

"Think of it," I wrote my brother. "After eight years of cultivation, father's farm possesses neither tree nor vine. Mother's head has no protection from the burning rays of the sun, except the shadow which the house casts on the dry, hard dooryard. Where are the 'woods and prairie lands' of our song. Is this the 'fairy land' in which we were all to reign like kings? Doesn't the whole migration of the Garlands . . . seem like madness?"[13]

Garland's critique was superficial and sentimental, with an implied nostalgia for pastoralism and the shattered dream, yet at the same time he could wonder if it was all "madness."

While the immediate cause of hardship on the rural scene might have been grasshoppers, drought, low prices, high railroad rates, or a combination of all of these factors, these vicissitudes were usually translated into another worrisome consideration: the mortgage. The fear of the mortgage has been dramatized in still another folksong:

But the Mortgage Worked the Hardest

We worked through spring and winter, through summer and the fall
But the mortgage worked the hardest and the steadiest of all
It worked on nights and Sundays, it worked each holiday
It settled down among us and never went away. . . .

The chickens left and scattered, when they hardly yet were grown
My wife she pined and perished, and I found myself alone
What she died of was a "mystery"—the doctors never knew
But I knew she died of mortgage, just as I wanted to.

If to trace the hidden arrow was within the doctor's art
They'd ha' found a mortgage, lying on that woman's broken heart
Worm or beetle, drouth or tempest on a farmer's land may fall
But for first class ruination, trust a mortgage 'gainst them all.[14]

It was the constant threat of foreclosure, even if it did not materialize, which was the cause of anxiety; and in times of crisis, the threat did materialize with great frequency. In the early days, even a small loan for a few hundred dollars by which a farmer might secure chattel property often required a mortgage on real estate. The loans ran for one year or two at the most. Thus, there was always a chance of losing the entire investment in land and labor for just a small loan for seeds, a plow, and horses. Snorri Thorfinson, presently the secretary of the North Dakota Historical Society, recalls that in the early 1900s his own father lost a one thousand-acre farm on which he had spent most of his lifetime because of a five hundred-dollar mortgage after two years of dry weather.[15]

In 1932 in North Dakota, Usher Burdick, the manager of a branch bank, won fame and affection among farmers when he refused to foreclose on mortgages before crops were harvested. Instead, he permitted farmers to harvest their crop with the chance of making payments on their mortgages, an act which caused his dismissal as the bank manager but which also propelled him first into the chairmanship of the state Farm Holiday movement and later into a career in the United States Congress.[16]

These examples provide some sense of the upheaval in emotions and outlook of great numbers of people as the myth of the Golden West gave way to the hard realities of privation, failure and isolation. Disillusionment with the American Dream has never been absolute in its impact nor total within an entire population. At worst, there is the example cited by Hicks of a large migration of people from Kansas going "back East" in the late 1880s, leaving their homes, schools, and towns deserted.[17] More typically, a smaller proportion of the population was affected at any given time, causing within communities and within regions a polarization between those who were "making it" and the so-called marginal people. This was especially so when the latter organized around radical aims. Even within each individual, the movement from illusion to disillusionment and to radicalism was never complete, since the commitment to the Dream died slowly and painfully; and this became a major source of ambivalence in the populist mentality.

It seems fair to note a cyclical eruption of disillusionment tied to the business cycle, producing vacillation as people responded variously to good times and bad times. From my own conversations with a host of rural people in the upper Midwest, I am led to say that it was a rare farmer or small businessman who was not on the verge of or directly involved in bankruptcy at some time in his lifetime. For many, the nadir of their lives was the time of the Cleveland panic, creating an antipathy to Cleveland and the Democrats which was equalled only by the blame later heaped upon Herbert Hoover for "causing" the depression of the 1930s. It does not necessarily follow that there is a close correlation between the depth of the business cycle and populist radicalization; for, as we shall see, cognitive reorientation is usually a slow process on a mass basis, as people respond in complex ways to distress and anxiety, at times clinging desperately to an old truth in their most anxious moments.

If objective social factors produce tendencies toward marginality and hence anxiety and disillusionment, it is not permissible to suggest that populism is "caused" by anxiety or disappointment. While anxiety may provide a trigger or a spur for a person to resolve dissonance, the specific resolution is shaped by the person's prevailing psychological tendencies, by his ideological framework, and by the degree of plasticity in the external environment. A response to any given type of anxiety can vary from passivity to rebellion, from political radicalism to conservatism, or from suicide to changing life goals and outlooks, all depending on the particular antecedent influences which form the total history of any one person.

As suggested above in the chapter dealing with social psychology, one's antecedent influences are not held abstractly in self-contained isolation; rather, these influences, whether ideological outlooks or psychological typologies, are imbedded in social organizations, such as churches, nationality movements, and prevailing political parties. These movements are the carriers of traditions. While any one person is born into tradition and thus tends to adopt from family and peers a pattern of responses to life's problems, in society at large, traditions (from present and past paradigms) are various, permitting people to pick, choose, and invent new responses for solving problems and reaching goals. However, to the extent that a certain tradition or a certain personality type is shared by a movement, a social stratum, or even a nation, it is possible to view such a tradition as a mass antecedent influence on subsequent thought and behavior; and it is with this assumption of a relative fixity of tradition that one can generalize about the influences of culture on behavior. Yet, there are many traditions imbedded in social institutions, traditions which seem to have contradictory effects in their influences on new responses; and thus, it is helpful to think of antecedent culture as a prism which emits many "colors" on the behavioral and ideological spectrum, the subject matter of the chapter which follows.

NOTES

1. Richard Hofstadter, *The Age of Reform* (New York: Knopf, 1955), p. 101.

2. Nils Runeby, "The New World and the Old," *American Studies in Scandinavia,* no. 5 (Winter 1970), pp. 3-23.

3. George M. Stephenson, *The Religious Aspects of Swedish Migration* (Minneapolis: University of Minnesota Press, 1932). See chapter 3, "The Lasere," pp. 24-48.

4. John Anthony Scott, *The Ballad of America* (New York: Grosset and Dunlap, 1967), p. 161.

5. Elwyn Robinson, *History of North Dakota* (Lincoln: University of Nebraska Press, 1966), p. 265.

6. Rhoda Gilman and Patricia Smith, "Oliver Hudson Kelley: Minnesota Pioneer 1849-1868," *Minnesota History,* 40:330-338, Fall 1967.

7. See Martin Ridge, *Ignatius Donnelly, the Portrait of a Politician,* for a narrative account of Donnelly's life (Chicago: University of Chicago Press, 1962).

8. Robert O. Parkinson, "Biography of Richard F. Pettigrew" (Unpublished master's thesis, University of Iowa, 1938). This thesis, on file with the Pettigrew Museum at Sioux Falls, South Dakota, covers the early years of Pettigrew's life until 1900. See also Richard Pettigrew's *Imperial Washington* (published privately, 1922) for autobiographical details.

9. Edward Blackorby, *Prairie Rebel: The Public Life of William Lemke* (Lincoln: University of Nebraska Press, 1963). While one need not share Blackorby's rather glowing attitude toward Lemke, this book fills a void in regional history.

10. For a brief documentary account of the agony of frontier living, see Gilbert H. Fite, "Some Farmers' Accounts of Hardships on the Frontier," *Minnesota History,* 37:204-211, March 1961.

11. Richard E. Lingenfelter, et al., ed., *Songs of the American West* (Berkeley: University of California Press, 1968), pp. 458-59.

12. Brown University Collection, *Series of Old American Songs,* p. 234.

13. Hamlin Garland, *A Son of the Middle Border* (New York: Macmillan, 1917), pp. 403-404.

14. Lingenfelter, p. 475.

15. Personal interview with Snorri Thorfinson, October 1969.

16. Ibid.

17. John D. Hicks, *The Populist Revolt* (Minneapolis: University of Minnesota Press, 1931), pp. 32-33.

5

*Naar det regner paa presten saa dryper
det paa klockern.*

*— A Norwegian epigram, meaning
"When it rains on the preacher,
it drips on the sexton," often
quoted by Governor Floyd Olson
to explain the tendency for
middle-class people to kow-tow to
upper-class conservatism for small
favors.*

CULTURE AS A PRISM

POPULISM AS ONE COLOR
OF THE SPECTRUM

The role of such cultural factors as ethnicity and religion as influences within the social process have long been a matter of debate among social scientists, witness the lively polemic flowing from Max Weber's thesis on religion and the rise of capitalism. More recently, there has been a revolt against progressives' melting pot assumptions and the neglect of the ethnic pluralism which inhabits American life. Michael Novak, in *The Rise of the Unmeltable Ethnics,* is especially vehement about the fact that the stamp of Anglo-Protestant culture has been imprinted by high culture while so-called low culture traditions have been devalued. However, the fact that we now identify ethnic traditions and can speak of a "Slavic" identity or a "black" identity does not in itself confer specific meaning upon these traditions; for any ethnic tradition exists always in the context of a larger orientation toward social reality. Generally, the new pluralists are committed to the progressive paradigm. They see a new institutional dimension to American social structure, and they raise questions over division of the "pie" along ethnic lines rather than class lines. Insufficient study has been made of the ways in which ethnic traditions either impede or accelerate paradigm revolutions in history as ethnic groups respond to American reality and to the American Dream.

The view in this study is that intellectual paradigms might be viewed as the independent variables in relation to ethnicity and religious factors as dependent variables. Thus, it will be possible to observe that ethnic assertions of identity might in one time and place support populist tendencies and at another time and place be associated with a very conservative outlook. This apparent paradox is most visible among black Americans, some of whom are committed to "black capitalism" while others seek alternatives to the industrial culture around quasi-socialist goals. Recently, I heard Barbara Mikulski, who describes herself as an ethnic populist from Baltimore, assert that blue collar ethnic people, sometimes described as hardhats, are politically progressive even though culturally conservative. On the contrary, it might be argued that these ethnic groups are politically conservative in their adherence to middle-class goals and to cold-war labor leadership but that they are culturally radical in rejecting "progress," in clinging to a sense of community which is threatened by freeway building, city redevelopment and high mobility in general. It is clear that debates over the role of ethnicity in culture are confused and unresolved. It is hoped that a discussion in this study of certain ethnic traditions which have contributed to the rise of populism will produce enlightenment over populism and also serve as a model for understanding ethnicity as a part of social dynamics.

To repeat, it is a central thesis of this study that paradigm revolutions in response to changing social reality provide a blueprint for understanding history. In this view, the dominant cluster of ideas in any era assumes deterministic proportions as people interpret their reality in typical fashion, leading in turn to typical behavior patterns, value syndromes and psychological complexes, all of which also become imbedded in cultural institutions. The persistence of various past traditions imbedded in institutions makes for a variety of responses which seem to flow from any given social situation as conflicting world views are generated. In other words, inherited culture serves as a storehouse of social responses from which people, depending on their special cultural roots, variously refashion present culture—either to restore a previous state of harmony or to search for a new resolution of social dissonance.

Since this chapter will examine in part certain religious traditions which have contributed to the rise of populism, it is well to point again to the various values and psychological syndromes imbedded in western religious movements, some of which promote reform and others of which deter change. There are such offense mechanisms as withdrawal, fatalism, confrontation, rebellion and millennialism, each of which influences people's responses to stress and anxiety as they attempt to resolve social problems. To make matters more complex, a given person or group may derive contradictory "messages" from their cultural traditions, perhaps a tendency for withdrawal from religion but a thrust toward confrontation or rebellion from a trade union or political movement, causing a state of dissonance. In this instance such a person or group might repress one side or the other of his traditions, always leaving the possibility that the repressed and unrepressed aspects might subsequently trade places, making for vacillation in behavior patterns between the "fight" and "flee" tactic.

94

The complexity of cultural impact upon behavior makes it difficult to predict the specific resolution of a given kind of dissonance, other than to gauge the persistence of certain social pressures once certain responses begin to form. The resolution of ambivalence which leads to one person's becoming a socialist or a populist while another recomes a right-wing bryanist may in fact depend on variations in the cultural traditions of the two persons as one accepts and the other rejects movement toward a new paradigm. It is especially difficult to single out a specific cultural trait as leading either toward or away from radicalism because a certain trait may operate in one way at one time and in an opposite way at another time. For example, a so-called religious fundamentalist might often be seen as a potential conservative; yet examples abound in populist circles of Christian socialists' being sustained by a literal adherence to the Sermon on the Mount. It is the failure to see the potential for this kind of variation which mars Paul Kleppner's study, *The Cross of Culture,* in which he makes much of the distinction between pietism and ritualism as causal explanations for divergent political behavior.

Kleppner argues that the pietists displayed behavioral tendencies toward asceticism, including prohibition, which moved them into Republican voting circles in the post-Civil War period. There is no allowance in the Kleppner model for prohibitionists' becoming socialists, as in fact happened with the Finnish temperance advocates. He singles out the Haugean Norwegians for being especially pietistic as he notes the close correlation of Haugeans with a pro-Republican voting pattern; yet he fails to note that the Hauge tradition in Norway was one of peasant political activism as well as religious pietism, making it possible for certain midwestern populists to hail Hans Nielson Hauge as a populist prototype. Although we will refer again to the Kleppner study to indicate its place in contemporary historiography, it is sufficient at this point to note that his model, which makes cultural factors (such as pietism and ritualism) the independent variables in history, is open to serious criticism.

A view of culture as an important dependent variable for explaining behavior is at odds with much received social science analysis. As was suggested above in chapter 2, the nineteenth-century petty capitalist paradigm built on a foundation of atomic individualism denied in its conception a sense of tradition and an existence of community. A partial denial of culture continued after the progressive revolution in social science outlooks, but for different reasons. With the assumption of the "melting pot" theory, which presumed a general "Americanization" of immigrant groups toward a caste-free, middle-class society, progressives tended to be blind to the impact of cultural influences upon historical development; indeed, the progressive outlook tended to view lower-class ethnicity as "foreign" and "un-

American." There were exceptions, to be sure—for example, the work of Theodore Blegen with Norwegian immigrants and Carl Wittke with German immigrants; but men such as these tended mostly to record the immigrant story with an air of nostalgia without incorporating their findings into a general view of American history.

As the progressive view of history as continual conflict between "the people" and "the interests" gave way to various consensus theories after World War II, an interest in cultural traditions came to the fore. Newer historians tended to find the source of observed social friction in varying cultural traditions, even as they denied deeper strains arising from paradigmatic conflict. Most prominent among these historians was Oscar Handlin, who in *The Uprooted* assigns much importance to the alienation and loneliness among immigrants as a factor in ethnic adjustment to American society. A consensus historian, Handlin makes a monumental error in his judgment that immigrants in their search for security rejected radical and populist leadership in the United States; he states, for example, that "the populists made no headway at all in districts where the newcomers were numerous."[1] In the upper Midwest, populism existed almost exclusively among the Norwegian, Finnish, German, and Irish settlers at various times. Likewise, the labor movement in this country has been fueled by immigrant groups, especially those of Irish, Jewish, Slavic, German, and Italian backgrounds.

Another consensus historian, Lee Benson,[2] has challenged Arthur Schlesinger, Jr.'s view of the Jacksonian era with a voting analysis. He properly refutes the notion of the Jacksonian revolution as a "radical" movement of "parasites" against "producers," or "people" against "interests." Benson seems to confirm the theory of William Appleman Williams that the Jacksonian revolution was essentially an intra-capitalistic shift from a mercantilist to a laissez-faire paradigm. Yet Benson himself is content to rest with a consensus outlook, seeing the voting variations in the Jacksonian period *only* as a reflection of cultural differences which predisposed certain groups to vote with the Jacksonians and others to stand in opposition.

Benson's outlook and method have been continued by Paul Kleppner in a voting analysis of Ohio, Michigan, and Wisconsin. Kleppner undertook this analysis to find the basis for adherence to the Democratic and Republican parties in these states from 1859 to 1900, with special reference to the Bryan vote in 1896. Like Benson, he finds that class or economic status does not offer an explanation for voting patterns but that cultural, especially religious factors, do seem meaningful. As noted above, Kleppner postulates pietism versus ritualism as the variables which explain adherence to either the Republican or Democratic parties. He proceeds to demonstrate that Democrats tended to coalesce around Catholic (ritualistic) outlooks and the Republicans around the pietistic movements, with a significant reversal in 1896 when the Democrats nominated a pietist, William Jennings Bryan. It was the impulse among pietists for imposing moral behavior on society at large which caused them to sponsor prohibition and nonparochial education, which in turn led to divisions between Catholics and Protestants and between Democrats and Republicans as well, While one can agree that there have been religious factors influencing adherence to the Republicans and Democrats, my own reservations stand that studies such as this one by Kleppner fail to sense the potential for either pietists or ritualists to become radicalized under certain circumstances out of their ambivalence toward overlapping paradigms in history. There is little point in developing in more detail a critique of his work other than to note that even well-designed statistical studies seeming to deal only with "facts" can serve to obscure rather than illuminate the process of social change.

Once cultural traditions are seen for their prism effect, capable of projecting a variety of responses, it is difficult to single out any single trait or tradition as a simple, positive influence for the rise of populism. It is even more difficult to quantify the impact of cultural influences, whether one is weighing the influence of Ralph Waldo Emerson on the rise of American individualism or that of Marcus Thrane on Norwegian radicalism. Often an obscure and small cultural trend will blossom under favorable conditions into a major social force in ways one would never suspect in its period of latency, as was the case with a small minority of rural Norwegians who became socialists in North Dakota and who in turn became the base for the Nonpartisan League. These observations serve to buttress the view stated in a previous chapter that one must deal somewhat impressionistically and by "feel" for the immigrant and religious traditions which have in some way helped spark the rise of a populist consciousness in the upper midwestern states.

Though he emphasizes in a simplistic way the role of culture in contributing to political polarization, Kleppner is nevertheless to be praised for bringing to light certain aspects of immigrant traditions which have been ignored. One of these is the Hauge movement of Norway. Hans Nielson Hauge was an itinerant preacher in the early nineteenth century in Norway who organized the rural poor into a Peasants Party,[3] organizing his missionary movement around communitarian life styles at times. Hauge became a martyr after serving time in prison on charges of violating laws against giving sacraments outside of the state church. In America, the Haugeans organized a special synod of the Lutheran Church noted for its asceticism and fundamentalism in interpreting Scripture. Kleppner may be quite right that the Haugeans initially were Republicans, coming as they did after the Civil War, when the illusion of the American Dream was widely held and when the

Republican Party was highly regarded for championing the fight against slavery and for sponsoring the Homestead Act. But there are bits of evidence that as time passed some Haugeans drew upon the tradition of Hauge himself as justification for engaging in political action, notably in populist activity. One of the leading persons who thus emerged in Minnesota was Mrs. Susie Stageberg, a leader first in the women's suffrage and temperance fight, then in the Nonpartisan League, in the Minnesota Farmer-Labor Party and finally in the Henry Wallace movement of 1948. An advocate of gentle persuasion, she reminded people of the coda from the temperance movement, "Hate the sin, but love the sinner." She lived in Red Wing, Minnesota, where her husband taught mathematics at Hauge Seminary, a school supported by the Hauge Synod.[4]

There were other influences upon the Norwegian people which propelled them toward political activism. The long struggle for independence, first from Denmark and then successfully from Sweden in 1905, produced an early tradition in Norway of a parliamentary democracy among all classes and also a heritage of resistance and courage to agitate for change. Marcus Thrane led an abortive revolutionary movement, a movement to which Henrik Ibsen was briefly attached. Thrane today is hailed as the founder of the Norwegian Labor Party for his role in organizing a peasant and labor movement which attempted a revolutionary overthrow of the government at the time of the general European unrest in 1848 and 1849.[5] He was jailed for his participation in the ill-fated attempt; and after some vacillation over the morality of whether to "fight" or "flee," he emigrated to the United States and lived both in Chicago and Wisconsin, editing iconoclastic newspapers in the Norwegian language and writing and performing plays with his family.[6]

Aloof as a popular leader, Ibsen nevertheless made a mark among Norwegian intellectuals. Once his initial revolutionary ardor had cooled after his narrow avoidance of arrest with Marcus Thrane, Ibsen's more typical outlook was that of a progressive reformer, exposing certain unpleasant realities in society and hoping thereby to prick the conscience of his age into striving toward the finer moral ideals of high bourgeois culture. A more important cultural hero in a popular sense was Bjornstjerne Bjornson,[7] first a writer of romantic stories celebrating peasant life and later a progressive reformer and religious freethinker. Bjornson was a man of great vitality who became a national hero in Norway and also among Norwegian immigrants in the United States. In 1880 and 1881, he visited in the United States. His visit was reported by Marcus Thrane in a weekly column, "The Wisconsin Bible," written in mocking style of the Bible. An excerpt from Thrane's account reflects Thrane's acerbic language along with a sense of Bjornson's iconoclastic tendencies:

And the great singer Bjornson travelled a thousand miles from Boston on a road laid with iron rails and came into the vicinity of the great city of Chicago. . . .

. . . Bjornson . . . entered into the city and took lodging in Palmer's Temple. All the people rejoiced and spread palm branches before him and the young maids kissed him (in their minds).

. . . And Bjornson preached his Sermon on the Mount to the Prophets, to the fear and trembling of all that were in the house. He taught that Moses had not written the Holy Book of Moses and that the Prophets did not know the History of Creation . . . and he taught that Abraham, Isaac, Jacob and Sarah were the old Folk's gods, that Jacob was the Sun God Orion married to the Virgin Moon and that from them descended the twelve children, January, February, March, and so forth; and he taught that Samson means "righteous sun," having his strength in his hair, which means sunbeams, and that Delilah is the sun of the winter. . . .

. . . This was horrible talk, Oftedal's chest began to heave and Skandinaven became so sick to its stomach that no quantity of Stomach Bitters was of any use and the Lord finally sent a "Delerium Hypocriticum" over them so that they became converted to sackcloth and ashes and swore allegiance to Moses and the Prophets and to Emperor Alexander the Third.

. . . And Bjornson's words were spread throughout the whole of Westerheim, from Chicago to Fargo and from the holy places of Eau Claire and Albert Lea to the borders of Iowa and Kansas.

And the word became flesh and dwelt among them, and the Word bore fruit . . . .

. . . But he was a very much disputed person. Some said this and some said that; but all said that he was the real Anti-Christ and Oftedal discovered that it was a Freethinkers' Conspiracy that had called Bjornson to the West and Stub added: "Certainly, verily a Conspiracy."

. . . And this happened during Caesar Garfield's first year of rule, which was the year the stars were to fall on the water and much trembling. Selah![8]

In view of the special history and experiences of Norwegian immigrants, it is possible to suggest that there were special influences which propelled them into radical political movements in the first place and that once in the movements they tended to persevere as radicals. It is possible to observe, for example, that the Nonpartisan League first flourished in northwestern Minnesota and in northeastern North Dakota, areas in which Norwegian settlement was predominant. Pending a closer study, it is possible to suggest from my own impressions only that leaders in populist movements came from Norwegian backgrounds far more frequently than from other ethnic groups. Just to list several of the prominent persons of Norwegian descent in Minnesota Farmer-Labor politics is partially to sustain this observation.

Congressmen O.J. Kvale and Knud Wefald along with United States Senator Henrik Shipstead, all three first elected in 1922 and all three coming from the heavily populated Norwegian areas of western Minnesota, were of Norwegian descent. Governor Elmer Benson was also a Norwegian and Governor Floyd Olson was half-Norwegian and half-Swedish. Henry Teigan, a congressman in the 1930s from Minnesota, who had his initiation in politics as the secretary of the North Dakota Socialist Party, was a son of Norway. I have already referred to Susie Stageberg, a pietistic Haugean who embraced a version of Christian socialism.

LaFollette's initial progressive coalition in Wisconsin was cemented with Norwegians through his choice of Nils Haugen as his first running mate for lieutenant governor; and in turn, the LaFollette movement was nearly derailed in 1906 when he insisted upon a Swede, Carl Davidson, as his running mate to replace Haugen, since this came in a year when feelings were running especially high between Swedes and Norwegians over the victory of the Norwegian independence movement in 1905.[9] In North Dakota, Norwegian Henry Martinson was the chief organizer of the Norwegian-American Socialist Party in the 1908-1912 period;[10] and it was these socialist clubs among Norwegians which became the base for the later Nonpartisan League. This catalogue of Norwegians who assumed leadership in populist movements of the states under consideration could be expanded to great length; however, the point to be emphasized is not simply the fact that they were Norwegian as such but the special cultural background of the Norwegian people which propelled many of them into reform and radical movements.*

In contrast to the Norwegians, Swedish immigrants seemed to be less inclined to participate in reform agitation. The pietistic Lasere movement of Sweden flourished in the mid-nineteenth century, but there is little evidence that it took a political form before the large waves of emigration as had been the case with the Hauge movement of Norway.[11] The reason for this failure for a lower-class political movement to emerge in Sweden much before the turn of the century is complex and beyond the scope of this study. O. Fritiof Ander notes that Swedish society was more class-ridden in the nineteenth century than was the case with other European countries and

*A number of historians have offered observations linking Scandinavians with a readiness to engage in political activity. Among them are Jon Wefald, *A Voice of Protest: Norwegians in American Politics 1890-1917* (Northfield, Minn., 1971); Sten Carlsson, *Scandinaviska politiker i Minnesota 1882-1900* (Uppsala, 1970); Richard B. Lucas, *Charles August Lindbergh, Sr.: A Case Study of Congressional Insurgency, 1906-1912* (Uppsala, 1974). While these studies tend to concur with the notion that Scandinavians were prone to politicization, they do not make the distinction between populism and progressivism and hence do not examine the argument of this study that a current in Norwegian culture propelled some Norwegians in a populist or socialist direction more than was the case with Swedes, for example.

that servants were abused and looked down upon as "dumbbells."[12] It might be inferred that a combination of repression and internalized self-deprecation created a marked degree of peasant obsequiousness among Swedish poor people. In any event, it seems clear that Swedish immigrants, both from cotter and landless classes, came without a tradition of parliamentary democracy or of overt resistance toward authority on a political level. It was not until after 1900 that urban socialism took root in Sweden under the leadership of Hjalmer Branting, and it was not until 1921 that Branting was elected the Swedish prime minister. Some Swedes, like other nationality groups, continued to read foreign language newspapers, and some of these in turn may well have been drawn toward a radical outlook as they watched developments in Sweden. In Minnesota alone, it is possible to identify several Swedes who rose to leadership as populists.

John Lind campaigned for governor in Minnesota in 1896 as a populist-Democratic fusion candidate. He lost, but two years later, he was elected and served a single term. In 1913, he served as President Wilson's special envoy to Mexico. Another person of Swedish background was Charles Lindbergh, Sr., who began a political career in 1908 as a progressive Republican congressman in rural Minnesota. Lindbergh moved increasingly leftward under socialist influence, opposing the Federal Reserve Act of 1913 as a "bankers' bill." He opposed Frank Kellogg, a Theodore Roosevelt progressive, for the United States Senate in 1916; he campaigned as a GOP peace candidate for governor during the hysteria of 1918; and finally he turned to the Farmer-Labor Party and was a candidate for governor in 1924 at the time of his death. There was a sprinkling of Swedish socialists, one group of which elected the mayor and city council of Two Harbors, Minnesota, in 1916. Another Swedish socialist, Carl Carlgren, a Saint Paul cabinet-maker and union leader, was one of the founders of the Farmer-Labor Party.

In spite of this catalogue of Swedish people who became involved in populist movements in Minnesota, the observation stands that the Swedes were less inclined to participate in populist movements and likewise less prone to rise to political leadership. A leading historian of Swedish immigration, George Stephenson, refers to the allegation that Swedes were "voting cattle" because of their "blind" support of the Republican party in the 1890s.[13] At the time that John Lind was proposed for governor of Minnesota on a fusion ticket in 1896, it was hoped that he could draw wavering Swedes onto the Democratic ballot. Stephenson reports that the Swedish language papers remained loyal to the Republicans with the exception, interestingly, of the paper published by the pietistic Mission Friends (from the Lasere movement), which urged that a vote for Lind could be safely cast without one's being considered a detested Democrat.[14] It was assumed during this campaign that the Norwegians were safely in favor of the fusion ticket. "Political observers reported that the Norwegians were going into the Farmers Alliance, whereas the Swedes remained loyal to their old allegiance," observes Stephenson.[15]

Pietistic revival movements swept through Finland, too, in the late nineteenth century, stressing the temperance and asceticism so common to these movements which served to rationalize a life style enveloped by poverty yet with middle-class aspirations. Finnish history in the eighteenth and nineteenth century was turbulent, as the Finns had struggled for national independence first from Sweden and then from Czarist Russia; and so, like the Norwegians, there was a tradition among them of agitating for national independence.[16] In view of the later radicalization of Finns in the United States, the question arises as to whether or not they came as immigrants with an ingrained radical tradition. While this question cannot be clearly resolved at this point, it seems fair to assume that the great proportion of immigrants from rural Finland were probably not especially aware of newer radical currents even though a socialist movement did exist in Helsinki by the late nineteenth century. With political attitudes shaped by agitation around nationalism, many Finns felt a special experience in the United States, especially in northern Minnesota and Wisconsin, where one-third of all Finnish immigrants settled.

Arriving later (largely in the 1890s) than the other Scandinavian immigrant groups, the Finns were recruited to work in mines and lumber camps in the northern states. When they were defeated in a Minnesota strike effort in 1907,[17] they were locked out of the iron mines, after which Slavic and Italian immigrants were recruited for mining. Without employment, many Finns were forced to settle as subsistence farmers in areas of especially poor land. In response to these experiences, Finnish fraternal movements flourished, the temperance societies were converted into socialist clubs, and the Rochdale cooperative movement developed strong roots as a profit-sharing device among Finnish people. In the 1910s the miners of all ethnic groups were radicalized as they turned to the Industrial Workers of the World for support in renewed conflict with the mine companies; this alliance peaked with a massive IWW-sponsored strike in 1916, which again was defeated with violence and bloodshed.[18]

Apart from a certain amount of draft evasion during World War I resulting in the imprisonment of several dozen Finns from an IWW background, the Finnish group was politically quiescent during the high period of Nonpartisan League organizing elsewhere. While it will be taken up again in the following chapter, it is noteworthy in this context that a large number of Finnish socialists identified with the Communist Party after 1920 and served as the major base for this party into the 1930s. This development contributed to much polarization in Finnish communities, first between the conservative "church Finns" and the "Red Finns" and later among the "Red Finns" as debates arose over the role of the cooperative movement—for example, whether or not the co-ops should help to subsidize the Communist Party.[19]

While an especially large proportion of the Finnish people were radicalized by their experiences as miners and subsistence farmers, this radicalism has always been sustained by a strong sense of ethnic solidarity as the Finns have tended to retain their language, newspapers, and customs up to the present day.

Arriving too late to participate in the populist movements of the nineteenth century, Italian and Slavic immigrants who labored for the iron mining industry also were radicalized by their experience as workers, and the mining communities were polarized along class lines. Unionization, strikebreaking and violence were all part of the scene in the mining areas.* The Slavs and Italians generally were ambivalent about World War I, many of them retaining old-country fears of Prussian expansionism; and thus, they were not inclined to join with the Nonpartisan League or the LaFollette movement in opposition to the war.[20] As with the Finns, the radicals among them tended to move into the IWW and later into the Communist Party without significant involvement in populist coalition politics in Minnesota and Wisconsin until the Popular Front period of 1935.

The Jews were numerically one of the smallest of the immigrant groups to settle in the upper midwestern states. As was often the case with other immigrant groups, they came with bad memories of Europe, especially those who came from Russia with its history of pogroms. Like other immigrants, they, too, were enraptured by the American Dream with its aspiration for middle-class status; consequently, many Jews, finding employment only as laborers in the needle trade industry in New York, migrated westward hoping for self-employment as small shopkeepers.[21] In addition, there was a movement to the land on the part of some who sought escape from city slums, a movement which materialized most fully in New Jersey. Joseph Brandes, in *Immigrants to Freedom,* notes that Jewish agricultural colonies were formed in Kansas and in Dakota Territory; however, there is no imme-

*A Slavic woman who prefers to be unnamed recalled for me the persistence of the *droit de seigneur* tradition on the part of mine foremen in the mining towns of Minnesota. She told of a foreman coming into her own home on a New Year's Eve when she was a small girl, demanding that the father leave the house for the night. The father returned two days later in a drunken stupor.

diate record of these particular Jewish people's participating in populist movements.[22]

The same political currents developed in Jewish circles as in American society generally, notably a reform tradition analogous to the progressivism and a more radical outlook more generally akin to populism and socialism. In a doctoral thesis on the evolution of Jewish political currents in Minneapolis, Herbert Rutman notes that Jews from Russia tended especially to respond to the appeal of socialism, even the small shopkeepers and the artisans.

Coming as these Jews did from lands where they were not accepted, where they were marginal and often persecuted, it would be natural for them to identify, as they frequently did, with the radical, revolutionary movements which were identified with change and with an overthrow of oppressive governments and systems which had for so long made their existence miserable.[23]

As small shopkeepers with upward aspirations, they found that life in western America was not in accord with the myth of the American Dream of democracy, tolerance and free enterprise. Jews soon discovered that doors were closed to them and that overt and covert social discrimination against them ran deeply. Minneapolis was a case in point. Rutman notes that the Yankee business interests who had first settled in Minneapolis kept a tight control in elite circles against aspiring outsiders. The American Dream was a sham; and in disillusionment many Jewish people turned to radical political alternatives, to socialist ideology, and to cooperation with the populist movements. These tendencies were most pronounced in Minnesota.

One person of the radical Jewish tradition in this state was Sender Genis, who campaigned for Eugene V. Debs as a youth in the campaign of 1912. After serving in World War I, he was refused his former job in a garment factory; and in response he organized the plant, launching himself into a lifetime career as a union organizer. Genis was one of the socialists who helped to organize the Farmer-Labor Party in the early 1920s; and he was instrumental as one of the international vice presidents of the Amalgamated Garment Workers Union in working toward the formation of the CIO in the 1930s.[24]

Other Jews of radical persuasion were active in Farmer-Labor Party circles. Among them were Abe Harris, a boyhood friend of Governor Floyd Olson, and Roger Rutchick, a leader in the fight against compulsory ROTC while he was a student at the University of Minnesota.[25] Harris became the editor of the *Farmer Labor Leader,* the house organ for the Farmer-Labor Party, while Olson was governor; and Rutchick was for a time assistant attorney general under Governor Olson and then secretary to Governor Benson. A prominent Jewish lawyer, George Leonard, was appointed by Benson as the first Jew ever to serve on the University Board of Regents.[26]

The forces of bigotry organized a backlash against the Farmer-Labor Party in 1938, making much of the presence of these Jews in influential circles. Rutman describes a widely circulated cartoon which portrayed Governor Benson as a donkey being ridden by his Jewish advisers. Pro-nazi Silver Shirts flayed the Jews and communists allegedly running the state of Minnesota.[27] The House Committee for the Investigation of Un-American Activities unloosed verbal barrages from Washington regarding the peril in Minnesota. John Gunther, in *Inside USA,* reprints a piece of doggerel which was circulated against the Farmer-Labor Party in 1938: "Hi Ho, Hi Ho, We join the CIO, We pay our dues, To the goddam Jews, . . .Hi Ho, Hi Ho, Hi Ho."[28]

It is fair to note in passing that Harold Stassen did not participate directly in the anti-Semitism of 1938, even though he was a beneficiary of it in winning the governorship from Elmer Benson in 1938. All in all, the Minnesota 1938 campaign stands as one of the most bigoted in the annals of American political history and as an example of populists as victims of bigotry and nativism rather than the reverse as Hofstadter alleges. It should be noted, however, that not all the hate mongering originated within the Republican opposition; for in that year there was a schism within the Farmer-Labor Party between forces led by Elmer Benson and those of Tory populist Hjalmar Petersen. As a result of this schism, there was a primary election contest between these two men, with Benson emerging victorious in this test of strength within the Farmer-Labor Party.

The largest ethnic group in the upper midwestern states was German. There were several waves of immigration from Germany and several ideological currents as well. In the 1830s a wave of German settlers came, fleeing from feudal oppression and embracing the "freedom" of Jacksonian individualism and petty capitalism. As good Democrats, many of these "dreizigers" eventually acquiesced to slavery.[29] Later, there were the "forty-eighters," refugees from the attempted revolution in Germany in 1848, a group who tended to be intellectuals and who gravitated to the emerging Republican Party and to an anti-slavery position and thus were in conflict with the earlier "dreizigers." It was in the context of this polarity that early intellectual currents formed among German immigrants. Some of the "forty-eighter" intellectuals settled on Wisconsin farms in the 1850s, writing articles on Hegelian philosophy, organizing debating societies, and generally promoting a high culture, coming to be known as "Latin farmers" as a mark of their erudite interests.[30] The Germans also brought with them

the Turnverein movement, organized originally during the Napoleonic invasion of Germany as patriotic, nationalistic, athletic clubs. In the United
States, the Turnverein movement served to keep German culture and language alive, through meetings, debates, and athletic contests; and, as with
the Finnish Temperance clubs, the Turnverein in some cases developed a
tradition for sponsoring socialism and "freethinking," especially wherever
the influence of the "forty-eighters" was pronounced. This was the case in
Milwaukee, where Victor Berger was first defended by the Turnverein when
he was dismissed as a schoolteacher for his "radicalism" and where he later
built the socialist movement partly within the Turnverein structure.

While the most significant radical influence of persons with German background lay with the Berger group in Milwaukee, examples of radical persons
of German background are abundant in other states as well. This was especially the case when the drums began beating for war against Germany prior
to World War I. Many Germans turned to populist and socialist outlooks
for a justification of their own hesitancy in going to war against the land of
their forebears. The repression and hysteria directed especially against
Germans during this war had the effect of driving them en masse into these
movements and in effect helped to build the movements in areas where
recent German immigrants lived.

In North Dakota, the Germans and German-Russians living in the southern and western part of the state had been notably conservative and reluctant to join the Nonpartisan League until wartime, when they gravitated to
the League and made possible an overwhelming League victory in 1918.[31]
It is notable that Governor-elect Frazier resisted all attempts to institute
witch-hunts during the war and that Charles Amidon, sitting as a federal
judge at Fargo, won national fame for his decisions upholding civil liberties
and the right of the League to institute economic reforms of a quasi-
socialistic nature in North Dakota.[32]

After war was declared in 1917, the predominantly German population
of New Ulm, Minnesota, held a "loyalty day" with parades and speeches.
The loyalty professed in New Ulm in 1917 did not suit the Committee of
Public Safety; for the Committee continued to single out Mayor Fritsche
and others as potential "traitors."[33] Fritsche emerged from this experience
a supporter of the forming Farmer-Labor Party, and he was a runner-up in a
Farmer-Labor primary contest for governor in 1924.

In the 1930s, John Bosch, a freethinker of German socialist background,
was elected the state chairman of the Farmers' Holiday movement in Minnesota. Bosch recalls that in the 1890s his own father was burned in effigy in
a nearby churchyard for his iconoclasm and that the father singly challenged
the crowd, cutting down the effigy and putting out the fire. The son initiated the first successful stoppage of a bank foreclosure on a chattel mortgage

in Minnesota in 1932; and, winning attention for his leadership, he traveled from state to state addressing Farmers Union conventions, calling for concerted action to halt foreclosures.[34] It was out of Bosch's agitation that the National Farmers Union finally spawned the Farm Holiday movement as a satellite under Milo Reno of Iowa, setting in motion a grassroots movement including rural bankers on the one hand and communists on the other.[35] With the death of Reno in 1936, Bosch was elected national chairman of the Holiday Association; however, by this time the movement was declining after it had served as an effective catalyst in prodding Franklin Roosevelt and the New Deal toward specific measures for farm relief.

With an eight-hundred-year tradition of hating and fighting English landlord rule, Irish settlers were easily attracted to populist movements both in cities and in rural areas. This tradition even inspired Irish settlers to support Irish insurrectionary movements in Canada, with the hope that this embarrassment to the British government would lead Britain to grant independence to Ireland. James Manahan, in *Trials of a Lawyer,* recalls that he had found a cache of rifles in Omaha in the home of a deceased uncle, rifles which had been intended for Irish freedom fighters in Canada.[36]

Especially during World War I, the Irish, like the Germans, were reluctant to take sides with England against the Central Powers. In Minnesota and North Dakota, many Irish turned to the antiwar Nonpartisan League at this time. In winning election to the United States Congress in 1922 from western Minnesota, O.J. Kvale gave credit for his Farmer-Labor victory to the inclusion of Irish Catholics into his coalition,[37] even though he himself was a Lutheran minister and might normally have been a symbol of one side of Catholic-Protestant polarity. Two key Nonpartisan League organizers under Townley were George and Chester Griffith, brothers from an Irish settlement in North Dakota. Later, George served as state oil inspector during the administration of Elmer Benson in Minnesota; he was later jailed on trumped-up charges when the subsequent Stassen administration needed a scapegoat to "prove" charges of "corruption" which had been leveled against Elmer Benson.[38]

Since the Irish population in these states was sparse as compared with that of the Scandinavians and Germans, it is difficult to find large numbers of them in key positions of leadership in populist movements here. Outstanding, perhaps, were two lawyers. One was Tom Sullivan, who campaigned for the position of Minnesota attorney general in Republican primaries in 1920 as a part of a ticket headed by Henrik Shipstead with designs to capture the Republican electorate. The other Irish lawyer of importance was James Manahan, attorney for the Nonpartisan League, member of Congress for one term, and generally a progressive iconoclast. Manahan's autobiography, *Trials of a Lawyer,* provides a colorful account, not only of his own life but also of the milieu of the 1910s and 1920s in the upper mid-western states, with tension between LaFollette-type progressivism and a more radical populism influenced by socialists.

The Irish, mainly adherents to the Catholic faith, were also influenced by the example of Archbishop John Ireland of Saint Paul, who worked to propel Catholics into the mainstream of American life. As a young priest, Father Ireland fought as a Union Army chaplain, in contrast to the reticence of many eastern priests who were sensitive to proslavery sentiment among their parishioners; and after the war he was an active Republican, contrary to tendencies for the Catholic population to form a Democratic Party nucleus in many areas. Archbishop Ireland was a close friend and confidante of Pope Leo XIII and a warm supporter of this pope's social encyclical, *Rerum Novarum.* He was disturbed by the anti-Catholic sentiments aroused during the crisis with Spain and Cuba, and he strongly opposed the Spanish-American War as a needless slaughter of faithful people.[39] The Archbishop was closer to the political position of the later peace progressives than to that of social radicalism. However, his example of political independence and social concern analogous to the Protestant Social Gospel movement seemed to encourage a variety of political currents among the Catholics, including a proclivity for joining with cooperative and populist movements.

The example set in Minnesota by Archbishop Ireland was quite contrary to that established by the Catholic clergy of Milwaukee, who carried on an unremitting opposition to the "freethinking" German socialists and thus contributed to a polarization in the city between socialists and the Catholic ethnic groups of Polish and Bohemian backgrounds. Hence, in Milwaukee and in Wisconsin generally, the weight of the Catholic Church moved against Catholic participation in populist movements and especially against coalition with the German socialists.[40]

It is clear from this discussion of the factors predisposing various nationality groups toward populism that religious outlooks were an important factor. At this point some additional observations should be made regarding the contribution of religious factors to the rise of populism.

In an age when "fundamentalism" is often identified with conservative social or political biases, it is important to recall the rationale of the Social Gospel movement, which gave support to reformism from the "original teaching of Jesus," as the rhetoric went, often pointing to the example of Jesus' throwing the money changers out of the temple. Even though the Social Gospel movement generally gravitated toward a system of Christian capitalism, the rationale did in some cases lead adherents into a socialist outlook. The most notable example of this group was the Reverend George Herron, professor of applied religion at Grinnell College in Iowa, who joined with Eugene Debs and Victor Berger in organizing the Socialist Party in 1901. There is no ready catalogue of others who followed in the steps of Herron; however, a person of my own acquaintance comes to mind—namely, Robert Duel, a Methodist minister at Ortonville, Minnesota, during the 1910s. When Duel's congregation divided over his sympathy for the Nonpartisan League, he took half of the congregation with him to another building, which he used as both a church and a League headquarters and for publishing a newspaper. Duel lived to be a candidate for lieutenant governor of Minnesota on the Henry Wallace ticket in 1948. When asked at this later time how he could be part of a movement supported by communists, he asked rhetorically, "Jesus and Marx weren't far apart, were they?"[41]

It seems fair to generalize that religion, more than any other cultural institution, functions as a storehouse of possible responses and that certain responses tend to become associated with certain paradigms. Because religion tends to provide a visible community around certain tendencies, it also provides psychic support for persevering in a given choice and also a tendency for justifying that choice in moral terms.

During periods of emerging radicalism, as with the rise of populism, there were abundant justifications from the Social Gospel for a radical outlook. For example, Ignatius Donnelly, in *Caesar's Column*, focused on the failure of industrial society to adhere to the teachings of Jesus as the cause of social decay. This observation could sustain either a socialist outlook or a belief in pastoral capitalism, as was reflected in the vacillations of Donnelly himself. Henry George, of single-tax fame, grounded his dream of an equalitarian society upon injunctions from the Christian Gospel. John Hicks, in *The Populist Revolt*, cites a version of an old hymn turned to radical ends:

> There are ninety and nine who live and die
>   In want, and hunger, and cold
> That one may live in luxury,
>   And be wrapped in a silken fold.
> The ninety and nine in hovels bare,
> The one in a palace with riches rare.[42]

At the same time that most populists tended to fall into the Social Gospel category, a minority could be found, often influenced by one of the Marxist currents, which was critical of religious sentiments generally. While there was a "freethinker" tradition with roots in the French Enlightenment, as exemplified in Thrane and Bjornson, a more virile strain of antireligious sentiments blossomed, especially within the Industrial Workers of the World, who saw middle-class culture, including religion, as a roadblock to revolution. The old Joe Hill song, with the lines "there'll be pie in the sky, by and by," is well known. A piece of doggerel with reference to North Dakota and

Minnesota probably also expressed an IWW bias:

The Swede from North Dakota

I bin a Swede from Nort Dakota
Work on a farmstead 'bout two yars
Tank I go to Minnesota
Go to Minneapolis to see a great fair.

I buy me a suit, I buy me a bottle
Dress me up way out of sight
Yump on the tail of a Yim Hill wagon
Yesus Christ, I feel for fight.

I go down to Seven Corners
Where Salvation Army play
One dem womans come to me
This is vat dot womman say

She say: "Will you work for Yesus?"
I say: "How much Yesus pay?"
She says: "Yesus don't pay nothing."
I say: "I won't work today!"[43]

While the overtly antireligious people, such as the IWW members, were ordinarily not a part of the populist coalitions, their influence was felt. Socialist mayor Arthur LeSueur of Minot, North Dakota, joined the IWW there in the free-speech movement and was arrested himself and served from jail as legal counsel for the group.[44] Floyd Olson, Farmer-Labor governor of Minnesota, is said to have worked with IWW lumberjacks in northern Minnesota after he was forced to drop out of the university for lack of funds.[45]

In the 1930s, persons with recollections of IWW experiences rose to prominence in the Minnesota Farmer-Labor Party, among them Mrs. Vienna Johnson Hendrickson, who served for many years as secretary of the Farmer-Labor Association, and later as United States Commissioner of Internal Revenue after the fusion of the Democratic and Farmer-Labor political movements. A participant in the Finnish IWW movement on the Minnesota Iron Range, she served when a young girl as an interpreter in court during World War I when IWW draft resisters were on trial for refusing army induction.[46] *

---

*Two acquaintances of mine in Minnesota both were part of the IWW movement in the early days. I. G. Scott, long time Hennepin County commissioner, was an IWW organizer in the Dakota wheatfields before coming to Minneapolis to win a seat as a socialist on the Minneapolis City Council in 1917. Walfrid Engdahl, for years the secretary of the AFL Carpenters Union in Minneapolis, immigrated from Sweden at the age of 17 in 1909. His first step was to join the IWW, because of his radical-anarchist beliefs, which were spread in Sweden by refugees from the abortive 1905 Russian revolution.

Generally, the religious and antireligious currents within the populist movements of the upper midwestern states seemed to exist with a high degree of mutual tolerance, as Irish Catholic radicals, Protestant Social Gospel adherents, socialist freethinkers, and Marxist materialists tended to find common ground many times. It is true that there were schisms, often so deep that a particular organization dissolved; however, it is my observation that these schisms were rooted in the first place in ideological differences, as when there was polarization between Tory populists and socialists, rather than in ethnic or religious animosities.

This chapter has surveyed the many factors which strengthened the populist impulse as a response to discontent. The approach here has been overtly impressionistic, merely citing suggestive examples of each significant factor. While we have emphasized those influences which seem to have nourished populism, care must be exercised not to obscure the many cultural influences which have contributed toward conservative or antipopulistic political and social movements. If there were Social Gospel populists, there were also deeply religious people who adhered to the Gospel of Wealth suitable for those bent upon economic success in a capitalistic world. If there were those who read Scripture to find sympathy for the poor and oppressed, there were also those, especially within the Wisconsin and Missouri Synods of the Lutheran Church, who reacted against the attempted revolutionary movements of 1848 in Europe and who preached that political engagement was sinful and that a narrow, individualistic interest in life after death was paramount. It is abundantly evident that while certain national and ethnic influences propelled some people toward populism, there were other aspects in the ethnic backgrounds of upper midwestern settlers which influenced them to stick with the American Dream and to be content with the more normative progressive or conservative outlooks in pursuit of middle-class success.

As we proceed into a new chapter dealing more directly with the rise of populism in the upper midwestern states in the late nineteenth and early twentieth centuries, continued references will be made to ethnic and religious influences. In a fundamental sense, the old traditions which have abetted populism have been carry-overs from previous efforts at the resolution of social and paradigm conflicts, especially from peasant revolts in the mercantilist era. While it is always possible to trace ideological threads into the past and to label new expressions of rebellion or reform simply as neo-reformist, this approach is inadequate in that it tends to ignore the dynamics of a later period in which old traditions are refashioned in a new setting and in a new stage of paradigm revolution. Certainly the impetus toward dissent and populism may have been greatly enhanced by cultural carry-overs from the past; however, an understanding of populism depends on viewing the movements in their own cultural gestalt, even while recognizing that the past serves both as a storehouse of responses from somewhat analogous situations and as an ideological prism, from which new responses fan out to meet new social stimuli. It is now appropriate to examine the main currents within populism as these currents swirled into action in the upper Midwest in the late nineteenth and early twentieth centuries, bearing in mind that these populist movements bore the imprint of antecedent culture even while responding to the problems of their own time.

NOTES

1. Oscar Handlin, *The Uprooted* (New York: Grosset and Dunlap, 1951), p. 218.
2. Lee Benson, *The Concept of Jacksonian Democracy* (Princeton: Princeton University Press, 1961). See especially chapter 15, "Jacksonian Democracy, Concept or Fiction."
3. For a biographical study of Hans Nielson Hauge, see Wilhelm Pettersen, *The Light in the Prison Window* (Minneapolis: K.C. Holter, 1921). Also see Theodore C. Blegen, *Norwegian Migration to America* (Northfield, Minnesota: The Norwegian-American Historical Association, 1931), pp. 161-163.
4. I had numerous discussions with Mrs. Stageberg while she lived. For years she published a column in the "Farmer-Labor Leader," the organ of the Farmer-Labor Party, under the heading, "As a Woman Sees It," excerpts of which are reprinted in *Third Party Footprints,* edited by myself.
5. Blegen, pp. 323-330.
6. Further biographical material on Marcus Thrane is contained in a mimeographed booklet circulated privately by his granddaughter, Mrs. F.H. Krook of New Ulm, Minnesota. This booklet also reprints excerpts from his newspaper columns, published as "The Wisconsin Bible."
7. See the chapter entitled "The Warmth of Life: Bjornstjerne Bjornson," in Halvadan Koht and Sigmund Skard, *The Voice of Norway* (New York: Columbia University Press, 1944), pp. 235-259.
8. Krook (n. 6 above), pp. 26-34.
9. Roger Wyman, "Voting Behavior in the Progressive Era: Wisconsin as a Case Study" (Unpublished doctoral dissertation, University of Wisconsin, 1970), pp. 277-278.

10. Personal interview with Henry Martinson, October 1970.

11. George Stephenson, *The Religious Aspects of Swedish Migration* (Minneapolis: University of Minnesota Press, 1932). See chapter 3, "The Lasere," pp. 24-48.

12. O. Fritiof Ander, *The Building of Modern Sweden* (Rock Island, Illinois: Augustana Book Concern, 1958), pp. 241-245.

13. George Stephenson, *John Lind of Minnesota* (Minneapolis: University of Minnesota Press, 1938), p. 118.

14. Ibid., p. 120.

15. Ibid., p. 119.

16. For a discussion of the rise of Finnish nationalism, see John I. Wourninen, *Nationalism in Modern Finland* (New York: Columbia University Press, 1931). The latter parts of this book explore tendencies for Czarist Russia to restrict Finnish autonomy after the attempted Revolution of 1905, which helps account for polarization of Finnish people in the United States at the time of the Bolshevik Revolution.

17. Neil Betten, "Strike on the Mesabi, 1907," *Minnesota History*, 40:340-347, Fall 1967.

18. Hyman Berman, "Education for Work and Labor Solidarity: The Immigrant Miners and Radicalism on the Mesabi Range" (Unpublished manuscript, University of Minnesota, 1964). This entire ms. provides an account of ethnic currents and of the various strike crises on the Minnesota iron range during the first two decades of this century.

19. I thank Michael Karni, University of Minnesota doctoral candidate, for discussions of his thesis material dealing with Finnish radicalism in the United States. Also see John I. Kolehaimainen, "The Finns of Wisconsin," *Wisconsin Magazine of History*, 27:391-399, June 1944.

20. Carl H. Chrislock, *The Progressive Era in Minnesota, 1899-1918* (St. Paul: Minnesota Historical Society, 1971), p. 178.

21. Herbert S. Rutman, "Defense and Development: A History of Minneapolis Jewry, 1930-1950" (Unpublished doctoral dissertation, University of Minnesota, 1970), pp. 5-7.

22. Joseph Brandes, *Immigrants to Freedom* (Philadelphia: University of Pennsylvania Press, 1971), p. 47.

23. Rutman, p. 55.

24. Personal interview with Sender Genis, October 1970.

25. Personal interviews with Roger Rutchick at various times in the 1950s.

26. Rutman, p. 117.

27. Ibid., p. 125.

28. John Gunther, *Inside USA* (New York: Harper and Bros., 1947), p. 301.

29. M. Hedwigis Overmoehle, "The Anti-clerical Activities of the Forty-Eighters in Wisconsin, 1849-1860" (Unpublished doctoral dissertation, St. Louis University, 1941). See early material dealing with the German immigrants of the 1830s (hence the term "dreizigers").

30. Carl Wittke, *Refugees from Revolution* (Philadelphia: University of Pennsylvania Press, 1952), p. 116.

31. Elwyn Robinson, *History of North Dakota* (Lincoln: University of Nebraska Press, 1966), chapter 16, "A Socialist State in the First World War," pp. 352-370. Also: personal interview with Henry Martinson, October 1970. Martinson recalled that the League won its conclusive state wide victory in 1918 after German-Russians in the southern counties of North Dakota flocked to the League. Also see Edward C. Blackorby,

Prairie Rebel (Lincoln: University of Nebraska Press, 1963), p. 65, for evidence that League leaders were careful not to offend German sensibilities on the war issues.

32. Robinson, pp. 364-367.

33. Chrislock, p. 141.

34. Personal interview with John Bosch, October 1970.

35. John Shover, *Cornbelt Rebellion* (Urbana: University of Illinois Press, 1965). Throughout this book, Professor Shover stresses the polarization between Milo Reno supporters and communists, but he fails to stress a more conservative current in the Farm Holiday movement, as, for example, the presence of Usher Burdick, an old line progressive, as the president of the North Dakota Farmers' Holiday Association.

36. James Manahan, *Trials of a Lawyer* (published privately by Kathryn Manahan, 1932), pp. 25-26.

37. Interview with Paul J. Kvale, 1946. The son of Congressman O.J. Kvale, first elected in 1922 on the Minnesota Farmer-Labor ticket, Paul served in Congress from 1929 to 1938 after the death of his father in a fire.

38. Personal interview with Elmer A. Benson, August 1968.

39. James H. Moynihan, *The Life of Archbishop John Ireland* (New York: Harper and Bros., 1952). See chapter 8, "The Spanish-American War and Its Aftermath," pp. 162-210. Note reference to Father Ireland's opposition to the United States' going into the "colony business," p. 172.

40. Personal interview with Frank Zeidler, formerly a socialist mayor of Milwaukee, October 1969.

41. Personal interview with Robert Duel, January 1949.

42. John D. Hicks, *The Populist Revolt* (Minneapolis: The University of Minnesota Press, 1931), p. 81.

43. Richard Lingenfelter, ed., *Songs of the American West* (Berkeley: University of California Press, 1968), p. 493.

44. Personal interview with Henry Martinson, October 1970. In 1916 Martinson was the editor of *The Iconoclast,* a prosocialist weekly.

45. George H. Mayer, *The Political Career of Floyd B. Olson* (Minneapolis: University of Minnesota Press, 1951), pp. 9-10.

46. Personal interview with Mrs. Vienna Hendrickson, October 1970.

Ethical Problem

Should one deflea the neighbor's dog
And stop his frantic scratching?
Or should one just quote "laiseez
faire"
The while more fleas are hatching;

Should one lay hands on neighbor's
dog
Defying all conventions?
Or should one quote a moral law
And curb one's good intentions.

Alas, alack! How fleas do flit!
While one is moralizing
Now fleas are biting all our dogs—
Our laws and codes defying.

— Henry R. Martinson
(Organizer of Scandinavian-
American socialist clubs in
North Dakota, 1908-09)

MAIN CURRENTS
WITHIN POPULISM

In earlier chapters dealing with a view of history and social psychology on a theoretical level, I have stressed the choice-making quality in human history as people develop strategies and outlooks from their cultural storehouses for dealing with social problems as they perceive them. Linked with new strategies and outlooks are new prescriptions for reform insofar as social reform emerges as a resolution for problems. It is the general thrust of this study that the new strategies and reforms which we have come to identify as populism have moved toward some type of social intervention and thus toward a new paradigm and away from notions of minimal government, the invisible hand of the marketplace, and the imperial self of autonomous individualism.

However, populism itself has not been monolithic. The process of moving away from the individualist bryanist syndrome has prevailed within populist movements in the form of three currents—Toryism, socialism and radical neomercantilism. It is the intent of this chapter to examine the presence of these three currents in upper midwestern states and also the movement of people from one current to another, yet with a tendency for radical neomercantilism to serve as a focal point of populism, especially in the twentieth century.

While there was a general tendency for the populist movements to move from "right" to "left," notably in the twentieth century, there was also the perennial tendency for ambivalence and vacillation, as people responded variously to the admitted and the repressed sides of their allegiances to ideological paradigms. Thus it is possible to observe populists moving at times from left to right, to use the political vernacular, even though the main drift was in the opposite direction. It is the vacillating movement to the right on the part of some populists which provided grist for the Hofstadter thesis that they were little more than frustrated bryanists, responding angrily and badly to the impact of corporate industrialism on their lives.

As I have stressed earlier, especially in the previous chapter on culture as a prism, there were many preexisting outlooks and movements from older traditions of dissent, all of which helped shape specific movements in the upper midwestern states, movements which were made up of coalitions of differing interests or ideological tendencies toward populist rebellion. Often the nature of the coalition provides important clues to its ideological trends, as, for example, when socialists were included in populist coalitions. On the other hand, those populist decisions to fuse with the Democrats, as in 1896 or in the Minnesota fusion in 1944, speak for a tendency to vacillate into "normal" progressive political channels and away from populism altogether.

The decisive coalition within populist movements has often been between farmer- and labor-based movements, beginning with early attempts on the parts of the Knights of Labor and the Grangers to coalesce under the banner of antimonopolism in company with certain businessmen (Peter Cooper, for example) intent upon restoration of a climate fair to small enterprise. The Farmers Alliance became politicized in many states in 1888 and 1890, again cooperating with remnants of the Knights of Labor.[1] It was a few Congressmen elected as Alliancemen who were instrumental in the formation of the Populist Party in 1892.[2] The most notable farmer and labor coalition at a later time was the Farmer-Labor Party of Minnesota. The willingness of farmers to identify with labor, especially in strike situations, can be seen as an ideological watershed for rural people as they rejected the "normal" anti-labor sentiments of those who aspired to entrepreneurial success.

Two other movements which at times coalesced with populism were those of temperance and woman suffrage, even though these coalitions produced tensions as well. The most notable example of the temperance movements' flowing into populism stands with the conversion of the Finnish Temperance societies into Socialist Party units, beginning in 1906. On the other hand, prohibitionists and populists clashed in Wisconsin, where German socialists and populists preferred their beer-drinking traditions to the crusade against alcohol. The bias of the German socialists and populists on this matter probably permitted the elder Robert LaFollette to capture the support of temperance-minded citizens for progressivism; however, it should be noted that even LaFollette, with his tendencies as a moral reformer, tempered his outlook with "political realism" by not opposing beer on Sunday when this was a vibrant issue.[3]

The Prohibition movement was not initially or inherently a part of populist or socialist dissent but, rather, arose as a moral crusade associated with the asceticism of people with middle-class aspirations; however, the potential for a political shift on the part of these people existed whenever asceticism seemed to fail as a formula for achieving middle-class status. An early example of prohibitionist-populist fusion was the attempt of the two groups to take control of North Dakota in 1890, a move which succeeded two years later as a still wider coalition, including the Farmers Alliance and certain Democrats, to elect Eli Shortridge as governor.[4] Prohibitionists were active in the formation of the Farmer-Labor Party of Minnesota around such persons as W.G. Calderwood, also a Bellamy socialist, and Mrs. Susie Stageberg, also a leader in the fight for woman suffrage. The last Farmer-Labor Party governor, Elmer A. Benson, was noted for his strong support of temperance, feeling that drinking and drunkenness were diversions from efforts for social reform.[5]

The other crusade which at times fused with populism was that of woman suffrage. Susan B. Anthony spent much of her time from 1865 until 1900 working in the western states to get woman suffrage incorporated into the constitutions of these states as they were organized. She was buoyed by the examples of populist movements. The Farmers Alliance, the Grange and the Prohibition Party all admitted women to membership and were friendly to woman suffrage.[6] While only Wyoming adopted female suffrage at the time of statehood, Mrs. Anthony's efforts were almost successful in both North and South Dakota. Her efforts were often linked with those of the Prohibition Party, which helped in some circles but hurt among anti-temperance Germans. Her biographer, Alma Lutz, has noted: "Stirred by the liquor interests to believe that woman suffrage meant prohibition, the foreign born proved to be increasingly formidable foes not only in South Dakota but in every state voting on the question."[7] In spite of the setback in the two Dakotas, it is significant that both states adopted woman suffrage prior to the federal amendment—North Dakota in 1916 under the first impact of the Nonpartisan League, and the sister state in 1918 under the ultraprogressive leadership of Republican Governor Peter Norbeck.

Having observed that the significant populist movements have been coalitions, it is appropriate now to examine the manifestations of the three ideological components of populism: Tory (laissez-faire), socialist and radical neomercantilist. It is in terms of these categories that populism can be defined and in terms of which the problems of holding coalitions together can better be understood. A word of caution is in order against viewing these ideological categories as water-tight compartments, for populists were often in flux from one category to another. Also, it is important to understand that these three currents within populism are generalizations, established to aid in understanding the cognitive tensions within populism, even as it showed tendencies to become a major paradigm in its own right. As analytic constructs, these categories are imposed by the historian and did not necessarily enter into the perspective of those human actors we have come to know as populists.

A question might arise as to whether the shifting ideological commitments within populism were derived primarily from a shifting of submovements in and out of the populist stream or from a shifting consciousness on the part of individuals. Both processes were at work; however, in final analysis, every shift in ideological structure is rooted finally in an individual experience. Thus, it is not enough to say that the Nonpartisan League was influenced by an input from the socialist movement, but we must also understand that the socialist movement itself arose among individuals as a resolution for dissonance when a gap developed between the promise of America and their perception of reality.

As I have already noted, the early populists in the late nineteenth century were men and women still hoping deeply to cash in on the Dream, only reluctantly becoming dissenters. Thus, they often displayed great ambivalence as they broke with the nineteenth-century laissez-faire mentality and bryanist negativism. At times, it is difficult to distinguish between a Tory populist and a bryanist; however, the Tory populist was one who was willing to join in coalitions with trade unionists, socialists, or radical reformers around demands for institutional reform, even though he himself might veer to bryanism and find the Jeffersonian dream to be attractive. Likewise, although the distinction between a Tory populist and a progressive is also difficult to make, nonetheless, it is possible to suggest certain differences, notably the willingness of the populist to coalesce with ethnic groups, trade unions or socialists with a goal of economic egalitarianism in contrast with more typical progressive elitism.

Just as populists, both as individuals and as movements, tended to vacillate in their ideological commitments, the same process went on among progressives, a process which brought a few progressives into populist or radical ranks. I have already pointed to the case of United States Senator Richard Pettigrew of South Dakota, who traversed the spectrum from the Republican Party, to progressivism, and then to socialism in his lifetime. While the shift in the case of the elder LaFollette is less dramatic, it appears that he too moved leftward a bit from progressivism and functioned in effect as a Tory populist as he accepted socialist support in his reelection campaign of 1922 and in his presidential bid of 1924. A number of studies document this shift in LaFollette's outlook. David Thelen has pointed to the existence of well-defined municipal reform movements in Wisconsin by the time LaFollette became governor,[8] dispelling the myth of his being initially far-sighted, courageous or "radical." While he at first endorsed Wilson's goals for New Freedom, he broke with Wilson over the Mexican War for typically conservative-isolationist reasons that eastern big business interests were supporting the war and reducing "our State Department into a trading post for Wall Street interests"[9] while midwestern small business interests were being ignored. The elder LaFollette persisted in his views in opposition to entering World War I, aligning himself on a parallel course with socialists and carrying on a last-ditch fight for peace even while most other progressives marched to the beat of the drums.

When LaFollette emerged with a peace progressivism contrary to the more "normal" progressive jingoism of Woodrow Wilson and Theodore Roosevelt, his constituency changed, as Herbert Margulies has pointed out:

. . . in truth the post war movement was substantially a new and different phenomenon, born, bred and shaped by the war. The original grassroots progressivism, the vibrant, grassroots progressivism of Congressman LaFollette and the "university boys" had faded and died of internal contradictions and external pressure by 1916.[10]

By 1920, the German population was solidly in his camp, the socialists were ready to mute their previous criticisms of his state regulatory commissions, and LaFollette himself endorsed limited forms of public ownership. This view of the elder LaFollette as moving in effect toward Tory populism and anti-imperialism by virtue of his new coalition is not one which necessarily alters the characterization of him as essentially conservative in consonance with the analysis of Gabriel Kolko and others; for by definition, even a Tory populist is primarily interested in restoring the laissez-faire order through regulatory or antitrust intervention. In any event, his honeymoon with socialists was most cautious and circumspect; and he was hostile to efforts of Minnesota socialists to form a national third party around his candidacy in 1924, partly so as not to endanger support from Samuel Gompers for his presidential attempt of that year.

Tory populism was the pervasive current in the early movements after the Civil War, notably the Grange and the Farmers Alliance. Even when Grangers sponsored cooperatives, there is no evidence that they saw them as a mode of social reconstruction; rather they saw them as a purchasing club for financial benefits only. The Grange sponsored producer cooperatives for manufacturing plows, seeders and other farm tools, aiming to cripple the "machinery trust"[11] as part of their initial aim to restore competitive capitalism. In his *History of North Dakota,* Elwyn Robinson refers to the early efforts of farmers to secure competitive bidding on their wheat through legislation requiring at least two grain buyers at every country elevator.[12] Railroads were under attack for discriminating against "scoopers," independent grain buyers who bought from farmers at a railroad siding.[13] The first efforts toward state-owned terminal elevators, dating to the 1880s, were geared not toward socialism but simply toward by-passing the monopoly role of railroads and commission men so that farmers might secure a larger slice of the world price for wheat. As a matter of fact, the Dakota Alliance in 1888 began to negotiate with English milling interests to invest in Minneapolis as a way for farmers to evade the local milling trust,[14] a move which provoked political responses and defeat for this plan to entice "foreigners" into the Midwest.

In Minnesota, Haldor Boen was elected to Congress as a populist with Alliance support in 1890, representing the northwestern wheat-growing area of the state.[15] Boen was strictly a Tory populist. When the national Populist Party was formed in Omaha in 1892 with its subtreasury plan for circumventing the free market, Boen denounced the plan with vigor. He argued that farmers were simply asking for a "special privilege" for themselves contrary to the prescription of "Equal rights for all; Special privileges for none," so often on the lips of free enterprisers. Boen was supported in his stand by Sidney Owen, who clashed with Ignatius Donnelly for leadership of the movement in Minnesota. A three-way schism developed between (1) Boen and Owen, (2) Donnelly, and (3) William Dobbyn, editor of a prohibitionist-socialist magazine, *The Progressive Age;* consequently, the Populist Party failed to prosper. However, it is noteworthy that all three factions warmly supported Eugene V. Debs's leadership in a successful strike against Hill's Great Northern Railroad in 1893.[16] The schism in Minnesota populism was finally healed somewhat around the candidacy of silverite John Lind for governor in the fusion movement of 1896 and around his election in 1898. While Lind was more a progressive than a populist, his election was a watershed in Minnesota politics, establishing reformism as a norm for both the Democratic and the Republican parties and establishing an anti-imperialist tradition, as well, from his opposition to the Spanish-American War during his term in office. Lind's subsequent career is of interest, for he was a Wilsonian progressive after 1912, serving as Wilson's special minister in Mexico during the revolutionary upsurge there in 1913. Lind served briefly on the Minnesota Loyalty Committee in 1917, but he resigned in protest and supported the quasi-socialist candidates, Charles Lindbergh, Sr., and W.G. Calderwood, for governor and senator, both endorsed by the Nonpartisan League. Thus, Lind is another example of a person who vacillated between a populist and a progressive outlook.

There are further examples of Tory populism in Minnesota. The editor of the Nonpartisan League paper and the business manager of the quasi-socialist *Minneapolis Star,* founded in 1920, was A.B. Gilbert. During the formation of the Farmer-Labor Party in the early 1920s, Gilbert vigorously opposed the third-party effort; and once it was formed he turned to the far right, expressing antilabor and antiradical sentiments the remainder of his life. In the 1930s Tory populism blossomed within the Farmer-Labor Party, especially during the campaign of 1938, when former Lieutenant Governor Hjalmar Petersen rallied persons fearing "radicalism" and CIO labor influences against Governor Elmer Benson, taking advantage as well of covert anti-Semitism directed against Benson's administration. While Governor Benson won the primary race between the two men, the effect was one of disuniting the party and allowing Harold Stassen to be elected in November.

Like that of their father, the stand of the LaFollette sons in Wisconsin in the 1930s was at best an ambiguous one between progressivism and Tory Populism. The story of Philip LaFollette is most instructive as an example of vacillation in a political career. Elected governor as a Republican in 1930, he was defeated in the Democratic landslide of 1932. Under pressure from certain quasi-socialist populists, organized as the Farmer-Labor Progressive League for promoting a third-party movement in Wisconsin, Philip acquiesced in organizing the Progressive Party as a third party in the state. However, he and a small coterie of friends excluded the Farmer-Labor Progressive League from a meaningful role, preferring to run the Progressive Party as a personal campaign committee for the LaFollettes.[17] Howard Y. Williams, the national secretary of the League for Independent Political Action, was active, along with Tom Amlie, who later was elected to Congress, in promoting the third-party effort. Williams recalls that Philip was most reluctant to leave the Republican Party and that he was most undemocratic in his decision making.[18] While Philip LaFollette deserves credit for certain legislation passed while he was governor, notably a system of unemployment insurance earlier advocated by socialists and later copied by the New Deal,[19] he continued to reject coalition with populists, including socialists, calling the latter a "rabid clique."[20]

In 1935 a populistic Farmer-Labor Progressive Federation was organized in Wisconsin to create a movement for mass participation; however, it failed to emerge as a major political force. Organized primarily by trade union socialists, the Federation excluded communists at a time when the Communist Party had about-faced to the popular front position, making for debilitating controversy as certain communists were elected to the Federation from local levels by labor and farm organizations. At the same time, the Federation drew fire from Philip LaFollette, especially for the code phrase employed by many socialists, "Production for use, not profit."[21] The Federation did manage to elect Tom Amlie to Congress in 1936 on the Progressive Party ticket, but he was defeated in a bid for a United States Senate seat in 1938 in a Progressive Party primary race with Thomas Ekern, a close friend of Philip LaFollette.[22]

The Wisconsin political scene was further muddied by Philip's attempt to organize a national right-wing third party in 1938 in opposition to Franklin

Roosevelt. LaFollette's National Progressives of America was launched in Madison with all of the trappings of the Hitler and Mussolini movements of Europe. Before long, Philip was traveling in circles with right-wing businessmen associated with the America First isolationist movement prior to World War II.[23] No longer even faintly a populist or a progressive, Philip LaFollette reverted to mugwump negativism, and he came soon to look upon Douglas MacArthur, an army general famous for his rightist and imperialist views, as his hero. Even before this open turn to the right, Philip had displayed an autographed picture of Mussolini in his office.[24]

There is a certain logic for the argument that the Tory populists would be the most susceptible to vacillating out of the populist movement altogether into "normal" political channels; for the Tory component is most attached to "normal" cultural values, having moved less to the left on the political spectrum. There are other cases within the populist movements of the upper Midwest of persons who followed the example of Georgia's Tom Watson in reverting to a far right mugwump or bryanist outlook. In addition to A.B. Gilbert and Philip LaFollette, there was Henrik Shipstead, who served as a Farmer-Labor senator from 1922 until 1940, at which time he switched to the Republican Party to give vent to his isolationism and distrust of Franklin Roosevelt.

The Nonpartisan League in North Dakota always remained nominally Republican, contesting primary elections with a more conservative Republican Organizing Committee (ROC). Thus, there were not dramatic shifts in party affiliation when Leaguers occasionally vacillated back into conservatism. The name of William Langer stands out in North Dakota politics as a maverick and as an astute political leader. While Langer was briefly associated with the Nonpartisan League in its formative period, he helped undermine the movement in 1919 and 1920 as copublisher of *The Red Flame,* an inflammatory magazine warning of "bolshevism" and "free love" if the League were to continue in power.[25] In 1929 and 1930, Langer and his friends took control of the League and used it as a personal campaign vehicle for his own stormy rise to the governorship and to the United States Senate.[26] Langer often sounded "militant" in his rhetoric in the 1930s, for example, shouting at Roosevelt with clenched fist, "You son of a bitch, we put you here and we'll get you out of here,"[27] at a time when several governors were imploring the President to provide farm relief at the behest of the Farm Holiday movement. Yet it seems inappropriate to regard Langer as a populist in the terms of this study. Like Philip LaFollette, he turned to right-wing isolationism; but as a less doctrinaire person, he maintained political popularity by balancing popular rhetoric with a conservative bias.

Most inexplicable of those who vacillated from a populist-progressive outlook back to the Republican Party was Robert LaFollette, Jr., who won fame as a conscientious supporter of New Deal reforms and as a champion of civil liberties. He led an exposé of corporate murder and violence against labor organizers as chairman of a Senate committee to investigate the state of civil liberties in America.[28] Although invited by national Democratic leaders to come into the fold of the New Deal, he chose to engage in a Republican primary contest in 1946, and he suffered defeat from a certain Joseph McCarthy, who paradoxically campaigned at this time as an advocate of Soviet-American friendship. It was McCarthy's position on this issue along with certain anti-Soviet expressions by LaFollette which propelled the Communist Party to support McCarthy in 1946, a case of the popular front tactic going awry.

In pointing to Tory populists as being the most prone to regress into nonpopulist political currents, it should not be assumed that such regression did not occur among socialists and radical neomercantilists. There was vacillation of this kind along the entire populist spectrum, most dramatically the case of A.M. Simons, who left the Socialist Party to serve on the wartime Loyalty Board in Wisconsin in 1918.[29]

As was suggested in chapter two, the normal political behavior and thought of the nineteenth-century individualist, who lacked a theory of social forces and process, resulted at best in promoting movements for moral regeneration on an individual basis and at worst in employing dragons or scapegoats as explanations for "evil." The choice of dragons for those who lived in a Manichean intellectual world could vary from time to time, but there has been a pervasive tendency in America to single out unions, radicals, Negroes and/or Jews as symbols of evil in the so called conspiracy view of history. Only as Tory populists came to accept a view of society amenable to institutional reform were they *free* to move beyond their individualistic cultural heritage, including its negativistic demonology; but always there was cultural lag, a tendency for the Tory side of their value system to exert itself. Thus we find, for example, Ignatius Donnelly supporting the positive reforms of the Omaha platform yet continually printing anti-Semitic cartoons in his monthly publication, *The Representative,* which he published in the late 1890s.[30]

A special dragon in the laissez-faire mythology was that of a "decadent, feudal Europe," often expressed as an anti-British outlook known as "twisting the lion's tail." At one level, this mentality served the interests of business investors, who found American nationalism a weapon in their competition with European interests. For these, warnings of the Monroe Doctrine and Washington's Farewell Address against foreign alliances have served as a screen behind which a private, business-dominated internationalism has operated in the context of isolationist rhetoric. Thus, the dichotomy between isolationism and internationalism has been essentially a false one in that both are opposite sides of the same coin, both representing different tactics for international expansionism.[31] However, on a cultural level isolationism has encouraged the dragon-chasing mentality by contrasting a unique America of self-made men with a corrupt and undemocratic Europe ruled by parasitical kings and nobility, as the rhetoric went. It was easy for Tory populists to carry on with this outlook and even to adapt it to an attack on finance capitalism in terms of "foreign, Jewish Rothschild international bankers" as the villains of society, a view adopted precisely by Ignatius Donnelly.

One of the most interesting representatives of Tory populism, Ignatius Donnelly was as much bryanist as populist. He is most famous as the author of the preamble to the People's Party platform of 1892, in which he inveighed against corruption dominating the ballot box, the legislatures and the Congress, against a subsidized and muzzled press, and against a hireling army established to shoot down workmen who protest. "The fruits of toil of millions are boldly stolen to build up colossal fortunes, unprecedented in the history of the world, while their possessors despise the republic and endanger liberty," declared Donnelly. The preamble continues: "A vast conspiracy against mankind has been organized on two continents and is taking possession of the world. If not met and overthrown at once it forebodes terrible social convulsions, the destruction of civilization, or the establishment of an absolute despotism." This was typical bryanist rhetoric; however, Donnelly, to his credit, also supported the positive planks for reform in the Omaha Platform, such as government ownership of railroads and utilities, the progressive income tax and the cotton warehousing plan. Yet, he was clearly committed to the dream of petty capitalism and Tory populism as well. In *Caesar's Column,* he outlined his vision of utopia as a Jeffersonian world of small enterprisers:

A thousand men in a community worth $10,000 or $50,000 or even $100,000 each may be a benefit, perhaps a blessing; but one man worth fifty or one hundred millions . . . is a threat against the safety and happiness of every man in the world. I should like to establish a maximum against which no man could own property . . . I would not stop his accumulation . . . but I would require him to invest the surplus under the direction of a governmental board of management, in great works for the benefit of the laboring class. . . .

I would fix a maximum of, say, 100 or 150 acres, or whatever amount might be deemed reasonable. I should abolish all corporations or turn them back into individual partnerships. Abraham Lincoln in the Great Civil War of the last century gave the Southern insurgents so many days in which to lay down their arms or lose their slaves. In the same way, I should grant one or two year's time in which the great owners of land should sell their estates, in small tracts, to actual occupants, to be paid for in installments, on long time, without interest. . . .[32]

Donnelly's *Caesar's Column* was a direct response to Bellamy's *Looking Backward,* in which Bellamy predicted a socialist evolution within a century, a view Donnelly did not share. Lacking any hope in social reform, Donnelly predicted an apocalyptic destruction of modern society. At best he could invent suggestive epigrams, which tended to serve as his mode of social analysis.*

At the time he died, Donnelly was still dreaming of becoming the presidential candidate of the almost defunct People's Party, rejecting at the same time the emerging socialist alternative. It seems possible to extrapolate a picture of Donnelly suffering from a double frustration in the decline of the populist movement by 1900 and the impossibility of the Jeffersonian dream, becoming a thoroughly ill-tempered and reactionary bigot like the later Tom Watson or Bryan, had he lived another ten years.

Even though populists at times engaged in the dragon-chasing tactic so common in American culture, the argument of this study must be repeated: namely, that populism tended to break with the nineteenth-century world view based on the petty capitalist mentality. In moving toward a socialist outlook, even when stopping at radical neomercantilism, populism began to see social forces in tension and to foster proposals for institutional reform rather than engaging in some form of bryanistic negativism.

Another carry-over of nineteenth-century mentality was the tendency on the part of some to endorse monetary panaceas or "funny money" schemes as a single cure-all for social ills. Banking reform and regulation of credit have frequently been needed to help iron out instability in the industrial marketing system. These reforms have usually materialized in the context of the progressive movement, for example, the Federal Reserve Act of 1913. As was argued earlier, money and credit reforms, while necessary, have often been advocated with the hope of achieving economic stability with mini-

---

*A few Donnelly quips follow: "From the same prolific womb of government injustice, we breed two great classes, paupers and millionaires. . . . Building a farm movement that does not engage in politics is like making a gun that does not shoot. . . . History is simply *his story* and depends on who tells it. . . . Great thoughts are like pearls; one must dive deep into the sea of suffering to bring them up. . . . Every political party has its helpless infancy, its gallant and chivalrous youth and its corrupt and selfish old age. . . . Man separated is man savage; man gregarious is man civilized. . . . Jesus was only possible in a barefoot world, and he was crucified by the few who wore shoes. . . . What we need in religion is a remedy for abuses, not an anaesthetic." A collation of such epigrams was published by Donnelly's friend Everett Fish, under the title *Donnellia* (Chicago: F. J. Schulte Co., 1896).

mum disturbance to the economic structure and with the least urgency to restructure income distribution patterns. Thus, Tory populists especially, with their commitment to minimal economic intervention, could easily join the ranks of the money panacea advocates. On the other hand, such a socialist as Henry Demarest Lloyd, with an interest in economic leveling, denigrated this issue with the charge that the money reformers were the cowbirds of the movement, laying the egg of monetary adjustment in the nest of reform organizations to squeeze out consideration of other possible institutional changes.

The Tory populists, then, opposed trusts and monopolies and signs of governmental favoritism to big business interests; and they sought to bolster the cause of petty enterprise under the flag of minimal government. Their rhetoric could sound most class conscious as they lamented the rise of the industrial behemoth; yet, in positive outlook they were geared to Jeffersonian values. They shared the cultural styles of an individualistic society, which often devolved into demon chasing and money schemes as a response to anxiety and frustration. If the populist movements had been composed only of Tory populists, Hofstadter would have been right in viewing them simply as a "heightened expression" of unfortunate tendencies endemic in middle-class America. However, there is more to populism than the Tory variety. And even though there was always an influx of new Tory populists into mass movements during periods of growth, causing tension and schismatic tendencies in the twentieth century as well as the nineteenth, the laissez-faire populists receded in importance as new populist movements evolved.

If Tory populism represented one pole of values and outlooks within populist movements, the opposite pole was that of socialism. I am not viewing socialism here narrowly as the Socialist Party or the Communist Party or as any other doctrinaire organization. The doctrinaire groups were part of the picture, but a socialist perspective extended beyond the confines of the specific organizations flying the flag of socialism. The many currents which went into the socialist tradition have been discussed in Howard Quint's *The Forging of American Socialism.* Quint refers to the Christian Gospel tradition, to Bellamy's nationalist movement and to Henry George's tax plan, which at different times were incorporated into a socialist outlook. He points to the early Marxist movements, which flowered in the person of Daniel DeLeon; and he notes the formation of the less doctrinaire Social Democratic Party in 1901 under Eugene V. Debs, Victor Berger, and Morris Hillquit. Among populists of the upper Midwest, A.R. Wayland's newspaper, *Appeal to Reason,* published for years in Girard, Kansas, was widely read; and the dream of the cooperative commonwealth as a goal for a transformed society had great impact.

It is well to stress the importance of the cooperative commonwealth as only one variety of socialist thought. Adherents to this point of view sought to universalize the profit sharing and the economic democracy inherent in Owen's Rochdale Plan developed in England. Yet, not all cooperators shared the larger ideal of social reformation. Many people adhered to the co-op movement only for its immediate profit-sharing benefits; and these men could often embrace Tory populism in all respects. However, a significant outlook, often projected by ex-socialists, developed both in the Nonpartisan League and later in the Farmers Union movements calling in effect for Owenite socialism under the banner of the cooperative commonwealth. In the 1930s, it was not unusual for the "left wing" of the Farmers Union to post large banners in their convention halls saying: "Toward a Cooperative Commonwealth of America."[33] This outlook found its most dramatic expression in the Farmer-Labor Party platform of 1934, written by a committee headed by Howard Y. Williams. The following passage from that platform is an excellent illustration of the ideal of a cooperative commonwealth as a basis for social reconstruction:

The Farmer Labor Party of Minnesota recognizes that the United States has the most wonderful resources, great factories, machinery of production. . . . At this time when all of us could live in prosperity and happiness, we find that there are millions of working men and women in poverty . . . also hundreds of thousands of farmers, business and professional people who have become poverty stricken and bankrupt. . . .

Palliative measures will continue to fail. Only a complete reorganization of our social structure into a cooperative commonwealth will bring economic security and prevent a prolonged period of further suffering among the people.

We, therefore, declare that capitalism has failed and immediate steps must be taken to abolish capitalism in a peaceful and lawful manner and that a new, sane and just society must be established, a system where all natural resources, machinery of production, transportation and communication shall be owned by the government and operated democratically for the benefit of the people and not for the benefit of the few. . . .[34]

The adoption of this platform followed Governor Olson's ringing declaration: "I am not a liberal . . . I am what I want to be; I am a radical." While the *Farmer Labor Leader* carried articles during the campaign of 1934 "explaining" the intent of this platform as favoring the goals of the Scandinavian "middle way," still the platform was never formally repudiated and Governor Olson was reelected, although with a reduced plurality.

The advocates of a cooperative commonwealth could usually be found as exponents of an evolutionary rather than revolutionary path to socialism; yet, as they set out to organize their cooperatives across the farmlands of the Midwest, they often became involved in serious conflict between farmers and town businessmen. Several leaders of the Nonpartisan League have suggested to me that it was the town merchants' fear of co-op competition which provoked violence against League organizers as much as the foreign policy issue during World War I and that farmers in many areas began to patronize mail-order houses in retribution.

In the 1920s and 1930s, Finnish socialists and communists in northern Minnesota and Wisconsin placed great emphasis on organizing cooperatives as profit-sharing devices; as a matter of fact, a large cooperative wholesale house (Central Cooperative Wholesale—CCW) was established at Duluth. The CCW endured sharp inner schisms, as communists expected the co-ops to help finance and advance the communist plan for revolutionary reform while the evolutionary-minded socialists insisted upon a more neutral political role for the organization.[35]

While Henry George was interested in achieving a utopia of Christian petty capitalism,[36] certain aspects of his analysis, especially his strictures against the concentration of wealth and income, were sufficiently close to socialist analysis that a coalition of Single Taxers and socialists at times developed within populism, witness George's own coalition in his mayoralty race in New York City in 1886.[37] The Single Tax movement had a great impact upon reform movements everywhere, even after George formally dissociated himself from the socialist movement. It is difficult to pinpoint the influence of Henry George on the upper Midwest other than to note that his book *Progress and Poverty* was regularly listed for sale in reform publications and that the national monthly *The Single Taxer* was published in Minneapolis for two years, beginning in 1896. It is noteworthy that Victor Berger was first a disciple of Henry George before he became a full-fledged socialist and that George Norris of Nebraska found the George analysis a good explanation of the rise of nineteenth-century millionaires, such as the Astor fortune.

A parody on "Mary Had a Little Lamb" dramatizes the radical potential in Henry George's theory in its attack upon unfairly earned income from land value increments.

Mary's Little Lot

Mary had a little lot
The soil was very poor
But still she kept it all the same
And struggled to get more.

She kept the lot until one day
The people settled down
And where the wilderness had been
Grew up a thriving town.

Then Mary rented out her lot
(She would not sell you know)
And waited patiently about
For prices still to grow.

They grew, as population came
And Mary raised the rent
With common food and raiment now
She could not be content.

She built up her mansion fine
Had bric a brac galore
And every time the prices rose
She raised the rent some more.

What makes the lot keep Mary so?
The starving people cry;
"Why Mary keeps the lot you know,"
The wealthy would reply.

And so each one of you might be
Wealthy, refined and wise
If you had only hogged some land
And held it for the rise. . . .[38]

These sentiments expressed in "Mary's Little Lot" run counter to those of early immigrants with townsite fever and dreams of getting rich from appreciation of land values. For Henry George and his adherents, this dream was a curse, the basis for the glaring unequal distribution of income in America.

Regardless of the many differences and sharp debates among socialists, a general observation stands that this tradition tended to abandon the notion of the self-made man inherent in the American Dream. Instead, socialists saw man as a "victim" of institutions, capitalist institutions to be sure; nonetheless, they generally saw man as a product of a social environment amenable to reform. This shift is fundamental, for it signifies a dramatic turning away not only from the myth of rugged individualism but also from the cultural qualities, such as demon chasing, manifest in a view of social structure defined in terms of atomic individualism.

The earliest socialist sentiments in the upper midwestern states might possibly be traceable to Father Haire, a radical Catholic priest in Aberdeen, South Dakota, who organized for the Knights of Labor in that state in the 1880s and who helped organize the Socialist Party there in 1901.[39] But the movement did not seem to flourish immediately among the first generation of rural or small-town pioneers. In Milwaukee, on the other hand, a socialist movement did take root, especially among the German immigrants there in the late 1890s.

The emergence of the socialist movement in Milwaukee provides a study of the transformation within populism from right to left on the political spectrum. The details are best provided in Frederick I. Olson's unpublished thesis on the Milwaukee socialist movement. Briefly, it seems that three persons emerged in Milwaukee as populist leaders in the 1890s. Robert Schilling, a former Greenbacker and Knights of Labor leader, who organized a Union Labor Party in Milwaukee in 1888, continued to be active in the 1890s. The second leader was Edward Heath, a Universalist minister and Fabian socialist influenced by Bellamy's *Looking Backward*. Victor Berger, moving from a commitment to Henry George to Edward Bernstein's Marxian revisionism, became a third leader of a loose coalition which operated in the name of the Populist Party.

A crisis arose in 1896 over the operation of the street railway system of Milwaukee, and this issue colored Milwaukee politics for a decade. Issues involved were a strike over wages and working conditions, fares for the public, and the ownership of the system by the Villard interests of New York.[40] In the course of a drawn-out controversy, the populist coalition divided between those who favored immediate public ownership and those satisfied with a resolution of the wage and fare issue. In the settlement, fares were reduced from five to four cents a ride, wages were adjusted, and a new franchise was granted the owners for twenty-five years. This settlement left the advocates of public ownership disgruntled and laid the ground for the formation of the Socialist Party in that city.

Under the leadership of Victor Berger, the Milwaukee socialists hoped to convert the American Federation of Labor into a socialist political movement while maintaining its trade union functions. The attempt on the part of Berger to win the AFL away from Gompers's theory of business unionism led him to make compromises and to mute his feelings about AFL racism in pursuing the "working from within" tactic. Yet, in later life Berger clearly repudiated racism and the Ku Klux Klan movement. In speaking of the tendency for people to be diverted by racism, he pointed to southern slavery as the root of it:

This is partly due to the system of slavery which prevailed in the South before the Civil War. The bulk of the white people of the South, who had no slaves, had no chance for industrial or economic development. It did, however, give them a false notion of superior "race consciousness."

Southern folks are well meaning, but as a general rule they are woefully

lacking even in elementary information about economics, history and eth-
nography. Where modern economic development is taking place in the
South, they are making headway in many directions. The South will for
some time, nevertheless, remain in the backbone of reaction in our country.
Nowhere is the percentage of illiteracy greater and the progress of new ideas
slower. The South has not produced a great writer, artist, poet, inventor or
even statesman in 75 years, but it has produced the Ku Klux Klan.[41]

The Milwaukee socialist movement, organized primarily around German
ethnic groups, elected Emil Seidel as mayor in 1910 and elected Berger to
Congress in the same year. Berger was defeated two years later, but for fifty
years the city usually elected socialists to manage their city government.
Frank Zeidler, the last of the socialist mayors, observes that the voting
electorate preferred the socialists for their honesty and efficiency, not for
any plans to socialize industries.[42] In spite of the reluctance of local voters
to support socialist reforms, the Milwaukee movement, nevertheless, served
to produce a socialist spin-off with a wide impact.

Berger claims to have been instrumental in converting Eugene Debs to the
socialist outlook during a visit with Debs in prison after the ill-fated Pullman
strike. Carl Sandburg served as secretary to Mayor Emil Seidel for a time,
leaving the post when the Socialist Party denounced World War I in 1917.
Oscar Ameringer began his career as a journalist on the *Milwaukee Leader*.
He left in 1917 to conduct a fund-raising drive in Oklahoma, and he stayed
to found the *American Guardian* and to preach socialism in the style of
religious revivals in that state.[43] It was a residue of Ameringer's efforts
which made possible the fairly successful Southern Farmers Tenants Union
in Oklahoma and Arkansas in the late 1930s; this union was an integrated
movement of black and white tenant farmers.[44] E. Haldeman-Julius, famous
for his publishing of the Little Blue Books at Girard, Kansas, after the death
of Wayland, also began as a writer for the *Milwaukee Leader*.[45] It is difficult
to trace all the waves which led from Milwaukee, but it is fair to estimate
that the pamphlets, speeches, and the *Milwaukee Leader* emanating from this
center of socialism made ripples far and wide.

While an image has emerged of the Milwaukee socialists as "good government reformers" lacking in doctrinal insights, this image is hardly tenable.
It is true that Berger was a leader of the "possibilists," who sought to influence mass movements, notably the American Federation of Labor, in
popular-front fashion in contrast with the "impossibilist" Marxists around
DeLeon, who advocated an exclusive radical movement aiming toward a
proletarian revolution. However, the evolutionary approach of the Milwaukee group ought not to be interpreted as nonideological pragmatism.
On the contrary, the Berger position represents a recurrent outlook in socialist circles, analogous to the Communist Party's popular front outlook of

the late 1930s (of course, this analogy suffers in that socialists and communists in the 1930s were at odds over other matters).

The image of the Milwaukee socialists as simple reformers has led to a notion that they were little different in their outlook from the LaFollette progressives. This notion is inaccurate. As a matter of fact, Daniel Hoan, the city attorney and later the mayor of Milwaukee, published a booklet in 1914 entitled *The Failure of Regulation,* in which the progressive LaFollette formula for regulating trusts was roundly attacked. Hoan cites LaFollette's charges that Theodore Roosevelt's antitrust record was mostly myth; but then he proceeds to indicate that LaFollette's own record in Wisconsin was equally devoid of performance. Hoan goes on to argue that the regulatory commissions established by LaFollette, Sr., as governor were welcomed by utility companies, that utility stocks rose in value after state regulation was instituted, and that the state regulatory commission helped to enforce anti-labor and no-strike working conditions. After reviewing the shift in industrial society from laissez-faire to a monopolized economic system, Hoan asks the question: "Shall we regulate, smash or own the trust?" His answer, of course, calls for public ownership. He concludes his brief with a heuristic appeal for readers to join the movement:

Better things are in store for us. The world ever moves onward. Get into the fray. Do your part, and you will soon see the results of your efforts. Don't expect all Socialists to be either perfect human beings or to think exactly as you do. Learn to overlook the shortcomings of your comrades. Remember they are fighting for a better system, not to make all men uniform or perfect. Filled with a conviction of right, resolved with a determination to win, nothing can stop the onward march of civilization until final victory is achieved.[46]

It is clear from this booklet by Hoan that the gulf between the socialists and the LaFollette movement was a wide one, which was reciprocally recognized. Even though the two movements ran on parallel courses in opposition to World War I and engaged in covert cooperation in 1922 and 1924,[47] it is clear that they operated from differing world views.

In Minnesota and North Dakota, the socialist movement took deeper roots in rural areas than seems to have been the case in Wisconsin. One of the few living socialists from the pre-World War I period, Henry Martinson, now living in Fargo, North Dakota, recalls that he participated in organizing a Norwegian-American branch of the Socialist Party in northern North Dakota in 1908 or 1909 and that it was these socialist clubs which transferred their membership to Townley's Nonpartisan League, making it possible for the League to appear to spread like a "prairie fire."[48]

A brochure published in 1915 telling the history of Ada, Minnesota, a

small county-seat town in Mahnomen County in northwestern Minnesota,
notes the presence of well-organized socialist clubs throughout the county
and in the town as well:

Ada has a little body of socialists who were affiliated with the Socialist
Party and who have been holding meetings since 1902. They began as a club
which made a study of socialism and most of its members soon became socialists. The organization meets once a month and has two special meetings
a year. There are thirty-two members of the local organization, ten of
whom are farmers, but the average attendance is only about eight. It has no
president and elects a chairman for each meeting. . . . A holiday supper or
dance is generally given, and an annual picnic is held during the summer.
These functions are exceptional in that the farmers and town people mix
freely. As one of the leaders put it, "Socialism seems to be the only bond
that brings country and town people together socially". . . . Since its organization in 1902 socialism has not gained in Ada; it has been gaining steadily,
however, in the country, and in other villages in the county. In fact there
are eleven locals in the county, some of which are fairly strong.[49]

The potential threat of the socialist movement was dramatized by the
creation of a nonpartisan legislature as a part of 1913 constitutional reforms
in Minnesota. It was feared that the Socialist Party, linked with Prohibitionists, would elect a bloc of legislators under a three-party system; whereas
socialists would be certain to be defeated in the final runoff in November if
they did survive a primary race and if they confronted a single conservative
candidate from either Democratic or Republican circles. While the trend to
nonpartisanship was abetted by the progressive notion of elevating "principle above party," it seems that the threat of "troublesome socialists" in
the legislature was the decisive factor in abandoning the traditional role of
the political parties in electing legislators.[50]

In both Minnesota and North Dakota, many socialists were initially integrated into the staff of the Nonpartisan League. The League's founder,
A.C. Townley himself, was head of a Socialist Party farm department in
1914. Even though Townley was soon dismissed from this post for the
reason that he knew nothing about socialism, he initially looked to the
socialists for help in getting the League started.[51] As the League grew from
its socialist base, Henry Teigan resigned as editor of a socialist weekly, the
Iconoclast, published in Minot, North Dakota, to become the editor of the
North Dakota League paper. Later, Teigan moved to Minneapolis as the
general manager of the National Nonpartisan League to direct activities in a
number of states. Also serving in the Minneapolis office, as director of organization, was Joseph Gilbert, who had previously been active in the socialist movement in several states.[52] While Townley was the national president
of the League and its leading spokesman, the role of Teigan and Gilbert in

the Minneapolis office was that of hiring socialist organizers as much as possible and incorporating socialist arguments into the practical demands of the League. Showing no isolationist fears of foreign ideas, the League leadership was intent upon socialist education. For example, a Nonpartisan League song book published in 1918 carried a two-page reprint of a statement of principles of the British Labor Party clearly calling for a socialist reorganization of society. A portion of the Labor Party statement follows:

But unlike the Conservative and Liberal parties, the Labor party insists on democracy in industry as well as in government. It demands of the progressive elimination from the control of industry of the private capitalist, individual or joint stocks and the setting free of all who work, whether by hand or by brain, for the service of the community, and of the community only. And the Labor party refuses absolutely to believe that the British people will permanently tolerate any reconstruction or perpetuation of the disorganization, waste and inefficiency involved in the abandonment of British industry to a jostling crowd of separate private employers, with their minds bent, not on the service of the community, but—by the law of their being— only on the utmost possible profiteering.[53]

As Townley increasingly looked to William Lemke for aid and advice, he broke with his socialist backers. In North Dakota, the more militant socialists eventually felt they had made a mistake in coalescing with Townley. In reaction, they made Henry Martinson, a Marxist with DeLeon sympathies, the new editor of the *Iconoclast.*[54] With the help of a Swedish printer, a revolutionary who kept three rifles shined up for the final assault on Minot, Martinson edited the paper with a good deal of financial help from Arthur LeSueur, the socialist mayor. However, too many of the former socialists were now committed to the League; and so the *Iconoclast* failed when LeSueur left in 1917 to become the chancellor of the People's College, a socialist correspondence school founded by Eugene Debs at Fort Scott, Kansas.

In Minnesota, the rift between Townley and the socialists took the form of a difference over whether or not to strive for the formation of a third party. Townley argued for Gompers's policy of rewarding friends and punishing enemies, but the socialists, notably Henry Teigan and William Mahoney, insisted upon the third-party route.

Socialist leadership in the Twin City labor movement emerged at the same time as socialist leadership within the Farmers League. This made possible the formation of the Minnesota Farmer-Labor Party as an equivalent of the European labor party pattern. While the Party was organized with much input from socialists, in final analysis it was an eclectic movement of many currents and deserves special attention as a case study in the next chapter.

After 1920, the Communist Party became a factor in the general socialist movement. Most often, the role of the Party in the populist movements of the upper Midwest has been overdramatized. Clarence Hathaway, a Minnesota communist who later became the national editor of the *Daily Worker* in the 1930s, was involved with the attempt to form a national third-party movement initiated by Mahoney in 1923 and 1924. He came on the scene after plans were well under way, and his role was not decisive. However, his importance was inflated by the fact that his presence was used by the LaFollette and Townley forces, who opposed a third party, as a basis for blasting the Mahoney dream of a national farmer-labor party. This matter will be treated more fully in a following chapter.

The relationship of the Communist Party and other smaller parties of Marxist parentage to the broadly based populist movements is a matter of perennial interest. It is sufficient at this point to observe that the Communist Party has fluctuated in its history between the popular-front evolutionary strategy and a proletarian based revolutionary strategy for influencing the social process. In its popular front phase, notably after 1935, and when practicing coalition politics with mass movements, the Party must be viewed as a part of the larger populist impulse. On the other hand, in its revolutionary phases, the Communist Party, along with the DeLeon and Trotsky movements, can hardly be viewed as populist in the definition of the term employed in this study. A significant exception to Trotskyism as isolated radicalism occurred in Minneapolis when Teamsters Local 574 came under the leadership of the Dunne brothers and Farrell Dobbs, who then led the truck drivers strike there in 1934. This strike was famous for the strikers' rout of the police in "The Battle of Deputies Run"; and two months later, for "Bloody Friday," when the police retaliated; and for Governor Olson's deployment of the state militia against both employers' and strikers' headquarters.[55]

Generally, the Communist Party during the late 1920s and the early 1930s worked to develop a "proletarian" movement in the trade unions with the hope that the day of revolution, Russian style, would dawn. In spite of the party line of the communists, there is one piece of evidence that Finnish communists did in fact participate in the Farmer-Labor Party in Minnesota in the 1920s. A letter written by Leo Mattson, a leftist editor of *Uusi Kotimaa* (New Homeland) published in New York Mills, a small Finnish community in western Minnesota, indicates that rural Finns were involved:

Uusi Kotimaa was especially devoted to serve the Farmer Labor Party cause. We organized local FLP club in Mills and helped in organizing such clubs in Sebeka, Menagha, Wolf Lake, Henning and Perham. Preparing for 1928 national election from our initiative, we held Otter Tail County convention that was very well attended (delegates from every part of the county). Many of the party candidates visited us. Knut Wefald (ex-congressman) was frequent visitor and after election told that probably election returns would have been different without *Uusi Kotimaa.* And I recall a lengthy debate with Senator Henrik Shipstead about crises in Nicaragua where United States troops were sended [sic]. As a member of Senate Foreign Relations Committee, Mr. Shipstead had voted for sending our troops to Nicaragua. Our policy in the paper was to oppose or criticize such interference. We departed discontented but Mr. Shipstead won nomination at the state convention in St. Paul and was reelected. In 1928 state convention, I was elected to FLP state committee from our congressional district. . . . I recall that in our first meeting Floyd B. Olson was present. He was called to our meeting in hope that he would be candidate for governor. He declined stating that he can't fulfill the great responsibility . . . for personal reasons (his mother was seriously ill). But in 1930 he accepted nomination and was elected . . . governor, winning respect and being in high esteem of all common people.[56]

During this period (1920s–early 1930s), it was not unusual for communists who adhered closely to the party line to denounce the populist movements for their petty capitalist tendencies and to refer, for example, to Governor Floyd Olson as a "social fascist" along with Huey Long and Father Coughlin. But with the switch in policy to that of the "popular front" late in 1935, communists took a direct interest in the populist political movements in 1936 and afterwards. An immediate result of this new policy in Minnesota was the election of John Bernard to Congress from the Minnesota Iron Range district. Bernard won fame as a freshman Congressman for his lone vote against the Neutrality Act in the Spanish Civil War, a war which was already internationalized, he argued, by the massive intervention of the fascist powers in behalf of General Franco's rebellion against the constitutional government.[57]

In Wisconsin, the attempt of the communists to break out of their political isolation after 1935 caused a great deal of conflict between them and the socialists as these two groups vied for power within unions and in political organizations. The struggle was especially bitter within the Progressive Farmer-Labor Federation, which was organized as a coalition of farm and labor organizations, including socialists but excluding communists. The Federation, under the guidance of Andrew Biemuller, was continually in a turmoil as persons of communist persuasion came into the structure through union connections or as farm delegates. In this situation, the case of the widow of Victor Berger became a cause célébre for her support of the more militant communist position and of the emerging CIO.[58]

In addition to communist influence in the labor movement, especially in the CIO in the latter half of the 1930s, the United Farmers League, organized in isolated counties in the upper midwestern states in the mid 1920s, generally reflected the communist position. This League published a weekly newspaper, *The Producers' News*, at Plentywood, Montana, during the 1920s and later, beginning about 1930, in Minneapolis. The communists who were affiliated with the United Farmers League played an active role in the Farm Holiday Association of the early thirties, often setting an example with farm strikes and penny auctions.[59] The idea of "enforcing" sales of mortgaged property and land for a few pennies at mortgage foreclosures and returning the property to the former owner title free is credited to a communist club in Madison County, Nebraska, headed by Harry Lux, and the practice came to be known as the Madison County Plan.[60] It should be noted that similar pressure on banks to renegotiate mortgages was simultaneously initiated in Kandiyohi County, Minnesota, under the leadership of noncommunist John Bosch, who became the national president of the Farm Holiday movement in 1936.[61] Communists were active as well in the famous milk strike in Wisconsin of 1933, which set the pattern for farm strikes and milk dumping in other midwestern states.[62]

With the advent of the popular front position, many of these communists gravitated into the Farmers Union movement, generating a debate between themselves and the Milo Reno group with its bias toward Lemke-Huey Long bryanism. In Minnesota, for example, this conflict took the form of a contest between two groups for the right to be recognized as the official Farmers Union organization of the state, one group headed by John Erp and the other by Oscar Christianson, the "right" and the "left," respectively.[63]

A consideration of the various socialist currents within the populist movements is not complete without reference to the foreign policy outlook of socialists. While the Tory populists tended toward a traditional isolationism rooted both in the economic interests of the business community and in demon chasing psychology, the socialists were committed to a special form of internationalism, to the idea of a common bond of the masses transcending the nationalism of business competitors in the world market. The Socialist Party resolution against World War I, adopted in April 1917 after war was declared, is a good illustration both of their rhetoric and of their pacifistic internationalism:

Modern wars as a rule are caused by the commercial and financial rivalries and intrigues of the capitalist interests of different countries. Whether they have been frankly waged as wars of aggression or have been hypocritically represented as wars of "defense," they have always been made by the classes and fought by the masses. War brings wealth and power to the ruling classes and suffering, death and demoralization to the workers. . . . They [wars] breed a sinister spirit of passion, unreason, race hatred and false patriotism. They obscure the struggles of the workers for life, liberty and social justice.

They tend to sever the bonds of solidarity between them and their brothers in other countries, to destroy their organizations and to curtail their civil and political rights and liberties. . . . We, therefore, call upon the workers of all countries to refuse to support their governments in their wars.[64]

This was a courageous stand to take after the passions of war were already inflamed, a position of note partly for its variance with the tendencies of German and French socialists to endorse their own nations' war efforts. Some American socialists resigned from the movement, Carl Sandburg and A.M. Simons among them. More seriously, government denial of mailing permits and a general mood of repression virtually destroyed the rural socialist movement in the United States,[65] crippling socialism as an alternative paradigm to mainstream progressivism.

There were nonsocialist currents with a close affinity to the socialist internationalism. Certain of the peace progressives developed an antiwar rationale based on what they regarded as the baneful influences of business interests, an outlook implicit in the Nye Committee's 1935 investigation of the influence of munitions industries in World War I. Charles Beard developed a serious critique of imperialist internationalism in *The Open Door at Home,* which called for restricting foreign investments in favor of domestic development. However, it was easy for peace progressives to be influenced by the socialists. Most notably, there is the example of Charles Lindbergh, Sr., whose books and pamphlets were widely read. He wrote of a four-class structure: labor, farmers, small businessmen and financiers, the first three opposed to the last as "producers against parasites," a cliché employed by many dissenters, including mugwumps. However, this analysis in the hands of persons leaning to socialism formed a basis for an argument to nationalize banks and big business while permitting capitalism for farmers and small businessmen, in effect a quasi-socialist program. Lindbergh, Sr., was explicit about his commitment to the socialist position: "The socialist view of war is, in my judgment, the correct view"; and in speaking before a 1916 Conference on Real Preparedness, he called for reform "so that toilers would be the beneficiaries of their own toil."[66]

The point to be stressed is that there were two distinct antiwar positions: Tory isolationism on one hand and socialist internationalism on the other. Both points of view were to be found in that eclectic mixture of world views which operated within populist movements. In commenting on the antiwar tradition of the Farmer-Labor Party in Minnesota, George Garlid has noted the differences over foreign policy within the Party without tracing these differences to their respective roots in socialist internationalism and Tory isolationism: "The isolationism of Congressmen Henry C. Teigan and John T. Bernard—and neither would have called it such—differed significantly from that of Senators Shipstead and Lundeen."[67] Garlid notes, however, that these differences in emphasis did not result in an open schism within the Farmer Labor Party over foreign policy since both outlooks tended to use identical antiwar rhetoric, including Anglophobia. Yet, in a larger context, Garlid is incorrect; for there was a deep schism in the Farmer Labor Party in the 1938 primary contest in which isolationists led by Hjalmar Petersen and Senator Henrik Shipstead (the "neurotic neutrals," in Garlid's phraseology) opposed internationalists led by Elmer Benson, Abe Harris and John Bernard, who consistently warned against Hitlerism as a reactionary force and supported collective security as evidenced by Bernard's opposition to the Neutrality bill. While the group led by Governor Benson was anti-Hitler, Senator Ernest Lundeen was hardly even a "neurotic neutral," for he permitted a Nazi agent, George Sylvester Viereck, to use his Senatorial mailing privileges.[68]

In examining the role of socialists in the twentieth-century populist movements of the upper Midwest, we have witnessed the vital role of the socialists in providing ideological leadership within the movements. However, there is danger of overstressing the role of the socialists. It should not be assumed that large numbers of people were consciously socialist or belonged to the Socialist Party. In 1914 the membership of the Socialist Party was only 4,965 in Minnesota and 1,644 in North Dakota.[69] My own assumption is that these statistics understate involvement in the socialist movement at this time; for it seems unlikely that these few people could have promoted five to ten percent of the voters to mark their ballots for Eugene Debs in the presidential election of 1912. But in any event, the fact remains that the socialist movement was not a mass movement as was the Nonpartisan League later.

Even though socialists gravitated into leadership in both the Nonpartisan League and the Farmer-Labor Party, the rank and file of these movements, and some leaders as well, were not ordinarily socialists. Yet, they clearly were something more than Tory populists in tending to accept socialist leadership. These people in the middle, so to speak, serve as the base for the third current in populist ideology.

The term "radical neomercantilism" is indeed an awkward one; yet it expresses well the central thrust of populism in the model presented in this book. This outlook represents a halfway step between Tory populism and socialism; and it combines elements from both poles. Generally, it calls for regulation of business and for interfering in the free market with a leveling intent rather than simply with an intent of rationalizing and smoothing out the economy in the interests of corporate business, which was the chief aim of the progressives. It might seem adequate to define populism simply as radical neomercantilism. However, this definition would ignore the Tory and socialist edges of the populist spectrum; and it would ignore the tendency for populism to move from right to left through time, in effect moving toward a more firmly established radical neomercantilist view as the socialist view came to counteract the influence of the Tory view within the movements.

Radical neomercantilism by definition embodies cognitive dissonance and ambivalence. Thus, it was possible for populists within this central outlook to be vacillators, to move into the socialist outlook at one time and to swing back to a Tory populist view at another time. Furthermore, in case after case individuals vacillated completely out of the populist orbit and ceased being populists at all. In this group, none stands out more than Tom Watson of Georgia, who, after a decade as a principled populist in the 1890s, moved into the ranks of the Democratic Party and displayed all of the bigoted and ill-tempered characteristics so common in frustrated bryanists. In addition to those midwestern populists already cited who reverted to an extreme right-wing political position, there were others who joined the parade to the right. Among them was A.C. Townley, the charismatic leader of the Nonpartisan League.

After Townley broke with his original socialist backers and after he had served a prison term for allegedly preaching wartime disloyalty, he organized a new movement, The Producers League, which in the 1920s offered competition to the failing Nonpartisan League.[70] The Producers League, a forerunner of a larger movement of the 1960s and 1970s, the National Farmers Organization (NFO), aimed to promote collective bargaining among farmers. However, Townley's new movement foundered and finally merged with the Farmers Union in 1926, when the latter organization was in the process of shifting from the South to a new base in the wheat belt. In 1934, Townley, living in Minnesota, filed in the Farmer-Labor primary against Floyd Olson for governor and criticized the famous 1934 platform of the Farmer-Labor Party, calling for a cooperative commonwealth type of social reconstruction. In 1938, Townley boasted to Governor Elmer Benson that he had been paid $2000 by the steel companies to expose the "kommunists" in the Farmer-Labor Party, including one of Townley's best friends, who had repeatedly given him gifts during the depression.[71] In the 1950s, Townley attacked alleged communist influences in the Farmers Union and caused a $25,000 libel suit to be filed against a Fargo radio station as a consequence of a Townley radio speech.[72] He died in the late 1950s, far removed ideologically from the populist movements of which he had once been a part. At the end, he made a living practicing "quack medicine" as a faith healer. This was the final enterprise in life of one who probably never lost the dream of again becoming the "flax king" of North Dakota under conditions of free enterprise.

There were others who moved in effect from left to right and out of the populist spectrum. As already noted, Henrik Shipstead, first elected to the United States Senate in 1922 by the farmer and labor coalition in Minnesota, emerged as an anti-Roosevelt isolationist in the 1930s and finally suffered his demise in a Republican primary contest in 1946. More poignant is the case of William Mahoney, a labor socialist who quite properly is considered the father of the Minnesota Farmer-Labor Party but who came in later years to associate with a Constitutional Money League with anti-Semitic overtones and with a general anticommunist ideology.

These examples of persons who have vacillated as populists, at times leaving the populist movements, seem to sustain the Hofstadter characterization of populists. However, we have already observed that a number of people moved in the opposite direction, from right to left, from Tory populism to socialism or quasi-socialism, including George Norris of Nebraska, Richard Pettigrew of South Dakota and Elmer Benson of Minnesota. More important, however, than a cataloging of individuals who vacillated one way or another in their ambivalence is the argument that radical neomercantilism became the central thrust of populism. This shift was evident as the Tory populist formula of simple trust-busting receded in emphasis and various proposals for institutional reform came to the forefront. One of the earliest and most important of these proposals was the cotton warehousing plan developed by Dr. C.W. McCune, a Texas Farmers Alliance leader. Other proposals set forth in the Omaha Platform of 1892 included those of the progressive income tax, government ownership of noncompetitive utilities, legislation protecting the right of labor to organize and strike, freedom from repressive use of police or the army in farmer or labor confrontations with establishment forces, and other measures implying governmental intervention in behalf of "the people."[73]

As progressives began to utilize the rhetoric of reform and regulation, populists were often co-opted, and there was always a tendency for potential populists to be attracted to the progressive camp, especially to the various governors in the upper midwestern states, such as LaFollette of Wisconsin, Cummins of Iowa, Crawford of South Dakota, Burke of North Dakota and John A. Johnson of Minnesota. This tendency for progressives to co-opt potential populists is well documented in a recent study of progressive voting patterns in Wisconsin. In his chapter entitled "Progressives and the Middle Class," Roger Wyman shows that LaFollette, Sr., consistently drew his support from less prosperous farm areas and from urban labor wards.[74] This pattern is at odds with the definition of progressivism as an upper middle-class movement to "save capitalism," as projected by most revisionist historians. However, a distinction must be made between the constituency and the intellectual intent and social impact. The revisionists are quite right in their assessment of progressive intent and impact.

Whatever the performance of progressivism, in the final analysis it did not always satisfy its constituency; for populist movements dramatically exploded in the wake of midwestern progressivism. Thus the Nonpartisan League, the Farmer-Labor Party, the Farmers Union and the Farm Holiday movement emerged as major populist expressions of the 1910s, 1920s and 1930s. If some populists were won over by progressives, either through co-optation and/or as an aspect of the vacillatory nature of populism, this shift should not obscure the difference in the intent of the two movements as developed in chapter two. One was a movement to rationalize the corporate system; and the other, a movement aiming to harness and even change the structure of corporate business. In view of this difference in intent, it is most misleading to characterize progressives as "populists dressed up with the hayseeds combed out of their hair." Furthermore, this difference in intent supports the view that the central thrust of populism was *radical neomercantilism* as distinguished from the Hamiltonian neomercantilism of progressivism.

Since radical neomercantilist populists are by definition eclectic and ambivalent, it is difficult to find any "grand theorist" who embodies the contradictions inherent in this point of view. I have already suggested that on a national level Henry Demarest Lloyd might be considered an intellectual theorist for populism in its main thrust, even though he leaned toward socialism.

One notable radical neomercantilist in the upper midwestern states was George Loftus, a small grain buyer at Stillwater, Minnesota. Loftus went bankrupt as a result of railroad discrimination in offering cheaper freight rates to bigger buyers associated with the Minneapolis Chamber of Commerce.[75] This experience galvanized Loftus into a lifelong career of fighting railroads, the grain exchange and big business in general. In time, he became the northwest organizer for the American Society of Equity, a movement that originated in Indiana in 1902, first with a collective bargaining approach and later with an aim to build farmer cooperatives to develop power in the marketplace. It was largely under the leadership of Loftus that the Equity movement took root in Minnesota from 1912 to 1916. As a matter of fact, it was in response to an Equity demand for a state-owned terminal elevator in North Dakota that a member of the legislature allegedly told a farm delegation to "go home and slop your hogs," which in turn became the rallying cry for Townley and the Nonpartisan League.

Loftus was a warm admirer of LaFollette, Sr., and the Wisconsin Plan; however, his desire to regulate and even cripple "big business," the grain trade in particular, seems to have been more far-reaching in intent than ever dreamed by LaFollette. Loftus, through his attorney Jim Manahan, was continually bringing suits against railroads before the federal Interstate Commerce Commission. One of his more famous cases was his successful litigation forcing the Pullman Company to charge less for an upper bunk than a lower one on grounds that an upper bunk was unhandy and uncomfortable, thus rendering less service to the user. In this case, he brought several Negro porters to testify as to working conditions on Pullman cars; and as their testimony became embarrassing, the Pullman Company, headed ironically by Robert Lincoln, son of the Great Emancipator, chose to concede rather than prolong the hearings.[76]

Loftus at one time attempted to organize a Minneapolis Grain Exchange of his own as a terminal through which farmers' cooperative elevators might market their grain on the national and world market, by-passing the alleged chicanery in the private grain trade. Loftus may have been a LaFollette admirer until his premature death in 1916, but his efforts to reform the grain selling system became a populistic war against the grain "robber barons" rather than a progressive legitimating of the system with a dose of honesty here and a pruning away of a special abuse there.

Jim Manahan, the attorney for both the Society for Equity and the Non partisan League, is an interesting example of a person who seemed to move finally toward a position of radical neomercantilism. His colorful career began as a Bryan Democrat in Nebraska, followed by an interlude as a progressive Republican in support of LaFollette, Sr., and ending in the populist movements of the upper Midwest. Although tempted toward socialism, he did not embrace a socialist viewpoint, even though he realized that the progressive dream had become "regulation that did not regulate." In his autobiography, *Trials of a Lawyer,* he wrote:

Somehow, and in some way, the Interstate Commerce Commission gradually drifted, as new appointments were made, from its old position as guardian of the people's rights, into the trustee for safeguarding the dividends of investors in railroad securities. . . . But I still clung, with the memory of our victories in the Express and Pullman cases sustaining me, to my old faith in government regulation. I was frankly afraid of socialism, and I was skeptical of government ownership, with its inevitable bureaucracy. . . . I reasoned in a circle, endlessly, on regulation that did not regulate.[77]

Even though Manahan rejected socialism himself, he was friendly with many socialists and quasi-socialists. He represented socialist Joe Gilbert at Red Wing, Minnesota, after Gilbert had been arrested for sedition while speaking at a Nonpartisan League meeting. Manahan's account of the trial is interesting both for its reflection of contemporary attitudes toward radicals and for Manahan's candid appraisal of his own behavior.

145

During the first day of the trial, the courtroom was packed with friendly farmers, and Manahan's defense of Gilbert seemed to be going very well. However, the judge called for a night session of court, which meant that the farmers would be home milking their cows. A highlight of the night session came during a temporary recess in the trial when the prosecuting attorney auctioned off a parrot named Kaiser Bill for the benefit of the Red Cross. Manahan bid on the bird lest he be accused of being unpatriotic.

When the trial recessed, a mob of "patriots" were waiting for Manahan. He ran down a back alley but was caught and taken toward the Mississippi River. His own words tell of the experiences of the next few minutes:

From the mob that followed close, someone kicked me twice. A voice shouted, "Get a Rope!" A smell of hate came from the heavily breathing crowd . . . I found myself saying a little prayer.

We came to a cross road and the leaders hesitated. In the pause my mind automatically functioned, professionally. I heard myself saying, "Boys, I am only a lawyer, trying a case for a living," and oh, for the pity of it, I heard my lying tongue say "I have no use for those damn socialists." I cursed.

My cowardice and betrayal caught the sympathy of the cowardly mob. I was one of them, after all. The leader gruffly scolded, "Why in hell did you threaten to boycott our town?" Thrice I lied that night. I said I did not mean it.[78]

Manahan was allowed to take the next train back to Minneapolis, admitting to having been a frightened man and bitter over his own cowardice. Yet, it is clear that he gravitated toward the socialists, even though he lied under duress that he had no use for them. The Gilbert case finally went to the U.S. Supreme Court. The majority upheld Gilbert's conviction, with Justice Brandeis dissenting. Since the conviction was under a Minnesota statute that forbade interference with enlistments through acts or speech, Brandeis argued that the federal government should interpose itself against this state violation of free speech rights. Brandeis also reasoned that the due process clause should apply not just to property but to the right of speech as well. An entire chapter in *Free Speech in the United States,* by Zechariah Chaffee, Jr., is devoted to this case and the Brandeis dissent, noting that the dissent later became a precedent in other cases where constitutional rights were abridged by state statutes.

In Governor Floyd B. Olson, who served in Minnesota from 1930 until his death in 1936, we have a radical neomercantilist who acted as a political pragmatist. He was inclined toward wanting far-reaching reforms but was always ready to compromise out of necessity. Generally, he supported the direction of the New Deal. He opposed, in the process, the rightist-bryanist Lemke third-party venture in 1936, and he also throttled down impulses of the American Commonwealth League, an outgrowth of the League for Political Democracy, to found a "production for use" third party in 1936. Olson feared that a serious third-party movement would permit the election of a Republican and open the door to American style fascism. Yet, he was often critical of Roosevelt liberalism, especially its tardy response to human suffering, and of the capitalistic system in general. Olson's 1934 keynote speech before the Farmer-Labor Party convention is an example of his more radical rhetoric:

Now all this destitution that confronts us in this nation certainly must suggest to every thinking man and woman that the system under which we have operated is a poor system . . . that a nation cannot endure, as has been fittingly said, part rich and almost entirely poor. . . . Now I am frank to say that I am not a liberal. I enjoy working on a common basis with liberals for their platforms, but I am not a liberal. I am what I want to be—I am a radical —I am not satisfied with tinkering, I am not satisfied with patching. I am not satisfied with hanging a laurel wreath upon burglars and thieves and pirates and calling them code authorities or something else. . . .[79]

A fourth person who fits the radical neomercantilist category is Elmer A. Benson, who was appointed by Governor Olson to fill an unexpired Senate term upon the death of Thomas Schall in 1935. Benson was elected governor in 1936 and served only one term. His 1938 defeat by Harold Stassen was due in part to the division in the labor movement caused by the formation of the CIO and in part to an unusually vehement attack from the far right in Minnesota, an attack utilizing the slogan "Jews, Communism and Corruption" as its war cry against the Benson Administration. While Stassen did not join in this bigotry, he capitalized on people's discouragement during the depression years by promising jobs, not relief, a promise which materialized later with war spending. The only employment which the Stassen administration provided was in hiring new state employees to replace Farmer-Labor appointees en masse, down to janitors and cleaning women—all in the name of Civil Service Reform.

The Benson administration was most unusual for the radical leadership offered by Benson himself. One of his first acts upon taking office was to call upon the University Board of Regents to reinstate political science professor William Shaper, who had been dismissed without a hearing in 1917 for alleged disloyalty. On several occasions, the governor called out the national guard to support the demands of unions on strike, contrary to the traditional tactic of using militia to suppress strikes. He called a special session of the legislature in 1937 and secured a highly progressive income and profits tax program for the state. Benson was friendly toward New Deal efforts to cure the depression; but he, along with other midwestern governors and Governor Lehman of New York, was sharply critical of President Roosevelt's 1937 retrenchment of federal spending on the assumption that the depression was over; and he was at odds with New Deal authorities over the administration of work projects, which were directed in Minnesota by a former Republican congressman, Victor Christgau. In general, Benson hewed to the left of the New Deal, a radical populist who was noted for speaking his mind bluntly.

The men cited here—George Loftus, James Manahan, Floyd Olson and Elmer Benson—serve as examples to demonstrate that radical neomercantilism was indeed a viable current within populism. None of these men was an overt socialist; yet all subscribed to practical proposals which ran counter to the free-market assumptions of classical economics. Their proposals for regulated farm prices, regulated currency, regulated working conditions in industry and government ownership of utilities proved to be a consensus position for rallying and unifying the movements. As antitrust action failed over the early years of the twentieth century, and as the Jeffersonian dream of a society of small entrepreneurs seemed to become a lost cause, the Tory populists could move toward these programs of a regulated economy, perhaps without completely shedding their cultural adherence to rugged individualism and the American Dream. At the same time, socialists could subscribe to a program of regulating business as a stepping stone toward a full-fledged program of socialist reform; and thus they too tended to concur with the radical neomercantilist position.

As has already been noted, there was a shift through time; for as a socialist outlook developed substance in the twentieth century, radical neomercantilism was strengthened as the central thrust of populism. This perspective on populism as a shifting spectrum is central to my differences with both Hofstadter and Pollack. Hofstadter defines populism almost exclusively in terms of the Tory current; whereas Pollack tends to idealize all populists as if they were quasi-socialists. Neither man allows for a median position, a point between Tory populism and socialism, a point shifting its emphasis through time away from Tory populism.

While the lines between progressivism and populism have often been blurred, especially at those times when the two movements were competing for the same constituencies, it has been possible to view them as conceptually distinct. Both began to view society in terms of institutions in mutual interaction, but they held different ideas about reforming the social structure. Both movements at their best echoed the altruism of John Winthrop's "Model for Christian Charity," but with a difference. The progressives were content to remain advocates of Christian capitalism, still retaining the spirit of nineteenth-century moral reformers. The populists, in effect, were attempting to turn the much maligned John Winthrop on his head, stressing egalitarianism and economic leveling with an anticapitalistic bias, contrary to the elitism explicit both in Winthrop and in progressivism.

NOTES

1. Donald F. Warner, "Prelude to Populism," *Minnesota History*, 32:129-145, September 1951.

2. John D. Hicks, *The Populist Revolt* (Minneapolis: University of Minnesota Press, 1931), p. 222.

3. David Thelen, "LaFollette and the Temperance Crusade," *Wisconsin Magazine of History*, 47:291-300, Summer 1964.

4. Elwyn B. Robinson, *History of North Dakota* (Lincoln: University of Nebraska Press, 1966), pp. 221-225.

5. Personal interview with Elmer A. Benson, August 1958.

6. Alma Lutz, "Susan B. Anthony in the Dakotas," *North Dakota History Magazine*, 25:119-125, October 1958.

7. Ibid., p. 122.

8. David Thelen, "The Social and Political Origins of Wisconsin Progressivism, 1885-1890" (Unpublished doctoral dissertation, University of Wisconsin, 1967). This important study focuses on the shift from mugwump negativism to progressive municipal reformism in several Wisconsin urban centers.

9. Padriac C. Kennedy, "The Progressives and American Foreign Policy, 1898-1917: From Imperialism to Anti-Imperialism," *Wisconsin Magazine of History*, 46:289-291, Summer 1963.

10. Herbert Margulies, *The Decline of the Progressive Movement in Wisconsin, 1890-1920* (Madison: State Historical Society of Wisconsin, 1969), pp. 281-282.

11. Solon Buck, *The Granger Movement* (Cambridge: Harvard University Press, 1913). See chapter 7, "Business Cooperation in the Midwest in the Granger Era, 1865-1875," *Agricultural History*, 37:187-205, June 1963.

12. Robinson, p. 185.

13. Robert Bahmer, "The Economic and Political Background of the Nonpartisan League" (Unpublished doctoral dissertation, University of Minnesota, 1941), p. 104.

14. The attempt of the Farmers Alliance to interest English investors is described in a pamphlet, *Our Daily Bread*, published privately in 1919 by

H.L. Loucks in Watertown, South Dakota. Loucks was the chairman of the Dakota Farmers Alliance in the late 1880s and early 1890s.

15. A basic source of information on populism in the 1890s in Minnesota is to be found in a study by Professor Chrislock of Augsburg College, Minneapolis: Carl H. Chrislock, "The Politics of Protest in Minnesota 1890-1901, From Populism to Progressivism" (Unpublished doctoral dissertation, University of Minnesota, 1954). This thesis deals with the three-way tension between Donnelly, Owen and Dobbyn at various times in the decade.

16. Carl H. Chrislock, "Sidney M. Owen, an Editor in Politics," *Minnesota History*, 36:120-122, December 1958.

17. Charles H. Backstrom, "The Progressive Party of Wisconsin" (Unpublished doctoral dissertation, University of Wisconsin, 1956), p. 34.

18. Personal interview with Howard Y. Williams, October 1969.

19. Personal interview with Elizabeth Brandeis Rauschenbush, September 1969. Mrs. Rauschenbush recalled that her father, Judge Louis Brandeis, was instrumental in calling Franklin Roosevelt's attention to the need for unemployment insurance legislation and for the desirability of drafting a federal plan based on the Wisconsin law.

20. Backstrom, p. 146.

21. Ibid., p. 143.

22. Ibid., p. 483.

23. Ibid., pp. 426-427.

24. Personal interview with Elmer A. Benson, August 1968.

25. Robert L. Morlan, *Political Prairie Fire* (Minneapolis: University of Minnesota Press, 1955), pp. 266-268.

26. Robinson; see pp. 345-346 regarding Langer's role in publishing "The Red Flame"; also see pp. 409-416 for an account of his administration as governor and for allegations of fraud levied against him.

27. This account of Langer's confrontation with President Roosevelt was related to me by John Bosch in a personal interview October 1969.

28. Jerold C. Auerback, "The LaFollette Committee and the CIO," *Wisconsin Magazine of History*, 48:3-20, Autumn 1964.

29. Lorin Lee Carey, "The Wisconsin Loyalty Legion, 1917-1918," *Wisconsin Magazine of History*, 48:35, Autumn 1969.

30. Copies of the *Representative* are on file with the Minnesota Historical Society. A perusal of these files brings to light numerous front-page cartoons of capitalistic Jews, usually labeled as the "Rothschild banking interests." Yet, it should be noted that Donnelly deplored the anti-Catholicism of the American Protective Association and that he published a novel, *Dr. Huguet,* a plea for racial tolerance utilizing the device of a white man's skin becoming black.

31. William Appleman Williams, "The Legend of Isolationism in the 1920's," *Science and Society*, 18, Winter 1954. This article presents the isolationism of the 1920s as a myth, using the context of my argument here.

32. Ignatius Donnelly, *Caesar's Column* (Cambridge: Harvard University Press, 1960), pp. 104-105.

33. A number of people have told me of the cooperative commonwealth slogans employed by the "left" in the 1930s; among these people was Einar Kuivinnen, for several years the president of the Minnesota Farmers Union in the 1930s.

34. The *Farmer Labor Leader* issue of March 30, 1934.

35. For certain observations about Finnish radicalism, I am indebted to

Mike Karni for permission to read materials assembled in preparation for his doctoral dissertation, including an unpublished paper, "Cooperatives versus Communism: The Demise of Finnish Political Radicalism," on file with the Immigrants Archives, University of Minnesota Library.

36. Fred Nichlason, "Henry George: Social Gospeler," *American Quarterly,* 22:649-664, Fall 1970.

37. Arthur N. Young, *The Single Tax Movement in the United States* (Princeton: Princeton University Press, 1916), pp. 118-119.

38. John Greenway, *American Folksongs of Protest* (Philadelphia: University of Pennsylvania Press, 1953), p. 51.

39. Herbert Schell, *History of South Dakota* (Lincoln: University of Nebraska Press, 1968), p. 241.

40. Forrest McDonald, "Street Cars and Politics in Milwaukee, 1896-1901," *Wisconsin Magazine of History,* 39:212, Spring 1956.

41. Anthology, *Voice and Pen of Victor L. Berger,* published by the *Milwaukee Leader,* 1929, p. 226. Also printed in *Third Party Footprints* by James M. Youngdale (Minneapolis: Ross and Haines, 1966), p. 204.

42. Personal interview with Frank Zeidler, October 1969.

43. Ibid.

44. Donald H. Grubbs, *Cry from the Cotton* (Chapel Hill: University of North Carolina Press, 1971), p. 27.

45. David V. Hintgen, "Victor L. Berger and 'The Milwaukee Leader'" (Unpublished master's thesis, Marquette University, 1962), pp. 81-83.

46. Daniel Hoan, *The Failure of Regulation* (Chicago: Socialist Party of the United States, 1914), pp. 97-98.

47. Scott P. Johnson, "Wisconsin Socialism and the Conference for Progressive Political Action," *Wisconsin Magazine of History,* 37:97, Winter 1953-54.

48. Personal interview with Henry Martinson, October 1970.

49. Louis Dwight Weld, *Social and Economic Survey of a Community in the Red River Valley* (Minneapolis: University of Minnesota, 1915), p. 83.

50. The debate over electing members of the Minnesota Legislature on a nonpartisan ballot is described in an article by Charles Adrian, "The Origin of Minnesota's Nonpartisan Legislature," *Minnesota History,* 33, Winter 1952.

51. Bahmer, p. 442. Bahmer quotes Henry Teigan as saying that the original five-point platform of the League was actually drafted in the office of the Socialist Party in Minot.

52. Davis Douthit, *Nobody Owns Us: The Story of Joe Gilbert* (Chicago: Cooperative League of the USA, 1948). This book provides a narrative account of Gilbert's life from an English immigrant and his rise as a young lawyer, his rebellion against middle-class values, and his experience as a lifelong socialist thereafter. His role in the Nonpartisan League is central to this biography. See pp. 92-161.

53. Nonpartisan League Anniversary Song Book, 1918. Copy on file with Nonpartisan League papers, Minnesota Historical Society.

54. Henry R. Martinson, "Comes the Revolution," *North Dakota History Magazine,* 36:41-109, Winter 1969.

55. Charles Walker, *American City* (New York: Farrar and Rinehart, 1938). See chapter 7, "The First Challenge" and chapter 8, "Battle in the Streets," pp. 93-128.

56. Personal letter from Leo Mattson to James Youngdale, dated January 15, 1969.

57. Personal interview with John Bernard, January 1970. The Minnesota Historical Society also has tapes of Bernard in the oral history department.

58. Frederick I. Olson, "The Milwaukee Socialists—1897-1941" (Unpublished doctoral dissertation, Harvard University, 1952), pp. 537-538.

59. John Shover, *Cornbelt Rebellion* (Urbana: University of Illinois Press, 1965), pp. 70-72.

60. Ibid., p. 71.

61. Personal interview with John Bosch, October 1969.

62. Shover, p. 91.

63. Personal interview with Oscar Christianson, August 1971.

64. Gilbert C. Fite and H.C. Peterson, *Opponents of War, 1917-1918* (Madison: University of Wisconsin Press, 1957), p. 50.

65. James Weinstein, *The Decline of Socialism in America, 1912-1925* (New York: Monthly Review Press, 1967), p. 144.

66. Robert Seager II, "Progressives and American Foreign Policy, 1898-1917: An Analysis of the Attitudes of Leaders of the Progressive Movement toward External Affairs" (Unpublished doctoral dissertation, Ohio State University, 1956), p. 314. Socialist influence upon Lindbergh, Sr., was confirmed by Joe Virnig of Fargo, North Dakota, who recalled that his father, who was a socialist, spent entire days discussing politics and socialism with Lindbergh. Personal interview with Mr. Virnig, September 1969.

67. George Garlid, "The Antiwar Dilemma of the Farmer-Labor Party," *Minnesota History*, 40:369, Winter 1967.

68. Walter Johnson, *The Battle Against Isolation* (Chicago: University of Chicago Press, 1944), p. 161.

69. Theodore Saloutos and John D. Hicks, *Agricultural Discontent in the Middle West, 1900-1939* (Madison: University of Wisconsin Press, 1951), p. 156.

70. Theodore Saloutos, "The National Producers' Alliance," *Minnesota History*, 28:37-44, March 1947.

71. Personal interview with Elmer A. Benson, August 1968.

72. Personal interview with Quentin Burdick, November 1971. Burdick was the attorney for the North Dakota Farmers Union in bringing this suit to court.

73. John D. Hicks, *The Populist Revolt* (Minneapolis: University of Minnesota Press, 1931), pp. 439-444.

74. Roger Wyman, "Voting Behavior in the Progressive Era: Wisconsin as a Case Study" (Unpublished doctoral dissertation, University of Wisconsin, 1970), see chapter 18.

75. See Usher Burdick, *The Life Story of George Sperry Loftus* (Baltimore: Wirth Brothers, 1944) for a brief narrative of Loftus's life.

76. James Manahan, *Trials of a Lawyer* (autobiography), published privately by Kathryn Manahan, Minneapolis, 1933, pp. 116-122.

77. Ibid., p. 200.

78. Ibid., pp. 237-238.

79. The *Farmer Labor Leader,* March 30, 1934.

7

"*Vote as you would strike*"

> —*W. W. Royster, railroad engineer, active in the Minnesota farmer-labor coalition.*

"*Vote as you would shoot*"

> —*From an 1918 editorial from the* Bismarck Tribune *equating the Nonpartisan League with the wartime enemy.*

A CASE STUDY

THE GENESIS OF THE MINNESOTA
FARMER-LABOR PARTY

Among the many attempts to organize populist third-party movements in
the United States, the Minnesota Farmer-Labor Party stands out as by far
the most significant and the most successful. It was not officially formed
until 1924, even though two United States Senators and two Congressmen
had been elected in 1922 as independents around a loose farmer and labor
coalition. During the ensuing twenty years, the Party elected two governors,
another United States Senator, several other Congressmen, and a host of
lesser officials. This is an amazing record in view of the tendency for dissenters to be co-opted by progressive rhetoric and by small favors from the
establishment, by the "drips on the deacons," to quote from the epigram
so often repeated by Governor Floyd B. Olson.

A thorough account of the period of Farmer-Labor ascendancy in Minnesota history is yet to be written. An unpublished doctoral dissertation written by Arthur Naftalin is widely quoted in academic studies. However,
Naftalin's study, while offering an adequate narrative account of the rise of
Farmer-Laborism, suffers as a product of cold war mentality, in that alleged
communist influences are highlighted without corresponding attention to
other ideological currents in this important populist movement. In contrast,
the aim of this chapter is to identify all currents within the movement, noting especially the important socialist outlook which prevailed among the
founders of the Party. The focus here is on the internal currents and tensions, with no pretense of offering a comprehensive view of the full political
spectrum in Minnesota during the 1916-1924 period, when the Farmer-
Labor Party came into being.

The very name of the Party suggests that it was formally composed of a coalition of farmer and labor elements. Indeed this was the case; for it was in this period that the famous Farmers Nonpartisan League was sweeping like a "prairie fire," (quoting from James Morlan's title, *Political Prairie Fire)* especially across North Dakota and Minnesota, where the labor movement also associated itself with the farmers' movement. It is helpful to recall that the Farmers Nonpartisan League originated in North Dakota in 1914 in response to farmers' frustration over their failure to secure a state-owned terminal elevator from the legislature. In that year, A.C. Townley and four socialists drafted a five-point platform on a scrap of brown paper. Their five points were: state-owned terminal elevators, packing plants and flour mills; state inspection of grain and grain dockage; exemption of farm improvements from taxation; state hail insurance; and a state bank to operate at cost. This platform was fully adopted, along with pro-labor legislation, when the League took complete control of the North Dakota government in 1918. (League members gained control technically as Republicans by winning in Republican Party primary election contests.) Very quickly, the League spread into other states; and in 1916, the national Farmers Nonpartisan League office was established in Saint Paul, Minnesota.[1]

Although the Farmers League was active in Minnesota prior to the formation of a similar Working People's Nonpartisan League organized in 1918, and although electoral victories for independent candidates were first visible in rural areas, the successful formation of the Farmer-Labor Party can be credited more to the labor than the farmer side of the coalition. The drive to form a distinct third party was led by William Mahoney, the editor of the *Minnesota Union Advocate,* the organ of the Saint Paul labor movement. He was instrumental in the formation of the Working People's Nonpartisan Political League, and he, more than anyone else, can rightly be called the "father" of the Farmer-Labor Party. It was Mahoney who almost single-handedly stuck to the goal of organizing a third-party movement in the face of defections among his colleagues, and it was he who sparked the ill-fated attempt to organize a national farmer-labor party to give support to LaFollette in 1924.

Coming from a Kansas farm with experience in the populist movement of the 1890s, Mahoney briefly studied law and then attended a trade school to learn printing. As a printer, he gravitated both to the union movement and also to the Socialist Party. In 1917, he became the editor of the *Minnesota Union Advocate.* He declared later that he left the Socialist Party because of its strong antiwar resolution of that year; however, he continued to be obliquely critical of the war as a breeder of autocracy, and he continued to work with socialists in his political activity. He was a candidate for mayor of Saint Paul in 1920 and 1922, castigating the "O'Conner machine" for ballot box stuffing and for serving as a haven and headquarters for gangsters and criminals who then plundered other cities and who raised the cry of "socialism" to hide their iniquities.[2] Mahoney was elected mayor in 1932 for one term and later served in several appointive positions in the Farmer-Labor administrations.

While stressing the role of Mahoney and the labor movement in the formation of the party, we should not ignore the Farmers League. For although A.C. Townley, the colorful head of the Farmers League, was opposed to third-party activity, the national secretary of the League, Henry Teigan, worked with Mahoney to organize the party; however, Teigan was in Washinton, D.C., as Senator Magnus Johnson's secretary in 1923 and 1924, a crucial period in the final crystallization of the party. Furthermore, the Farmers League splintered after 1920. Certain socialists, such as Joe Gilbert, national director of the League, and Arthur LeSueur, formerly an attorney for the organization, were supportive of Teigan; but other leaders of the Farmers League, along with the quasi-socialist *Minneapolis Star,* edited by A.B. Gilbert, clearly sided with Townley against a third party in the 1920-1924 period when the issue was being hotly debated.

Even though it was apparent in 1923 and 1924 that a majority of farm delegates to League meetings might favor the third-party direction, the main organ speaking for this move was the *Minnesota Union Advocate* edited by Mahoney; this paper, therefore, provides most of the printed documentation illuminating the emerging political coalition which became the Farmer-Labor Party.

Without labor, it seems unlikely that the party would have been formed; and without mass farm support, it would never have elected candidates. It appears that the fortuitous circumstance of a labor and farm movement arising together, both partly under socialist leadership, accounts for the formation of the Farmer-Labor Party in Minnesota; and perhaps it was the absence of this circumstance which precluded success in other states of the union.

To understand better the rise of the Farmer-Labor Party, it is helpful to review briefly the political background of the state. From 1900 until 1918, many Republican leaders in Minnesota enjoyed a reputation as progressives, especially after a revolution in 1914, in which Young Turks in the party, who spoke in radical rhetoric about defending the masses against plutocracy, took control of party affairs. Earlier a progressive Democrat, John A. Johnson, had served as governor from 1904 to 1909, having been elected at a time when the Republicans were feuding between their progressive and stalwart wings. Even earlier, the progressive impulse was first generated with the election of John Lind in 1898.[3] Lind was both an anti-imperialist and a reformer, a product of the fusion of populist and Silver Democrats in the election of 1896. It seems evident that sentiment in the state was deeply committed to progressivism, regardless of party label. But the halfway measures of progressives were not always enough to satisfy the fundamental demands for reform.

In 1916, the progressives were threatened by the growing appeal of socialists; for in that year, several socialist mayors were elected in Minnesota, including Thomas Van Lear in Minneapolis. It seems likely that the appeal of the socialists was due in part to their opposition to war. Carl Chrislock suggests that Woodrow Wilson nearly carried Minnesota in 1916 because socialists supported him as the man who "kept us out of war" in Europe.[4]

Apart from the election of these socialists in 1916, there were few signs on the horizon of an impending political upheaval that would lead to the formation of a third party in the state of Minnesota. Labor leaders seemed satisfied with the progressive image of Republicans J.A.A. Burnquist and Frank Kellogg, candidates for governor and United States Senator, respectively. There was a ripple in rural areas as Charles Lindbergh, Sr., challenged Kellogg in the Republican primary for the Senate. While Lindbergh was well known for his opposition to the progressive Federal Reserve Act, charging that it was a bankers' bill, Kellogg was even more famous as Theodore Roosevelt's choice as chief counsel in several of the trust-busting cases during the Roosevelt administration. Despite support from the fledgling Farmers Nonpartisan League, Lindbergh lost badly.

In 1917, everything changed. Early in the year, representatives of the Farmers Nonpartisan League made overtures to the labor movement for mutual support. One speaker called upon labor to support farmers in their efforts to end chicanery in the marketing system dominated by "parasitic speculators," and another speaker called upon labor to help expose the lie that "farmers are rich and labor greedy."[5]

In September of that year, a further identification of the common cause of farmers and labor developed when the Farmers' League called a mass Producers and Consumers Conference in Saint Paul in September. Speakers at the conference sought to develop the theme that farmers and labor had a common interest in reforming the profit system of the commercial-industrial economy. This conference received national attention because the keynote speaker was Senator Robert LaFollette, Sr., who had been one of the "willful six" opposed to a declaration of war the previous April.

LaFollette was misquoted by the press as declaring that the United States had "no grievances" against Germany. This report caused a furor in the nation and in the United States Senate; and it was not until six months later that the press services admitted that he had been completely misquoted. As a consequence of this incident the Farmers Nonpartisan League was also propelled into the limelight and also attracted the wrath of patriotic organizations.

Later in 1917 a labor dispute arose between the unions and the Twin City Street Car Company. By this time, Governor Burnquist had appointed a Public Safety Commission, headed by Judge McGee, for the purpose of securing social tranquility and patriotic support for the war effort. Burnquist turned the streetcar dispute over to the Public Safety Commission for resolution. The dispute was exacerbated when the commission ruled that union members were not allowed to wear union buttons on their clothing during work while the dispute was being arbitrated. This ruling aroused a storm of protest.

Early in December, a rally of 15,000 was held in Saint Paul in support of the streetcar workers. The mayors of both Saint Paul and Minneapolis addressed the rally. Joseph Gilbert spoke, representing the Farmers Nonpartisan League. James Manahan, attorney for the Farmers' League, warmly defended the right to wear a union button. "The Union stands for patriotism, true democracy and the soul of civilization," declared Manahan; and he continued, "that button does not irritate anyone except businessmen like those who own West Publishing Company."[6]

After the rally, Manahan and two other speakers were arrested for incitement to riot. Even though the charge was dismissed two months later, the political gain for farmer and labor cooperation was tremendous because of Manahan's close association with the Farmers' League. At this time the Farmers' League was being harassed in rural areas by the McGee Commission. Several antiwar farmers were tarred by patriotic vigilante committees; and Republican Congressman Ernest Lundeen was abducted in Ortonville, Minnesota, and shipped out of town in a boxcar. It was reported that Judge McGee advocated using the firing squad overtime to take care of the "disloyal vipers" in German and Swedish communities in the state.[7] While this repression was in force, there were advertisements by farmers in the labor papers appealing for labor support for civil rights.

It seems clear that Judge McGee's enthusiasm for combating "disloyalty" played a decisive role in bringing the farm and labor movements together in 1917 and 1918. In the process Governor Burnquist became persona non grata with labor and farmers as well. The charge was made that "a vote for Burnquist is a vote for McGee."[8] In the 1918 elections, Lindbergh, Sr., filed against Burnquist in the Republican primary election. The Lindbergh challenge was a heated one. In the course of the campaign, he was stoned, egged and shot at. The story is told that he instructed his driver as they were fired upon while leaving a small town: "Don't drive too fast; they'll think we're scared."[9] This show of courage failed to win enough votes. In the midst of nationwide hysteria against "war slackers" and "Hun lovers," Lindbergh was again defeated.

After the primary election, the Minnesota Federation of Labor held its annual convention and organized a Working People's Political League as a counterpart of the Farmers' League. William Mahoney was made the chairman of the workers' league, and socialist mayor Thomas Van Lear was elected secretary.

The Farmers' and Workers' Leagues met jointly in 1918 and filed an independent slate in the general election, a slate headed by a rather conservative rural town businessman, David Evans, who had been a friend of Ignatius Donnelly. Evans filed against Burnquist for governor, while W.G. Calderwood, a prohibitionist and Bellamy socialist, filed for the Senate seat against the popular progressive Republican Knute Nelson. The entire slate lost, but Evans was the leading opponent against Burnquist, with 112,000 votes as compared with 166,000 for the incumbent governor.

In 1919, the Minnesota Federation of Labor convention was held in New Ulm, Minnesota. On the evening prior to the convention, the Working People's Political League met under the chairmanship of Mahoney. In addressing the meeting, Mahoney warned of twin dangers to the labor movement:

The two dangers are "restoration" instead of "reconstruction," which is all that the privileged classes are striving to bring about in order that they may restore the very evils the war was fought to free us from, and the tendency of the radical element toward direct action, or what in Europe is called "syndicalism."[10]

This point of view in Mahoney fairly defines his outlook as one of abjuring the left or the IWW tradition while affirming a "parliamentary" socialist path to reform. This outlook was dramatically expressed by another labor leader, W.W. Royster of Glenwood, Minnesota, who was a railroad engineer and an officer in the Brotherhood of Locomotive Engineers: "Labor is learning it can accomplish more by voting than by the strike. Vote as you would strike."[11]

At the 1919 New Ulm Convention, the Minnesota Federation of Labor moved officially to support the political league as a separate entity. The name of the political committee was changed to the Working People's Nonpartisan Political League, a name evidently designed to provide a parallel with the Farmers Nonpartisan League. Mahoney continued to be the chairman of the reorganized committee, and former Mayor Van Lear was again elected secretary. By this time, the pattern of cooperation between the Workers' Nonpartisan League and the Farmers' League was firmly established, and this pattern was to continue through 1924.

The regular convention of the Minnesota Federation of Labor, held during the following days at New Ulm, gave its official stamp of approval to the Working People's Nonpartisan Political League, urging locals to join the League as bodies and to contribute funds on a per capita basis. The Working People's League launched a campaign to organize on a statewide basis, sending teams of organizers to towns of a thousand or more to recruit members, individuals as well as union locals. It is difficult to assess their success in rural Minnesota towns, but they did organize in every Congressional district, and they did provide representatives from each district to meet with counterparts of the Farmers' League in joint conferences. The presence of W.W. Royster, a railroad engineer from Glenwood, Minnesota, as a leader in the Workers' League provides a clue that one object of their rural town membership drive was to enlist railroad workers. A news item in the *Minnesota Union Advocate* a year later announced: "Numerous letters pledging support of the League ticket and policies have been received from railroad conductors, firemen, switchmen and other brotherhood members."[12] It seems to be a fair conjecture, supported by my personal observations, that railroad workers were instrumental in bringing not only the political League to rural towns in Minnesota but also a certain amount of Debsian socialism as well.

After the 1919 convention, the Working People's League printed a statement in pamphlet form, entitled "A New Political Alignment for Minnesota." The first printing was 100,000 copies, indicating an intention toward a massive campaign. The opening section of the pamphlet describes the political scene as a contest between capital and labor:

Labor of Minnesota is going into politics. For years labor has been influenced into staying out of politics by those who have been in politics and who have understood the power of controlling politics. . . . Those who own and control industry in which labor produces great wealth which enormously enriches those who own, find it necessary to control political parties and candidates in that they may not be hampered in freely exercising their great profit making schemes. . . . Had the steel trust not been in control of the political state of Minnesota, through control of its governor, who vetoed the tonnage tax bill, the steel trust is enabled to save for the individual members of the corporation $10,000,000 which the people must now pay. The steel crowd saved $10,000,000 BY BEING IN POLITICS. The people lost $10,000,000 by following the advice of the steel trust and NOT BEING IN POLITICS. . . .[13]

The pamphlet recalled the victories of the Farmers Nonpartisan League in North Dakota, where the Farmers' League had taken control of the state including the governorship in 1918, and it pointed to the prolabor legislation passed in that state. Noting that anti-injunction legislation, an eight-hour day, minimum wages for women and mine inspection laws passed when the Farmers' League took control of North Dakota, the pamphlet declared that

161

labor in no other state could claim as much to compare with North Dakota.

The platform adopted by the Working People's League in 1919 illustrates the capacity of populists to produce a serious and comprehensive statement of political goals in a quasi-socialist vein, quite the opposite of the "zany" or "comic" side of populism stressed by Hofstadter. Key planks of the platform are as follows: eight-hour day and forty-four-hour week; reduction of cost of living through cooperatives to eliminate useless middlemen and profiteering; state compensation system for injured workers; abolition of unemployment; public ownership of railroads, banks, terminal grain elevators . . . and all public utilities; equality of men and women and equal pay; federal department of education; and full freedom of speech and the press.[14] This platform was the prototype for later platforms adopted in 1924 and again in the 1930s.

Membership dues were set at three dollars per year for individuals and twenty-five cents per capita for union bodies. Along with a membership, an individual also received a year's subscription to one of several labor papers published in the state. A clause in the plan of organization prohibited any member of the governing committees of the League from being affiliated with any existing political party, even though the Farmer and Labor committees had used the Republican Party primary the previous year and were to do so again in 1920.

This platform is significant for its far-reaching attention to various practical issues and also for its long-range proposals for revamping the social structure; for example, it juxtaposed demands for an eight-hour day with a "gradualist" vision of a socialist utopia. The platform might fairly be called "Fabian" in its stress on "progress" and "harmony"; yet it was un-Fabian in the sense that it emanated from working people, not middle-class intellectuals.

It is apparent that the organization of two Leagues, one by farmers and one by workers, was a cause for concern in conservative circles. In the fall of 1919, Governor Burnquist called a special session of the legislature, with a view to passing certain legislation. For one thing, the governor wanted to change the election laws of the state to forbid a losing candidate in a primary election from filing for the same office by petition as an independent in the final election. The governor also asked for a double primary election, so that the two top contenders would contest for the nomination in the second primary. Both of these proposals were aimed directly at the Leagues. Both of them were defeated; and the very next year, the Leagues filed candidates in Republican primaries and then as independents after losing in the primaries. In the Seventh Congressional District, the Reverend O.J. Kvale even won the Republican primary, but he was later disqualified through a libel charge for having called his opponent, A.J. Volstead of Volstead Act fame, an atheist.

In March 1920, the two Leagues met in Saint Paul, each group in a separate convention but working together through a committee consisting of one person from each Congressional District for each League. Out of these negotiations, a slate of candidates was selected to file in the Republican primaries. The Workers' League at first declared its support for Van Lear for governor, but it acquiesced to the Farmers' League choice of Henrik Shipstead, a Tory populist dentist from Glenwood, Minnesota, who had identified with the Farmers' League by obliquely criticizing the war. After losing the primary election, the Shipstead slate filed as independents and lost the final election as well; but the independent vote increased measurably over the vote of the David Evans slate in 1918. Shipstead received 281,000 votes as compared with 112,000 for Evans.

In July of 1920, the Workers' Nonpartisan League held its annual convention in conjunction with that of the Minnesota Federation of Labor. In one year's time, three hundred unions had joined the League, accounting for 45,000 members. The platform of 1920 repeated much of the 1919 platform, calling, for example, for the eight-hour day, government ownership of utilities and a federal department of education. The League was buoyed by a sense of progress, which was to be confirmed by the relatively good showing of the Shipstead slate in November.

According to Mahoney, the dream of a fully formed third-party movement was about to be fulfilled after the strong showing of the Shipstead ticket. Once the political power of the two Leagues working in unison had been demonstrated, discussion developed over the desirable tactics for 1922. Mahoney strongly urged the formation of the third party and an end to the tactic of filing in the Republican primary; but A.C. Townley, president of the Farmers Nonpartisan League, was unyeilding in wishing to follow a Gompers line and stay within the two-party structure. The Leagues were approached by Mrs. Anna Dickey Olesen, a progressive Democratic leader who urged fusion with the Democrats.[15] Van Lear reported in a Workers' Nonpartisan League newsletter that the Farmers' League desired to support the Democratic nominee for governor, Edward Indrehus; but the Workers' League refused to back a Democrat at all, especially since the Democratic Party was very weak in Minnesota, having received only 81,000 votes out of 700,000 cast for governor in 1920. In 1921, while Townley was serving a prison term for his "seditious utterances" during the war, Henry Teigan undermined Townley's influence among farmers against a third-party approach. Finally, the notion of fusion with the Democrats was rejected, and a full independent slate was filed, headed by Shipstead for the United States Senate and Magnus Johnson for governor. Johnson was especially popular among farmers because of his position as the state manager of the Equity

League, which was engaged in organizing farm cooperatives.

During the campaign of 1922, Van Lear, as secretary of the Working People's Nonpartisan League, sent out a newsletter on an irregular basis. In one letter, he reported on the key resolutions passed at the convention at which Shipstead and Johnson were nominated:

Nationally, we demanded the revival of the National Corporation, the restoration of the power of the government to issue currency and credit, the repeal of the Esch-Cummins law, government control of natural resources, Soldier's bonus from excess profits, relief of unemployment through useful public work by direct employment of home labor, abolition of government by militia and injunction. Our state program recommends economy in public service, state owned cement plants, enlargement of our state owned flour mills, recall of the Brooks-Coleman law, ten percent royalty and tonnage tax on iron ore, laws providing for co-operative banks, loan and credit associations, initiative referendum and recall.[16]

In other newsletters, Van Lear sounded a note of alarm over attempts to repress organized labor and to introduce "slavery." In commenting on the forthcoming meeting of the legislature early in 1923, he said:

There is going to be an effort to pass a state constabulary bill, like the Cossacks of Pennsylvania; no working man wants this bill but we are going to have to live with it unless every workingman immediately protests against it.[17]

Van Lear called attention to another danger:

Another bill will be a Motor Corps bill, for quick transportation of military and home guards. They will tell you that this is to prevent trouble in riots. The fact of the matter is that these bodies usually consist of hired thugs and rioters and will cause more riots than they will quell.[18]

In the same newsletter, Van Lear warned of the "industrial court" system:

A bill will be introduced providing for an industrial court like that of Kansas; an industrial court means industrial slavery . . . there is a lot of propaganda out about the advantages of the industrial court but the fact is that in Kansas the industrial court was going to throw the miners in jail for striking and the miners went back to work. The flour mills closed down and shut out the workers, simply because they wanted to hire them back at lower wages. They took their case to the industrial court; the flour mill people just said that they could not manufacture flour at a profit, so they had to close down.[19]

It is not possible to determine whether or not these specific pieces of antilabor legislation were an immediate threat in Minnesota, but apparently the labor leaders saw a straw in the wind, at least, from the fact that Kansas and Pennsylvania had enacted repressive laws. The general tenor of the resolutions passed in 1922 appears to be consistent with the platform of 1918; however, the selection of Shipstead and Johnson as candidates suggests a concern with electability in picking men with a more conservative public image. It is difficult to elicit documentary proof of the Tory populist outlook of Shipstead and Johnson, but Shipstead, in particular, never distinguished himself as a vigorous advocate of reform. Later, he was cool toward Franklin Roosevelt, turning Republican in 1940 as an isolationist on the right.

Regardless of Shipstead's basic conservatism, he nevertheless symbolized third-party insurgency. His 1922 victory over Frank Kellogg stunned the nation. Shipstead's running mate, Magnus Johnson, was barely defeated in the governor's race; but he, too, was elected to the United States Senate in 1923 to fill an unexpired term after the death of Knute Nelson. Also elected in 1922 were two Congressmen, O.J. Kvale in the Seventh District and Knud Wefald in the Ninth District. It was almost unthinkable that a fledgling third party should enjoy such initial success. After this success, several important decisions had to be made. Should they organize a permanent third party or should they continue as nonpartisan leagues, free to operate as a faction within one of the existing parties?

In April, 1923, a conference of the Farmers Nonpartisan League and the Working People's Nonpartisan Political League was held to discuss the future of the movement. Also included in the conference was a third group calling itself the Farmer-Labor Party, representing a group of individuals outside of labor and farm circles who had paid three dollars for an individual membership. This Farmer-Labor Party group was headed by F.A. Pike, a Saint Paul attorney for the Farmers' League. At this conference several points of view were presented. In opposing the formation of a permanent third party, former mayor Van Lear, now siding with the Townley forces, argued that farmers and workers could not successfully work together and that a nonpartisan approach of supporting the best candidates in primaries would be preferable. It was apparent that there was friction at this time between Van Lear and Mahoney, in view of the fact that Mahoney rebuked Van Lear in the *Minnesota Union Advocate* for having opposed a third party the previous year at Cleveland, contrary to instructions.[20] It appears that Van Lear had been a delegate to the Conference for Progressive Political Action the previous year and that his violation of instructions had occurred at this conference. Another man who spoke against a third party was W.W. Royster, railroad engineer from Glenwood; but William Mahoney and Carl Carlgren, speaking for the Saint Paul labor bodies, both supported the formation of a permanent Farmer-Labor Party.

Whereas the reports on this debate in the labor papers are very sketchy, it is apparent from the alignment of forces that it was the solid resolve of the Twin City labor movement that carried the day for the decision to form the Farmer-Labor Party, in view of the fact that some leaders of the Farmers' League were cool to the idea of independent political structure.

It is interesting that the Twin City labor bodies stuck to their resolve in the face of Samuel Gompers's efforts to discourage third-party movements within labor circles. In an editorial in the *Minnesota Union Advocate,* Mahoney took note of an ultimatum issued by Gompers to the Seattle Central Labor body, demanding: 1) a withdrawal of support for the Washington Farmer-Labor Party, 2) a renunciation of industrial unionism, and 3) ceasing to urge recognition of Russia. Mahoney observed in his editorial that the Minnesota Federation of Labor held exactly the same position on these issues as did the Washington body. He noted without explanation that the Minneapolis Trades and Labor Assembly also had been subjected to an "extraordinary experience recently" by representatives of the American Federation of Labor but that nothing so sweeping as Gompers's ultimatum in Seattle had taken place. Tongue in cheek, Mahoney concluded his editorial:

We cannot give credence to the report, as the officials of the AFL surely cannot be behind the trend of the times. The industrial struggle for plutocracy during the past few years has demonstrated the weakness of the trades unions to meet the class conscious solidarity of big business. Every fight in which any craft or union engaged was against "the one big union" of capitalism backed up by the government. How can this be met? Certainly not by the puny disjointed craft unions and the non-political trading tactics of the old-time organization.[21]

However, within a month the Minneapolis Trades and Labor Assembly did expel certain communists, probably as a result of pressure from the AFL. Mahoney approved of this expulsion, citing material from a Trade Union Educational League publication to the effect that the communists considered themselves to be the "natural leaders of the Union movement," which Mahoney felt was unwarranted and arrogant.

While this tension existed between the AFL and the local labor bodies, the 1923 special election was being held to fill the seat of the deceased Senator Knute Nelson. After three candidates filed on the Farmer-Labor ticket—Magnus Johnson, Charles Lindbergh, Sr., and Dr. L.A. Fritsche, mayor of New Ulm—the problem arose as to whether or not the various bodies in the Farmer-Labor coalition should make an endorsement of a favorite candidate. Mahoney editorialized against an endorsement, urging that each voter "cast his vote for the candidate that he believes will serve his cause."[22] Mahoney noted, however, that the Farmers' League and the Railway Unions already had endorsed Magnus Johnson, a move he criticized. In any event, Magnus Johnson won the primary and went on to win the final election as well.

On August 11, 1923, a call was issued by the Workers' and Farmers' Leagues and by the special Farmer-Labor group under Pike for a convention to formalize plans for a Farmer-Labor Party in Minnesota. The new convention was to be held on September 8. Mahoney's enthusiasm for this convention was reflected in the *Minnesota Union Advocate,* as he ran front-page stories three weeks in a row hailing the importance of this meeting. He sought to obviate the problem between communists and noncommunists which had arisen in Chicago for Fitzpatrick* by ruling that the new party was to be a coalition of economic groups, not of political creeds; and using this formula, he ruled that the Workers' Party would not be eligible to participate as an entity. This formula did not preclude communists from participating providing they came as delegates from a farm or labor organization.

The September 8 convention was successfully held. The Farmers' Non-partisan League held its convention in one hall and the Working People's Nonpartisan League met in another. Each League made proposals and counterproposals, which were mediated by a committee of members from both Leagues. One issue at stake was the question of a tight federated organization versus a continuation of the Leagues in loose affiliation. The labor league favored federation, but there was hesitation among the farmers who were allied with former mayor Van Lear. After the convention was over, Van Lear, in the "socialist" *Minneapolis Star,* attacked the new Farmer-Labor Federation for being ruled by radicals; but Mahoney fired back editorially that the "Farmer Labor Conference was a complete success and that the convention was not ruled by any 'ism' as the *Daily Star* charges."[23] On September 20, Mahoney unloosed another blast at his former friend Van Lear, who had served with him as secretary in the Working People's Nonpartisan League.

Will Mr. Van Lear, the erstwhile Socialist Mayor and leader of the "radicals" of Minneapolis with his holier than thou attitude, point out the terrible plotters and show that they have not joined wholeheartedly in all the economic and political activities of the producing classes of the state?[24]

---

*Reference here is to the attempt in 1923 on the part of the Illinois Federation of Labor led by John Fitzpatrick in coalition with leaders of the "Committee of 48" to initiate a national third-party movement. Due to differences in outlook, two organizations emerged from this effort—a procommunist Federated Farmer-Labor and a noncommunist Farmer-Labor Party.

The Farmer-Labor Party was not officially formed at the September meeting in 1923. A committee of seven was elected who were to promote ratification of a full fusion by the movements. This fusion was consummated in March 1924. Throughout this period, it appeared likely to many that fusion would never occur, judging from the editorial position of the *Daily Star,* which represented the Townley outlook for "balance of power" politics. In his dissertation on the Farmer-Labor Party, Arthur Naftalin approvingly quotes the *Daily Star* and the *Minnesota Leader,* edited by A.B. Gilbert, both of which were wary of the third party for fear of communist influence in the labor movement.[25] Naftalin misses the point. It is true that the *Star* was critical of communists, especially after the LaFollette open letter in May of 1924; but already in 1923, the *Star* was flailing at any and all "radicals" who favored a third party. Joseph Gilbert and Arthur LeSueur were especially singled out. Both men had previously held high positions in the Farmers Nonpartisan League; both had broken with Townley over his autocratic management of the League, and both were socialists. The *Daily Star* also attacked Mahoney's *Minnesota Union Advocate* in October of 1923, long before the Hathaway issue provided grist for charges of communist infiltration. At one point, Mahoney in return charged that Van Lear maintained connections with the Minneapolis underworld and that the former editor of the *Star,* Herbert Gaston, had resigned to go to the *New York World* because of Van Lear's odious connections.[26] There is no surviving evidence from which to make a judgment about these charges. In any event, the feud was not a simple one of communism versus anticommunism; there was the larger debate over a third party versus the balance of power tactic, a debate which had begun in 1918 and 1920, before the communists were even on the scene.

The September 1923 meeting drafted a constitution and a platform, both of which were submitted to the various local bodies for consideration and ratification pending final adoption at a later date. The proposed constitution provided for an untraditional political party. It was to be a federation of farmer, labor, cooperative, women's and other social and economic groups, with delegates to conventions to be elected from these various groups as well as from precinct and county organizations. The proposed platform was very much in the tradition established by the platform of the Working People's Nonpartisan League in 1919. Various sections of the platform called for public ownership of transportation, anti-injunction legislation, free speech guarantees, fixed farm prices, equal rights for all regardless of sex and color, workmen's compensation, conservation of natural resources and government aid to the cooperative movement. The platform as adopted the following March concluded: "We affirm that war is a crime. A war-less world is a prime necessity if civilization is to endure.. . . we would extend the hand of fellowship and recognition to all sister nations working out their own destinies in their own way."[27] The last sentence no doubt referred to recognition of the Soviet Russian government.

It was not until March of 1924 that conventions of the Farmers' and the Working People's Nonpartisan Leagues met again to form the Farmer-Labor Party. Even though certain Townley followers fought the fusion of the two Leagues to the bitter end, a majority of the Farmers' League responded to an appeal by Carl Carlgren, a Saint Paul carpenter using his best "Swedish brogue knowing that the majority of farmers were Scandinavian,"[28] to adjourn and move to the labor convention for the fusion. In various analyses of the Farmer-Labor Party in Minnesota, there is a good deal of imprecision. For example, Theodore Draper, in *American Communism and the Soviet Union,* is incorrect in placing the date of fusion as 1923 and in describing the outcome as a "united front of a type by now familiar between communists and 'left' Farmer-Laborites."[29] In support of this assertion, Draper quotes an exaggerated claim by Ruthenberg from the *Daily Worker* that the Farmer-Labor Federation in Minnesota was organized "largely through the efforts of our party."[30] In the same paragraph, Draper quotes Clarence Hathaway, also a communist, as claiming to have been the only communist within the Farmer Labor Party in Minneapolis, noting that the Workers Party existed at the time primarily among rural Finns interested in building cooperatives. Draper makes no attempt to reconcile the contradictory statements by Hathaway and Ruthenberg. In general, Draper tends to inflate the role of the communists without seeming to realize that there were well-organized farm and labor movements in Minnesota which had been gathering momentum for several years and which had developed a fairly sophisticated leadership aiming toward a third-party coalition.

While the Farmer-Labor Party was being formed, Mahoney and others were engaged in an effort to organize a national third party based on the Minnesota model. This attempt, which will be treated in the following chapter, ended in disaster. In spite of failure on the national level, the Minnesota Farmer-Labor Party held together fairly well in the 1924 campaign. Floyd Olson came within a few thousand votes of being elected governor. Magnus Johnson, the butt of much ridicule for his Scandinavian speech and style, lost the Senate seat by fewer than 10,000 votes; but O.J. Kvale and Knud Wefald were both reelected to Congress in the Seventh and Ninth Districts, respectively. The successes in 1922 and 1924 were sufficient to provide momentum for the Farmer-Labor Party until 1930, at which time it secured a new lease on life with the election of Floyd B. Olson as governor. Olson himself and many of the men who were active with him in the 1930s were spawned politically in the earlier period with Mahoney.

After the election of 1924, Mahoney dropped out of a leadership position in the Farmer-Labor Party, but he was elected mayor of Saint Paul in 1932 for one term. Thereafter, he served in appointive capacities with the Farmer-Labor state administration, concluding as state liquor commissioner under Governor Elmer Benson. After the defeat of the Farmer-Labor Party in 1938, Mahoney began to dissociate himself from the movement on grounds of "communist infiltration." It is significant to note that while Mahoney was making these charges against the Farmer-Labor Party, he was also corresponding on friendly terms with a Constitutional Money League of America, an organization which in addition to talking about "funny money" also spread anti-Semitic virus by criticizing Franklin Roosevelt for having men like "Frankfurter, Cohen, Baruch, Lubin and Ginsburg" as advisers.[31]

Floyd Olson was elected governor in 1930 and served almost six years in office until his death from cancer in 1936. Elmer Benson, who was elected the next governor, had been slightly active in the 1924 campaign as chauffeur for Burt Wheeler, vice-presidential candidate on the LaFollette ticket, during a campaign tour of North Dakota. Shipstead served in the United States Senate until 1940, at which time he switched to the Republican Party; he was defeated in a Republican primary contest in 1946. Vince Day, Floyd Olson's secretary, had served as an attorney for the Farmers Nonpartisan League in 1920. Carl Carlgren, a close associate of Mahoney in the Saint Paul labor movement, served first on the Industrial Commission and then on the State Board of Control, during the administrations of Olson and Benson. In an interview in 1969, Carlgren pointed to the many administrative reforms which were instituted while the Farmer-Labor Party had control of the Industrial Commission and the Board of Control, the latter with supervisory power over prisons and mental institutions. He recalled such matters as strict enforcement of industrial safety regulations, adequate medical staffing in prisons—especially for treatment of venereal disease—and the decision to abandon the term "insane asylum," with its negative connotations.[32]

Previously, we have noted A.C. Townley's flip-flop to the far right, as he adopted the Joe McCarthy anticommunist mentality of the 1950s, and his final career as a faith healer, "laying hands" on anyone needing medical help. Clarence Hathaway returned to Minnesota in the early 1940s after working as the editor of the communist *Daily Worker* during the 1930s. Having been expelled from the Communist Party, he became active in the merged Farmer-Labor and Democratic parties after 1944. Possibly in reaction to the narrow outlook of the communists in the 1924 campaign, he was a vigorous champion of coalition politics in the 1940s. He was a strong supporter of Hubert Humphrey during this period when many other radicals from the former Farmer-Labor Party, such as Governor Benson, refused to support Humphrey. As a matter of fact, Hathaway was highly vocal in arguing that Orville Freeman (later governor of Minnesota and secretary of agriculture under Presidents Kennedy and Johnson) be permitted to be secretary of the merged DFL Party in 1946, a position from which Freeman moved to secure organizational control of the party for the Humphrey faction.[33] The irony of this situation is that Orville Freeman became a most vigorous crusader against communism among the Humphrey group, even though he owed much to Clarence Hathaway.

Many others who were active in the formative period of the Farmer-Labor Party emerged as leaders in the 1930s. This brief catalogue of persons whose influence persisted into the 1930s, 1940s and 1950s is sufficiently large to indicate that the early third-party insurgency in Minnesota has cast a long shadow upon subsequent history.

In retrospect, it seems fair to observe that the Working People's Nonpartisan Political League headed by Mahoney from 1918 until 1924 served as a stabilizing influence around which the Farmer-Labor Party took form. Mahoney himself was certainly the key person in holding the Working People's League together, and for this role he rightly deserves to be credited as the "father" of the Farmer-Labor Party.

Even though the effort to initiate a national third party failed, the group of socialists around Mahoney and Teigan were eminently successful in putting a populist third party on its feet within Minnesota. By seizing the initiative, these socialists probably attracted potential progressives into their quasi-socialist populist movement. Under other circumstances, Shipstead would likely have been a peace progressive; however, in the context of the farmer and labor coalition in Minnesota, he can be viewed as a populist, even though as a Tory populist at best. In Wisconsin, on the other hand, LaFollette's leadership pulled the same social constituency into the progressive camp and inhibited the growth of a populist farmer-labor movement by isolating the socialists from the political mainstream.

By seizing the initiative, the socialist leadership in the Minnesota farm and labor movements contributed toward a transformation of ideology toward the left. The emerging farmer-labor coalition cannot be viewed as a fully socialist movement as far as rank and file people were concerned. It was a time when working people could fully realize that the hope of becoming an independent artisan was dwindling, and it was a time when farmers realized that they must influence the marketplace either through cooperatives or government programs. These realizations made it possible for both groups to accept socialist leadership for practical, narrow objectives. But they also came into contact with wider socialist views as well. Even though the Minnesota Farmer-Labor Party was less than a socialist party throughout its history, it always bore the imprint of socialist proposals for institutional reform and socialist internationalism.

In Minnesota as elsewhere in populist movements, there was ambivalence, making it possible to find individuals who have moved from left to right in the pattern of Tom Watson of Georgia. We find persons such as Senators Shipstead and Lundeen, both deeply committed to bryanistic isolationism and to the prewar America First movement and both confusing the anti-bourgeois rhetoric of fascism with "radicalism." Persons of former socialist persuasion were not immune to the attraction of the political right, as the case of Mahoney himself dramatizes when he finally went the "funny money" route. Possibly it was Mahoney's frustration which caused his shift as his dream of parliamentary socialism seemed to fade with the communists' increased influence in labor and political movements on the radical end of the political spectrum.

During World War II and afterwards, the leadership of the Farmer-Labor Party was influenced by the hope that a revived New Deal in the postwar years would serve as a satisfactory avenue for reform; consequently, former Governor Elmer Benson was instrumental in arranging the merger of the strong Farmer-Labor Party with the traditionally weak Democratic Party in the state. While there was some foot dragging on the part of some "dry" Farmer-Laborites and some anti-Roosevelt Democrats, the fusion was consummated in 1944 with firm support both from Benson and from Franklin Roosevelt. Benson soon began to have doubts; for Roosevelt permitted the power brokers of the Democratic Party to substitute Harry Truman for Henry A. Wallace as the vice-presidential running mate that year, indicating a retreat from vigorous New Deal reformism and concessions to the conservative southern bloc of the Democratic Party. This fact was dramatized for Governor Benson during the campaign when he asked Harry Truman to pose for a picture with a leading Negro clergyman of Minneapolis, only to have Truman refuse, saying: "I don't mind having my picture taken with a nigger but I guess I'd better not; I was made the candidate to take the curse off the party on this issue."[34] Benson broke with Truman over cold war initiatives signaled by Winston Churchill's Fulton, Missouri, speech; and in 1948, Benson served as national co-chairman of the Henry A. Wallace attempt to form a new third party,* primarily in protest against the hardening attitudes toward Soviet Russia and against the remilitarization of America.

---

*It was at this time, when many former Farmer-Laborites moved to support Henry Wallace, that Hubert Humphrey captured control of the center-right spectrum of the DFL Party in Minnesota. This occurred in spite of the fact that the Wallace supporters attempted to stay within the DFL Party structure, aiming to make Wallace the presidential candidate of the DFL Party. After 1948, the Party was polarized for several years between the leadership of the Hubert Humphrey-Truman and the Elmer Benson-Wallace factions, a polarity which reemerged among a new generation of voters in 1968 at the time Eugene McCarthy challenged the Democratic Party establishment.

The three ideological currents have been clearly visible in the Minnesota Farmer-Labor Party: the Tory populists on one side and the socialists on the other, with a central thrust of radical neomercantilism. In the case of the Farmer-Labor Party, the role of socialist leadership, both in farm and labor circles, was pronounced, making for a greater counterweight to the Tory outlook and making for a vigorous radical neomercantilism pulled toward a socialist outlook. This meant a quasi-socialist leadership as well, in such persons as Governors Floyd Olson and Elmer Benson. It was the socialist input into Minnesota populism which gave it its distinctive character and which provided the early leadership in organizing the successful coalition of the farmer and labor movements.

The socialist input as an integral part of the populist movements in the twentieth century has been ignored by historians, especially those in the Hofstadter school, who view populism in terms of a conceptual framework which limits perception of the more radical currents. The Minnesota experience, more than any other sector of populism, contributes evidence which contradicts the Hofstadter thesis and supports a perspective on populism as having a potential for moving toward a quasi-socialist outlook as a microparadigm in American history and as the equivalent of the European labor party tradition.

NOTES

1. For a thumbnail history of the Farmers Nonpartisan League, see a *Guide to a Microfilm Edition of the National Nonpartisan League Papers,* edited by Deborah K. Neubeck (St. Paul: Minnesota Historical Society, 1970), pp. 3-5.
2. See Mahoney papers, undated file, Minnesota Historical Society, for a more complete description of the O'Conner machine in Saint Paul as seen by Mahoney.
3. Carl H. Chrislock, *The Progressive Era in Minnesota 1899-1918* (St. Paul: Minnesota Historical Society, 1971), p. 14.
4. Ibid., p. 124.
5. *Minnesota Union Advocate,* January 19, 1917.
6. Ibid., December 7, 1917.
7. Ibid., April 26, 1918.
8. Ibid., June 14, 1918.
9. Bruce L. Larson, *Lindbergh of Minnesota* (New York: Harcourt, Brace, Jovanovich, 1973), p. 237.

10. *Minnesota Union Advocate,* July 25, 1919.
11. Ibid., October 3, 1919.
12. Ibid., February 27, 1920.
13. Minneapolis Central Labor Union papers filed with the Minnesota Historical Society.
14. Ibid.
15. Arthur Naftalin, "A History of the Farmer Labor Party" (Unpublished doctoral dissertation, University of Minnesota, 1948), pp. 71-73.
16. Undated newsletter from 1922 file, Minneapolis Central Labor Union papers, Minnesota Historical Society.
17. Ibid.
18. Ibid.
19. Ibid.
20. *Minnesota Union Advocate,* April 9, 1923.
21. Ibid., May 3, 1923.
22. Ibid., May 31, 1923.
23. Ibid., September 13, 1923.
24. Ibid., September 20, 1923.
25. Naftalin, p. 113.
26. *Minnesota Union Advocate,* September 20, 1923.
27. Mahoney papers.
28. Personal interview with Carl Carlgren, September 1969.
29. Theodore Draper, *American Communism and the Soviet Union* (New York: Viking Press, 1960), p. 101.
30. Ibid.
31. Mahoney papers, Minnesota Historical Society. See letter from C.G. Binderup to William Mahoney, dated June 15, 1942.
32. Personal interview with Carl Carlgren, September 1969.
33. James Shields, *Mr. Progressive: A Biography of Elmer A. Benson* (Minneapolis: T.S. Denison Company, 1971), pp. 297-308.
34. Personal interview with Elmer A. Benson, August 1970.

*"Would you please tell me which
way I ought to walk from here?"
said Alice.*

*"That depends a good deal on
where you want to get to," said
the Cat.*

— *Lewis Carroll*

A CASE STUDY
IN POPULIST DISASTER

THE NATIONAL FARMER-
LABOR PARTY OF 1924

While circumstances were favorable for the formation of a Farmer-Labor Party within Minnesota, an attempt to organize a similar coalition on a national scale failed miserably in 1924 when William Mahoney and other Minnesotans tried to launch a national third party around the LaFollette candidacy. There were new factors involved: namely, the ambivalent Robert LaFollette, Sr., and the rigidly Marxist Workers (communist) Party on the left. This attempt to found a national Farmer-Labor Party is the subject of much speculation in various studies of radical and labor history covering this time period. Such an historian as Theodore Draper, in *American Communism and the Soviet Union*, tends to overplay and thus distort the role of the communists; and at the same time, he underestimates the difficulty of working with LaFollette, Sr., who was at best a Tory populist at this point, unwilling to break sharply with his older progressive outlook. It is helpful to review this episode in populist history, both to correct certain distortions and, in the context of this study, to observe the clash of ideological currents within populist ranks which precluded success.

As soon as plans were completed for the proposed Farmer-Labor Federation in Minnesota, Mahoney and a number of friends, especially Henry Teigan, serving as secretary to Senator Magnus Johnson and also as executive secretary of the failing Farmers Nonpartisan League, made plans to coalesce a national Farmer-Labor Federation for the purpose of supporting LaFollette for President in 1924. The intent of the Mahoney group was explained in a letter (dated November 8, 1923) from Henry Teigan to Jay G. Brown, secretary of the struggling noncommunist Farmer-Labor Party in Chicago, which had emerged from an attempt to form an Illinois third party the previous year.

I think William Mahoney wrote you some time ago relative to a proposed conference of FARMER-LABORITES to be held in the Twin Cities in the middle of November. We have called the conference for November 15th and it will be held at the Labor Temple in St. Paul.

The attendance will be small—perhaps thirty or forty all told. It will, however, be quite representative of the states of the Northwest. We should like very much to have you come with us, and also the Chairman of the Farmer-Labor Party, if he can come with you. As I do not know his name or address, I am unable to reach him by letter.

The purpose of the conference is to discuss plans for launching in the most effective way possible a third party movement next year. This doesn't mean that we disregard the standing of the existing Farmer-Labor Party or other Third Party organizations. The thing we have in mind is to bring these elements together and to secure the issuance of a joint-call for a convention next year. There is all kinds of third party sentiment, but there is considerable confusion as to the methods and plans. I think that no one will deny that the FARMER-LABORITES have succeeded to a point where their movement can be regarded as quite successful. However, I am confident that the States of the Northwest can make as good a showing as Minnesota has made . . . please do not give any publicity to the call as we have no desire to have any mention made of it until after it has been held.[1]

The committee meeting was held in Saint Paul on November 15 and 16, and plans were laid for a national convention to be held May 30, 1924. A committee of five was appointed to arrange for the forthcoming convention. A reading of Theodore Draper's *American Communism and the Soviet Union* gives the impression that the decisions of the November 15 meeting were those reached by an executive meeting of the Workers Party two days earlier, in which the communists had taken a pro-LaFollette stand. In any case, this position was in line with the long-held outlook of Mahoney and Teigan; so it made little difference. Draper overplays the role of communists at this point in suggesting that their decisions two days prior to the November 15 meeting were crucial, when the planning had been underway for two months on the part of the Mahoney group. The Workers Party role at this time was irrelevant as far as plans for the May 30 meeting were concerned.

The committee of five were clearly noncommunists. Four of the five were from Minnesota, including Mahoney, Henry Teigan, W.A. Shaper, an unemployed professor since his dismissal as head of the Political Science Department of the University of Minnesota during the hysteria of 1917, and Robley Cramer, editor of the *Minneapolis Labor Review*. The fifth member of the Arrangements Committee was J.A.H. Hopkins, a New York lawyer and chairman of the almost defunct Committee of 48, a movement of middle-class populists who had tried to draft LaFollette, Sr., to become a presidential candidate in 1920 around such issues as public ownership of railroads, public control of natural resources, and equal rights for all citizens. An active chapter of the Committee of 48 existed in Minnesota for several years, which explains the presence of the national chairman in the Mahoney group.[2]

The proposed third-party meeting was immediately in conflict with the Conference for Progressive Political Action (CPPA), which had been formed in 1922, primarily by the railroad unions. Mahoney lost no time in criticizing the CPPA. "The Conference for Progressive Political Action is an attempt by certain would-be progressives to inaugurate an assumed nonpartisan movement. This is a dual movement as the AFL already has such an organization."[3] Other editorials by Mahoney commented on news stories that the CPPA was organized to provide support for McAdoo for President on the Democratic ticket in 1924.

Within Minnesota, Mahoney also encountered opposition from F.A. Pike, the chairman of the Farmer-Labor Federation, which was composed of individual members not in farm or labor bodies. Mahoney thought Pike was trying to build support for McAdoo on a national level also.

Mr. Pike is a former Democrat who never has fully divested himself of his old party allegiance. He was brought into the Farmer-Labor movement as an attorney for the Non-Partisan League. . . . He has shown a virulent hatred for the League and the activity of economic organizations in politics. He has sought to build a movement independent of organized labor and farmer movements.[4]

The editorial appeared under the caption, "Boss Rule Pike." This feud between Mahoney and Pike simmered on for several months.

On February 12, 1924, the CPPA held a meeting in Saint Louis, also to plan for a national convention. Four labor leaders from the Twin Cities attended, including Mahoney. Efforts were made to get the CPPA to join with the third-party convention planned for Minneapolis on May 30. The CPPA rejected these overtures, not surprisingly in view of Mahoney's previous antipathy to the CPPA and in view of the prior existence of the CPPA. The CPPA planned its own convention for July 4, 1924 in Cleveland, to which they in turn invited the Minnesota group.

In March, the Arrangements Committee for the Minnesota Farmer-Labor Convention met and changed the date from May 30 to June 17, with the hope that LaFollette might be endorsed in Minneapolis on June 17 and in Cleveland by the CPPA on July 4. At this March meeting, the steering committee was enlarged to include representatives from several other states, including South Dakota, Montana and Washington, states in which there were embryonic third-party movements. After the committee was enlarged, there was discussion as to whether or not communists from the Workers Party should be included. In the discussion, Mahoney opposed their inclusion, but Robley Cramer, editor of the *Minneapolis Labor Review,* favored including communists, noting their positive support for a third party within Minnesota. On a motion by Cramer, communist Clarence Hathaway was elected national secretary of the Arrangements Committee, to serve with Mahoney as chairman. Hathaway, at this time, was a vice-president of the Minnesota Federation of Labor, having risen in the ranks of the International Association of Machinists.[5]

It is difficult to evaluate the significance of the decision of this group to elect Hathaway to a key position on the committee. No doubt the Workers Party was interested in playing a dominant role in projecting a third-party movement at this time; however, it should not be construed that the members of the committee were members of the Workers Party, even though these people did support a coalition including communists. At this point in history, the polarization between communist and noncommunist socialists had not sharply developed. As a matter of fact, the logic of events seemed to support the more acerbic evaluation of American society projected by communists, an evaluation which found a ready ear among many who had been moderate socialists committed to parliamentary reform. It was difficult for moderates in this period to deny the Marxian argument that the state is the "executive committee for the bourgeoisie," especially as the moderate leaders themselves had been the victims of jailing, repression, deportations, tarring and feathering. Robley Cramer had himself served a jail sentence for violating an injunction against picketing in a strike against a downtown theater in Minneapolis.

From 1919 to 1923, the pages of the *Minneapolist Labor Review* reveal the presence of a number of noted radicals in Minneapolis, apparently sponsored by the Minneapolis Trades and Labor Assembly. William Z. Foster spoke several times, either about his problems in leading the steel strike or about his trip to Russia, where the "workers had assumed control." Kate Richards O'Hare came to Minneapolis to speak; and Clarence Darrow was there as well. Milwaukee socialist Victor Berger addressed three thousand people in Minneapolis, asserting in anger that the congressmen elected from North Dakota by the Nonpartisan League had not voted to support him when he was denied his seat in Congress in 1919, and thus he implied that the Farmers' League was not far enough to the left. At a time when the IWW were being excoriated and singled out as "wild anarchists," Berger came to their defense and at the same time criticized the AFL for its conservative stance.

I want to say that I am not an IWW. They are desperate proletarians fighting for the right to organize. I have contributed to their defense and will do so again. I am a member of the American Federation of Labor, but know that as managed at present it is the tail end of capitalism.[6]

The parade of socialist and communist speakers was less evident in Saint Paul during this period; however, late in 1922, Saint Paul radicals sponsored an address by Jean Longuet, son-in-law of Karl Marx and son of a famous French socialist, at the Garrick Theater. Longuet assailed the Versailles Peace Treaty and the system of indemnities imposed upon Germany as leading to still another war. A digest of this speech was prominently reported in Mahoney's *Union Advocate.*

During this period, the Twin Cities labor movement reflected the disillusionment with World War I which was emerging in American culture. At the behest of a socialist radical, Julius Emme, the State Federation of Labor established a permanent "Anti-Militarism Committee" as one of the standing committees of the organization. In 1922, the Saint Paul Trades and Labor Assembly was addressed by three European women touring for the Women's International League for Peace and Freedom. Under the headline "United States Bills Hit Common People," Mahoney published an article on the per capita cost of war expenditures:

According to the United States Bureau of Standards, 93 cents out of every dollar of Uncle Sam's money goes for war, past, present, or to come. Only one cent of every dollar goes for education and the improvement of public health. . . . Whereas cities spend an average of $6 per capita for education in one year, and the states and local government about $3 per capita for education. Uncle Sam only spends 6 cents per capita for education . . . and some of that goes to the land grant colleges for military drill.[7]

In addition to this general interest in radical currents in American life within the labor movement, as reflected in the two Twin Cities labor papers, there was also support expressed for the idea of industrial unionism, justified in terms of giving strength to labor in its contest with collective capital. Mahoney was very explicit in rejecting the "pure and simple" unionism of Gompers in favor of the industrial unionism then advocated by radicals throughout the nation.

The evidence here points to a general acceptance of radical views within the Minnesota labor movement rather than undue influence of communist leaders. This view would deemphasize the importance of Clarence Hathaway's inclusion on the Arrangements Committee for the June 17 meeting. Theodore Draper alleges that a formal agreement was reached between Mahoney and the communists.[8] Rather, it seems that Mahoney, in inviting representatives from a number of embryonic Farmer-Labor Parties, included some communists who had risen to leadership in this period, and that Mahoney himself was outvoted on the issue of seating Hathaway as secretary. Draper may be right in finding that William Z. Foster and other communist leaders held talks with Mahoney, but such meetings do not necessarily imply a vast amount of communist influence upon plans for a third party at that time.

The next month, after the inclusion of Hathaway on the Arrangements Committee, the house organ of the railway unions, *Labor,* attacked the forthcoming Saint Paul meeting as "communist controlled," at the same time boosting McAdoo for President on the Democratic ticket. Mahoney denied the allegation about communist control, saying that the communists would be a small minority in the Saint Paul meeting, and at the same time, he renewed his support for LaFollette for President.[9] The position on McAdoo by *Labor* further confirmed charges made all along by Mahoney that the CPPA was intended to be another pressure group and not a vehicle for a third party. In February, Mahoney and ex-professor W.A. Shaper were in Washington and talked with Senator LaFollette, and apparently they went away satisfied that they had the senator's blessing.[10]

Throughout April and May, Mahoney ran weekly headlines and articles reflecting euphoria over the prospects of the coming convention. It was to be the largest convention in the history of the Twin Cities. Fifty thousand invitations were mailed throughout the nation, and one would almost think that the sponsors dreamed that 50,000 people would attend. Mahoney saw this third-party movement supporting LaFollette for President as grounded on a five-point program: (a) public ownership of monopolies, (b) government banking, (c) restoration of civil liberties, (d) public control of all natural resources, and (e) abolition of the injunction in labor disputes.

The official formation of the Minnesota Farmer-Labor Party provided a basis for enthusiasm that the year of the national third party had arrived. Throughout much of May in 1924, Mahoney's *Minnesota Union Advocate* continued to publish articles with headlines reflecting great optimism over the June 17 meeting. But in the May 29 issue, it was apparent that a deep chill had overtaken the editor. "It is clear that LaFollette is cool to the June 17th convention,"[11] began a news story vastly understating the impact of LaFollette's open letter blasting the forthcoming Saint Paul meeting for its communist "taint." The Arrangements Committee put on a brave front and announced that their proposed third party was not to be a "one man" but rather a "bottoms up" movement. Mahoney wrote a pessimistic editorial suggesting that "it is not possible to build a homogeneous party out of the divergent elements which will be represented in Saint Paul on June 17." His pessimism proved to be well founded, as cancellations began to pour in from potential delegates who objected to communist participation and/or who preferred to identify with LaFollette, Sr. At the same time, Mahoney blasted LaFollette as a tool of the CPPA for trying to cripple the attempt to organize a new political party of the real producers of wealth, and he denounced LaFollette for wanting to be an independent candidate without jeopardizing his position in the Republican Party.[12]

The June 17 meeting was duly held in Saint Paul. It was apparent from the beginning that communists were in control of the convention. They delivered a stinging defeat to Mahoney by electing Charles Taylor of Montana instead of Mahoney as permanent convention chairman by a vote of 718 to 116.[13] At one point, William Z. Foster spoke to allay the fears of those concerned with the communist takeover, saying that the new Farmer-Labor Party was not and should not be a duplicate of the Communist Party. The convention endorsed an Illinois miner, Duncan McDonald, for President and a western farm leader, William Bouck, for Vice-President. A four-point program for action was adopted:

1. Delegates would attend the CPPA Convention in Cleveland July 4.
2. McDonald and Bouck would withdraw in favor of LaFollette if the latter ran.
3. The third-party organization would be completed after the election.
4. A national committee of two persons per state was to guide the new party until after the election.[14]

The platform of the June 17 convention included:

1. Repeal of the Federal Reserve and National Bank Act, to be replaced with a federally operated banking system
2. Freedom for the Philippines
3. Recognition of the Soviet Union
4. Use of the army to protect strikers, not vice versa
5. No military intervention in behalf of foreign investment
6. Equality with men for women and Negroes
7. Abolition of the power of the courts to issue antistrike injunctions
8. Nationalization of all monopolized industries.[15]

It was clear that persons close to the Communist Party were in predominance in the new governing board of the national Farmer-Labor Party, formed on June 17. It also happened that the "party line" had changed at the end of May when William Foster was in Moscow for discussions. The new "party line" called for a narrow proletarian party rather than the kind of middle-class party forming around LaFollette; and so LaFollette's snub of the Mahoney committee caused no pain for the communists. With this new strategy, the communist-controlled Farmer-Labor Party later withdrew

McDonald and Bouck in favor of two outright communists, William Foster and Benjamin Gitlow, as national candidates. The experience of the previous year was repeated, with another "still-born" Farmer-Labor Party, as Theodore Draper has described the 1923 communist takeover of the Fitzpatrick movement in Chicago.

In response to the fait accompli which confronted Mahoney, he commented editorially: "No attention will be given to their action, as it is beyond the scope of their authority, and an attempt to speak for the Farmer-Labor convention is a fraudulent misrepresentation."[16] While Mahoney was flaying the left, he swallowed his pride and went to Cleveland to the CPPA Convention on July 4. He was denied a seat. A news item in the *Minnesota Union Advocate,* probably written by himself, tells the story:

There was one brand of thought that the convention wanted the world to know was anathema, and to make this fact known a special victim was selected. Mr. Mahoney, who dared to lead a coalition convention at which so-called communists participated, was denied a seat and was publicly excoriated for his "depraved" association.[17]

Ironically, the CPPA Convention seated as a Minnesota delegate A.B. Gilbert, who was associated with Van Lear and the *Minneapolis Star,* still presumably a socialist daily paper. However, even the CPPA was too far left for Gilbert. Within a month after his return to Minneapolis, Gilbert announced his support for the Republican Party, and he remained a far-right Republican the rest of his life, another case of flip-flop.

Mahoney found what comfort he could in the situation. He hailed the candidacy of LaFollette, even though the LaFollette forces worked outside of the established Farmer-Labor Party in Minnesota. LaFollette himself, however, did finally endorse Floyd Olson for governor after Olson emerged as the winning candidate in the Farmer-Labor Party primary in 1924.

Within Minnesota, Mahoney steered a middle course during the 1924 elections, a course between his new enemies on the *Daily Star,* Van Lear and Gilbert, and his adversaries on the left, former friends who were now promoting the more left outlook of the Workers Party. After the election was over, Mahoney derived some satisfaction from reprinting the "confessions" of Clarence Hathaway from the *Daily Worker.* In this article Hathaway charged the communist leadership with suffering from serious illusions in thinking that they could promote a communist ticket against LaFollette in 1924. "We had found that all we had was a house of cards," said Hathaway, "that crashed on our heads as soon as the LaFollette wind came up. Communism made no inroads among the masses. We had captured conventions, but we had not succeeded in winning the worker to a revolutionary program."[18] Hathaway was especially vehement toward a Comrade Wicks, who had been sent to Minnesota from Chicago and who knew nothing about the history of protest politics in Minnesota and was too lazy to learn. Hathaway, however, agreed with the position taken by the Workers Party during the 1924 campaign that Coolidge and Davis were the candidates of big business and LaFollette the candidate of small business, and that both outlooks should be rejected in favor of a working-class party.

The failure to launch a national Farmer-Labor Party in 1924 was a major disappointment to Mahoney and his associates. Looking back, it seems that Mahoney had been over-optimistic and even unrealistic to imagine that a national third party could be launched from one state alone. One can always speculate about what "might have been." The effort might have been successful beyond Minnesota if LaFollette had been less inclined to win the favor and support of Samuel Gompers in 1924 and had been willing in turn to associate with those forces in the labor movement advocating industrial unionism. The third-party effort might have done better if the Workers Party had not changed its line on advice from the Comintern in May 1924, just before the communists were to become the overwhelming force in the June 17 meeting in Saint Paul. Even if these "ifs" had been fulfilled, this new movement would still have had a problem with the Tory populist/progressive views of LaFollette.

Some historians, such as Theodore Draper in his study of the communist movement in the United States, have been facile in fixing the blame for the failure of the third-party effort on communist influences. It is essential to weigh all of the factors and all of the ideological currents which contributed to the failure. Perhaps the central factor was the essential conservatism of Robert LaFollette, Sr. A Tory populist/progressive, he was unwilling to work with the more radical socialist labor and farm leaders; he did, however, work out informal relations with the Milwaukee socialists, who did not try to push him toward a national third party as the Minnesota socialists had done. LaFollette's philosophical conservatism made him a hard man for Mahoney to deal with; it seems that LaFollette had no intention of organizing a quasi-socialist third party on the Minnesota pattern, even if the presence of Clarence Hathaway had not provided a target for labeling the movement as "communist influenced." The LaFollette attempt to organize a third ticket in 1924 was a reflexive action on the part of a dying progressivism; and in rejecting an open coalition with radical populist forces, LaFollette hurt the possibility of establishing a movement which might have developed roots in states other than Minnesota.

Apart from the difficulties posed by LaFollette, Sr., on one side and the dogmatic communists on the other, Mahoney failed to perceive that other states lacked the kind of politicized mass movements among farmers and workers which had emerged previously in Minnesota; hence, other areas lacked a foundation of organized popular support for the national third party he hoped to launch. Even in failure, however, this attempt to organize a populist coalition serves as a laboratory example for studying populism in American history; in this example the more radical populists saw their constituency melt away toward the less radical LaFollette, Sr., who emerged from the 1924 elections with a respectable four million votes for a third ticket.

Mahoney's failure reflects upon the frequent lament among radicals over the absence of a socialist or labor party tradition within the working class in the United States. It has been observed repeatedly that working people generally are committed to some form of bryanism or progressivism or the two in some combination. As long as a socialist/populist outlook is absent, it is implicitly clear that mass movements are certain to be co-opted by such progressives as LaFollette, at best, or by bryanist types, such as a Huey Long or a George Wallace, who project some form of simplistic rhetoric. It is inadvisable to idealize "the working class" or the yeoman farmer as "the man with the hoe" without examining first the ideological premises of the class or of particular sectors or groups. Discontent causes movement, but ideology provides direction.

If Minnesota and North Dakota stand out as exceptions to the national tendency toward forms of conservatism in farmer and labor circles, one can only repeat the observations made earlier that repression of socialism was ineffective in these two states during World War I and that large numbers of people in these states, especially, teetered on the brink of marginality and that certain immigrant groups brought with them a tradition of political activism. Of course, even in these two states there was ambivalence and vacillation in outlooks between petty bourgeois bryanism and socialism in some form; however, the radical neomercantilist/socialist views were predominant at certain times, giving these two states a special place in the annals of American populism.

In addition to the conflicting outlooks of individuals and groups in the progressive and populist movements at this time, external factors entered the picture as well. Consumer spending deferred during the war years fueled the economy and accelerated both investment and employment. Thus, economic and social pressures were relieved, at least after recovery from the 1921 slump, on lower middle-class people; and by the same token, potential progressives within middle-class circles were satisfied with the counter-reform rhetoric of "back to normalcy." If "normalcy" turned out to be an illusion, it was not until the end of the decade that this illusion was punctured, as the Great Depression gathered momentum and as new populist expressions developed.

NOTES

1. Henry Teigan papers, letter from Teigan to Jaye G. Brown, November 8, 1923, on file with the Minnesota Historical Society.
2. Committee of 48, Minnesota State Central Committee, papers on file with the Minnesota Historical Society.
3. *Minnesota Union Advocate,* December 6, 1923.
4. Ibid., December 27, 1923.
5. Theodore Draper, *American Communism and the Soviet Union* (New York: Viking Press, 1960), p. 100.
6. *Minneapolis Labor Review,* February 13, 1920.
7. *Minnesota Union Advocate,* November 12, 1920.
8. Draper, p. 101.
9. *Minnesota Union Advocate,* April 17, 1924.
10. A more complete account of the pressures and counter-pressures on LaFollette, Sr., is found in a chapter, "The Minnesota Farmer-Laborites and the 1924 Election," in James Weinstein's *The Decline of Socialism in America, 1912-1925* (New York: Monthly Review Press, 1967).
11. *Minnesota Union Advocate,* May 29, 1924.
12. Ibid.
13. Mahoney papers, "Report on the National Progressive Farmer Labor Convention," Minnesota Historical Society.
14. *Minnesota Union Advocate,* June 19, 1924.
15. Ibid.
16. Ibid., July 24, 1924.
17. Ibid., August 10, 1924.
18. Ibid., January 1, 1925.

9

This country is going so far to the right you are not even going to recognize it.

I'll tell you who's not informed, though. It's these stupid kids. Why, they don't know the issues.... Why, I talked to the kids from the Harvard Law School in my office and I was flabbergasted at how uninformed they are about what's going on inside government. And the professors are just as bad if not worse. They don't know anything. Nor do these stupid bastards who are ruining our educational institutions.

— *John Mitchell, United States Attorney General*

NOTES ON HISTORY AS OVERLAPPING PARADIGMS

This study began with an explication of a theory of history based on the assumption that the past and the present can only be understood in terms of a series of overlapping and competing paradigms. Each paradigm offers in idealized form special and normative definitions of "proper" behavior and "good" values as a part of a general perception of social reality, which in turn is assumed to be in a state of change or evolution. In the terminology of this theory, a major problem of human life is to choose between paradigms or else invent a compromise outlook to resolve or soften paradigm conflict, often as some form of ambiguity. In modern civilization, ambivalence, paradox, vacillation, co-optation and ambiguity all characterize the functional relations of people toward paradigm conflict. To this catalogue one must add the striving for a sense of harmony by psychological repression of one side or the other of conflicting world views; and such repression implies a redefined sense of the "unconscious" with social rather than instinctual content.

Rollo May notes dramatically in the opening passages of *Love and Will* the symptoms he finds in people which reflect cultural dissonance in the modern world.

The striking thing about love and will in our day is that, whereas in the past they were always held up as the *answer* to life's predicaments, they have now themselves become the *problem.* It is always true that love and will have become more difficult in a transitional age; and ours is an era of radical transition. The old myths and symbols by which we oriented ourselves are gone, anxiety is rampant; we cling to each other and try to persuade ourselves that what we feel is love; we do not will because we are afraid that if

we choose one thing or one person we'll lose the other, and we are too insecure to take the chance. The bottom then drops out of the conjunctive
emotions and processes—of which love and will are the two foremost examples. The individual is forced to turn inward; he becomes obsessed with
the new form of identity, namely, Even-if-I-know-who-I-am, I-have-no-
significance. I am unable to influence others. The next step is apathy.
And the step following that is violence. For no human being can stand the
perpetually numbing experience of his own powerlessness.[1]

While May is sensitive to the experience of the neurotic personality and
while he speaks of living in a transitional age, his perspective generally lacks
a view of history as overlapping paradigms, a view which helps explain the
inability of many persons to find a solid anchor in some belief system. May
speaks of living in a "schizoid world," but lacking a theory of history, he is
unable to define the deeper roots of the cultural schizophrenia which im-
mobilizes people. There is nothing new in May's observations; for we have
seen apathy, nihilism and pessimism before in history, at least among intellectuals. The difference, perhaps, is that in the modern world, apathy has
spread into everyday culture to a degree not previously experienced, as
greater numbers of people are left without a traditional meaningful "frontier" to which they might apply their energies.

The views here represent a conflict theory of history, with conflict occur-
ring either between competing world outlooks or as a contradiction between
reality and a given world view in the form of anomalies. In the long run,
both forms of conflict merge. A hungry person may tolerate his distress
under one paradigm even while being aware of the gap between promise and
reality; but if he shifts to a new world view, he may find that hunger is intolerable and that he is also in conflict with the cultural and intellectual
aspects of his previous outlook. This principle has been implicit in the discussion of populism in this study. A frontier farmer believing in the American Dream could long tolerate deprivation, poverty and a sod house; however, once committed to a radical outlook, he would look upon his fading
expectations as intolerable and as cause for political protest. "Once your
point of view changes, everything changes," as Abraham Maslow has
observed.

A social observer, whether historian, social critic, or literary critic, operates within the confines of some paradigm in terms of which he perceives
his subject matter and exercises selectivity as to "facts" deserving emphasis.
In this view, social observers are never "value free" and never partake of
Olympian detachment. At best, the function of the social critic is one of
making sound judgments of the social scene, a function shared by every
person in some way and especially by those known as creative artists. The
social critic has an additional obligation beyond that of the man on the

street or the artist, namely, that of making explicit his methodology, the spectacles through which he defines "social reality" and offers judgments and advice. In this study of populism, I have stressed a methodology described in terms of history as overlapping paradigms; and I wish to suggest that this view of history is useful generally for other time periods or as a basis for literary criticism.

A view of overlapping paradigms is evident in such an important recent study as Michael Kammen's *People of Paradox,* in which the author notes conflicting tendencies in the colonial and revolutionary period of American history. After examining the legacy of Samuel Johnson, Jonathan Edwards and Benjamin Franklin, Kammen observes: "In America, henceforth, there could be no singular society—only societies conceived by communities of unlike minded men."[2] Kammen is describing the paradigm conflict between mercantilism and petty capitalism in terms of the shift from concern for the "gracious community" in Edwards to "personal nurture" in Franklin, even though Kammen himself is committed only to a vague theory of pluralism as a basis for methodology.

It is not practical to cite here numerous examples which overtly or covertly illustrate the principle of history as overlapping paradigms. Rather, it is more helpful to focus briefly on certain currents of thought which lack a historical perspective and which thereby suffer from limitations. In general, those currents which stress a concern with presocial human nature as forms of primitivism or innate determinism tend to lose sight of the dynamics of culture. We have already discussed the asocial conservatism implicit in Freud; and we have noted these same tendencies in linguistic and anthropological circles in which man is treated as the "naked ape" or in which myths and symbols are regarded as imprinted codes, especially when interpretations of these so-called innate aspects of life are treated ahistorically. Alfred Adler's view of the relation between inherited capabilities and the social milieu is superior to that of other formulations. Adler's view is that inherited capacities, generally defined, are employed variously by persons in differing life situations and/or with differing outlooks as strategies for dealing with life's problems. While Adler made his point most explicitly around the notion of organ inferiority, this theory is all the more appropriate in regard to myth and symbols, certainly more appropriate than the notion of genetic transmission as projected by Carl Jung and persons influenced by him or by the highly abstract treatment of myths and symbols by Levi-Strauss and his followers. Even though there is an apparent universality in certain myths, it seems sufficient to suggest that there is a universality of certain human experiences: life, death, the life-giving power of the sun, and more; however, even so-called universal myths are constantly transformed and retranslated as an individual moves from one paradigm to another or from one social class to another, especially when differing social classes reflect different paradigm commitments.

It is perfectly true that the outward forms of myths and symbols are transmitted from one era to another in a way which might give superficial credence to the notion of the universality of myths as archetypal mental forms; however, it is almost irrelevant simply to trace the persistence of the outward manifestations of myths and symbols without also analyzing the changing functional relationship of each one to the paradigm conflicts of an era. It is not enough simply to identify or to describe various forms of certain myths, as Henry Nash Smith has done in *Virgin Land* with the concept of "the West." The more tantalizing problem is one of searching for the changing meanings of myths and symbols as paradigm revolutions occur and overlap in a world of social reality. Freedom could mean one thing for a plantation owner, another for the slave. Jesus could be a socialist for radicals and a capitalist for conservatives. The pastoral dream could be a nightmare for a bankrupt farmer even while the dream might serve as an escape from unpleasant realities for the romantics. The cowboy, far from perceiving himself as a romantic hero in the individualist tradition, was a down-and-out migrant worker who often sought refuge from nature in such institutions of civilization as the whorehouse and the bar, and who usually was prohibited even from carrying a gun, contrary to the myth of a later time. In a more esoteric vein, Reuben A. Brower, in "Visual and Verbal Translation of Myth: Neptune in Virgil, Rubens and Dryden" illustrates the principle of transformation of myth discussed here. Brower begins:

Although we commonly speak of "The Oedipus Myth" or "The Hercules Myth" and though anthropologists refer to mythical "archetypes" or "structure," it can be said that there are no myths, only versions. To put it another way, there are only texts for interpretation, whether the text is written or oral, a piece of behavior—a dance or a cockfight—a drawing or a painting.[3]

Although the pastoral myth has become a mechanism by which social conflict has been resolved into a "higher" harmony in apotheosized Nature, this is not a resolution at all in a social sense but rather an ambiguous resolution of conflict, a key intellectual construct in the literary convention known as naturalism. It is in this context that I have criticized Hofstadter's misreading of the pastoral myth as the soft side of populism; he was, in my view, seeing a phenomenon widely held within modern culture, a phenomenon which has served to obfuscate rather than to resolve conflict and which has displayed itself as bryanism, not populism, in politics.

For social and literary critics, there is always the double problem of analyzing conflict as a reflection of clashing paradigms and of noting tendencies toward conflict resolution and homeostasis at the same time, the latter most often as forms of ambiguity. In regard to ambiguity, we are aware of the stereotype of the politician who employs rhetoric vaguely so as to mean all things to all people; however, artists and academicians often display similar tendencies in dealing with myths and symbols in overly abstract ways divorced from the experiences of time and place. To the extent that the abstract manipulation of myths and symbols becomes a game, so to speak, it is a short step into the symbolist or surrealist genre in which the world is cynically conceived to be absurd, a genre which, when conventionalized, serves as a sign of disintegration of the current paradigm even though it contains little prescription for reform other than futility. In the surrealist genre, there is a devaluation of values as a form of exaggerated irony but never an attempt toward a revaluation of values in a new world view.

Given the definition of a paradigm as a pattern or holistic world view including life styles, manners, moral attitudes and ideals for social and economic organization, it is apparent that paradigm revolutions involve the full range of human experience. Yet, it happens that special perspectives or "schools of thought" for viewing tension, and resolution of tension, develop in literary and social science circles. For example, in the novel we have the genre of "manners and morals" often pitted against "social realism"; yet, both modes reflect a different angle of vision upon a given paradigm conflict, each mode in its own way being "realistic." Such a novel as William Dean Howells' *The Rise of Silas Lapham* incorporates both genres; for Howells cherishes the dream of a morally decent and honest capitalism which is threatened by financial manipulators after the "fast buck." Even while Howells was engaged in holding high the torch of bourgeois idealism as a guide for practical behavior, any number of other observers were sipping the sour dregs of a culture corrupted by materialism. Among these were Henry Adams and Mark Twain, the intellectual mugwumps of their time, who could only imagine an apocalyptic destruction of modern civilization as if by a massive suicidal impulse. These pessimists, who can see only the decadent or the ironic aspects of culture, always seem unable to formulate a new dream for a viable society; hence, they can be regarded in final analysis only as reactionaries tied to an outmoded paradigm and unable to embrace either a socialist, populist or progressive world view as a basis for a new optimism.

The upholders of the paradigm built around autonomous individualism have made a special imprint upon American culture; for in denying institutions and thereby a sense of human community, they have left man dangling in intellectual space, with a theory of each-on-his-own and without a thrust toward community or gemeinschaftsgefühl. Generations of scholars have been intellectually crippled by the persistence of Emerson and Whitman as

American heroes, neither of whom had a vision of social structure between the discrete individual and God, a void filled in their scheme only by the individual hero. From this individualism flows the well-known concept of the "American Adam," who lacks social roots and who is often portrayed in literature as an orphan hero without family ties, past or present. In *The Imperial Self,* Quentin Anderson exposes the Achilles heel of nineteenth century individualism in terms of the works of Emerson, Whitman, and Henry James, arguing that "all three believed that the worst thing a man could do was to accept the conditions of action in the society or the community, to pin himself to a particular role."[4]

For Henry James, especially, a possibility of new or different roles existed only for a person of wealth, the source of which was best left obscure. James's intent was to "educate" the innocent, nouveau riche American with a sophisticated sense of tradition and good manners often associated with Europe. James was realist enough to sense that this formula could not work in the social milieu which he constructed in his fiction; thus, the tragic note in his writing. Yet his commitment to this formula precluded him from imagining a new social paradigm as the basis for new roles and new values for a society drugged with commercialism.

On a popular level, there are many cultural tendencies which reflect existential concerns for finding a real self, as opposed to a false self, as a remedy for alienation and apathy in the modern world. These tendencies take many forms, such as a return to nature, encounter-group experiences or religious introspection fostered by new cults. In all cases, persons who move in this direction strive to reject, ignore or escape from history and culture as if it is possible for a real self to exist in the abstract apart from a social setting of some sort. These pursuits are supported by the theories of third force psychologists, such as Abraham Maslow, who stresses a neoromantic concern for the achievement of "feeling" and "peak experiences" as means of gaining better adjustment in immediate personal relationships; but again, the role of the larger paradigm conflicts of the age as a source of confusion and alienation is ignored. These outlooks reflect a renewal of a transcendental stress on individual perfectionism, even though people with such outlooks may perceive themselves variously as being counter culture, new left, or plain social dropouts. It is not amiss to suggest that the "flower people" can become victims of the pathology of perfectionism which we have discussed earlier and that they, too, can become addicted to violence as an art form, violence for violence's sake, as it were.

The doctrine of individualism was obviously most satisfying to those who were successful in reaching their goals and who could imagine themselves as a part of an elite; and the doctrine was most debilitating to the "losers," the marginal people who could only feel defeated and who could easily embrace the negativistic, bryanistic mentality which emerged so strongly out of the petty capitalist era. As a part and parcel of bryanism, there has been in American popular culture a heavy strain of Manicheanism, with allegorical myths celebrating "good" over "evil," often with religious overtones. This outlook encourages a definition of "evil" in terms of symbolic scapegoats rather than as institutional dysfunction as a facet of the much celebrated American innocence.

There is logic to the assertion that various forms of racism have found a fertile soil in our culture where innocence of social process is well rooted, an innocence which reflects primitivism in some way as I have previously argued. Lacking theories to explain social complexity, genetic factors have been employed to rationalize variations in intelligence, behavior and moral attitudes. These rationalizations reinforce a Manichean view of a natural opposition between genetic "misfits" and those endowed with the "good" genes. In a more subtle way, genetically based instinctualism in psychology easily develops into a monocausal explanation for behavior, enabling persons to make rationalizations to support political and social biases that are actually rooted in a commitment to a particular paradigm. Freud's reactionary attitude toward female creativity and Jung's flirtation with fascism in Germany are examples of instinctually (primitivist) based justifications for attitudes on social questions.

The concept of history as overlapping paradigms is patently in contradiction to the outlooks of consensus historians and functionalist (Parsonian) sociologists. These groups can speak of social change only as technical alterations in social relationships, while ignoring the implications of conceptual revolutions for new perceptions and behavior. For example, Neil Smelser's *Social Change in the Industrial Revolution,* a study of the industrial revolution in England, views the emergence of new social organizations, such as the trade unions and cooperatives, simply as new "structural differentiation," as if there were no cultural or ideological (paradigm) implications associated with the formation of these new movements. Likewise, consensus historians, such as Hofstadter, have tended to idealize the progressive world view as the unfolding of such American ideals as equality and brotherhood, pointing to the mote in the eye of the petty capitalist outlook while not noticing the beam in progressive ideology. Later, such thinkers as Reinhold Niebuhr, unable to conceal from overt consciousness the contradictions in progressivism, have attempted to justify contradiction as "irony," or "sin" as an inherent ingredient in history. (Rosa Parks did not see the irony in rhetoric about "freedom" juxtaposed with the reality of sitting in the back of the bus as an "inherent" aspect of history!) It is difficult to concur with Gene Wise, who argues in *American Historical Explanations* that recognition of irony in history reflects the formation of a new counter-progressive paradigm. Rather, it might be noted that recognition of irony or absurdity simply speaks for acknowledgment of an anomaly or falsification in the Kuhnian sense and not at all for a new outlook per se. Rather, I suggest that William Appleman Williams, in *Contours,* has initiated the movement toward a new model for viewing history; not Reinhold Niebuhr, who in the name of irony justified the cold war and the warfare state, the Achilles heel of progressivism.

* * *

In a study such as this, with its stress upon an explicit conceptual model for viewing history, questions arise as to the implications of applying this model in the present. Such questions relate to my initial argument in chapter one that there is always a concern with the present in both the subject matter and the treatment of historical material. Many popular appeals, notably *The Populist Manifesto* by Jack Newfield and Jeff Greenfield, cause many people to ask whether a new populism might not be on the horizon; furthermore, many protest movements or episodes have emerged in the last two decades which might portend the rise of a new populism. In many cases there is much confusion over the meaning of the term, as is the case with Greenfield and Newfield. These authors include Harry Truman as a populist, presumably because he used "down to earth rhetoric." They ignore the fact that Truman rose through the Kansas City Pendergast machine, not through any kind of farmer or labor popular coalition; and they ignore Truman's role in launching the cold war, a policy contrary to the anti-jingoist tradition of American populism.

Some academic observers, especially consensus historians, are negative about the possibility of a new populism. Louis Hartz, for example, in *The Liberal Tradition,* argues that the United States has not developed a radical ideology because we emerged as a nation without a feudal past and hence without cause for ideological polarization. The Hartz argument for the inevitability of a liberal consensus is faulty in a number of respects. While the existence of the frontier did prolong and solidify the petty capitalist era and its counterpart liberal culture (with both idealistic and ugly facets), this country has experienced ideological watersheds, first from mercantilism (with domination by a tidewater aristocracy) toward petty capitalism, and later from petty capitalism to corporate capitalism (with progressive reformers in the vanguard). Not only does Hartz fail to take note of major paradigms, but he ignores the lesser radical ideologies and movements related to the major watershed developments as well. He asserts that radicalism is somehow alien to the great liberal tradition of this country.

The Hartz thesis has been questioned by Kenneth McNaught, who argues that socialism was co-opted too easily, not as a matter of historical inevitability but because of a lack of intellectual discipline among such early socialists as Walter Lippman.[5] However, McNaught is too much concerned with the fate of a few intellectuals, like Lippman; and thus he fails to observe the various spin-offs from socialism into popular movements, such as the Minnesota Farmer-Labor Party and the Southern Tenant Farmers Union, to name but two examples.

A more balanced view of populist radicalism in America has been projected by Christopher Lasch, in *The Agony of the American Left.* Lasch is fuzzy in his definition of populism, stressing the ideological commitment of populists to Jefferson, Jackson and Lincoln without adequately noting the tendency for populists to break with the petty capitalist point of view symbolized by these three presidents.[6] Also, Lasch is technically incorrect when he says that the People's Party gave way to the Farm Bureau Federation, becoming simply another special interest group[7]; for the Farm Bureau was not organized until 1919, twenty years after the demise of the People's Party. Moreover, as I have noted heretofore, the more typical pattern for populists after the turn of the century was one of being co-opted by progressives, with a minority turning to the newly formed Socialist Party or to cooperatives. Lasch seems to miss the point that while certain populist movements may wither away, new ones emerge among a new generation of marginal people seeking redress of grievances, often with new ideological perspectives as well. However, in spite of these criticisms, Lasch's observations are often acute, especially his contention that the concept of "radical-liberalism" projected by Arnold Kaufman is inherently self-contradictory, in that radicalism implies institutional alterations while liberalism denotes only a restoration of personal freedom and rational choice.[8]

Linked with speculation over a possible resurrection of populism in the United States are other related questions: Is progressivism terminally sick? (Or would we rather repress the notion of a "sick society"?) Might a new bryanism be the wave of the future? Is it possible that political polarization will develop more clearly along class lines, as predicted by Marxist theory? Might the American labor movement alter its traditional political outlook and move instead toward the goal of a populist or socialist labor party, more in the European tradition? These kinds of questions can be both subdivided and multiplied. It is not my intent here to offer definitive predictions as answers to these questions; rather, it is preferable to clarify the choices facing institutions and individuals in the context of the current state of paradigm conflict, adding a prophetic note at times, with the hope that my own prophecies might be self-fulfilling.

It seems hardly necessary to belabor the argument that the progressive paradigm celebrating progress, optimism and an orderly middle-class society is in many ways at odds with social reality. For in spite of a series of "New Freedoms," "New Deals," and "New Frontiers," old problems of poverty, racism, corruption, and international warfare are pervasive in western society. While progressives have frequently co-opted populist and even socialist proposals for limited domestic reform, they have remained singularly committed to capitalist internationalism, with its built-in need for exporting investment and for importing raw materials, as the keystone of the United States' social structure. This kind of expansionism seemed relatively harmless when it was perceived as liberation and freedom for European immigrants filling a frontier; perhaps it was harmless except for American Indians, who were ruthlessly pushed aside, and except for Mexicans, from whom a large area of the Southwest was taken by force of arms.

Today, while expansionist attitudes and patterns persist, the external situation is changing in ways which challenge a 350-year-old frontier tradition. For example, with a growing sense in the world that certain resources are finite, many of the Third World nations are resisting rapid industrialization on United States investors' terms and the loss of precious raw materials to the "mother country." This resistance, as dramatized by the Vietnam War, has provoked military intervention by the "mother." (Perhaps the metaphor of capital punishment by an autocratic "father" is more appropriate!) The paradoxical effect has been that the ideal of a welfare society has been transformed into the reality of a warfare society, in which war production has become a pump-priming device for jobs, bringing with it a corrosive inflation which is forcing new groups of people into economic marginality.

The growth of warfare spending has meant that social investment for health, education and public transportation has lagged far behind the needs of a modern economy. American progressivism, with all of its fine but ambiguous phrases, seems to stand impotent before problems facing this country and the world at large. Possibly, the New Frontier proclaimed by John Kennedy will prove to be the "last hurrah" for the progressive movement; perhaps it will be the last attempt to breathe life into the United States economy via the investment frontier, by such devices as giving corporate giants an investment credit tax break in the hope that economic growth for the giants will somehow trickle down to the common citizen. The impotence of progressivism is most clearly discernible in the field of economics. Formulae for reform, such as the cruel policy of trading off unemployment for inflation control, are patently inoperative; and the traditional Keynesians are unable to imagine new courses of action which might reverse simultaneous tendencies toward both stagnation and inflation (stagflation).

The current crisis in the progressive paradigm has already produced and will continue to produce a variety of new political strategies. In intellectual circles there is a revival of many outlooks, on both the right and the left of the political spectrum. The decisive factor for future political direction is the ability of persons committed to these outlooks to generate mass movements. Already, we can observe a new version of bryanism around such a person as Governor George Wallace as an important force in American politics. We can wonder if there will also emerge a new populism in the form of radical neomercantilism. If such a new populism should emerge on a massive basis, we can also wonder if there would again be co-optation, or whether establishment forces faced with a chaotic breakdown of the social system might panic, leading to a polarization which would confirm the classical Marxist version of class conflict. To raise these questions is not to provide easy answers; for in the long run, the answers will be provided by individuals operating within various political movements.

In making speculative projections, it is unsound to assume that history repeats itself. It never does. While we can identify similar social forces in the late nineteenth and the late twentieth century, there is one significant difference which may contribute to quite different political and cultural developments in the two periods. Throughout the late nineteenth century, there was a shift from small enterprise to corporate industrialism and an ideological shift from the petty capitalist paradigm to progressivism (with prodding from populism). During this shift, there was a variegated assortment of backward looking responses in both political and cultural life, most notably a sour mugwumpism and an intolerant bryanism along with modes of nihilism and despair in artistic circles, arising among frustrated individuals whose world view was disintegrating. Now in the late twentieth century, we can observe vast numbers of people for whom the progressive trickle-down theory has been a fraud and a snare, people ranging from the unemployed to the underemployed, to small farmers, and to shopkeepers struggling long hours for poor financial returns. It is easy for victims of progressivism to celebrate the spirit of rugged individualism and self-help associated with the petty capitalist paradigm. They are often quick to condemn the various forms of progressive intervention as "socialism for the rich", and they react to the decline of progressivism with a reaffirmation of a bryanistic outlook as their definition of utopia couched in nostalgia for "old time religion" and for minimal government.

Alongside these bryanistic tendencies in the marginal strata of our society, individualistic (privatist) outlooks are prevalent in upper-class, intellectual and artistic circles as forms of modern day mugwumpism. Even while committed to progressive economic intervention, upper-class persons have traditionally maintained their right to the best personal life style money can buy, often following the implied admonitions of Henry James to dabble in high culture in the art for art's sake tradition. Privatism is implicit in many existential tendencies in philosophy and psychology, especially in the search for an elusive inner self. This search for self may be pursued through drugs, through a return to nature, or through the pessimism of Kierkegaardian despair. The outlook in any event is asocial and ahistorical. Privatism takes another form in the heroic vitalism of a Hemingway or a Mailer or the violence of Mickey Spillane's Mike Hammer. Heroic vitalism reflects American innocence, even when the hero might (as with the nouveau riche Jay Gatsby) come to a tragic demise as a symbol of the failure of individualism. Privatism leads to an amoral unconcern for social problems; at best it produces an absence of scapegoatism among liberals in the tradition of John Stuart Mill; but at worst, privatism is the seedbed for an ugly mugwumpism or bryanism when frustration and anxiety mount.

It is conceivable that new forms of mugwumpism and bryanism, as reactions against progressivism, might become a more powerful force in the late twentieth century than these same reactions were in the late nineteenth century, when a culture based on atomic individualism was overwhelmed (but not destroyed) by the rise of populism and progressivism. It seems safe to make the prophecy that nostalgia for nineteenth-century individualism is certain to come to a dead end and that sour, hateful persons are in prospect as a continuation of the anti-FDR bryanism of the 1930s and of the mccarthyism of the 1950s. It is my hope that this prophecy will not be self-fulfilling; however, it is well to be prepared for the reality that on a popular level bryanism has the potential for becoming a major current within the larger climate of opinion, a potential which is already evident in the popularity enjoyed by Governor George Wallace during the past decade in both the North and South.

If this projection of bryanism as a major current in the culture of the United States is valid, any new populistic or radical movements will have to deal with this phenomenon. It is well to be reminded that while bryanism is most often overtly reactionary in looking back to a lost utopia, there is also a potential in the outlook for movement in a radical direction, if at first only into the camp of Tory populism. For certain bryanist elements, especially those with trade union or populist experience, sooner or later are attracted to *some* platform of reform beyond that of vituperative rhetoric or nostalgic sentiments. Whether or not certain bryanist types are eventually pulled into the populist or radical orbit depends in large part upon the skill, artfulness, and knowledge of the organizers of populist coalitions, especially their knowledge of history and of those ethnic traditions that reinforce tendencies toward radicalism. In modern democratic society, populist organizers must necessarily strive toward a mass movement; hence, they must also understand the repressed as well as the overt outlooks of their potential constituency. The alternative to seeking a viable mass movement is to be condemned to sectarian ineffectiveness or to abandon ideological concerns for an aimless exploitation of popular discontents, with a tendency to slip into episodic protest efforts with little effect upon ideology. These kinds of protest are often called populistic; but, in the context of this study, bryanism is the better term. Senator Pettigrew's observation about Bryan himself describes the weakness of this tendency: "He yielded to the necessity of the moment, trusting that all would be well in the end, but without foreseeing the end or understanding its import."

Examples of episodic protest movements, including outbursts of violence, abound in American history. Episodic protest of whatever variety lacks the perspective for forming an ongoing mass movement and lacks the possibility of institutionalizing any gains which are achieved. These lacks are often applauded by certain romantic or anarchistic radicals who fear or reject the possibility of bureaucracy. It is true that bureaucracies at times can be both repressive and regressive; but any movement perforce must exist in a world of power relations and must strive to exercise organized power to alter these relations. Individualistic decentralization in the name of democracy leads to ineffectiveness and finally despair. The traditional liberal identification of individualism with democracy is an exercise in contradiction, for no man by himself can practice democracy; Robinson Crusoe is a case in point. In the modern world, the pressing problem is that of democratizing bureaucracies, not one of returning to the petty capitalist past with its culture of autonomous individualism and romantic protest.

A well known kind of episodic protest is that promoted by followers of the late Saul Alinsky, a self-styled radical community organizer who stressed "protest from below" among the have-nots of society. These reformers focus upon narrowly defined local problems with confrontative tactics while abjuring an interest in the larger significance of local issues in the context of paradigm conflicts and while taking little interest in forming ongoing populist movements. The upshot is typically a pragmatic type of reformism which serves to make progressive capitalism viable even though the rhetoric can sound quite radical. This kind of reformism does produce gains in concrete situations; however, such gains persist at the whim of social circumstances and can be lost in the winds of an ensuing crisis, leaving followers confused and adrift in an ideological fog. Much closer to genuine populist-type movements have been the protest efforts among black people during the past two decades; however, there has been much variation in ideological outlook from movement to movement and much episodic protest as well.

During the 1960s, a new organization sprang up in rural America, the National Farmers Organization. Essentially, this organization was formed to protest against economic decisions during the Kennedy and Johnson administrations to roll back or suppress farm prices in order to average down the rate of inflation at the expense of farmers. For a time, the NFO massively captured members from the Farm Bureau and the Farmers Union, especially the latter with its close ties to Democratic Party progressivism. By and large, the NFO can be described as a version of Tory populism, demanding farmer collective bargaining on one hand, while employing typical petty capitalist rhetoric and toying with the politics of George Wallace on the other hand.

Generally, the protest movements of the last two decades have failed to forge the kind of coalition which would move into a quasi-socialist or radical neomercantilist direction. The gluing together of coalitions is always difficult at best, and it is a skill which has been practiced badly in the United States, where the concept of "front" organizations has been more often in operation. The important distinction between a front and a coalition deserves attention. The front idea has somehow become associated with the "communist front" as a tactic in radical politics; however, the tactic is obviously employed across the political spectrum; for example, the Committee for Economic Development (CED) as a front for pro-business associations, the Committee on Political Education (COPE) as a political arm of the trade union movement, or the National Rifle Association (NRA) as a front for the Pentagon. There is nothing inherently wrong with a front tactic, and it often helps a parent organization to focus sharply on an issue or to engage a larger public into supporting the parent's aims. On the other hand, the coalition approach implies a modification of the aims of various federated groups or movements in the interest of a larger unity; and it is the give and take in this kind of modification that requires a certain political skill, which in turn contributes to success for a political movement where the aim must be one of organizing a majority coalition among the electorate.

Organizing a coalition is especially difficult among movements which are essentially amorphous and lacking in clearly defined leadership. Bryanism poses a particular problem for a potential populist coalition, for it requires that populist organizers deal not only with an amorphous structure but also with the limited radical potential within the divided mind of bryanism, which harbors radicalism only as a repressed social consciousness, if at all.

In a larger sense, the organization of coalitions involves a process of mutual co-optation, always with the hope that a central thrust will be able to be maintained and that unity will overcome schismatic tendencies. Observers often point to the skill of President Franklin Roosevelt in keeping together a disparate progressive coalition of reactionary southern Democrats, union labor, black movements and western family farmers. By the same token, it is possible to point to the relative success of the Minnesota Farmer-Labor party as an example of a populist coalition which persisted for over twenty years, part of this time as the dominant party of the state. Those who would engage in neopopulism might well find the Farmer-Labor experience instructive both for its successes and also for its difficulties, as schismatic tendencies finally did polarize the Party in 1938. This is not to say that schisms can or should be avoided at all costs; for social realities change, new outlooks arise, and new prescriptions for reform are advocated which may well be in sharp, unresolvable conflict with older outlooks.

It is not my intent here to outline programmatic content for a new populism in such areas as taxation, price and wage policy, foreign policy, public ownership, land policy, and more. Various outlooks on these questions will be negotiated toward a common ground when any populist coalition forms. It is sufficient to stress the problems inherent in building coalitions, with the hope that a new populism will make a mark in United States history now in the last third of the twentieth century. Whether a new populism will survive to become a new paradigm cannot be determined in advance. Perhaps "establishment forces" will successfully co-opt a new movement. Even co-optation is a partial success; yet it is such a limited success that historically new populist revolts have repeatedly erupted within a decade after co-optation occurred. We should be ever mindful that "it can happen here," that forms of overt fascism are possible at times when conservative forces panic. This was the case during the repression of 1917-18, the McCarthy era of the 1950s, and most recently in the Watergate episode, which revealed overreaction in the White House to the threat of mild progressivism as personified in a McGovern or a Muskie.

In speculating about a possible new populism, it is difficult to predict whether or not such a new movement will emerge as a new form outside of existing political organizations or whether it will gestate within Democratic and Republican ranks. This study, with its empirical references to upper midwestern populism, suggests that populist movements arise first within an existing party, as was the case in Minnesota, North Dakota and Wisconsin, where insurgent or third-party movements all were born among the ranks of the disaffected within the Republican Party. If this precedent is repeated it is likely that future populist expressions will be generated within the Democratic Party, which has replaced the Republicans as the party of the "common people." It seems most likely that new structures or "factions" will arise within the Democratic Party for the reason that the Party for too long has rejected a radical-populist input while it has juxtaposed jingoistic progressivism with bryanistic rhetoric. It is symbolic of this juxtaposition that the annual shakedown of Democratic fat cats occurs at an annual dinner dedicated to the memory of Jefferson and Jackson, our two presidents most associated with the pastoral myth, with unfettered petty capitalism and with geographic expansionism. It seems incongruous that the Democrats might consider dedicating their cause to the memory of Eugene V. Debs. The fact of this perceived incongruity speaks for the distance between the Minnesota Farmer-Labor tradition, with its roots in Debsian socialism, and ailing Democratic progressivism.

If a new populism begins to arise, the role of the "humanists" in academia will be an interesting one to observe, especially in view of the academic tendency to obfuscate conflict with ambiguity (a tendency I have noted above). It has been popular in academic circles to deprecate the pastoral myth of nineteenth-century individualism and to view lower-class bryanism as a modern form of know-nothingism. Yet, many of these same academics are often engrossed in the pessimism of a Nietzsche, T.S. Eliot or Ezra Pound and in other forms of intellectual nay saying, often little more than sophisticated forms of the know-nothingism feared in bryanism.

The pastoral myth is not the only form of innocence in the modern world. New myths have achieved credence within the progressive paradigm, such as the myth of progress, defined around corporate economic growth, and the myth of instinctualism, observed in Freudian form, for example. If the progressive world view is in a state of disrepair, as I allege, it is these progressive myths which need to be replaced by new truths, new ideas for achieving social order. We may well experience a form of "future shock"—not a shock arising from rapid technological change as such, but rather a trauma of confronting a new paradigm as the old progressive one seems to suffer from senility. The trauma of confronting new ideas is exacerbated partly because older populistic and socialistic traditions have been repressed and unadmitted as legitimate alternatives for America in the years since World War II. William Appleman Williams is most perceptive when he observes: "Yesterday is not dead and gone. We are just meeting it head on for the first time in a hundred years." (Amend to read "350 years.") Will we meet yesterday and today and tomorrow honestly and humanely? We have choices to make.

CODA

"The Past is Prologue"—Motto engraved on the National Archives Building, translated by an anonymous Washington, D.C. taxi driver as "You ain't seen nothing yet."

NOTES

1. Rollo May, *Love and Will* (New York: Norton, 1969), pp. 13–14.
2. Michael Kammen, *People of Paradox* (New York: Random House, 1973), p. 94.
3. Reuben A. Brower, "Visual and Verbal Translation of Myth: Neptune in Virgil, Rubens and Dryden," *Daedalus*, Winter, 1972, p. 155.
4. Quentin Anderson, *The Imperial Self* (New York: Alfred Knopf), p. ix.
5. Kenneth McNaught, "Socialism and the Progressives: Was Failure Inevitable?" in *Dissent: Explorations in the History of American Radicalism*, Alfred F. Young, Ed. (DeKalb: Northern Illinois University Press, 1968), pp. 251-271.
6. Christopher Lasch, *The Agony of the American Left* (New York: Alfred Knopf, 1969), p. 6.
7. Ibid., p. 16.
8. Ibid., pp. 190-192.

SELECTED BIBLIOGRAPHY

By and large, the sources which have been most helpful in this study have been incorporated into chapter footnotes. It would be redundant to repeat these citations in toto. Rather, I will cite only key references which have served either as supportive or as counterpoint outlooks, especially in the many disciplines which are tangential to this study, such as history, social psychology, political sociology, social criticism and sociology of knowledge. However, in a final section of this bibliography, I will provide a somewhat more detailed catalogue of sources referring to midwestern populism. Interviews and discussion with people who have been in populist movements have been so numerous that I am making no attempt to list them other than those quoted and cited in footnotes.

In the text, I have referred to William Appleman Williams' *The Contours of American History* (Cleveland and New York: World Publishing Co., 1961) as a source of methodological inspiration for understanding American history. Likewise, Thomas Kuhn's *The Structure of Scientific Revolutions* (Chicago: University of Chicago Press, 1966) is another foundation stone of this study. Kuhn's views are sharply debated in articles reprinted in I. Lakatos and A. Musgrave, eds., *Criticism and the Growth of Knowledge* (Cambridge: Cambridge University Press, 1970). A well developed argument for employing the Kuhnian model for understanding social process is made in Bruce Kuklick's "History as a Way of Learning," *American Quarterly*, 22 (Fall 1970).

In the field of American Studies, a number of scholars have raised questions regarding method. An early article was that of Henry Nash Smith, "Can American Studies Develop a Method?" *American Quarterly*, 9 (Summer 1963). A number of essays on this question have been reprinted in Robert Meredith's *American Studies Essays on Theory and Method* (Columbus: Charles E. Merrill, 1968). Most recently, Cecil F. Tate's *The Search for Method in American Studies* (Minneapolis: University of Minnesota Press, 1973) provides a survey of the various ways for achieving perspective on culture which have been employed by leading American Studies scholars.

An important study of movement among marginal people in Europe is E.J. Hobsbawn's *Primitive Rebels* (Manchester: Manchester University Press, 1957). A collection of sociological essays assembled by Hans Peter Dreitzel titled *Recent Sociology No. 1* (London: Macmillan, 1969) focuses on the dynamics of mass movements. Samuel Hays' *Response to Industri-*

alism, 1885-1914 (Chicago: University of Chicago Press, 1954) points to
the variety of outlooks generated among those who suffered in some way
from the later industrial revolution. A sharp critique of Parsonian sociology
is developed in Alvin Gouldner's *The Coming Crisis in Western Sociology*
(New York: Basic Books, 1970). Ethnic influences in politics are stressed
in Samuel Lubell's *The Future of American Politics* (New York: Harper,
1965) and in Lawrence H. Fuchs, ed., *American Ethnic Politics* (New York:
Harper, 1968).

In developing a version of psychohistory based on the theories of Alfred
Adler, I have found his own work the most directly useful; Alfred Adler,
Understanding Human Nature (New York: Greenberg, 1925) and Alfred
Adler, *What Life Should Mean to You* (New York: G.P. Putnam, 1958).
Adler's colleague and interpreter, Rudolph Dreikurs, has published much,
notably *Fundamentals of Adlerian Psychology* (Chicago: Alfred Adler Institute, 1950). Two publications edited by Heinz and Rowena Ansbacher
provide further source material from the writings of Adler: Heinz L. Ansbacher and Rowena R. Ansbacher, *Superiority and Social Interest* (New
York: Viking Press, 1970) and *Adler* (New York: Harper, 1956). In addition to footnoted references to Freud, Erikson, Jung and neo-Freudians,
there are numerous standard references in which their views are explicated.

Of special interest in this study has been Leon Festinger's *A Theory of
Cognitive Dissonance* (Stanford: Stanford University Press, 1966), and
Viktor Frankl's *The Will to Meaning* (New York: World, 1969). Fred
Weinstein and Gerald M. Platt's *Psychoanalytic Sociology* (Baltimore: Johns
Hopkins Press, 1973) integrates Freudian and neo-Freudian psychology with
Parsonian sociology. The interaction of the individual with the cultural
milieu has been treated in C. Wright Mills and Hans Gerth's *Character and
Social Structure* (London: Routledge and Kegan Paul, Ltd., 1965) and
Peter L. Berger and Thomas Luckman's *The Social Construction of Reality*
(New York: Doubleday, 1967). A chapter, "The Use and Abuse of Psychol-
ogy in History," in Frank Manuel's *Freedom from History* (New York: New
York University Press, 1971) deserves attention, especially Manuel's critique
of Erik Erikson. Bruce Mazlish in *Psychoanalysis and History* (Englewood
Cliffs: Prentice-Hall, 1963) reprints a number of articles which reflect a bias
toward either Freud or Erikson in the field of psychohistory.

It is useful to review the Hofstadter-Pollack debate in considering my
reinterpretation of populism. See: Richard Hofstadter, *The Age of Reform*
(New York: Alfred Knopf, 1955) and Norman Pollack, *The Populist Response to Industrial America* (Cambridge: Harvard University Press, 1962).

This debate peaked with a series of articles in the April 1965 issue of *Agricultural History*. In *The Burden of Southern History* (New York: New American Library, 1969) C. Vann Woodward softens the Hofstadter analysis of populism in a chapter, "The Populist Heritage and the Intellectual." Little was added to the dimensions of this dialogue until the publication of an article by Martin Ridge, "The Populist as a Social Critic," in *Minnesota History* 43 (Winter 1973).

It is only possible to interpret populism in juxtaposition with progressivism. For an interpretation of progressivism, I have depended upon views which originated in Gabriel Kolko's *The Triumph of Conservatism* (New York: Free Press of Glencoe, 1963). David W. Noble in *The Paradox of Progressivism* (Minneapolis: University of Minnesota Press, 1958) has pointed to the contradictions in the progressive paradigm as it continued to incorporate ideological baggage from the era of individualism. The argument that progressivism has been a new form of conservatism has been advanced also by James Weinstein in *The Corporate Ideal in the Liberal State,* 1900-1918 (Boston: Beacon Press, 1968).

Much of the raw evidence for this study has been gleaned from biographies, autobiographies, articles, anthologies, unpublished theses or books dealing directly with the upper Midwest. While many of these sources lack an interpretive framework, they still provide valuable documentation for the ethnic influences and the currents within both populism and progressivism. In most cases, the title explains the nature of the source sufficiently for scholars; and hence, only a bare catalogue of these sources is provided.

BOOKS

Ameringer, Oscar. *If You Don't Weaken.* New York: Henry Holt, 1940.
Berger, Victor L. *The Voice and Pen of Victor L. Berger.* Milwaukee: *The Milwaukee Leader,* 1929.
Blackorby, Edward. *Prairie Rebel.* Lincoln: University of Nebraska Press, 1963.
Blegen, Theodore. *Norwegian Migration to America, 1825-1860.* Northfield, Minnesota: The Norwegian-American Historical Association, 1931.
Bryn-Jones, David. *Frank B. Kellogg.* New York: G.P. Putnam and Sons, 1937.
Buck, Solon J. *The Granger Movement.* Cambridge: Harvard Press, 1913.
Burdick, Usher. *The Life Story of George Sperry Loftus.* Baltimore: Wirth Brothers, 1944.
Chrislock, Carl H. *The Progressive Era in Minnesota, 1899-1918.* St. Paul: Minnesota Historical Society, 1971.

Donnelly, Ignatius. *Caesar's Column.* Cambridge: Harvard University Press, 1960.

Douthit, Davis. *Nobody Owns Us, The Story of Joe Gilbert.* Chicago: Cooperative League of the USA, 1948.

Fish, Everett. *Donnellia.* Chicago: F.J. Schulte Co., 1896.

Fite, Gilbert C., and H.C. Peterson. *Opponents of War, 1917-1918.* Madison: University of Wisconsin Press, 1957.

Haines, Lynn and Dora Haines. *The Lindberghs.* New York: Vanguard Press, 1931.

Hicks, John D. *The Populist Revolt.* Minneapolis: University of Minnesota Press, 1931.

Hoan, Daniel. *The Failure of Regulation.* Chicago: Socialist Party of the U.S., 1914.

Iowa Farmers Union, Ed. *Milo Reno, Farmers Union Pioneer, 1866-1936.* Iowa City: Athens Press, 1941.

Janson, Florence E. *The Background of Swedish Immigration, 1840-1930.* Chicago: University of Chicago Press, 1931.

Kramer, Dale. *The Wild Jackasses.* New York: Hastings House, 1956.

Larson, Bruce. *Lindbergh of Minnesota.* New York: Harcourt, Brace, Jovanovich, 1971.

LeSueur, Meridel. *Crusaders.* New York: The Blue Heron Press, 1955.

Lindbergh, Charles A., Sr. *The Economic Pinch.* Philadelphia: Dorrance Press, 1923.

Lucas, Richard. *Charles August Lindbergh, Sr., A Study of Congressional Insurgency.* Uppsala: Historiska Institutionen vid Uppsala Universitet, 1974.

Manahan, James. *Trials of a Lawyer.* Published privately by Kathryn Manahan, 1932.

Mayer, George H. *The Political Career of Floyd B. Olson.* Minneapolis: University of Minnesota Press, 1951.

McCoy, Donald R. *Angry Voices.* Lawrence: University of Kansas Press, 1958.

Mordell, Albert, Ed. *The World of E. Haldeman-Julius.* New York: Twayne, 1960.

Morlan, Robert L. *Political Prairie Fire.* Minneapolis: University of Minnesota Press, 1955.

Moynihan, James H. *The Life of Archbishop John Ireland.* New York: Harper and Brothers, 1952.

Nelson, Bruce. *Land of the Dacotahs.* Lincoln: University of Nebraska Press, 1946.

Norris, George. *Fighting Liberal.* New York: Macmillan, 1945.

Nugent, Walter T.K. *The Tolerant Populists.* Chicago: University of Chicago Press, 1963.

Nye, Russel B. *Midwestern Progressive Politics.* New York: Harper Torchbooks, 1959.

Pettigrew, R.F. *Imperial Washington.* Chicago: Charles Kerr, 1922.

Qualey, Carlton C. *Norwegian Settlements in the United States.* Northfield, Minnesota: Norwegian-American Historical Association, 1938.

Ridge, Martin. *Ignatius Donnelly, the Portrait of a Politician.* Chicago: University of Chicago Press, 1962.

Robinson, Elwyn. *History of North Dakota.* Lincoln: University of Nebraska, 1966.

Rogin, Michael Paul. *The Intellectuals and McCarthy.* Cambridge: The MIT Press, 1967.
Ross, Martin. *Shipstead of Minnesota.* Chicago: Packard and Co., 1940.
Saloutos, Theodore and John D. Hicks. *Agricultural Discontent in the Middle West, 1900-1939.* Madison: University of Wisconsin Press, 1951.
Schell, Herbert. *History of South Dakota.* Lincoln: University of Nebraska Press, 1968.
Shannon, James P. *Catholic Colonization on the Western Frontier.* New Haven: Yale Press, 1957.
Shaw, Joseph M. *Pulpit under the Sky: Life of Hans Nielson Hauge.* Minneapolis: Augsburg Publishing House, 1955.
Shields, James. *Mr. Progressive, a Biography of Elmer A. Benson.* Minneapolis: T.S. Denison Co., 1971.
Shover, John. *Cornbelt Rebellion.* Urbana: University of Illinois Press, 1965.
Stephenson, George. *A History of American Immigration, 1820-1924.* Boston: Ginn, 1926.
_____. *The Religious Aspects of Swedish Migration.* Minneapolis: University of Minnesota Press, 1932.
_____. *John Lind of Minnesota.* Minneapolis: University of Minnesota Press, 1938.
Stiller, Richard. *Queen of the Populists, the Story of Mary Elizabeth Lease.* New York: Thomas Y. Crowell and Co., 1970.
Tindall, George B., Ed *A Populist Reader.* New York: Harper and Row, 1966.
Walker, Charles. *American City.* New York: Farrar and Rinehart, 1938.
Wittke, Carl. *Refugees from Revolution.* Philadelphia: University of Pennsylvania Press, 1952.
Young, Arthur Nichols. *The Single Tax Movement in the United States.* Princeton: Princeton University Press, 1916.
Young, Donald, Ed. *Adventure in Politics, the Memoirs of Philip LaFollette.* New York: Holt, Rinehart and Winston, 1970.
Youngdale, James M. *Third Party Footprints.* Minneapolis: Ross and Haines, 1966.

JOURNAL ARTICLES

Acrea, Kenneth. "The Wisconsin Reform Coalition, 1892 to 1900: LaFollette's Rise to Power." *Wisconsin Magazine of History,* 52 (Winter 1968-69).
Adrian, Charles. "The Origin of Minnesota's Nonpartisan Legislature." *Minnesota History,* 33 (Winter 1952).
Armin, Calvin Perry. "Coe I. Crawford and the Progressive Movement in South Dakota." *South Dakota Historical Collections,* 32 (1964).
Auerback, Jerold C. "The Lafollette Committee and the CIO." *Wisconsin Magazine of History,* 48 (Autumn 1964).
Betten, Neil. "Riot, Revolution, Repression in the Iron Range Strike of 1916." *Minnesota History,* 41 (Summer 1968).
Carey, Loren Lee. "The Wisconsin Loyalty Legion, 1917-1918." *Wisconsin Magazine of History,* 48 (Autumn 1969).
Cerny, George. "Cooperation in the Midwest in the Granger Era, 1869-1875." *Agricultural History,* 37 (October 1963).

Chrislock, Carl H. "The Alliance Party and the Minnesota Legislature of 1891." *Minnesota History,* 35 (September 1957).

————. "Sidney M. Owen, an Editor in Politics." *Minnesota History,* 36 (December 1958).

Cosmos, Graham A. "The Democracy in Search of Issues: The Wisconsin Reform Party, 1873-1877." *Wisconsin Magazine of History,* 46 (Winter 1962-63).

Dodd, James W. "Resolutions, Programs and Policies of the North Dakota Farmers' Holiday Association, 1932-1937." *North Dakota History Quarterly,* 28 (April-July 1961).

Fite, Gilbert H. "Some Farmers' Accounts of Hardship on the Frontier." *Minnesota History,* 37 (March 1961).

Garlid, George. "The Antiwar Dilemma of the Farmer Labor Party." *Minnesota History,* 40 (Winter 1967).

Gates, Paul W. "Frontier Land Business in Wisconsin." *Wisconsin Magazine of History,* 52 (Summer 1969).

Gilman, Rhoda and Patricia Smith. "Oliver Hudson Kelley: Minnesota Pioneer 1849-1868." *Minnesota History,* 40 (Fall 1967).

Griffith, Robert. "Prelude to Insurgency." *Wisconsin Magazine of History,* 49 (Autumn 1965).

Halbo, Paul S. "The Farmer Labor Association, Minnesota's Party within a Party." *Minnesota History,* 38 (September 1963).

Hendrickson, Kenneth E., Jr. "Some Political Aspects of the Populist Movement in South Dakota." *North Dakota History Quarterly,* 34 (Winter 1967).

————. "The Public Career of Richard F. Pettigrew of South Dakota, 1848-1926." *South Dakota Department of History Collections,* 34 (1968).

Johnson, Scott P. "Wisconsin Socialists and the Conference for Progressive Political Action." *Wisconsin Magazine of History,* 37 (Winter 1953-54).

Kennedy, Padriac. "LaFollette's Foreign Policy: From Imperialism to Anti-imperialism." *Wisconsin Magazine of History,* 46 (Summer 1963).

Klotsche, J. Martin. "The United Front Populists." *Wisconsin Magazine of History,* 20 (Winter 1936-37).

Kohlehaminen, John I. "The Finns of Wisconsin." *Wisconsin Magazine of History,* 27 (June 1944).

Korman, Gerd. "Political Loyalties, Immigrant Traditions and Reform: The Wisconsin German Press and Progressivism, 1909-1912." *Wisconsin Magazine of History,* 40 (Spring 1957).

Lutz, Alma. "Susan B. Anthony in the Dakotas." *North Dakota History Magazine,* 25 (October 1958).

Martinson, Henry R. "Comes the Revolution." *North Dakota History Magazine,* 36 (Winter 1969).

McDonald, Forrest. "Street Cars and Politics in Milwaukee, 1896-1901." *Wisconsin Magazine of History,* 39 (Spring 1956).

Morlan, Robert L. "The Nonpartisan League and the Minnesota Campaign of 1918." *Minnesota History,* 34 (Summer 1955).

Muzik, Edward J. "Victor Berger: Congress and the Red Scare." *Wisconsin Magazine of History,* 47 (Summer 1964).

Naftalin, Arthur. "The Tradition of Protest and the Roots of the Farmer Labor Party." *Minnesota History,* 35 (June 1956).

Nash, Roderick. "Victor L. Berger: Making Marx Respectable." *Wisconsin Magazine of History,* 47 (Summer 1964).

Nelson, Daniel. "The Origins of Unemployment Insurance in Wisconsin." *Wisconsin Magazine of History,* 51 (Winter 1967-68).

Nicklason, Fred. "Henry George: Social Gospeler." *American Quarterly,* 22 (Fall 1970).

Olson, Frederick I. "The Socialist Party and the Unions in Milwaukee." *Wisconsin Magazine of History,* 44 (Winter 1960-61).

Saloutos, Theodore. "The National Producers Alliance." *Minnesota History,* 28 (March 1947).

Shannon, David A. "Was McCarthy a Political Heir of LaFollette?" *Wisconsin Magazine of History,* 45 (Autumn 1961).

Shannon, James P. "Bishop Ireland's Connemara Experiment." *Minnesota History,* 35 (March 1957).

Shenton, James P. "Fascism and Father Coughlin." *Wisconsin Magazine of History,* 44 (Autumn 1960).

Shideler, James H. "The LaFollette Progressive Party Campaign of 1924." *Wisconsin Magazine of History,* 33 (June 1950).

Thelen, David. "The Boss and the Upstart, Keyes and LaFollette, 1880-1884." *Wisconsin Magazine of History,* 47 (Winter 1963-64).

_____. "LaFollette and the Temperance Crusade." *Wisconsin Magazine of History,* 47 (Summer 1964).

Warner, Donald F. "Prelude to Populism." *Minnesota History,* 32 (September 1951).

Wefald, Jon M. "Knud Wefald, a Minnesota Voice for Farm Parity." *Minnesota History,* 38 (December 1962).

Wilkins, Robert P. "Tory Isolationist: Porter J. McCumber and World War I, 1914-1917." *North Dakota History Quarterly,* 34 (Summer 1967).

Wyman, Roger E. "Wisconsin Ethnic Groups and the Elections of 1890." *Wisconsin Magazine of History,* 51 (Summer 1968).

UNPUBLISHED DISSERTATIONS

Backstrom, Charles H. "The Progressive Party of Wisconsin." Unpublished doctoral dissertation, University of Wisconsin, 1956.

Bahmer, Robert. "The Economic and Political Background of the Non-partisan League." Unpublished doctoral dissertation, University of Minnesota, 1941.

Chrislock, Carl H. "The Politics of Protest in Minnesota, 1890-1901." Unpublished doctoral dissertation, University of Minnesota, 1955.

Goldstein, Jerrold. "Reform Rabbis and the Progressive Movement." Unpublished master's thesis, University of Minnesota, 1967.

Hingten, David U. "Victor L. Berger and the Milwaukee Leader." Unpublished master's thesis, Marquette University, 1962.

Jenson, Carol E. "Agrarian Pioneer in Civil Liberties: The Nonpartisan League in Minnesota during World War I." Unpublished doctoral dissertation, University of Minnesota, 1968.

Naftalin, Arthur. "A History of the Farmer Labor Party." Unpublished doctoral dissertation, University of Minnesota, 1948.

Nydahl, Theodore. "The Diary of Ignatius Donnelly, 1859-1884." Unpublished doctoral dissertation, University of Minnesota, 1941.

Olson, Frederick I. "The Milwaukee Socialists, 1897-1941." Unpublished doctoral dissertation, Harvard, 1952.

Overmoehle, M. Hedwigis. "The Anti-clerical Activities of the Forty Eighters in Wisconsin." Unpublished doctoral dissertation, St. Louis University, 1941.

Parkinson, Robert O. "Biography of Richard F. Pettigrew." Unpublished master's thesis, University of Iowa, 1938.

Rutman, Herbert S. "Defense and Development: A History of Minneapolis Jewry, 1930-1950." Unpublished doctoral dissertation, University of Minnesota, 1970.

Seager, Robert II. "The Progressives and American Foreign Policy 1898-1917: An Analysis of the Attitudes and the Leaders of the Progressive Movement toward External Affairs." (Volumes I and II) Unpublished doctoral dissertation, Ohio State University, 1956.

Smemo, Irwin. "Progressive Judge, the Public Career of Charles Fremont Amidon." Unpublished doctoral dissertation, University of Minnesota, 1967.

Thelen, David. "Prelude to Populism: A Study of Six Wisconsin Cities, 1891-1900." Unpublished doctoral dissertation, University of Wisconsin, 1969.

Wyman, Roger Edward, "Voting Behavior in the Progressive Era: Wisconsin as a Case Study." Unpublished doctoral dissertation, University of Wisconsin, 1970.

INDEX

217

Index

Home Fire

Also by Kamila Shamsie

Home Fire

Kamila Shamsie

RIVERHEAD BOOKS
New York
2017

RIVERHEAD BOOKS
An imprint of Penguin Random House LLC
375 Hudson Street
New York, New York 10014

Library of Congress Cataloging-in-Publication Data

Names: Shamsie, Kamila [date], author.
Title: Home fire : a novel / Kamila Shamsie.
Description: New York : Riverhead Books, 2017.
Identifiers: LCCN 2017003238 | ISBN 9780735217683 (hardcover)
Subjects: LCSH: Families—Fiction. | Domestic fiction. | Political fiction. |
BISAC: FICTION / Family Life. | FICTION / Political. |
FICTION / Cultural Heritage. | GSAFD: Love stories.
Classification: LCC PR9540.9.S485 H66 2017 | DDC 823/.914   dc23
LC record available at https://lccn.loc.gov/2017003238
p.   cm.

International edition ISBN: 9780525533269

Printed in the United States of America
3   5   7   9   10   8   6   4

BOOK DESIGN BY LUCIA BERNARD

For Gillian Slovo

The ones we love . . . are enemies of the state.

—Sophocles, *Antigone*
(translated by Seamus Heaney)

Home Fire

Isma

1

ISMA WAS GOING to miss her flight. The ticket wouldn't be re-
funded, because the airline took no responsibility for passengers who
arrived at the airport three hours ahead of the departure time and
were escorted to an interrogation room. She had expected the interrogation, but not the hours of waiting that would precede it, nor that
it would feel so humiliating to have the contents of her suitcase inspected. She'd made sure not to pack anything that would invite comment or questions—no Quran, no family pictures, no books on her
area of academic interest—but even so, the officer took hold of every
item of Isma's clothing and ran it between her thumb and fingers, not
so much searching for hidden pockets as judging the quality of the
material. Finally she reached for the designer-label down jacket Isma
had folded over a chair back when she entered, and held it up, one
hand pinching each shoulder.

"This isn't yours," she said, and Isma was sure she didn't mean *because it's at least a size too large* but rather *it's too nice for someone like you.*

"I used to work at a dry-cleaning shop. The woman who brought

this in said she didn't want it when we couldn't get rid of the stain."
She pointed to the grease mark on the pocket.

"Does the manager know you took it?"

"I was the manager."

"You were the manager of a dry-cleaning shop and now you're on
your way to a PhD program in sociology?"

"Yes."

"And how did that happen?"

"My siblings and I were orphaned just after I finished uni. They
were twelve years old—twins. I took the first job I could find. Now
they've grown up; I can go back to my life."

"You're going back to your life . . . in Amherst, Massachusetts."

"I meant the academic life. My former tutor from LSE teaches in
Amherst now, at the university there. Her name is Hira Shah. You can
call her. I'll be staying with her when I arrive, until I find a place of my
own."

"In Amherst."

"No. I don't know. Sorry, do you mean her place or the place of my
own? She lives in Northampton—that's close to Amherst. I'll look all
around the area for whatever suits me best. So it might be Amherst,
but it might not. There are some real estate listings on my phone.
Which you have." She stopped herself. The official was doing that
thing that she'd encountered before in security personnel—staying
quiet when you answered their question in a straightforward manner,
which made you think you had to say more. And the more you said,
the more guilty you sounded.

The woman dropped the jacket into the jumble of clothes and shoes and told Isma to wait.

That had been a while ago. The plane would be boarding now. Isma looked over at the suitcase. She'd repacked when the woman left the room and spent the time since worrying if doing that without permission constituted an offense. Should she empty the clothes out into a haphazard pile, or would that make things even worse? She stood up, unzipped the suitcase, and flipped it open so its contents were visible.

A man entered the office, carrying Isma's passport, laptop, and phone. She allowed herself to hope, but he sat down, gestured for her to do the same, and placed a voice recorder between them.

"Do you consider yourself British?" the man said.

"I am British."

"But do you consider yourself British?"

"I've lived here all my life." She meant there was no other country of which she could feel herself a part, but the words came out sounding evasive.

The interrogation continued for nearly two hours. He wanted to know her thoughts on Shias, homosexuals, the Queen, democracy, *The Great British Bake Off*, the invasion of Iraq, Israel, suicide bombers, dating websites. After that early slip regarding her Britishness, she settled into the manner that she'd practiced with Aneeka playing the role of the interrogating officer, Isma responding to her sister as though she were a customer of dubious political opinions whose business Isma didn't want to lose by voicing strenuously opposing views, but to whom she didn't see the need to lie either. ("When people talk

about the enmity between Shias and Sunnis, it usually centers on some political imbalance of power, such as in Iraq or Syria—as a Brit, I don't distinguish between one Muslim and another." "Occupying other people's territory generally causes more problems than it solves"—this served for both Iraq and Israel. "Killing civilians is sinful—that's equally true whether the manner of killing is a suicide bombing or aerial bombardments or drone strikes.") There were long intervals of silence between each answer and the next question as the man clicked keys on her laptop, examining her browser history. He knew that she was interested in the marital status of an actor from a popular TV series; that wearing a hijab didn't stop her from buying expensive products to tame her frizzy hair; that she had searched for "how to make small talk with Americans."

You know, you don't have to be so compliant about everything, Aneeka had said during the role-playing. Isma's sister, not quite nineteen, with her law student brain, who knew everything about her rights and nothing about the fragility of her place in the world. *For instance, if they ask you about the Queen, just say, "As an Asian I have to admire her color palette." It's important to show at least a tiny bit of contempt for the whole process.* Instead, Isma had responded, *I greatly admire Her Majesty's commitment to her role.* But there had been comfort in hearing her sister's alternative answers in her head, her *Ha!* of triumph when the official asked a question that she'd anticipated and Isma had dismissed, such as the *Great British Bake Off* one. Well, if they didn't let her board this plane—or any one after this—she would go home to Aneeka, which is what half Isma's heart knew it should do in any case. How much of Aneeka's heart wanted that was a hard question to answer—she'd

been so adamant that Isma not change her plans for America, and whether this was selflessness or a wish to be left alone was something even Aneeka herself didn't seem to know. A tiny flicker in Isma's brain signaled a thought about Parvaiz that was trying to surface, before it was submerged by the strength of her refusal ever to think about him again.

Eventually, the door opened and the woman official walked in. Perhaps she would be the one to ask the family questions—the ones most difficult to answer, the most fraught when she'd prepared with her sister.

"Sorry about that," the woman said, unconvincingly. "Just had to wait for America to wake up and confirm some details about your student visa. All checked out. Here." She handed a stiff rectangle of paper to Isma with an air of magnanimity. It was the boarding pass for the plane she'd already missed.

Isma stood up, unsteady because of the pins and needles in her feet, which she'd been afraid to shake off in case she accidentally kicked the man across the desk from her. As she wheeled out her luggage she thanked the woman whose thumbprints were on her underwear, not allowing even a shade of sarcasm to enter her voice.

⁂

The cold bit down on every exposed piece of skin before cutting through the layers of clothing. Isma opened her mouth and tilted her head back, breathing in the lip-numbing, teeth-aching air. Crusted snow lay all about, glinting in the lights of the terminal. Leaving her suitcase with Dr. Hira Shah, who had driven two hours across Massa-

chusetts to meet her at Logan Airport, she walked over to a mound of snow at the edge of the parking lot, took off her gloves, and pressed her fingertips down on it. At first it resisted, but then it gave way, and her fingers burrowed into the softer layers beneath. She licked snow out of her palm, relieving the dryness of her mouth. The woman in customer services at Heathrow—a Muslim—had found her a place on the next flight out, without charge; she had spent the whole journey worrying about the interrogation awaiting her in Boston, certain they would detain her or put her on a plane back to London. But the immigration official had asked only where she was going to study, said something she didn't follow but tried to look interested in regarding the university basketball team, and waved her through. And then, as she walked out of the arrivals area, there was Dr. Shah, mentor and savior, unchanged since Isma's undergraduate days except for a few silver strands threaded through her cropped dark hair. Seeing her raise a hand in welcome, Isma understood how it might have felt, in another age, to step out on deck and see the upstretched arm of the Statue of Liberty and know you had made it, you were going to be all right.

While there was still some feeling in her gloveless hands she typed a message into her phone: Arrived safely. Through security—no problems. Dr. Shah here. How things with you?

Her sister wrote back: Fine, now I know they've let you through,

      Really fine?

           Stop worrying about me. Go live your life—
               I really want you to.

The parking lot with large, confident vehicles; the broad avenues beyond; the lights gleaming everywhere, their brightness multiplied by reflecting surfaces of glass and snow. Here, there was swagger and certainty and—on this New Year's Day of 2015—a promise of new beginnings.

||||||||||||||||||||||||

Isma awoke into light to see two figures leaving the sky and falling toward her, bright colors billowing above their heads.

When Hira Shah had brought her to see this studio apartment, the morning after her arrival in America, the landlord had drawn attention to the skylight as a selling point to offset the dank built-in cupboard, and promised her comets and lunar eclipses. With the memory of the Heathrow interrogation still jangling her nerves, she had been able to think only of surveillance satellites wheeling through the sky, and had rejected the studio. But by the end of the day's viewings it had become clear that she wouldn't be able to afford anything nicer without the encumbrance of a roommate. Now, some ten weeks later, she could stretch out in the bed, knowing herself to be seeing but unseen. How slowly the parachutists seemed to move, trailing golds and reds. In almost all human history, figures descending from the sky would have been angels or gods or demons—or Icarus hurtling down, his father, Daedalus, following too slowly to catch the vainglorious boy. What must it have felt like to inhabit a commonality of human experience—all eyes to the sky, watching for something mythic to land? She took a picture of the parachutists and sent it to Aneeka with the caption Try this someday? and then stepped out

of bed, wondering if spring had arrived early or if this was merely a lull.

Overnight the temperature had climbed vertiginously, melting the snow into a river. She had heard it at her first waking, for the dawn prayer, as it rushed down the gentle slope of the street. It had been a winter of snowstorms, more than usual, she'd been told, and as she dressed she imagined people exiting their homes and, on patches of ground glimpsed for the first time in months, finding lost items—a glove, keys, pens, and pennies. The weight of snow pressing familiarity out of the objects, so that the glove placed beside its former pair looked no more than a distant relative. And what then do you do? Throw away both gloves, or wear them mismatched to acknowledge the miracle of their reunion?

She folded her pajamas and put them under her pillow, smoothed out the duvet. Looked around the clean, spare lines of her apartment—single bed, desk and desk chair, chest of drawers. She felt, as she did most mornings, the deep pleasure of daily life distilled to the essentials: books, walks, spaces in which to think and work.

When she pushed open the heavy door of the two-story stone-veneer house, the morning air was free of its hundred-blade knife for the first time. The thaw had widened the streets and sidewalks, and she felt—what was the word?—"boundless"! as she set off walking at a pace that didn't worry about slipping on ice. Past double-storied colonial houses, past cars announcing all their political beliefs on bumper stickers, past vintage clothing, past antiques and yoga. She turned onto Main Street, where City Hall with its inexplicable Norman towers inset with arrow slits gave the vista an edge of hilarity.

She made her way into her favorite café and walked down the stairs with a mug in hand to the book-lined basement—a haven of warm lamplight, worn armchairs, and strong coffee. Punched keys on the keyboard to wake her laptop, barely registered from overfamiliarity the desktop picture of her mother as a young woman of the 1980s, big hair and chunky earrings, dropping a kiss on Isma's infant scalp. As a matter of morning routine, she opened the Skype window to check if her sister was online. She wasn't, and Isma was about to click out when a new name appeared on the online contacts list: *Parvaiz Pasha*.

Isma lifted her hands off the keyboard, set them down on either side of the laptop, and looked at her brother's name. She hadn't seen it here since that day in December when he'd called to tell them the decision he'd made for his life without any consideration of what it would mean for his sisters. Now he would be looking at her name, the green check mark next to it telling him she was available to chat. The Skype window was positioned so that her mother's lips were touching it. Zainab Pasha's slim, fine-boned features had skipped Isma and passed on to the twins, who laughed with their mother's mouth, smiled with their mother's eyes. Isma maximized the Skype window so it filled the entire screen, encircled her throat with the palms of her hands, and felt her heart's reaction to the sight of his name in the high-speed propulsion of blood through her arteries. The seconds passed, and there was nothing from him. She kept watching the screen, just as she knew he was watching his, both for the same reason: waiting for Aneeka.

A few weeks earlier, at Hira Shah's condo, a strange music had cut through the sound of Hira slicing potatoes—a whistling, high-pitched

twang. Isma and Hira checked phones and speakers, placed ears against walls and floorboards, stepped out into the corridor, opened closets, entered empty rooms, and still it kept on, eerie loveliness, impossible to pinpoint as any known instrument, voice, or birdcall. A neighbor stopped by, looking for the source. "Ghosts," he said with a wink before leaving.

Isma laughed, but Hira drew her shoulders in tighter, reached out to touch the evil eye that hung on her wall, which Isma had always assumed to be merely decorative.

The music kept on, coming from everywhere and nowhere, following them as they moved through the apartment. Hira, gripping her knife, whispered something that turned out to be the Lord's Prayer— she'd been educated at a convent school in Kashmir. Finally, the supremely rational, razor-minded Dr. Shah said they should go out for dinner despite the unpleasant hail. Perhaps the sound would have stopped by the time they returned. Isma went upstairs to the bathroom to wash the grime of concealed corners off her hands. While standing at the sink, looking out of the window beside it, she saw the source of the music.

Running down, she caught Hira's arm and pulled her out of the backdoor entrance, ducking her head against the hail. All along the redbrick building, end to end, icicles hung from the eaves, a foot or more in length. Against these broadswords, pellets rained down and made music. The acoustics of ice on ice, a thing unimaginable until experienced.

Pain swerved at her then, physical, bringing her to her knees. Hira moved toward her but Isma held up a hand, lay back in the snow, and

allowed the pain to roil through her while the hail and icicles continued their synthetic-edged symphony. Parvaiz, a boy never seen without his headphones and a mic, would have lain out here for as long as
the song continued, the wet of snow seeping through his clothes, the
thud of hail beating down on him, uncaring of anything except captur-
ing something previously unheard, eyes hazy with pleasure.

That had been the only time she had truly, purely missed her
brother without adjectives such as "ungrateful" and "selfish" slicing
through the feeling of loss. Now she looked at his name on the screen,
her mouth forming prayers to keep Aneeka from logging on, the adjectives thick in her mind. Aneeka must learn to think of him as lost
forever. It was possible to do this with someone you loved, Isma had
learned that early on. But you could learn it only if there was a complete vacuum where the other person had been.

His name vanished from the screen. She touched her shoulder,
muscles knotted beneath the skin. Pressed down, and knew what it
was to be without family; no one's hands but your own to minister to
your suffering. *We'll be in touch all the time,* she and Aneeka had said to
each other in the weeks before she had left. But "touch" was the one
thing modern technology didn't allow, and without it she and her sister had lost something vital to their way of being together. Touch was
where it had started with them—as an infant, Aneeka was bathed and
changed and fed and rocked to sleep by her grandmother and nine-
year-old sister while Parvaiz, the weaker, sicklier twin, was the one
who suckled at their mother's breast (she produced only enough milk
for one) and cried unless she was the one to tend to him. When the
twins grew older and formed their own self-enclosed universe, there

was less and less Aneeka needed from Isma, but even so, there remained a physical closeness—Parvaiz was the person Aneeka talked to about all her griefs and worries, but it was Isma she came to for an embrace, or a hand to rub her back, or a body to curl up against on the sofa. And when the burden of the universe seemed too great for Isma to bear—particularly in those early days after their grandmother and mother had died within the space of a year, leaving Isma to parent and provide for two grief-struck twelve-year-olds—it was Aneeka who would place her hands on her sister's shoulders and massage away the ache.

Clicking her tongue against her teeth in remonstration of her self-pity, Isma pulled up the essay she was writing and returned to the refuge of work.

ı111ıı1ıı1ıı11ıı1ıı11

By midafternoon the temperature had passed the 50 degree Fahrenheit mark, which sounded, and felt, far warmer than 11 degrees Celsius, and a bout of spring madness had largely emptied the café basement. Isma tilted her post-lunch mug of coffee toward herself, touched the tip of her finger to the liquid, considered how much of a faux pas it might be to ask to have it microwaved. She had just decided she would risk the opprobrium when the door opened and the scent of cigarettes curled in from the smoking area outside, followed by a young man of startling looks.

His looks weren't startling because they were exceptional—thick dark hair, milky-tea skin, well-proportioned features, good height, nice shoulders. Stand on any street corner in Wembley long enough

and you'd see a version of this, though rarely attached to such an air of privilege. No, what was startling was the stomach-turning familiarity of the man's features.

In her uncle's house—not an uncle by blood or even affection, merely by the habitual nature of his presence in her family's life— there was a photograph from the 1970s of a neighborhood cricket team posing with a trophy; it was a photograph Isma had sometimes stopped to look at as a child, wondering at the contrast between the glorious, swaggering boys and the unprepossessing middle-aged men they'd grown into. It was really only the ones she knew as middle-aged men she paid much attention to, and so she'd never given particular thought to the unsmiling one in the badly fitting clothes until the day her grandmother stood in front of the picture and said, "Shameless!" poking her finger at the young man.

"Oh yes, the new MP," the uncle said, coming to see what had drawn out a pronouncement of such uncharacteristic venom. "On the day of the final we were a player short and this one, Mr. Serious, was visiting his cousin, our wicketkeeper, so we said, *Okay, you play for us,* and gave him our injured batsman's uniform. Did nothing all match except drop a catch, and then ended up holding the trophy in this official photo- graph, which went into the local newspaper. We were just being polite to offer it to him, since he was an outsider, and only because we were sure he'd have enough manners to say thanks but the captain—that was me—should be the one to hold it. We should have known then he would grow up to be a politician. Twenty pounds says he has it framed on his wall and tells everyone he was man-of-the-match."

Later that day, Isma overheard her grandmother talking to her best

friend and neighbor, Aunty Naseem, and learned the real reason for that "Shameless!" It was not the unsmiling one's choice of career but a cruelty he'd recently shown to their family when it would have been easy for him to act otherwise. In the years after that, she'd paid close attention to him—the only one in the picture to grow up slim and sharp, bigger and brighter trophies forever in his sights. And now here he was, walking across the café floor—not the hated-admired figure he'd grown into but a slightly older version of the boy posing with the team, except his hair floppier and his expression more open. This must be, had to be, the son. She'd seen a photo that included him as well, but he'd ducked his head so that the floppy hair obscured his features—she'd wondered then whether that was by design. Eamonn, that was his name. How they'd laughed in Wembley when the news-paper article accompanying the family picture revealed this detail. An Irish spelling to disguise a Muslim name—"Ayman" become "Eamonn" so that people would know the father had integrated. (His Irish-American wife was seen as another indicator of this integrationist posing rather than an explanation for the son's name.)

The son was standing at the counter, in blue jeans and a quilted olive-green jacket, waiting.

She stood up, mug in hand, and walked over to him. "They only open up this counter when it's busy."

"Thanks. Kind of you to say. Where is—?" His vowels unashamedly posh where she had expected the more class-obscuring London ac-cent of his father.

"Upstairs. I'll show you. I mean, I'm sure you understand 'up-

stairs.' I should have said, I'm going there myself. Coffee's cold." Why so many words?

He took the mug from her hand with unexpected familiarity. "Allow me. As thanks for rescuing me from being the Englishman Who Stood at the Counter for All Eternity. Who you could be forgiven for confusing with the Englishman Who Gets Lost Going Upstairs."

"I just want it heated up."

"Right you are." He sniffed the contents of the mug, another overfamiliar gesture. "Smells amazing. What is it? I wouldn't know an Ethiopian from a Colombian if . . ." He stopped. "That sentence doesn't know where to go from there."

"Probably just as well. It's the house brew."

She stood where she was a moment, watching him walk up the stairs, which were bracketed on one side by potted ferns and on the other by a wall with ferns painted on it. When he glanced down toward her, mouthing "Not lost yet," she pretended she had simply been preoccupied by her thoughts and returned to the little table in the alcove, angling her body so that her own shadow kept the sunlight from her computer screen. Slid her fingers over the wooden tabletop, its knots, its burns. Guess who, she started to type into her phone, then stopped and deleted it. She could too easily imagine the tone of Aneeka's response: Ugh! she'd say, or Why did you even talk to him?

He didn't return. She imagined him seeing a short line at the counter and placing her mug down with a shrug before walking out the upstairs exit; it left her both vindicated and disappointed. She

went up to buy herself another coffee and found that the machine had broken down, so had to settle for hot water and a tea bag that leaked color into it. Returning downstairs, she saw a mug of fresh coffee at her table and a man folded into the chair next to it, legs thrown over the arm, reading a book in the shape of the gap in the bookshelf above his head.

"What is it?" he said, looking at the cup of tea she set down on an empty table. He examined the tag at the end of the tea bag. "Ruby Red. Not even pretending it's a flavor."

She held up the mug in thanks. The coffee wasn't as hot as it could have been, but he must have had to carry it down the street. "How much do I owe you?"

"Five minutes of conversation. That's what I spent standing in the queue. But after you're finished with whatever you're doing."

"That could be a while."

"Good. Gives me time to catch up on essential reading about . . ." He shut the book, looked at its cover. "*The Holy Book of Women's Mysteries. Complete in One Volume Feminist Witchcraft, Goddess Rituals, Spellcasting, and Other Womanly Arts . . .*"

One of the undergraduates looked up, glared.

Isma slung the laptop into her backpack, downed her coffee. "You can walk to the supermarket with me."

iiiiiiiiiiiiiiiiiiiiii

During the short walk to the supermarket, she learned that he'd quit his job with a management consultancy and was taking some time to live life beyond office walls—which included visiting his maternal

grandparents in Amherst, a town he loved for its association with childhood summer holidays.

While she tried to choose between one variety of unconvincing tomato and another for tonight's pasta sauce, Eamonn wandered off and brought back a can of plum tomatoes, as well as leaves for the salad she hadn't intended to make. "Arugula," he said, rolling the *r* extravagantly. "Halfway between a Latin American dance and an ointment for verrucas." She couldn't tell if he was trying to impress her or if he was the kind of man in love with his own charm. When she had finished placing the shopping in her backpack he picked it up from the checkout counter and looped it over one shoulder, saying he liked the schoolboy feeling of it, would she mind very much if he carried it for a while? She thought he was making a show of the polished manners that passed as virtue among people like him, but when she said there was no need for such chivalry he said it was the opposite of chivalry to burden a woman with his company just because he was feeling lonely and a London accent was the best possible antidote. So they continued on together, walking toward the nearby woods since the day was so lovely. On the way he asked for a detour via Main Street (he said the name with the slight deprecation of someone newly arrived from a metropolis) so they could stop at an outdoor-clothing store, and in little more than the time it took her to cross the street and withdraw twenty dollars from the ATM he was out again, wearing expensive walking shoes, the backpack more weighed down than previously.

The woods were slushy, but the light piercing through between scrabbling branches was a pleasure, and the river, swollen with snow-melt, roared. They turned up their collars against the dripping from

the branches; he didn't seem to mind yelping when fat, cold drops fell on his head, merely commented on the stylish protection of her wool turban and called her "Greta Garbo." Every now and then they heard the *whump!* of a section of dislodged snow landing on the ground, but they felt safe enough to keep going. Their talk was insubstantial—the weather, the overfriendliness of strangers in America, favorite London bus routes (which revealed nothing so much as the distinct geography of their lives)—but even so, the Englishness of his humor, and his cultural references, were a greater treat than she would have expected. Small talk came more naturally to him than to her, but he was careful not to dominate the conversation—listening with interest to even her most banal observations, asking follow-up questions rather than using her lines as springboards to monologues of his own in the manner of most of the men she knew. *Someone raised him the way I tried to raise Parvaiz,* she couldn't stop herself from thinking.

Along one of the calmer stretches of water, a fallen tree extended out twenty or more feet from the bank. Isma walked across it, arms out for balance, while he remained behind, making noises that were half anxious, half admiring, wholly pleasing to hear. The sky was a rich blue, the water surged like blood leaving a heart, a lean young man from a world very distant from hers was waiting for her to walk back to him. She breathed in the moment, tried to catch her reflection in the water, but it was too quick, nothing like the slow-moving waterways to which she was accustomed.

She came from a city veined with canals: that had been the revelation of her adolescence while her school friends were embarking on other kinds of discovery that discomforted more than appealed to her.

In Alperton, two miles from her old home, she could descend into waterside avenues of calm, unpeopled in comparison to the streets, thick with noise, she'd traveled to arrive there. She knew her mother and grandmother would say it was dangerous, a lone girl walking past industrial estates and along silent stretches with no company other than the foliage, as in the countryside (to her family nowhere was more dangerous than the countryside, where you could scream for help without being heard), so she never said anything more specific than "I'm going for a walk," which they found both amusing and un-threatening.

Her foot slipped on the slick surface of the branch, and she had to drop to her knees to keep from falling in. The cold water a spray on her hands and sleeves. She walked back cautiously, registering the anxiety in Eamonn's expression.

After that, he asked more direct questions about her life, as though seeing her walk away from him across a fallen tree had brought her into focus. She gave him the easiest version: Grew up in North Lon-don, as he already knew because of the bus routes—the Preston Road neighborhood to be precise, which was obviously too precise for him. Two siblings—much younger. Raised by her mother and grandmother, now both dead; she'd never really known her father. She was here for a PhD program, fully funded, with a stipend from a position as a re-search assistant that would give her enough to live on. She'd applied too late for the autumn semester, but her former tutor Dr. Shah had arranged permission for her to start in January, and here she now was.

"And so you're doing what you want to be doing? You lucky thing!"

"Yes," she said. "Very lucky." She wondered if she should respond to his questions about her life with some about his. But then he might mention his father, of whom she couldn't pretend to be unaware, and that might lead them down a road she didn't want to travel.

The river was dark now, the first indication that the day was ending although there was still abundant light in the sky. She led the way back onto the road, bringing them out near the high school, where long-limbed teenagers were running on the outdoor track, piles of muddy snow pushed to the corners of the field.

"Can I ask you something?" he said. "The turban. Is that a style thing or a Muslim thing?"

"You know, the only two people in Massachusetts who have ever asked me about it both wanted to know if it's a style thing or a chemo thing."

Laughing, he said, "Cancer or Islam— which is the greater affliction?"

There were still moments when a statement like that could catch a person off-guard. He held his hands up quickly in apology. "Jesus. I mean, sorry. That came out really badly. I meant, it must be difficult to be Muslim in the world these days."

"I'd find it more difficult to not be Muslim," she said, and after that they walked on in a silence that became more than a little uncomfortable by the time they were back on Main Street. She had assumed that in some way, however secular, however political rather than religious, he identified as Muslim. Though what a foolish thing to assume of his father's son.

"Well, good-bye," she said as they approached the café, holding out

a hand for him to shake, aware that the gesture was strangely formal only after she'd made it.

"Thanks for the company. Perhaps we'll run into each other again," he said, extracting his shoes and delivering the backpack into her extended hand as though that's what it was there for. Assuming women who wore turbans as "a Muslim thing" couldn't possibly shake hands with men. As she walked home she thought how much more pleasant life was when you lived among foreigners whose subtexts you couldn't hear. That way you didn't need to know that "Perhaps we'll run into each other again" really meant "I have no particular wish to see you after this."

||||||||||||||||||||

Aunty Naseem, the neighbor who had taken the place of their grandmother when she died and with whom Aneeka was now staying, called to say she didn't want to worry Isma but could she check on Aneeka? "She stays out so often now, and I thought she was with her friends, but I just saw Gita and she says the friends don't see her very much at all anymore."

Gita of Preston Road was a link between Aneeka's home and university lives—a year older than the twins and with a new stepmother who didn't want her around, she had a room in student halls to which Aneeka had a spare key; Gita herself never used the room because she was living with her boyfriend, though none of the older generation of Preston Road knew this.

When Aneeka had first started staying over at Gita's, because Aneeka was in the library or out socializing in one way or another

until after the tube stopped running, Isma hadn't been happy about it. All those boys at university, whose families no one knew. And unlike Isma, Aneeka had always been someone boys looked at—and someone who looked back. More than looked, though Aneeka always guarded that part of her life from her sister, who was, perhaps, too inclined to lecture. It was Parvaiz who had talked Isma into accepting it—if there was anything worrying going on with Aneeka he'd know, and would tell Isma if he needed backup in talking sense to his twin. But there was no need to start having nightmares about Aneeka out alone in the cold, impersonal heart of London—she'd always been good at finding people who would look out for her. There was an instant appeal in her contradictory characteristics: sharp-tongued and considerate, serious-minded and capable of unbridled goofiness, as open to absorbing other people's pain as she was incapable of acknowledging the damage of having been abandoned and orphaned ("I have you and P. That's enough"). Whereas Parvaiz and Isma stayed at the margins of all groups so that no one would start to ask questions about their lives ("Where is your father? Are the rumors about him true?"), Aneeka simply knew how to place herself in the middle of a gathering, delineate her boundaries, and fashion intimacies around the no-go areas. Even as a young girl she'd known how to do this: someone would approach the subject of their father, and Aneeka would turn cold—an experience so disconcerting to those accustomed to her warmth that they'd quickly back away and be rewarded with the return of the Aneeka they knew. But now Parvaiz was a no-go area too, and not one that Aneeka could confine to a little corner of her life.

After the conversation with Aunty Naseem, Isma called her sister repeatedly, but it was late at night London time before she replied. The lamp at her bedside cast a small pool of light that illuminated the book resting on her chest—an *Asterix* comic, an old childhood favorite—but left her face in darkness.

"The Migrants have a new car. A BMW. A BMW in our driveway. What next? A pony? An AGA? An au pair?" When the tenants had moved into the house in which the siblings had grown up, and replaced the net curtains with obviously expensive blinds that were almost always lowered, Aneeka said she sympathized for the first time with residents of a neighborhood who felt aggrieved when migrants moved in. The nickname had stuck despite Isma's attempts to change it.

"I'm surprised you noticed—Aunty Naseem says she hardly sees you. And neither do your uni friends."

"I must really be behaving badly if Aunty Naseem is driven to complaining," Aneeka said.

"She's concerned, that's all."

"I know. I'm sorry. I don't mean to worry her. Or you. It's just easier being on my own these days. I suppose I'm learning why solitude has always been so appealing to you."

"I'll come home. Spring break is starting soon. We can at least have a week together." The thought of London was oppressive, but Isma kept that out of her voice.

"You know you can't afford it, and anyway, you don't want to have to go through that airport interrogation again. What if they don't let you board this time? Or if they give you a hard time when you return

to Boston? Also, I've got papers due. That's the main reason why no one's seen me. I'm working. The law makes you work. Not like sociology, where you get to watch TV and call it research."

"Since when do we lie to each other?"

"Since I was fourteen and said I was going to watch Parvaiz at cricket nets, but instead I went to meet Jimmy Singh at McDonald's."

"Jimmy-Singh-from-Poundland Jimmy Singh? Aneeka! Did Parvaiz know?"

"Course he knew. He always knew everything I did."

The night they discovered what Parvaiz had done, Aneeka had allowed Isma to brush out her long dark hair as their mother used to do when she had a daughter in need of comforting, and partway through Aneeka leaned back into her sister and said, "He never explained why he didn't tell me about the Ibsen tickets." Months after their mother died, Parvaiz, a boy suddenly arrived into adolescence in a house where bills and grief filled all crevices, had decided he needed a laptop of his own so that his sisters wouldn't disrupt his work on the sound projects that had recently become an obsession. One night he sneaked out of the house when everyone had gone to sleep, took the bus to Central London, and waited from midnight until mid-morning outside a theater in the West End for return tickets to the opening night of an Ibsen play that an actor recently elevated, via a superhero role, to the Hollywood A-list was using to reestablish his credentials as a serious thespian. Parvaiz bought two tickets with money he'd "borrowed" from the household account using Isma's debit card, and quickly sold them both for an astronomical sum. He announced all this, sauntering into the house like a conquering hero, only to be confronted with his sisters' rage. Is-

ma's anger came from the thought of the overtime she worked to keep the debt collector from the door, and from the thought of every horror that could befall a young boy in a world of racists and pedophiles; but Aneeka's rage was far greater. "Why didn't you tell me? I tell you everything—how could you not tell me?" Both Parvaiz and Isma, accustomed to Aneeka's being the buffer between them, had been completely unprepared for this. Six years later, that story was all Aneeka could grasp to help her understand her brother's subterfuge. Isma had an easier answer: his father's son; a fecklessness in the gene pool.

"Boys are different from us," Isma said. "They see what they want through tunnel vision."

The screen became a place of confusion, all motion and shapes, for a few seconds, and then she saw her sister lying in bed, face turned toward the phone that had been settled in its dock.

"Maybe if we start looking now for cheap flights I could come to you for my Easter break," Aneeka said, but Isma shook her head firmly before the sentence was finished.

"Don't want me telling the security monkeys at Heathrow how much I admire the Queen's color palette?"

"I do not." Her muscles tightened at the thought of Aneeka in the interrogation room. "Are we really not going to talk about the fact that Parvaiz has reappeared on Skype?"

"If we talk about him we'll argue. I don't want to argue right now."

"Neither do I. But I want to know if you've spoken to him."

"He sent a chat message just to say he's okay. You get the same?"

"No, I got nothing."

"Oh, Isma. I was sure you had. I would have told you otherwise.

Yes, just that. He's okay. He must have assumed I'd tell you as soon as I heard."

"That would imply he remembers how to think about anyone other than himself."

"Don't, please. I know anger is the way you express your concern but, just don't."

Anger is the way I express my anger, she would have said on another night, but tonight she said "I miss you."

"Stay with me until I fall asleep," Aneeka said, her hand reaching toward Isma, swerving to switch off the light.

"Once upon a time, there lived a girl and a boy called Aneeka and Parvaiz, who had the power to talk to animals."

Aneeka laughed. "Tell the one with the ostrich," she said, voice muffled by her pillow.

She was asleep before Isma was done telling the childhood story their mother had invented for her firstborn and Isma had modified for the twins, but Isma stayed on the line, listening to their breath rise and fall together as in all those times when Aneeka would crawl into Isma's bed, awakened from or into some night terror, and only the older sister's steady heartbeat could teach the younger one's frantic heart how to quiet, until there was no sound except their breath in unison, the universe still around them.

2

ALL MORNING SHE PRETENDED not to notice him sitting across the café basement, working on a crossword. But when she ordered a sandwich for lunch and brought it to her table, he came over and said he was about to have a bite himself, would it be all right if he sat with her.

"Preston Road," he said, returning a few minutes later with a plate of pasta. "It sounded familiar when you said that's where you grew up but I didn't know why until I looked it up on a map. That's in Wembley. My father's family lives somewhere around there. I used to visit every Eid."

"Oh, really?" she said, choosing not to mention that she knew exactly where his father's family used to live, and that she also knew, as he seemed not to, that they'd moved away, to Canada.

"There was a song my cousins used to sing to my little sister when the adults weren't around. I've had a line of it stuck in my head for years. Drives me crazy that I can't remember the rest, and my sister has no memory of it. Do you know it?" Unexpectedly he broke into a Pakistani pop song that predated his birth—he was four years her

junior, she'd discovered. She recognized the song by the tune more than the words, which came out as gibberish tinged with Urdu. He sang two lines, softly, face turning red—a self-consciousness she wouldn't have expected, particularly given how pretty his voice was. She pulled up a song for him from the music library on her phone and watched as Eamonn plugged in his headphones—unconscionably expensive; Parvaiz had coveted such a pair. He listened, eyes closed, recognition rather than pleasure in his expression.

"Thank you," he said, when he was done. "What does it actually mean?"

"It's in praise of fair-skinned girls, who have nothing to fear in life because everyone will always love their fair skin and their blue eyes."

"Oh, yes," he said, laughing. "I knew that once. They sang it to tease my sister, but she just treated it as a compliment and made it one. That's my sister for you."

"And you? Are you like that too?"

He frowned a little, sliding the tines of his fork into the little tubes of pasta. "No, I don't think so," he said in the unconvinced manner of someone who isn't accustomed to being asked to account for his own character. He raised the fork to his face and with little sucking sounds drew the pasta into his mouth. "Oh, sorry. My table manners are usually better than this."

"I don't mind. Do you know any Urdu?" He shook his head, a response his singing had anticipated, and she said, "So you don't understand 'bay-takalufi.'"

He sat up straight and raised his hand like a schoolboy. "I do know that one. It's informality as an expression of intimacy."

She experienced a brief moment of wonder that a father who hadn't taught his son basic Urdu had still thought to teach him this word. "I wouldn't say intimacy. It's about feeling comfortable with someone. Comfortable enough to forget good table manners. If done right, it's a sort of honor you confer on the other person when you feel able to be that comfortable with them, particularly if you haven't known them long." The words rushing out to cover how her voice had caught at "intimacy."

"Okay," he said, as if accepting a proposition. "Let's be comfortable with each other beyond table manners." He pushed his plate toward her. Extravagantly, she dipped the crust of her sandwich into his pasta sauce and leaned forward over his plate to bite into it.

At the end of lunch—a lunch that was relaxed, swift-flowing—he stood up and said, "See you here again one of these days? I've discovered that when the coffee machine is working, this place has the best cappuccino in town."

"I only have afternoon classes, and this is my favorite place to spend my mornings," she said. In fact, she sometimes went to her second-favorite café when it seemed too crowded in here, but really, what was the need for such fussiness?

||||||||||||||||||||||

The siblings watched one another, and watched one another watching one another. At least it felt that way, though in all probability she was far more aware of the twins than they were of her. She raised her eyes briefly from the screen to see Eamonn at a table neither too close nor too far away from her, so intent on some story in the local paper that

he didn't take his eyes off the page even as he lifted his mug of coffee and drank. Existing in another world entirely from the one she now inhabited for these few seconds each morning at eleven a.m. Her brother had always been a creature of habit, and that at least was something to be grateful for, else hours of every day might go like this: watching Aneeka waiting for Parvaiz to come online, then that moment when the green check mark appeared next to his name, Isma wondering, *What is he saying is he telling her something that will upset her is he asking her to become part of this madness he's joined oh no please he wouldn't do that but why can't he just leave her alone*; but every day it was only a few seconds before his name moved into the offline column again. Just after, Aneeka would text Isma to say: he checked in. *Check in,* one twin used to say to the other when there were school trips or sleepovers that kept them apart, and at some prearranged hour a text would arrive saying nothing more than checking in.

When Parvaiz logged off, followed shortly by Aneeka, Isma felt herself released of the day's burdens and texted a steaming-mug emoji across the room to Eamonn, who in response went upstairs to buy them both fresh cups of coffee. This too had become part of the morning routine over the last week or so—why pretend she wasn't keeping track? It was nine days since he decided they should be informal in intimacy together. "What's happening in the world today?" she asked when he returned and sat down across from her, and he presented her his highlights of the local news stories: a bear was reported clawing at a garage door, traffic in the adjoining town was briefly held up because of a three-car accident in which no one was injured, a statue of Ronald McDonald was reported missing from a family's garden. She said it

was clear the Ronald won gold medal for "most local" of the local news stories, but he disagreed on the grounds that Ronald was a global icon.

Daily, after their elevenses, he'd set off to "wander" by wheel and on foot, a Christopher Columbus of modest ambitions, retracing childhood paths and discovering new ones. He would sometimes arrive at the café the next morning with an offering from his journey: a jug of maple syrup from a sugarhouse, a one-dollar bill he'd found nailed to an oak tree with an oak-leaf shape cut out of it, a rubbing from Emily Dickinson's gravestone, with its peculiar wording— "CALLED BACK"—which he said made Dickinson sound like a faulty product. She learned more about this part of the world from his retelling than from her own living, but when she asked him the point of it all—imagining a travel book—he said surely experience and observation were point enough. What would happen when his savings ran out, she asked, and he said, actually, those savings he'd mentioned were his mother's—she had recently semiretired and decided that people gave too much of their lives and relationships to work; while there was no talking her daughter out of her seventeen-hour days, she had quite easily convinced her son to try to find other ways of constructing meaning in life than via paychecks and promotions. Isma found this idea compelling and Eamonn's less-than-halfhearted pursuit of it disappointing. Surely he should be learning a new language, or piloting a ship through waters where refugees in search of safety were known to capsize in their pitiful dinghies.

In the first few days she had thought he might suggest they do something together past elevenses—a movie, a meal, another walk—

but she now understood that she was just part of the way he divided up his days, which had structure in place of content. Between "morning newspaper" and "daily wander" there was "coffee with Isma." Even the fact that spring break had now started and she'd made it clear she had time on her hands hadn't changed that.

His father was often a topic of conversation during coffee, but always as "my father," never as a man in the public eye. The picture Eamonn conjured up, of a devoted, indulgent, practical-joking parent, was so at odds with Isma's image of the man that she sometimes wondered if the whole thing were an elaborate fiction to disguise the truth about his father. But then she'd observe Eamonn's unguarded manner and know this wasn't true.

One morning he was late to the café. She thought it was because of the weather —winter had returned. Snow slashed across the windowpanes, the sky was white, cars alerted cops that they'd overstayed their two-hour parking limit by the depth of snow on their roofs. Just as she'd got past the distraction of his absence and submerged herself in the problem of missing variables for her statistics course, a text arrived from Aneeka:

Have you heard? Lone Wolf new home secretary.

She must have said something out loud because the woman sitting next to her asked, "Are you okay?" but she was already clicking on a bookmark in her browser, pulling up a news site with a BREAKING NEWS banner announcing a cabinet reshuffle, the most significant change of which was the appointment of a new home secretary. There

he was—the man whom she had thought Eamonn looked just like before she'd spent enough mornings noticing the particulars of his face, his mannerisms. The accompanying article described the newly elevated minister as a man "from a Muslim background," which is what they always said about him, as though Muslim-ness was something he had boldly stridden away from. Inevitably, the sentence went on to use the phrase "strong on security."

She felt sick before she could form the thoughts to understand why. Her phone buzzed and she looked down to a series of messages.

> It's all going to get worse.
>
> He has to prove he's one of them, not one of us, doesn't he? As if he hasn't already.
>
> I hate this country.
>
> Don't call me, I'll say things I shouldn't.
>
> Stop spying on our messages you arseholes and find some bankers to arrest.

"Hey, Greta Garbo, why so serious?"

He sat down across from her, one arm slung over the back of the chair. Such a languid contrast to the coiled spring of his father. She slammed the lid of the laptop, flipped the phone screen over.

"You're late," she said.

"Big family news." He leaned forward, smiling, a proud son. The table was so small his knees knocked against hers. "My father's just been appointed the new home secretary. Karamat Lone. You know who he is, right?" She nodded, took a sip of coffee for something to

do. "I guess you're one of the people who doesn't see my face, hear the surname, and put two and two together."

"It's not an uncommon Pakistani surname." An evasion rather than a lie, she told herself.

"I know. Anyway, I'm glad I can finally tell you. Also, this is why I haven't been able to answer your question of how long I'm staying. I hate all the old muck they scrape up about him every time he's in the headlines, and this time it'll be worse. I came to avoid it. He's good at dealing with it; I'm not. So if you see me obsessing over stuff they're saying online, take my phone away from me, would you?" He tapped her fingers with his as he spoke to emphasize the final point.

All the old muck. He meant the picture of Karamat Lone entering a mosque that had been in the news for its "hate preacher." LONE WOLF'S PACK REVEALED, the headlines screamed when a tabloid got hold of it, near the end of his first term as an MP. The Lone Wolf's response had been to point out that the picture was several years old, he had been there only for his uncle's funeral prayers and would otherwise never enter a gender-segregated space. This was followed by pictures of him and his wife walking hand in hand into a church. His Muslim-majority constituency voted him out in the elections that took place just a few weeks later, but he was quickly back in Parliament via a by-election, in a safe seat with a largely white constituency, and the tabloids that had attacked him now championed him as a LONE CRU-SADER taking on the backwardness of British Muslims. Isma doubted very much that "the old muck" would rise again—oh, unless he meant the opposing side of that story: all the accusations she'd heard, and that seemed entirely accurate, that Karamat Lone had precisely calcu-

lated the short-term losses and long-term gains of showing such contempt for the conventions of a mosque. Sellout, coconut, opportunist,
traitor.

"You're close to him, aren't you?"

"You know what fathers and sons are like."

"Not really, no."

"They're our guides into manhood, for starters."

She'd never understood this, though she'd heard and seen enough
anecdotally and academically to know there was something to it. For
girls, becoming women was inevitability; for boys, becoming men
was ambition. He must have seen her look of incomprehension, because he tried again.

"We want to be like them, we want to be better than them. We
want to be the only people in the world who are allowed to be better
than them." He gestured at himself and around the café with a shrug
that encompassed the mediocrity of everything. "Obviously, I worked
out long ago that such an attempt would be futile."

"That's not true. You're a much better person than he is."

"What do you know about it?"

She didn't answer, didn't know how to, and he said, "Why were
you acting so furtive when I came in?"

She hesitated, turned her laptop around so it faced him, and
opened the lid.

"You were reading about him. Isma, did you already know he was
my father?"

"Yes."

"Why did you lie about it?"

She clasped her hands together, looked down at the interlacing of her fingers, which he'd touched so familiarly just a few moments ago.

"You're one of them? The Muslims who say those ugly things about him?"

"Yes."

He waited, but there was nothing more she could say.

"I see. Well, I'm very sorry to hear it." She heard the scraping of the chair and looked up as he stood. "I suppose one day I'll see the irony in running here to try and escape certain attitudes only to find myself having coffee with their embodiment." Gone was the friendly, considerate boy, and in his place a man carrying all the wounds his father was almost certainly too thick-skinned to feel as anything more than pinpricks. When he said good-bye there was no mistaking the finality of his tone.

||||||||||||||||||||

The wind had dropped, and the snow drifted down in large flakes that retained their shape for a moment on her sleeve before melting into the fabric. Isma walked the short distance home, but as she approached her front door the thought of her studio with its clanging pipes was intolerable. She carried on down to the tree-lined graveyard at the end of the street, unexpectedly positioned beside a nursery school, across the road from a baseball diamond. In the summer it must be a place of shade, in autumn a feast of color; but she had known it only as the white of snow, the gray of stone.

She started on a cleared pathway before cutting across a snowdrift that came halfway up her knee-high boots, and pulled herself onto a

nineteenth-century gravestone, feet dangling. Sometimes the dead were a friendly presence, but today they were only dead, and every chiseled slab was a marker of someone's sorrow. She kicked her heels against the gravestone. "Stupid," she said.

That was the only word for this sense of enormous loss where there had been so very little to lose.

||||||||||||||||||||||

"You don't have to decide that's the end of it," Hira Shah said that evening, when they sat down together for a typically elaborate meal. A single woman in her mid-fifties who had never had to cook on a regular basis for anyone, Hira retained the idea that company for dinner must be occasion for pyrotechnics in the kitchen, no matter how frequently company was over—or perhaps she did that only when her company hadn't had anyone to mother her in a long time. "You should at least try explaining why you feel the way you do. What is there to lose?"

"What is there to gain? He'll be going back to London soon in any case."

Hira looked at her over a forkful of rogan josh. "Do you know when you were at LSE I thought you found me offensive?"

"That's ridiculous. Oh, you mean that first term. When I rolled my eyes at you?"

It overturned seven hundred ninety years of precedent in British law, the Kashmiri lecturer had been saying during an impassioned presentation on control orders and their impact on civil liberties when Hira saw the quiet girl in the third row roll her eyes. *Would you like to say some-*

thing, Ms. Pasha? Yes, Dr. Shah, if you look at colonial laws you'll see plenty of precedent for depriving people of their rights; the only difference is this time it's applied to British citizens, and even that's not as much of a change as you might think, because they're rhetorically being made un-British. *Say more.* The 7/7 terrorists were never described by the media as "British terrorists." Even when the word "British" was used, it was always "British of Pakistani descent" or "British Muslim" or, my favorite, "British passport holders," always something interposed between their Britishness and terrorism. *Well, you have quite a voice when you decide to use it.*

Isma had gone home that evening and stood in front of the mirror, pressing down on her larynx, and felt the slight tremor of something on the cusp of waking. And wake it had—her suppressed anger distilled and abstracted into essays about the sociological impact of the War on Terror. Then Isma's mother died, and that voice was lost until now. Dr. Shah was coaxing it back with the shared paper they were working on—"The Insecurity State: Britain and the Instrumentalization of Fear"—which took Isma's experience in the interrogation room and made it research.

"No, not then. All the way through until you graduated. I thought you disliked something in me personally, and that's why you acted so distant when I tried to talk about anything other than work. It was only after your mother died and you told me everything that you made sense."

How she'd wept that day in Hira Shah's office. For her mother, for the grandmother who had predeceased her daughter-in-law by less than a year, for her father, for the orphaned twins who had never

really known their mother before bitterness and stress ate away the laughing, affectionate woman she'd once been—and, most of all, for herself.

"I don't want Eamonn's pity, if that's what you're driving at here."

"I'm driving at the fact that habits of secrecy are damaging things," Hira said in her most professorial voice. "And they underestimate other people's willingness to accept the complicated truths of your life."

"So—what? I should just call him up—" She held the saltshaker to her ear, miming a phone. "Eamonn, here's a funny story about my father."

"Maybe without the word 'funny.'"

"And then? Do I follow up with the even funnier story of my brother? To the son of the new home secretary?"

"Mmm. Maybe start with your father, and see how it goes from there. And one other piece of advice. Reconsider the hijab." She pointed at the turban that Isma had left near the door along with her shoes, the latter out of consideration for Hira's hardwood floors and Persian carpets, the former out of consideration for her sensibility.

"Don't miss an opportunity with that one, do you, Dr. Shah?"

"It might be keeping your young man at a distance. He'll read things into what it means."

"He's not my young man and his reading won't be so wrong. And when did I say I wanted anything from him in that way?" It had been so long since anything approaching "that way" that she didn't know if she knew how to want it anymore. Mo at university had been the last and—barring some forgettable fumbling—the first man with whom

she'd known any physical intimacy. Perhaps if they'd gone further than they had she'd have a sense of missing something, but Mo worried about their eternal damnation and Isma thought you should at least be able to imagine marrying someone before doing something so significant with them. In retrospect, it was a mystery they'd stayed together almost their entire second year of university.

"You know the Quran tells us to enjoy sex as one of God's blessings?" Hira said.

"Within marriage!"

"We all have our versions of selective reading when it comes to the Holy Book."

Isma laughed and stood to clear the plates. From her greathearted vantage point Hira Shah saw Isma clearly—so careworn, so blemished by all the circumstances of her life that certain options had simply crossed their arms and turned away from her. But when a boy stepped into Isma's path, his laughter trailing a promise that life could be joyful if you stayed near enough to him, Hira turned her attention to a piece of fabric and said, *There, that and an untold story are the only obstacles between you and him.*

For a moment Isma stood in the kitchen, with its familiar scents and the warm glow of its lamps, and allowed herself to believe it. There was perfectly good cappuccino near his grandparents' house; he didn't have to drive twenty-five minutes every morning to the same café. She caught her reflection in the window. She had no idea where he went in the evenings, where he spent his nights. Where he was right now.

"Stupid," she said, and turned her attention to loading the dishwasher.

⁓⁓⁓⁓⁓⁓⁓⁓⁓

Eamonn opened his mouth and the sound that came out was that of a grasshopper. *Say something,* she said. *Chirp.* Isma opened her eyes from one darkness into another that was interrupted by a rectangle of light. It was 2:17 a.m. Why was Aneeka calling at this hour? No, no, no, no, no. Her baby, her brother, the child she'd raised. She grabbed at the phone—images in her mind of his death, violent, unbearable—and pressed the answer button. Aneeka's face a death mask.

"It was you," her sister said.

"Parvaiz?" her own voice strange with sleep and fear.

"You were the one who told the police what he'd done."

One kind of panic ending, another beginning. "Who told you that?"

"Aunty Naseem is on the phone talking to Razia Apa about it. So you admit it?"

"They would have found out anyway."

"You don't know that." Her sister's voice all hurt and confusion. "They might not have. And then he could have come home. He could just have turned around the moment he knew he'd made a mistake and come home. You've made him not able to come home." She cried out, as if she'd only just then felt the wound that had been delivered to her. "Isma, you've made our brother not able to come home."

Isma touched her sister's face on the screen, felt the cold glass. "Shh, listen to me. People in the neighborhood knew. The police

would have found out. There was nothing I could do for him, so I did what I could for you, for us."

"For me?"

"We're in no position to let the state question our loyalties. Don't you understand that? If you cooperate, it makes a difference. I wasn't going to let him make you suffer for the choices he'd made."

"Is this me not suffering? Parvaiz is gone."

"He did that, not me. When they treat us this way the only thing we can do for our own sanity is let them go."

"Parvaiz is not our father. He's my twin. He's me. But you, you're not our sister anymore."

"Aneeka . . ."

"I mean it. You betrayed us, both of us. And then you tried to hide it from me. Don't call, don't text, don't send me pictures, don't fly across the ocean and expect me to ever agree to see your face again. We have no sister."

One moment her face was there, enraged, and then it was replaced by Isma's phone's wallpaper; yellow and green leaves floating on the surface of the Grand Union Canal. Isma tried FaceTime, Skype, WhatsApp, and even the expense of an international phone call, not with any hope of Aneeka answering but to let her sister know how desperately she wanted to communicate.

Finally, when the sound of ringing became more than she could bear, she lay back in bed, wrapping the duvet tightly around her. The stars were cold above her head. A verse from the Quran came to mind: *By the sky and the night visitor! / And what is the night visitor? / A piercingly bright star.* She got up, pulled the prayer rug out from under

her bed, and knelt down on it. "Bismillah ir-Rahman ir-Rahim." The Arabic words her companions since childhood, passed on to her within her grandmother's embrace when no one thought she was old enough to learn them. *In the name of Allah the Beneficent, the Merciful.* This rocking motion that accompanied her prayers was her grandmother rocking her to sleep, whispering these verses to protect her. At first the words were just a language she didn't know, but as she continued, closing her eyes to shut out the world, they burrowed inside her, flared into light, dispelled the darkness. And then the light softened, diffused, enveloping her in the peace that comes from knowing your own powerlessness.

At least, that's how it usually worked. But today she couldn't make them anything other than words in a foreign language, spoken out loud in a room that didn't anticipate anyone's being out from under covers at this hour, and so was too cold. She returned to bed, hugged a pillow close to her chest, placed another against her back. She had only been fooling herself that night when she thought she still knew how to calm the frantic pacing of her sister's heart. Aneeka's had learned to beat in the company of her twin brother, in the world of their mother's womb. As children the twins would lie in the garden, fingers on each other's pulses, listening to the trains go by on the tracks behind their house. Waiting for those moments when their hearts were synchronized, first with each other and then with the sound of the train pulling out of Preston Road station.

Please call me please call me please call me she Skyped, WhatsApped, texted her sister.

Aunty Naseem called, horrified at her own role in what had hap-

pened. She and her daughter Razia had been discussing something in the news and she had said what a good thing it was, in this climate, that Isma had reported what Parvaiz had done. She hadn't heard Aneeka come in the night before and assumed she was miles away, at Gita's. "She was rude to me," Aunty Naseem said, the sentence conveying a whole universe and its behavior patterns upturned.

So then Isma had to convince her that it was a mistake easily made, and that there was nothing to forgive, and Aneeka would come around eventually, when really she wanted to shout into the phone *How could you have been so careless!* When the call finally ended she felt as tired as she'd ever been. She leaned into the pillow against her back, Eamonn holding her tight. "Oh," she said, surprised and not. This wasn't the first time she'd found him there, but she'd always banished him before. Now she pressed herself closer, taking the comfort it was suddenly obvious only he could give. At first, and for a long time, it was warmth that spread through her limbs, then, eventually, heat. She turned toward him in the darkness. By the time the first light appeared in the sky she felt herself transformed by the desire to be known, completely. Before the day and its realities could dispel this headiness, she reached for the phone and sent Eamonn a text: I'm sorry. I envy you your father. Mine died while being taken to Guantánamo. I want to explain it all to you.

He answered, earlier than she imagined he would be awake: Tell me where to meet you.

From Aneeka, no word. FaceTime, Skype, WhatsApp, phone call. Nothing.

||||||||||||||||||||||

Isma looked at her reflection in the mirror, hair "texturized" into "beachy waves," as Mona of Persepolis Hair in Wembley had promised when she recommended a product that could counter frizzy, flyaway hair without attaining the miracle of straightening it. Her hair said "playful" and "surprising." Or it would if it didn't come attached to her face. She opened the drawer in which she kept her turbans and headscarves, closed it, looked in the mirror once more, opened it again.

A diffidence of knuckles on her door. She had expected him to call when downstairs, but one of her neighbors must have left the front door open, and now he was here, sooner than she'd anticipated, and she was still in her bathrobe. "Wait," she called out, and grabbed the nearest clothes at hand. Jeans, bra discolored in the wash—for heaven's sake, what difference did that make?—and fleece-lined sweatshirt.

She opened the door, a little breathless, as self-conscious as on the day she'd offered to walk him upstairs to the coffee counter. There was a slight, spiced scent of aftershave coming off him. Specially for this meeting, or did she usually not see him until late enough in the day that it had worn off?

"Hello," he said, in a tone that wasn't unfriendly but more formal than his usual "hey." Was it because of their last conversation or because she was without a turban? His eyes slipped across her face and beyond it, as if he thought it might be impolite to look straight at her while she was uncovered. She saw him take in the glass and plate in

the drying rack, the bare walls, the single bed with its white duvet and sheets.

"It's nice," he said. "Uncluttered." He unbuttoned his coat, the popping sound intimate in the silence of the studio. She wondered if "uncluttered" was a polite word for "austere," or if he really saw the studio as she had until that moment—a home that made almost no demands on you, allowed you simply to be. Now she wished she'd put a little more care into it, and that the single bed wasn't so determinedly single.

"Sorry about yesterday," he said.

"I'm the one who should be saying that. Tea?"

He kicked off his Wellies, and while she was filling the kettle she could hear him walking over to the desk, then a low whistle telling her he'd seen the photograph of Aneeka.

"That's my sister," she said.

He turned toward her, photo frame in his hands. The picture had been taken the previous year, soon after the twins graduated. Aneeka was dressed to go out in her favorite ensemble: black knee-high boots, black leggings, and long white tunic, a black bonnet cap accentuating the angles of her face, a scarf of black and white gauze wrapped loosely over it. One hand on hip, jutting her chin in a show of attitude to her twin behind the camera while Isma, elbow resting on her sister's shoulder, smiled indulgently. How broad her face looked next to her sister's, how washed-out her features compared to the lipstick-and-mascara enhancements at which Aneeka was so skillful.

"How old is she?"

"Nineteen." A woman-child, a mature-immature. Isma couldn't think of any words that would reach her.

He put the photograph down. "Attractive family," he said. He finally looked straight at her. "You have nice hair." The remark followed the one before it in going straight to her stomach, but he'd already turned his attention to the other frame on her desk, which contained an Arabic verse, handwritten on lined paper. "And this?"

"It's from the Quran. La yukallifullahu nafsan ilia wus-ahaa. Allah does not burden a soul with more than it can bear." When her grandmother died she had found this taped inside her bedside-table drawer.

He looked at her with more pity than she could endure, which he must have seen, because when he spoke his tone was lightly wry: "Here ends the small-talk part of the conversation, then."

She sat down on her bed, wondering if he'd sit next to her or choose the desk chair several feet away. He did neither, settling himself on the floor instead, knees drawn up to his chest.

"Tell me about your father," he said.

"I don't really know what to tell you about him, is the thing. I didn't know him. He tried his hand at many things in his life—guitarist, salesman, gambler, con man, jihadi, but he was most consistent in the role of absentee father."

She told him everything as she remembered it, without evasion. The first time her father had abandoned his family she was too young to remember either his departure or his presence before it. So she grew up in a house with her mother and grandparents, unaware that her heart was missing anything. When Isma was eight years old, he

reappeared—Adil Pasha, known to his friends as "Pash, short for Passion," a laughing, broad-shouldered man who delighted in her resemblance to him. Like every woman in his life she quickly fell for his charm, which was so devastatingly effective it gained his readmittance to the marital bed, even though when he first walked through the door her mother overrode her in-laws and insisted he sleep on the couch. He stayed long enough to impregnate his wife with twins and to ensure his daughter found the thought of his ever leaving again unbearable, and then he was gone once more. This time his excuse for going wasn't a get-rich-quick scheme but an aid convoy to Bosnia, which was then in the final months of war, allowing him to cloak his departure in righteousness. The convoy returned a few weeks later, but he didn't, and Isma never saw him again.

Every so often a card in his scribbly handwriting would arrive to say how invaluable he was to some fight or other against oppression, or a bearded man would appear at the doorstep with some small amount of money and the name of wherever Pash was fighting—Kashmir, Chechnya, Kosovo. In October 2001 he called. He was in Pakistan, en route to Afghanistan, and had heard of his father's death. He wanted to speak to his mother, and also to hear his son's voice. His wife hung up without waiting to find out if he might also want to hear Isma's voice—the voice of the only one of his children he'd ever known.

Eamonn shifted, rested his ankle against hers, an act of sympathy just small enough for her to bear.

"A few months later MI5 and Special Branch officers came around, asking about him, though they wouldn't say why. We knew something

was wrong, and my grandmother said maybe we should try to contact someone—the Red Cross, the government, a lawyer—to find out where he was. If my grandfather had still been alive that might have happened, but he wasn't, and my mother said if we tried looking for him we'd be harassed by Special Branch, and by people in the neighborhood, who would start to suspect our sympathies. My grandmother went to the mosque looking for support, but the Imam sided with my mother—he'd heard too many stories of abuse suffered by the families of British men who'd been arrested in Afghanistan. One of my grandmother's friends had said the British government would withdraw all the benefits of the welfare state—including state school and the NHS—from any family it suspected of siding with the terrorists."

Eamonn made a face of distaste, clearly offended in a way that told her he saw the state as part of himself, something that had never been possible for anyone in her family. She raised a hand to hold off his objections. "My mother knew that wasn't true, but she allowed my grandmother to believe it. So that was that until 2004, when a Pakistani man released from Guantánamo contacted my father's family in Pakistan to say he had been imprisoned at Bagram with my father from early 2002. In June that year both he and my father were among the men put on a plane for transport to Guantánamo. My father died during takeoff, some sort of seizure. He said other things also, about what happened to my father in Bagram, but the family in Pakistan said no one needed those images in their head, and didn't tell us."

"No one told you he was dead for two years?"

"Who was going to tell us? The Americans? British intelligence? We weren't told anything. We still haven't been told anything. They

haven't released records of Bagram from that time period. We don't even know if anyone bothered to dig a grave."

"I'm sure they dug a grave," he said.

"Why? Because they're so civilized?" She had promised herself she wouldn't lie to him, and that included not curtailing her rage.

"I'm sorry. I was trying to . . . I'm sorry. I can't imagine what that must have been like for you, for your whole family."

She made a helpless, hopeless gesture. "We didn't talk about it. We were forbidden to talk about it. Only Aunty Naseem and her daughters who lived across the road knew because we were essentially one family divided into two households. Other than that there was only one other person who was told—a man who my grandparents had known since they first moved to Wembley and there were so few Asian families around that all of them knew each other. On my grandmother's behalf, this man went to visit his cousin's son, a first-term MP, and asked if the British government could find out any information about Adil Pasha, who died on his way to Guantánamo, and whose family deserved answers. 'They're better off without him,' the MP said, and left the room."

"That was my father?"

"Yes."

He slumped forward, his face in his hands.

She wanted to run her fingers through his thick hair, stroke his arm. There was a lightness inside her, entirely new, that made the whole world rearrange itself into a place of undreamt-of possibilities. In this lightness Aneeka's anger was short-lived, Parvaiz's choices reversible.

He looked up, held her gaze. "Can I?" he said, pointing to a spot on the bed next to her. She nodded, not trusting her voice enough to use it.

The mattress dipped slightly beneath his weight. He took her hand, looked at her with deep feeling in those brown eyes of his. "I'm so sorry for everything you've suffered," he said. "You're a remarkable woman." And then he patted her hand, once, twice, and let go of it. "You need to understand something about my father."

She didn't want to understand anything about his father. She wanted his hand back sending currents through her, including in the most intimate places. Almost as if he'd touched her there.

"It's harder for him," he said. "Because of his background. Early on, in particular, he had to be more careful than any other MP, and at times that meant doing things he regretted. But everything he did, even the wrong choices, were because he had a sense of purpose. Public service, national good, British values. He deeply believes in these things. All the wrong choices he made, they were necessary to get him to the right place, the place he is now."

There he sat, his father's son. It didn't matter if they were on this or that side of the political spectrum, or whether the fathers were absent or present, or if someone else had loved them better, loved them more: in the end they were always their fathers' sons.

"I'm not saying that makes it okay," he said. He touched two fingers to his temple, rubbed. Perfect half-moons in his fingernails. "I'm not very good at this. He should be the one explaining. I'll tell you what— next time you're in London, you two can meet. I'll set it up. Confront him with this—make him account for it. He'd be up for that. My guess is, you'll feel more favorably about him at the end."

"Me? Meet Karamat Lone?"

Mr. British Values. Mr. Strong on Security. Mr. Striding Away from Muslim-ness. He would say, *I know about your family. You're better off without your brother, too.* And Eamonn, his devoted son, would sadly have to agree.

"Don't sound so worried about it. He'll be nice. For my sake." He took hold of a strand of her hair, pulled it lightly. "Now that I've seen your head uncovered, I'm practically your brother, aren't I?"

"Is that what you are?"

"Sorry, is that too presumptuous?"

She stood, turned, shrugged. "No, it's fine," she said, making her voice light, making him seem absurd for sounding so serious about it. "Oh, look, I never made you that cup of tea, and now I have to go out. Appointment."

"Will you come to the café after?"

"Probably not today. Actually, maybe not for a while. A friend has invited me to come and spend the rest of spring break at her place." Not strictly untrue. At the end of their meal the previous night Hira had said, *You're welcome to move into my spare room for a few days if you want company. Don't be heartbroken alone.*

"Oh, but then we won't see each other. I'll be leaving in the next day or two. News cycle already moving on from my father. And to tell you the truth, I think I'm cramping my grandparents' social life."

"Well, then. I'm glad we cleared the air," she said, holding herself straight-backed, upright.

"Me too. Well. Good-bye. Thanks for being such a fantastic coffee companion." He stepped forward and held his arms out slightly awk-

wardly. What followed was not an embrace so much as two bodies knocking into each other then moving away. He smiled, pushed his hair back from his face in a way that already felt as familiar to her as the tics of people she'd grown up with. She watched him put on his Wellies, button up his coat, smile again, turn to go. His hand reached for the doorknob, and then he paused.

"Isma?"

"Yes?" The trace of hope still working its way through her veins.

He picked up the padded envelope from the kitchen counter, which was filled with M&M's—there was a long-running joke between the neighboring households about Aunty Naseem's sweet tooth for American confectionery after a vacation there in the 1980s.

"This the same package you had in the café last week? Weren't you going to the post office with it?"

"Keep forgetting," she said.

He tucked it under his arm. "I'll post it from London."

"There's no need."

"It's really no problem. Cheaper and quicker."

"Oh, okay. Thanks."

"Bye, sis," he said with a wink. Then he stepped through the door and closed it behind him.

She ran over to her balcony. Moments later, he stepped out onto the street, rolling back his shoulders as if released from the weight of her company. He walked away without looking up, his stride long.

Isma knelt down on the snow-dusted balcony floor and wept.

Eamonn

3

A KAYAK GLIDED high above the stationary traffic of the North Circular Road, two ducks paddling in its wake. Eamonn stopped along the canal path, looked over the edge of the railing. Cars backed up as far as he could see. All the years he'd been down there he'd taken this aqueduct for just another bridge, nothing to tell you that canal boats and waterfowl were being carried along above your head. Always these other Londons in London. He typed "canal above north circular" into his phone, followed a link that led to another link, and was soon watching news footage of a bomb planted on this bridge by the IRA in 1939. When the newsreader came to details of what would have happened if the bridge had been destroyed, he clicked pause midsentence, and hurriedly strode on.

But today was not a day to worry about the precariousness of things. It was the start of April, and London was bursting into spring, magnolia flowers opening voluptuously on the trees in Little Venice where he'd entered the tow path. Now he was walking along a wilder terrain, weeds and bushes growing in all directions, sometimes tall enough to hide the industrial blight that lay beyond, sometimes not.

And then it changed again, became beautiful, almost rural—swans on the bank, yellow buds studding the trees, a man and his dog both snoring on the roof of a canal boat, the sky an expanse of blue smeared with white. Isma the invisible presence walking alongside him, her expression intense except when he could make her smile. He wondered if she would get in touch next time she was in London. Probably not. Despite their attempt to clear the air, the history of their fathers had made things between them far too strange. He tried to imagine growing up knowing your father to be a fanatic, his death a mystery open to terrible speculation, but the attempt was defeated by his simple inability to know how such a man as Adil Pasha could have existed in Britain to begin with.

He left the canal path near high-rises embodying the word "regeneration" and was soon on Ealing Road, walking past Gurkha Superstore, Gama Halal Meat, a Hindu temple intricately carved of limestone, cheerful stalls and restaurants. He couldn't point to anything in particular he recognized, yet he had complete certainty that he had looked out a car window onto this street many times in his childhood. "We're going," is all his father would say before the annual outings to Eamonn's great-uncle's house every Eid, a holiday that his mother explained as "marking the end of the month of not observing Ramzan for all of us." On that one day of the year, his father became someone else, and it was this that he knew his mother hated as much as he did. Surrounded by his extended family, Karamat Lone disappeared into another language, with its own gestures and intonations— even when he was speaking English. One year, when Eamonn was nine or ten, Eid fell just after Christmas. The American family was

visiting, and there were plans every day for outings with cousins. "You don't have to come this year," his father agreed after some judiciously timed postprandial Christmas Day pleading, and went on his own. The next year it was "Do you want to come?" and he didn't seem to mind when his wife and children said no. Just when Eamonn was becoming old enough to want to know the part of his father's life that remained so mysterious, there was the whole business with the mosque photographs and a falling-out with the cousins over the necessary damage control.

He was nearing a mosque, crossed the street to avoid it, then crossed back so as not to be seen trying to avoid a mosque. Everyone always went on about the racism his father had had to face when a section of the press tried to brand him an extremist, but it was London's Muslim population who had turned their back on Karamat Lone and voted him out, despite all the good he'd done for his constituents. All because he'd expressed a completely enlightened preference for the conventions of a church over those of a mosque and spoke of the need for British Muslims to lift themselves out of the Dark Ages if they wanted the rest of the nation to treat them with respect.

On the High Road now, with its pound stores and pawnshops, glancing up every so often at the bone-white rainbow of Wembley Stadium for its reassuring familiarity—and then north toward Preston Road, where everything turned residential, suburban. Any one of these semidetached houses could be the home in which he'd spent all those Eid afternoons, sitting pressed against his mother in an alliance she tried to push him out of, knowing that he would rather be in the garden playing cricket with the boy cousins whose invitations to join

them were located confusingly at the border between the merely polite and the genuine. His sister, habitually free of the burden of alliances, would be upstairs with the girl cousins, throwing herself into a
rapture of family feeling that would disappear as soon as they were
back in Holland Park. She was, everyone said, her father's daughter, a
claim she was proving with her determined ascent, at twenty-two,
through the world of investment banking in Manhattan.

On the rare occasions he remembered his father's family it was
only to recall the feelings of estrangement that visits to them brought
up, but spending time with Isma had reminded him that there were
other, more familial feelings. She evoked in particular his father's
youngest cousin, the one who once affixed a Band-Aid and a healing
kiss on his elbow when he took a tumble in the garden, gashing open
his skin. He wondered if, in turn, he reminded Isma of Parvaiz, the
younger brother to whom she referred only in passing, twin to the
beautiful woman in the photograph.

He was walking past curving side streets that he seemed to know
had been laid directly over country roads more recently than a person
might assume. The distance between his father's life and his own revealed itself here more acutely than in West London. This was the
London of Karamat Lone's childhood, these were the homes of the
affluent relatives whose lives his father had aspired to when he sat up
all night in his cramped flat in Bradford, studying for exams. Late at
night was the only time he could spread his books onto the surface
that was kitchen counter, dining table, and workspace for his seam-
stress mother. On the wall across from him a large poster of the

Ka'aba, the faithful prostrating themselves around it. Eamonn knew this from a photograph, one of the few his father had from his childhood, about which he had always been too embarrassed to ask.

Finally, he approached the street on which Isma had grown up, just off a commercial stretch of Preston Road. Now that he was here he felt awkward about not simply posting the package, and he walked up Preston Road for a while—past a Jewish bakery beside an Islamic bookshop beside a Romanian butcher—before turning back toward Isma's street again. He was unable to let go of the feeling that behind these doors existed a piece of his childhood—of his father—that he'd been too ready to forget. He knocked on the door of a pebble-dash house and an elderly woman made small by age answered, wearing a shalwar kameez with a thick cardigan that signaled her internal thermometer was still set to another country. This must be the old friend and neighbor, Aunty Naseem, in whose house Isma's sister was living while studying law at LSE. He said he had brought something for her from Isma, which made her open the door wide and reach up to place the palm of her hand against his cheek before turning to walk back inside with the words "Come, have some tea."

The Arabic calligraphy on the wall, the carpeted stairs, the plastic flowers in a vase, the scent of spices in the kitchen despite there being nothing on the stove: all brought back his great-uncle's home, and with it the shameful memory of his own embarrassment about it.

He took Isma's envelope out of his satchel and handed it to the old lady, who laughed in delight when she shook it, guessing the contents. "Such a thoughtful girl, that girl. Tea—with sugar?" At his response

she said, "You British, never any sugar in your tea. My grandchildren are all the same. My daughters, half-and-half—one yes, one no. How did you meet Isma? What do you do for a living?"

She was amused by the story of the man who needed rescuing from an unmanned coffee counter but made a disapproving face at "taking a year off," which made him say "probably return to consultancy but perhaps a more boutique firm." "One of those personal shoppers?" she asked, and it took him a moment of placing together "consultancy" and "boutique" to understand how she'd reached that conclusion. When he explained, she laughed, slapping his hand in a show of mirth, and he laughed too, wishing he'd known a paternal grandmother—a dadi. His had died the year before he was born, and her husband—a newspaper-kiosk vendor—had followed soon after, "dead of helplessness," as Eamonn's father explained.

Soon she was frying samosas for him, as though determined to inhabit a stereotype, while, as instructed, he licked the end of a thread and guided it through the eye of a needle. She had moved to London from Gujranwala in the fifties, she said; his grandparents had come then from Sialkot, he said. No, he didn't speak Punjabi. No, not Urdu either. "Only English?" Some French. She said, "My father fought in the British Indian army during World War One. He was in France for a while, billeted with a family there—the sons and husband were soldiers, so it was just the women he lived with. *Je t'adore*, he used to say to his children years later. After he died, I wondered who had taught him those words. Here, hold out your arm."

The threaded needle was for him, it turned out. She had noticed the loose button on his sleeve, and he found himself looking at the

parting of her dyed black hair as she bent down to set it right, still talking away. "Shukriya," he said, the Urdu word clumsy on his tongue, and after a moment's pause in which something else seemed necessary he added "Aunty," and was rewarded by another pat on his cheek. He assumed all this affection and the generosity of her welcome was just the famed Pakistani hospitality his father sometimes sighingly spoke of when regretting how "English" his children's lives had turned out (to which Eamonn's mother would reply, "It's wonderful in the abstract but when you actually encounter it you call it intrusive and overbearing"); but then she said, "So, Isma sent you to meet us."

He set down the samosa, which, it was suddenly clear, had been given to him under a false assumption. "Not exactly. In fact, no. I told her I would post the package, but it was such a nice day I thought I would take a long walk and drop it off."

"You walked here? All the way from Notting Hill, to see us."

"It's a nice walk. I like discovering new bits of London—in this case, the canal," he said, which seemed an effective way of dispelling her misconception without either of them actually mentioning it.

"Oh, she told you how much she loves walking along the canal." He picked up the samosa and bit into it. Isma could set her straight when they spoke—he didn't doubt Aunty Naseem would be on the phone to her as soon as he left. "You know, I've known her since the day she was born. Her grandmother was my first friend—we were living off the High Road, nothing like today. There were no other Asians at all. And then one day, across the street I saw a woman in a shalwar kameez. I ran across, in the middle of traffic, and caught her by the arm, and we stayed there talking for so long my husband came out looking

for me. When we moved to this street, we said to them, Come on, we can't separate. So they came. And here Isma was born, and grew up. So much sadness in her life, looking after the twins from such a young age. It's time someone looked after her."

He was spared the further embarrassment of this conversation by the sound of footsteps coming down the stairs.

"We have a guest. A very nice young man. Isma sent him." The footsteps retreated up the stairs and the old woman's voice dropped. "Aneeka. She'll come down again once she's fixed herself up. In my days either you were the kind of girl who covered your head or you were the kind who wore makeup. Now everyone is everything at the same time."

He had been about to leave, but instead he reached for another samosa. A few minutes later, the footsteps approached again. The woman who walked in was smaller than he'd expected from the picture—petite, really, and without any of the sense of mischief he'd seen in the photograph—but just as beautiful. Eamonn stood up, conscious of his greasy fingers and of the question of how he might use them to unpin the white hijab that framed her face. She greeted him with a puzzled look, which confirmed how unlikely it was for Isma to have sent someone like him to meet her family. The old lady introduced him by his first name—which was all he had given her—and Aneeka's expression didn't so much change as ossify.

"That's spelled with an *e*, not an *a*, Aunty. Eamonn Lone, isn't it?"

"Isma told you about me?"

"What do you want here? Why do you know my sister?"

"He met Isma in Northampton. At a café," the old woman said,

coming to stand next to Eamonn and place a hand on his arm, looking at him apologetically, not only for the girl's behavior but for her own "oh" of disappointment when the girl mentioned his surname. "He walked all the way from Notting Hill to bring me M&M's from Isma. Along the canal."

The beautiful girl looked at the envelope with Isma's handwriting on it and then at him, her face confused.

"It's a lovely walk. The canal flows above the North Circular, along an aqueduct. I never knew that. The IRA tried to bomb it in 1939. It would have flooded all of Wembley." He had no idea if this last detail was actually true, but he wanted to say something interesting so the girl would see that he might be the kind of person her sister would choose to have coffee with, not just the posh toff who seemed so out of place in this kitchen and in Isma's life. "You can see news footage about it. Just search for 'north circular canal bomb' or something like that and it'll come up."

"Right—because that's a good idea if you're GWM, isn't it?"

"I don't know what that is."

"Googling While Muslim. Aunty, did Isma tell you anything about this person?"

"Why don't we all call her now?" Aunty Naseem said brightly, and the girl—who made less sense with every second—said, "Please stop trying to make me speak to her. Anyway, I have to go out now. And Mr. Lone, since you've delivered the M&M's you can leave with me."

Despite Aunty's noises of protest, he followed the girl out. She didn't say anything until they were at the end of the street, and then she turned sharply on her heels to face him.

"What's going on here?"

"I really don't know what you mean," he said, holding up his hands. "I was just delivering a package for Isma. As your . . . aunty said, we met in a café. In Massachusetts. Became friends, sort of. Two-Brits-abroad kind of thing."

A man in a bright red suit that appeared not to have been washed in several years stopped next to Aneeka and held out a filthy square of fur. "Have you met my cat?"

Before Eamonn could chivalrously interpose himself, Aneeka was reaching out to stroke the matted fur as if it were the smoothest mink. "Of course I've met Mog, Charlie. She and I are old friends." The man made happy noises, tucked the fur into his jacket against his heart, and carried on.

After that moment of gentleness, the harshness of her voice when she turned her attention back to him was particularly unsettling. "That doesn't explain why she asked you to come here."

"She didn't. I offered to post it." He couldn't imagine articulating to this woman his curiosity about a lost piece of his father, so instead he said, "Okay, this is embarrassing, but I saw a photograph of Isma's sister, and wanted to know if anyone could really look that beautiful in person."

She gave him precisely the look of disgust he deserved for such a statement, and strode away without another word.

||||||||||||||||||||

The train pulled out of Preston Road station, and he turned in his seat to look out at the houses alongside the tracks. Beyond the back wall

and garden sheds of one property a girl flew up, hovered for a moment, fell, flew up again. A trampoline. She made her body a starfish, and though he knew she couldn't see him, he raised his own hands to mirror hers. He continued to look through the window after the train picked up speed and left Preston Road behind.

When he finally turned to face forward, a woman standing farther along the mostly empty carriage came over and sat next to him.

"Do you live alone?" Aneeka said.

"Yes."

"Take me there."

||||||||||||||||||||||||

After the boldness of that line, she barely spoke all the way from Preston Road to Notting Hill. At first he tried to fill the silence with conversation about Isma, but her response made it clear theirs was not the relationship of closeness Isma had portrayed. "Did she tell you—" he started to say, and she replied, "I'm discovering the list of things Isma hasn't told me is far longer than I would have believed," which made any further conversation along that line impossible.

On the walk from the tube station to his home she looked around like a tourist, and he was embarrassed by the affluence of the neighborhood he lived in while unemployed. It was an embarrassment not aided by entering his flat, which was paid for and decorated by his mother, with its central open-plan space that combined kitchen, living room, and dining area in an expanse that could double as a playing field and provoked Aneeka to say, "You really live here alone?"

He nodded, offered her tea or coffee. She asked for coffee, before

turning to walk the length of his flat, looking at the framed photographs on his shelves—family picture, graduation picture, his friends Max and Alice's engagement-party picture.

"One of these your girlfriend?" she asked, looking up from the last photograph.

He was all the way at the other end of the flat, by the coffee machine, but his emphatic "No, I'm single" would have carried down a room twice as long. He waited for her to return to the kitchen end and slide onto a high stool at the counter before asking, "And you? Boyfriend?"

She shook her head, dipped a finger into the coffee foam, checking its depth, didn't meet his eye. *Why are you here?* didn't seem like a question he could ask, and might make her leave, which he didn't think he wanted, although it was hard to know what to want of a silent, beautiful woman in a hijab sipping coffee in your flat.

"Isma prefers turbans," he said, to say something, indicating her head covering.

She unpinned the hijab, folded it carefully, and placed it between the two of them on the counter, then pulled off the tight-fitting cap beneath it. She shook her head slightly and her hair, long and dark, fell about her shoulders like something out of a shampoo advertisement. She looked at him, expectant.

Eamonn knew what to do when a woman asked to come home with him and began to undress. It was not a situation he was unfamiliar with. But he didn't know if this was that situation. Though what was it, if not that?

He leaned forward, placed one elbow on the counter, and ex-

tended the rest of his arm across the glass-topped distance between them, palm up, resting it close enough to her hand to be an invitation, but distant enough to be ignored without too much awkwardness. She downed the rest of the coffee in a gulp, wiped the back of her hand across her mouth, which slightly smeared her lipstick, and placed the hand on his wrist. Coffee foam and lipstick on her skin. He was conscious of the hammering of his heart, the pulse leaping out at her. She smiled then, finally. Taking his other hand, she placed it on her breast but over her shirt. That too was confusing until he realized, no, not her breast, she had placed his hand on her heart, which was beating frantically too.

"We match," she said, and the promise of her voice made the situation familiar, and thrillingly new.

iiiiiiiiiiiiiiiiiiii

The next morning, he is pressing his nose against the sofa, breathing in the smell of her. All these surfaces of his home—walls, bed, sofa— marked with her scent. He walks from one surface to the next, his senses still filled with her.

He glances around the room. How is it possible that it appears exactly the same as yesterday? It should look as though a storm has been through. There should be broken vases, torn blinds, upturned furniture. Something to mirror this feeling of turmoil, of everything having changed. He stands in front of the mirror, touches the scratch on his shoulder as though it's a holy relic. At least there's this. Cups his hands and lifts them to his face, breathing in. His personal act of prayer.

To start with she'd been hesitant, tentative. During their first kiss, she'd broken away and started to put her hijab back on, before his entreaties convinced her to stay. Then things swung the other way, and she seemed to think she had to prove to him that she really wanted to stay, in the way of a certain kind of adolescent girl who had always made him uncomfortable in his teenage years—the ones who thought they were required to give to the older boys without anything in return. So he stopped her, showed that wasn't how this would work, and she said, "You're nice," as if that was a surprise, and they set about discovering each other in that slow-quick way of new lovers—testing, exploring, building on what each was learning about the other.

At daybreak he woke to discover she'd risen from the bed, to which they'd finally made their way. Hearing the sound of the shower, so early, he thought she was planning to leave without saying goodbye. But when she left the bathroom her footsteps didn't move in the direction of the door. Eventually he swung himself out of bed and walked into the living room to find her praying, a towel as her prayer mat, the hijab nothing more alien than a scarf loosely covering her head without the elaborate pinning or the tightly fitted cap beneath. She made no sign of being aware of him except a slight adjustment of her shoulders, angling away from his naked form. He should have left immediately, but he couldn't help watching this woman, this stranger, prostrating herself to God in the room where she'd been down on her knees for a very different purpose just hours earlier. Finally, the depth of her immersion in a world other than that of bodies and senses made him go back to the bed, wondering if she'd return.

"What were you praying for?" he asked when she came back in and started to unbutton her long-sleeved shirt, starting at the base of her neck.

"Prayer isn't about transaction, Mr. Capitalist. It's about starting the day right."

"You had to put on a bra for God?" he said, as she unbuttoned further, needing her to laugh with him about it. "Did you think He might get distracted by your . . . distractions?"

"You do other things better than you do talk."

That burned in ways both good and bad. He held back from mentioning that he could say the same for her. When openings for conversation had arisen she preferred to pillow her head in her arms and look up at the ceiling, or doze with her back to him, the soles of her feet pressed against his legs, combining rejection and intimacy. He watched as she continued to undress until there was nothing left but the white scarf covering her head, one end of the soft fabric falling just below her breast, the other thrown over her shoulder.

"Leave this on?" she said. He had learned already that everything new she offered was posed as a question. It was not because she doubted his desire, as he'd thought the first time, but because it seemed important to her to hear the "yes," its tones of want and need. Now he hesitated, though his body's reactions were answer enough as she touched her nipple through the white cotton, colors contrasting. He reached a hand out to her, but she stepped back and repeated the question. "Yes," he said, "please."

Now he picks the white fabric off the sofa, wraps it around himself

like a loincloth, beats his chest, and makes gorilla sounds. Just before leaving she had put on that tight-fitting object she referred to as a "bonnet cap," ignoring his comment that this was as superfluous a name as "chai tea" or "na'an bread," and taken a blue scarf from his hall closet, which she started to wrap around her head. "Why'd you have to do that?" he said, and she brushed the end of the scarf against his throat and said, "I get to choose which parts of me I want strangers to look at, and which are for you." He had liked that. Against his will, against his own self, he had liked it. Dumb ape.

After breakfast they lay together on the sofa in a square of sunlight, and either the dimensions of the cushions, or the thought that she soon had to leave, made her finally curl up against him, her head on his chest.

"So, Isma," he said tentatively. "She speaks about you as if you're close."

There was silence for a while, and he wondered if mentioning Isma had been a bad idea. He felt strangely guilty about her; straitlaced, pious Isma. She wouldn't approve of what they had done here. If he was thinking that, surely Aneeka was too. He threaded his fingers through her hair, wondered if her sister's disapproval would be a reason for her never to come to him again, held her tighter.

"We used to be close," she said. "But now I don't want her anywhere near my life. Are you in touch with her?"

"Not since I left. But I thought I'd drop her a line to say I'd been to Aunty Naseem's. Why, would you rather I wasn't in touch with her?"

"Would you do that for me if I asked?"

"I think I would do any number of outrageous things for you if

you asked," he said, tracing a beauty mark on the back of her hand. "But don't give me too much credit for this one—it's not as if she's written to me. I think we both recognize it was just one of those holiday friendships which there's no point trying to carry into the rest of your life." The complication of fathers was not an issue he felt any need to bring up while they were lying naked together.

There was another stretch of silence, then she said, "When I leave, will you want to see me again?"

"That can't possibly be a serious question."

"If this is something that's continuing, then I do want you to do something outrageous for me. Let me be your secret."

"How do you mean?"

She placed her open palm against his face and dragged it slowly down. "I won't tell anyone about you, you don't tell anyone about me. We'll be each other's secret."

"Why?"

"I don't ask 'why' about your fantasies, do I?" she said, sliding a bare thigh between his legs.

"Oh, this is a fantasy, is it?" Distracted by the beginnings of a rocking motion she was making, the friction of her skin against his.

"I don't want my friends wanting to know when they can meet you. I don't want Aunty Naseem inviting you round for a meal. I don't want Isma thinking she can use you as a conduit to me. I don't want other people interpreting us. I don't want you wanting any of those things either. Just want me, here, with you. Say yes."

"Yes." Yes, yes, yes.

||||||||||||||||||||

Over the next few days he discovered her version of secrecy meant he didn't have her phone number, couldn't contact her online (couldn't find her there, in fact), wasn't permitted to know when she was planning to come and go. She'd simply turn up at some point in the day, sometimes staying for so short a time they never even got completely undressed, other times remaining overnight. Secrecy was an aphrodisiac that gained potency the longer it continued, every moment filled with the possibility that she might appear, so there was no time when he was away from home that he didn't want to return there, and no moment at home when he didn't race to the front door at every imagined footstep, every pressed buzzer. Soon he found himself almost incapable of thinking about anything but her. And not just the sex, though he thought about that often enough. The other things also: the concentration with which she brushed her teeth, her fingers tapping on the sink, counting out the number of strokes up and down and to the side; her habit of spraying on his aftershave before showering, claiming the scent would linger under the shower gel, so subtle only she would know it; the way her face transformed into a cartoon— eyes narrowed, lips pressed together, nose wrinkled—when she ate slices of lemon with salt with her morning tea; the precision with which she followed recipes, one tooth biting her lip as she measured out ingredients, even while praising his skill at culinary improvisation. Aneeka drying her hair with a towel, Aneeka balanced cross-legged on a kitchen stool, Aneeka's face settling into contentment when he took hold of her feet and massaged them.

In the beginning, he was afraid she might choose simply to stop coming around one day. There was a skittishness to her manner, now passionate, now distant. Once she'd even broken off at a moment that left him crying out in dismay to say, "No, I can't," dressing quickly and leaving, refusing to explain. He suspected it was her God and His demands that made her want to deny what she clearly had no wish to be denied; he knew he couldn't win an argument on that score, so there was nothing to do but stay quiet and trust that her headstrong nature ensured that no abstract entity would set the rules for her life.

Sometimes he thought of calling Isma, just to speak to someone who knew Aneeka, just to hear her name. But Aneeka didn't want him to, and he wasn't going to get caught in the rupture between sisters that, it turned out, centered around some issue of inheritance. "There was something that belonged to me. She had some claim on it, but mostly it was mine. From our mother. And she took it away from me." Although he couldn't believe that Isma would steal something, he could imagine her deciding to sell some family heirloom for financial reasons and seeing no reason to discuss it with the sister whom she sometimes spoke of as though she were still a child in need of parenting.

"And what does your brother say about this?" he asked.

In Eamonn's mind this brother—Parvaiz—was a slippery ghost, sometimes an ally, sometimes a rival. The slipperiness came from the fractured nature of Aneeka's stories about him. In her tales of growing up he was her ever-present partner in crime, the shadow who sometimes strode ahead, sometimes followed behind, without ever becoming detached from their twinness, an introspective boy who

disapproved of her relationships ("always with older boys, of course") but helped her keep them hidden from her sister and Aunty Naseem, while remaining perpetually in love with one or another of Aneeka's friends, who all insisted they loved him as a brother. (Eamonn knew well the pain of this, thanks to his sister's childhood friend Tilly, of the long legs and bee-stung lips—"I don't want to know about it," Aneeka said, which was a balm to her mention of the older boys.) But after school, their lives diverged. Unlike Aneeka, Parvaiz hadn't received any scholarships; unwilling to start his adult life by taking on crippling loans, he'd instead gone traveling, in the time-honored fashion of drifting British boys. Here he disappeared from her stories.

"I haven't told him what she did. When he comes back, I will."

"And when is he coming back?"

She shrugged, and continued clicking through the photographs on his computer, watching his life from childhood to the present day—all the family holidays, all the girlfriends, all the hairstyles and fashion choices and unguarded moments.

"I can't actually tell if you're on better terms with him than you are with your sister."

She zoomed in on a picture of Eamonn with his arm around his father's shoulder, both in matching T-shirts with the words LONE STAR written on them, the resemblance between them everywhere, from smile to stance. Unlike her sister, Aneeka didn't seem to have much of an opinion of his father as a political figure, and he sometimes wondered if she'd been too young when her own father had died to have been told what Karamat Lone had said about him.

"He knew Isma was leaving and then he went and left too. It's nothing I won't forgive when he comes back. Until then, I'm holding it against him."

It struck him as unfair to take issue with a nineteen-year-old boy wanting to see the world instead of sitting at home keeping his sister company. But then Aneeka clicked to the next photograph—the Lone parents and children hamming it up for the camera in Addams Family Halloween costumes—and he reminded himself that growing up an orphan obviously created an interdependence between siblings that he, with his affectionate yet disengaged relationship to his sister, couldn't understand.

There was, in fact, a great deal about her he didn't understand. Most days that was part of her allure, but one morning, less than two weeks after they'd first met, he woke up resentful. The previous afternoon he had returned from the bakery around the corner to find a note she'd slipped through the communal letter slot in the front door saying "Was here. Left." He canceled his evening plans in case she came back, but she hadn't, and all that secrecy he'd been enjoying suddenly seemed a tiresome game in which she held all the power. Impulsively, he packed his bags for a week away and caught the train to an old school friend's home in Norfolk. To begin with, he enjoyed the thought of her returning repeatedly to his front door only to find him gone. Let her know what it felt like to be the one who did the waiting around. But on the second night, when his hosts were asleep, he called his father's personal assistant and asked him to find a cab company nearby that could get him back to London.

He arrived home at nearly three a.m., half asleep as he came up the stairs to his front door, and saw a figure curled up on the landing, his doormat rolled up as a pillow. He crouched down next to her, and when she opened her eyes her relief was both shaming and thrilling.

Once they were inside he walked straight to the living room, withdrew a set of keys from a ceramic bowl on a shelf, and handed it to her, saying it was hers to use anytime, day or night. She butted her head against his shoulder and said, "Don't be this nice." He asked her what she meant and she replied by kissing him, slow and intense.

Something shifted between them that night. When he woke up the next morning and walked toward the sound of Aneeka making breakfast in the kitchen, she left off blending a smoothie to show him the chart she'd made of all the blocks of time when he shouldn't expect to see her—times when she was on campus, or in study groups, or the Wednesday evenings when Aunty Naseem insisted on a family dinner, and any day between three and five p.m. "Why not then?" he said, and she nipped his shoulder and said, "Let a woman hold on to her mystique!"

"Okay, okay. Block out Sunday afternoons too," he said.

She kissed his shoulder where she had nipped at it. "The weekly Lone family lunch in Holland Park. Is it very civilized? Do you say 'please' and 'thank you' and 'sorry' and talk about the weather?"

"Why don't you come some Sunday and see for yourself."

She stepped back. She was wearing nothing but his T-shirt, and the tightening of her shoulders transformed the look from sexy to vulnerable. So she did know about her father and his. He caught her hands in his, reassuring them both that they could survive the conversation he

knew they had to have. "I know that'll be difficult for you. Isma told me. About your father. And about what my father said about him."

"You know about my father?"

"Yes."

"Why did she tell you? We don't talk about that to anyone."

"If you ever speak to her again you could ask."

She walked away, poured out a smoothie, left it next to the blender, and returned to him. Shoulders still held in, looking at him with some of the mistrust she'd shown at their first meeting.

"Who else did she tell you about?"

"What do you mean?"

"Not who else. I meant what else. What else did she tell you about him?"

"It's okay," he said, touching her hand. "It'll be okay. You never even met him. No one will judge you by him."

"Not even your father?" She sat down on one of the high stools next to the kitchen counter, looking at him very seriously.

"Especially not him. He says you are what you make of yourself." He raised and lowered his shoulders. "Unless you're his son. Then he indulges you even if you don't make anything of yourself."

"He indulges you?"

"Yes. My sister's like him, so she gets all the expectation. I get the pampering and the free passes."

"Do you mind that?"

"I mind a lot. And you're the first person to ever guess that might be the case."

She hooked her feet around the back of his legs and drew him to

her. "I never held it against your father that he said what he did about mine. He was right—we were all better off without Adil Pasha. But now I mind. Because when I think about it, he comes across as unforgiving. I don't like the idea of you having a father who is unforgiving. I want to know he's different with you." She kept kissing him as she spoke, light kisses on his mouth, his neck, his jaw, slightly frantic.

He drew back, took her hands in his. "It's fine to talk about this. It's true, he can be unforgiving, particularly of people who betray his country."

"What if you were the one asking him to do the forgiving?"

"You want me to ask him to find out what he can about your father?" But she was shaking her head emphatically. No, she didn't want to know. Her father was nothing to her   it was her grandmother who had needed to know what had happened to her son; maybe her mother, maybe Isma. But not her, not Aneeka. She wanted to know about him, about Eamonn. She would like to have a picture of what it meant to be Karamat Lone's son beyond what the photo album revealed.

"He's one kind of person as a politician. Another kind as a father. There's nothing he wouldn't do for me."

"That's good," she said, a new note in her voice, one he couldn't place. "That's how it should be." She put her arms around him, and he tried to ignore how relieved he felt at knowing she didn't expect him to raise the issue of her father with the home secretary. Of course if this continued—and he desperately wanted it to—Eamonn would eventually have to tell his father that he was involved with the daughter of a jihadi. Not now, though, not yet. Let Aneeka's game of secrecy allow things to remain simple for as long as they could.

IIIIIIIIIIIIIIIIIII

The weeks went by. Life adjusted around the rules she set. In the hours when he knew Aneeka wouldn't visit, he went to the gym, did his shopping, dropped in on his mother to prevent her dropping in on him. He fired his cleaning lady, who also worked for his parents, claiming it was a temporary situation until he started earning again— then hired someone else, whose details he found in a corner shop window. In the time he had at home without her he started learning Urdu, the difficulty of it made worthwhile by her delight in his growing vocabulary, which she augmented with words no online tutorial would ever teach. She started e-mailing him surprisingly interesting articles related to contract law, and they were both pleased to discover that his short time in the working world had given him insights she wouldn't necessarily find in course reading. They cooked together, alternating roles of chef and sous-chef with perfect good cheer. Parallel to all this, his friends' teasing about his "double life" faded away— as did their invitations to join them on weekends in the country, Friday evenings in the pub, picnics in the park, and dinners within the two-mile radius in which they all lived. He knew it was a paramount failure of friendship to disappear into a relationship, but to be in his friends' company now felt like stepping back into the aimlessness that had characterized his life before Aneeka came along and became both focus and direction.

"When you're ready for reentry let us know," his ex-girlfriend, Alice, now engaged to his best friend, Max, said sympathetically one Wednesday evening when he was over at their place with the rest of

the old school gaggle, the discomfort of the patio furniture dulled by Pimm's. A few glasses in he learned that his friends had decided he was in a slump brought on by unemployment, his feeling of failure exacerbated by his father's continued conquest of the world. This midweek gathering in Brook Green, consequence of Alice calling up and demanding a date from him, was an intervention. Helen recommended a doctor who would prescribe pills without making a fuss, Hari invited him to join a rowing club on the Thames, Will offered to set him up with a "fantastic" work colleague who wouldn't expect anything serious, Alice proffered a job in her family's PR company, and Max rested a hand on his shoulder and reminded Eamonn that he was as good at listening as he was at creating distractions.

"I love you all," he said, meaning it. He felt in love with everything: the Pimm's, the furniture, the ironic gnomes in the garden, the sky with its bands of sunset colors. "But I'm really fine. Just doing my own thing, under the radar."

"I don't know," Max said. "Twenty-something unemployed male from Muslim background exhibits rapidly altered pattern of behavior, cuts himself off from old friends, moves under the radar. Also, are we sure that's an evening shadow rather than an incipient beard? I think we may need to alert the authorities."

"Take it straight to the home secretary," Hari said. "At least he's drinking Pimm's, so we know we haven't lost him completely."

He hardly drank anymore. Aneeka hadn't told him not to, but the first time he'd moved in for a kiss with alcohol on his breath she'd recoiled. Even after he'd brushed his teeth, she said she could still

smell it. "Sorry," she'd said. "We can do the other things, but just don't kiss me." That distilled the issue in a way that made only one outcome possible. He leaned back in his chair, looked at his friends and tried to imagine walking into this garden with Aneeka—the hijab, the refusal of alcohol, Wembley. Everyone would be perfectly polite, but at some point the following day, either Max or Alice would call him up to say, "Lovely girl. I hope she didn't mind our sense of humor?" No relationship had ever withstood "hope she didn't mind our sense of humor."

"What would you have done if I had walked in with a full beard?" he said, picking a piece of apple out of his Pimm's and chucking it at Max.

Alice made one of those annoying humming sounds of hers that was meant to, and did, stop Max from reacting, and came around to pull Eamonn's head to her stomach, stroking his hair as if he were a child.

"We'd hold you down and shave it off, my darling. Friends don't let friends become hipsters." It was the kind of glib answer he'd previously have found amusing, but now he was impatient with it, with her, with the stale dynamic of all of them. What was the point of surrounding yourself with other versions of yourself all the time?

He allowed Alice to hold his head against her almost concave stomach, so that his friends could exchange whatever glances they needed to, and all the while he was thinking, before Aneeka there was Alice. This body, these hands, this scent. Less than two months after it ended he had given his blessing when Max wanted all that for himself, and he'd meant it. How had he ever imagined what he'd felt was passion,

let alone love? Before Aneeka, there was only the facade of feeling. And now he was in so deep that everyone but Aneeka was blurred and indistinct, poor creatures of the surface, their voices receding.

⸻

Every so often there were times she would switch out of the frequency of their relationship. That was the only way he knew to describe it to himself; a sudden transformation, as if an elbow had accidentally pressed against a radio button and, mid-note, jazz became static. She'd turn cold, or sad, sometimes angry, and any attempts to talk to her about it were futile. One particularly strange night he woke up in the early hours of the morning to see her standing at the foot of the bed, staring at him with one of her unreadable expressions. When he called to her she said, "Go back to sleep and tell yourself you dreamed it." He tried talking to her instead—demanding to know what was wrong, made angry by his own inexplicable fear—and she ended up leaving, Eamonn following her on the street in boxers and flip-flops to make sure she was safe until a cab came along and she stepped into it.

Worse followed just a few days later. They were having a languorous afternoon, lying on a thick-pile rug, playing favorite songs from their childhood for each other, swapping stories of growing up. Aneeka was teasing him gently for thinking that his was the more "normal" life despite his millionaire parents, both of whom regularly appeared in the newspapers. The trace unpleasantness of that strange night had finally disappeared, and they were both grateful for this return to happiness, slightly silly with each other. Her mouth against his

arm, blowing out to make trumpetlike noises in time with the music, when her phone announced an incoming Skype call. She always ignored calls, no matter who it was—from one particular expression of distaste he guessed it was often Isma—but even so, she had to check her screen when she heard the sound.

"You're not going to answer it. Stop with the Pavlovian response," he said, pretending to grab for her ankle as she scrambled to her feet. He was too lazy, though, to turn and watch her reach for the phone. The next track that came on was one he loved and hadn't heard in ages, and he turned up the volume and sang along. It was a few seconds before he realized she had left the room, and he went in search of her to apologize for raising the volume just as she answered the phone, which is what must have driven her away.

She wasn't in the hall or the bedroom, but the bathroom door was closed and through it he could hear sounds but not the words they formed. He stepped up to the door and put his ear to it.

"I'm making sure of things here," he heard her say.

At the end of the sentence her voice seemed to move closer to the door, and he backed away and quickly returned to the living room. It was a long time before she joined him there, and when she did her eyes were bloodshot, as if she'd been crying, but also glinting with a kind of frenzy that he'd only ever known in the manic or the high.

"Who were you talking to?" he said.

"One day you'll know," she replied. She burst into laughter and wrapped her arms around him. "Soon, please God, soon."

She was a weight against him, unwanted, clinging. In that moment he could imagine not loving her; he could imagine wanting her gone

from his life, with her secrets and her strangeness, her swerves of mood, the sheer inconvenience of her. But then she pulled away, put a hand over her eyes, and when she looked at him again she was Aneeka once more.

"I'm acting a little crazy, aren't I?" she said. "I'm sorry. Please bear with me. Please." She rested the back of her hand against his cheek, a touch he'd never had from her before. He bowed his head and rested it against hers, a moment of love between them that made all obstacles surmountable, even the ones around her heart.

4

Cocooned in white sofa cushions and the sound of rain outside, Eamonn watched a man dancing on the top of a train, declaring in Urdu, with subtitles, that if your head is in the shade of love then surely your feet are in paradise. It was a sentiment Eamonn would have sung along with, trying to get the accent right by the time Aneeka arrived, but today the world was sitting a little too heavily on his shoulders. He clicked out of the video and returned to the clip of his father addressing the students at a predominantly Muslim school in Bradford, which counted among its alumni Karamat Lone himself and two twenty-year-olds who had been killed by American airstrikes in Syria earlier in the year. There he was, no notes in hand, the lectern ignored as he stood front and center on the stage, the old school tie drawing attention to how little he'd changed physically from the head boy whose image was projected onto the screen behind him, other than a graying around the temples, a deepening of character in his face. "There is nothing this country won't allow you to achieve— Olympic medals, captaincy of the cricket team, pop stardom, reality TV crowns. And if none of that works out, you can settle for being

home secretary. You are, we are, British. Britain accepts this. So do most of you. But for those of you who are in some doubt about it, let me say this: Don't set yourself apart in the way you dress, the way you think, the outdated codes of behavior you cling to, the ideologies to which you attach your loyalties. Because if you do, you will be treated differently—not because of racism, though that does still exist, but because you insist on your difference from everyone else in this multi-ethnic, multireligious, multitudinous United Kingdom of ours. And look at all you miss out on because of it."

More than twenty-four hours after the speech that ended with those sentences, the media attention had barely died down. Across the political spectrum, except at its extreme edges, the home secretary was being lionized for his truth-telling, his passion, the fearlessness with which he was willing to take on both the antimigrant attitudes of his own party and the isolationist culture of the community he'd grown up in. #YouAreWeAreBritish was trending on social media, as were #Wolfpack and its Asian offshoot, #Wolfpak. The phrase "future prime minister" was everywhere.

The Eamonn of a month ago would have been proud. Now, he kept imagining a meme of his father's voice saying "Don't set yourself apart in the way you dress" played over a video of Aneeka standing up from her prayer mat and walking into his embrace, shedding her clothes along the way until only the hijab remained. The video wouldn't reveal the things that were most striking about her in those moments: the intensity of her concentration, how completely it could swerve from her God to him in the time she took those few footsteps, or her

total lack of self-consciousness in everything she did—love and prayer, the covered head and the naked body. He heard the door open— Aneeka entered and called out from the hallway to say she was taking a shower.

He no longer had feelings of dread if she didn't turn up when he expected, or of relief when she did—he had come to accept that he was who she wanted to be with. The joy of that moved through the days with him, burnishing every moment, even this one in which he stretched out on his sofa, listening to the different tones of the rain— clattering against windows, slapping against leaves, pinging off bricks. In Aneeka's company he'd learned to listen to the sounds of the world. "Hear that," she used to say in the beginning, somewhere between a command and a question. Soon he learned the pleasure of being the one to say it to her, hear that, the London we never enter together: the lawn mower rattling against pebbles at the edges of the garden; the differing weight of vehicles on the street outside—the swoosh of the motorcycle, the trundle of the van; the voices of drunk English lovers, matched in pitch though not in tone by caffeinated Italian tourists. Hear that, the varied creaks of the bed frame: the short cry of disappointment when you leave, the long groan of pleasure when you return. Hear that, the quickening of my breath, my blood, when you touch me, just so. At her urging, he started to record snippets of the time he spent without her, playing them back and asking her to identify the sounds he linked together to form a narrative of life without her: tube barriers opening and closing, his mother's pruning shears cutting through stems in the rose garden, the heavy thud of the door

to the newly constructed panic room in his parents' house, a row of men on treadmills at the gym engaging in unacknowledged competitions of speed and stamina, conversations with the interactive Urdu learning tutorial, his hand bringing himself to climax while he thought of her. When he asked her why she didn't bring him the soundscape of her days, she shrugged and said he'd have to think up a game of his own for her to play, he couldn't simply borrow hers. But his mind didn't know how to do that.

"Caught in the rain?" he said, going over to kiss her when she entered the room in his blue-and-white-striped dressing gown, carrying an armload of wet clothes. She pulled away almost immediately, holding up the wet clothes as explanation. When she'd deposited them in the dryer, she sat down on one of the stools at the kitchen counter, and he walked over to dry her hair with a towel.

"Does anyone give you a hard time because of the hijab?" he said.

She tilted her head back to rest it against his chest and look up at him. "If you're nineteen and female you'll get some version of a hard time for whatever you wear. Mostly it's the kind of thing that's easy to shrug off. Sometimes things happen that make people more hostile. Terrorist attacks involving European victims. Home secretaries talking about people setting themselves apart in the way they dress. That kind of thing." He didn't say anything to that, just gripped a fistful of her hair and squeezed while moving his hand down along the length of it, water dripping onto the wood floor. "And no, I wasn't showering because I got caught in the rain. Some guy spat at me on the tube."

"Some guy what?"

She swiveled the stool around. "What do you say to your father

when he makes a speech like that? Do you say, 'Dad, you're making it okay to stigmatize people for the way they dress'? Do you say, 'What kind of idiot stands in front of a group of teenagers and tells them to conform'? Do you say, 'Why didn't you mention that among the things this country will let you achieve if you're Muslim is torture, rendition, detention without trial, airport interrogations, spies in your mosques, teachers reporting your children to the authorities for wanting a world without British injustice'?"

"Wait, wait. Stop it. My father would never . . ." He had never heard her speak of any of this since the first time they met, when she'd made her Googling While Muslim comment, which he'd managed to put out of his mind until now. "Do you think he doesn't know what it is to face down racists? He wants people like you to suffer less from them, not more. That's why he said what he did, even if it wasn't the best way of phrasing it."

A small, sad smile. "'People like you'?"

"That came out wrong."

"No, I don't think it did. There are people like me and people like you. I've always known it. Why do you think I did all this 'Let's be secret' stuff? I wouldn't have lasted five minutes in your life if you had to tell your family and friends about me."

"I know." The admission surprised them both. "But that was before. Now if the world wants to divide into Aneeka and everyone else, there's no question where I'm standing. Or kneeling, which is really what I'd like to do right now, but I don't know if you're anywhere near ready for me to do that."

"Do what?"

"I just proposed proposing to you."

For a moment he thought he'd made a terrible mistake, Aneeka looking at him as though he'd said the craziest thing in the world. And then her mouth was on his, his hands on her shower-warm skin, everything he wanted in the world right here, right now, this woman, this life, this completeness.

|||||||||||||||||||||

Although they never went as far as the private communal garden, the flat roof jutting out a few feet from Eamonn's bedroom window, which he'd failed to turn into a terrace in the four years he'd lived here, had become a favorite retreat. With a little nudging from Aneeka, he had bought a variety of tall plants—cactus, chili, kumquat—which they placed along the edge of the roof, and although they shut out the view of the gardens below, they also made privacy possible while alfresco.

The morning after the "proposed proposal," as she enjoyed calling it, they sat outdoors pitting cherries for jam, the sun beating down almost as palpably as the previous day's rain. Eamonn in a pair of khaki shorts and Aneeka once again in the blue-and-white dressing gown, now hiked above her knees. The concrete warm on their skin as they sat cross-legged at the very edge of the janglingly colorful floor cushions that had been her way of objecting to the muted tones of Eamonn's flat. She'd carried them in a couple of weeks earlier, her glare daring him to comment on the fact that she was claiming his space as hers, as he'd wanted her to do almost from the start. He placed a cherry in his mouth, considered kissing her, the cherry passing be-

tween them, but settled for watching her instead, enjoying her evident satisfaction at the clean workings of the cherry pitter she'd mocked not an hour earlier as an accessory of the rich who don't know what else to do with their money. *It's a cherry pitter. It pits cherries. How is that some wild extravagance?* In response she'd opened a kitchen drawer and held up one utensil after another: *A cherry pitter to pit cherries, a garlic peeler to peel garlic, a potato masher to mash potatoes, a lemon zester to zest lemons, an apple corer to core apples.* She'd grinned at him. *All you need is basic cutlery and a little know-how.* But here she was now, making a small satisfied noise with every cherry pit she neatly punched out using the gadget in her hand. She'd gathered up the dark weight of her hair and twisted it into a loose knot at the base of her neck. A temptation to tug just so and watch it tumble down.

"Whatever you're thinking, the answer is, not until we've finished with the cherries."

He grinned, stretched out a leg, laid it over her knee, part of her thigh, and picked up the knife he was using to cut into the cherries and flip out the stones with his thumb. "This reminds me of a summer holiday in Tuscany when I was ten or eleven. Cherries and gelato, that's all my sister and I ate the whole summer. At least in my memory."

"What do people do when they go away on holiday? Other than eat cherries and gelato."

"You've never . . . ?"

"There was a trip to Rome once, the year before my mother died. The travel agency she worked for gave her free tickets—but it felt more like a school trip than a holiday. She thought we should see as many sights and spend as little money as possible."

"What was she like, your mother?"

"Stressed. Always. It's what killed her. Isma said she used to be different—when my grandfather was alive and paying the bills, when my father wasn't yet a terrorist who could have us all driven out of our homes if any of us said the wrong thing to the wrong person."

"I really don't know how you survived your childhood."

"Didn't feel like it was something that needed surviving until she died. Everything else you can live around, but not death. Death you have to live through." She smiled, shrugged. "But then again, no one told me I was missing out on holidays with cherries and gelato raining down. If I'd known that, I would have been much more disgruntled."

"Well, we should go somewhere together. As soon as your summer holidays start." She gave him the look of exasperation he was accustomed to receiving every time he suggested anything that involved leaving his flat. "Come on, it's time we entered the world together. We can start with Max and Alice rather than my parents if you want to ease into things. And isn't it time you told Isma? Maybe even that brother of yours?"

"Not yet," she said.

Exasperated, he threw a cherry pit into the bowl with such force that it bounced out and landed on the dressing gown, leaving a crimson stain on a white stripe.

"Let's go back to pretending it's a game," she said, flicking the stone onto his bare leg. "Who needs other people? Who needs to leave London on a vacation when everything we want is right here in this flat?"

"I'm not bloody spending my summer locked up in here. Neither

are you. Come to Tuscany with me. Come to Bali. You don't want other people, fine. We'll find a remote island somewhere."

"If we try to leave the country together the people who work for your father will know." At his puzzled look: "MI5. They listen in on my phone calls, they monitor my messages, my Internet history. You think they'll think it's innocent if I board a plane to Bali with the home secretary's son?"

It was a mark of his love for her that he felt nothing other than protective about the Muslim paranoia she'd revealed the previous day. Gently he said, "My love, I promise you MI5 isn't watching you because of your father."

"I know. They're watching me because of my brother. Ever since he went to Syria, to Raqqa, last year."

"I don't understand," he said automatically.

"Yes you do."

He rubbed at the cherry mark on his leg. It was something to do while his brain sat inert in his skull, offering him nothing that would make this explicable.

"He's fighting there?"

"Parvaiz, fighting? God, no! He's with their media unit."

Their. The black-and-white flag, the British-accented men who stood beneath it and sliced men's heads off their shoulders. And the media unit, filming it all.

He stood up, walked to the edge of the roof. As far from her as it was possible to go. In his life he'd never known anything like this feeling—rage? fear? What is it, make it stop. He kicked out, knocked over the kumquat tree. Shoved with his hands, toppled the cactus

plant. The kumquat fell straight, flower pot shattering as it hit the ground; for an instant the root-entangled soil held its shape, then the plant leaned forward and collapsed, orange fruit rolling around the garden patio. The cactus, by contrast, wheeled in the air, upturning itself as it fell, never before so anthropomorphized as with arms outstretched in a headfirst plummet, its neck snapping in two on impact.

He became aware of everyone in the communal garden looking up to see the madman on the terrace, the woman in a dressing gown stepping forward to take him by the hand and pull him toward the window. He allowed himself to be led, but once indoors he shook himself free of her, strode into the kitchen area, and opened a bottle of beer, which he downed in two long drafts, maintaining eye contact with her the whole while.

"Fight like a man, not a boy," she said.

"That the kind of advice that gets passed down from father to son in your family?"

The words hung horribly in the beer-stenched air. He put down the bottle and hunched onto a stool, looking at the cherry stains on his hands. Through the open window he could hear the raised voice that was his neighbor coming outside to see the carnage on his patio. Aneeka sat down on the stool facing him, the long room with its tasteful decorations extending behind her, its track lighting in the ceiling, its expensive art. All of it his mother's handiwork. Every part fitting seamlessly together except this woman whom he'd allowed in.

"He wants to come back home," she said.

"Well, he can fuck off and stay in the desert he chose, can't he?"

"Please, Eamonn."

"Please, what? Oh, god." His thumb bit into the corrugated edge of the bottle cap, deep enough to draw blood. "Why did you get into the tube with the home secretary's son that day?"

She took his hand and placed his thumb in her mouth, drawing his blood into her. He pulled away with a *No.*

"I got into the tube because I thought you were beautiful."

"Don't lie to me." He slammed his hand on the kitchen counter, making the fruit bowl jump, making Aneeka jump.

In a voice so low he could barely hear it she said, "I got into the tube because I thought the home secretary's son could help my brother come home and avoid charges."

No pain had ever felt quite like this. "That's what this has all been about?"

"No!" She tried to take his hand again, and this time he physically pushed her away from him. "I know you don't have reason to believe me, but the truth is . . . the truth is . . ."

"Give me enough respect to avoid the 'From the first time we kissed I fell in love with you' line. Do that much for me."

"You were hope," she said simply. "The world was dark and then there you were, blazing with light. How can anyone fail to love hope?"

"A love that's entirely contingent on what hope can do for your brother."

"I couldn't have done this, for all these weeks, if my feelings for you weren't real. You'll have to choose whether you believe that or not. No words I say here will convince you."

"Get out."

She went, without another word. He could hear her in their—his—bedroom, and could imagine too clearly her body as she unbelted the bathrobe and bent to open her drawer of silky underwear. He put on a shirt, walked downstairs with a dust pan and brush, and rapped on his neighbors' door. He had accidentally knocked over the plants, he said to Mrs. Rahimi, surprised to hear how ordinary his voice sounded, and yes, it was fortunate he hadn't fallen himself, and yes, she had warned him that he needed to build a proper terrace or this kind of accident could occur. Despite her protestations he insisted on helping her un-protesting husband clear up the mess on the patio. Even with his vigor-ous, concentrated sweeping it took longer than he expected, shards of pottery and clumps of soil everywhere. The kumquat plant was recov-erable, Mr. Rahimi said, but the cactus, poor thing, was for the compost. There followed a conversation about the absurd smallness of the com-post bin the council had provided, which Eamonn threw himself into with great verve. They moved on to kumquats after that—there was a Persian tangerine stew that might work very well with kumquats, Mrs. Rahimi said. Eamonn told her there was an old Notting Hill saying, "If you drop a tree on your neighbor's patio, all the fruit it ever bears is theirs by right—particularly if that stops them from suing you." Even Mr. Rahimi was won over by that, and Eamonn remembered how easy it was to be a social being, well liked, surrounded by uncomplicatedness.

Eventually Mr. Rahimi said he was returning to watch the test match, and would Eamonn care to join him. Eamonn said he would. He still hadn't heard the sounds telling him she'd left the flat.

"When I first arrived in England as a student I decided I had to understand cricket in order to come to grips with the subtlety of English character," Mr. Rahimi said, ushering Eamonn into the TV room. Holding a finger to his lips he withdrew two bottles of beer from a mini fridge, and handed one to Eamonn. "Then I encountered the figure of Ian Botham and discovered that the English aren't nearly as subtle as they want the world to believe. You Pakistanis, on the other hand, with your leg glances and your googlies."

Eamonn's response to statements like that had always been, "I've never even been to Pakistan." But he didn't want to say that now.

Mrs. Rahimi walked in, took the beer bottle out of her husband's hand, and replaced it with a glass of something yogurty. Mr. Rahimi said something in Farsi, his tone one of affectionate protest. They'd married over thirty years earlier, despite the disapproval of their families—a difference of class, more insurmountable than any other difference in his family's eyes. Better you had married a Sunni from Iraq, Mr. Rahimi's mother had said, the same mother who now spent months in London, telling anyone who'd listen how all her other daughters-in-law took such little care of her compared to this one, whom she'd treated so badly at first.

Eamonn stood up, apologizing. He had to go, he said. He was sorry, he'd forgotten in the warmth of his neighbors' hospitality that he was expecting someone. He left the Rahimis sitting in front of the TV, Mr. Rahimi drinking from Eamonn's bottle of beer, Mrs. Rahimi sipping from the bottle she'd confiscated from her husband.

He took the stairs two at a time, calling Aneeka's name as he

opened the door. When there was no answer he thought she'd left, but he found her sitting on the edge of their bed, still in the stained dressing gown.

He sat down next to her, for once not touching. She held her hand out to him. Within it, the phone with the factory-set picture for a home screen and security settings that ensured no one without the passcode could see who had called or texted. She tapped in the code and pulled up a photograph. A boy with headphones on turned toward the camera with an open smile and a thumbs-up gesture. He had Aneeka's skin tone and her fine bones—but while hers made her look fierce, like a panther, his gave him a breakable air. His eyes were sleepy, his shoulders narrow. If he was standing in a room with his sisters, your eyes would go straight over him to Aneeka's beauty, Isma's gravitas. "That's Parvaiz," she said unnecessarily, and leaned into him. "That's my twin. I've spent every day the last six months sick with worry about him. Now he wants to come home. But your father is unforgiving, particularly about people like him. So I'm not going to get my brother back. And I don't really know what to do . . . half of me is always there, wondering if he's alive, what he's doing, what he's done. I'm so tired of it. I want to be here, completely. With you."

It was what she'd say if she were still only trying to manipulate him. It was what she'd say if she'd really fallen in love with him.

You think marriage is in the large things, Mrs. Rahimi had once said. *It's in the small things. Can you survive the arguments about housework, can you learn to live with each other's different TV viewing habits.* He thought of Aneeka opening his kitchen drawers, mocking the cherry pitter that

pits cherries, the apple corer that cores apples. A life of small things forming between them.

"I've broken us, haven't I?" she said.

He put his arm around her and kissed the top of her head. "No," he said, and felt the relief go through her body, and his own. "Tell me everything about your brother."

ıllıllıllıllıllıllıllı

His mother had warned him about increased security following the attention brought on by the Bradford speech, but that didn't make it any less strange to see SO1 officers where previously there'd been trees at the bottom of the garden. Makes it less likely for a terrorist to get in undetected, his mother had said on the phone when he asked if he could stop by for breakfast, and she told him the noise he was hearing in the background was his beloved childhood tree house and its support structure being sacrificed. She had sounded unbothered, but there were dark smudges around her hazel eyes, and she was crossing her arms with hands tucked beneath her armpits as she did when she wanted to hide her usually immaculate nails bitten down to stubs. She was the portrait to his father's Dorian Gray—all the anxiety you'd expect him to feel was manifest in her.

Terry Lone, mistaking the uneasy looks her son was directing at the officers, turned her back on them and slipped a check into his pocket. When he shook his head and returned it to her, she raised her eyebrows. "You mean that's not why you've stopped by at this ungodly hour? That shouldn't have come out as an accusation—you know I'm happy to help."

He draped his jacket over his mother's shoulder, as a show of affection rather than a response to any sign of her feeling the early-morning cold. "You're magic. But some of the bonds you bought for me years ago just matured. And anyway, I'm going to get back to work soon. Alice thinks PR and I will be a good fit—she has a job waiting for me." He wasn't at all sure that was what he wanted to be doing, but he knew he couldn't turn up at Aunty Naseem's door as Aneeka's intended if he didn't have a job.

"Well, you know my thoughts on the matter of employment for the sake of employment. But your father will be pleased," his mother said, allowing him to ask where the man in question was.

"In his study, of course. See if you can drag him out, while I consider the roses." He watched for a moment while she walked toward the rose bushes: Terry Lone, née O'Flynn, of Amherst, Massachusetts, one of Europe's most successful interior designers, with a chain of stores from Helsinki to Dubai bearing her name. When she was sixteen, her parents pulled her out of school a few weeks before the end of the semester to travel to London with them, hoping the visit to a city of "real culture" would cure her growing interest in the worrisome feminist movement that was so active on the nearby Smith College campus. They arrived to stay at the Savoy on April 29, 1978, and the next morning, while her parents slept off jet lag, she dutifully walked down to Trafalgar Square to see the National Gallery, and ran into the thousands gathered for a Rock Against Racism march, which was just setting off for Victoria Park to hear the Clash and other musicians raise their voices louder than the racist chants of the National Front. "You coming?" said a Spanish boy with dark hair falling around

the shoulders of his black leather jacket covered in badges letting on-lookers know NAZIS ARE NO FUN and RACISTS ARE BAD IN BED. They'd been marching awhile by the time she discovered his parents were from Pakistan, a country she'd never heard of. Considerably later that day, when the compliant side of her personality asserted itself and she said she had to return to her parents, he insisted on accompanying her all the way to the Savoy, even at the risk of missing the Clash, and when she burst into tears at the thought of saying good-bye to some-one so thrilling, he vowed to marry her one day. For the next two years they communicated by letter, until she enrolled at Chelsea School of Art, by which point he'd left university and swapped his leather jacket for a banker's suit, which she found both a disappoint-ment and a relief.

Terry Lone picked up a yellow petal, brushed the smoothness of it against the tip of her nose. It was only now that Eamonn understood how you could decide you wanted to marry someone in the course of an afternoon, and without drugs being the primary factor, as he and his sister had concluded many years ago. Did she ever wish she'd con-tinued on to the National Gallery, he wondered. His parents weren't unhappy together, but there was a separateness to their lives. His mother winding down her daily involvement in her business just as his father became too busy for holidays or even breakfast—that seemed somehow apt for the state their marriage had reached. Today particu-larly, he wished they were more like the Rahimis.

Glancing around the terrace, he tried to imagine an occasion later this summer when two families might be sitting out for dinner on a balmy evening. Karamat and Terry and Emily and Eamonn, Aneeka

and Isma and Aunty Naseem, and maybe even Parvaiz. He acknowledged to himself he had no idea how the world might take him from this moment to that imagined one—he knew only that they all would have to find a way to make it happen.

He entered the house and made his way to his father's basement office, a room that lacked his mother's signature spare style and featured instead dark wood and solid lamps and windowlessness. Those years of nocturnal study had left their mark—Karamat Lone was at his most productive when there was no glimmer of natural sunlight.

"Since when does my son knock before entering?" he said, standing up to kiss and embrace Eamonn, a form of greeting that had embarrassed him for years, until one day it didn't.

"Since my father started bringing home top-secret documents. Do they actually have 'top-secret document' written on them?"

"No, they have 'If you aren't important enough to have clearance for this, you'll be dead soon' written on them. In very, very small print, otherwise there wouldn't be room for anything else. Why are you awake, let alone here?"

"There's something I wanted to talk to you about. Can we sit a minute?" He gestured his father back to his worn leather chair and perched on the edge of the desk, facing him—the position in which he'd spent so much time in tense arguments with his father (his GCSE subjects, backpacking with Max, arrangements for his girlfriend's abortion) through that period of adolescence when Karamat Lone was a backbencher with more time for parenting than his wife had. Terry Lone was the one to whom Eamonn and his sister would turn when they wanted new gadgets, cars, and, later, a flat each of their own—

the relationship's binary options of "yes/no," usually "yes," giving it solidity. But with father and son everything was more abstract, the baseline love threaded through with contradictory emotions that left the women of the family exhausted by the up-and-down of it all. *Who is this posh English boy with my face,* the father would say, sometimes with disappointment, sometimes with pride. Who *you made me, so blame yourself,* the son would reply, and his father would respond with either *There is no blame, my jaan, my life* or *That was your mother's doing, not mine.*

"I'm seeing someone," he said, and watched his father's eyebrows lift. One morning, in the brief period when Eamonn was pining over Alice, the door of his bedroom had been kicked open and Karamat Lone had walked in, knees buckling slightly under the weight of the halibut in his arms, ice chips glinting on its skin. He had lowered the massive fish onto his son's bed, with the single word "replacement." It was the coarsest thing anyone in his family had ever known him to do, and Terry and Emily Lone were both horrified, words such as "misogynist" and "chauvinist pig" echoing around the house. Eamonn pretended to side with them, but he had been more amused than he'd ever admit, and the act put a decisive end to his pining. Though it was only since Aneeka that he'd come to agree, yes, Alice really had been a cold fish.

"Don't look at me like that," Eamonn said. "She's not like the others."

"How so?"

"For starters, she's not from around here."

"She's not British?"

"She's not West London."

This was received with his father's extravagant snort, which his children were always amazed he could restrain from in public life. "Well, that is a change. Where's she from then? Cheltenham? Richmond—my god, not south of the river!"

"Wembley."

His father looked surprised, and pleased to be surprised. Eamonn picked up a paperweight with a lion and unicorn etched on it, turned it in his hands, a little shy, all the other concerns pushed to the side as he told the man he loved most in the world about the woman he loved most in the world. Aneeka, he said. Yes, Pakistan—her mother raised in Karachi, her father a second-generation Brit whose parents were originally from Gujranwala. An orphan at the age of twelve, raised by her sister. Preston Road. Beautiful, and so smart, Dad, on a scholarship to LSE for law. Only nineteen but far more mature than that. Yes, very serious. Yeh ishq hai. His father took his hand and squeezed it when Eamonn spoke the Urdu words, beaming at his son.

"Well, if it's love you'd better bring her around. Next Sunday?"

"There's one thing I should warn you about. She's a bit, well, Muslim."

"How 'well, Muslim,' exactly?"

"She prays. Not five times a day, but every morning, first thing. Doesn't drink or eat pork. She fasts during Ramzan. Wears a hijab."

"Uh-huh. But she has no problem—" He brought the palms of his hands together and then separated them.

"What? Opening a book?"

"Sex."

"Dad! No, she has no problem with that. There is no problem with that at all. And if you want hand gestures for sex, try one of these."

"Those could be useful in Parliament, thank you. So, she's no halibut. Glad to hear it." He grinned in the way that had earned him the Wolf part of his nickname.

"You're taking all this much better than I thought."

"What? You think I have a problem with you dating a Muslim? I have a lot more trouble with all the double-barreled girls whose fathers don't waste a minute telling me of their family's long association with India—governor of this province, aide-de-camp to that viceroy. Helped quell the Mutiny. Helped quell the Mutiny! All delivered in a way that sounds perfectly polite, but everyone knows I'm being informed that my son isn't good enough for their daughter." Eamonn waited for the Chip to play itself out. Alice's poor father would be mortified if he had any idea how much offense he'd caused with his "helped quell the Mutiny" line about his namesake. That's what Alice had said, and only Hari had rolled his eyes in response, but then Hari had a little version of the Chip himself. "Anyway, if she's only nineteen, I suspect she can be persuaded out of the hijab in time. Get your sister to take her off to the hair salon next time she comes to visit. I'm mostly joking. You know I grew up a believing Muslim. Didn't harm anyone but myself with it."

"I didn't know that, actually. I mean, I knew your parents made you go to the mosque and fast and stuff, but I didn't know you really believed."

"No? Well, I did. That's how I was raised. There are still moments of stress when I'll recite Ayat al-Kursi as a kind of reflex."

"Is that a prayer?"

"Yes. Ask your girlfriend about it. Actually, no, I'd prefer it if you didn't mention it to anyone."

"You shouldn't have to hide that kind of thing."

"I'd be nervous about a home secretary who's spoken openly about his atheism but secretly recites Muslim prayers. Wouldn't you?"

"Do I look nervous?"

"You've been looking nervous throughout this conversation. Son, she's your girlfriend. I'll be on my best behavior, as always. What I might say when you break up is another matter."

"There's one other thing. There's a boy she was close to at school. He's gone to Syria—I don't mean on humanitarian work."

"Parvaiz Pasha."

"How do you know?"

"I know all their names. Where they come from. Who they were before they went. There's only one from Preston Road. It's the last place in England I'd expect to find that kind of thing happening. But that one, he had exceptional circumstances. Terrorism as family trade. Illustrative of how much you need to do to root out this kind of thing. I mean, literally, grab by the very roots, and pull. Pull the children out of those environments before they're old enough for the poison to seep in."

"No, it's not like that."

"What's not like what?"

Eamonn stood up; it was warm in here, oppressive. Already the

script he'd plotted in his head was beginning to unravel by the sheer fact of his being in his father's presence. *He knows he was wrong. He was brainwashed but now he understands, and he wants to come back. He didn't take part in the fighting, never actively recruited anyone. He's only nineteen. No reason to ruin his life over this. His name has never been in the papers, you can make it stay that way. He just needs a new passport, and to slip quietly back into the country without any charges against him. His friends all think he's been in Pakistan this whole time; no one will ever know. It's best for everyone—imagine the media storm if anyone finds out your son is planning to marry the sister of a boy who went to Raqqa. You'd never survive it.*

Trust me, he'd said to Aneeka. *I know my father. I know how to spin it so he'll agree.* But that wasn't spin, it was a threat. How could he possibly do that to this man who had always offered him the most unconditional of loves? And why was his father looking at him so strangely, as if he knew his son had come here with betrayal in his heart?

"Orphaned at the age of twelve, and raised by her sister?"

"Yes."

"Just like Parvaiz Pasha."

"All right, yes. She's his twin."

"Eamonn!" His father caught hold of him around the neck, half headlock, half embrace. "You stupid, stupid boy. My stupid boy."

Jaan, she had called him, kissing his eyes, his mouth, his cheeks, his nose, when he'd said he would speak to his father. *Jaan, my life.* A word his father was now saying as he held his son. And just as suddenly, Karamat Lone disengaged, stepped back, and wiped a hand across his face. Where there'd been a father, now there was a home secretary.

"You will have no more contact with this girl. I'm setting up a security detail for you."

"Dad! Look, just, meet her. All right? I'll bring her over. Tonight, this evening, and . . . what's so funny?"

"All this security around the house, and the nexus of al-Qaeda and the Islamic State is just going to waltz in on the arm of my son."

"Don't you ever refer to her in that way again. She's the woman I'm going to marry."

Nothing moved in his father's face. "Stay here."

"Or what, you'll arrest me?" But the home secretary was gone before the end of the sentence, door slamming behind him.

Eamonn sat down in his father's chair, looked at the computer screen, which asked for a password. Riffled through the file of news clippings from this morning's papers. Wished he hadn't left his phone in his jacket—Aneeka was at his flat, waiting for him to call and tell her what had happened. She'd finally given him her number, but he hadn't thought to memorize it. If only he hadn't laughed off the suggestion when his mother said he should have a landline.

I could just leave, he kept telling himself. *I could at least go up and eat something.*

He had a small moment of satisfaction when he realized he could use his father's phone to call directory assistance and ask for the Rahimis' number.

"It's Eamonn," he said, his voice fissured, when Mrs. Rahimi answered. "Could you please do me a vast favor? There's a friend of mine upstairs, in my flat. Would you call her down. I really have to speak to her."

"The beautiful one in the hijab, you mean? I'm sorry, she just left. Almost knocked me over as I was taking the rubbish out. She seemed in a great hurry. Are you all right?"

He walked over to the sofa and lay down on it, curled up like an animal protecting its soft parts. A few minutes later, his mother entered the study and sat down beside him. No, she wouldn't bring him his phone. No, he really should just stay in here until his father said otherwise. She told him to close his eyes, and stroked his back until he fell asleep. When he woke up, feeling he'd slept a long time, his father was sitting at his desk, watching him.

"My fault," his father said. Eamonn sat up, rubbed his hands across his eyes, tried to understand what that meant.

"My fault," his father repeated sadly. "I say it's your mother's doing, but I'm the one who never wanted you to know what it feels like to have doors closed in your face. To have to fight your way in. I didn't think it would make you so sure of yourself, so entitled, that you wouldn't stop to ask why a girl like that would have time for a public-school boy who lives off his mother because he can and has no ambition beyond beating his own high score in computer games."

"What have you done?"

"I haven't done anything. The officers who were called in when her brother left were concerned about her. They said she was clearly shocked by what he had done, but seemed more upset about being kept in the dark than the fact of his going. They thought she might be at risk of trying to join him. So there've been some people keeping an eye on her, for her own safety. But apparently there've been no phone calls, no texts, no communication of any kind that could be inter-

cepted to suggest she was in touch with my son. Nothing to set off alarm bells. Which sets off alarm bells. And now, this." He placed Eamonn's phone on the desk. "Twenty-three missed calls from Aneeka Pasha."

Eamonn stood up. "Something's wrong."

"On that, at least, we agree."

Parvaiz

5

THE TWO MEN WALKED into the electronics store in Istanbul with near-identical attitudes of ownership, though their South Asian features marked them as foreign. Their white robes, shoulder-length hair, and long beards further distinguished them as men whose attitude of ownership you don't contest. The younger of the two walked over to the wall of mics and scanned the empty display boxes. His companion leaned against the counter behind which the shopkeeper was standing and flipped his phone from hand to hand while looking at the other customers. They filed out quickly in response, leaving the two men and the shopkeeper alone in the cavernous store.

"Look at all this!" the younger man said. "The RØDE SVMX. The Sennheiser MKH 8040. The Neumann U 87."

"Uh-huh. Just get what Abu Raees asked for, and let's go. I'm starving."

The shopkeeper reached beneath the counter and pulled out a box. "The Sound Devices 788T. Didn't Abu Raees receive my message? I've had it for over two weeks."

"Should I tell Abu Raees he needs to dance in Raqqa when you snap

your fingers in Istanbul?" The older man turned his muscular bulk toward the shopkeeper, who paled and started to stammer an apology that was cut short by the younger man's whoop of delight as he took the box containing the 788T into his hands, testing the weight of it.

"Sorry, Farooq. This will be a while. Abu Raees said I should try out some different mic combos with this to see which works best." He walked back to the wall of mics and started to pull empty boxes off the shelves, tossing them back toward the shopkeeper, who cried out, "Just tell me which ones you want! You're ruining my display."

Farooq made a noise of disgust. "I'm going to that café on the corner. You have half an hour before we go to the airport."

"Okay. Pick up some takeaway for the new recruits. You didn't give me anything to eat for hours after I arrived."

Farooq grinned. "What a baby you were, Parvaiz—afraid to ask for a slice of bread."

"I'm not Parvaiz anymore."

"Ma'ashallah," said the older man, his voice tinged with irony.

"Ma'ashallah," said the younger one, placing his hand on his heart.

||||||||||||||||||||||

His journey to the electronics store in Istanbul had started the night last autumn when Isma walked into the kitchen and said she was going to America and so it was time for all three of them to leave their home.

Nothing in the early part of that evening had suggested what it would become. It was just a few weeks after Aneeka had started university, and Parvaiz hadn't, but already the old routines of their lives

had become a thing of the past, so there was a feeling of celebration
about Aneeka being home to cook dinner for the first time that week,
consulting the grease-stained recipe book with her usual intensity of
concentration, as though a recipe might have changed between the
forty-ninth time she followed it and the fiftieth. Parvaiz was sous-
chef, cutting onions with his swimming goggles on to prevent tears.
The playlist compiled by their guitarist cousin in Karachi streamed
through the speakers—chimta and bass guitar, dholak and drums;
overlaid onto it, the sound of Parvaiz's knife cutting through the
yielding onions, hitting the hardness of the board beneath; two slim
bracelets on Aneeka's wrist clinking together as she measured out ingredients; low hum from the refrigerator; a train pulling into Preston
Road station almost precisely at the same moment another train
pulled out; the banter of twins. Tonight's version centered around
Aneeka pretending to craft Parvaiz's profile for an Asian marriage site:
Handsome Londoner who loves his sister that sounds incestuous *ugly Londoner who loves his sister* that sounds desperate *handsome Londoner with
strong family ties* why do you have to be in the first sentence how about
broodingly handsome Londoner with *no, broodingly handsome is a euphe-
mism for dark-skinned* how is it that *Heathcliff* he was also violent and a
bit mad *yes but know your audience, dark-skinned is the real problem.*

Isma walked into all this, preceded by the smell of dry-cleaning
solvent, and said, "A total lack of career prospects is the real problem."
Parvaiz pushed the chopping board to a side, took off the goggles, and
picked up his phone, its screen without message notifications from
Preston Road friends, now scattered emotionally and geographically
by the demands of post-school life. "Turn the volume down and listen

to me," Isma said. She had a serious look about her that made him do as she asked even though ordinarily he would have turned the volume up in response. Aneeka saw it too, and reached out to put a hand on their sister's wrist: "Tell us," she said.

Isma had been issued her visa for America. She would leave for Massachusetts in mid-January. She announced all this in the way another woman would have announced an engagement—proud, shy, worried about her family's reaction to news no one had anticipated.

Aneeka stepped forward and wrapped her arms around her. "We'll miss you, but we're so pleased for you. And proud of you. Isn't that right, P?"

"America," Parvaiz said. The word felt strange in his mouth. "They really gave you the visa?"

"I know, I didn't think they would either."

When she'd first come to the twins to discuss the letter Dr. Shah had written to her, with its suggestion—almost a command—that she apply for the PhD program, Parvaiz had said, "What's the point?" And Isma had immediately agreed yes, he was right. Neither Parvaiz nor Isma had come right out and actually said it was the unlikelihood of a visa that made the whole thing futile, but they all recognized well enough when their father was subtext to a conversation. Still, Aneeka was adamant that she apply. "Sometimes the world surprises you," she said, "and more to the point, if you don't even try, you'll always wonder what might have happened." After enough of Aneeka's badgering, Isma finally said that it would seem ungrateful to Dr. Shah if she didn't at least try. She clearly had a greater capacity for hurling herself at

disappointment than he'd known, Parvaiz had thought at the time with both irritation and regret.

"So," Aneeka said. "What are we going to do about the house?"

Parvaiz shoved his twin's shoulder. "I'm getting her bedroom. I need a studio, and you're not around nearly as much as I am anymore."

The sisters looked at each other and back at him. Isma said a number. It was the household's monthly expenditure. She invoked this number every time she wanted to remind Parvaiz that his earnings as a greengrocer's assistant were insufficient, that the time he spent building up his sound reel rather than chasing after job postings was wasteful. She didn't believe he was good enough to find work doing what he loved, didn't see that his sound reel was as much an investment in the future as Aneeka's law degree was. *She doesn't think our lives allow for dreaming*, Aneeka had said, in a way that rang as both indictment of and justification for Isma's position.

They'd been all right so far, Isma continued. But in America she would have only enough from the university to sustain herself, just as Aneeka had only enough from her scholarship for the most basic living expenses. The mortgage alone would become impossible.

"Don't go, then," he said. Aneeka threw a cube of potato at him, and he head-butted it back at her—reflex rather than play.

Isma opened the crockery cupboard and started unloading plates and glasses for dinner. She'd just stopped in across the road, she said; Aunty Naseem was getting older, she needed help around the house, and even though her daughters and grandchildren were often around to help out, she was struggling to keep up. Some extra hands about

the place would be a huge assistance. That's how Aunty Naseem had presented the option.

"What option?" said Parvaiz.

"We'll move in with Aunty Naseem, and sell the house." Aneeka said this as if it were a matter as small as buying a new set of towels. Now it was Isma who looked stricken; she said she was only thinking they'd rent it out. With the new French school opening in Wembley the following year, property values were going to go up and up, so it would be foolish to sell now. And anyway, in a few years, when she had her PhD and Aneeka was a lawyer, they'd be able to move back in. Ordinarily, Parvaiz would have felt the blade of being omitted from the conversation. But just then Aneeka shrugged in response, and he experienced one of those terrifying moments in which a person you thought you knew reveals a new aspect of their character that has taken hold while you weren't looking.

Aneeka would leave them. That's what the shrug said. After university she had no intention of continuing to live in this house and remain a sibling rather than anything else that a law degree made possible.

"You can't just decide this for us," Parvaiz said to Isma. But the "us" carried no weight with his twin helping her sister set the kitchen table, refusing to meet his eye.

"Traitor," he said, pushing away from the counter. He made enough of a production of looking for keys and phone and mic that anyone who had wanted to stop him could have, but when they didn't, he had no option but to walk out, though the night looked less than inviting.

An autumn evening that carried more anticipation of winter than memory of summer. Cold seeped in through his badly chosen jacket,

and his skin quickly speckled with goose bumps. The neighborhood lights captured by the clouds turned the sky a pale red. The sound of the world turned up just that little bit. One of the first occasions he'd become aware of the acuteness of his hearing was when he had asked a teacher why planes sounded louder on overcast days, and the teacher said they didn't, to the laughter of his classmates, only to return the next day to tell Parvaiz he'd been right.

His mother's old friend Gladys stopped him halfway down the street to talk about the ongoing library campaign, and to ask him if his doorbell had rung differently at any point today. Hers had—the usual chimes replaced by a gonglike sound. When she'd gone to answer the door there was no one there so she'd returned indoors, switched on the TV, and there was that psychic she liked to watch, saying that if ever your doorbell rings with a different sound that means it's the devil and you mustn't answer.

"Do you think the devil's in your house now, Glad?" he said, smiling. "Isma will know some exorcism prayers."

"I hope to find out when I go to bed tonight—keep that sister of yours away!" He held up three fingers in a Scout's sign and noticed the deepening lines around Gladys's eyes when she laughed. She and his mother had been only a few months apart in age.

Leaving Gladys to entertain the devil, he walked down to Preston Road, mostly shuttered and quiet. He dipped his head in acknowledgment at the curved spine of the stadium arch as he always did, and rapped his knuckles affectionately on the door of the notary's office, which had housed a pop-up library during one stage of the library campaign, before continuing on to the sports ground—it had rained

for most of the day and perhaps he could improve on the "shoes on wet grass" segment of his sound reel, which he was overlaying on footage of a video game that had won sound awards. By early next year he'd start sending it out to both the big and the little gaming outfits, and—please God!—work offers would come in.

He was walking across the car park, attaching the mic and its homemade windscreen to his phone, paying no attention to the lone car until its doors opened and three boys he knew from football games on this ground stepped out. Designer sneakers, pristine white robes, ecosystem beards (Aneeka had named them: *large enough to support an ecosystem*, she'd said). They hung around the neighborhood trying to look troublesome, not understanding they'd done themselves no favors with the name they'd chosen· Us Thugz. A shortened form of the Arabic astaghfirullah. What exactly are you seeking Allah's forgiveness for, Isma had asked them when they accosted her in the street one day and told her that sisters should cover up more. Their response made it clear they had no idea what astaghfirullah meant.

"Give it," one of them said, holding out an upturned palm for Parvaiz's phone and mic.

"I'll tell your mother," Parvaiz said.

The boy—Abdul, his childhood friend—lowered his hand and mumbled something about Parvaiz's phone being too old anyway, but the older boy standing next to him, who wasn't from the neighborhood, stepped forward, kneed Parvaiz in the groin, and, when he doubled over in pain, took the phone from his hand, tossing aside the expensive mic as if to prove his own stupidity.

Parvaiz lay on the ground of the car park, waiting for the pain to pass, as the boys' car screeched past him. The sound envelope: slow attack, short sustain, long decay. Nothing to hear that he hadn't heard before. How he hated his life, this neighborhood, the inevitability of everything.

||||||||||||||||||||||||

Farooq found him the next morning, standing among empty crates around the back of the greengrocer's, trying to remove a splinter from his palm.

"Asalaamu Alaikum," said an unfamiliar voice in the faux-Arabicized accent of a non-Arab Muslim who is trying too hard, and Parvaiz looked up to see a compact but powerfully built man, muscles distorting the shape of his tightly fitting bomber jacket. Somewhere around thirty years old, with hair that fell in ringlets to his shoulders offsetting a beard neither hipster nor ecosystem but simply masculine. An instant glamor to him that excused all accents. He was holding out the tweezer component of his Swiss Army Knife, a surprising delicacy in the gesture. Parvaiz took it and tried to capture the splinter, but his left hand felt clumsy, and he kept pinching his skin instead. Without saying anything, the man took the tweezers from him, rested his hand beneath Parvaiz's to steady it, and plucked out the splinter with a flourish and a wink. Then he pressed his thumb against the drop of blood that appeared, stanching the inconsequential wound.

"My kutta cousin took something of yours. I apologize. He didn't

realize who you were." He reached into a pocket of his combat trousers and handed back the stolen phone. *Who am I?* Parvaiz wanted to ask, but he knew the answer already. He was Aneeka's brother. When older boys, the kind you would die to be friends with, paid attention to him, it was always because he was Aneeka's brother. Aneeka never liked the ones Parvaiz tried to nudge her toward, though; she preferred the quieter boys she could boss around.

"You know my sister?"

The man looked displeased. "What are sisters to do with me? I know of Abu Parvaiz."

"I'm Parvaiz. I don't know any Abu Parvaiz."

"Don't you know your own father's name?"

Parvaiz assembled his features into neutrality with a tinge of bewilderment. Who was this man—MI5? Special Branch? They too had seemed so friendly that time they'd come to the house in his childhood. One of them had entered his room and played racing cars with him on the track that took up all the space between his bed and Aneeka's—then he'd picked up the photograph album that Parvaiz's father had sent him and walked out with it. They'd returned most of the items they took, but not the pictures of Adil Pasha climbing a mountain, sitting beside a campfire, wading across a stream— sometimes alone, sometimes in the company of other men, always smiling, always with a gun slung over his shoulder or cradled in his lap. *When you're old enough, my son,* his father had inscribed inside it, which made Parvaiz's mother furious for reasons he didn't then understand. Although his grandmother had intervened to prevent her daughter-in-law from taking the album away from him when it had

first arrived, he'd always suspected his mother had told the friendly man about it so he would remove those images of Adil Pasha from his son's life. It was discomforting to remember that and, with it, how early on he'd started to look at his always harried mother and think, *No wonder he left.*

"I never knew my father." This was what he'd been taught to say, over and over, by his mother and grandmother. There were whispers in the neighborhood about Adil Pasha, he knew, and one day in the school playground a group of boys had accosted him to ask if it was true his father was a jihadi who'd been killed in Guantánamo. *I never knew my father,* he had replied weakly. The boys walked over to Aneeka and asked the same question. She shrugged and turned away, disdain already perfected at the age of nine, but later she whispered to the most loose-lipped of her friends, *It makes him sound like someone in a movie, doesn't it? More interesting than a father who died of malaria in Karachi.*

"He regretted that," the stranger said. "That you never knew him. He fought with my father; I heard all the stories of the great warrior Abu Parvaiz."

"That wasn't my father's name. It was Adil Pasha."

"It was his——" the man said something that sounded like *numb digger.* "That's French for 'jihadi name.' Superhero name is how I think of it, though some of the brothers don't like that. But, yeah. Your dad. When he entered the fight for justice he called himself Father of Parvaiz. That was his way of keeping you close. So anytime someone said his name—his enemies, with fear; his brothers, with love; his comrades, with honor—they were saying your name too."

Horribly, Parvaiz felt tears come to his eyes in the company of a man who probably wouldn't cry if you drove a tank over his legs. But the man didn't seem to think any less of him for it. Instead he drew Parvaiz close, in a cologne-scented embrace, and said, "I'm glad I've found you, brother."

Parvaiz went home that evening with the incandescence of a beautiful secret in his heart. He did all the cooking, didn't take his plate off to the TV room while his sisters ate at the kitchen table, teased Isma about the American accent she would acquire in Massachusetts.

"What's happened to you?" Aneeka asked, and he had the satisfaction of having a hidden corner of his life that his sisters didn't know about.

||||||||||||||||||||

Late that night, Farooq called.

"I've been thinking about you all day," he said. "I've been thinking, why does the son of Abu Parvaiz seem to know so little about his father?"

Parvaiz had no words with which to answer this. The question had never been a question before. He'd grown up knowing that his father was a shameful secret, one that must be kept from the world outside or else posters would appear around Preston Road with the line DO YOU KNOW WHO YOUR NEIGHBORS ARE? and rocks would be thrown through windows and he and his sisters wouldn't receive invitations to the homes of their classmates and no girl would ever say yes to him. The secrecy had lived inside the house too. His mother and Isma both carried an anger toward Adil Pasha too immense for words, and as for

Aneeka, her complete lack of feeling or curiosity about their father had been the first definite sign that he and his twin were two, not one. His grandmother alone had wanted to talk about the absence in their lives, and part of their closeness came from how sometimes she would call him into her room and whisper stories about the high-spirited, good-looking, laughing-eyed boy she'd raised. But the stories were always of a boy, never of the man he became. *Oh, something happened, I don't know,* she'd say whenever Parvaiz tried to find out who his father had become by the time his son entered the world.

"Because no one ever told me," he said now.

"Do you want to know?"

"Of course."

"Don't answer so quickly. Once you know, you'll have to think about what it means to be that man's son. Maybe it's easier never to think about him."

He had always watched boys and their fathers with an avidity composed primarily of hunger. Whenever any of those fathers had made a certain kind of gesture toward him—a hand placed on the back of his neck, the word "son," an invitation to a football match—he'd retreat, ashamed and afraid in a jumbled way that only grew more so as the years passed and as the worlds of girls and boys grew more separate; there were times he was not a twin but rather the only male in a house that knew all the secrets women shared with one another but none that fathers taught their sons.

"I think about him every day," he said, whispering it.

"Good. Good man. What time are you done with work tomorrow?"

||||||||||||||||||||

And so it began. At some point mid-morning, every morning, Farooq
would text with a location: sometimes a kabab shop, sometimes a
street corner—but more often than not, a betting shop on the High
Road. That was usually where he was when Parvaiz finished work.
Regardless of location, they'd talk and talk. Or Farooq would talk and
Parvaiz would listen to those stories of his father for which he'd always yearned—not a footloose boy or feckless husband but a man of
courage who fought injustice, saw beyond the lie of national boundaries, kept his comrades' spirits up through times of darkness. Here was
Abu Parvaiz, the first to cross a bridge over a ravine after an earth-
quake despite continuing aftershocks, to deliver supplies to those
stranded on the other side; here was Abu Parvaiz using the butt of his
Kalashnikov as a weapon when the bullets ran out; here was Abu Parvaiz dipping his head into a mountain stream to perform his ablutions
and coming up with a beard of icicles, which lead to dancing on the
riverbank as if he were Adil Pasha at a discotheque rather than Abu
Parvaiz in Chechnya, whose every shake of the head produced the
sound of wind chimes. Of all the stories this was the one that most
clearly evoked the father he'd never known: the rushing stream, the
dancing icicles, the men around him similarly braving the cold water
so they could provide the jester-warrior Abu Parvaiz with an accompanying orchestra.

"The father every son wishes he had," Farooq said.

"But I never had him as a father," Parvaiz replied, tracing the lines

of his own palm with the grenade pin—was it really?—Farooq had brought along to the kabab shop.

"Do you think he wanted the world to be as it is? No. But he saw it for what it is. And having seen it he understood that a man has larger responsibilities than the ones his wife and mother want to chain him to."

To help Parvaiz understand those responsibilities, Farooq talked to him of history: the terror with which Christendom had watched the ascent of Islam, the thousand years of Muslim supremacy, which was eventually squandered by eunuchlike Ottomans and Mughals who had lost sight of the moral path, and then the bloodlust with which the Christians had avenged themselves for their centuries of humiliation; imperialism, with its racist underpinnings of a "civilizing mission," followed by the cruel joke of pretending to "give" independence when really they were merely changing economic models via the creation of client states, their nonsensical boundaries designed to cause instability. There didn't seem to be any part of the Muslim world Farooq didn't know about—Pakistan and India and Afghanistan and Algeria and Egypt and Jordan and Palestine and Turkey and Chechnya and Kashmir and Uzbekistan. If ever Parvaiz started to lose his concentration, Farooq would swerve the conversation toward football (he supported Real Madrid, Parvaiz Arsenal, but they agreed on the greatness of Özil) or the tiniest details of Parvaiz's life (*What did you have for dinner? Any interesting characters at the greengrocer's? Let me listen to another one of your recordings—this time, I'll guess what it is*) or the American reality TV show Farooq watched devotedly and that Parvaiz started

watching too, in order to talk to him about it. But no matter what the topic of conversation, it always returned to the central preoccupation of Farooq's life, the heart of all his lessons: how to be a man.

"It's your sisters' fault," Farooq said one afternoon when they were sitting side by side in green bucket seats in the betting shop, watching a bank of screens with greyhounds racing around a track and sweating men in another time zone walloping a cricket ball in the direction of sponsors' billboards. The volume was off, allowing for some pleasing moments of synchresis, such as when the dogs were released from their cages just as the front door was hurled open by a drunk, or when the strip light overhead started to buzz and the on-field umpire batted midges away from his face. Farooq had placed three phones on Parvaiz's leg between knee and hip, and each time one pinged with a text message he'd glance down and go to the counter to place another bet. It was good training for Parvaiz to stop fidgeting, he said the first time he did it. Parvaiz always kept his legs so tensed up during those betting shop sessions he had trouble walking afterward. "They want you in the house, doing their shopping and mowing the garden, so they've tried to keep you a boy, a child in need of a mother. That older one particularly, you know what I mean? The one who claims to be a good Muslim, and thinks she has the right to decide whether or not you can live in your own house. Tell her it is written in the Quran, 'Men are in charge of women because Allah has made one of them to excel the other.' And by Allah's law, you, not your women, dispose of your property."

Your women. Parvaiz turned the phrase in his mouth while Farooq placed another bet. He liked how it felt. Though that didn't mean he'd

be stupid enough to try to quote the Quran to Isma, particularly when it came to the roles of men and women. He was a Muslim, of course; he believed in God, and went to the mosque for Eid prayers, and put aside 2.5 percent of his income for zakat, which he split between Islamic Relief and the library campaign, but beyond that, religion had, since early childhood, been a space he'd vacated rather than live in it in the shadow of Isma's superiority. But in Farooq's company he came to see there was such a thing as an "emasculated version of Islam, bankrolled in mosques by the British government, which wants to keep us all compliant," and there was more than a little satisfaction in knowing this.

"Where are you these days?" Aneeka asked him one night, climbing up the ladder he'd propped against the garden shed to get onto the roof with his phone, headphones, and pride and joy, the secondhand shotgun mic. A favorite perch since childhood that allowed a clear view of the trains pulling in and out of Preston Road. The bodies of the trains were shadows in the darkness but the long windows revealed illuminated snapshots of life passing by. Every so often there was a jagged break in the conventions of tube behavier: a man throwing a punch, a kiss so concentrated that train carriage or gondola ride or bedroom were irrelevant details, someone pressing a palm against the glass, leaning toward the boy on the garden shed as though fate wanted them together but the wheels of plot weren't allowing it. Nearly two years ago he had started working on a project that would eventually be a 1,440-minute track that his ideal listener would play between midnight of one day and the next—a soundscape of every minute of a day from this perch.

He stopped the recording, took off his headphones, scribbled in his notepad. It might be nice to leave in that *Where are you these days* between 20:13 and 20:14. Aneeka's was the only human voice scattered through his audio files of *Preston Road Station Heard from the Garden Shed*.

"I'm here. You're the one who's hardly around."

"I meant where are you here?" She reached out to tap his head. "And here." She rested her hand on his wrist, at his pulse point, in the old childish way, but he didn't reciprocate. "Is this about moving to Aunty Naseem's? I know you're upset about losing this spot, but at least we'll still be in the neighborhood."

We, she said, but he wondered how often she'd be around. There was hardly a week when she didn't spend at least one night at Gita's. He knew Aneeka well enough to recognize she was laying the groundwork for staying out more and more often—and it wouldn't always be with Gita either.

"This is our home," he said.

She clicked her tongue against the roof of her mouth. "Always so senti. You should join me in convincing Isma we should sell. You could afford to go to uni with the money we'd get. That'd make up for the loss of *More of the Same Heard from the Garden Shed*, wouldn't it?"

"They only gave you a scholarship because you tick their 'inclusive' and 'diverse' boxes," he said, wounded enough to vocalize a sentiment Farooq had recently dredged out of his unconscious.

"Since when are you so white?" She flicked his earlobe with her thumb and forefinger.

"Muslim women, particularly the beautiful ones, need to be saved

from Muslim men. Muslim men need to be detained, harassed, pressed against the ground with a heel on our throat."

"None of these things has ever happened to you."

"How many times have I been stopped and searched by police? Compared to you?"

"Twice. Only twice, P. And you said yourself it was no big deal either time, so stop whining about it after the fact." She jumped down from the ladder, with that physical confidence that always made his breath stop in terror for her safety. "Isma's right, you know. It's time for you to grow up."

Previously he would have gone after her and turned it into a shouting match that would continue until they'd exhausted themselves into reconciliation. But now he remained where he was, watching all the lives within their narrow frames slide past on the tracks in the darkness, allowing the wound to fester so that tomorrow he could tell Farooq about it and receive the antiseptic of his new friend's indignation.

⎮⎮⎮⎮⎮⎮⎮⎮⎮⎮⎮⎮⎮⎮⎮⎮⎮⎮

Farooq sent a text asking him to come to the flat in Wembley where he lived with two of his cousins, though not the one who had mugged Parvaiz. It felt momentous enough for Parvaiz to go home from the greengrocer's, scrub the dirt out from beneath his fingernails, and put on a fresh shirt.

When he pushed open the unlocked door at Farooq's address he smelled chicken grease from the fast-food joint downstairs, and familiar cologne. A window was rattling in its frame, not because of any

breeze but as a consequence of the traffic on the street below. Farooq's baritone voice told him to stop waiting for a gold-plated invitation and come in.

The furnishings consisted of three mattresses piled on top of one another and pushed against a wall and two green plastic chairs, which faced a flat-screen TV hooked up to a video game console. The kitchen area had a microwave and an electric kettle, the open door of a cabinet offering a glimpse of rolled black T-shirts and black socks. A punching bag hung from a thick bolt in the ceiling, a slight creaking as it oscil lated almost imperceptibly. There was a bolt in the floor, similar to the one in the ceiling, that didn't seem to serve any purpose. He remembered Farooq's texts—the ones he didn't know how to respond to—about wanting to chain up women from the American reality TV show, and looked away. An ironing board served as makeshift table for a lamp and a pair of boxing gloves. On the floor beside it, an iron rested on a base the size of a bread box.

"It's the Ferrari of irons," Farooq said, proudly, seeing Parvaiz looking at the appliance. "Only one setting so you never burn your clothes You ever want to iron something, bring it here. Sit, sit, make yourself at home. You are at home. No, on the chair, on the chair."

Parvaiz sat down, tried to smooth the creases of his shirt. Farooq smiled, cuffed him on the side of the head, and handed him a mug of tea.

"Wait for me. I'll be back in a few minutes," he said, and walked out.

Parvaiz sipped the tea—too weak—and looked around the flat, trying to find any further clues to his yaar's life. The Urdu word came

closer than "friend" to explaining how he thought of Farooq. Or even better, jigari dost—a friendship so deep it was lodged within you, could not be cut out without leaving a profound, perhaps fatal, wound.

A photograph was taped to the wall just above the ironing board. Three men with their arms around one another's shoulders under a DEPARTURES sign at an airport—Adil Pasha; Ahmed from the fabric shop, who had convinced Parvaiz's father to come with him to Bosnia in 1995; and a stocky third man. That must be Farooq's father. The man who fought for less than a week in Bosnia before running back home, a broken creature with night terrors who embarrassed his young son. Farooq had revealed all this only a few days ago—*Ahmed from the fabric shop would come to visit, and every time he brought more and more stories of the heroism of the man who had become Abu Parvaiz, which my father never wanted to hear, but I did.* Ahmed had moved away a few years ago—Parvaiz knew him only as the man his mother crossed the street to avoid.

He reached out to touch his father's arm in the photo, searched his face for signs of similarity. But he and Aneeka took after their mother's family; it was Isma, unfairly, who had their father's wider face, thinner lips. He leaned in closer to the photograph, the only one he'd ever seen of his father at the moment he set off on the path that would become his life. He looked excited. It was the first time in years Parvaiz had seen a photograph of his father that he hadn't already committed to memory. He found himself staring at the paler band of skin on his father's wrist. Where was his watch? Had he taken it off to go through the metal detector and failed to put it back on? Did they have metal detectors at airports back then? Perhaps at the moment the

picture was taken he hadn't yet realized that he'd left his watch in the security screening area. Once he realized, he would have gone back, perhaps with the slightly anxious expression Parvaiz knew from an Eid photograph, in which he looked off to the side, away from the camera. He thought of all the photographs of his father, the ones before Bosnia, and the very few ones after. Yes, he still had the watch with the silver band afterward. It was a triumph to remember this, to piece together this tiny truth.

It felt neither and both a long and a short time that he stood there, memorizing his father's image, before the door opened and two strangers entered, one of them bearing enough resemblance to Farooq for Parvaiz to work out that they were the cousins he lived with.

His words of greeting went unanswered. Instead the cousins walked over to the bolt in the floor and looped a chain through it.

"Come on," one of them said impatiently. Parvaiz approached them, uncertain what it was they needed his help with.

Then he was on the ground, one cousin straddling his legs, the other his chest. The one on his legs tied the chain around his ankles, the one on his chest slapped him to stop him from struggling, and then both of them maneuvered him into a squatting position and used the chain to shackle his wrists to his ankles. When he called out Farooq's name they laughed in a way that made him stop.

"What are you going to do to me?"

"We've done it already," one of the cousins replied.

They both stood up, walked over to the TV, and started to play a video game, the volume turned so high that even if he shouted again no one would hear. It didn't take long to understand what the cousin

meant. The chain so short that it was impossible either to straighten up or topple over entirely, and he could only remain hunched in a squatting position, the pressure on his back increasing by the minute. What started as discomfort eventually became pain, shooting from his back down through his legs. When he tried to move—tried to find a way to roll onto his side—the chains cut into his flesh. Layered into the pain was the torment of not understanding why he deserved it and what he could do to make it stop. He heard his voice begging to be set free, but the two men didn't even look in his direction. The video game sound designer hadn't accounted for cheap speakers, and the crackling and distortion were more intolerable than the gunfire and death screams. He tried prayer but it did nothing.

Sunshine left the room. Clouds or evening, he couldn't tell. Even the relief of unconsciousness eluded him. Scorpions of fire were under his skin, frantic to escape—they raced from his shoulders to his calves, their stingers whiplike. Every crackle from the speakers was magnified until it became a physical force attacking his ears. He was screaming in pain, had been screaming in pain for a long time.

One of the cousins pressed pause.

The sounds of the everyday rushed to embrace him—rattling windows, traffic, his breath. The two men walked over, unshackled him. For a moment there was release, his body collapsing onto the ground, but then they picked him up, carried him to the kitchen sink, which was filled with water, and dunked his head in.

So, he was going to die. Here, above a chicken shop, just a mile or so from home. How would his sisters bear it, after all they'd lost? The men pulled his head out, he breathed in a lungful of air, they dunked

him again. This went on. He told himself he wouldn't breathe in next time, but his body wanted to live. They pulled him out; the air had an increased concentration of Farooq's cologne in it; he braced himself for the next immersion, but instead they carried him over to the pile of mattresses and threw him facedown on it.

A hand touched his head, tenderly. "Now you begin to see," Farooq's voice said, full of sorrow.

The only response Parvaiz had was tears, and Farooq turned him over so that Parvaiz could see that the older man was crying too.

"They did this to your father for months," Farooq said.

The cousins had left the flat. There was only Farooq, stroking Parvaiz's arm, helping him into a sitting position. When Farooq stood up, Parvaiz reached out and held his leg.

"No, I won't leave you again," Farooq said. "I'm just getting something from the kitchen."

If he turned his head he'd be able to see what Farooq was doing, but all he could do was stay as he was, breathing in and out, feeling the stabbing, shooting pain move from back to lungs to legs. Farooq returned, held a hot water bottle to his back, handed him an ice cream stick wrapped in a chocolate shell. He bit down into it, felt sweetness spread through his mouth, remembered pleasure.

When he'd finished, licking every clinging bit of ice cream off the stick, Farooq took the photograph off the wall and placed it into his hands.

"How much do you know about what they did to prisoners in Bagram?"

Parvaiz shook his head. It was all he was capable of doing.

"You've never tried to find out?"

A shorter shake of the head, ashamed now. It had always been there just out of the corner of his eye, the knowledge of "enhanced interrogation techniques," but he had never looked closely. Because he didn't want anyone to ask why he was so interested. That was the reason he'd always given himself.

Farooq rested a hand on his shoulder. "It's all right. You were a child, alone. You weren't ready for it. But that's changed now, hasn't it?"

A child, alone. He'd never been alone. There had always been Aneeka. Even when she was different, she was still there. He looked at the iron bolt in the floor, thought of Aneeka saying they should sell the house. She was unlinking the chains that held them together, casting him into darkness without the accompanying sound of her heartbeat for the first time since his heart had clenched in terror to find itself dividing into chambers, becoming an organ with the capacity to feel, then relaxed, knowing there was another heart experiencing every moment of fear, every second of wonder alongside it.

Legs still wobbly, he stood up. "I have to go."

Farooq stood with him and drew him into an embrace. "You're strong enough to bear this. You're his son, after all."

Parvaiz pulled away, walked out without saying anything. Please come home, he texted his twin while going down the stairs.

He was on the 79 bus home, just a few minutes later, when she texted back. Urgent? Class ends in 20.

He rested his temple against the window of the bus and watched the familiar world pass by. "Sicko," "creep"—those would be the words she'd use about Farooq, and she'd make him swear on their mother's grave never to see the man again. But the farther the bus took him from Farooq's flat the more he felt he was in the wrong place. The ache in his back had begun to recede and he remembered how, before the pain had become too unbearable for any thought beyond his own suffering, he had turned his head toward the wall, toward the photograph of his father, and there was this understanding, *I am you, for the first time.*

He texted back: Haha just testing your devotion. Don't make me have another night of takeaway and Isma.

Idiot, you worried me, she responded. Paper due tomorrow so working late in the library. Will stay at Gita's tonight.

He slid the phone into his pocket. Near the front of the bus a man was tapping his wedding ring against a yellow handrail. The sound, metal on metal, was chains unlinking.

ıııııııııııııııııı

Parvaiz sat down on the stool near the till in the greengrocer's, wiping the back of his hand against his mouth, surrounded by a lie. Asparagus and plantains and okra and Scotch bonnet peppers and bird's-eye chilis and samphire and cabbage and bitter gourd. Nat, the greengrocer, said the world was divided into two kinds of people: those who regularly ate fresh food, and those who didn't. With each new influx of migrants to the neighborhood, he'd ask, What do they eat? and add to his stock accordingly. Pakistanis, West Indians, Albanians—

they were all fine by Nat. His shelves bursting with freshness and color, the promise of family meals and welcoming neighbors.

Parvaiz set Nat's phone down on the weighing scale, surprised by how light it was. In his hands it had felt like an iron bar. He'd taken it out of the pocket of Nat's winter coat, which hung in the back room, when Nat went to the café next door for his morning toast and tea. He'd switched the browser into private mode and typed "Bagram abuse" into the search bar. Then he'd read, and looked at images, until he'd had to run outside and throw up in an empty crate that smelled of cabbage.

He'd always told himself a story, which came from nowhere he could now recall, that said Guantánamo was the place where really bad things happened, and at least his father had been spared that. Such a clever little lie, neat as the piles of fruit and vegetables he'd so carefully arranged this morning, as if the placement of a pear were something that mattered.

Nat returned, took one look at him, and said, "What's happened?"

Parvaiz stood up. "Not feeling well. Can I go?"

"Of course. Should I call Isma? You need something from the pharmacy?"

He shook his head, unable to bear Nat's kindness.

A short while later he was at Farooq's flat. He walked over to the shackles, lifted their weight in his hand. The cool steel harmless in his palm, link clinking against link.

"Tie me again. I want to feel my father's pain."

"My brave warrior," Farooq said, as Parvaiz knelt down and waited for the agony to resume.

ıııııııııııııııııı

"Are you finally ready to tell me about her?" Aneeka said, perched on the arm of the sofa, her foot tapping against Parvaiz's ankle inquiringly as he lay prone beneath his favorite blue blanket, a hot water bottle against his back.

"Her who?"

"Really? You going to tell me you aren't lying here looking so wounded because of whoever you've been going off to meet every afternoon and texting deep into the night for—what—a couple of weeks now? Longer? Who is she? Why all the secrecy?"

"Why the law?"

"What?"

"Why is that what you've decided to do with your life? What does the law count for? How did the law help our father?"

She raised her eyebrows at him, unbothered. "You could just say you aren't ready to tell me who she is. Is she married? Oh god, she's not from one of those crazy honor-killing type families, is she?"

"Why are you pretending I'm not asking you a valid question?"

"Well, you aren't, really. What has Adil Pasha ever had to do with our lives?"

He turned away from her, his face pressed against the sofa cushions. "You're just a girl. You don't understand."

She held his foot in her hands, pressing her thumbs into his sole. "Don't get your heart broken."

"Shut up. Leave me alone. You don't know anything."

IIIIIIIIIIIIIIIIIIIIIII

A few days later there was a fund-raiser for the library campaign. Parvaiz had been involved with the campaign through his adolescence, ever since the council had announced that the local library, to which his mother had taken him and Aneeka after school at least once a week, would have to close. He'd handed out leaflets, written letters to the local newspaper, attended meetings with Gladys where strategies were discussed; when it became clear the council was going to go ahead with the closure he'd seamlessly moved into the next stage of the campaign, to set up and keep going a volunteer-run library. He'd sung carols outside the tube station to raise money, helped transport books local residents donated, volunteered at the library every Sunday. But as the day of the fund-raiser drew closer, he became increasingly worried that one of the Us Thugz boys might see him at the cake stall with Gladys, selling Aneeka's chocolate brownies, Aunty Naseem's Victoria sponge, and Nat's apple pie, and report back to Farooq that with the world ablaze with injustice Parvaiz Pasha thought the cause to which he should devote his time was a local library. The only way to limit the damage was to break the news himself.

He found Farooq ironing in his underpants, the windows of the flat thrown open to allow in the sunshine of the unseasonably warm day and the chicken-grease-scented air. A pile of freshly laundered clothes lay in a basket near his feet. Squares of sunlight fell like epaulets on his chiseled shoulders. He was in a boisterous mood, instructing Parvaiz how to roll up the ironed clothes, asking him if he knew that was the

best way to keep them from creasing, and deriding the "idiots" who chose to fold instead. Parvaiz found himself imagining Farooq working with Isma at the dry-cleaning store, swapping tips about stain removal.

Tentatively, Parvaiz mentioned the library campaign, which he described as a "habit" carried over from adolescence. Farooq upended the iron and pointed to a spot in the center of the ironing board.

"Put your hand there. Palm up. I'm going to press this iron on it."

Parvaiz looked from the hissing iron to Farooq's face, but there was no hint of a joke. Just a watchfulness, a judgment waiting to be made. He stepped forward, placed both palms on the ironing board, forced himself into stillness as Farooq lifted the iron, feinted, smiled when Parvaiz didn't flinch, then lightly touched the wedge-shaped weapon to Parvaiz's palms. It was hot but not unbearable.

"Uses steam pressure more than heat. It won't burn even the flimsiest silk," Farooq said, with the air of a salesman. He caught Parvaiz by the back of the neck and kissed his forehead. "My faithful warrior." He resumed his ironing, and Parvaiz jammed his hands into his pockets.

"The library," Farooq said. "Of course it matters. Same as what they're doing to the NHS, welfare benefits, all the rest of it. You know this country used to be great."

"When was that?"

"Not so long ago. When it understood that a welfare state was something you built up instead of tearing down, when it saw migrants as people to be welcomed not turned away. Imagine what it would be

like to live in such a nation. No, don't just smile. I'm asking you to do something: imagine it."

Parvaiz shook his head uncertainly, not sure what he was being asked.

"There is a place like that we can go to now. A place where migrants coming in to join are treated like kings, given more in benefits than the locals to acknowledge all they've given up to reach there. A place where skin color doesn't matter. Where schools and hospitals are free, and rich and poor have the same facilities. Where men are men. Where no one has to enter haram gambling shops to earn a living, but can provide for his family with dignity. Where someone like you would find himself working in a state-of-the-art studio, living like a prince. Your own villa, your own car. Where you could speak openly about your father, with pride, not shame."

Parvaiz laughed. He'd never seen Farooq so light, so playful. "So what are we still doing here? Let's follow the yellow brick road, or is it the White Rabbit who takes us there?"

"What rabbit? What are you talking about rabbits for when I'm trying to tell you something serious."

"Sorry. You're talking about a real place?"

"You know where I'm talking about. The caliphate."

Parvaiz raised his hands defensively. "Come on, boss. Don't mess with me."

Farooq switched off the iron, stepped into cargo pants, pulled on his T-shirt. "I've been there. I'd just come back from there when we met. Who are you going to believe about what it's really like? The

same people who said Iraq had weapons of mass destruction, the ones who tortured your father in the name of freedom, or me?"

Parvaiz's heart seemed to have taken up his entire chest cavity, hammering so furiously he was surprised his shirt wasn't moving. Farooq's expression became gentle.

"Believe the evidence of your eyes. Wait." He went into the kitchen area and came out a little while later with a tablet. "Don't worry, no one will know you're looking at this—it's all offline. I'm going to finish ironing. You have any questions, ask."

Parvaiz sat down on the piled-up mattresses, rested the tablet on his knee. Farooq had pulled up the photo browser to show him the image of the black-and-white flag he'd first seen only a few months ago and that he'd learned to glance quickly away from in newspapers on the tube so no one would think the Muslim boy looked too interested. He looked up at Farooq, who made a swiping gesture with his finger. Parvaiz flicked forward through the images. Men fishing together against the backdrop of a beautiful sunrise; children on swings in a playground; a man riding through a city on the back of a beautiful stallion, carts of fresh vegetables lining the street; an elderly but powerful-looking man beneath a canopy of green grapes, reaching up to pluck a bunch; young men of different ethnicities sitting together on a carpet laid out in a field; standing men pointing their guns at the heads of kneeling men; an aerial nighttime view of a street thrumming with life, car headlamps and electric lights blazing; men and boys in a large swimming pool; boys and girls lined up outside a bouncy castle at an amusement park; a blood-donation clinic; smiling

men sweeping an already clean street; a bird sanctuary; the bloodied corpse of a child.

Parvaiz didn't know he'd said anything in response to the last, but he must have, because Farooq asked, "What?" and came to see what he was looking at. "The Kurds, those heroes of the West, did that. Her name was Laila, three years old."

"And the men about to be executed in the other picture?"

"The men who did that to her, or those just like them."

"These other images, are they real?"

"Of course they're real. Look!" He cycled back to the fishing image, and Parvaiz saw that one of the men—the one whose large muscles were straining with the weight of the catch he was trying to reel in— was Farooq.

"Okay, there's a little bit of a lie in there. That giant fish you think I've hooked—it was a waterlogged jacket. This is the Euphrates we're fishing in. You want to come and fish in the Euphrates with me? And with your other brothers? That's Abu Omar, that's Ilyas al-Russ, and this one is my sweet Abu Bakr, who was martyred by the FSA."

"So it's not true then? About all the violence? Only if they're enemy soldiers, is that what you're saying?"

Farooq sighed heavily and sat down beside him, hooking his arm around Parvaiz's neck. "What do they teach you in history?"

The French Revolution. That was Farooq's lesson of the day. The cradle, the bedrock, the foundation of enlightenment and liberalism and democracy and all the things that make the West so smugly superior to the rest of the world. Let us agree to accept for a moment that

the ideals that came from it were good. Liberty, equality, fraternity—
who could argue against that? Well, Farooq could, but that was another day's lesson. For the moment, accept those ideals as ideal. But
where would those ideals be without the Reign of Terror that nur-
tured and protected them with blood, eliminating all enemies, internal and external, that threatened the new utopia, and did so in full
view of the public? It might have been regrettable—a man would
rather fish with his friends than cut off the heads of his enemies—but
it was necessary. Eventually the terror ends, having served its purpose
of protecting a new—revolutionary—state of affairs that is besieged
by enemies who are terrified of its moral power.

"So the question for you is this: Will you protect the new revolution? Will you do the work your father would have done if he'd lived?"

Parvaiz looked from Farooq back to the screen, flicking through
the remaining images. A land of order and beauty and life and youth.
A Kalashnikov resting on one shoulder, a brother's arm around the
other. It was another planet, one on which he'd always be the boy
from Earth whose lungs don't know how to breathe this wondrous,
terrifying atmosphere.

IIIIIIIIIIIIIIIIIIIII

But increasingly, his lungs didn't know how to breathe the air of
London. MI5 officers were present at Bagram, Farooq told him, and
showed him evidence to corroborate that. Your government, the one
that took taxes from your family and claimed to represent the people,
knew what was going on. How can you live in this place, accepting,
after all that you now know? How can you live in this mirage of de-

mocracy and freedom? What kind of man are you, what kind of son are you?

The questions followed him through his days now. Everywhere he saw evidence of rot and corruption, lies and cover-ups. His two sisters had allowed themselves to become part of it too: one preparing to go to America, the nation that had killed their father and hundreds of thousands of other Muslim fathers; the other propping up the lie that theirs was a country where citizens had rights and courts of appeal.

At night, via the proxy servers Farooq said he could rely on, he went deeper and deeper into the Web, to stories of dogs raping prisoners at Bagram, pictures of tortured bodies, medical accounts of what the different forms of "enhanced interrogation techniques" could do to a body and mind. One night he lay in bed with his desk lamp directed straight at his eyes, his most powerful headphones blasting heavy metal into his ears—he managed for no more than twenty minutes before, whimpering, pathetic, he had to restore his room to darkness and silence. Increasingly, during the day he would stop in the middle of the smallest action—handing a bag of celery to a customer, waiting for a bus, raising a cup of tea to his mouth—and feel the wrongness of it all, the falseness of his life.

"You need to break up with her, she's no good for you," Aneeka kept saying, unable to imagine any pain in the world larger than a bad love affair. More than once he found her trying out different password combinations on his phone—he'd changed it from their joint birthday to the day he first met Farooq.

One day Farooq showed him a photograph that he recognized. A white man kneeling in the sand just prior to his execution, an image

that encapsulated for the world the barbarity of the caliphate. When he'd first seen it he'd felt sorrow for the man with the courage to try to look brave with a blade at his throat, whose only crime was the nation he'd been born into. But this time what struck him most powerfully were the man's clothes, the same shade of orange as the prison jumpsuit in which his father had died. His vision expanded; he saw beyond the expression of the individual kneeling in the desert to the message the caliphate sent with his death: *What you do to ours we will do to yours.*

So this was how it felt to have a nation that wielded its sword on your behalf and told you acquiescence wasn't the only option. Dear God, the vein-flooding pleasure of it.

ııııııııııııııııı

And then he found himself preparing to leave.

How exactly it happened he couldn't have said. He had been too busy changing to stop and chart the change. It had been a long time since he and Farooq had discussed football, reality shows, life at the greengrocer's. There was only one subject, and eventually he understood that the subject was a destination.

"You're sure I can come back if I don't like it?"

"Of course you can. I'm back here, aren't I?"

"You've never said why."

"Had to deal with family stuff. Then you happened."

"What do you mean?"

"Should have left weeks ago. But thought if I waited, maybe you'd come too."

"You stayed for me?"

"Yes."

"And you'll really help me find people there who knew my father?"

"I really will."

"You're the best friend I've ever had."

"I'm your brother."

"Yes. I know. Thank you."

||||||||||||||||||||

He called his cousin, the guitarist in Karachi—the one he'd hated because on the only occasion they'd met the other boy had said, "I'm a
Pakistani and you're a *Paki*"—and said he was going to take up the
offer, proffered by the guitarist's mother, to spend some months in
Karachi working on a popular music show to build up his professional
credentials. He sorted out his paperwork, one half of his brain believing he really would end up in Karachi, and booked a flight with a
connection in Istanbul that would arrive in the old Ottoman capital
soon after Farooq's flight. When Aneeka talked about meeting him in
Karachi over Easter he enjoyed making travel plans with her, their
heads bent together over maps of Pakistan. Badshahi Mosque and
Kim's Gun, the ruins of Taxila, the Peshawar Museum, with the
world's largest Gandhara collection, and in Karachi the studio of the
music show they'd been listening to since its inception a few years
ago, where Parvaiz would soon be working.

"If I like it there, maybe I'll stay awhile and you can visit too," he
said to Isma the December night before he was due to leave, the state-

ment brought on by the smell of the masala omelet she was cooking for his final dinner at home.

The first weekend after their mother died, Parvaiz had stopped eating. He was unable to explain to himself why he was rejecting every item of food Aunty Naseem and her daughters and Aneeka offered him, and even Aneeka was at a loss to understand it. It was Isma, who disliked cooking above all other domestic chores, who had come into his room with a masala omelet such as their mother used to make for breakfast every Saturday. She had cut it into pieces and fed it to him, forkful by forkful.

Now she looked up in surprise and smiled in a way usually reserved for Aneeka. "I'd like that," she said.

Her smile sent him out the door into the cold December night, head tipped back to count the stars and keep the tears from falling. It was there that Aneeka found him a short while later.

"You're going to have to get rid of that growth on your face," she said, maybe or maybe not noticing the hand he quickly rubbed across his eyes at her approach. "The Heathrow officials might mistake what is fashionista for fundo and decide not to let you board the plane to Pakistan. Particularly if you're flying through Istanbul. Jihadi alert!"

He laughed too loudly, and his twin touched his arm. "You sure you want to go? You know I'm only allowing you to do it because you obviously have to get away from *her*. Will you never tell me who she is? I promise I won't beat her up too badly."

"I'm going in order to improve my career prospects for that Asian

marriage site. Though the bio should still start *Handsome Londoner who loves his sister.*"

She stepped forward until there was almost no space between them, butted her head against his shoulder. "Both you and Isma leaving. What will I do all alone?"

He held her earlobe between thumb and finger. He knew she had wanted to say this since he first announced he was going. There was no living person for whom he'd leave her just weeks before she had to say good-bye to the older sister who had raised her—raised them both—as much as their mother ever had. But the dead made their own demands, impossible to refuse.

iiiiiiiiiiiiiiiiiii

While the plane was taxiing he ignored the instructions to turn off his phone and listened, instead, to the audio track "Twin Heard from the Garden Shed."

These were the things her voice said:

It's getting late; even the birds have gone home.

Oh god, I'm interrupting you again.

Couldn't you have found a less solitary obsession?

Where are you these days?

Regardless, dinner's ready. Might as well come in.

The wheels left tarmac. He uploaded the track to her account on the Cloud and deleted her from his phone.

6

PARVAIZ PAID THE MAN in the electronics store with the Turkish liras he was carrying in his knapsack, and then asked, as if it were an afterthought, if he sold phones with SIM cards that allowed international calls.

"The new arrivals will have to call home, and there's always one who weeps into the phone and covers it with snot. So they're not getting my phone again," he said.

"I don't need to know your business," said the shopkeeper, moving over to the glass-topped display case housing cell phones. "Here." He pulled out a bricklike handset that belonged to a time when calls and texts were all anyone expected from a phone, and that continued to exist, Parvaiz was sure, only because people in high-crime areas liked to carry around a decoy phone to hand over to muggers. "No charge," the man said expansively, as he slipped the SIM card into its compartment.

"Jazakallah khayr," Parvaiz said, scooping up the pile of boxed equipment for which he'd just paid a small fortune. "Do you have a back door? My car's parked behind your shop."

"Can you carry all that? Do you want to call your friend to help you? I would, but my back . . ."

"This is nothing after what they made us do in military training," he said.

"You're a fighter? I thought you were with Abu Raees in the studio."

"I am. But that doesn't mean they didn't teach me how to fight in the way of Allah in preparation for a time when I can be more useful that way. Why is it, my friend, that you're still living in Turkey?"

The man blanched. "I do my part from here. The back door— through there. I'll open it for you."

Parvaiz stepped out into the sunlight and started to walk toward the row of parked cars until he heard the door close. He turned, made sure the man had gone back inside, then set the pile of boxes down on the side of the road, placed his traceable smartphone on top of the pile, and began to run.

‖‖‖‖‖‖‖‖‖‖‖‖‖‖‖‖

Six months earlier he had entered Raqqa in the late afternoon, his stomach contracting with excitement and terror. A motorcycle back- fired as it drove past an antiaircraft gun mounted on the back of a pickup truck; the soldier swiveled the weapon in the motorcyclist's direction. A joke, Farooq told him, relax! A row of palm trees slapped their fronds against one another in a breeze that wasn't felt at street level. The driver of the car, one of the two men who had picked Fa- rooq and Parvaiz up at Istanbul airport, insisted you could hear the palm fronds whisper *Allah* if your ear was good enough. His ear was

better than anyone else's in the car, Parvaiz said; he meant good as in "holy," Farooq explained. The colors of the buildings were sunbleached, but there was a brightness in the call of the birds. A polyethylene bag caught in the electric wires strung across the street made shivering sounds. A man juggled a flattened loaf of bread the size of his arm that made all the saliva rush to Parvaiz's mouth; a *fwump!* sound as the oven-hot bread was dropped onto a table on the pavement. Bearded men stood around a cluster of motorcycles, two in long robes with bomber jackets, the others in jumpers and trousers, arguing in Arabic. Minarets reached high into the sky—at prayer time the azaan would bounce between one slim tower and the next. A tank rumbled past a monument with two headless statues. A very young girl in a green-and-yellow dress walked behind two women in black niqabs, even their eyes invisible beneath a face veil; Farooq hummed the music from a popular ninja video game until one of the men in the car warned him to stop disrespecting sisters or he'd have to report him to the Hisba—this was the first Parvaiz heard of the morality police, and he saw how mention of them strained Farooq's expression.

The soundscape changed around the central square, or perhaps Parvaiz stopped listening so acutely because of the distraction of heads of enemy soldiers mounted on spiked railings. It was curiously unmoving, something you might see in a TV show. One day, inshallah, there would be no enemy and children would play in the square, Farooq said. In the company of the other men his English conversation had become peppered with Arabic, and perhaps this was what made his words sound false. Then a different part of town, more affluent:

villa-like houses, tall apartment blocks, the yellow and white paint on the facades brighter here. The car pulled up in front of one of the double-storied villas, and Farooq said, "This is our stop."

"Who lives here?" Parvaiz asked, stepping out of the car, taking in the sprawling luxury of the house, the size of three homes in his neighborhood put together.

"One of the perks of the media arm," Farooq said, nudging him, laughing at his disbelieving face.

Two men only a few years older than Parvaiz appeared in the door way of the villa. One Scottish, one American. They introduced themselves by their noms de guerre, embraced him formally, greeted Farooq in the manner of friends. Cameramen, both of them, and yes, those were their SUVs in the driveway—another perk of the media arm.

Inside, the house had marble floors and faded places on the walls where once must have been photographs or artwork. There was a very large room with stiff-backed chairs and sofas with flower-patterned cushions, and beside it a formal dining room with a long table. Boxes lined the hallways—"our equipment," said one of the men, whose names he had already forgotten, so that he referred to them mentally as Abu Two Names and Abu Three Names. It was like an icebox, the lowered blinds adding to the mortuary atmosphere. But then the two men led him upstairs, saying this was the part they actually lived in. Here it was light and airy, pleasingly informal.

The American—Abu Two Names—ushered him onto a wrap-around balcony that overlooked a garden dense with color. It was still afternoon, but he gratefully huddled into the shawl the Scotsman—

Abu Three Names—offered him to counter the cold breeze, "from the Euphrates," that reached him as he sank down into the surprising blue beanbag. A man appeared from somewhere—"This is Ismail, he came with the house"—and offered him tea and biscuits on a silver tray. From up here you could make out the sounds of motorcycles and cars, hammering, birdsong, the wind through the branches of trees, fallen bougainvillea flowers dancing in the breeze along the balustrade of the balcony. Despite his disquiet at the spiked heads and veiled women, the blue skies and camaraderie of the men slumped in beanbags promised the better world he'd come in search of.

"One day you'll tell us the story behind your name," the American said. He was black, very tall, and had a wide smile. His friend was quieter, bespectacled, mixed-race Pakistani-Scottish. The name he meant was Parvaiz's nom de guerre—Mohammad bin Bagram. Farooq had written it onto Parvaiz's registration form at the first checkpoint with an air of pride at having chosen it for his friend. It was both a reminder of what his father had suffered and an acknowledgment that this new Parvaiz was born out of vengeance and justice, Farooq said—which made it impossible for him to say he hated it. And anyway he'd quickly been distracted from questions of naming when Farooq had reached into Parvaiz's knapsack, taken out his passport, and handed it to the man at the registration desk, who had the soulless look of bureaucrats everywhere. *Relax,* Farooq said. *If you ever need it back I'll get it for you. But you won't need it back. You're now a citizen of al-Dawla—the State.*

Parvaiz tried not to think about the passport and asked the cameramen how long they'd been living here. They said they'd been sharing

this house for over two months, though their friendship had assumed an instant depth that told them their souls must have met in Jannah well before the will of Allah brought them back together in Raqqa. They touched each other's arms and shoulders, unself-consciously affectionate, which made the whole thing moving instead of absurd.

"It was the same with this young warrior and me," Farooq said, ruffling Parvaiz's hair. "It'll be strange not seeing him every day."

"Where you going?"

"To the front. I'm a fighter, aren't I?"

"You won't be living in Raqqa?" He saw the American shake his head in that schoolyard way boys signaled to each other that too much emotion was being revealed, usually around a girl, and Parvaiz attempted to undercut the pleading tone of his voice with a chin-jut that said *Huh, interesting, why didn't you say before?*

"I'm mostly away fighting the kafir bastards so you boys can be safe in your air-conditioned studios."

"Big-talking man. If you fighters are so important, why do we get paid more?" the American said.

The Scotsman put up a hand to stop the conversation. "Alhamdu lillah, we all play our part in the way of Allah. Who is better or worse is judged only by the quality of his faith."

"Brother, you can always be relied on to remind us what's important, Ma'ashallah," Farooq said, in a tone that managed to sound genuine. "No, man. I'll mostly be gone. And when I'm here, I've got my wife and kid, haven't I?"

"You have?"

"Of course. They gave me a wife almost right away—these two

highly paid men are still waiting to be approved by the marriage bureau."

"You just got here earlier, that's all," the American said. "The waiting time is up to six months these days. Anyway, I'm talking to a girl in France. She's almost ready to come over."

"No, but——" He heard his own voice coming out in a whine, but he couldn't help it. "You said you'd help me find people who knew my father."

Farooq shrugged. "You'll run into some of the old jihadis at the training camp. Tell them who you father was, and they'll hook you up with people who knew him."

"What training camp?"

"Didn't you tell him anything?" the Scotsman said.

What Farooq hadn't told him was that all new arrivals were required to undergo ten days of Shariah camp ("It would have been longer, but I put down your level of Shariah knowledge as 'intermediate' when I filled out your form"), followed by six weeks of military training. After that, assuming he was accepted into the media wing ("And of course you will be," said Farooq, but the other two were quiet), there'd be another month of media training. It all sounded a little overwhelming, Farooq knew, but soon enough he'd be placed in a studio, earning a salary, and would have his own SUV and portion of a house—maybe he'd even have a share of this villa if the marriage bureau or the French girl saw fit to move either or both of its present occupants into married quarters by then.

It would have been stupid to say he thought he'd been brought to this house because this was where he was going to live right away,

un-Muslim to say he didn't want to go to Shariah camp, unmanly to say he didn't want military training, petulant to accuse Farooq of anything when he had been the one who hadn't thought to ask the practical questions about the life he was entering. He shrugged and said that was fine by him, although no one had asked.

"And once you're settled in you can put in a request with the marriage bureau too," the American said. "Though my advice is, try and find a European girl online. They know how to do more things than the Arabs, if you get my drift, though my bonnie friend here doesn't like it when I speak that way."

"Speaking of talking to girls, should we tell your sisters where you are?" The cascading noise from the beanbag was Farooq shifting his weight, reaching for the phone in his back pocket.

Parvaiz had sent Aneeka a series of texts since his arrival in Istanbul the previous afternoon. Cheerful lying messages about sightseeing during his daylong stopover en route to Karachi. Near the Syria–Turkey border he said his battery was dying, it hadn't charged overnight, so she might not hear from him for a while. Then Farooq had taken the phone from him, jerked his wrist, and sent the phone flying out of the car window. He knew Farooq's tests well enough by now to merely smile, shrug, and think of the new phone he'd buy in Raqqa with the income he'd receive for his work as a sound designer.

He took the phone from Farooq, was surprised by the time on the home screen—later than he'd thought. The flight from Istanbul to Karachi would be en route; soon his cousin would call Aneeka to say he was at the airport, the passengers had exited, but there was no sign of Parvaiz.

"Stay here while you speak to her," Farooq said when Parvaiz started to get up.

He logged on to Skype and called Aneeka, imagining the bubbling sound of an incoming call bouncing around the interior of her tan-colored handbag slung on the handle of the door leading into the living area. He wiped the palms of his hands on his trousers, waited.

When Aneeka answered, his first thought was that her strange expression could be explained by the fact that she expected him to still be on a flight. "Where are you?" she said, voice catching.

"Hey. Before I answer that, promise you'll . . ."

"Who's Farooq?"

He glanced at Farooq, who took hold of his wrist and seemed about to pivot the phone toward himself, but the Scotsman quickly caught his shoulder. "Not if she's unveiled," he said.

"Who are you with? P, where are you?" she said.

"Why are you asking about Farooq?"

"You should be on a plane. The plane left on time. I checked. Why aren't you on the plane?"

"Calm down, it's okay. Why are you asking about Farooq?"

"Abdul told his mother you've gone with his friend's cousin Farooq. To Raqqa. Where are you really?"

"Can't even trust your own family to keep secrets anymore," Farooq said, but without looking unduly displeased.

"I would never go to the place you think Raqqa is. But it's not that place."

Something was squeezing his voice box, making the words come out funny. The American was giving him that look again, that shake of

the head. Aneeka's face was unfamiliar to him for the first time in his life—an expression there he hadn't seen before and didn't know how to interpret. Her mouth a strange shape, pursed, as though she were eating something awful that she could neither spit out nor swallow. Then she vanished, and Isma was there.

"You selfish idiot," she said. This was easier to contend with—he rolled his eyes at Farooq, placed two fingers against his temples to mime a gun firing into his brain. "Watch your manners, brother. We have company." She swiveled the phone, and two men were standing in their living room, everything surrounding them as familiar as his own heartbeat. "Say hello to the men from the Met," Isma's voice continued, conversational. "They're going to turn our house and our lives upside down. Again. Do you have anything you want to say to them?"

He was conscious of the three men on the balcony watching him, waiting to see his response to the news that the police knew where he was and now there was no going back.

"My sisters didn't know anything," he said to the men from the Met whose faces were made of stone.

Farooq took the phone from him. "I will plant the flag of the caliphate on Buckingham Palace myself," he said, and jabbed the phone to end the call. "What?" he said, in response to Parvaiz's cry of outrage. "I should've said Downing Street instead?"

The Scotsman leaned forward, touched Parvaiz's knee sympathetically. "It's all right. Allah will protect them while you're here doing His work. Inshallah."

Parvaiz looked at the man's shining eyes, his certainty, and lowered his head as if in prayer so that the others couldn't see his panic.

|||||||||||||||||||

Panic was a familiar companion, months later, of the man who sat at the back of the café, where the bright light of the June afternoon couldn't reach. Every so often he reminded himself to look down at the tourist guidebook, sip the apple-flavored tea.

The open-fronted café allowed him to observe life along the narrow Istanbul street that carried tourists and residents between Galata Tower and the Golden Horn. The tiniest things seemed exceptional: a silver bracelet catching the light on a woman's wrist; a woman's wrist itself. Voices speaking over the azaan from the city's mosques, the sounds of trade continuing undisturbed, as though muezzins demanded as little attention as car horns.

The tray on the table provided a reflective surface, allowing him to see the slight, unremarkable boy from Preston Road whom the barber a few streets away had sheared back into existence. His face was deceptive now with its promise of familiarity to those who had known him when he still was that boy. He ran his hand along the clean-shaven chin, its contrast to the rest of his skin tone worrying him, pulled the baseball cap lower over his close-cropped hair, hunched. *Take me somewhere far from here where I can buy clothes,* he'd said to the cabdriver he'd frantically hailed after running away from the electronics shop. Then he'd phoned Aneeka.

A voice from the outdoor table, raised, spoke excitedly of "the meeting point of Asia and Europe." Such outmoded concepts, why did people still think they meant anything? The language of violence, spoken by the powerful of all nations, erased the distinctions beneath the

surface. Two girls walked past, laughing, uninhibited. The sound—continuing on, burrowing down from the girls' throats to their bellies—was more remarkable than bracelets or wrists. Perhaps surface was all there was to fight for. He remembered how it felt to float on a surface of freedom and safety, to feel himself buoyed up by it, and longing tugged at his heart.

He looked down at his book again. The words on the page, dimly lit by the overhead lamp, made no sense. *Leave Nizam Caddesi to head down to the shore via Hamlacı Sokağı and eventually you will come to Leon Trotsky's house, standing ruined in its wild garden.* How was it possible, this invitation to a world in which you might spend an afternoon meandering toward a shore, stopping at a ruined house in which someone important once lived. No, not an invitation; the words assumed you already were of that world: *you will come to Leon Trotsky's house.* That promise, that certainty. Had there ever been a time when he could have slipped into such a life—a cheap flight, a youth hostel? Why not? In the company of Aneeka he could have left Nizam Caddesi to head down to the shore. But no, Isma would have stopped it. *I gave up my life to work in a dry-cleaning store and put food on this table; now it's your turn. If you can't get yourself a scholarship, at least pay some bills.* The depth of his homesickness announced itself with the realization that he was looking forward to sparring with Isma in the familiar, inconsequential way. If they allowed him back, that is, instead of handing him over to their allies in a prison somewhere outside the law. Perhaps they were better at keeping people alive now; or perhaps life and death weren't outcomes of any interest. They cared only about information, of which he had too little for anyone to believe he didn't have more. Or per-

haps they cared only about inflicting pain. The one thing that the violent respect is more violence, Farooq had said last autumn, in those weeks when every word that tripped off his lips was wisdom and beauty. He pressed the soles of his feet into the carpet. Stillness—external stillness—was one of Farooq's lessons too.

Just when he felt he would have to scream to relieve the pressure in his chest, there was Aneeka, lighting up the screen of the phone:

HAVE PASSPORT AND TICKET. FLIGHT IN
THREE HOURS. RUSHING TO AIRPORT.

> Turn off your CAPS LOCK, Shouty.

DON'T THINK YOU CAN START BOSSING
ME AROUND, IDIOT.

> Love you too.

Until soon, Senti.

> Until soon, Mental.

He ordered a coffee, some bread. Perhaps when she arrived there'd be time to go look for the ruined house in the wild garden. A bearded, broad-shouldered man appeared in the doorway, his shadow extending deep into the café. Someone asking the waiter for directions. There were houses and gardens enough in London. The British consulate, the airport: that was all he wanted to see of Istanbul. Tomorrow at this time he'd be back in Preston Road. Inshallah.

His phone buzzed again, making him smile. Aneeka the Anxious.

He raised himself off the seat, pulled the phone out of his back pocket, read:

You're a dead man, my little warrior.

ıııııııııııııııııı

The man knelt in the sand, motionless except for the movement of his lips.

"Find something to gag him with," said Abu Raees, the head of the Raqqa sound studio. "We don't want that interference."

Parvaiz ran back to the SUV in which he and Abu Raees had only minutes ago driven up to this scene out of a movie. Blue winter sky, a day so still not a single speck of sand moved in the desert landscape, no sign of life other than the kneeling man and the executioner sitting a few feet away, turning his sword this way and that so it caught the sun and became a dancing beam of light. Parvaiz opened the passenger door of the SUV and ducked inside. Hidden from view, he rested his head against the leather interior, tried to stop the shaking of his hands that had started the moment they stepped out of the SUV and he understood what was going to happen.

It was late March. He had survived the tedium and affront of Shariah classes, in which he learned that everyone he loved was either an infidel or an apostate, and that both categories deserved to die, and that it was against Allah's will to wear T-shirts with slogans on them, or to give anyone the wrong directions, or to allow your women to sit down in public. He had survived military training, during which he learned that fear can drive your body to impossible feats, and that the

men of his father's generation who fought jihad in Bosnia, Chechnya, Kashmir, all went home to their families for the winter months. That piece of information had made him blubber into his pillow at night, not because it made him understand that his father had never loved him (though he did understand that) but because he finally saw that he was his father's son in his abandonment of a family who had always deserved better than him. He had survived all that, and even though he knew by then the nature of the joyless, heartless, unforgiving hellhole for which he'd left his life, he believed he had survived the worst. The media wing had accepted him, trained him (and he had found pleasure in the learning), and now he had a position at the Raqqa sound studio and had taken the Scotsman's place in the villa (the marriage bureau had found him a wife, but the American's French girl had backed out of coming—the only piece of news that had actually made Parvaiz feel happy in the last three months). In his two weeks at the sound studio he'd been assigned mainly low-level tasks—editing distortions out of speeches, cataloging Abu Raees's haphazard sound files—but today Abu Raees, a man who was known to prefer working alone, had asked him to come along and help set up an important field recording. He had felt proud, even though after Farooq—whom he hadn't seen since that first day in Raqqa—he'd learned to mistrust his need for an approving father figure.

He heard Abu Raees calling the name he'd learned to answer to, and pulled a cloth out of the glove compartment. The sand shifted beneath his feet as he trudged back, hands fisted in pockets. The executioner lifted his blade, brought it down onto the kneeling man's neck. Parvaiz bent over, stomach emptying. When he straightened,

wiping the back of his hand across his mouth, the executioner was lifting the blade again, bringing it down to within a few inches of the man's neck again. Abu Raees, headphones on, was checking the DAT levels. The executioner pointed off to the side and Abu Raees walked in the direction he was gesturing, just a few feet away. They were anticipating the trajectory of the man's head when it left his shoulders. Working out where to place the mics.

He reached the kneeling man, bent down to place the cloth in his mouth. The man's lips still moving, the words now discernible. He was praying. Ayat al-Kursi, the prayer Parvaiz's grandmother had taught him to say in times of distress. The prayer he too had been whispering on the walk from the SUV to the kneeling man. The man looked up. Parvaiz wouldn't remember anything of the man's face afterward, only his expressive eyes.

"Come here, listen to this," Abu Raees said, holding out his headphones. Parvaiz reached for them, dropped them. "What's wrong with your hands?"

He shook his head, picked up the headphones again, and managed to fit them onto his head. Abu Raees, eyes narrowed, handed him a mic. What he heard through the headphones was the sound of the mic juddering in his hand. The tremors had moved all the way up to his elbow.

"I can't stop it," he said. And then, "I'm not feeling so well."

"Go and lie down in the SUV," Abu Raees said, turning away.

He did as commanded, lay sealed up in the back of the car, imagining it again and again: the blade cutting through air, cutting through flesh and bone, the body slumping, the head bouncing on the sand, rolling to a stop. The eyes still open, not afraid but accusing.

How long does it take to cut off a man's head?

When Abu Raees finally returned to the car, Parvaiz said, "I don't know why Allah made that happen. My will was in one direction, but my hands couldn't follow. I must have failed Him in some way."

Abu Raees gave him a long, considered look as he invoked the will of Allah as explanation for his failure. A lapse in loyalty could see a man stripped of his privileges and sent to dig trenches on the outskirts of town, where he would be an easy target for aerial bombing. "You should stay up all night praying for forgiveness," Abu Raees said.

"I will," he answered. It was unclear if the taciturn Iraqi believed him or just didn't want to do without such an efficient worker. Impossible here to know who was a true believer and who was playing along for any of a host of reasons, from terror to avarice. The price of letting your mask slip was far too high for anyone to risk it.

For days and days after that, he worked in the studio on sound effects of beheadings, crucifixions, whipping. This was both a test and a punishment. In the studio, he had control of himself. Abstracting himself to that place where nothing but getting the sound right mattered. The fascination of discovering the different pitch and timbre of a nail through flesh, a blade through flesh. Some men were men in their dying screams, some were animals. He, Mohammad bin Bagram, now numbered himself among the animals.

And that's why, although he'd been given his own phone since joining the studio and could finally speak to his sister without a minder standing within earshot, he hadn't called her. Just daily chat messages to let her know he was alive, then he'd log off. Conversation had

become unimaginable. What have you been up to? How was your day? How are you doing?

But then, in the early days of April, he logged onto Skype to quickly send his daily message and there was one from her: Call me. I'm working on a plan to get you home.

Home. A place from a past he'd turned his back on, and to which MI5 would make sure he never returned.

I'm fine here, he wrote back.

And she replied, Liar.

||||||||||||||||||||

He left the café, head bent, walk altered. Keeping watch for Farooq's white SUV, he shuffled past Galata Tower to the broad pedestrianized Istiklal Caddesi, where the presence of a clothing shop he knew from London was a comfort. He entered, bought a pair of blue jeans, a gray T-shirt, a black baseball cap with the shop's name stitched on it. Changed into the new set of clothes, left the ones he had bought just a couple of hours earlier in the changing room, and walked out.

The next shop he went into sold cell phones. He'd destroyed the SIM card from the brick handset in case it could be used to locate him, but buying a new SIM card required identification. Or, he discovered, part of the large wad of Turkish liras left over from his shopping spree in the electronics store. He fitted the SIM card into the brick and texted Aneeka to let her know how to contact him. Her flight would be leaving soon.

Doing something other than waiting for Farooq to walk into the

café and find him made him feel briefly in control, and for a few minutes he walked unconcernedly among the camouflage of crowds of people, looking at the elegant facades of the buildings lining the street. The bookshop tempted him, as did the movie theater, but it felt safer to be in public, among people, with more than one direction in which he could run. From the corner of his eye he caught a flash of white sleeve and his legs turned to water before his gaze traveled up the arm to an unfamiliar face.

He sat down on a step leading into a shop. Closed his eyes, forced himself to remember the song playing in the kitchen the day Aneeka joked with him about Asian wedding sites. Chimta and bass guitar, dholak and drums, a man's voice carrying a song that arose from a place deeper than the currents of history. He drew his knees up to his chest. Just across the street was a narrow road. If he cut down it he would be at the British consulate. Perhaps he should just do it. Why wait for Aneeka, why embroil her in this? He could simply present himself there: I made a mistake. I'm prepared to face trial if I've broken laws. Just let me go to London. But he was the terrorist son of a terrorist father. He rested his head on his knees. He didn't know how to break out of these currents of history, how to shake free of the demons he had attached to his own heels.

꙼꙼꙼꙼꙼꙼꙼꙼꙼꙼꙼

The MiG dropped its payload close enough to rattle the windows and the plates in the studio's communal lunch room.

"Go," Abu Raees said. "Hurry. Take this." He pulled the Zoom H2

out of his pocket, but Parvaiz was already on his feet, reaching into his own pocket to demonstrate he hadn't forgotten the most basic lesson: always have a portable recorder on you. "Good! Now go."

He drove in the direction of the plume of smoke, one hand pressing the horn to move other vehicles out of the way. Before he reached the place where the smoke was densest—a market—he slowed, switched off the air-conditioning, and rolled down the windows to let in the blast of hot May air and the sounds of the city. Across Raqqa, the roar of power generators provided an aural map of where the members of the State lived and worked, but he was too accustomed to the inequality between the locals and those who ruled over them to pay it much attention anymore. Before long he heard a loud, repeated cry that came from a street so narrow he had to park his SUV around the corner and enter on foot. There were men standing on the corner, facing away from the street. All locals, who knew him at a glance by his foreign features, his white robes, as a member of the State. They looked at him, a couple seemed about to speak, but he brushed past them. By now he could make out the word "help" in a woman's voice.

The narrow street was deserted, even the shops along it empty. Parvaiz ran, able now to see the collapsed section of a wall even though he couldn't see what was pinned beneath it.

A voice called out sharply. The door opened to a van he'd assumed empty, one he now identified by the writing on its side as belonging to the Hisba, the morality police. The man who emerged—only a little older than Parvaiz—spoke to him first in Arabic and then, seeing he didn't understand, English.

"She has taken off her face veil. You can't approach her. We've

called the women's brigade." He was holding his hand against the side of his face so that no inadvertent movement of his eye muscle might cause him to look upon an unveiled woman.

"Please," she called out. "Please, please help me." Oh god, a Londoner's voice. A young voice, maybe his age, Aneeka's age.

"If we go to her to help, surely that isn't a greater sin than leaving a sister to suffer?"

"She is being left to suffer because she removed her face veil."

"She may have needed to do it to breathe properly."

Could she hear him, he wondered, as he raised his voice? Could she hear the London in him? "Please," she was still crying out, "please help, it hurts." And then, jolting his heart, "Mum! Mum, I'm sorry."

A memory then of arms lifting him up when he fell off the garden shed, a cheek pressed against his. His mother. Or Isma. There was a woman without a face veil just a few feet from him. A woman's face, the softness of her cheek. She might have bad teeth, a crooked nose, chicken-pox scars, and she would still be the most remarkable, the most dangerous thing in the world.

"Brother, watch yourself."

There were a great many things he could say right then, and all but one of them would get him killed. "Jazakallah khayr, brother. Thank you for correcting me. And for preserving our sister's modesty from the gaze of strangers."

The man took his hand, squeezed it. "Are you married? No? You should be. We will find you a wife. Alhamdullillah."

"Alhamdulillah," he replied, disengaging his hand as soon as, but not before, it seemed inoffensive to do so.

"Please don't go," she called after him. "Please, brother. Why won't you help me?"

Oh, to be deaf. Allah, take away my hearing. Take away the memory of that voice.

What was in his face that made the men on the street corner back away, frightened? At nineteen he was terrifying to grown men. He was the State.

He strode onward to the SUV. Once inside he rolled up the windows he'd left open, knowing no one would dare touch what belonged to a man like him. These were the kinds of things he'd learned to take for granted, the small privileges he enjoyed. Whispering a prayer, he logged onto Skype. Her status was DO NOT DISTURB, but that was never meant for him. It would have to be a voice call rather than a video call so that no one might look in through the window and see him talking to an unveiled woman.

"P! Thank god. Oh, thank god."

Her voice, so long unheard, broke him open. He leaned his forehead on the steering wheel so that no one could see the tears he thought he'd stopped being able to cry.

"What's happened? Are you in trouble?"

The things you forget. How it feels to hear someone speak to you with love.

"No, I just. I can't stay here. I can't do it. They're taken my passport so I have to but I can't. I thought if I learned the rules . . . but I can't. I can't. I just want to come home."

He could hear her exhale on the other end, understood that she

had been waiting for this admission since he'd left, and that failing to make it had been just another way he'd caused her pain. He started to apologize but she cut him short, her voice taking on the brisk efficiency of the women of his family, which he loved, which he missed, which he should never have left.

"You have to get to Istanbul. Can you do that?"

"I don't know. Maybe. Yes, eventually. When they trust you enough you can get a pass if you have a reason."

"Find a reason. And then go to the British consulate and tell them to give you a passport."

"Aneeka, I'm the enemy. You know what they do to the enemy. Do you? Do you know? You said you had a plan—please tell me you have a plan."

"What happened to our father won't happen to you."

"You don't know that."

"I'm making sure of things here."

"What does that mean?"

"Explain when I see you. Some things need to be explained face-to-face. But trust me."

"What are you up to?"

"It's funny. I thought I was doing something for you. But it's turned out nice for me. Remember that when I explain it to you, okay?"

"Oh god, what? You shagging the head of MI5?"

The joy of teasing her, of finding that voice still lived in his throat.

"Shut up. Come home."

"Okay."

|||||||||||||||||||||||

People were beginning to look at the man with the trembling hands sitting on a step while everyone else on İstiklal Caddesi was moving. He stood, walked a short distance, and crossed into a shop that had books and old maps in its windows. Inside, an old man behind the counter looked up, nodded, looked down again at his newspaper. There was a quiet inside here of the sort other people would call "atmosphere," but he knew it was all about the way the carpet muffled footsteps, and the closed door blocked out noise from the outside, and the tiny hum of the air conditioner. He walked over to the wooden map display cabinet with four drawers, each containing dozens of old maps. The Ottoman Empire, Konstantinopel, La Turquie en Asie, Asia Minor, Egypt and Carthago, The Dardanelles, The Abbasid Caliphate in the Ninth Century.

He handled the maps with one hand, the other holding tightly to the brick handset. Aneeka should have texted back by now. Something was wrong at her end, he didn't know what, but when he'd called as his cab sped away from the electronics shop and said he was in Istanbul she sounded first incredulous, then irate. *Why didn't you give me any advance warning?* I didn't want to get your hopes up in case something went wrong. *Today of all days!* Why, what's so special about today? *Nothing, never mind, it'll be fine. Today is perfect. Just, it's all being sorted out right now. It'll be fine.* Which one of us are you trying to convince? What's going on? *Look, I need to call someone, I'll call you back.*

But when she called back a few minutes later she was anxious, didn't directly answer his question about whether she'd arranged

whatever she was trying to arrange. He'd said perhaps he'd be safest returning to Farooq, maybe trying this again some other time. *No, just go to the consulate.* I can't. I'm scared of what they'll do to me. *No, wait, give me five minutes, I'll call you back.* No—if I'm going back I have to go back now, before he realizes I've run away. *No, no, no. Don't. I'll come to you. I'll get the next flight. Just find someplace he won't find you, and stay there until I arrive. We'll go to the consulate together.* And all he could think was at least that way he'd see her. Whatever they did to him once he arrived at the consulate, at least he would see her first. He could bear anything else, as long as he saw her first.

A little space of clarity opened up in his brain. Of course they wouldn't allow her to board a flight to the very place from which her twin had disappeared into the world of the enemy. She was probably still arguing the point, refusing to leave the airport until they gave her a boarding pass. Isma's voice in his head calling him selfish, irresponsible, and she was right.

He wrote to her: You don't need to come here and hold my hand. It'll be ok. I'm going to the consulate now. Will be home soon—biryani when I get there? Page 131 of the recipe book.

He pressed send, his hands steady.

||||||||||||||||||||

It was Farooq, in the end, who was his means of escape. He turned up at the villa-cum-studio one afternoon, catching Parvaiz in a headlock as he stepped off the prayer mat in the covered veranda at the end of Zuhr prayers, and kissing him hard on the temple.

"My little warrior's grown up," he said. "Do you get a lunch break?"

Abu Raees, who had been praying alongside Parvaiz, tapped Farooq on the arm. "Who are you? What are you doing here?"

"I'm a fighter," Farooq said, moving his shoulders back, his chest forward in a way Parvaiz had once thought of as impressive and now saw as ridiculous. "And I'm his sponsor."

Abu Raees looked as uninterested in this as he did in all conversations suggesting any of his employees had a life beyond the studio. "Early for lunch," was all he said.

"I'm driving out soon," Farooq said, with a tone of self-importance. "Picking up new recruits in Istanbul tomorrow." Glancing at Parvaiz, he said, "The cousins are getting good at it."

Parvaiz forced his face into a look of appreciation. A few weeks earlier, during a dinner of kebabs at a restaurant overlooking the Euphrates, the Scotsman confirmed what Parvaiz already half knew: when they'd met, Farooq had been in London to train his cousins as recruiters. Parvaiz had appeared at just the right time to serve as guinea pig. The Scotsman hadn't really said "guinea pig." The word "pig" was too haram to pass his lips. Instead, he'd found some other way of expressing it that made Parvaiz out to be an instrument of Allah's will. From Farooq's manner now it seemed this was a line Parvaiz was expected to have taken too. Parvaiz imagined running a sword through Farooq's throat, hearing the gurgle of blood.

"Take him with you," Abu Raees said, jerking a thumb at Parvaiz. "I need some equipment for the studio."

"If you can organize a pass before I leave," Farooq said doubtfully, looking at his watch.

"Of course I can," Abu Raees said.

That easy.

||||||||||||||||||||||

He stood on the pavement of Meşrutiyet Caddesi, looking at the brick wall with black spikes rising from it that allowed only a partial glimpse of the facade of the consulate. But the view of the red, white, and blue flag that fluttered from the roof, cheerful in all its colors, was uninterrupted. Mo Farah at the Olympics, Aunty Naseem's commemorative cake tin from the Queen's Golden Jubilee.

London. Home.

Aneeka

7

i.

It was not a possibility her mind knew how to contain. Everyone else in the world, yes. Everyone else in the world, inescapably. Some in stages: their grandfather, for weeks half paralyzed, unable to speak, even his breath unfamiliar. Some in a thunderclap: their mother, dropping dead on the floor of the travel agency where she worked, leaving behind the morning's teacup with her lipstick on the rim, treasured until the day one of the twins stood up in a rage and swung the cup by its handle, smashing their mother's mouth (Aneeka thought it was her; Parvaiz insisted it was him). Some in a sleight of hand: their grandmother, awaiting the test results that they had already decided would be presented as a death sentence, crossing the road as a drunk driver took a turn too fast; the doctor called two weeks later with the good news that the tumor was benign. Some as abstraction: their father, never a living presence in their life, dead for years before they knew to attach that word to him. Everyone died, everyone but the twins, who looked at each other to understand their own grief.

Grief manifested itself in ways that felt like anything but grief; grief obliterated all feelings but grief; grief made a twin wear the

same shirt for days on end to preserve the morning on which the dead were still living; grief made a twin peel stars off the ceiling and lie in bed with glowing points adhered to fingertips; grief was bad-tempered, grief was kind; grief saw nothing but itself, grief saw every speck of pain in the world; grief spread its wings large like an eagle, grief huddled small like a porcupine; grief needed company, grief craved solitude; grief wanted to remember, wanted to forget; grief raged, grief whimpered; grief made time compress and contract; grief tasted like hunger, felt like numbness, sounded like silence; grief tasted like bile, felt like blades, sounded like all the noise of the world. Grief was a shape-shifter, and invisible too; grief could be captured as reflection in a twin's eye. Grief heard its death sentence the morning you both woke up and one was singing and the other caught the song.

When she received the words that made her singular for the first time in her life, she pushed them away. It was not true, they meant someone else, it wasn't him. Where was the proof, bring him to me. No, they couldn't do these things because it was not him. If it had been him it wouldn't be this man sitting in Aunty Naseem's living room bringing the news, a plastic comb sticking out of his breast pocket. He wasn't one of yours, she told the man; we aren't yours. Then she left him downstairs, went to her room to catch up on the reading for class she had neglected since her brother had called earlier that day. And now he was sulking because she hadn't come to him though she promised she would. She locked her door against Aunty Naseem's knocking and entreating. It wasn't her fault, they hadn't let her through. *For your own protection,* they'd said, taking her passport away, refusing to say when she could get it back. Or no, he wasn't

sulking, he was on his way to her, the texts he had sent stuck somewhere in a foreign network, this happened sometimes, a logjam of communication unable to cross borders for hours or days at a time and then the onslaught of pinging that was every message arriving in triplicate. It had happened with her aunt texting from Karachi six months ago: Where is he? When is he coming? He could at least call to explain, don't they teach manners in England? He was on his way to her, flying home, watching the stars from his window seat—Castor and Pollux holding hands through the cold, dark night.

She fell asleep and at some point there were arms around her in that childhood familial way. It wasn't a surprise, but that made it no less a pleasure to curl into the warmth of a twin and slip deeper into that level of sleep where nightmares can't reach, held fast by love, a foretaste of heaven.

ii.

The sunlight across her eyes was late morning. She turned in bed, her body heavy with sleep and anticipation. No one there but an indentation on the pillow. Out of bed and down the stairs she went, to the voices of Aunty Naseem and her two daughters and sons-in-law, all of whom had skipped work to come over and welcome home the boy whose absence they'd carried as a secret these past six months when everyone else thought he was in Karachi. Kaleem Bhai—Aunty Naseem's older son-in-law—had even given Aneeka the handset he used on trips to Pakistan so she could send occasional messages seemingly from Parvaiz to his friends missing home not missing the weather camels look so surly because they can never escape their own smell sorry trying to stay off the grid—exploring my inner ascetic. *Someone will find out eventually,* Kaleem Bhai had said, but she'd known from the start that her brother would never stay away very long.

But why was it Isma coming toward her—liar, betrayer, but now that Parvaiz was home she could be forgiven. But even so, why was it Isma catching her in a familiar familial embrace, and why the face she knew too well the one that had said Ama's dead Dadi's dead, why her

voice heavy with tears saying, "I took the first flight when Aunty Naseem called," and "We'll always have each other," when Isma had never been "always"; "always" stretched both forward and back, womb to tomb, "always" was only Parvaiz.

And why was he back, the man with the plastic comb in his pocket, the representative of the Pakistan High Commission, holding his hands up as she entered the room, apologizing for yesterday, which should have meant apologizing for bringing them someone else's grief but instead meant apologizing that he'd failed to lift his cupped hands and recite Inna lillahi wa inna ilayhi raji'un—We surely belong to Allah and to him we return.

"No," she said to the man. "You're confusing him with someone else. He's a British citizen; he has nothing to do with you."

"I'm sorry," the man said, miserably, looking at Isma, who had taken Aneeka's hand as if one of them were a child in need of help crossing the road. "You're obviously a good, pious family. You don't deserve this treatment from your government. This home secretary has a point to prove about Muslims, no?"

She'd been so preoccupied with waiting to hear from Parvaiz she'd failed to notice Eamonn hadn't called back.

iii.

The Turkish government confirmed this morning that the man killed in a drive-by shooting outside the British consulate in Istanbul yesterday was Wembley-born Pervys Pasha, the latest name in the string of Muslims from Britain who have joined ISIS. Intelligence officials were aware that Pasha crossed into Syria last December, but as yet have no information about why he was approaching the British consulate. A terror attack has not been ruled out. The man in the white SUV who shot Pasha has not been identified, but security analysts suggest he could have belonged to a rival jihadi group. The home secretary spoke just minutes ago to our political correspondent, Nick Rippons, about Pervys Pasha:

—So we have yet another case of a British citizen who

    —I'm going to cut you off there, Nick. As you know, the
    day I assumed office I revoked the citizenship of all dual

nationals who have left Britain to join our enemies. My predecessor only used these powers selectively, which, as I have said repeatedly, was a mistake.

—And Pervys Pasha was a dual national?

—That's correct. Of Britain and Pakistan.

—Practically speaking, does this have any consequences now that he's dead?

—His body will be repatriated to his home nation, Pakistan.

—He won't be buried here?

—No. We will not let those who turn against the soil of Britain in their lifetime sully that very soil in death.

— Has his family in London been informed?

— That's a matter for the Pakistan High Commission. Excuse me, Nick, that's all I have time for.

iv.

#WOLFPACK

Just started trending

#PERVYPASHA

Just started trending

#DONTSULLYOURSOIL

Just started trending

#GOBACKWHEREYOUCAMEFROM

Just started trending

v.

The kitchen filled with food for mourners who didn't come.

Only Gladys phoned. Her daughter had arrived in the afternoon to bundle her in the car and take her to Hastings, where she wasn't supposed to leave the house until the news cycle stopped replaying the woman with mascara-stained cheeks telling news cameras: "He was a beautiful, gentle boy. Don't you try to tell me who he was. I knew him from the day he was born. Shame on you, Mr. Home Secretary. Shame on you! Give us our boy to bury, give his mother the company of her son in the grave."

vi.

@gladysinraqqa

Tweets 2   Following 0   Followers 2,452

Ooh such beautiful boys, let me lift my veil to see them better—oh, I'm being gently #crucified.

Come on boys, look at me, I can do things those 72 virgins don't know about. #MaybeThisIsntHeaven

vii.

What was this? Not grief. Grief she knew. Grief was the stepsibling they'd grown up with, unwanted and inevitable. Grief the amniotic fluid of their lives. Grief she could look in the eyes while her twin stared over its shoulder and told her of the world that lay beyond. Grief changed its shape to fit your contours—enveloping you as a second skin you eventually learned to slip into and resume your life. Grief was the deal God struck with the angel of death, who wanted an unpassable river to separate the living from the dead; grief the bridge that would allow the dead to flit among the living, their footsteps overhead, their laughter around the corner, their posture recognizable in the bodies of strangers you would follow down the street, willing them never to turn around. Grief was what you owed the dead for the necessary crime of living on without them.

But this was not grief. It did not cleave to her, it flayed her. It did not envelop her, it leaked into her pores and bloated her beyond recognition. She did not hear his footsteps or his laughter, she no longer knew how to hunch down and inhabit his posture, she couldn't look into a mirror and see his eyes looking back at her.

This was not grief. It was rage. It was his rage, the boy who allowed himself every emotion but rage, so it was the unfamiliar part of him, that was all he was allowing her now, it was all she had left of him. She held it to her breast, she fed it, she stroked its mane, she whispered love to it under the starless sky, and sharpened her teeth on its gleaming claws.

viii.

The police came around, notepads on knee, recorders in hand, received as their due Isma's thanks for not insisting on an interview at Scotland Yard.

"Why won't you let him come home? He wanted to come home, he was trying to come home."

They weren't there to talk about Parvaiz, they were SO1, Specialist Protection, assigned to the home secretary.

"Oh. This is about Eamonn?"

Isma had lifted the teapot to pour a cup for the policemen and seemed to forget what she intended to do with it, holding it motionless just a few inches off the table, looking at her sister, color rising from her throat to her face.

"I was with him because I thought he could help. Ask him, he'll tell you, I wanted my brother to be able to come back. It's all I want now. Why the secrecy? Why do you think? Because of men like you with your notepads and your recorders. Because I wanted him to want to do anything for me before I asked him to do something for my brother. Why shouldn't I admit it? What would you stop at to help the people

you love most? Well, you obviously don't love anyone very much if your love is contingent on them always staying the same."

Watching Isma, who had set the teapot down without pouring it and was staring at her. Suspecting something that had never occurred to her before. What might she have felt about it were there space for other feelings?

"There's no need for any such warning. What good would it do me to contact him now?"

When they left there was Isma, wounded and appalled.

"Don't look at me like that. If you liked him you should have done it yourself. Why didn't you love our brother enough to do it yourself?"

ix.

"Aneeka. Can I come up?"

"Why? I don't want to see you, and now you know about Eamonn you don't want to see me either."

"You're the only family I have left. There's nothing bigger than that."

"What's that noise?"

"The movers packing up inside."

"Have they left? The Migrants?"

"Yes. We have their expensive blinds and an electric kettle with four heat settings in place of next month's rent."

"You're blaming him, aren't you? For the loss of your posh tenants."

"Stop acting as if you're the only one whose heart is broken. He was my baby boy."

"And Eamonn? What was he? I think you mind about him more than Parvaiz."

"Why do you want to be so hurtful? He was five minutes of my life. You two were my life. I'm coming up."

"You never did when he was sitting here."

"Move up a little, won't you?"

"I don't think he wants you here."

"He's beyond wanting now."

"I don't want you here. You betrayed him."

"That isn't why he's dead. That has nothing to do with why he's dead. You have to forgive me. Please, I'm sorry, forgive me."

"Do you believe in heaven and hell?"

"Only as parables. A god of mercy wouldn't condemn any of his creation to eternal suffering."

"So what happens after death?"

"I don't know. Something. Our dead watch over us, I know that. They're trying to speak to me today, to tell me what I can do for you."

"Nothing. There is nothing to do for me. What are you willing to do for him?"

"I pray for him, for his soul."

"What about his body?"

"That's just a shell."

"Hold a shell up to your ear and you can still hear the ocean it came from."

"Hmm. So, what do you believe happens after death?"

"I don't know the things you know. Life, death, heaven, hell, god, soul. I only know Parvaiz."

"What does he want?"

"He wants to come home. He wants me to bring him home, even in the form of a shell."

"You can't."

"That isn't reason not to try."

"How?"

"Will you help me?"

"Why can you never understand the position we're in? We can't even say the kinds of things Gladys said, we don't have that liberty. Remember him in your heart and your prayers, as our grandmother remembered her only son. Go back to uni, study the law. Accept the law, even when it's unjust."

"You don't love either justice or our brother if you can say that."

"Well, I love you too much to see anything else right now."

"Your love is useless to me if you won't help."

"Your love is useless to him now he's dead."

"Get off his shed. Your voice doesn't belong here."

"Aneeka. I need my sister—how can either of us bear this alone?"

Isma's hand stroking her hair, trying to take her away from Parvaiz.

"Go."

"SHATTERED AND HORRIFIED":
SISTER OF PARVAIZ PASHA SPEAKS

Early this morning, Isma Pasha, the 28-year-old sister of London-born terrorist Parvaiz Pasha, who was killed in Istanbul on Monday, read a statement to journalists outside her family home in Wembley. She said, "My sister and I were shattered and horrified last year when we heard that our brother, Parvaiz, had gone to join people we regard as the enemies of both Britain and Islam. We informed Counter Terrorism Command immediately, as Commissioner Janet Stephens has already said. We wish to thank the Pakistan High Commission in Turkey for the efforts they're making to have our brother's body sent to Pakistan, where relatives will make plans for his burial, as an act of remembrance to our late mother. My sister and I have no plans to travel to Pakistan for the funeral."

Pasha's local mosque has also issued a statement to clar-

ify it does not intend to hold funeral prayers for the dead man, and condemned rumors to the contrary as "part of a campaign of hatred against law-abiding British Muslims."

Pasha's body is in a mortuary in Istanbul, and sources say it could be several days before it is released for repatriation to Pakistan.

Istanbul police have said the dead man was not carrying any weapons at the time of his death. His reasons for approaching the British consulate when he was killed remain unknown, as does the identity of his killer—described by eye witnesses as an Asian male in his 30s. Commissioner Janet Stephens has said Pasha was working with the media wing of ISIS, which is responsible for the recruitment of fighters and of so-called "jihadi brides." Tower Hamlets resident Mobashir Hoque, whose daughter, Romana, left for Syria in January to marry an ISIS fighter, told reporters, "My daughter was tricked into going by the lies and propaganda of men such as Parvaiz Pasha. My only disagreement with the Home Secretary's decision is that it deprives me of the chance to spit on the terrorist's grave."

Sources in the Home Office say the Immigration Bill due to go before Parliament in the next session will introduce a clause to make it possible to strip any British passport holders of their citizenship in cases where they have acted against the vital interests of the UK. Under present rules only dual nationals or naturalized citizens with a claim to another nationality can have their citizenship revoked. The Home Sec-

retary has repeatedly expanded on his predecessor's claim that "citizenship is a privilege not a right" to say "citizenship is a privilege not a right or birthright." The human rights campaign group Liberty issued a statement to say: "Removing the right to have rights is a new low. Washing our hands of potential terrorists is dangerously shortsighted and statelessness is a tool of despots not democrats."

xi.

Woke up to rain gusting in through the windows broken by rocks. Isma had said at least it meant they spared Aunty Naseem's house. Isma, shattered and horrified, playing the good citizen even now, dragging her sister's name into that shameful act. Isma, traitor, betrayer.

Alone now in the house they'd grown up in, empty, the Migrants gone with all their furniture, only a mattress for furnishing, which Kaleem Bhai and Isma dragged across the street, *since you insist on sleeping here*, a double mattress for both sisters but this house was for the twins only now. Made Isma leave with a shrieking flapping of arms madwoman behavior that finally drove her away. Downstairs a pounding sound, what? Someone trying to break in, to break the house from inside for the crime of having been a roof over the terrorist's head. Picked up the electric kettle with four heat settings the closest thing to a weapon that remained. Opened the door to David Beckham, the Queen, Zayn Malik boarding up the broken windows. Beckham almost hammered his thumb in surprise. "Didn't

think anyone was here," he said from behind the mask with the voice of Abdul.

"Better go inside there may still be journos lurking," said Zayn Malik, who was really David Beckham's father.

"Cuppa would be lovely, though," said the Queen aka Nat the greengrocer, jerking her tiaraed head toward the kettle.

xii.

Countless hours of recording, and never his own voice. As though he'd started to practice disappearing long ago. Now he wouldn't even enter her dreams. Too angry.

xiii.

HOW MANY PARVAIZ PASHAS WILL IT TAKE
FOR THE GOVERNMENT TO WAKE UP?

The revelation that Adil Pasha, the father of recently dead terrorist Parvaiz Pasha, abandoned his family in order to take up jihad has not entirely come as a surprise to one former classmate of the Preston Road resident.

"There was a rumor that his father had been a jihadi in Afghanistan who died in Guantánamo," said the classmate, who wished to remain unnamed. "His sisters always denied it and said he'd died of malaria while abroad, but Parvaiz never did. I didn't think anything of it at the time, but looking back it's obvious he thought jihad was something to boast about when he was still just a little kid."

Sources at the Met say Adil Pasha fought with jihadi groups in Bosnia and Chechnya in the '90s, and traveled to Afghanistan in 2001 to fight with the Taliban. He is believed to have died soon after. "We have no idea if he was killed in

a battle or died of malaria or from other causes. But if he'd ever been in Guantánamo there would have been records, and there simply aren't," said a retired Special Branch officer who interviewed the Pasha family in 2002. "I remember the son, Parvaiz. He was very young but was already being allowed to idolize the father who fought with Britain's enemies. I took away the photograph album he had with pictures of his dad holding a Kalashnikov, and an inscription saying 'One day you'll join me in jihad.' I recommended CPS keep a close eye on him, but unfortunately this recommendation was never taken up."

It's a cause of profound concern that the children of jihadis, many of them British-born, are not closely watched by the state. How many more Parvaiz Pashas will it take for things to change?

xiv.

He'd returned from the Pakistan High Commission that day to say he didn't have to pay the exorbitant visa fees for British nationals or go through bureaucratic processes in order to work in Karachi because turns out he had something called a NICOP.

"Oh yes," Isma said, "I got them for all of us when I was planning that trip to Pakistan which never happened, remember?"

Up to the attic Parvaiz went, and down he came triumphant. One for you and one for me, he said, handing Aneeka the laminated card with NATIONAL IDENTITY CARD FOR OVERSEAS PAKISTANI printed on it. She glanced at the picture, remembered then how sullenly she had accompanied her sister to the High Commission to have the card issued, hating the idea of missing a summer in London, to spend it in a country teeming with relatives who thought blood ties gave them the right to interrogate and lecture and point to the sisters' hijabs as proof that British Pakistanis were "caught in the past" then point to their jeans to prove they were "mixed up." It didn't improve her mood to see that the card insisted on listing NAME OF FATHER. In the end, though, something in the phone conversations with the rich relatives

who had promised to fund the trip had gotten Isma's back up, and the cards were dispatched to the filing cabinet in the attic along with birth certificates and NHS cards and X-rays of broken bones.

"What is an Overseas Pakistani, exactly?" she asked.

Parvaiz shrugged. "Think it just means your family's from there so you're exempt from visas. Anyway, that's the only part that's relevant to me."

"To us," she said. "I'll need it when I come to visit you. Put it in my purse, would you? I don't want to have to go up to the spidery attic to find it when you're gone." She had no memory of his expression as he did as she asked.

Now the laminated card with her sullen fourteen-year-old self sat on the desk at the High Commission while the man with the plastic comb in his pocket looked sadly down on it.

"You should do what your older sister says, and stay away," he said. "Ladies don't go for the burial anyway, so you would only be praying at home, which you can do just as well in London as in Karachi—Allah would hear even a prayer whispered by a mute from the bottom of the world's deepest ocean."

"Am I or am I not entitled to a Pakistani passport?"

"Yes."

"I have a bank draft for the urgent-processing fee. Please tell me who I should give it to."

XV.

HO-JABI! PERVY PASHA'S TWIN SISTER ENGINEERED SEX TRYSTS WITH HOME SECRETARY'S SON

Aneeka "Knickers" Pasha, the 19-year-old twin sister of Muslim fanatic Parvaiz "Pervy" Pasha has been revealed as her brother's accomplice. She hunted down the Home Secretary's son, Eamonn, 24, and used sex to try and brainwash him into convincing his father to allow her terrorist brother back into England.

"Knickers" kept her true identity hidden from her lover until hours before her twin brother was fortunately killed while trying to enter the British consulate in Istanbul. Eamonn Lone quickly informed the Home Secretary that the woman he had allowed into his bed wanted him to use his influence with his father to bring her evil brother back into Britain. Karamat Lone immediately contacted the security services, but before any actions could be taken Pervy Pasha was killed.

The brave Home Secretary, who has taken a strong stand against extremists at risk to his own life, had kept quiet while a police investigation was taking place. This morning his office issued a short statement revealing the sordid affair and promised "full transparency." Although the terrorist's Twisted Sister cannot be proved to have broken any laws, she has been told to keep her distance from the Home Secretary's son, who is understood to be staying with friends in Norfolk. "She was barking up the wrong tree. The Home Secretary would never compromise this nation's security for any reason," say sources close to the Lone family.

INSIDE: DAUGHTER AND SISTER OF MUSLIM TERRORISTS, WITH HISTORY OF SECRET SEX LIFE— THE EXCLUSIVE STORY OF "KNICKERS" PASHA

xvi.

He looked like a taunt
tasted like a world apart
felt like barriers dissolving

He looked like opportunity
tasted like hope
felt like love

He looked like a miracle
tasted like a miracle
felt like a miracle

A real
actual
straight from God
prostrate yourself in prayer
as you hadn't done since your brother left
miracle.

xvii.

Packed a suitcase, wheeled it outside, the first time leaving the house in days, cameras, microphones, police holding them back. Isma rushing out from Aunty Naseem's house across the road "where are you going." Isma not someone she ever had to answer to again.

Kept walking, police flanking her "miss please go back inside" stepped into the waiting car, Dame Edna this time aka Abdul who had become chief protector, ally, jumping garden walls to enter her house unseen by the press outside. Abdul, who had taken her token and picked up the passport, booked her ticket, paid for it so that Isma wouldn't receive an alert from the credit card company.

Joined quickly by a police escort, TV vans following, never mind, nothing to hide, better this way.

"Why are you helping me, Abdul?"

"Something about me you don't know."

"I've known you're gay since before you did, probably."

"Not that but thank you for never mentioning. I told that Farooq's cousin who Parvaiz was, the rumors about your father, I mean. I think that's why Farooq came for him."

"It's not your fault he went."

"Why did he go?"

"I don't know exactly. I stopped asking it. He wanted to return home, that's what mattered."

"If he comes back, Farooq, I'll kill him."

"No, don't kill him. Take his skin off with the world's smallest scalpel, remove his eyes with an ice cream scoop, drip slow-working acid on his tongue."

"You've thought about this, I guess."

"It's one of the few things I can concentrate on."

"I don't think I could do any of that."

"I know. It's okay."

"One other thing you don't know."

"What's that?"

"Really fancied your brother." Said in a Dame Edna voice.

"Thank you, Abdul. I'd forgotten what it felt like to smile."

At the airport she expected the interrogation room again, but the man at the security checkpoint looked over her shoulder at the police, then down at her new passport and the boarding card to Karachi, and nodded her through.

"Why are you going?" one of the journalists called out from across the barrier, just before she walked into the departure lounge.

"For justice," she said.

xviii.

Karachi: colorful buses, colorless buildings, graffitied walls, billboards advertising cell phones and soft drinks and ice cream, birds circling in the white-hot sky. Parvaiz would have wanted the windows down to listen to every new sound, but she sat back in the car in silence disrupted only by the rattling vents of the air conditioner, a silence not of her own devising but of her cousin's, the guitarist, who refused to explain why she had been escorted off the plane by airport officials who drove her to the cargo terminal where he was waiting to pick her up in a beige car with a sticker on its windscreen announcing its membership to a golf club; it looked more suited to a businessman than a musician.

"Take off the hijab and put these on," was the only thing he'd said, passing her a pair of oversize glasses. She refused, but eventually the sun's glare made her change her mind about the glasses.

The silence continued until he turned into the driveway of a tall white hotel, cleared an ineffectual security check, and pulled over, waving away the valet who came around to take his keys.

"You can get out here," he said.

"For what?"

"Entrance to the hotel is through there. I've checked you in for three days. Under the name Mrs. Gul Khan. His body arrives tomorrow, he'll be buried by the evening. We've arranged a funeral plot, I'll send a car to take you there the next morning. Nine a.m. You can pray over the grave, and leave. Okay? Do not call me. Do not call my mother. You understand?"

"You're the one who needs to understand. He isn't going to be buried. I've come to take him home."

The cousin held his hands up. "I don't want to know. Crazy girl. I don't want to know anything. My sister lives in America, she's about to have a child there—did you or your bhenchod brother stop to think about those of us with passports that look like toilet paper to the rest of the world who spend our whole lives being so careful we don't give anyone a reason to reject our visa applications? Don't stand next to this guy, don't follow that guy on Twitter, don't download that Noam Chomsky book. And then first your brother uses us as a cover to join some psycho killers, and then your government thinks this country can be a dumping ground for its unwanted corpses and your family just expects us to jump up and organize a funeral for this week's face of terrorism. And now you've come along, Miss Hojabi Knickers, and I have to pull strings I don't want to pull to get you out of the airport without the whole world's press seeing you, and it turns out you're here to try some stunt I don't even know what but my family will have nothing to do with it, nothing to do with you."

"I don't want you or your family to have anything to do with it.

Just tell me what time tomorrow he's arriving, and who to speak to about where to bring him."

"What do you mean, where to bring him? You planning on checking a corpse into your hotel room?"

"You really want to know?"

"No. Get out."

"Who do I speak to about where to bring him?"

He reached into his wallet, pulled out a business card, and threw it at her.

"Thank you. By the way, how far are we from the British Deputy High Commission?"

"Look at a map," he said, leaning across to open her door.

xix.

The British Deputy High Commission compound was surrounded by barbed wire, vans bristling with guns, and roadblocks to prevent any stranger's approach. But just a few minutes' walk away there was a park lined with banyan trees, their ancient overground roots more enduring than wire rusting in the sea air or guns that jammed with dust or the calculations made today by politicians looking to the next elections.

Here she would sit with her brother until the world changed or both of them crumbled into the soil around them.

Karamat

8

KARAMAT LONE IGNORED the unusual twitchiness of the shadow stretched out alongside his on the Thames path and poured a second shot of coffee from the thermos into a paper cup. On two separate occasions Eamonn had given him one of those insulated mugs as a birthday present, well intentioned but oblivious to the mug's inability to keep a man's hands warm while doing the same for the coffee. When it came to his son, Karamat had always treated "well intentioned" as good enough. With his daughter, the only other possible candidate for such preferential treatment, there'd never been any need. Poor fellow, he used to think, considering the gap in abilities and achievements between Eamonn and his younger sister. It had never occurred to him that Eamonn alone was blind to his own—the word hurt in relation to a man's only son, but nothing else would do—inadequacy. All the good cheer Karamat had admired as a front became an embarrassment when revealed to be a genuine attitude. *She loves me!* he had continued to insist in the face of all evidence to the contrary. *Why is that so impossible to believe?* A question Karamat had hated answering. He held the paper cup to his face, allowing the steam

to enter his nostrils, warm his cheeks. There was a precise calibration to how long you could do this before the coffee dipped below optimum drinking temperature.

He gulped down the coffee, felt it burn its way pleasingly through him while he continued to look at the Palace of Westminster and its watery reflection, the yellow stone pink-gold in the interlude of sunrise. The heart of tradition, everyone agreed, but few understood Britain as well as Karamat Lone and knew that within the deepest chamber of that heart of tradition was the engine of radical change. Here Britain whittled down the powers of the monarchy, here Britain agreed to leave its empire, here Britain instituted universal suffrage, here Britain would see the grandson of the colonized take his place as prime minister. The most constant criticism against Karamat Lone was that his positions flip flopped between traditionalist and reformer—but the critics learned nothing from their own inability to know which was which. Take, for instance, his intention to expand the home secretary's power to revoke British citizenship so that it applied to British-born single passport holders. It was, clearly, the sensible fulfillment of a law that was so far only half made. You had to determine someone's fitness for citizenship based on actions, not accidents of birth. An increase in draconian powers! said one set of his opponents on the left; a renewed assault on true Englishmen and -women by Britain's migrant population, said another set on the far right. Both sets probably drank coffee out of insulated mugs.

You're doing the contemptuous thing again, Terry would say.

It was one of his wife's few remaining misconceptions about him. Contempt, disdain, scorn: these emotions were stops along a closed

loop that originated and terminated in a sense of superiority. In their preservation of the status quo they were of no use to Karamat Lone. A man needed fire in his veins to burn through the world, not ice to freeze everything in place. He'd thought he had mastered the art of directing the fire, but yesterday, with TV cameras on him, he'd heard the girl's one-line explanation for leaving England and hadn't been able to stop himself from responding: "She's going to look for justice in *Pakistan?*" That final word spoken with all the disgust of a child of migrants who understands how much his parents gave up—family, context, language, familiarity—because the nation to which they first belonged had proven itself inadequate to the task of allowing them to live with dignity. At some point, he'd have to respond to the foreign secretary's irate message about his comment. Or not, if the PM kept up his silence—a silence Karamat worried had less to do with favoring his home secretary than with the PM's irritation at how Pakistan's prime minister was trying to make political capital of the situation. He'd sanctimoniously explained that Pakistan, as a matter of state policy, shouldered the cost of repatriating its citizens while the UK government expected the bereaved to pay thousands of pounds to have the remains of their loved ones returned to them.

A Lycra-covered runner approached, swerved skin-scrapingly close to the Thames path barrier as soon as he was close enough to recognize the home secretary, and held up a hand to the officers to indicate he wasn't a threat. Brown skinned. Karamat clicked his tongue against the back of his teeth.

He twisted off the thermos cap again, shook the container gently, considered the liquid swishing around the glass-lined interior. He

didn't seem to need it despite his total lack of sleep the previous night. The wonders of adrenaline—it had been a long time since he'd stayed up all night wondering what his opponent was going to do. People were usually so predictable.

"Sir," cautioned Suarez behind him.

"That one too Muslim for comfort?"

"That one was Latino."

"You always insist the good-looking ones are your cousins rather than mine."

"We really should go, sir."

Karamat turned to look at the head of his security detail. From the start, Suarez had understood the home secretary's insistence that he didn't want to know anything at all about the threats against him; *You do your job and let me do mine,* Karamat had said. Of course when they cut down trees in his garden and put officers in their place it was obvious there'd been some "development," but Suarez maintained an air of calm through everything. Today, though, he was visibly anxious, and although Karamat had managed to insist on this riverside coffee, a post-sleepless-night tradition stretching back to his earliest days as a backbencher, it was clear that he wouldn't win the argument twice.

He was about to stand up when his phone rang, and the screen told him it was his son. He cradled the phone in his hands for a moment, found the old empty habits forming the word "Bismillah" before he answered.

"Hi, Dad. Thought you'd be up." Eamonn's voice was calm, affectionate, nothing like that of the crazed thing who'd had to be physically restrained from returning to the arms of that manipulative

whore. Well, "arms" wasn't really the bit of her he wanted to return to, was it? Though Karamat probably shouldn't have said so at the time.

"You okay?" He hadn't spoken to Eamonn since Terry had arranged for Max and Alice to take him away to one of Alice's family estates after he'd moved from hysteria to a listless resignation—the press assumed the estate was the one in Norfolk, though it could just as well be Normandy. Karamat hadn't asked Terry not to tell him where their son was, but she knew well enough that it was information better kept from him in case someone asked him a direct question, which he'd have to answer honestly. His wife had always had a perfectly judged sense of who he was, who he had to be, as a public figure, which made it all the more mystifying when she packed up a segment of his wardrobe and moved it down to the basement bedroom in response to his office's breaking the story of Eamonn's involvement with the girl. *You could have protected him,* she'd said, as if her husband were the kind of man either stupid or unethical enough to try to organize a cover-up. She hadn't relented when most of the newspapers correctly portrayed Eamonn as a dupe, and some even managed to suggest he'd turned on the girl as soon as he'd realized what she wanted.

"Yes. I'm sorry how I behaved the other day."

Karamat crossed a foot over his knee, considered the open-mouthed sturgeons with bulging eyes and entwined tails at the base of the nearby lamppost. Usually grotesque, they now appeared winningly comical to his benevolent gaze. "I'm sorry you're going to have a rough ride for a bit. Perhaps that move to New York your sister suggested might not be the worst idea."

"I worry about you more than me."

Karamat stood up and walked to the lamppost, leaned against it, and turned away from his security detail. "That's nice to hear, but unnecessary."

"It's just that from where you're sitting it may not be clear how this looks. A government that sends its citizens to some other country when they act in ways we don't like. Doesn't that say we can't deal with our own problems? And stopping a family from burying its own—that never looks good. That's what people are beginning to say around me. If your advisers won't tell you this, your son will."

"My son, schooling me in politics from his vantage point among the landed gentry," he said, pressing his knuckles into the bulging eyes of the fish.

"I'm saying this because your reputation matters to me. More than you know."

"She told you to say all this, didn't she?"

"I haven't heard from her. You know that. I've done what you asked. I haven't called or texted. You said if I agreed, you would help her. How have you helped her?"

"She's had police protection stationed outside her house. I haven't let the world see the kinds of videos her beloved brother worked on. She hasn't been locked up in an interrogation room for fourteen days without charge, not even after admitting that she seduced my son in order to help a terrorist. You saw that transcript, didn't you? She admitted it."

"Of course she said that once she thought I'd abandoned her."

"Do you hear yourself?"

"Do you hear yourself? You think you're doing someone a favor by not locking them up for fourteen days without reason?"

"Please don't try to develop a spine. You weren't built for it. Did she give you your first really great blow job, Eamonn? Is that what this is about? Because trust me, there are better ones out there."

A pause, and then his son's voice at its most cuttingly posh: "I think we're done here, Father."

The call went dead and Karamat turned around, crumpling the empty paper cup in his fist. Suarez stepped forward and extended his palm to take the cup, teeth marks visible on his thumb. He saw Karamat's eyes on the indentations and folded his thumb over his palm to hide the visual reminder of Eamonn kicking wildly at the air, teeth clamped on Suarez's gag-hand.

Pivoting away from Suarez, he sent the paper cup flying in the direction of the garbage can. It hit the rim, bounced up, plummeted into the receptacle.

Take out the trash. Keep Britain clean.

||||||||||||||||||||||

Mid-morning in London, mid-afternoon Karachi, someone called @CricketBoyzzzz uploaded pictures of a woman in the white of mourning, sitting cross-legged on a white sheet covered in rose petals. The sun-singed grass and the patches of damp on her kameez conveyed an extraordinary heat despite the banyan tree under whose spreading branches and beardlike aerial roots she'd arranged herself. #Knickers #FoundHer

All the press assigned to the Pasha story, scattered among upscale

hotels and graveyards and family homes and airport terminals, descended on the park, only to be met by the blank stare and silence of a girl whom Karamat was beginning to suspect of being as unhinged as she was manipulative.

"Find out where the body is," Karamat instructed his assistant, James, eyes moving between the two TV screens in his Marsham Street office, one tuned to a Pakistani news channel, the other to an international one.

The Pakistani channel had a split screen. One side showed scenes from the park, as increasing numbers of onlookers arrived to cluster around the girl, as if she were the site of an accident; the other showed a studio in which the urbane host of a religious discussion program explained what Shariah law had to say about the Pasha case. The man had slicked-back hair and a black mark on his forehead — the latter a sign of piety, helped along by banging one's head against a stone or rough surface during the daily prostration of prayer. Karamat picked up a lion-and-unicorn paperweight, pressed it to his forehead. First, said the man, the boy had joined those modern-day Khajarites who were a greater enemy of Islam than even America or Israel, and so he should never be described as a "jihadi." Second, he should have been buried before sunset on the day he died, no matter how far from home he was, and anything else was un-Islamic. Third, by her own admission to the UK police, the girl was a sinner, a fornicator, and should be flogged.

Karamat made a note of the man's name and turned his attention to the international channel, where the anchor had pulled up a digital 3-D map of the area surrounding the park and was describing the lo-

cation as "significant" as red circles appeared on the map identifying the gas station next to the park, the convent school and Italian consulate across the street, and the busy roundabout a stone's throw away. The 3-D models of buildings and trees collapsed into the ground as if from a powerful detonation, and what remained was the figure of a girl facing the British Deputy High Commission.

Karamat pressed the mute button and watched the doe-eyed girl in white, head covered, surrounded by bloodred rose petals, the park railings looking like a backdrop of prison bars in close-up shots of her. Nothing accidental in any of it, but what was all the iconography of suffering meant to achieve?

James returned to say the Turkish embassy could confirm only that the body had arrived in Islamabad, but had no details of how or when it would be transported to Karachi, and the Pakistan High Commission had made it clear they expected an apology from the home secretary before they would reveal any information about their citizens to him. Karamat handed him the piece of paper with the urbane host's name and said, "If he has a UK visa, find a reason to cancel it."

"There are some people who think you're wanting a reason to strip her of her citizenship too," James said, indicating the girl on the screen, his accent turning more pronouncedly Scottish and working-class, as it always did when he thought he might be about to enter into a disagreement with Karamat. It was a tic James was almost certainly unaware of, but Karamat had always found it winning that the young man's unconscious played his outsider status up rather than down when he challenged the home secretary.

"And what do you think of that?"

"I think it's a terrible idea. Everyone will think it's because of Eamonn."

"Everyone should know better," Karamat said. He stood up and approached the split screen. "Damned if I know what she's planning next. Would you be standing as near her as all those people in the park?"

"You think she's wearing a suicide vest under those clothes?"

"No, I think she turns everything around her toxic. Look, it's all gone a bit yellow around her, hasn't it?"

"Must be something wrong with the camera lens. I'm sorry, sir, about the suicide vest comment."

"Don't be silly, James. These are the times we live in."

The girl stood up fluidly from her cross-legged posture and stepped off the sheet. A single rose petal adhered to the top of her slim, bare foot. He imagined his son's mouth pressed where the petal was, made a flicking-away motion with his hand. Both TV channels were showing the same scene, from slightly different angles, the air clearly yellow with an impending dust storm. The park—no more than twice the size of the Lone family garden—was bound in by railings and banyan trees, with an open gate toward which she was walking. A van had pulled up outside—an ambulance.

"No. Oh, come on, no."

The driver of the ambulance opened the back doors, called out for some of the onlookers to help him. Far more men than was necessary lifted out the unadorned casket and carried it on their shoulders behind the girl, who, pale but composed, led them back to the white sheet and rose petals—the scene of martyrdom now complete. The

men laid the casket down, but the girl wanted something more from them. She spoke to the man who had driven the ambulance; he shook his head vigorously, pointed to the hazy sky—indicating either the Almighty or the afternoon sun. She knelt beside the casket, placed the palms of her hands, one on top of the other, against the lid, near the corner, and pressed down with all her weight, her knees lifting off the ground with the effort.

"Move the cameras away," he heard himself say.

The wood buckled, splintered.

"Jesus," James said. "Jesus, no."

The dupatta had fallen from her head, long hair whipping across her face as the wind picked up. The casket revealed its flimsy construction, nails ripping out of wood as the girl set to dismantling it with her bare hands. One by one she collapsed the sides until what remained was a shape sandwiched between the coffin's base and a top layer of plywood. The girl sat back on her heels, as if only now, at this moment, had she stopped to consider what she was asking her own eyes to look at. Or maybe she was waiting for what happened next: the yellow-brown wind picked up the plywood and flung it into the air with a whipping sound.

The girl lowered herself to her knees, placed her hands on the ground on either side of her, and leaned forward, as a child might examine some unknown animal found in the garden. Her brother, embalmed, looked *not right*. How else to say it? Dead.

She lifted a hand, looked at it as if she wasn't sure what it was about to do, and watched as her palm came to rest on the forehead of what had once been her twin. The hand jerked away, settled back

down, slid along his skin toward his temple. Karamat and the cameras saw the stitches before she felt them, the place where death entered him. Her expression when she touched the thread was irritated, as if objecting to the untidiness, nothing more. The hand lifted again, moved down to the corpse's wrist, two fingers pressed against what would have been a pulse point. Her mouth opened and a small word or sound may have come out, nothing the mics could pick up.

James said the words "broadcast regulations" with nothing around them. Every phone in the room was ringing. Someone was knocking on the door. "Shut up," Karamat shouted, to everything.

The dust storm that had sent its advance guard now arrived in a hurtling, pelting wind. The white sheet flew up at its corners, tossing aside the rectangles of wood that had weighed it down; rose petals pitched up into the air, came down muddied; leaves were ripped from the banyan trees; the world tilted this way and that; the women wound their dupattas around their faces, the men made themselves small. One camera recorded only the flattened grass through a cracked lens. The other, moving closer to the girl, showed her dupatta fly toward it, a close-up of the tiny embroidered flowers on the white cloth, and then a battering darkness.

For a few moments there was only a howling noise, the wind raging, and then a hand plucked away the white cloth and the howl was the girl, a dust mask on her face, her dark hair a cascade of mud, her fingers interlaced over the face of her brother. A howl deeper than a girl, a howl that came out of the earth and through her and into the office of the home secretary, who took a step back. As if that were the only thing the entire spectacle had been designed to achieve, the wind

dropped as suddenly as buildings collapse in 3-D models, and the girl stopped her noise, unlaced her fingers. The cameras panned, then zoomed. In the whole apocalyptic mess of the park the only thing that remained unburied was the face of the dead boy.

"Impressive," said the home secretary.

‖‖‖‖‖‖‖‖‖‖‖‖‖‖‖‖

The girl licked her thumb, ran it over her mouth, painting lips onto the dust mask. Then she looked directly at the home secretary and spoke:

"In the stories of wicked tyrants, men and women are punished with exile, bodies are kept from their families—their heads impaled on spikes, their corpses thrown into unmarked graves. All these things happen according to the law, but not according to justice. I am here to ask for justice. I appeal to the prime minister: Let me take my brother home."

Karamat spun the paperweight on the desk, watched the lion and unicorn animate, smiled. After all the noise and spectacle, she was just a silly girl.

‖‖‖‖‖‖‖‖‖‖‖‖‖‖‖

Prime Minister's Questions was usually an embarrassment. Childish jeering and taunts, the PM parading his ability at that facile talent, the put-down, the chancellor—or "chancer," as Karamat preferred to think of him—sitting beside him with an expression both obsequious and smug close up but that managed to look just the right degree of supportive on camera. Parliament reduced to a playground. Karamat

had been particularly dreading today—the first PMQs since the Pasha affair began. The PM, who had been abroad and out of touch the last few days, had been worryingly quiet on the whole matter, and any withholding of support from his home secretary would be a victory for the chancer and his leadership bid. But then the girl had opened her mouth.

"Heads impaled on spikes. Bodies thrown into unmarked graves. There are people who follow these practices. Her brother left Britain to join them."

The PM rose above party politics; the leader of the opposition rose to join him. There were "hear, hears" on either side of the aisle. The home secretary was lauded for the difficult decisions he had to make and the personal trials he'd undergone that had in no way affected his judgment or commitment to doing the right thing. Even the chancer had to lean across the space vacated by the PM as he stood at the dispatch box and pat Karamat appreciatively on the shoulder, a tiny nerve pulsing near his eye, which he saw Karamat recognize as defeat.

ıııııııııııııııııııı

James was waiting for him in his room behind the Speaker's Chair, mimicking some awful footballer's goal celebrations as he entered, the right mix of genuine and ironic. Not for the first time, Karamat wished his daughter and James would get together. But that set him off thinking about his children and their choice of partners—you could see Aneeka Pasha was the kind of girl who would do anything. A girl who looked like that and was willing to do anything. His poor

boy never stood a chance. He sat down heavily in his chair, missed his wife—not in the ways he used to miss her when he was Eamonn's age but in the way that only one parent can miss another, when their child is in pain.

He nodded at James to make the required call, and chose to speak in Urdu when his assistant handed him the phone, purely because he knew that puffer fish in human form who was the Pakistan high commissioner would assume it meant the home secretary believed his English was inadequate.

"What mischief are you people up to now?" Karamat asked.

"That's a strange way to start off an apology," the HC replied, in English.

"I'm not the one who has to apologize. That body would never have made it to the park if your government hadn't agreed to it. Or engineered it."

"Come, come," the HC said, unconvincingly. "The closest living relative asked for the body to be brought to a particular spot—on what grounds should the driver have refused? As for my government, it has bigger things to worry about than the logistics of a corpse."

"I assume someone is going to remove the body from the park. On the grounds of hygiene, if nothing else."

"I'm my nation's representative to the Court of St. James's. Do you think I go around talking to municipal councils in Karachi? But maybe things are different in Britain, in which case please tell my bin man not to make such a clanging noise when he comes round in the morning."

"How's your son's student visa application coming along?"

"Actually, he's decided to go with Harvard rather than Oxford. The girl made some interesting points, don't you think?"

It was beginning to stop being enjoyable, so he switched to English. "Fine, I spoke out of turn. Pakistan's judiciary is a credit to your nation."

"Bunch of bastards," the high commissioner said unexpectedly. And then he was the one to switch languages—not to Urdu but Punjabi. "Listen, I'm a father too. I would want her off the news as well."

"It's not that."

"Oh shut up, friend, I'm being sympathetic." Punjabi allowed this breach of etiquette, and Karamat felt something in his whole body shift, become looser. He tightened his shoulders against it. "The issue is, my government has no reason to intervene."

"Intervene on decency's behalf. What kind of madness makes someone leave a corpse out in the heat to putrefy?"

"The madness of love. Remember your Laila-Majnu, Karamat? The lover so grief-stricken at the loss of the beautiful beloved that he wanders, in madness, in the desert. This beautiful girl in a dust storm has managed to become Laila and Majnu combined in the nation's consciousness. Or Sassi and Punnu in parts of the nation—same story, except it's the girl who runs grief-crazed through the desert in search of her love."

"This nation, which has decided to cast her as a romantic heroine, is the same one that wants her flogged?"

"Oh, people are already saying your government made up the whole story about her relationship with your son to discredit her,

though opinion is divided whether it was you or one of your enemies who was behind it. Either way, for us to act against her now is difficult."

"For god's sake, man, do you really expect me to believe your government makes decisions based on a combination of folktales and conspiracy theories?"

"You really are as British as they say you are. Let me put it in language you'll understand: The people, and several opposition parties, have decided to embrace a woman who has stood up to a powerful government, and not just any powerful government but one that has very bad PR in the matter of Muslims and as recently as yesterday insulted us directly. So, now it's political suicide for my government to get involved. I hope we'll see you at our Eid reception. Until then, Allah hafiz."

The door swung open. The expected supporters, and some unexpected ones too, entered, bowing and throwing imaginary hats in the air. Karamat rubbed the back of his hand against his mouth, tasting dust.

⁣⁣⁣||||||||||||||||||||||||

He was in a coffin made of slabs of ice, a prince in a fairy tale. The owner of the city's largest ice factory said he would supply his product free of charge, a truck driver said he would transport it as a religious duty. Everyone who had gathered in the park took turns unloading the ice slabs and passing them along a conveyer belt of human hands to the white sheet, now soaked through. When the ice left their hands they touched their red palms to their faces, the burn of cold against the burn of heat. Those nearest the corpse wrapped their faces in cloth.

The translucency of the ice made it possible for the news channels to continue their live coverage without worrying about meeting broad-cast standards: the corpse was little more than a blurry outline. The girl didn't assist with the continual rebuilding of the melting ice cof-fin, nor did she stop it. Her only insistence was that his face should remain uncovered. Now, as sunset bruised the sky, she stood with her back pressed against the banyan tree, her eyes never moving from that face.

"Is This the Face of Evil?" a tabloid asked, illustrating the question with a picture of the girl howling as dust flew around her. "Slag," "ter-rorist spawn," "enemy of Britain." Those were the words being used to describe her, the paper reported, placing inverted commas around the words as proof. Would the home secretary strip her of her citizenship for acting against the vital interests of the UK, as surely she had done by giving ammunition to the enemies of Britain?

The home secretary set the paper aside with a sound of irritation and resumed looking at Aneeka Pasha. Even when there was nothing new to report there was always someone new to interview, and so the TV journalists were thrusting microphones into the faces of the "rep-resentatives of civil society" who had shown up in support of the be-reaved girl and were now starting to light candles in the deepening twilight.

There was no need to do anything so dramatic as strip her of her citizenship, a move that could be traced back to personal motivations. She couldn't return to the UK on her Pakistani passport without ap-plying for a visa, which she was certainly welcome to do if she wanted to waste her time and money. As for her British passport, which had

been confiscated by the security services when she tried to join her brother in Istanbul, it was neither lost nor stolen nor expired and therefore there were no grounds for her to apply for a new one. Let her continue to be British; but let her be British outside Britain.

The candles threw their reflections onto the ice coffin. Flames trembled along its length, creating the impression of something stirring inside. Karamat walked over to the blinds, opened them to let in the afternoon sunlight, and looked down at the familiar scene of Marsham Street, suddenly so moving in all its quotidian details, cars parked in parking spots, a woman walking by with shopping bags braided around her wrists, trees with thin trunks standing side by side. His London, everyone's London, everyone except those who wanted to harm it. He touched a vein in his neck, felt the reassuring warmth of his own blood.

IIIIIIIIIIIIIIIIIIIIII

He returned home to Holland Park after *Newsnight*, a tough interview as expected, but he'd maintained his calm, clarified that he had never made a decision about a corpse—his decision had been about a living "enemy of Britain" (he used the expression three times, which seemed just right, though he might have been able to get away with a fourth). The very word "repatriation," which is what the girl wanted for her brother's corpse, rested on a fact of citizenship that had ceased to exist the day he, Karamat Lone, took office and sent an unequivocal message to those who treated the privilege of British citizenship as something that could be betrayed without consequences. No, he didn't think it was harsh to send that message even to the girls who went as so-called jihadi brides.

It was well past the point when anyone could pretend they didn't know exactly what kind of death cult they were joining. The British people supported him, and that included the majority of British Muslims. The news anchor had raised his eyebrows at that.

Are you sure? he'd said. *There seems to be a common view, repeated on this program just yesterday by a representative of the Muslim Association of Britain, that you hate Muslims.*

I hate the Muslims who make people hate Muslims, he'd replied quietly.

Up the stairs he went to the bedroom he'd been exiled from. Terry would have been watching, and she'd know how much that question wounded him. He was aware she would still be angry about what she saw as his failure to protect Eamonn, but even so, she would have softened toward him. All he asked for was to be allowed to lie down next to her, not quite touching—unforgiven but not unwanted. At some point in the night she'd touch her foot to his—the once involved rituals of making up pared down to this single gesture over their more than three decades together. *Our love is almost middle-aged now,* she'd said to him a few weeks earlier, at the anniversary of their first meeting, trying to hide how much she minded that he'd returned home very late from Marsham Street having forgotten the date they always celebrated privately, unlike the wedding anniversary, which was generally a family, or more widely social, affair. His memory lapse was particularly blundering given that it came just months after she'd moved herself to a ceremonial role in her business, something she'd often talked about but that he didn't think she'd ever do. *One of us has to be a fixed point in the universe, otherwise we'll keep missing each other,* she'd said when she announced the decision, the only indication that

she'd done it because his promotion to home secretary was imminent. The least he could have done in exchange was to remember the damn anniversary. He was generally a man to acknowledge a mistake the moment it was made, correct it (he had brought her breakfast in bed the next morning, and before leaving for work was attentive in other ways that pleased her), and never think of it again—this raking over a past failure was disquieting, adding to the wrongness of every part of the day, from Suarez's jumpiness to the conversation with his son to the question about hating Muslims to the girl, that fucking girl.

"No," Terry said when he pushed the door open. "No. Out."

"I'll sit there," he said, pointing to the stool next to her dressing table.

"I spoke to our son. He told me what you said. About the blow job. Are you an expert on the better ones out there?"

"Whatever my failings are you know that isn't one of them," he said, loosening his tie, kicking off his shoes.

"Karamat, I mean it. Out."

There was no arguing with her in this mood. Unbelievable that his son should have repeated that part of the conversation to his mother— did he know nothing about the rules between men? Down the stairs he went again to the consolations of a laughably expensive bottle of red wine, a gift that Terry had been saving for a special occasion. The ground floor was the place for formal entertaining, the basement the space in which he shut himself away from his family—each as alienating as the other, in the circumstances. He took the wine outside to the patio, where the moving shadows made him drop into a squat to offer as small a target as possible before he realized they were there for his

protection. He finally ended up in the kitchen, sitting on the counter, swinging his legs as his children used to do when he would prepare breakfast for them while his wife was on a business trip somewhere. The kitchen table had long since been removed and a gleaming chrome island was in its place to allow more space for cheese boards, platters of canapés, glasses—sorry, children, "flutes"—of champagne. He rolled up his sleeves, picked up the wineglass. The first Indian crick-eter to be loved by the English, Ranjitsinhji, always wore his sleeves buttoned at the wrist to hide his dark skin—something about holding an expensive glass of wine made Karamat understand how he'd felt. He let the wine sit in his mouth before it slid down with all the lan-guor of the overpriced.

There was a gentle knock on the door leading outside, and a mo-ment later Suarez entered.

"You're supposed to be off duty."

"My men called. There's someone who's been walking repeatedly up and down the street. Jones finally asked her what she wanted and she said she knew you lived on this street but didn't know which house, and thought if she loitered long enough your security detail would identify themselves."

Karamat grunted in amusement. "Who is she?"

"Isma Pasha. The sister—"

"I know who that is. Bring her in."

"In here, sir?"

"My mother didn't raise me to turn women out onto the street at midnight. And Suarez, there are only male officers tonight, aren't there? Keep the pat-down minimal."

"Too late for that, sir. Your security comes first."

When she entered her eyes scanned the dimensions of the kitchen and Karamat could already feel a judgment being passed. He poured wine into a second glass and slid it across the chrome island toward her.

"No thank you," she said, instead of the expected purse-lipped *I don't drink*. She looked nothing like the girl—not just a matter of coloring and features but also the way she was holding in her body, as if aware enough to understand she was in the presence of a man who had all the power and might just choose to exercise it. *Probably a virgin*, he thought, and wondered when he'd become the kind of man who reacted in this way to the sight of a woman with a covered head who made no effort to look anything but plain.

"It may just be worth going to hell for," he said, taking a long sip.

She picked up the glass with both hands and sniffed its contents. "Smells like petrol."

There had been a moment, experienced in the pit of his stomach, in which he'd thought she was going to take a sip because she believed he was demanding it as the price of listening to whatever she had to say. "What do you want?" he said, the tone of his voice making Suarez step forward from his post near the door to see what the girl had done.

"I want to fly to Karachi in the morning without anyone at the airport stopping me from going."

He took her glass and poured it into his. "Your statement to the press was exactly as it should have been. It made me think you were reasonable."

"She's my sister. Almost my child."

"She doesn't show much concern for you, though, does she?"

"Do you love your children based on how much concern they show for you?"

"Watch yourself." Not a girl, this one. An adult, far more dangerous than that banshee in the dust.

"Eamonn worships you. And you've allowed the world to think he's a fool."

"That was his doing, not mine. A girl that obsessed with her brother never said anything about him that should have raised suspicions? Or about her father?"

She leaned back against the fridge, her elbow pressing a button on the LED panel that smoothly ejected two cubes of ice from the dispenser before she jerked away. The noiseless efficiency had always been a disappointment—in his childhood he coveted the rattling, groaning ice dispenser in the fridge door of one of the Wembley relatives. Isma Pasha of Preston Road, the upmarket end of Wembley, picked up one of the ice cubes from the grille onto which it had been deposited and briefly became the embodiment of all his childhood ambitions. Surely she was among those who could be saved, despite the wreckage of her family.

"Eamonn knew about our father all along. I told him, before he even met Aneeka."

She was standing there with an ice cube melting between her fingers, not knowing what to do with it now that she'd picked it up. A picture of harmless awkwardness. A wolf in lamb's clothing.

"You've been sensible so far. Keep being sensible," he said, swirling

the wine in his glass, looking contemplatively into the miniature blood ocean.

"What? No, I didn't mean . . ." She placed the ice in the empty wineglass, where it soaked up the color of the remaining droplets of red. "Do you think I'd try to make it my word against the office of the home secretary? Or that I'd try to make things worse for Eamonn? I only meant to suggest your son has more character than you give him credit for. There's strength where you think there's weakness."

"You're very impassioned on the subject of my son. Pity he didn't end up with you instead of that sister of yours. You I'd accept."

"He didn't want to end up with me," she said, her tone flat.

He raised his eyebrows at her over his wineglass. "Was that an option?"

"No."

"There are interesting shades of 'yes' in that 'no.' We may have to return to it one day. But first let's deal with the situation in which we find ourselves. You're here to ask a favor. All right. Let's see how sensible you are. Will you convince her to let the body be buried, in Karachi? No airline would carry it in the state it's now in anyway." He couldn't take his eyes off the ice cube in the glass, now pinkly melting.

"There's no convincing her. I want to be with her, that's all."

Those were almost exactly the words Eamonn had used. *I only want to be with her.* Meaningless words from a weak boy. He had been repeating that word to himself endlessly about his son: "weak." He took hold of the almost-emptied glass on the chrome island, swallowed the numbingly cold water with its tinge of something else. A foreign body in ice.

"Suarez, where is my son?"

"Normandy, sir. On Miss Alice's estate."

"Is someone watching him?"

"Sir, no. I thought it would be enough to watch his . . . Aneeka Pasha . . . to ensure there was no further contact, as you asked. Would you like me to—"

"No, no. You've done the right thing. Well, thank you, Suarez, for coming out so late. You can leave me here with her. I'm closer to the knife block than she is."

When the door closed behind Suarez, Isma Pasha said, "Eamonn has your sense of humor."

"He's funnier."

"Yes."

He took his phone out of his pocket, texted James: Find out if my son's used his passport in the last few days. Discreetly.

He folded his arms, leaned back. He heard a tiny sigh from Isma Pasha and tilted his head forward to see her replicating his posture, the fridge her headrest. Curious woman. She was quite clearly besotted with Eamonn, but that seemed to make no difference to her devotion to her sister.

"Why sociology?" he said. He shouldn't have opened the wine—it would only make Terry angrier. There was never anything to be gained from pettiness.

"I wanted to understand why the world is so unfair."

"Shouldn't your God give you those answers?" he said, surprised by the slight teasing of his own tone.

"Our God did, in a roundabout way."

"How's that?" he said. She was pretty when her face was at rest, wiped clean of the encroachment of anxiety.

"For starters, He created Marx."

"So you have a sense of humor too."

"Only assuming I meant that to be a joke." She looked directly at him, and something passed between them—it wasn't about sex, but something that felt more dangerous. She was familiar to him, a reminder of a world he'd lost.

He flexed his shoulders, trying to loosen them, looked at the microwave clock, wondered how it was still today. "You must have seen what was happening to your brother. Why didn't you say something? How do I get people like you to say something when it's still early enough to act?"

"We saw something was happening, my sister and I. We thought it was some kind of secret affair, his first time in love. In a way, it was. What else explains a person being turned inside out in the space of just a few weeks? Did you see what was happening with your son?"

He could feel the muscles of his face contract. "Let me tell you this: If it turns out you're right, and I'm wrong. If there is an Almighty and He sends His angel Jibreel to lift up your brother—and your sister—in his arms and fly them back to London on his wings of fire, I will not let him enter. Do you understand? Not Jibreel himself."

"A pair of nineteen-year-olds, one of them dead," was all she said.

The quietness of her tone made his rhetoric of angels and wings of fire—the language of his parents—sound exactly as hysterical as it had been. He touched his tongue to his incisor to help him formulate a response that would decimate both Isma Pasha and his own momen-

tary lapse, but was distracted by James calling. He answered the call, said "Yes" and "Thank you." Hanging up, he poured the contents of his wineglass back into the bottle without wasting a drop. He'd need a clear head in the morning.

"Will you allow me to leave tomorrow?" she said.

"You won't matter tomorrow. Do what you want."

He left the kitchen, headed down to the basement. Along the way he passed a console table with a smiling picture of Eamonn. He picked it up and kissed his son's cheek. *My beautiful boy.* One final lingering moment in which he allowed himself the luxury of being a father to a son—a son who was moving in the opposite direction of home, burning bridges in his wake, a trail of fire in the sky.

9

KARAMAT NEVER REMEMBERED the tiniest shred of his dreams, so when he was awakened in the middle of the night his first thought was that it must have been some unwanted presence making his heart race so fast it woke the rest of him up. But the silence of the spare bedroom in the basement was so complete it was obvious nothing had disturbed it. The sliding glass door with its rolled-up blinds looked onto a light well composed of a glass platform overhead and carefully angled mirrors that were reflecting a confusing, cold light into the bedroom. In his pajamas he walked out into the light well. The moon was full and low overhead. He lay down on the wooden bench built into the wall at the insistence of his heat-seeking boy, who used this space as a sunroom. But now it was cold—the light cold, his skin cold, the emptiness cold. He stood up on the bench, on the tips of his toes, pressed his palm flat against the glass platform. A subterranean creature reaching for the moon. He shuddered, felt a terrible loneliness. "Terry," he said, in the way that as a child he had mouthed prayers to ward off the darkness of the world.

A short while later he was climbing into bed with his wife, travers-

ing the sheets to fit himself to her as she lay on her side. He hiked up her silk nightdress so he could rest his hand on the warmth of her inner thigh, a place he particularly loved, heard her breathing change to tell him she was near enough waking to know he was there. "Let me stay, jaan," he whispered. She relented, as she almost always did when he used that tone of need, shifting against him, a minor adjustment that increased their points of contact. Her foot pressing against his. Tomorrow he would have to tell her that Eamonn had gone to Karachi to prove to his father he had a spine. He inhaled the scent of his wife, slid his hand up to the source of her heat. After tonight, who knew when she'd allow him to do this again? He touched his mouth to Terry's bare shoulder, rolled away, and got out of bed, ignoring her muffled noise of protest. Too distracting. He needed to keep his mind clear.

|||||||||||||||||||||

He went back to sleep in the basement, and when he woke there really was an unwanted presence in the room, and it was James, a mug of coffee in his hand. Karamat sat up. It wasn't yet light outside.

"Eamonn's landed?" he said.

"Just boarded the connecting flight," James said, handing Karamat the coffee. "Someone recognized him at the boarding gate and tweeted a picture, so the media will probably get it soon. Have you spoken to the ambassador yet?"

"About what?"

"I thought you might have asked the Pakistanis to put him on a plane back home when he arrives."

"Would I do that if he weren't my son?" He wondered if Eamonn was counting on this—the father watching over him, not allowing things to go too far.

"With respect, sir, he is your son."

"With respect, James, he's a British national who made a choice and has to face the consequences. As any other British national would."

"There's something else the media will get soon. It went online just a few minutes ago." The little folder James was carrying under his arm turned out to be his tablet. He proffered it to Karamat, who shook his head and got out of bed, reaching for his dressing gown. A man couldn't be prone in his pajamas when something important happened. James followed him into his office, and although there was a desktop computer with a large monitor he set up his tablet on a stand on Karamat's desk.

"So bad I shouldn't look at it in large scale?" Karamat said, and James didn't meet his eye.

In that way the mind has of focusing on trivial details to avoid the enormity of what it has to bear, Karamat spent the first seconds of the video feeling irritated that his son hadn't sat down with a journalist but had decided instead to speak directly to a camera and upload the whole thing to a website. It was the kind of choice that wanted to come across as honest and direct but was really just controlling. Or lazy.

"There's been some speculation about my whereabouts these last few days," Eamonn said, handsome and well rested. The close-up shot showed nothing of his surroundings, only a white wall behind him, his shoulders broad and trustworthy in a button-down navy blue shirt.

His eyes moved—to whom?—then settled back on the camera lens. "I admit, I've been paralyzed by indecision"—he made it sound like an actual ailment—"caught between the two people I love most in the world: my father and my fiancée."

"Ah, no," said James, moved beyond expletives by the damaging awfulness of the word "fiancée."

"I had hoped my father would change his thinking about this, but I understand now that won't happen. Let me clear something up. Aneeka Pasha didn't come looking for me. I went to her house looking for her. While carrying a gift of M&M's from her sister, who I had had the privilege of spending some time with in America."

Nice touch there, the M&M's. Who was it behind the camera whom Eamonn just looked at again?

"It's true I didn't know right away about her brother, but I did know that her father had been a jihadi, that he'd gone to Afghanistan to fight with the Taliban, was held—and possibly tortured—at Bagram, and died on his way to Guantánamo. Like almost any other Brit, I despise the choices Adil Pasha made, and I despise the manner of his dying. But the indefensible facts of his life and death make Aneeka and her sister, Isma, extraordinary women. In the face of tremendous difficulties—including the death of their mother when they were very young . . ."

How earnest he looked, how *good*, as he continued to speak of the trials and glories of the Pasha sisters. Faith in human nature positively rolling off him. Silly clot, as if this were a time in which anyone would trust the idealistic.

"We fell in love. God, all my friends are going to have a go at me

for that—we don't just come out and say things like that in public, do we? But there we are. It's my truth."

When had this phrase become so popular, "my truth"? Hateful expression, something so egocentric in it. And something so cynical, also, about all those absolute truths in the world.

"I don't know why I was lucky enough for her to feel that way about me—my father, who knows me well enough to know that I don't deserve a woman that wonderful, tells me she must have been pretending—"

"Ouch," said James under his breath.

"—but there was never any pretense between us. And that's why she told me about her brother when she agreed to spend her life with me. I can't tell you how hideous it's been to see how that admission—which took so much courage for her to make, and showed such trust in me—has made people paint her as . . . as . . . I can't really say the words."

Embarrassing. That's all this was. "How much more of this is there, James?"

"Don't know, sir. Didn't seem right to watch it before you did," said James, furiously examining the pattern on the carpet.

"It's true that I went to my father, the home secretary, almost immediately to talk to him about Parvaiz Pasha. Not because my fiancée had asked for any favors but because, as a son, I felt honor-bound to tell my father that my personal life and his professional life were bound to collide. You see, I knew Parvaiz Pasha was trying to get to the British consulate in Istanbul—not for some act of terrorism, but because he wanted a new passport that would allow him to return

home. I have shared this information with Counter Terrorism officials—I'm sure Aneeka has done the same—and it's unclear to me why the British public has been allowed to continue thinking that terrorism was his motive for being where he was at the time of his murder—which I'm sure was carried out by those he almost succeeded in escaping."

Oh don't, son, don't make him out to be a hero. They'll never forgive you that.

"But Parvaiz Pasha is not my concern. I never met him and it's true, I don't know what he did, what crimes he might have committed while in Syria. I do, though, know his sister. The woman you've been watching on your TV screens is a woman who has endured terrible trials, whose country, whose government, and whose fiancée turned away from her at a moment of profound personal loss. She has been abused for the crime of daring to love while covering her head, vilified for believing that she had the right to want a life with someone whose history is at odds with hers, denounced for wanting to bury her brother beside her mother, reviled for her completely legal protests against a decision by the home secretary that suggests personal animus. Is Britain really a nation that turns people into figures of hate because they love unconditionally? Unconditionally but not uncritically. While her brother was alive that love was turned toward convincing him to return home; now he's dead it's turned to convincing the government to return his body home. Where is the crime in this? Dad, please tell me, where is the crime?"

So this was what heartbreak felt like. Karamat acknowledged it, allowed it, arms dangling helplessly from his side. *Personal animus.* That

was an arrow dipped in a poison only those closest to him could know
to use. Whoever was standing behind the camera, whoever had honed
Eamonn's words, whoever had chosen that particular shade of blue
that the color psychologists insisted instilled confidence and trust—it
didn't matter. It was Eamonn who mixed the poison, fired the arrow.
He knew it to be a lie, he knew that of all lies it was the one that
would hurt his father the most, he knew that once he'd said it he gave
carte blanche to every one of Karamat Lone's political opponents to
repeat the claim. If a son doesn't recognize personal animus, who
does? Fathers and sons, sons and fathers. An Asian family drama
dragged into Parliament. He clenched his fists, pulled them up to rest
on the arms of his chair, muscles taut along his back and shoulders.
Where the body leads, the mind learns how to follow. He breathed in
slowly, pacing his thoughts along with his breath, the chess player in
him seeing the move just made then examining the whole board.

James waited silently until the home secretary turned to look at
him. "What do we do now, sir?"

"We do nothing. He's, excuse the expression, digging his own
grave." He looked at his watch. "Let's go to the office and watch it
unfold."

"Will you be wanting a few minutes with your wife before we
leave?"

"James, until this thing is over I don't have a son and I don't have a
wife. I have a great office of state. Are we clear?"

"Yes, sir. Sorry, sir."

Karamat returned to his room, opened the cupboard, and looked
at his tie rack. There were more blues than any other color, but today

his hand reached for a matte red—strong but subtle, the tie of a man assured of his own power.

||||||||||||||||||||

He arrived at Marsham Street along with the first editions of the morning papers, which he still insisted on reading in print. His face, half in light, half in darkness, like some comic book villain, was above the fold of the newspaper most closely allied to his party. NATIONAL INTEREST OR PERSONAL ANIMUS? asked the headline.

"Someone must have leaked the video to them ahead of time," James said unnecessarily.

"Stand outside the door and don't let anyone in. I don't care if it's the Queen herself." The building was empty, most of London asleep. He simply wanted to be left alone.

The first paragraph gave him the phrase "anonymous cabinet member," which, when put together with the name of the journalist, almost certainly meant the chancer. The anonymous cabinet member reflected on the irreversible damage to the home secretary if his son had been seen attending the funeral of a terrorist—"of course he'd do everything in his power to prevent that from happening." Such a simple line of attack, as the most effective ones always were.

Piece by piece the article dismantled yesterday's principled man of action and remade him: an ambitious son of migrants who married money and class and social contacts in order to transform himself into an influential party donor, which allowed him to be selected ahead of more deserving candidates to run in his first election. He used his identity as a Muslim to win, then jettisoned it when it started to dam-

age him. It remained a mystery how he had had the privilege of running in a by-election for a safe seat after his constituents threw him
out following Mosquegate; it had led to resignations within the party.
Rather than fully address the questions regarding his connections to
known terrorists in the mosque he frequented, he'd taken on a new
role as the loudest voice of criticism against the community that had
voted him out. Working-class or millionaire, Muslim or ex-Muslim,
proud son of migrants or antimigrant, modernizer or traditionalist?
Will the real Karamat Lone please stand up? And the final blow, again
from Anonymous Cabinet Member: "He would sell out anyone, even
his own son, if he thought it would move him closer to number 10."

It escalated from there. Britain woke up to a chorus of tweets,
hastily written online columns, and morning TV interviews all placing
the home secretary on trial. "Personal animus" the phrase they all
picked up on, which one wit turned into #PersonalEnemas.

A professional, coordinated effort, all in all. Why had it taken him
so long to work out who was behind the camera?

"Alice, you've never liked me, have you?" he said, when the Halibut
deigned to answer her phone on the fifth ring.

"Mr. Lone, your son hired my family's PR firm," she said, in a tone
of warm honey dripped onto cold fish scales. "This is purely professional. No personal animus."

He hung up, laughing, and unbuttoned his cuffs. "Hold your nerve,
marshal your forces," he said to James. It wasn't quite eight a.m. yet.
Plenty of day yet to come, and there was only so much the Halibut
could spin.

He clicked on the video file on his desktop. A shadow on the desert

sand of a man kneeling, a curved sword like a crescent moon above his head. Exceptional production values, the work of people who cared about camera angles and light and—he pressed a key repeatedly to increase the volume of God's name being sung in praise—sound. This came from the media unit for which Parvaiz Pasha had been working. He didn't want to release it to the British public—barbaric, nightmare-inducing stuff. He shouldn't have to. If he had gauged the situation correctly—and he was sure he had—it would take only the sight of Eamonn walking into that most un-British spectacle in the park to switch the conversation from personal animus to Eamonn Lone's clear lack of judgment. But just in case it didn't work that way, it was useful to have a backup plan to remind the public that the only story here was that of a British citizen who had turned his back on his nation in favor of a place of crucifixions, beheadings, floggings, heads on spikes, child soldiers, slavery, and rape. And did Karamat Lone take this personally? By god, yes, he did! He thumped his hand on the desk, practicing, wondered if "by god" was a good idea, as a head rolled in the desert sand.

The first time he'd watched the video he had been unable to eat meat the rest of the week. Had barely been able to shave without thinking of that blade on flesh. Now it was his weapon. He looked up from the computer screen to the television, which he'd switched on as soon as he'd entered the office. The girl was cross-legged beside the ice coffin, hair still caked with mud, once white clothes soiled, every-thing about her older and more tired. *Do you even know the man you're mourning?* he wondered.

His phone buzzed with a text message from Terry: Get home now or

the next news headline with your name in it will have the story of your wife moving out to a hotel.

He ran his hands through his hair, not knowing whether to be admiring or despairing that she'd written to the politician rather than the father or husband. Not even a video of a beheading would shift the story away from the Asian family drama if Terry Lone, celebrity interior designer, style icon, the most admired of Westminster wives by a mile, according to a recent poll, backed up her son's story of personal animus.

Checkmated, Teresa. I'm on my way.

|||||||||||||||||||||||

Terry's signature aesthetic was muted colors, sleek-lined furniture, and wooden floors, on display in every room of the house except her husband's lair and the family room with its red walls, deep carpet and sofas, and white bookshelves filled with the family's best-loved books. As Karamat approached this room he heard an unexpected voice telling him his footsteps had started to sound more portentous since he'd become home secretary.

He covered the remaining distance in the largest possible strides and held his arms out to his second-born, Emily the Uncomplicated, the son he'd never had.

"I'm here to find out if any of that racist, misogynistic ho-jabi nonsense is coming from your office, and to fire whoever is responsible," she said, pulling away and beaming at her father. Beautiful Emily, physically her mother's child, with the light brown hair and hazel eyes, the delicate hands with their quick gestures.

"Oh and here I thought you had come to support your old man," he said, tugging at her nose.

"My old man will be fine. He always is. But my brother's turned a little loopy, hasn't he?" She threw herself down on a sofa and resumed attacking a half-eaten croissant. "Still, he is my brother. And he is your son. I thought I'd come and remind you what parental feeling feels like. And then I can whisk him off to New York until this whole thing goes away."

He was aware of Terry in her dressing gown with her back toward them, her fingers moving along the spine of the children's books as though they were piano keys. It was cowardly, but easier, to talk through Emily. He sat down next to his daughter, took a sip from her teacup, and wrinkled his nose at the lack of sugar.

"You know what he's done, don't you?"

"Mum just showed me the video. That was stupid of him. How are you going to fix it?"

Astonishingly, the story about Eamonn traveling to Karachi hadn't yet become public knowledge. Whoever had tweeted the picture of him at the departure gate had since taken it down—whichever branch of the security services was responsible for that, Karamat was grateful. He must remember to thank James, the only one to notice it because he was the only one who had thought to include among his Google Alerts the misspelling #EamonLone. Not that it mattered very much—everyone would know soon enough. But at least he could be the one to tell his wife, who had finally turned around, her expression making it clear what a terrible idea it had been to leave the

house this morning without waking her up first. "Get some rest while I talk to your father," she said.

Emily sat up straight, looked from one parent to the other. "Sorry," she said, kissing her father's cheek.

When she had gone Terry walked over to the balcony doors and opened them. Her fresh-air mania undeterred by the early-morning cold. Some irritations dissipate in a marriage, some accumulate.

"Sometimes I forget how much like you she is," she said.

"Only compared to her brother, who's nothing like either of us."

"That's not true. He's who I was. Before you. Before I concentrated my life on making myself good enough for you."

He had to laugh at that. "I think you have that the wrong way round, my blue-blooded East Coast heiress. Remember the first time I took you out for dinner?"

But she shook her head, wanting to be alone in some distorted version of their life together. He tossed the remnants of Emily's tea into the flowerpot with the money plant and poured himself another cup. No sugar in sight so he dropped in a teaspoon of jam and stirred vigorously. But not even that outrage reached her. Instead she stayed at her end of the room, gnawing at whatever remained of her thumbnail.

"You used to ask me what I thought," she said. "Every campaign, every bill, every speech."

This, again. In all the times she'd brought it up he'd always stopped himself from pointing out that in the early days it was her because there was no one else. He was the boy from Bradford who'd made his

millions and bought his way into the party no one expected someone like him to join. "Is it so terrible that I want my home to be a haven away from the noise of Westminster?"

"Don't you talk to me as if I'm some housewife here to bring you your slippers at the end of your working day. Have you even stopped to wonder what I think about this business with the boy?"

He watched the bits of jam bobbing in the tea, felt mildly revolted, but took a sip rather than admit it. "You want to protect your son. Of course you do. It's your job. But it can't be mine, not in these circumstances."

"I'm not talking about Eamonn, you self-important idiot. I'm talking about a nineteen-year-old, rotting in the sun while his sister watches, out of her mind with grief. He's dead already; can't you leave him alone?"

His family. His goddamned family and they were the ones least able to understand. "This isn't about him. It isn't about her. It isn't about Eamonn. Perhaps I don't ask your advice anymore because your political mind isn't as sharp as it was. And close those doors—my tea's turned to ice already." A way to stop drinking the jammy liquid and make it her fault. Satisfying, that, even though she seemed entirely oblivious to the whole thing.

"Sharp enough still to see what you don't. That within the party you have enemies rather than rivals, backers rather than supporters. That brown skin isn't made of Teflon. Why do you think I really stepped away from my business?"

The question was a surprise, and he followed it back along the thread of conversation to understand its logic rather than admit as

much. Oh. "To spend your energies being—which one of us first came up with the phrase?—the silk draped over my too-dark, street-fighting muscles. As you did at the start." He held out his hand to her, prepared to be indulgent. "It's true I wouldn't be here without you. That's never forgotten."

She finally closed the balcony doors but only, it seemed, in order to slam something. "You arrogant idiot. You arrived at the foothills and your mind catapulted you to the summit. You're the one person who doesn't realize the article this morning was the beginning of an avalanche that it's already too late to stop." She finally came over to him, but it was to pick up the remote and point it at the television. There she was, the girl, still cross-legged, no change since he'd left the office. He looked at the clock on the mantelpiece. Eamonn would be landing soon.

"A few days ago your greatest rival was a man born with a diamond-encrusted spoon in his mouth, a party insider for years. And now it's this orphaned student, who wants for her brother what she never had for her father: a grave beside which she can sit and weep for the awful, pitiable mess of her family life. Look at her, Karamat: look at this sad child you've raised to your enemy, and see how far you've lowered yourself in doing that."

The ice coffin was sealed up now, slabs laid on top of the corpse, the face no longer uncovered. What state of decay had it reached for her to allow that? Where before there were people nearby, now she seemed to be alone with the body, in the singed grass, beneath the banyan tree, rose petals desiccated around her. The smell, Karamat guessed. It had pushed everyone to the periphery. Soon his son would

walk into this park, into the stench of death, the woman he loved at its center.

"Oh, god," he said, seeing it—his boy surrounded by the rot-drenched horror.

"And you've lost your son too," Terry said. She placed her hand over his eyes, and her touch made something in him stop, something else in him start. He bent his head forward, resting the too-great weight of it against his wife's palm. Once, on an afternoon when rain beat on the windows, he'd sat here with his arm around his son's shoulder, comforting him through his first heartbreak. Eamonn all of thirteen, just the age at which he'd stopped allowing a father's embrace, except in this moment of pain. The elements raging fierce outside, and Karamat helpless with love for the boy weeping into his shirt. He knew he should tell him to be a man, to take it on the chin, but instead he pulled him closer, grateful beyond measure that it wasn't mother or sister or best friend that Eamonn had turned to but his father, who loved him best, and always would.

Terry removed her hand. "Be human. Fix it."

A flutter of silk and she was gone. Now there was only him and the girl who reached out to touch the ice. He bunched his hands together, blew on his cold fingertips. The night his mother had died he'd kept vigil over her body until the morning, reading the Quran out loud because she'd have wanted him to although it touched nothing in his heart. How important it had seemed to do everything with unwavering devotion—not because he believed there was anything left of her to know either way but because it was the last thing he could do for her as a son.

It felt like an effort to reach into his jacket pocket and pull out the phone to call James.

"Thanks for having the tweet about Eamonn taken down, and get me the number of the British deputy high commissioner in Karachi," he said.

"It wasn't us who took it down, sir. I'll text you the number in a minute."

Hanging up, he considered going to his wife. No, he would fix it, for his son, for the girl, and then he would tell Terry. He stretched out on the sofa, arms crossed over his chest, eyes open. Who would keep vigil over his dead body, who would hold his hand in his final moments?

ııııııııııııııııııı

Thunder in the house, on the stairs, in the hall. He stood to meet it just as three men from his security detail charged into the room, a human wall around him, a moving wall running him down the stairs, lifting him off his feet and carrying him like a mannequin when he tried to veer away to find his wife, his daughter. Calling out their names, "Terry, Emily," the only two words in the world that mattered. "Behind you," his wife's voice, rapid footsteps following him down. "I have them, sir." Good man, Suarez! Sirens outside, the human wall moving away from the front door down toward the basement. Guns out, voices coming through the walkie-talkies, Suarez commanding: "Lock the door, don't let anyone in until we give you the all-clear." Into the safe room, wife and daughter behind, door pulled shut, Terry turning the multipoint lock.

"Why are we in the bathroom?" Emily said.

It took Karamat a moment to remember his daughter hadn't been back since he'd become home secretary. She was a visitor from the past, a reminder of a life before. "It's a safe room now."

"Oh my god we're going to die."

His daughter's face something he couldn't bear to look at so he busied himself running his hands along the doorframe. As if he were a father capable of finding a point of vulnerability and fixing it. "Suarez," he shouted, banging on the door. "What the hell is going on?"

A voice on the other side—Jones, was it?—said, "We'll get you out as soon as possible," as though the home secretary and his wife and daughter were in a malfunctioning elevator. The English, sometimes. Even when they were Welsh. He reached into his pocket, but the phone wasn't there. On the table waiting for James's text. Emily and Terry didn't have theirs either. Banged on the door again. "I'm going to need something more than that."

"Sir, we picked up chatter. About an imminent attack."

"This isn't helpful," Terry said, her arms around their daughter. He should go over to join them, think of something comforting to say, but instead he sat down, back to the tiled wall. What could he say? That they would be all right?

"I'm sorry," he said, and waited for one of them to tell him it wasn't his fault.

Terry turned her face away from him, started speaking in a clear, practical tone to their daughter, explaining security protocols, the safety features of this room, the likelihood that chatter meant nothing was going to happen because why would anyone broadcast plans of an

attack that they actually intended to carry out? "Blast-proof" . . . "bulletproof" . . . "air supply." These were the words with which she reassured their child.

How beautiful they both were, his wife and daughter. While his enemies were out there playing politics to bring him down—leaks and innuendos and muckraking, the stuff that gave Westminster a bad name—he was in a reinforced steel box with his wife and daughter while terrorists tried to kill him. He cupped his hands together like a man about to pray or a father cradling his infant son's head. Or a politician examining the lines of his palm. He didn't believe in any form of mumbo jumbo but someone once told him that according to palmistry the lines on your left palm represent the destiny you were born with and the lines on your right the destiny you make for yourself. It had since pleased him to note the wide divergence of the two. Heart line, head line, fate line, life line. At what point had he made himself into a man who thought of saving his political career while his daughter was in need of a father's reassurance? He patted the floor next to him and took her hand in his when she sat down, her head on his shoulder. Counted her fingers as he'd done when she was born, though until Eamonn he'd always thought that was some myth of parenting that no one actually did.

"Your mother's right," he said. "Those who can, do. Those who can't, go online." That got a small laugh. "To be honest, I'm pretty sure Suarez is pretending this is a bigger deal than it is as a sort of drill. That's the way he is. Likes to be very certain all his men—and women, before you correct me—know how to act under pressure."

"Are you saying this to make me feel better?"

"I'm the Lone Wolf. I don't say things to make people feel better." He bared his teeth at her, and she smiled at him, trustingly.

Still children into their twenties, this generation. By Emily's age he'd already faced down so much of the ugliness of the world. Had fun doing it too, in places. And for all the political wrongheadedness of the Anti-Nazi League, they'd won. Wasn't he proof of that? Who would have thought in the days he walked around with his RACISTS ARE BAD IN BED badge, spoiling for a fistfight or a fuck, whichever came along, that someone like him could end up where he was now? And if he had thought it, if someone had said he'd be the home secretary in a safe room while men prowled outside trying to kill him, he'd have known without asking that the men were neo-Nazi skinheads. But how dare they— how dare it be *his people*. After everything his generation did to make this country better for them, how dare they. Personal animus— hell, yes!

"Dad?" Emily said, and he loosened the pressure on her hand.

How were they planning to do it? A truck packed with dynamite on a parallel street, a detonation that would destroy the whole neighborhood? Were they in the sewer system? Had they infiltrated his security detail? He looked at Terry.

"Breathe," she mouthed, and came to sit on the other side of their daughter.

So he concentrated on that. On breathing; on holding his daughter's hand. On remembering that there was no correlation between evil and competence. On thinking how he could emerge from this a hero, the party leadership in his grasp. Then back to breathing, back to holding his daughter's hand.

After what seemed an endless time of silence Emily said, "If Eamonn were here he'd be telling us jokes."

Karamat glanced at his watch. His son was there now, in Karachi.

He cleared his throat. "Terry, there's something . . ."

There was a hammering on the door, Suarez's all-clear code, and then his voice saying it was safe to come out. Karamat stood up so fast he felt a moment of light-headedness. He turned the lock, heard all the bolts slide out from their positions of protection. Heard his daughter burst into tears of relief, and turned to help her up, Terry doing the same, the three of them clinging together for a moment. When they pulled apart there was Suarez, smiling in relief.

"Just some kind of a hoax, sir. Useful drill for all of us."

"How do you know?"

"Because they claim they've got you, sir, and clearly they haven't."

The crackle of a walkie-talkie. A voice on the other end—urgent, horrified.

|||||||||||||||||||||

Every television channel replayed it endlessly:

A man in a navy blue shirt walks into the park. He is recognized, the journalists race forward, he holds up his hand to them, calls out the name of the woman he's come for. The cameras turn to her. She is the only person unaware, her cheek resting on the lid of ice that has melted to near-transparency. The journalists move back, allow a path from him to her. Into this path step two men in beige shalwar kameezes. "At last you're here," says one, and opens his arms wide. The man in the navy blue shirt looks over to the woman, but he's in a new

place, he doesn't want to offend, he allows himself to be embraced. While one man pulls him against his chest, pinning his arms in place, the other encircles his waist. The two men step away, turn, run. They are climbing the railings out of the park before the man in the navy blue shirt understands the belt they've locked around him.

He tugs at it, he yells for a knife, something, anything to cut it off. But everyone is running, toward this exit or that, screams and voices raised to God, who else can save them now? One cameraman, a veteran of carnage, stops at the edge of the park, beyond the blast radius as well as he can judge, turns his lens onto the new emptiness of the field. The woman has stood up now. The man with the explosives around his waist holds up both his hands to stop her from coming to him. "Run!" he shouts. "Get away from me, run!" And run she does, crashing right into him, a judder of the camera as the man holding it on his shoulder flinches in expectation of a blast. At first the man in the navy shirt struggles, but her arms are around him, she whispers something, and he stops. She rests her cheek against his, he drops his head to kiss her shoulder. For a moment they are two lovers in a park, under an ancient tree, sun-dappled, beautiful, and at peace.

Acknowledgments

Jatinder Verma at Tara Arts gave me the idea of adapting *Antigone* in a contemporary context. Jatinder, many thanks, and apologies for doing so in the form of a novel rather than a play.

I'm fortunate to continue to have the Santa Maddalena Foundation in my life; thank you to Beatrice Monti for the space to work, and for her friendship and her dogs.

Thanks also to Dermot O'Flynn for the desk overlooking the sea.

Thank you, Victoria Hobbs, Alexandra Pringle, Becky Saletan, Angelique Tran Van Sang, Jennifer Custer, Faiza S. Khan, and everyone else at Bloomsbury, Riverhead, and A. M. Heath who has played a part in the life of *Home Fire*.

Thank you to my other publishers, and to my translators.

Thank you also to the translators of Sophocles: Anne Carson's *Antigone* (Oberon Books, 2015) and Seamus Heaney's *The Burial at Thebes: Sophocles'* Antigone (Faber & Faber, 2005) were my constant companions as I wrote this novel. I'm also grateful for Ali Smith's *The Story of Antigone* (Pushkin Children's Books, 2013), and for Ali Smith herself.

Thank you to Shami Chakrabarti for permission to use her words, spoken when she was director of Liberty (liberty-human-rights.org.uk), regarding plans to strip British nationals of their citizenship.

Elizabeth Porto remains as trusted an early reader as ever.

The Preston Road sections owe a great deal to Geraldine Cooke—friend, guide, fact-checker—who gave of her time unstintingly without demanding to know what I was up to. My thanks also to her many friends and acquaintances who spoke to me about their neighborhood.

Gillian Slovo's excellent verbatim play *Another World: Lossing Our Children to Islamic State* (Oberon Books, 2016) was commissioned shortly before I started to write *Home Fire*. Gillian showed extraordinary generosity and friendship in sharing her knowledge and resources, as well as in her reading of the first draft of this novel.

Spencer's underlings followed him, gaping.

Sally Jensen stood in the shade of the porch roof. Small fists on hips, she looked across the yard at the hands gathered near the breaking corral. Young Bobby had crowded in among them. Ordinarily, that would not trouble her. But of late, the boy had taken to the newcomers as his idols. It wasn't often that Sally questioned the judgment of her husband.

In his life of enforced caution, Smoke sometimes made bad judgments about people. Sally had recently begun to hold a mild distrust toward the drifters Smoke had sent with that note. At least, he would be in San Francisco the next day and she would know where to contact him. Only thing, would she pass on her distress to worry him? He would think her taken with old maidish vapors, she scoffed at herself. A loud shout drew her attention closer to the ranch hands.

At the urging of Buck Jarvis and Jason Rucker, the new hands, Bobby Jensen had climbed over the top rail and made for a particularly fractious young stallion who stood splay-legged at the tie-rail. Foam flecked its black lips and hung in strings

49

nearly to the ground. Its buckskin hide glistened with sweat and its bellows chest heaved from exertion. So far he had dumped three hands. A sharp pang of concern shot through Sally and she hoisted her skirts to make room for her boots to fly faster.

Running brokenly, Sally streaked toward the corral. "Bobby!" she yelled. "Bobby, don't you dare get on that horse."

Most of the hands, the old-timers, turned to look and said nothing. Buck and Jase sneered and Buck turned his head to shout encouragement to the boy. "Go on, Bobby. You know you can do it."

"That's enough!" Sally commanded. "If that boy gets on that horse, you can pick up your time as of now."

"Awh, come on, Miz Jensen. You're gonna make a sissy out of him," Jason Rucker brushed off the threat.

"Cole, you hear me?" Sally called to their winter foreman, Cole Travis.

"Sure do, Miss Sally," Travis responded, a tight smile on his face.

"I mean what I say. If Bobby gets on that horse, you throw them off the Sugarloaf."

An uncomfortable silence followed in which Sally reached the cluster of hands at the corral. Buck would not meet her eye.

Jase turned his back insolently. Sally marched to the gate, slid the bar, and entered. She raised an imperious hand toward the lad who stood before her, the pain of humiliation written on his face.

"Come on out of here, Bobby," she ordered quietly.

"But I *can* ride him. I know I can."

"I'm not going to argue with you. Come with me."

"Please? He's worn down some now. At least let me try?"

"Not another word. Come along."

Outside the corral again, with Bobby in tow, Sally had the first pang of regret as she looked at his miserable expression. Huge, fat tears welled up and threatened to spill down his face. She knew she had done right! Then another part of her mind mocked her; *How would Smoke have handled it?*

"Saaan Fraaaan-cisssco. Last stop. Saaan Fraaan-ciiisssco!" the conductor brayed as he passed through the cars of the *Daylight Express.*

Smoke Jensen, who had been snoozing, tipped up the brim of his hat and gazed out the window of the Pullman car. A row of weathered gray shanties — shacks, actually — lined the twin tracks. A gaggle of barefoot, shirtless boys of roughly eight to ten years old made impudent gestures to the passengers as the train rolled past their squalid homes. How different from youngsters in the High Lonesome, Smoke mused. There they would be clean as Sunday-to-meeting, bundled up to their ears in coats and scarves and in rabbit-fur-lined moccasins or boots to protect them from the cold. Already the car felt warm, after their descent from the low costal range. Gradually the speed drained off the creaking, swaying coaches.

Now grim factories and warehouses took the place of the shacks. No doubt those youngsters' fathers toiled in these places, Smoke reasoned. How could any man labor day after day with the only light from windows too high up to see out of and only dingy inner walls to look at. How could they stand it? He wondered again if Thunder had received proper care.

His twice-daily visits to the stock car had not provided time enough to make a thorough check. Smoke had acquired the 'Palouse stallion from an old Arapaho horse trader to add new vitality to the bloodline of his prize horses. The Arapaho had obtained Thunder from the Nez Perce who had raised him from a colt and gently broken him. The beast proved to be better as a saddle horse than as a breeder. Accordingly, Smoke had ridden him for more than three years now. A sturdy mountain horse, Thunder could cover ground with the best of them. For years Smoke had worn smooth-knob cavalry spurs out of respect for his horses. As a result, not a scar showed on Thunder's flanks. A huge rush of steam and a jolt of compressing couplers announced the arrival at the depot as the locomotive braked to a stop.

Smoke roused himself and retrieved his saddlebags from a rack overhead. At night, the same rack served as frame for the folddown bed that he had occupied for two nights. Not the most comfortable arrangement, Smoke acknowledged, but it beat the daylights out of a chair car. A trip back East with Sally several years ago had spoiled him. They had ridden in luxury in the private car of the president of the Denver and Rio Grande.

They had their own room, and a big, soft bed that did not even creak when they made love. Now, *that* was the way to travel. Until man learned to fly — a foolish notion! — Smoke would prefer the pleasures of a private car for long-distance journeys.

When the Pullman finally came to a jerking halt, Smoke walked down the aisle to the open vestibule door and outside, to descend from the train.

He had a short wait while the crew positioned a ramp and opened the stock car. A vague hunger gnawed him, so Smoke availed himself of a large, fat tamale from a vendor with a large white box fitted on the front of a bicycle. The thick cornmeal roll was stuffed with a generous portion of shredded beef and lots of spices, including chili peppers, Smoke soon found out. Mouth afire, Smoke rigidly controlled his reaction, determined not to give the Mexican peddler the satisfaction of seeing a *gringo* suffer.

Ten minutes later, as Smoke finished the last bite of the savory treat, a trainman walked Thunder down the ramp. Smoke hastened forward, but not fast enough. Typically, Thunder, like most 'Palouse horses, liked to nip. With a jubilant forward thrust of his long, powerful neck, Thunder sank his teeth into the shoulder of the crewman in a shallow bite.

A bellow resulted. "Tarnation, you damn nag!" the handler roared, as he broke free and turned to drive a clinched fist into the soft nose of the stallion.

Smoke Jensen's big hand closed on the offended shoulder in an iron clamp. "Don't hit my horse," he rumbled.

"I'll hit any damn' animal that bites me," the man snarled. Then he whirled and got a look at Smoke's expression. *Jeez!* It looked as though *he'd* bite him, too. "Uh — er — sorry, Mister. Here, you hold him an' I'll go fetch your saddle."

Somewhat mollified, Smoke accepted the reins from the trainman and walked Thunder down off the ramp onto the firm ground. Fine-grained, the soil held thousands of broken bits of seashell. Smoke studied the curiosity. The station was some distance from the bay and even further from the ocean. Could it be that this area had once been under water? He ceased his speculation, rubbed Thunder's nose, and slipped the big animal a pair of sugar cubes.

Crunching them noisily and with great relish, Thunder rolled his big, blue eyes. The pink of his muzzle felt silken to Smoke's touch. The 'Palouse flared black nostrils and whuffled his gratitude for the treat. Shortly the trainman returned with the saddle and blanket, which he fitted to Thunder's back with inexpert skill. Amused, Smoke wondered how someone could get through life without acquiring the ability to properly saddle a horse. He took over when the man bent to fasten the cinch.

"Here, I'll do that. You hold him."

With a dubious look at Thunder, the man hesitated. "You sure he won't bite me again?"

"Positive. I gave him some sugar cubes."

"That's all it takes?"

Smoke chuckled. "That's all it will take this time."

He tightened the cinch strap and adjusted his saddlebags, tying them in place with latigo strips. Then he swung into the saddle and rode off toward the far side of town.

Narrow, steep streets thronged with people made up the hilly city of San Francisco. Horse-drawn streetcars clanged noisily to scatter pedestrians from the center of the thoroughfares. Smoke Jensen steered his mount though the crowds with a calming hand ready to pat the trembling neck that denoted the creature's dislike of close places and milling, noisy humanity.

"Easy, boy, use your best manners," he murmured. "We'll be out of here soon."

The center of town consisted of tall

56

buildings, four and five stories each, like red-brick and wooden canyon walls. Even Smoke Jensen felt hemmed in. Too many people in far too little space. He passed the opera house, its marquee emblazoned with bold, black letters.

TONIGHT!
MADAME SCHUMAN-HINKE

Whoever she was, she must be important, Smoke thought. Those letters were big. Beyond the commercial district, which appeared to be growing with all the frenzy of a drowned-out anthill, tenements stood in rows, rising to small duplexes and single-family dwellings. Smoke found the street he sought and began to climb another hill. This one was wider, and led to a promontory that overlooked the bay. The higher he went, the better the quality of the houses.

At last he came to an opulent residence that had a spectacular view of the Golden Gate, as the harbor was being called lately. Tall masts billowed with white bellies, a stately, swift clipper ship sailed toward port, a snowy bone in her teeth so large it could be seen from Smoke's vantage point. He watched her for a while, captivated by her grace. Then he nudged Thunder and rode on to his destination.

When he got there, his instincts kicked in and his hackles rose. Smoke cast a guarded gaze from side to side and along the street. What roused his sixth sense was the sight of a black mourning wreath that hung below the oval etched-glass portion of the large front door of the stately mansion. He slowed Thunder and eased off the safety thong on the hammer of his right-hand Colt.

When he reached the wide, curving drive, he halted and looked all around. Not even a bird twittered. Smoke could feel eyes on him — some from inside the mansion, others from hidden places along the avenue. A cast-iron statue of a uniformed jockey stood at the edge of a portico. Smoke reined in there, dismounted, and looped his reins through the ring in the metallic boy's upraised hand. Four long strides brought him to the door. A brass knocker shone from the right-hand panel. Smoke had barely reached for it when the door opened.

A large, portly black woman, dressed in the black-and-white uniform and apron of a housekeeper, gave him a hard, distrustful look. "We's closed. Cain't you see the wreath?"

"I'm not a — ah — client. I'm Smoke Jensen. Here to see Miss Francie."

Suddenly the stern visage crumpled and large tears welled in the eyes. "Miss Francie, she dead, suh."

"What?" Smoke blurted. "When? What happened?"

"We's ain't supposed to talk about it, the po-lice said. Miss Lucy, she in charge now. Do you wish to talk to her?"

"Yes, of course."

He followed her into the unfamiliar hallway. Although Smoke had known of the place, and known Francie Delong for years, he had never visited the extravagant bordello. The housekeeper directed the way to a large, airy room, darkened now by the drawn drapes. A large bar occupied one long wall, a cut-crystal mirror behind it. Comfortable chairs in burgundy velvet upholstery surrounded small white tables.

"Wait here, if you will, Mr. Jensen. Miss Lucy will join you shortly."

"Thank you." Hat in hand, Smoke waited.

Lucy Delong arrived a few minutes later. She wore a high-necked black dress set off with a modest display of fine white lace. Her eyes, red and puffy from crying, went wide when she took in the visitor. "You have to be Smoke Jensen. Francie speaks — spoke — so highly of you." The tears came again.

"Miss Lucy, I'm sorry. I didn't know something had happened to Francie. Was she sick for long?"

"It — wasn't sickness. She was — she was run down by a stolen carriage." An expression of horror crossed her face and she covered it with both hands, sobbing softly.

So that's why the police said not to discuss it. Lips tight, Smoke laid his hat on the bar and stepped to Lucy, putting a big hand on her shaking shoulder. "It must have been terrible for you. For all the girls," Smoke said helplessly, unaccustomed to words of condolence. "When did it happen?"

"Three days ago. It was a foggy day. Francie went out to see her banker. She never came back." Lucy drew a deep breath and shuddered out a sigh in an effort to regain control.

"I received a note saying someone would meet me here."

"I don't know anything about that. I'm sorry."

"We'll wait here a while, then."

"Oh, we cannot. There's to be a reading of Francie's will at half past noon. I am to be there, and you are expected, too." She looked confused. "I sent you a telegram when I learned. We barely have time to get there as it is."

"I still want to confirm who wrote me to meet him here."

"I'll leave word with Ophilia as to where we'll be."

"Your housekeeper?"

"Yes. All the girls are to be at the reading of the will."

"All right. Let me write a little note."

Lucy took paper, a pen, and an inkwell from behind the bar. Smoke wrote briefly. He gave it to Ophilia and turned to Lucy. "How are you getting to this?"

"We have a carriage. You're welcome to come along."

"I have my horse outside. I'll accompany you."

"I'll be relieved if you do." She frowned slightly, her eyes gone distant. "Something doesn't seem . . . right about the way Francie died. It will feel nice to have a strong man around. We will meet you on the drive."

Raymond Wagner looked up from his study of the flake gold and several rice-sized nuggets he had retrieved from his sluice. The splash and rumble of water

61

racing down the riffles and screens of his sluice box had masked the sound of hoofbeats. He stared into the ugly, impassive faces of the three men whom he had run off his claim not four days ago. They had another one with them.

This time it was he who came forward and thrust the deed for him to sign. "Sign this," Tyrone Beal demanded.

"I told them fellers I would not and I say the same to you. Get off my claim."

"Sign it and save us all a lot of trouble."

"Gehen Sie zu Hölle!" a red-faced Wagner snarled in German.

Beal sighed. "Go to hell, huh? Well, I tried to be nice."

With that, he whipped the pick handle off his left shoulder and swung it at Wagner's head. The prospector ducked and lashed out a hard fist that caught an off-balance Beal in the chest. He staggered backward, recovered, and waded in on his victim. Another swing broke the bone in Wagner's upper left arm. Beal rammed him in the gut, then the chest, and cracked the dancing tip off the stout German's chin. Teeth flew.

Wagner had not a chance. Methodically, Beal beat him with the hickory cudgel. Driven to his knees, Wagner feebly raised his arms to shield his head. Beal broke three of Wagner's ribs with the next blow. Then came a merciful pause while Beal looked over his shoulder at the others.

"Don't just stand there. Give him a good lesson."

Kicks and punches pounded Raymond Wagner into a bleeding hulk curled on the ground in an attempt to protect his vital spots. The pick handle in Beal's hands made a wet smack against Wagner's back and the prospector rolled over to face upward. His eyes had swollen shut and a flap of loose skin hung down over his left eye. His mouth was ruined and large lumps had distorted his forehead. Beal prodded him with the bloody end of the handle.

"We'll be back when you've healed enough to sign this deed."

Without another word, they left. Raymond Wagner lay on his side again and shivered in agony. Slowly the world dimmed around him.

FOUR

Buck Jarvis and Jason Rucker looked up from the generous slabs of pie on their noon dinner plates. They fixed long, hungry, speculative looks on Sally Jensen as she distributed more of one of her famous pastries to the other hands. Only four days and Sally had grown to dislike them intensely. Forcing herself to ignore their lascivious stares, she turned away.

Jason leaned toward Buck and whispered softly into his ear, "Wonder what her body looks like under that dress?"

"I wonder what it would look like *without* a dress," Buck responded.

"I bet them legs go on forever," Jason stated wistfully.

"Shoot, man, she's too old for you."

Jason thrust out his chin. "I'm willin' to find out. Some of them older wimmin is the best ride you can get. They appreciate it more."

"You be blowin' smoke, Jason."

"Am not. My pappy tole me that when I was a youngin."

Buck sighed regretfully. "Well, neither one of us will get a chance to find out, you can be sure of that."

"Don't count on it, Buck. I reckon her man is gonna be gone a long time. Wimmin get to needin' things, know what I mean?"

Smoke Jensen had half the hall yet to cover when a loud pounding came on the door. Ophilia materialized out of a small drawing room and beat Smoke to the entrance. She opened the portal to reveal six tough-looking men.

"I wanna see whoever's runnin' this fancy bawdy house," a wart-faced man at the center of the first rank demanded.

"I'm sorry, we are not receiving clients at this time. There's been a death."

"Yeah. We know. An' we're here to throw you soiled doves out. This place don't belong to you."

Icily Ophilia defied them, drawing up her ample girth like a fusty old hen. "That is to be determined at the reading of Miss Francie's will this afternoon. Until then, no one is going anywhere."

"I have the say on that, Mammy," the unpleasant man barked, as he pushed past the housekeeper.

65

"I think not," Smoke Jensen's voice cracked in the quiet of the hall.

"Who the hell are you?"

"A man who does not like rude louts." Smoke advanced and the intruder retreated.

Back on the porch, the knobby-faced man regained his belligerence. "We come to evict them whores and we're gonna do it," he snarled.

"Who do you work for?" Smoke demanded.

"That's none of your business."

Smoke bunched the man's shirt in his big left fist and hauled him an inch off the ground. "I think it is. Is it the city? If so, by what right do they say these ladies must leave?"

A carriage had pulled around from the stable behind the house and nine lovely young women peered out with surprise at the scene before them. Lucy dismounted and stormed across the lawn and drive to the front steps. Hands on hips, she confronted the six unwelcome visitors.

"What exactly is going on here?"

"You're out in the street. My boss is taking over this place."

"Who is your boss?"

"Gargantua here asked me the same

thing. I didn't tell him and I won't tell you."

Smoke Jensen shook him like a terrier with a rat. "You do a lot of talking to say so little. Maybe I should loosen your jaw a little and rattle something out of you."

The thug turned nasty. "Put me down or I'll blow a hole clear through you."

If only to better get to his six-gun, Smoke set the man on his feet again. At once, the ruffian, a head shorter than Smoke Jensen, shot out a hand and pushed Smoke in the chest. Smoke popped him back, then two more of the evictors jumped him.

Smoke planted an elbow in the gut of one and rolled a shoulder in the way of the other so that he punched his boss instead of Smoke. He took in the remaining three standing in place on the bottom step, staring. That wouldn't last long, Smoke rightly assumed. Time to give them something to worry about.

Smoke Jensen spun to his left and drove a hard, straight right to the chest of the bruiser who kept punching him. He followed with a left, then swung his right arm in a wide arc to sweep the smaller man on that side off his feet. By then, their leader had recovered himself enough to return to the scuffle. He lowered his head and came at Smoke with a roar.

Roaring back, Smoke met him with a kick to one knee. Something made a loud pop and the thug howled in pain and abruptly sat down. Smoke returned his attention to the last upright opponent. He moved in obliquely, confusing the brawler as to his intent. The man learned quickly enough what Smoke had in mind when big, powerful hands closed into fists thudded into his chest and gut. Wind whistled out of his lungs and black spots danced before his eyes. Wobble-legged, he tried to defend himself only to be driven to his knees. Smoke finished him with a smash to the top of his bowed head. The other three, Smoke noted, had been suitably impressed.

They remained where they had been, eyes wide and mouths agape. Not so their leader. Unwilling to face that barrage of fists again, he decided to up the ante. A big, wicked knife appeared in his hand from under his coat. Sunlight struck gold off the keen edge as he forced himself upright, wincing at the pain in his leg. He took a wild swipe at Smoke Jensen, expecting to see his intended victim back up in fright.

Smoke obliged him instead with a swift draw of his .45 Peacemaker and quick discharge of a cartridge. The bullet shattered the thug's right shoulder joint.

"D'ja see that?" one of the less belligerent ones croaked. "Let's get out of here."

"Help me, you idiots!" their wounded leader bellowed. "Get me away from here."

They moved with alacrity, eyes fixed on the menace of the six-gun in Smoke's hand. Ignoring the continued yelps of discomfort, they dragged their leader away. With order restored, Smoke Jensen reholstered his revolver and tipped his hat to the soiled doves in the carriage.

"I apologize for the unpleasantness, ladies," he told them politely.

"Quite all right," Lucy replied. "I enjoy seeing scum like that get their comeuppance. We'll lead the way to Lawyer Pullen's office."

Brian Pullen had his office over the Bank of Commerce on Republic Street. Smoke Jensen was able to tie up at a public water trough, which Thunder appreciated. The ladies had to place their oversized vehicle in a lot next door to the bank. Smoke walked there and escorted them to the outside staircase that led to the lawyer's office.

The sight of all those painted ladies turned more than a few heads.

Rising from behind a cluttered desk, Brian Pullen extended a hand in greeting. "You must be Mr. Jensen. Lucy — uh — ladies, I'll send my law clerk for more chairs. Please, make yourselves at home."

The lawyer turned out to be younger than Smoke had expected. His well-made and stylishly cut suit showed his prosperity without being ostentatious. Pullen wore his sandy-blond hair in a part down the middle. Not one to make snap judgments, Smoke Jensen found himself liking the youthful attorney. Chairs began to arrive and with a twitter of feminine voices the soiled doves seated themselves.

Smoke noted that Pullen had mild gray-green eyes, which he imagined could become glacial when arguing before a jury, against a prosecutor in defense of a client. He spoke precisely, addressing them in an off-hand manner.

"There is another gentleman expected, though he appears to be late. We'll give him until one o'clock."

They passed the time in small talk. Pullen made an effort to draw Smoke out about his circumstances. "I understand you are in ranching?"

70

"Horse breeding. I have a good, strong line of quarter horses and another of 'Palouse horses."

"Weren't they first bred by Indians?"

"Yes, Mr. Pullen. The Nez Perce," Smoke answered precisely.

"Please, call me Brian. I'm not old enough to be *Mister* Pullen. You are in Montana, or Colorado, is it?"

"Colorado, Brian," Smoke replied.

Pullen frowned and checked his big turnip watch. These short answers weren't getting him anywhere. If only the other man would arrive so they could get on with the reading of the will. He'd give it one more try.

"You've been a lawman, is that right?"

"Yes. Off and on."

"On the frontier?"

"Of course."

Brian sighed. "I suppose you have some exciting tales to tell."

"Nothin' much to tell. At least, not in mixed company. Blood and violence tends to upset the ladies." Smoke gave Lucy a mischievous wink.

Another look at the watch. "Well, it's the witching hour, you might say. I don't believe we can delay any longer. Very well, then, let's proceed. We are here for the

71

reading of the last will and testament of Frances Delong. As her attorney, I am well aware of the contents, and feel she exercised excellent judgment in the disposal of her estate."

He paused and opened a folded document. From a vest pocket, he produced a pair of half-glasses and perched them on his generous patrician nose. Then he began to read in a formal tone. " 'I, Frances Delong, being of sound mind and body, do hereby bequeath all my worldly possessions as follows: to my dear friends at the San Francisco Home for Abandoned Cats, the sum of one thousand dollars. To my faithful employees,' " here, Brian Pullen read off the names. " 'I leave the sum of five hundred dollars each. To my ever faithful assistant, Lucy Glover, I leave in perpetuity the revenue from the saloon bar at my establishment. All my other property, liquid assets, and worldly goods I leave to the man who once saved my life, Kirby Jensen.' This was dated and signed six months ago," Brian added.

Smoke had always hated his first name and had not used it except under the utmost necessity for many years, so the shocking import of what the lawyer read did not strike him at once — not until the door opened and a jocular voice advised him, "What do you think of being the proprietor of the most elaborate sporting house in San Francisco, *mon ami?*"

Just as he had expected. Louis Longmont, his old friend and fellow gunfighter, stood in the doorframe with a broad grin on his face. Smoke came to his boots quickly and crossed the short space. Both men gave one another a back-slapping embrace.

"I thought it was you who sent me that mysterious message. Now, tell me about it."

"I will, *mon ami,* but not here or now. We need some place to be alone for what I have to say."

Sally Jensen stood over the boy seated at the kitchen table. Bobby had his face turned up to hers, though he would not meet her eyes. Not ten minutes ago Sally had caught the twelve-year-old behind the big hay barn, a handmade quirley in his lips, head wreathed in white tobacco smoke. Now, rather than the hangdog expression of shame, his face registered defiance. His explanation of the smoking incident had shocked and angered her.

"Buck made it for me. Jason said I was

big enough to take up smokin'.'"

She hadn't liked the looks of them when they'd first arrived, and she hadn't grown any fonder of them since. This was just about the last straw.

This morning, they had both remained in the bunkhouse, claiming sickness, when the hands had ridden out to check the prize horses on graze in the west pasture. Not long ago they had come out and moseyed around the barnyard. Bobby, who had been laid up with his bunged-up toe since three days ago, had joined them. The three of them had gone around behind the barn.

Sally, at work at the kitchen sink, had kept an eye on the barn, wondering what they might be doing. When enough time had passed to arouse her suspicions, she wiped her hands on her apron and walked out to check on them. She had found Bobby alone, smoking a cigarette. She descended on him in a rush and snatched the weed from his mouth. Crushing it with a slender boot toe, she had demanded to know what he thought he was doing. His explanation only increased her pique.

"Well, Buck Jarvis and Jason Rucker are neither your mother nor your father. Smoke would have a fit if he knew what you've done. Come with me to the kitchen."

Seated now, with Sally over him, Bobby said, "Does it mean you are not going to tell Smoke? You know? What you said? That he would have a fit if he *knew* what I had done?"

"I'm disappointed in you, Bobby. I don't know now if I will tell Smoke or not. But you are staying inside for the rest of the day, young man."

"Awh, Miss Sal— Mom, I feel okay now. No more sore toe. Please let me eat with the hands. It's goin' on noon anyhow."

Sally considered it. "All right. But you stay away from Buck and Jason, hear?"

"Yes, ma'am."

"You may go to your room now."

"Yes, ma'am." Feet dragging, Bobby headed for the staircase that led to the second-floor bedrooms.

Although he ordinarily slept in the bunkhouse with the hands, since the arrival of Buck and Jason, Sally had insisted that Bobby return to his room in the main house. Something about them made her mighty uncomfortable.

She had good reason to recall that when the hands arrived at noon. Buck and Jason joined them. The two drifters stuffed themselves, then begged off work on the pretext that they still ailed a mite. After the hands rode off and Bobby came back inside, they lounged around on a bench outside the bunkhouse. When she went outside to hang up a small wash, they gave her decidedly lascivious looks.

Aware of that, Sally thought to herself it was a good thing she was not entirely alone.

Dinner for Smoke Jensen and Louis Longmont was at the Chez Paris on the waterfront, near the huge pier that people were already calling Fishermen's Wharf. The fancy eating place catered to San Francisco's wealthy and near-wealthy. White linen cloths covered the tables, their snowy expanse covered with matching napkins in silver rings, heavy silverware, and tall, sparkling candleholders, complete with chalky candles. Thick maroon velvet drapes framed the tall windows, each foot-square pane sparkling from frequent cleaning. Paintings adorned the walls, along with sconces with more tapers flickering in the current sent up by scurrying waiters.

The staff wore black trousers and short white jackets over brilliant lace-fronted

shirts and obsidian bow ties. The maitre d'
was formally attired in tails. He led Smoke
and the New Orleans gunfighter to a table
in an alcove. Seated, they ordered good
rye. While it was being fetched, Louis pe-
rused the menu.

"I'll order for us both, if you don't mind,
Smoke," he offered with a fleeting smile.
The menu was in French.

Smoke took a glance and smiled back.
"Yes, that would be fine."

When the waiter returned with their
drinks on a silver tray, Louis was ready to
order. "We'll start with the escargots.
Then . . ." He went on to order a regular
feast. He added appropriate wines for each
course and sat back to enjoy his whiskey.

After an appreciative sip, he inclined his
long, slim torso toward Smoke, seated
across from him. "You are no doubt wondering why I so summarily summoned you
here, *non?*"

Smoke pulled a droll expression. "I will
admit to some curiosity."

Louis pursed his lips and launched into
his explanation. "Francie was still alive
when I sent that letter. It is not about her
rather — unusual — demise. Something is
afoot among the big power brokers of
Northern and Central California. There

are rumors of a secret cabal recently formed that includes Cyrus Murchison, the railroad mogul, Titus Hobson, the mining magnate, and Gaylord Huntley, the shipping king."

"Hummm. That's some big guns, right enough. Murchison is the biggest fish, of course. Even in Colorado we have read of his doings in the newspapers."

"Well, yes. Word is that they are out to establish a monopoly on all transportation and gold mining. But, that's not all, *mon ami.* Phase two of their scheme, I have learned since coming to San Francisco, is to then go after title to all of the land in private hands.

"They will strangle out all the small farmers and shop owners with outrageous shipping rates by rail, water, or freighting company." Louis paused and nodded sagely. "Part of it, too, is to take control of all forms of entertainment: theaters, saloons, and bordellos."

"Not too unusual for captains of commerce," Smoke observed drily. "A bit ambitious, but I'd wager any group of powerful men might seek to eliminate competition."

"Quite true," Louis agreed. "Yet this is no ordinary power play. The cabal is supposed to have made an unholy alliance, which has prompted me to seek your help. Murchison and company are believed to have made an accommodation with the dreaded Triad Society." At Smoke's quizzical expression, he explained, "The Tongs of Chinatown."

Smoke raised an eyebrow and his eyes widened. A certain darkness colored his gray gaze. "Of course I'll help, Louis. I think I've already had an encounter with some of the cabal's henchmen." He went on to describe the incident at Francie's.

Louis listened with interest and nodded frequently. "That sounds like their methods, all right. Must be the railroad police."

"Are you staying at Francie's?" Smoke asked, as the waiter arrived with their succulent, garlicky-smelling snails. Smoke took one look and made a face.

"Try them. You'll like them."

"I don't eat anything that crawls on its belly and leaves a trail of slime behind."

"Smoke, my friend, you must become more worldly. Escargots are a delicacy."

"Sally squashes them when they show up in her garden."

"These are raised on clean sand and fed only the best lettuce and other vegetable tops."

"They are still snails."

"Suit yourself," Louis said, as he picked up the tongs and fastened them onto one of the green-brown shells.

With a tiny silver fork he plucked the mollusk from its shelter and smacked his lips in appreciation. His hazel eyes twinkled in anticipation as he popped the snail onto his tongue. His eyes closed as he chewed on it thoughtfully. Smoke made a face and sipped from the glass of sherry the waiter had poured. Not bad. The aroma of the escargots reached his nostrils and they flared. His stomach rumbled. He had not eaten since the depot cafe that morning, he recalled. Tentatively, he reached for the tongs and clamped them on a snail shell.

"Aha! You have joined the sophisticates. Enjoy. Now, in answer to your question, no. I am staying at Ralston's Palace."

"I haven't taken a room. But I think one of us should stay at Francie's. The trash that showed up might come back."

"Since you own it now, it sounds reasonable to me that it is you who stays there, *mon ami*. I'll meet you there in the morning."

"Make it early. The way I see it, we have a lot to accomplish."

★ ★ ★

When they had finished the lemon *gelato,* Louis Longmont offered to accompany Smoke Jensen back to the bordello. Smoke gladly accepted; he enjoyed the company of his friend. Their route took them past the pagoda gateway that marked the entrance to Chinatown. Beyond it, a dark alley mouth loomed. They had barely passed it when the men in black pajama-like clothes attacked.

Tong hatchets whirred in the moonlight, striking a myriad of colors from the cheerful lanterns bobbing in the light on-shore breeze behind Smoke and Louis. Both gunfighters had been walking their horses and now mounted swiftly. A man on horseback had it all over one afoot. With eight Oriental thugs rushing at them, it became even more critical.

In the lead, one snarling, flat-faced Tong soldier swelled rapidly. Smoke reared Thunder and prodded with a single spur in a trained command. The black cap flew one way and the cue flung backward as Thunder flicked out a hoof and flattened the Tong face. Then the others swarmed down on Smoke and Louis.

FIVE

The Chinese gangsters soon discovered that their Tong hatchets might well strike terror into the merchants of Chinatown, but they proved no match for blazing six-guns in the hands of the two best gunfighters in the West. Smoke Jensen and Louis Longmont opened up simultaneously with their .45 Colts. Hot lead zipped through the air. Louis's first round rang noisily off the blade of a hatchet descending on the head of his horse.

Its owner howled in pain and dropped the weapon. Smoke put a bullet through the hollow of another Tong soldier's throat and blew out a chunk of his spine. Suddenly limp, the Asian thug went down to jerk and twitch his life away. Louis fired again. Another Tong fight master screamed and clutched his belly in a desperate attempt to keep his intestines from squirting through the nasty hole in his side where the slug had exited. Alarmed, others shrank back momentarily.

"Where did they come from, Smoke?" Louis asked cheerily, as he lined his sights on another enemy.

"I'd say that alley behind us." Smoke paused as Louis fired again. "I believe we can safely say you heard the right of it about the Tongs."

"Why is that?"

Smoke Jensen loosed a round at a squat Chinese who had recovered his nerve enough to foolishly charge the two gunfighters. "They don't even know I'm in town. You're the one who has been asking questions around San Francisco."

"I see what you mean, *mon ami*. Smoke, we had better make this fast, *non?*"

"Absolutely," Smoke agreed, as he dropped another hatchet shaker.

Wisely, the surviving pair, one of them wounded, turned and ran. The wide street held a litter of bodies and a sea of blood. Longmont's horse flexed nostrils and whuffled softly, uneasy over the blood smell. Both men reloaded in silence.

"Shall we go on to Francie's?" Smoke asked lightly.

"Hadn't we better report this to the police?" Louis asked.

"If the police haven't showed by now, I imagine they already know and don't want to get involved. We'll leave these here for whoever wants them."

★ ★ ★

Freshly ground Arabica beans usually made the day for Cyrus Murchison. This morning, his coffee tasted bitter in his mouth. The reason was the presence of Titus Hobson and Gaylord Huntley in his breakfast room — that, and the news they brought. The news came in the form of Xiang Wai Lee. The slight-statured Chinese could barely suppress his fury.

"The first time we are to perform a service for you, we are sent out against men of inhuman capability." His queue of long black hair bobbed in agitation as he hissed at Murchison. "You told us that Louis Longmont was a fop, a dandy, a gambler, an easy target. Not so," Lee informed the wealthy conspirators. "Then there was the other man with him. Such speed and accuracy with a firearm."

"Who was that?" Murchison demanded.

"What does it matter?" Xiang snapped. "Only two of the men sent after Longmont and his companion survived the encounter."

"That doesn't answer my question. Who is this other man?" Ordinarily, this Oriental would not be in this part of his house. Would not even gain access, except by the servants' entrance to the back

84

hallway and pantry. Murchison took his presence as an insult.

"My two soldiers who lived informed me that Longmont used the word 'smoke' as though it was a name."

Hobson paled and gasped. "He can't still be alive."

"Who?" Murchison barked.

"Smoke Jensen," Hobson named him. "He is reputed to be the best gunfighter who ever lived. If he still *is* alive, we have a major problem on our hands."

"Preposterous," Murchison dismissed.

Hobson would not let it go. "He has killed more men and maimed many more than any other three shootists you can name. His name is legend in Colorado. When I was there last, Smoke Jensen had devastated a force of forty men who hunted him through the mountains for a month. It was they who died, not Jensen. He has been an outlaw and a lawman.

"There are some who say he has back-shot many men he has killed." Hobson paused to catch his breath. "Personally, I don't believe that. I have also heard that to say so to his face is to get yourself dead rather quickly. He is mean and wild and totally savage. He's lived with the Indians. He was raised by another total barbarian, a mountain man named Preacher. The pair struck terror into the hearts of the men in the mountains for years."

Murchison snorted derisively, totally unimpressed. "What impact can a couple of aging gunfighters have on our project?" His small, deep-set blue eyes glittered malevolently in his florid face as he cut his gaze to Xiang. "If your men cannot handle this, Tyrone Beal and his railroad detectives can take care of a mere two men, no matter that they are good with their guns. Now, get out of here, all of you, and let me finish my breakfast."

Smoke Jensen punched back his chair from the round oak table in the breakfast nook of the Delong mansion. Frilly lace curtains hung over the panes of the bay window, with plump cushions on the bench seats under them. This excess of the feminine touch made Smoke a bit uneasy. If he kept the place, there would have to be some changes. No. That was out of the question. Sally would be bound to find out. When she did, she would skin him alive.

Amusement touched his lips as he recalled the time Sally had herself inherited a bordello from a favored aunt who had passed away. That and a big ranch that stood in the way of the ambitions of powerful, greedy men who needed some lessons in manners. Smoke Jensen had given those lessons, with fatal results. No, Sally would never favor him owning a bawdy house. Lucy Clover's entrance banished the images of the past.

"Mr. Longmont is here, Smoke."

"Thank you, Lucy. Have Ophilia show him in. Join us — we have a little strategy to discuss."

"Oh?"

"Yes. About protection for this establishment, among other things," Smoke informed her.

Lucy left him alone to return with Louis Longmont. *"Bonjour, mon ami,"* Louis greeted.

"Oui, c'est tres bon," Smoke answered back with almost his entire French vocabulary.

Louis chuckled. "They must have fed you well. What is in order for today?"

"First, we must make provisions for someone to protect this place." He paused to sip the marvelous coffee.

"You think there will be trouble?" Lucy asked anxiously.

"Those louts who came yesterday will be

back, count on it. And we can't stay here all the time. Now that I own the place, I want to make sure all of you are safe."

"You make it sound ominous," a pale-faced Lucy observed.

Smoke was disinclined to play it down. "Believe me, it is."

Ophilia appeared in the doorway. "Those nasty gentlemen from yesterday are here again, Miss Lucy. And they brung friends."

Smoke's lips tightened. "How many?"

"They's about a dozen, Mister Smoke."

Smoke came to his boots. Louis started to rise. "I'll take care of it, Louis."

"If you say so, *mon ami*," he answered with a shrug.

"This way, Mister Smoke," Ophilia directed. Although richer by $500, thanks to Francie, she still performed her duties as housekeeper flawlessly.

At the door, Smoke quickly counted the twelve men standing in a semicircle at the foot of the porch steps in three ranks. Several of them held stout hickory pick handles. Tyrone Beal, who had returned only that morning on the early train, acted as spokesman this time.

"Tell those girls that they are to be out of here within half an hour. This place has been sold for back taxes and the new owner, the California Central Railroad, wants immediate occupancy."

After seeing all the books and ledgers on Francie's establishment the previous day in Pullen's office, Smoke knew that there were no back taxes. "I have some bad news for you, whoever you are."

Beal drew himself up. "Captain Tyrone Beal of the Railroad Police. I'm not interested in any news you might have. I said out they go, and that's what I mean."

"The bad news, *Captain* Bean," and Smoke put a sneer on the title, "is that you are a liar. All taxes have been paid up through next year. I'm the owner now, so you had best back off so no one gets hurt."

Goaded by the insult, Beal launched himself at Smoke. Jensen waited for him to the precise second, then powered a hard right into the face of the railroad detective. Beal, his feet off the ground, flew down the steps faster than he had ascended them. His pick handle clattered after him. The others similarly armed, pressed forward, dire intent written on their faces.

Smoke turned slightly and called over his shoulder, "Louis, would you like to join the dance?"

"I would be delighted," Louis said from

the doorway, where Smoke had anticipated he would be.

Back-to-back, they met the railroad thugs. The first to attack came at Smoke. When he swung his pick handle, Smoke ducked and kicked him in the gut. The billet of wood went flying. Smoke finished him with a left-right combination to the right side of his head and jaw. He fell like a rumpled pile of clothes. Another stick-wielder went for Louis.

The New Orleans gunhand gave his hapless assailant a quick lesson in the French art of *la Savate*. He kicked the brawler three times before the man could get set to swing his hickory club. His swing disturbed, he staggered drunkenly when he missed. Louis kicked him twice in the back, once in each kidney. Grunting in misery, he went to his knees, one hand on the tender flesh at the small of his back. Louis swung sideways and put the toe of his boot to the bully's temple. He went down like a stone.

Smoke popped a hard right to the mouth of an ox of a man who only shook his head and pressed his attack. Smoke went to work on the protruding beer gut. His hard fists buried to the wrists in blubber. Still he failed to faze his opponent. Instead, he launched a looping left that caught Smoke alongside his ear. Birdies twittered and chimes tinkled in the head of Smoke Jensen. He shook his head to clear it and received a stinging blow to his left cheek that would produce a nasty yellow, purple, and green bruise.

Another pick handle whizzed past his head and pain exploded down his back when it struck the meaty portion at the base of his neck. Left arm numbed, he cleared tear-blurred eyes and snapped a solid right boot toe to the inner side of his attacker's thigh. A squeal of pain erupted from thick, pouting lips. Smoke sucked in air and stepped close.

With a sizzling right, he pulped those flabby lips. The blow had enough heft behind it to produce the tips of three broken teeth. *Finish him fast,* thought Smoke, as feeling returned to his left arm. Two powerful punches to the gut brought the man's guard, and the gandy stick, down. Smoke felt the cheekbone give under the terrible left he delivered below the man's eye. His right found the vulnerable cluster of nerves under the hinge of the jaw and the man went to sleep in an instant.

Louis had four men down in front of him and worked furiously on a fifth. Not bad, Smoke thought. He sought his fourth. The sucker came willingly to the slaughter. Wide-eyed and yelling, he rushed directly at Smoke. The last mountain man side-stepped him at the proper moment and clipped him with a rabbit punch at the base of his skull. His jaw cracked when he struck the lowest marble step. Suddenly Smoke had no more enemies. The remaining three thugs hung back, uncertain, and decidedly impressed by what these two men could do. Smoke gestured to the fallen men.

"Drag this trash off my property and don't bother to come back," he commanded hotly.

Satisfied with the results, he and Louis turned to walk back in the mansion. Enraged at this ignominious defeat, Tyrone Beal wouldn't leave it alone. Mouth frothing with foam, he shrieked at his henchmen. "What's the matter with you three? Finish them off. Kill the bastards!"

Six-guns exploded to life and a bullet took the hat off Louis Longmont's head. Instantly the two gunfighters turned to meet the threat. Crouched, they spun and drew at the same time. Smoke's .45 Colt spoke first. He pinwheeled the middle hard case, who did a little jig with the devil and expired on his face in the grass. Louis took his man in the stomach, doubling him over with a pitiful groan. Smoke's Peacemaker barked again.

The slug burned a mortal trail through the lower left portion of the railroad policeman's chest and burst his heart. He tried to keep upright, but failed. Slowly he sank into a blood-soaked heap. Powder smoke still curling from the muzzle of his Colt, Smoke Jensen addressed Tyrone Beal.

"Take this garbage out of here. You would be smart not to report this to the police. We have a building full of witnesses who saw what happened. If your boss wants to verify what I said about the taxes and owning this place, he can check with Lawyer Pullen." He turned away, then paused and spoke over his shoulder. "Oh, and don't bother coming back."

Up on the porch, Louis Longmont opened the loading gate on his revolver and began to extract expended cartridges. "Now that we have finished our post-breakfast exercise, what's next?"

"Easy," Smoke said with a slow grin. "We look into this Tong business from last night and find some reliable men to guard this place while we are gone."

★ ★ ★

"They did it again," Sally Jensen testily said.

Both of those saddle tramps, as she now saw Buck and Jason, remained behind, professing illness again. She looked up sharply from the elbows-deep soap suds when their coarse laughter reached her in the wash house attached to the outer kitchen wall. Through the small, square window she saw them lolling around, obviously in perfect health. She had sent Bobby out with the hands today. Now she was thankful she had. While she watched, Buck and Jason drew their lanky frames upright and ambled in the direction of the bunkhouse well pump. She gave her washing an angry drubbing on the washboard and abandoned it.

Wiping her arms, she headed to the kitchen. She had pies in the oven, and biscuits yet to do. When she stepped out of the wash house, Buck and Jason were nowhere in sight.

"What are they up to now?" she asked herself, mildly disturbed by this disappearance.

In the kitchen she pulled the four large deep-dish pies from the oven and slid in two big pans of biscuits. That accomplished, she dusted her hands together in satisfaction. Now, she had better cut vegetables for the stew. She strode to the sink and pumped water into a granite pan. Bending down, she pulled carrots, potatoes, turnips, and onions from their storage bins. As she came upright, her eye caught movement through the window.

Buck and Jason were back. The two young saddle tramps were headed directly toward the kitchen.

Tyrone Beal and his battered henchmen sat nursing their wounds in a saloon on Beacon Street. After they'd downed several shots of liquid anesthetic, their bravado found new life.

"We're not gonna let two country hicks get the best of us, are we, Boss?" Ned Parker growled.

"Not on your ass," Tyrone Beal growled.

Parker poured another shot from the bottle. "I want a piece of that Frenchie bastard."

"Me, too," Earl Rankin piped up.

"Sam's got a busted jaw," Beal reminded them.

"They say only sissies fight with their feet," Monk Diller observed.

"Maybe so, but that Longmont broke

five of Ham's ribs with a kick," Beal continued to list their injuries.

" 'Twern't nothin' compared to what the big guy with him did to the boys," Ned Parker summed up.

Tyrone Beal had enough of this. "No, boys, we're not going to let them get away with it. We'll get 'em both, even if we have to shoot them in the back."

Monk Diller's tone came out surly. "You tried that. There's three of us dead for it."

Tyrone Beal wanted to keep them on the subject. "What's done is done. The thing is, we drop everything else until we can fix their wagon."

Beal had no idea of how soon the opportunity would come. Even while he detailed a plan for ambushing Smoke Jensen and Louis Longmont separately, a young Chinese entered the saloon. The bartender noticed at once.

"Get out. We don't allow your kind in here."

"I got message for thisee gentleman, Bossee," he singsonged in pidgen, pointing to Tyrone Beal.

"Okay. Deliver your message and get out."

Walking softly in his quilted shoes, the Chinese youth approached the table. "Arrogant *qua'lo* disgust me," he muttered in perfect English, as he came before the railroad detective.

"What was that?"

"I said bigots like that bartender make me angry. I have a message for you from Xiang Lee. Here it is." He offered a scrap of rice paper.

Beal opened the folded page and read carefully. "*Smoke Jensen and Louis Longmont are strolling around Chinatown bold as brass dragons. It is an insult to the Triad. The Tong leaders have met and consider it wise, and more convenient, if other* qua'lo *take care of them. You and your railroad police are to come at once. The messenger who brought this will lead you to your quarry. Xiang.*"

Boyle looked up at the young Chinese. "This says you can take us to some men we want rather badly. Is that so?"

"Oh, yes."

"Then do so," he rumbled as he rose, and adjusted the hang of his six-gun.

The door to the Jensen kitchen flew open and the two young drifters swaggered in. Sally looked askance at them from where she stood washing vegetables. She dropped the paring knife in the bowl and

97

rubbed her arms furiously on her apron. Nursing her rising anger, she turned to them with a stony face.

"What is the meaning of this?" she demanded harshly.

Buck Jarvis cut his eyes to Jason Rucker. Then they both ogled her boldly, slowly, up and down in an insolent, lewd manner. "We're here to get some of what you must have under that dress," the smirking lout nearest to Sally brayed.

Sally took two purposeful steps to the table and picked up her clutch purse. Men had seen the expression in her eyes and known fear. This pair hadn't a clue. Her scorn aimed directly at Jason, she calmed herself as she shoved a hand into the open purse. Her voice remained level when she answered his insolence.

"No, you're not."

Buck, the bolder of the two, reached for her. His eyes, slitted with lust, widened to white fear and disbelief when the bottom of the purse erupted outward toward him, a long lance of flame behind the shattered material. An unseen fist slammed into Buck's gut an inch above his navel and an instant of hot, soul-shriveling pain raked his nerves raw. He doubled over so rapidly that Sally's second round, double-actioned from her Model '77 Colt Lightning .44, smacked into the top of his head.

A giant starburst went off in the brain of Buck Jarvis and he fell dead at her feet.

White men alone on the streets of Chinatown stood out markedly in the daytime. Particularly ones as big, strong, and purposeful as Smoke Jensen and Louis Longmont. The denizens of the Chinese quarter gave them blank, impassive faces. The few who would talk to them, or even acknowledge they understood English, made uniformly unsatisfactory replies.

"So solly, no Tongs in San Francisco," one old man told Smoke, his face set in lined sincerity. He was lying through his wispy mustache and Smoke knew it.

"I know nothing of such things, gentlemen," a portly merchant in a flowing silk robe stated blandly. "The Triads did not come with us from China."

More horse crap, Smoke and Louis agreed. They moved on, creating a wake behind them. More questions and more denials. One young woman in a store that sold delicate, ornately decorated china did register definite fear in her eyes when Smoke mentioned the Tongs. Like the rest, though, she denied their existence in San Francisco.

"This is getting nowhere," Louis complained. "We waste our time and make a spectacle of ourselves, *mon ami*."

"We'll give it another quarter hour, then try the local police," Smoke insisted.

When the quarter hour ended, they had come to the conclusion it would be a good idea to give it up. They had turned on the sidewalk to retrace their steps when Tyrone Beal and his black-and-blue henchmen located them.

"There they are! Let's get 'em!" Beal shouted. This time they had the forethought to bring along guns. A shot blasted the stately murmur of commerce in Chinatown. A piercing scream quickly followed.

SIX

Hot lead whipped past the head of Smoke Jensen. More screams joined the first as women, clad in the traditional Chinese costume of black or gray pegged-skirt dresses that extended to their ankles, awkwardly ran in terror from the center of violence. Louis Longmont overturned a vendor's cart heaped high with dried herbs and spices. A sputtering curse in Cantonese assailed him. Bullets slammed into the floor of the hand cart and silenced its owner.

"Smoke, on your left!" Louis shouted as he triggered a round in the direction of the shooter who riddled his temporary, and terribly insubstantial, cover.

Smoke Jensen reacted instantly, swiveled at the hips, and pumped a slug into the protruding belly of Ned Parker. Parker's mouth formed an "O," though he did not go down. He raised the Smith American in his left hand and triggered another shot at Smoke Jensen. Another miss. Smoke didn't.

His second bullet shattered Parker's

sternum and blasted the life from the corrupt railroad policeman. "We've got to move, pard," he advised Louis. "There's too many of them."

"*Exactement*," Louis shouted back over the pandemonium that had boiled along the street in the wake of the first shots.

With targets so plentiful, they had no problem with downing more of Beal's men as they emptied the cylinders of their six-guns. More Chinese women and children ran shrieking as havoc overtook their usually peaceful streets. Bent low, Smoke and Louis sprinted from cart to cart. They reloaded on the run. Chinese merchants yelled imprecations after them. Blundering along behind, the furious railroad police overturned carts of produce and dried fish. Smoke spotted a dark opening and darted into a pavilioned stall to replace the last cartridge in his .45 Colt.

A squint-eyed hard case saw Smoke duck out of sight and came in after him — his mistake. His first wild shot cut through the cloth of the left shoulder of Smoke's suit coat, not even breaking skin. Facing him, his face a cloud of fury, Smoke pumped lead into the chest of the slightly built gunman. Flung backward by impact and reflex, the dying man catapulted himself through the canvas side of the vendor's stall. The material tore noisily as the already cooling corpse sagged to the ground, partway into the street. It forced Smoke Jensen to abandon his refuge, though.

"He's over there," voices shouted from outside.

Smoke slid his keen-edged Green River knife from its sheath and cut his way to freedom through the back of the stall. The Chinese owner gobbled curses after him, his upraised fist and his long black pigtail shaking in rhythm. Smoke moved on. Then, from behind him, he heard yelps of pain and surprised curses. A quick glance over his shoulder showed him the cause.

Wielding a long, thick staff, the irate merchant took out his frustration on the rush of thugs who poured into his establishment. He struck them swiftly on shoulder points, legs, and heads. Two went down, knocked unconscious. Smoke produced a grim smile and moved on.

Tyrone Beal looked on in disbelief as his magnificent plan began to disintegrate. How could two lone men create such havoc among his men? Granted they were a wild, wooly lot, but he had managed to instill enough discipline in them that they fought together, as a unit. Yet here and now they seemed to forget all they had learned.

"Get them, you stumbling idiots!" he railed at his men, who darted around the central market square of Chinatown in confusion. "They went down the main street."

Five or six obeyed at once. Others continued to mill around. They poked six-guns into the faces of the frightened Chinese and overturned their displays of goods. "You'll not find them that way, you worthless curs," he bellowed at them.

He had sent to the railroad yards for reinforcements. It looked to Beal as though the stupidest of the lot had responded to the summons. He had no time to stay here and reorganize this mob-gone-wild. He headed along the central artery that led to this marketplace. Ahead he saw three of his better men closing in on the one called Longmont. Well and good. Put an end to him, and then go after Jensen.

Louis Longmont had a revolver in each hand, the left one a double-action Smith and Wesson Russian .44. He crouched, eyes cutting from one hard case to the other. Only one of them had a firearm.

The other two wielded knives and pick handles. One of those lunged at Louis and he leaped catlike to the side and discharged his right-hand Colt. The roar of the .45 battered at him from the wall to his left. His target fared far worse.

Shot through the hand, the bullet lodged in his shoulder, the railroad thug howled in agony and pawed at the splinters from the hickory handle that stuck in his face. On weakened legs he tottered to the side and sat down heavily on a doorstep. Believing Louis to be distracted by this, the remaining pair moved as one.

First to act, the gunman raised his weapon for a clear shot. He never got the sights aligned. Louis shot him in the forehead with the .44 Russian in his left hand. Automatically he had eared back the hammer on the .45 Peacemaker in his right and tripped the trigger a split second later. The fat slug punched into the belly of the other thug. Before he plopped on the street, Louis went into rapid motion.

A rickety cart piled high with racks of delicate bone china loomed in his vision. Louis jinxed to avoid it, only to feel the hot path of a slug burn along the outside of his left arm. That threw him off balance enough that he crashed into the mountain of tablewear. Cascading down, the fragile pieces gave off a tinkling chorus as they collided and rained onto the cobblestones to shatter into a million fragments.

"*Go, qua'lo!*" the owner shouted after Louis, uselessly shaking a fist. Then he repeated his insult as two of the railroad thugs blundered through the ruin. "Barbarian dog!"

Warned by this renewed outburst, Louis turned at the hips and fired behind him. The sprint of one of the hard cases turned into a stumbling shamble that sent him into the window of a shop that dispensed Chinese medicinal herbs. Shards of glass flew in sparkling array. The largest piece fell last and decapitated the already dying man. His companions hung back, mouths agape, while Louis disappeared from their view.

Slowly Smoke Jensen began to notice a change in the people of Chinatown. When they had recovered enough composure to look at the men being pursued and their pursuers, they recognized old enemies. Shouts of encouragement came from a trio of elderly men on one street corner when Smoke plunked a slug smack in the middle of one thug's chest. He had shot his one

Colt dry and now used the one from the left-hand holster, worn at a slant at belt level, butt forward. Singly and in pairs, Smoke noticed, he and Louis were gunning down the trash sent to kill them.

A volley of praise in Cantonese rose when Smoke shot a stupidly grinning hard case off the top of a Moon gate. The volume of gunfire had diminished considerably. Smoke found he had to look for targets. Unfazed by this, he continued on his way toward the main entrance to Chinatown.

"Impossible!" Tyrone Beal shouted to himself. It was all over. He could see that clearly. Only five of his men remained upright, and three of them had been wounded.

Self-preservation dictated that he get the hell out of there — and fast. He didn't delay. He would report to Heck Grange; Heck would know what to do. These two were inhuman. Nobody was *that* good. But his eyes told him differently. Quickly, Tyrone Beal turned away from the scene of carnage and broke into a trot, departing Chinatown by the shortest route.

His course took him to the railyard of the California Central. There he banged in the office of his superior, Chief of Railroad Police Hector Grange. "Heck, God damn it, we got wiped out."

Heck Grange looked up sharply, startled by this outburst. "Did the Chinks turn on you?"

"Some of them did, near the end. But it was Longmont and Jensen. I saw it with my own eyes. We've got to do something to stop them."

Heck considered that a moment. "We can start by filing a complaint with the city police."

"What good will that do?" Beal protested.

"You've got cotton between your ears?" Heck brayed. "Mr. Murchison is a pillar of the community, right? He owns the mayor, the police, the city fathers, even the judges. So you put together a story as to how these two troublemakers, wanted for crimes against the railroad, were located by some of your men. They opened fire without warning and killed our policemen. You follow so far?"

A light of understanding glowed in Beal's eyes. "Yeah, yeah. I think I do. We put the blame on them, send the regular police after them."

"And when we get them in court, they

get convicted and hanged. End of problem. Now, get on it."

Inspired by Heck's confidence, Beal departed faster than he'd arrived.

"Stay on your knees, if you want to live," Sally Jensen coldly told Jase, the would-be rapist.

The instant Buck Jarvis had fallen dead to the kitchen floor, Jason Rucker had gone alabaster white and dropped to his knees, his hands out in appeal, and begun to beg for his life. Sally had been sufficiently aroused by their brazen attempt that she had yet to simmer down enough to ensure that this worthless piece of human debris *did* survive.

"Oh, please, please, don't hurt me. We didn't mean nothin'."

The former schoolteacher in Sally Jensen made her wonder if Jase understood the meaning of a double negative. The wife of Smoke Jensen in her made her wonder why she had not already shot him. Driven by a full head of steam, she formed her answer from her outrage.

"If I turn you over to the sheriff, you will most likely hang. Why not take the easier way out with a bullet?" she coldly told him.

Jase cut his eyes to his partner, lying

dead on the floor. *"Please!"* he begged in desperation, "please. I'll do anything, take any chances with the law. Just — don't — shoot — me."

Sally considered that a moment, eyes narrowed, then told him, "Drag that filth out of my kitchen and clean up the mess while I think about it."

Gulping back his terror, he hastily crawled on hands and knees to comply.

Slowly at first, the solemn-faced residents of Chinatown came forward. Stooped with age, one frail man with a wispy, two-strand beard and long, drooping mustache approached Smoke Jensen.

"You were acting in defense of your life, honored sir," he said softly. "The damage done is inconsequential. I am Fong Jai. It shames me that our own people have not stood up to these *qua'lo* bandits like you have done."

"I am called Smoke Jensen, and this is Louis Longmont," Smoke introduced the two of them. "You know them, then?"

"Ah, yes. To my regret, we of Chinatown know them all too well. I recognized the one who led them. He is called Tyrone Beal. He is an enforcer for the greedy *qua'lo* who owns the California Central Railroad . . . and, regrettably, most of the land in Chinatown. He and his villainous rabble have broken legs and made people disappear for a long time."

Smoke gave him his level gray gaze. "Then I am doubly glad we could be of service."

Fong Jai folded his hands into the voluminous sleeves of his mandarin gown and bowed low. "It is we who have a debt to you. Earlier you asked about the Triad Society. We behaved badly toward one who is a friend. If you wish to confront the Tongs, the name to use is Xiang Wai Lee."

Smoke and Louis repeated the name several times, committing it to memory. It turned out Fong had more to say. "I would urge that you use that name cautiously. These Tong hatchet men are very dangerous."

"Thank you, Fong Jai," Smoke offered sincerely. He gestured around him. "You can see how we handle danger."

Fong smiled fleetingly and bowed low again. "It is the Tongs, I think, who should take caution if they rain trouble down on your heads. But my warning comes from another case. It is rumored that the Triad has made an arrangement with the villains of Murchison and his two devil allies, Hobson and Huntley. If that is the case, you will encounter them again."

Smoke placed a friendly hand on Fong's shoulder. "My friend, I — we — have every intention of doing so."

"Our great philosopher Confucius said, 'A wise bird never leaves its droppings in its own nest.' By arousing your wrath, I believe that the Triad should consider that carefully. Go in peace, Smoke Jensen, Louis Longmont. Ask what questions you wish. You will get answers."

It took them less than half an hour to learn all they could about the Tongs. Most people remained frightened of the Chinese gangsters and gave scant aid, and none claimed to know where Xiang could be found. When they had what could be gotten out of the residents of Chinatown, Smoke halted Louis on the street with a word.

"We have our name now, and some idea of how the Tongs work," he declared. "Now to get those bouncers for Fran — er — my new place."

"Where to, *mon ami?*"

"Why, to the dockyards, of course. There are always out-of-work longshoremen aplenty."

★ ★ ★

Tyrone Beal stood in the opulently furnished office he had never before visited. He held his hat in his hands, his head bowed, shame flaming on his cheeks as he repeated the account of his ignominious defeat at the hands of Smoke Jensen and Louis Longmont. Behind the huge desk centered between two tall, wide windows, Cyrus Murchison grew livid as each sentence tumbled out.

"You mean to tell me that twenty men could not stop those two?" Murchison roared. His thick-fingered fist pounded out each word on the desk top.

"Yes, sir. I'm sorry, sir."

"You will be sorrier if you fail again. You behaved stupidly in the matter involving Wagner. You should not have beaten him so badly he could not sign. And now this. Disgusting." He paused, poured a crystal glass full of water, and drank deeply. It successfully masked his ruminations over how to deal with Tyrone Beal. "I'm going to give you a chance to redeem yourself. You will return to the gold fields. Get me Wagner's signature on that deed. You do that, and all will be forgiven."

Relief flooded through Tyrone Beal. He had visions of ending up at the bottom of the bay, wrapped in anchor chain. "Yes, sir. Thank you, sir. I won't mess this one up. I promise you that."

Ice glittered in the deep-set eyes of Cyrus Murchison and his stunning shock of white hair shook violently. "See that you do."

With that dismissal, Tyrone Beal exited the office. When the huge door closed softly behind him, Murchison sighed heavily. "Now, we have to deal with these two gunfighters," he addressed Heck Grange. "I want you to drop everything else you're working on. Find a sketchmaker who can draw likenesses of Longmont and Jensen. Go to our company printing plant and have engravings made and flyers printed. I want them by tomorrow morning. Then," Murchison went on, ticking off his points on his stubby fingers, "circulate them to every employee, every informant you've developed among the low-lives of this town, every barkeep — flood the entire city with them." He paused, anger once more flushing his face. He poured and drank off more water and licked his lips fastidiously. "Anyone who finds them is to report directly to you. Then I want you to file a complaint with the police. I'll contact the chief personally, and get them looking for Jensen and Longmont."

"A tall order, sir. But, I am pleased you approve of my idea of bringing in the regular police."

"Harrumph! The idea occurred to me before that idiot Beal got the first two sentences out of his mouth," he dismissed the contribution of his Chief of Railroad Police. "Now, as far as your men are concerned, they are to have orders to shoot to kill Jensen and Longmont on sight. Finally, there are some dirt-scratching farmers in the Central Valley who need convincing that selling to the railroad or to Hobson's Empire Mining and Metal would be good for their health. Send some of Huntley's dockwallopers out there to impress it on them. See to all of it," Murchison commanded. "Jensen and Longmont first."

"This is going to be harder than I thought," Smoke Jensen admitted after their fourth profane refusal.

"It is strange that men out of work, waiting in a hiring hall, would refuse an offer so generous in nature," Louis Longmont agreed.

They had spent the past half hour along the harbor. With scant results, for all that. So far, only a single man had taken up the offer. A burly man with bulging forearms, bulldog face, and thick, bowed legs ambled along a careful two paces behind Smoke and Louis. He had a knit sailor's cap on his huge head, canvas trousers, and a blue-and-white-striped V-neck pullover. Smoke privately suspected he was not a long-shoreman, but that he had recently jumped ship. He would do, though.

"Over there," Louis pointed out. Two men sat astraddle a bench, a checkerboard between them. As Smoke approached, one picked up a black playing piece and made a triple jump.

"You're cheatin', Luke," his opponent growled. "I don't know how, but I know you are."

"No, I ain't," Luke responded. "You just make too many mistakes."

"I don't make mistakes."

"Yes, you do."

"No, I don't."

"Do."

"Don't."

"Now, boys," Smoke addressed them, in a tone he often heard Sally use on their children when they squabbled.

It brought up the both of them, red-faced, their disagreement forgotten. Luke gestured to the playing board. "Doin' nothin' for days on end gets to a feller," he apologized for them both.

"Out of work?" Smoke suggested.

"Sure am. We refused to turn back half our pay to the hall boss."

"Would you like to take a job?"

Luke studied the blue sky above. His eyes wandered to a wheeling dove. "Sure, if we get to keep what we earn and it ain't again' the law."

"It's not, I assure you," Louis Longmont added.

"So, what is this work you have? Cargo to unload? Sure. Warehouse to clean out? Sure. We can do anything."

"Speak for yourself, Luke," his companion snipped.

"This job does entail some danger. You may have to fight to preserve the peace."

"You ain't offering us a place with the police, are you?" Luke objected.

"Far from it," Smoke Jensen assured him. "I have recently inherited a famous sporting house in San Francisco. I need some strong, honest men to keep order. I know nothing about running such a place, but there is a nice young lady who is in charge. She can explain your routine duties to you. As for the other, there are some interests in town who don't want me to keep the place."

Louis joined the outline of what might be expected. "We will not be able to be there all the time. It would then be up to you to eject any of their convincers who happened around."

Luke squared his shoulders and gave them a roll suggestive of readiness. "A bouncer, eh? I've been one before. What's it pay?"

"Right now, fifty dollars a week."

Luke's jaw sagged. "I don't believe you. That's more than a month's wages."

"It is quite correct," Louis said sincerely.

"Why, sure, Mister," Luke addressed Smoke. "Far's I'm concerned, you got yourself another bouncer." He looked beyond Smoke to the big man who intently took in their conversation to illustrate his meaning.

"Count me out," Luke's surly friend stated flatly.

"That's two," Smoke agreed, lightly. "What we need is about six more."

Louis rolled his eyes.

Outside the next hiring hall, Smoke Jensen and his companions came face-to-face with a large group of longshoremen. Smoke noted their mood to be surly at best, if not downright hostile. A barrel-chested inverted wedge of a man stepped forward, a hand raised in a sign to stop.

"That's far enough. You fellers have been pokin' around here long enough. It's time for you to get yourselves out of here. And you, too," he gestured to Luke and the other dockworker. "You ain't workin' for them nohow. Come over here with us."

"Sorry," Smoke answered lightly. "Can't do that. I need about six more good men to work for me."

"Well, you can't have 'em," the spokesman snapped.

Smoke was quickly getting riled. First the running gunfight with the railway thugs in Chinatown, and now this. "By whose authority?" he asked with deadly calm.

Pointing to the sign over the doorway to the hiring hall, the aggressive longshoreman bit off his words. "D'you see that sign? This here's the North Star Shipping Company. Mr. Huntley heard what you two were up to and told me special to see you got run off from the docks. So take a hike."

Sharp-edged menace covered every word Smoke Jensen spoke. "I don't think so."

"Then we'll have to remove you."

Luke stepped forward and spoke uneasily in Smoke's ear. "What are we gonna do? They got us outnumbered five-to-one."

A taunting grin lighted Smoke's face. "Simple. We surround them."

No stranger to street fighting, Luke understood immediately. "Sure. We spread out and hit them from four places at once. But that don't make the numbers any less."

"I think we have the advantage," Smoke spoke from the corner of his mouth. "I failed to introduce myself and my friend. I'm Smoke Jensen. He's Louis Longmont."

"*The* Smoke Jensen?" Luke asked in an awe-filled tone.

"There's only one I know of."

"I've heard of you. Read about your doin's in the far mountains. Read about Mr. Longmont, too. The fast gun from New Orleans. I'm honored to be in such famous company." Luke dusted his hands together in eagerness. "We'd better get at it, right?"

"Yes. Before they take it on themselves to start the dance," Smoke agreed.

"Take 'em, boys," Huntley's lead henchman commanded.

At once, the phalanx of longshoremen

surged forward. Smoke and company separated. Before the dockworkers realized it, they had been flanked by the two most deadly gunfighters in the nation. Two of them turned to face Smoke Jensen. He stepped in and swiftly punched the nearest one in the mouth.

Shaking his head, the hard case threw a right at Smoke, which the last mountain man took on the point of his shoulder. He rolled with it and went to work on the mouth again. Lips split under a left-right combination. Blood began to flow in a torrent when Smoke hooked a right into the damaged area. His opponent tried for an uppercut and failed to land it. Smoke took him by the upthrust arm and threw him into his companion.

A quick glance told Smoke the other three had their hands full, though they managed to deal with it. Then two more came at him. As they closed in, Smoke extended his arms widely and jumped into the air.

Eager for a quick end to it, the thugs closed in, shoulder to shoulder. Smoke Jensen clapped his hands together, one to the opposite side of each of his attackers' heads. He slammed their noggins together and they went down groggy and aching.

Louis had two longshoremen at his feet, out of the battle. Luke had accounted for one and had another in an arm lock around his head. Methodically Luke pounded the man in the face.

Enough of that, the gang of thugs seemed to conclude at once. Fists rapidly filled with cargo hooks and knives.

SEVEN

One pug-faced grappler lunged at Smoke Jensen with a wicked long-bladed pig-sticker. Swiftly Smoke filled his hand with a .45 Colt Peacemaker. The hammer fell and brought a roar of exploding gunpowder. The long-shoreman went off to meet his maker. Smoke reckoned the meeting would not be a friendly one. He took note that Louis had his own six-gun in action. While those menacing him backpedaled, confused by this sudden turn of events, Smoke reached left-handed for his second revolver and freed it from leather.

A line of fire blew across Smoke's left forearm. He pivoted in that direction and jammed the muzzle of his right-hand Colt up under the knife-wielder's rib cage and squeezed the trigger. Hot gases shredded the thug's intestines, while the bullet punched through his diaphragm and exploded his heart before exiting his body behind his right collarbone.

"Luke!" he barked in warning as he tossed the Colt to the young dockworker.

Facing three men armed with deadly six-guns changed the outlook of the dock brawlers. Few of them owned a firearm, and fewer had ever been in a gunfight. With a curse, the leader called his men off. They fled down the bayside street. The fight ended as quickly as it had begun. Smoke Jensen had a shallow slash on his left forearm. Louis Longmont was bent slightly, one hand clutching at a ragged tear at the point of one shoulder, which he had received from a cargo hook. His remark showed he felt little of it.

"It is nothing, *mon ami*. A big steak and a shot of brandy will make everything right again."

"Wonder why they didn't stay around?" Smoke asked jokingly. "Let me wrap up that arm for you, Louis. And then it's time for us to find six more good men."

Smoke Jensen and Louis Longmont returned to Francie's with six big, capable men, two less than Smoke had wanted, yet enough, he felt sure, to do the job. He gathered them in the spacious former ballroom, which had been converted into a saloon. Lucy joined Smoke and Louis there. Smoke introduced her and began to outline their duties to the collection of seamen and dockworkers.

"Two of you will be on watch in alternating four-hour shifts, day and night. You are to hold this place against anyone who comes here fixing to throw the ladies out. The weakest places are the back door to the kitchen and the French doors to the drawing room. A twelve-year-old could knock them down. I suggest you put some heavy furniture in front of them. The kitchen door can be blocked with that butcher's block in the middle of the room when needed. No drinking on duty, and only two drinks while off. When the emergency is over, we'll have a rip-roaring party that will be the talk of the town. Until then, I want you all sober.

"In the event someone tries to break in, everyone will respond. You will all be given a rifle or shotgun. Make good use of them, if need be." He paused. "Any questions?"

"Why's someone want to take over this place?"

Smoke smiled at him. "It makes a lot of money. That's not all of it. There are some powerful men who aim to take over every saloon and bawdy house in town. I learned yesterday that they intended to start with this one. I also discovered that Miss Francie refused to sell at a piddling price. Later she was run down by a freight wagon no one saw. I own it now and I don't intend to let these ladies be turned into virtual slaves by anyone."

"Who are these men?" Luke asked.

"Cyrus Murchison, Titus Hobson, and Gaylord Huntley."

Luke's eyes narrowed at the list of names and he gave a slight start. "That's why Huntley's dockyard trash set on us, right?"

"We don't know that for sure," Smoke advised him. "Another thing — don't wear yourselves out on off-duty time. In other words, no sampling of the wares."

That brought six loud groans. Smoke suppressed a smile. He had chosen well, he concluded. "Any other questions?"

"Where will you be while we watch over these pretty doves?" a man called Ox asked.

"Louis and I will be out finding a way to put an end to this cabal's schemes."

"Sure you won't need some help?" Ox asked.

Luke answered for Smoke. "Ox, I know you saw how four of us took care of twenty of Huntley's bully-boys. What do you think?"

Ox produced a gap-toothed grin, the absent teeth the result of more than one brawl. "I think we'll be missing out on a lot of fun."

None of the newly hired protectors had more questions. Smoke Jensen released them to their tasks and strolled to the front door with Louis Longmont. "Old friend, we're going back to Chinatown. I want to get those Tong thugs off our back before we go after Murchison and company."

Monte Carson, hat in hand, stood on the porch of Smoke Jensen's home on the Sugarloaf. Earlier in the afternoon, Sally Jensen had sent a hand to town to summon the lawman. Now he listened to Sally's account of what had happened. His frown deepened and a flush rose to color his face darkly.

"Why, them rotten damn polecats!" he growled, then flushed deeper. "Pardon my language, Miss Sally. I can't help it. You say one's dead and the other is waiting for me inside? How'd that happen?"

"I shot Buck when he made lewd suggestions and took a grab for me."

"Good for you, I don't doubt he deserved it."

"It was not . . . pleasant, Monte."

"I understand. Well," he went on, gesturing to his deputy still astride his lathered mount at the tie-rail, "best put the other one in shackles and get him out of here."

Monte's deputy came forward with an armful of leg irons, chains, and handcuffs. He and Monte entered the house. Sally remained on the porch, preferring not to observe the conclusion of this affair. When the sheriff and his deputy returned, a crestfallen Jason Rucker accompanied them. His appearance shocked Sally.

Leg irons enclosed his ankles, a chain running from the midpoint to another set of links around his waist. His wrists were restrained by thick steel cuffs, and again extended from the coupling bar to his waist. Tear tracks streaked his sallow cheeks, the usual tan faded to a sickly yellow. The corpse of Buck Jarvis had been wrapped in a tarp and draped over his horse by Jason Rucker. The morgan stood knock-kneed at the tie-rail, its loose hide rippling nervously in the presence of death. Monte paused beside Sally while his deputy frog-marched Jase to his waiting mount. She wondered how she could explain all this to Bobby.

"What will happen to him now, Monte?"

Monte Carson paused, weighing how to tell her. "He'll be tried, of course. Most likely he'll hang."

Sally lowered her eyes. "I'm . . . sorry. Oh, not that he will be punished. But I am sorry that this happened in the first place. It seems that there is something terribly wrong with a lot of the younger people these days."

Monte scratched his graying head. "Don't I know it. Well, we'd best be movin' on. It's a long way to Big Rock. And, stop frettin' yourself, Miss Sally. You'll be safe enough."

"Oh, I have no doubt of that, Monte. Though I will need a new purse."

Tyrone Beal arrived in Parkerville on the late train. He located the incompetent henchmen in the nearest saloon. He accepted that philosophically. They could sober up on the ride to the Wagner claim. He'd be damned if he failed again.

"Why'er we goin' now?" Spencer demanded with a drunken slur.

"Because I say we are," Beal barked.

"It'll be dark before we get there," Quint objected with beery breath.

"That's why we're going now. We didn't do too well in daylight, did we?" Beal taunted.

"Bet your ass," Spencer muttered sullenly.

They rode out ten minutes later. Beal took the lead, the route burned into his mind. They began the climb into the foot-hills along the Sacramento River as the sun sank below the coastal range. That still left ample light, the afterglow would last for a good two hours. Grumbles came to Beal's ears from the whiskey-soaked hard cases behind him. He kept a strict silence, letting his irritation with these incompetents feed his anger.

That was the good part. Spencer had informed him that Wagner had taken on a partner, a man reputed to be good with a gun. That didn't set too well with Beal. It had caused him to make changes in his plan. He knew what he would do now. It varied little from his original. Of course, that could be a little rough on Wagner.

Ray Wagner had returned to his claim the previous day. Some of the bruises had faded slightly, and he wore his left arm, broken in two places, in a sling. His ribs had been tightly bound and he moved like an arthritic old man. He had taken the precaution to bring along a burly miner friend of his as a minority partner. Let them come again, he thought. Eli Colter had a small reputation as a shootist. He wore a six-gun slung low on his right hip, another tucked into the waistband of his trousers

130

on the left. And he could use them.

Ray had seen Eli face down three rowdy highwaymen who'd tried to rob him. He had killed two of them and wounded the third. Not a one of the robbers had gotten off a shot. He mused on this fact as he added another stick of firewood to the cookfire in a ring of stones. Above him, blue slowly faded into gray, and the first stars twinkled in the black velvet of the East.

A cloud of sparks ascended as he released the piece of firewood. He froze a second when his ears picked out the distinctive sound of a hoof striking a small rock. Slowly he uncoiled his body and came upright. A quick glance located Eli Colter.

"Eli," he cautioned tense and low. "I think we are about to have visitors. Be ready."

A gravelly voice answered him. "No problem, Ray."

"This ought to hold the fire until morning," Ray speculated, as he added another stick. When he came upright again, he directed his hand to the butt of the finely made Mauser revolver in a flap holster at his hip. Constantly alert, he went about preparing to roll up in his blankets.

He glanced away from the treeline for only a moment to do so, yet when he looked back, four men, led by Tyrone Beal, appeared as if by magic at the edge of the firelight. Wagner braced himself, certain a showdown was in the offing. Beal dismounted and came forward. Without a word, he thrust the quit-claim deed at Wagner.

"I told you I would never sign. You are trespassing. Get off my claim or I will bury you here."

Beal sighed gustily. "You failed to profit from my previous lesson, I see. You are feeling very cocky, eh, Fritzie?"

"I will not sign," Wagner ground out in a hard, flat voice, and went for his gun.

Eli Colter slapped leather a split second later. He never got off a shot. Two of the hard cases with Beal gunned him down before the muzzle could clear leather.

"You don't have a chance," Beal warned. "Sign it and be damned."

Raising his Mauser 10mm revolver to chest level, Wagner shook his head in the negative. "I will not."

At once, all four hard cases tore into him with hot lead. When they finished, eleven bullets had struck Ray Wagner. He lay at Beal's feet, quivering on the threshold of death. Tyrone Beal coldly stepped close to the dead man and rolled him over with the toe of one boot. He looked down at the deed in his other hand, shrugged, and signed it himself.

"Got that signed at last," he commented flatly as he walked away. "Mount up. We've got a long ride in the dark."

Smoke Jensen and Louis Longmont spent a fruitless afternoon and evening in Chinatown. They picked up Louis's belongings at the Palace Hotel and he moved into the bordello. Morning found them at the breakfast table. Louis took another long draw on his cup of coffee and smacked his lips.

"This is excellent coffee," he remarked.

"They're the same Colombian Arabica beans Cyrus Murchison prefers," Lucy Glover informed him.

That raised some eyebrows. "Murchison? How did Francie get her hands on anything he fancied?" Smoke asked.

"The captain of the ship that brings them to San Francisco was a great admirer of Francie's. He always saw to it that at least one full bag got delivered here. Murchison has never known."

Smoke joined Louis in laughter. When they subsided, Louis asked Smoke the key question. "What do we do today?"

"Go back and try to find a lead to Xiang Lee."

Louis made a face. Before he could make a response, Ophilia came to the doorway to the breakfast room. "Mistah Smoke, they's two po-lice here askin' for you."

Smoke and Louis exchanged glances. "We are not at home, Ophilia."

Eyes twinkling with approval for Smoke, Ophilia left to deliver this message to the lawmen. She liked a man with spunk. This would sure put those officious policemen in their place. Her enjoyment was dampened somewhat by their reaction.

"I'm not sure we believe that. You could be charged with harboring fugitives."

Ophilia controlled herself enough to not show any reaction to that. "What you callin' them gentlemen fugitives for?"

"They are wanted for the murder of fifteen railroad police officers and other crimes."

Ophilia let her outrage flow over. "That ain't true. No, suh, not one bit of it. I don' believe a word you said. Now, you get your flat feet off my porch before I throw you off." She turned her ample back on him and slammed the door.

When they learned the purpose of the visit by the police, Smoke Jensen produced a frown. This could complicate matters considerably. "Murchison is a powerful man. I reckon he's got some higher-ups in the police in his pocket. We'll have to be mighty careful going around outside here."

Louis nodded his understanding. "Perhaps a change of costume is in order," he suggested in a glance at Smoke's buckskin hunting shirt and trousers.

"Umm. I see what you mean. Sorta stands out around here, doesn't it? I don't cotton to the idea of fighting in fancy clothes, but the situation suggests I not look like myself."

"I, too, shall change my appearance," Louis offered. "Perhaps the clothing of a longshoreman would be advisable."

"What?" Smoke jibed. "And give up those fancy shirts you like so much?"

"It was Shakespeare who said, 'All the world's a stage.' In this case the actors must blend with the audience."

Smoke quipped back, " 'Faith, that's as well said, as if I had said it myself.' "

Delighted amusement lighted the face of Louis Longmont. "Jonathan Swift. *Polite*

Conversations, I believe. From Dialogue Two?"

"Yes," Smoke said with sudden discomfort. "Sally made me read a lot of Swift."

"And for good reason, I would say. His characters and you have a lot in common. Especially in *Gulliver's Travels.*"

"Are you comparing me to a giant among the Lilliputs? Don't wax too literary, old friend. It's too early in the morning." They shared a laugh, and Smoke went on. "Seriously, we're going to find ourselves with our tails in a wringer if the police get too involved in this."

"Why not talk to Lawyer Brian?" Lucy suggested, then flushed furiously.

Louis picked up on it at once. "Aha! So it's *Brian* now, eh?"

"He's been advising me on managing the — ah — business."

"And you have grown close? No doubt," Louis went on gallantly. "You're a lovely woman, *ma cherie.*"

Lucy hastened to protest. "It isn't — I'm just a client. He doesn't even look on me as a woman, let alone have a romantic interest."

Louis cocked an eyebrow and shaped a teasing expression. "Time for our friend Shakespeare again. 'Methinks the lady doth protest too much.' Yet it's entirely understandable, given the circumstances. What do you say, Smoke, my friend?"

"I think they deserve a tad bit less prying. Louis, can't you be serious for two minutes at a time? Lucy, I agree that maybe Pullen can help. I'd be obliged if you'd go see him about all this. As a lawyer, he can look into it, find out what the police have."

Lucy pushed back from the breakfast table, her meal forgotten. "I'll go right away."

"Finish your breakfast first," Smoke urged.

"But those policemen might come back. And they might bring more with them."

"It's a thought, Lucy. Though by then, Louis and I really will not be here."

Liam Quinn had been working for the California Central Railroad since he was a boy — first as a cook's helper and scullion, then as a switchman and telegrapher, and finally as a locomotive engineer. He was enjoying a day off with his buxom wife, Bridget, and their five dark-haired children. A small park, soon to be converted into office buildings and shops, stood across from the entrance to Chinatown.

Bridget had packed a huge picnic basket, with cold fried chicken, a small joint of ham, cheese, pickled herring, cold boiled potatoes, and hard-cooked eggs. Liam had sent his eldest, eleven-year-old Sean, for a bucket of beer.

Savoring the arrival of the cool, frothy brew, Liam tore off a hunk of sourdough bread and munched contentedly, a chicken wing in the other hand. Two men, quite tall, caught his attention across the street. Lord, they moved like panthers. A full head above other white men, head and shoulders topping the Chinese who milled about near the large Moon gate, they had an air about them that riveted Liam's attention. Something about them set off an alarm in his head.

Yes, that was it. Those men had the moves of gunfighters Liam had read of in the penny dreadfuls. And, yes, on those flyers that he had seen circulated early this morning when he had checked in at the yard office to be sure he could take the day off. These two sure resembled them. He studied them further, noting the rough dress of the bearded one and the somber cut of the other's suit. Certainty bloomed in Liam's brain.

"That's them, by St. Fiona!" Liam

138

shouted. There was a reward offered, Liam recalled. A fat bounty on those particular gentlemen, sure and wasn't it? He must get the word to Captain Beal or Chief Grange. "Sure an' then that gold will jingle in me pocket," he muttered gleefully.

His beer would have to wait. Nothing for it, though. He had to be the first to report them and where they might be found. Liam tossed a hasty word of explanation to his wife and promised to rejoin them within the hour, then hurried off down the street.

Smoke Jensen and Louis Longmont resumed their search for the elusive Xiang Wai Lee on one of the many bustling new side streets of Chinatown. One shopkeeper, fear clearly written in his seamed old face and tired, ancient eyes, spoke with them while he cast worried glances at the front of the shop.

"Nothing good can come of your search. You are not *Han*. You have no idea with what, and whom, you are dealing."

"Then the Tongs are here?" Smoke pressed.

"*Heyi!* Take care in what you say," the frightened elder warned. "They have ears and eyes everywhere. I do not want a hatchet painted on my door. You should not want one on yours, gentlemen."

"I agree," Louis hastened to put in. "What can you tell us of Xiang Wai Lee?"

Eyes wide with fear, the old man blanched so thoroughly that his complexion took on a waxen color. *"Buddah nee joochung!"* he wailed. "To speak the name is to ask for death. Buddha, fortify me," he moaned again.

Smoke Jensen found his patience wearing thin. "Look, this is getting us nowhere. You saw what happened yesterday?" Slowly the aged Chinese nodded. "Then I reckon you should rely upon us to protect you, instead of this Buddha feller. If you know anything at all, tell us how we can find Xiang Lee."

Drawing a shuddering breath, the old merchant stared at a spot above and beyond the shoulder of Smoke Jensen, while he spoke in quiet, broken words. "It is said that there is a secret place, near the opera house."

"The San Francisco Opera?" Smoke asked impatiently.

"No — no, the Chinese opera. It is that large building near the south end of Chinatown. You see it easy, big pagoda, with many peaks and dragon carvings. Near it, it is said, the Triads hold secret meetings. Some say underground. I not know more."

Smoke gave him a warm smile. "You've done enough, old-timer. More than you think. Thank you."

Outside the shop, Louis asked the question that had been troubling Smoke. "Shall we go there straightaway?"

"Don't reckon to. We need to know a lot more about the Tongs. How many are they, for one thing. We don't want to stumble into some nest of wasps. I've been thinking, maybe we're goin' at this the wrong way. There must be some whites who know something about the Tongs. What say we head for those offices built into the wall that runs along Chinatown?"

Louis shrugged. "It's worth a try."

Again, they drew blanks. Not until the fifth small, narrow office did Smoke and Louis come upon anyone with specific knowledge. The sign on the outside identified it as an import broker's office. Inside, dusty chairs were littered about and a large, desk-like table had been heaped with invoices and bills of lading. Seated at a cluttered rolltop desk, a slender, bookish young man in shirt sleeves and garters glanced up, his features shadowed by a green eyeshade.

"You here to pick up the shipment of spices? The paperwork's not done yet," he added without waiting for verification.

"No. Actually, we stopped in to ask you a little something about dealing with the folks of Chinatown," Smoke Jensen advised him.

Smoke kept his questions to generalities until the man had relaxed. At that point he directed their conversation toward the area of interest. "Tell me, when you bring in things from the Orient, China in particular, do you have to deal through — ah — shall we say — out-of-the-ordinary agents among the Chinese?"

"Exactly what do you mean?"

"Do you have to make payoffs to one or more of the Tongs?" Smoke asked bluntly.

The broker did not even blink. "Yes. Anyone dealing with Chinatown has to make their — ah — contributions. It's the way they do business. Even though I am not Chinese, I am not exempt from that rule. Tell me, why are you so interested in the Tongs?"

"Idle curiosity? No, you'd never believe that," Smoke went on, as though thinking out loud. "Actually, we need to talk to Xiang Lee."

Blinking, the import broker pushed up

his eyeshade and removed his hexagonal spectacles. He wiped the lenses industriously as he spoke. "Whatever for?"

"We have good reason to believe that the Tong hatchetmen are bent upon killing us," Louis informed him.

"Then the last thing you want to do is get anywhere near Xiang Lee. He's the most bloodthirsty of them all. Xiang Wai Lee is a deadly, silent reptile who gives no warning before he strikes. You wouldn't stand a chance."

"Perhaps. Though I would reserve judgment, were I you," Louis Longmont advised.

They got a little more out of the broker. Not enough, and no confirmation of the location of Xiang's lair. Back on the street, they headed again for Chinatown, armed with new facts to prod those they questioned. To appear to be armed with more knowledge than one had often resulted in gaining what one sought, Louis reminded Smoke. They had come abreast of the small park across the street when a shout thrust them into quick action.

"Jehosephat! There they are! There's the men I told you about," a voice, thick with Irish accent, shouted.

Smoke and Louis looked that way to see

143

a burly black-haired man. He stood at the curb, pointing directly at them. Half a dozen railroad police gathered behind him. Two of them carried carbine-length Winchesters, which they swiftly brought to their shoulders. The discharge of the rifles made a *crack-crack* sound. Before they heard the muzzle roar, the deadly bullets passed close enough beside the heads of Smoke Jensen and Louis Longmont that they felt the heat of the lead. It answered one question. These men had been ordered to shoot to kill.

EIGHT

Ten more of the railroad thugs swarmed out of the park. That put Smoke Jensen and Louis Longmont in considerable jeopardy. A quick evaluation of the situation decided Smoke on their wisest course of action.

"Let's get out of here," he said tightly.

With Murchison's hirelings streaming after them, Smoke and Louis bolted into Chinatown. The pursuers rapidly lost ground. Once they entered the throng of Chinese, the two with Winchesters did not fire again. Smoke led the way toward the central marketplace. He noted with satisfaction that many of the residents of the Chinese quarter bustled themselves into the street in a manner that would block the passage of the railroad detectives.

Cursing and shoving their way through the throng, the hired guns fell further behind. Finally the first one broke free of the obstacles and threw a shot in the direction of Smoke and Louis. His bullet passed the gunfighter pair far enough away not to be heard. Two more guns joined the fusillade.

145

Smoke and Louis led them by a block. It forced their attackers to halt to take aim.

Now the slugs cracked past uncomfortably close. One round kicked up rock chips from the cobbles beside Smoke's boots. He drew his Colt Peacemaker and returned fire. His target emitted a weak cry and pitched forward onto his face. It gave those behind him pause. Smoke pounded boot soles on the street as he led the way at a diagonal across the market square. Louis followed. In less than five strides, Smoke and Louis found themselves in even more trouble.

Another ten railroad thugs appeared on their left. They had even less distance to cover than those coming from behind. In an eyeblink, they had their six-guns in action. Before flame lanced from their muzzles, Smoke and Louis responded.

Smoke's .45 roared and sent a slug into the pudgy belly of a buck-toothed hard case who wore the round blue billcap and silver badge of a railroad policeman. He went down in a groaning heap of aching flesh. Smoke cycled the cylinder again and sought another target.

Louis already had his. He put out the lights for a red-faced gunman who bellowed defiance at the formidable pair facing him. He stopped in mid-bellow when Louis's bullet punched a neat hole half an inch below his nose. There was more hell to pay for the "detectives" as they closed on Smoke and Louis from two directions.

Smoke blasted a round into the chest of another of them who had ventured too close. He screamed horribly and flung his Smith and Wesson American high in the air. Beside him, a startled thug triggered a hasty, unaimed round. He did well enough, though, as his slug gouged a shallow trough along the left side of Smoke's rib cage. It burned like the fires of hell. All it did was serve to heighten Smoke's anger.

By then, so many of the hunters had weapons in action it sounded like the Battle of Gettysburg. A Chinese woman screamed shrilly as a slug from one of the hard cases struck her in the chest. An angry mutter rose among the fright-paralyzed onlookers. A quick glance indicated to Smoke that they had only one way out. A small pagoda fronted on the west side of a small park south of the market square. It rested in stately composure atop a gentle, grassy slope. Smoke touched Louis lightly on one sleeve and nodded toward the religious shrine. Louis understood at once.

Ducking low, the dauntless pair sprinted among the vendors' carts toward their only hope. Two bullets cut holes in the sailor's jacket worn by Louis Longmont and smacked into a cart wall. The pungent odor of spicy Szechuan food filled the air as the contents of a barrel inside poured onto the ground.

Once free of the closing ring of hard cases, Smoke settled in to pick individual targets while Louis dashed forward a quarter block. Smoke zeroed in on a florid face and squeezed off a round. The thug went down with a hole in his forehead and the back of his head blown off. Those around him ducked for cover. At once, Smoke set off to close the distance between himself and Louis.

Louis sighted on one of the more daring among the throng of hoodlums and sent his target off to pay for his sins. Smoke joined him a moment later. "Take off, Louis," Smoke panted.

Longmont left without a remark. Smoke turned at once to face their enemies. He had little time to wait for a new target. Two men loomed close at hand. The first shouted an alarm too late. Smoke pinwheeled the other railroad detective and spilled him over backward. Sweat stung the raw wound along Smoke's ribs.

No time to think about that. He banished the discomfort from his consciousness. Halfway to their goal, Louis Longmont took cover behind a cart piled with what looked like small gray-brown stones. A stack had been made on a counter outside one of the barrels from which they had come. Louis opened up on the charging gunmen and immediately Smoke Jensen made a dash to join his companion. Return fire shattered several of the stones and released an abominable odor.

Smoke's nostrils flared at the scent of sulfur and sea salt. He swiveled at the hips and fired almost point blank into the chest of his closest pursuer. The man's arms flung wide and his legs could no longer support him. He hit the ground in a skid. Two more long strides and Smoke rounded the odorous cart. More of the objects had been broken open by gunfire and three of the barrels oozed a malevolent ichor.

Through the distaste in his expression, Smoke asked Louis about them. "What are those?"

"Hundred-year-old eggs," Louis enlightened him. "They are not really a hundred years old, merely duck eggs preserved in sea salt and brine."

Before Louis started off on the next leg of their retreat, Smoke asked, "What are they for?"

"The Chinese eat them," Louis answered and began his sprint.

Left behind to hold off the hoodlums, Smoke could only repeat the last part of Louis's sentence: *"Eat them?"*

Without pausing to consider that, Smoke had his hands full of burly railroad detectives and uniformed yard police. He had emptied his Peacemaker and now used the left-hand Colt to hold them at bay. A well-placed round took down a skinny thug with a huge overbite that made him look like a rabbit. That scattered the two who had been beside him. One of the nearer hard cases caught a whiff of the broken eggs.

"Gawd, that's awful. What is that stink?"

"Them things there," a comrade answered. "Let's get away from here."

"Can't. That's where they're holed up."

"Only one of them, an' you're welcome to him," the disgruntled gunhawk offered. "That stuff would gag a maggot."

Louis had reached his latest shelter and taken the time to reload his six-gun. Now he opened up. Instantly, Smoke was on the run. He concentrated on their goal and found a final dash would make it. He advised Louis of that fact when he skidded to a halt behind a stone lion carved in the Chinese style.

"I figured it that way, too, my friend. Shall I give you time to reload?"

"It would be a good idea. I don't hanker to have them follow us into that place with my iron dry."

Swiftly, without a tremble to his hands, Smoke Jensen reloaded both revolvers. Louis kept up a steady fusillade until he had emptied his own, then ran for the beckoning archway that formed the entrance to the temple. Smoke laid down covering fire, and as soon as he glanced at the pagoda and saw Louis no longer in sight, he made his own hurried rush to the promised safety. Louis blasted two more thugs into perdition while he backed up Smoke. When the last mountain man disappeared into the shrine, a jubilant shout rose from their hunters.

"We got 'em trapped, boys!" Mick Taggart yelled gleefully.

"How's that, Mick?" one of his under-lings asked.

"That Chinee church ain't got no back door, that's how," Taggart told him angrily. He had lost too many men, too many good men at that.

Not all had died, though enough had to make him fume inside. He had heard of Louis Longmont; he was supposed to be a hotshot gunfighter from New Orleans. Well, he sure as hell proved that to be true. The other one really bothered him. Smoke Jensen. How many times had he read of that one's exploits? It was unnerving to see the fabled Smoke Jensen in action.

There had been a time when Mick Taggart had fancied himself good enough to go up against any gunhand west of the Mississippi — and where else were they? — then he had come across an account of Smoke Jensen. Overwhelming pride and self-confidence are necessities for a gun-fighter, and Taggart had his full share. Yet he recognized that if even half of what had been written about Smoke Jensen and his fight against the Montana ranching trust was true, he didn't stand a chance. Too late to worry about that secret knowledge.

Now he faced the only man he consid-ered his better. Think fast, he admonished himself. "Pass the word to the rest," he told Opie Engles. "We'll rush that place in a bunch. No way they can get away from us."

"When do we do it, Mick?"

"When you get back, you and me will open up. That'll be the signal."

It worked exactly as Mick Taggart had planned it. Opie returned to tell him the boys were ready. Then Taggart and Engles opened fire on the entrance to the pagoda. The entire force of railroad detectives and police charged as one toward the besieged building. To Taggart and his crew of hard cases and thugs, the shrine held no religious significance. What did it matter if they brought violence and death to its interior? They stormed through the gateway with a shout.

In no time they swarmed into the sanctuary and spread out. They ran and fired as they went. Then Mick Taggart skidded to a stop in the middle of the lacquered floor. A quick glance around verified his suspicion.

Only a smiling-faced Buddha witnessed their assault. Smoke Jensen and Louis Longmont had completely disappeared.

Jason Rucker looked up disbelievingly at his visitor to the cell in the Big Rock jail.

Dressed in the height of fashion, Sally Jensen cut quite a figure in the dingy corridor of the cellblock. She wore a high-necked, full-skirted dress of deep maroon, edged with black ostrich feathers. A matching hat, small and with only a hint of veil, sat perkily on her head, cocked forward in the latest style.

"Monte told me you were convicted. I — had no reason to stay for the rest of the trial."

"Yep. They're goin' to hang me," Jason said, without even a hint of self-pity.

"That's too bad. You know, this whole thing has broken a small boy's heart?"

Jase brightened, then his lips curled down in genuine sadness. "Bobby? He's a kid with a lot of spunk. He's got sand, that he does. How's it broke his heart?"

Sally hesitated, then forged ahead. "He hasn't spoken to me since he learned about the shooting. He won't even look at me, except with a sulky pout and eyes narrowed with hate."

"That's too bad," Jason said through a sigh. "We weren't neither of us worth that."

Sally's misery wedded the pent-up anger in her heart. "Why did you have to take him into your lives?"

Jason made a helpless gesture. "I ain't sure. It was Buck that shined up to the boy. Said it reminded him of himself at that age."

"Good Lord!" Sally expelled in a rush. "And he wanted to remake Bobby in his likeness?"

"I couldn't say . . . though I suspect you've got the right of it." Suddenly he wanted to change the subject. "You know, your husband is a good man, Miz Jensen. But, he ought to be more careful who he takes on as help. It could get him bad-hurt some time."

"I think not. Do you know who he is, Jason?" Sally responded.

"Just Mr. Jensen, I suppose."

Sadly, Sally shook her head. Maybe if Smoke did not cherish his privacy so much and had told the two of them his first name, none of what had followed would have happened. "His first name is Kirby, but everyone calls him Smoke."

"Oh, my God!" Jase paled and swallowed hard. "That's how come you shoot so good. Honest truth, Miz Jensen, I reckon it's a mercy I'll face the hangman, instead of your — Smoke Jensen."

Sally thought on it a long, silent minute. Slowly, she fixed her features into a mask of genuine concern. "You really regret what was done, don't you, Jason?"

Head hanging, he nodded in agreement. "Yes. Yes, I do."

"Well, then, there's something I must do. Your concern over Bobby and your show of remorse have convinced me that you deserve a second chance. Mind, I'm not promising anything. Nor am I given to feeling sorry for criminals. But you're young, with apparently a will of your own, although it has been long in the shadow of Buck Jarvis, I wager. I'll have a talk with Monte Carson and the judge. Perhaps we can get your sentence commuted to prison time only. Don't get your hopes up, but I will try. Goodbye, Jason."

Jason choked out a farewell through the flood of relieved tears that streamed down his suddenly gaunt cheeks.

"Come this way," a small, old monk in a saffron robe summoned Smoke Jensen and Louis Longmont when they dashed into the center of a large square area with wood floor, red lacquered walls picked out with gold leaf, and a blue domed ceiling.

They cut their eyes to the frail figure, his hands hidden within the voluminous sleeves of a plain yellow silk robe. Twin, wispy hanks of white hair sprouted from his chin to mid-chest, matched by a ghost of mustache the same color and thinness. When they hesitated, he withdrew one skeletal hand, parchmented with age, from the folds of his sleeve and beckoned.

"Come this way," he repeated.

Smoke and Louis shifted their gaze to the seemingly solid wall behind the old man. What good would it do to be against that wall, as opposed to any other? Impatiently the old monk gestured again.

"Hurry, there is little time."

"I'm willing," Smoke Jensen told him. "But I sure hanker to know what good it will do."

"I will take you out of the shrine to safety."

That was good enough for Smoke. He and Louis crossed the expanse of floor, their boot heels clicking on the high-gloss floorboards. When they neared the monk, he stepped away in the direction of a fat statue of a smiling Buddha. There, he pressed a spot on the wall that looked like any other.

A hidden panel swung open in the side wall of the pagoda. The priest-monk waited until they reached the opening and nodded to indicate they should enter. Smoke remembered the .45 Colt in his hand and thought well of keeping it there. With a small gasp of impatience at their hesitation, their host preceded them into a dark passageway.

There he used a lucifer to light a torch and return it to its wall sconce. Smoke and Louis stepped through into what they soon saw to be a tunnel. Behind them, the secret panel clicked back into place. Smoke tightened his grip on the plowhandle butt grip of his Peacemaker. The monk advanced down the tunnel, igniting more torches. When he had three burning brightly, he waited for his unexpected guests.

"I am Tai Chiu. I am the abbot of this temple. We have taken notice of your activities in the past few days. It became obvious that you are fighting the evil ones. When they outnumbered you, you took sanctuary in our humble shrine. It is our duty to protect you." He motioned with the same thin, frail hand he had used to summon them to the hidden passage. "Follow in my steps. I will take you to a hidden place and heal your wounds."

Smoke Jensen again became aware of the gouge along his ribs. The bleeding had slowed, but it still oozed his life's fluid. A quick glance apprised him that his wound did not show.

"How did you know we had been shot?"

"I . . . felt your agony. Please to come this way. Those who seek you will be befuddled."

Cyrus Murchison pushed back the picked-clean carcass of the half duck he had enjoyed for his noon meal. Silver bowls held the remains of orange sauce, fluffy mashed potatoes, thick, dark gravy, and wilted salad greens. Beyond this gastronomic phalanx sat a silver platter filled with melting ice and a pile of oyster shells, all that remained of a dozen tasty mollusks on the half-shell. Murchison hid a polite belch behind the back of his hand and dabbed at his thick lips with a white napkin.

"Well, then Judge Batey, did you enjoy your *canard à l'orange?*"

A similar array of plates and utensils covered the tablecloth in front of the judge. He patted a protruding belly and nodded approvingly. "Most excellent, my dear Cyrus. I always look forward to dining with you. Do you eat this well at night?"

Murchison produced a fleeting frown. "Alas, I have been constrained by my stomach, as well as my doctor, to curtail my epicurean adventures in the evening. A chop, a boiled potato, and some fruit and cheese is my limit of late. But I sorely miss the pig's knuckles, sauerkraut, and beer, or roasted venison with *pommes frites,* and strawberries in cream that I used to indulge in."

Judge Batey chuckled softly. "I know whereof you speak. Though I fear we digress."

"Oh? How's that?"

"You are not known to wine and dine persons of influence without some ulterior motive. What is it I can help you with this time?"

"Right to the point, eh? Your courtroom reputation has preceded you. That is why I dismissed the servants. We'll not be imposed upon." He paused, steepled his thick fingers, and belched again before launching into his proposition. "There are going to be some transfer deeds coming before your court in the near future. Some of them will no doubt be contested. I trust that you can recognize the genuineness of these instruments merely by examining them?"

Judge Batey nodded solemnly. "Is that all? Surely those excellent ducks will have gone begging for so small a favor."

Murchison wheezed stout laughter.

"You're the fox, right enough, Judge. You'll be hearing a criminal matter soon — two men charged with murder of railroad police and some of Hector Grange's detectives. The culprits are named Louis Longmont and Smoke Jensen. To be quite up front with you, Judge, I want to see them hanged."

Batey hesitated only a fraction of a second. "That will depend a lot upon the evidence."

A frown flickered on the broad forehead of Cyrus Murchison. "It need not. In order to provide binding evidence, some things might come out that would prove deleterious to the California Central. We like to keep a — uh — low profile. You understand?"

"Quite so." Judge Batey pursed his lips. "That is asking quite a lot, Cyrus." He raised a hand to stave off a protest. "Not that it is impossible. I shall have to examine the circumstances and evidence and perhaps find a way to accommodate you. Whatever the case, I will do my best."

"Fine, fine. Now, help yourself to some of that chocolate cream cake."

NINE

Tai Chiu led Smoke Jensen and Louis Longmont down a long incline that Smoke soon judged put them well below street level. The Chinese priest remained silent, husbanding his thoughts. As he progressed, he paused at regular intervals to light another torch. The flambeaus flickered and wavered, as though in a breeze. Yet the air still smelled dank and musty. Their steps set off echoes as they advanced over the cobblestone flooring of the shaft. When they reached a level space, they had only hard-packed earth beneath them. Their course took them through a twisting, turning labyrinth of intersecting tunnels. Even with his superb sense of direction, Smoke Jensen had to admit that he had not a hint of where the old monk was taking them.

"Where do you think he is taking us, *mon ami?*" Louis voiced Smoke's thoughts in a low whisper.

"I haven't the least idea."

"He could be taking us directly to Murchison," came the source of Louis's worry.

"I doubt that. He could have left us for those railroad thugs."

"Umm. You have a point."

They walked on in silence for a while, ignorant of their destination, or even of where they had been. Then Louis put voice to his concern again.

"He could be taking us to Xiang Lee," he proposed.

Smoke produced a wide, white grin. "Then all the better for us. We can gun down Xiang Lee and end of problem."

Louis got a startled expression. "You do not really mean that, my friend."

Smoke sobered and left only a hint of smile on his full lips. "Only halfway, old pard. I would never kill an unarmed man. But I could gladly tom-turkey-tromp the crap out of him."

Louis looked relieved and pleased. "Now, that's the Smoke Jensen I have always known. Only, I would feel better if I knew where we were going."

"As I said, we will have to wait and see."

They walked along in silence for several lengthy minutes. Suddenly Smoke received a hint of their destination. The sharp tang of salt air reached his nostrils. He cut his eyes to Louis, who nodded his understanding. They made another turn and it came to Smoke's attention that someone had come along behind them to snuff out the torches. Even if they tried, they could not find their way back through the mystifying maze of tunnels.

Ahead of them, Tai Chiu stopped abruptly before what appeared to be the inner side of the wall of a building. When Smoke and Louis came up to him, he lifted a thick iron ring and gave it a twist. A rusty bolt screeched in its latch. Then a section of the "wall" swung inward. Bright sunlight and the stinging tang of sea air, mingled with the fishy smell of the bay, poured in.

"This way, please," Tai urged.

They followed him out of the building onto a street that paralleled a section of San Francisco Bay. Tai Chiu directed them to a tall, wide wire gate in a high fence at the street end of a long pier. Tai used a key to open the fat padlock and ushered them inside. At the far end of the wharf Smoke saw an odd-shaped ship. Its sails had been furled and the masts were stepped at a steep backward angle. The stern rose in the likeness of a turret from a castle in the Middle Ages, even more so than the caravels of fifteenth-century Spain. On a large plank, mounted below the aft weather rail, picked out in Chinese ideograms and English letters, was the name of the ship, the *Whang Fai*.

The bow also jutted high and square, with murlons to accommodate archers. A likeness of a human eye had been painted a couple of feet above the plimsol line. Louis Longmont soon apprised Smoke of its origin and type.

"It is a Chinese junk. The largest one I have ever seen."

"How astute, Mr. Longmont," Tai Chiu complimented him. "It is an oceangoing junk. You will find it curious to see that it appears even bigger from inside. Our Chinese builders have a talent that way."

Tai led them to a rickety gangway that gave access to the deck of the junk. There, he directed them below decks to an aft cabin decorated in an opulent Oriental style. Statuary in the form of dragons and lions, several of them covered in gold leaf, ranged around the bulkheads, which had been hung with heavy silk brocade tapestries. These depicted various subjects, among them, lovely young ladies of the court, solemn mandarins, fierce warriors astride snorting stallions, bows drawn until the wicked barbs of the arrow heads touched the arms of the bow, and a lordly emperor. Incense burned in tall brass braziers. Cushions abounded, though there was nary a chair. Low tables held porcelain bottles and small, footed cups. It truly did look as if it were too large to fit into the junk's aft quarter.

Smoke took it in and found it a bit too fancy for his liking. Fringe-lined lanterns hung from the overhead in bright colors of red, yellow, and green. They swayed slightly with the movement of the water beyond the bulkheads. The junk creaked and groaned like any wooden sailing ship. From beyond the bulkhead that divided the cabin from the rest of the belowdecks area came the twitter of distinctly feminine voices. Tai Chiu clapped his hands in a signal and the owners of those voices appeared.

One bore a tray with a large, steaming pot, and small, handleless cups. The other had a plate of savory smelling tidbits of foods. "*Dim sum,* little bites," Tai explained. "There are Chinese dumplings, steamed wonton, oysters in peanut sauce — oh, and many more things. Refresh yourselves while I summon our doctor."

Lacking any chairs, Smoke and Louis made themselves comfortable on cushions around the low table on which the young women placed their tea and snacks. Louis made an attempt with chopsticks; Smoke settled for his fingers. He lifted a plump prawn from a scarlet sauce and bit off half of it. At once his tastebuds gave off the alarm. Sweat broke out on his forehead and his eyes began to water as he chose to chew rapidly as the best means of eliminating the fiery morsel. He did not want to spit it out; that, he knew, would be bad manners.

"Szechuan," one of the lovelies provided helpfully.

"I don't know what that is, but it sure is hot," Smoke responded.

They turned their heads away and covered their mouths and broke into a fit of giggles. Smoke noticed in detail how comely they appeared. More than twenty years of fidelity to Sally protected him from their blandishments, a fact for which he gave great gratitude. Louis, however, showed signs of becoming enthralled. He answered Smoke's unasked question in a distant voice.

"She said 'Szechuan.' It's the name of a province in China, and also a style of cooking that uses a lot of garlic and chili peppers."

"More than the Mexicans, I'll grant

you," Smoke gasped out.

"Don't use tea to douse the fire," Louis cautioned, "that would only make it hotter. Try some of that rice wine in the ceramic bottle."

Smoke shook his head in wonder. "Is there no place you have not visited, Louis, no one's food you have not sampled?"

Louis produced a deprecating smile. "*Oui.* There are many places I have never gone. Such as Greece, the principalities of Lesser Asia, the islands of the South Pacific, with their dusky maidens . . ." He would have gone on, except that Smoke raised a hand in a warding-off gesture.

"Enough. I get your point. I hope our gracious host hurries. That bullet I took along my ribs left a world of smarting behind it."

"Let me take a look at it."

When Louis removed Smoke's coat, the China dolls turned away in twittering honor at the sight of the bloody shirt worn by Smoke Jensen. Louis cut away the sodden garment and Smoke swore hotly.

"Damn, that's the only Sunday-go-to-meetin' shirt I brought from home."

Louis studied the wound. "Better it is for you that you had it along. Good, clean linen. Less chance of a suppuration. This should heal nicely. But it will leave another nasty scar."

Another scar, Smoke Jensen thought resignedly. His torso and limbs had accumulated a veritable criss-cross of the patterns of violence. He had received wounds from knife and tomahawk, bullet and buckshot, gouges from the sharp stabs of broken branches, flesh ground off by gravel, and painful burns. His body could serve as a roadmap of his many close encounters with death. He shook his head to dislodge the grim images from his mind.

Having recovered from their initial shock, the enchanting Chinese women — hardly more than girls — hovered over their guests once more. In halting English they urged each man to eat more of the delicacies, to drink their tea. There would be a sea of rice wine afterward, they promised. Half an hour went by, according to Smoke's big Hambleton turnip watch, before Tai Chiu returned with a black-clad, bowed older man, his lined face reminiscent of a prune in all but color. With only a perfunctory greeting he set right to work.

From a little, black bag — just like the kind a *real* doctor carried — he produced an assortment of herbs and lotions and a large roll of bandage gauze. He treated both Smoke and Louis, then leaned back on his small, skinny buttocks to chatter in rapid-fire Chinese at the priest.

Tai Chiu translated for the benefit of the Occidentals. "The doctor says you must take this powder in a little rice wine three times a day."

Smoke eyed the packet suspiciously. "What's in it?"

Tai Chiu smiled deceptively. "It is better that you are not knowing," he said through his spread lips.

"No. I want to know."

The priest sighed and named off the ingredients. "Ground rhinoceros horn, dried fungus from the yew tree, and processed gum of the poppy." He gave a little shrug. "There are, perhaps, other things, secrets of the doctor, you understand. The potion will ease any pain, strengthen you until your body overcomes the blood loss, while the unguents he put on the wound will prevent infection."

Dubious, Smoke responded uneasily. "I'm not so sure about all this."

Enigma coated the lips of Tai Chiu. "Do not your *qua'lo* doctors do the same? They mix roots, bark, and herbs and give them to their patients. The gum of the poppy, in your language, is called laudanum. And does it not ease pain?"

Smoke decided to make the best of it. "You've got me there. And, to top it off, our croakers give everything queer foreign names, so a common feller don't know what it is he's getting."

"Just so. There are no mysteries in Chinese healing. Now, to explain why I brought you here. Your courage and your skill with weapons have been observed and have convinced the high council of our humble order, and the elders of the community, that you have been sent by the ancestors to lead a great battle against the evil dragons of the Triad Society."

What a flowery way to say we're here to break up the alliance between the Tongs and Murchison's thugs, Smoke thought. A quick, silent counsel passed between Smoke and Louis. They acknowledged that they weren't too sure about that. The exchange also conveyed that both agreed to go along for the time being.

"How are we to go about this?" Smoke asked.

"You are to wait here. Men will come, young men who wish to rid Chinatown from the curse of the Tongs for all time. They are strong and good fighters. Students at the temple, for the most part.

Now that your wounds have been mended, you will eat and rest and wait for the others to join you."

"When will that be?" Louis inquired.

"Later. In the dark of night. It is our hope to catch Xiang Wai Lee by stealth and deal a death blow to his army of hatchetmen. Now, enjoy. These delightful young ladies have prepared a feast for you. And afterward, you may avail yourselves of the baths in another part of the ship. I will return with the last of our young warriors to make certain none were followed."

After Tai Chiu swept out of the cabin, Smoke Jensen went to one porthole to watch his departure from the wharf. Strangely, the frail old monk seemed to have completely disappeared. He turned to Louis, who pressed on him a plaguing question.

"What was that in service of, *mon ami?*"

Smoke flashed an appreciative smile. "I think we have found the key to dealing with the Tongs, and Xiang Lee in particular. For now, my stomach thinks my throat's been slit. Let's eat."

Steaming bowls and platters of exotic Chinese dishes came one course at a time, in a steady procession. Few, if any, did Smoke Jensen recognize. He enjoyed the pork and noodles, the egg foo yong, and the sweet-and-sour shrimp. He balked, though, at the baby squid in their own ink — another Szechuan delicacy, which he wisely avoided after his eyes watered from the chili oil and plethora of peppers, when he sniffed the pedestal bowl in which they were served. As was his custom, he tried to eat sparingly, yet when the parade of food at last ceased, he felt stuffed to the point of discomfort.

"That was some feed," he remarked, stifling a belch. "The soup was good, only why did they serve it last?"

"It is their custom," Louis informed him.

Smoke sucked at his teeth a moment. "Tasty, even if it came as dessert. What was in it?"

"It was bird's nest soup," Louis answered simply.

Smoke swallowed hard, as his stomach gave a lurch. "You're funnin' me, Louis. Aren't you?"

"Not at all. Of course, they clean them first. I won't go into how the nests are made."

"No. Please don't." Smoke said no more with the appearance of the sweet young ladies.

"You come bath now?" one of them chirped.

"Sounds good," Smoke agreed, as he came to his boots. All the way to the small, humid chamber that held the bubbling wooden bath, Smoke Jensen tried to puzzle out the slightly amused, esoteric smile on the lips of Louis Longmont.

When they reached the tiny cabin, Smoke quickly learned the reason why. "You undress now," the charming daughter of Han told them. Both girls and Louis began to remove their clothing.

"What! Whoa, now, hold it," Smoke pleaded. Images of the reaction Sally would have boiled in his mind.

Soft light glowed on the nubile bodies of the delightful creatures while Smoke Jensen continued to gobble his protests. With lithe movements, the girls became water nymphs as they climbed the two short steps and waded into the steaming water. Buck naked, Louis Longmont quickly joined them.

"Louis? What are you doing?"

"I have always appreciated a good bath, *mon ami*. You should join us. There are delights that surpass the imagination that follow the laving."

Smoke gulped down his trepidation and

174

pulled a somber face. "Thanks, partner, I think I'll pass."

Puzzled by this exchange, beyond their capacity for English, one of the girls cut her eyes to the other. "What is this? The barbarian will not clean himself?"

Although the language mystified him, Louis Longmont caught the drift of what had been said. It summoned a deep, rich guffaw. "I think the young ladies are disturbed over your aversion to taking a bath."

"I do have that gouge along my ribs. Wouldn't do to get that wet."

Louis sobered. "You have a point. Ah, well, *mon ami,* I suppose I can force myself to uphold the honor of Western man."

Confounded at last, Smoke Jensen stomped from the room, though not without a backward, longing glance at the precious physical endowments of the giggling girls.

Cyrus Murchison and Gaylord Huntley took their postprandial stroll through the minute park named after St. Francis of Assisi, patron of the city, in the center of the cluster of municipal buildings. Tall marble columns surrounded them, while pigeons and seagulls made merry sport of the imposing bronze figure on horseback that occupied the center of the swatch of green. It was there that Heck Granger found him and spoiled the repose Murchison had generated from this good meal they had consumed.

In fact, it soured Murchison's stomach. "They whupped the hell out of 'em."

"What?"

"Those two, Jensen and Longmont, blasted their way through twenty-seven of my men and flat disappeared."

Murchison's visage grew thunderous. "That is impossible. I will not accept that. No two men can outgun twenty-five plus."

Fearing the outburst that would be sure to follow, Granger answered meekly, "These two did. They ran into a Chinee temple and when my men got in there, they were nowhere to be seen."

"They went out a back door," Cyrus Murchison suggested.

"There weren't none. No side doors, either. There was . . . no place for them to escape."

"Nonsense. I want you to take more men, go there, and tear that place apart until you find how they got out of there."

"That — wouldn't be wise, Mr. Murchison. That temple is in Chinatown. Even the Tongs would turn on us if we did. We only got them behind us a little while ago. It's touchy, I say."

A ruby color suffused the angry expression on the face of Cyrus Murchison. "Damn the Tongs. I never approved of allying ourselves with them in the first place."

"I hate to mention it, sir. But there are more of them than there are of us. I won't risk my men for that. We'll find those two. And we'll do it our way."

It was blatant defiance, and Granger all but quailed at the boldness he had displayed. To his surprise, it worked. Murchison's expression softened. "All right, Heck. I understand your anxiety. Do it the way you see best. Only . . . don't fail this time."

Brian Pullen appeared before Judge Timothy Flannery in the judge's chambers. Aware of Flannery's aversion to wasting time on small talk, he came right to the point.

"Your Honor, I have reliable information that several powerful men in this community have conspired to wrest control of a building owned by a client of mine from him. In furtherance of this conspiracy, they have made false representations to the police of this city that the property had been sold for back taxes, which it had not. Also regarding acts committed by my client and an associate. These acts were, in fact, self-defense. The result is that the police are looking for my client and his associate as fugitives from justice."

Judge Flannery steepled his fingers. "What is it you wish me to do, Counselor?"

"Inasmuch as these persons are actively engaged in an attempt to seize my client's property and using police pressure to accomplish their goal, I have here a petition for a restraining order, which will relieve my clients from the loss of said property until such time as the matter can be resolved. It also asks that the police be restrained from hunting down my client and his associate, and to prevent agents of the conspirators from doing the same."

"I . . . see." Judge Flannery considered that a moment. "I'll see your brief and make my decision within two hours. By the way, who are these men you allege are co-conspirators?"

Brian Pullen swallowed hard. "Cyrus Murchison and Titus Hobson. Also Gaylord Huntley."

Flannery's eyebrows rose. "Your client

picked some big enemies, I must say."

Brian asked, "Will that have an effect on your decision, Your Honor?"

A frown creased Flannery's brow. "Certainly not. Come back in two hours."

Shortly after sundown, slim, hard-faced young Chinese men began to drift aboard the *Whang Fai*. Smoke Jensen and Louis Longmont inspected them critically. They exchanged worried glances over the odd assortment of weapons these volunteers possessed. Some carried pikes with odd-shaped blades. Several had swords with blades so broad that they resembled overgrown meat cleavers. A few had knives of varying blade length. More than half bore only stout oak staffs.

Smoke cut his eyes to Louis. "They expect to use those to fight the Tong soldiers and any of Murchison's railroad detectives we come across?"

Louis sighed. "It is a most discouraging prospect, *mon ami*."

Tai Chiu merely smiled and bowed. "Honorable warriors, it is my humble duty to introduce you to Quo Chung Wu." He indicated a fresh-faced youth who could not be past his twentieth year. "He is the leader of these students that it is my humble privilege to instruct."

"Students? Are they studying to be priests?"

"Yes, that, too. What I teach them is *Kung Fu,* which are our words for what you would call martial arts. The Way of the Warrior. Since they are destined to follow the religious life, most of what they learn is unarmed combat. Yet I believe that when you see Wu and his young men in action, you will both marvel at what can be done. Now, the time draws near. We must lay a course of action."

TEN

Tyrone Beal and six thick-muscled railroad detectives sat their horses outside the small, wooden frame building that had been sided with galvanized tin. A pale square of yellow light slanted to the ground from the window in an otherwise blank wall to their left. An angled layer of shingles formed a roof over the narrow stoop that gave to a door, the top third of which was a lattice of glass panes. A hand-lettered sign rested at the junction of porch roof and building front. It read in dripping letters: CENTRAL VALLEY FREIGHT. At a nod from Beal, the thugs dismounted.

"Don't look like much," one hard case grumbled.

"Heck Granger said Mr. Huntley don't want the competition, so we take care of it," Beal told him. "The sooner the better, I say. This is my last job up here in the nowhere, then it's back to San Francisco for me."

A local tough glanced at Beal quizzically. "You don't like it out here?"

"Nope. It's too wide open for me. I grew

181

up with buildings all around me. This kinda country makes me feel like I'm gonna fall right off the earth." Beal motioned to a pair of the local gang. "You two take the back. Make sure no one gets away."

Beal and the other four climbed the open, rough-hewn plank steps to the stoop. Beal took the lead, his big hand smacking the door hard enough to slam it against the inside wall. From behind the counter a man with the look of a farmer gave them a startled glance.

"Wh-what do you gentlemen need?" he asked shakily.

"You're out of business, Harper," Beal growled.

Gus Harper backed away from the counter that separated him from the hard cases. He raised both hands in protest. "Now, see here . . ."

"No, you listen and do as you are told."

"Who are you?"

Beal gave Harper a nasty smirk. "Names don't mean a lot."

"Then who sent you?"

"I think you know the answer to that. We come to give you a different outlook on what's what in this world. There ain't gonna be any competition in the freighting business."

"I have every right," Harper blustered. Then he weighed the menace in Beal's expression. His next words came in a stammered rush. "N-Now, let's not do anything hasty."

Beal pointed at the counter and rolltop desk behind. "We'll not, just so long as you put an end to this crazy notion of yours. You're a farmer, Harper. Go back to clod-hoppin'." He glanced left and right to the thugs with him. "Spread out, boys. This place needs a little rearrangin'."

Harper made a fateful mistake. "Stop right there. There's law in this valley, and it's on my side."

Beal nodded to a pair of thugs. "You two take ahold of him. Now, Mr. Farmer-Turned-Freight Master, for the last time, go back to your plow. There ain't gonna be another freight company in the Central Valley."

Harper made one final, weak effort to make reason prevail. "But the railroad and Huntley's Dray Service have raised rates twice this year already and harvest is three months away."

"Don't matter how many times the prices go up, you and all the rest are going to pay and keep your mouths shut."

Beal moved in then, through the small

183

gate at one end of the counter. He balled his big fists while the two thugs grabbed onto Harper. They spread the former farmer out so his middle was open to the vicious attack Beal leveled on him. Beal worked on Harper's belly first, pounded hard, twisting blows into the muscle of the abdomen, then worked up to the chest. A severe blow right over the heart turned Harper's face ashen.

For a moment he went rigid and his eyes glazed. Slowly he came around in time for Beal to start in on his face. Knuckles protected by leather gloves, Beal put a cut on Harper's left cheekbone, and a weal on his forehead. Beal mashed his victim's lips and broke his nose. Harper went limp in the grasp of the hard cases.

Beal showed no mercy. He went back to the gut. Soft, meaty smacks sounded with each punch. Harper hung from the grip of strong hands. Beal aimed for the ribs. He felt two give on his third left hook. It gave him an idea.

"Let him go," he ordered.

Harper sank to the floor, a soft moan escaped though battered, split lips. Beal toed him onto his back and began to methodically kick Harper in the ribs. The bones broke one by one. When all on the right side had been broken, Beal went around to the other side and began to slam the toe of his boot into the vulnerable ribs. They, too, snapped with sharp pops. When the last gave, Beal went to work on Harper's stomach.

Unprotected, the internal organs suffered great damage. Sometime while Beal worked on Harper's liver, the man died. The first Beal and his henchmen knew of it was when the body, relaxed in death, voided. The outhouse stench rose around them.

"He's gone, Mr. Beal," Spencer said quietly.

"Then drag him outside. Let that be a lesson for the others. The rest of us are going to torch this place."

It did not seem like much of a plan to Smoke Jensen. Tai Chiu had described to them the dens habituated by the Tong soldiers. One was an opium parlor. There, the wretched individuals in the thrall of the evil poppy idled away their lives, many filth-encrusted and never off their rude pallets, where they smoked the black, tarlike substance that gave them their life-sapping dreams. That is how Tai Chiu described them.

At least they sounded incapable of putting up any resistance, Smoke speculated. That still left some two hundred Tong members. Tai Chiu had been quite certain of the number. The count varied from time to time, though never exceeding a hundred members for each of the three Tongs. Tai Chiu had named them the Iron Fan Tong, the Blue Lotus Tong, and the Celestial Hatchets. Smoke considered the names odd and a bit pretentious. Louis had explained the reasoning behind them.

"These Tong members choose a name based on the power a Tong has. Some of them go back centuries. Anything with 'Celestial' in it is most powerful. It is likely that Xiang Wai Lee is from this Tong."

"Quite right, Mr. Longmont," Tai Chiu confirmed. "You know much about the darker side of our ancient culture."

"There were, for a time, some Tongs in New Orleans."

Tai Chiu's eyes danced with interest. "Might I ask what happened to them?"

"Myself, and some of my friends, ah, persuaded them to depart."

"I presume you did not use gentle persuasion on them?"

"Right you are, Mr. Tai. We used six-guns and some rope."

Tai Chiu's white eyebrows rose. "I think we have the answer to why they so readily came after you. No doubt some of the survivors came here, to San Francisco. You might have been recognized the first time you were seen."

Louis considered that. "Sounds reasonable. Now, as I understand it, each of the three of us will take on one of the Tongs. When one of their meeting places has been pacified, those of us who fought there will go on to another location."

"That is correct," Tai Chiu verified. "The Celestial Hatchets are currently the strongest of the three. You do not feel uncomfortable assuming that task, Mr. Jensen?"

"Not too much. Considering I'm going to have only fifteen of your student-fighters along," Smoke answered drily.

"Be advised that it is your prowess with firearms that will tip the balance. The Tongs are not loath to use modern weapons."

Smoke looked hard at the old priest. "Thanks very much, Mr. Tai. If I thought I was goin' up against fellers armed only with hatchets, I couldn't live with myself."

Tai Chiu studied Smoke's face a moment. "Your face tells me you are serious, yet your eyes speak of a jest. You are having fun with me, yes?"

"It's that or walk away from this whole thing. Sixteen against a hundred is mighty long odds."

"Bear in mind, not all of them will be there at one time. You must deal with them as they come in answer to the rallying call. That will make your task simpler, I think."

Smoke checked the loads in his right-hand six-gun. He slid a sixth cartridge into the usually empty chamber. Then he did the same for the second revolver. "All together, I have about thirty rounds. After that, it's going to get quite interesting."

"We go now," Tai Chiu answered simply.

To their surprise, Smoke Jensen and Louis Longmont found Chinatown brightly lighted even at the midnight hour. Families streamed in and out of restaurants, many with sleepy-eyed little tykes tugged along by their small hands. Westerners as well as Chinese thronged the shops, clutching their purchases by the strings that bound the gaudy red-and-gold or green-and-silver tissue paper. Musical bursts of conversation in Cantonese and Mandarin filled the air. All of that added an unexpected complication for Smoke

Jensen. Their small force had divided before entering Chinatown and Smoke felt uncomfortably exposed.

His target, the Celestial Hatchets, had a building on the far side of the market square, near the Chinese opera house. He and his volunteers would be in the open the longest. Quo Chung Wu took the lead as they rounded the corner. Two youthful Chinese lounged against the wall outside the door to the Tong headquarters. One of them roused himself when he caught sight of Quo in his saffron temple robe. He stepped out to block the walkway and raised a hand to signal that Quo should halt.

"You are in the wrong place, *shunfoo go*," he snarled insolently.

" 'Dog of a priest,' am I?" Quo Chung Wu rasped back.

Then, in only the time it took Smoke Jensen to blink, Quo made his move. His body pivoted and bent backward. A weird birdlike sound came from his throat as he lashed out a foot in a powerful kick that knocked the Tong thug back into his companion, who had only begun to straighten up, sensing at last that trouble had come to their lair. Quo followed up the unconventional kick with a full swing that brought him back face-to-face with the Tong soldiers. Elbows akimbo, he formed his long-fingered hands into the shape of tiger claws and darted one out to rake sharp, thick nails across the face of the slow-awakening Tong man. To Smoke's surprise, the youth did not scream as long, red lines appeared on his cheek. Quo's fist closed and he smashed the injured man in the nose with a back-blow.

His left elbow struck the chest next. Then he sent a side-kick that knocked the insulting one to his knees. A pointed toe rose under the Tong hatchetman's chin and stilled his opposition. His companion had regained his feet and leaped into the air to deliver a flying kick that rocked Quo back, though it did not faze him. He pivoted to the right and drove hard fists, the middle knuckles extended, into the breastbone of his attacker. Staggering back until his shoulders collided with the wall, the thug drew a hatchet.

It gave off a musical whistle as it swung through the air. When the blade passed him, Quo stepped in and drove an open palm to the already damaged nose. Bone and cartilage cracked and popped and sliced through the thin partition into his brain. He fell twitching to the ground.

Smiling sardonically, Quo stepped to one side and made a sweeping gesture of welcome to the door.

Smoke entered, his .45 Colt at the ready. Two more Tong henchmen sat on ornate plush chairs. One leaped up with a Smith American .44 in his hand. He didn't get to use it as Smoke upset him into a heap on the floor with a fat .45 slug in his chest. Beside him, his partner shrieked curses in Cantonese and loosed a round from his .38 Colt Lightning. It knocked the hat from the head of Smoke Jensen and smacked into the wall beyond.

Superior weapons skills put Smoke's round right on target. Eyes bulging, the Chinese hoodlum slammed back into his chair, which tipped over to spill him onto the hall carpet. Smoke stepped over his twitching legs and advanced along the hall. A steady drone of conversation in Chinese ended with the roar of the guns. How many would be waiting? Smoke didn't let it worry him. He stepped through the archway at the end of the hall with his Peacemaker ablaze.

A squat, rotund Chinese with a sawed-off shotgun discharged a barrel into the ceiling on his way over backward in his chair. To his left, another hurled a hatchet at the head of Smoke Jensen. Ducking below the deadly device, Smoke popped a hole in the Tong soldier's chest that broke his collarbone and severed the subclavian artery. Another Tong bully came at Smoke, his face twisted in the fury of his scream, at the same moment Quo Chung Wu stepped into the room beside Smoke.

Quo gave the thug a front kick, high in his throat, that cut off the scream like a switch. Then he pivoted and delivered a side-kick to the chest and a second to the descending head. To Smoke's surprise, he had accomplished this in less time than it took Smoke to cock his Colt. The Tong butcher dropped his hatchet and skidded on his nose to the feet of Smoke Jensen. Quo smiled and bowed slightly.

Stacks of coins and paper currency went flying as another Tong hatchetman leaped onto the table and jerked back his arm to unloose a hatchet. He pitched over on the back of his head when Smoke plunked a .45 slug into his belly, an inch above the navel. A scrabbling sound came from the corner of the room.

A youthful Tong henchman tried desperately to fling up the sash of a window. When the muzzle of Smoke Jensen's .45 Colt tracked toward him, his fear overcame him and he threw himself through the pane. Broken glass rang down musically. One of the student volunteers rushed to the gaping frame and drew a fancy carved bow. The arrow sped down the alley and took the fleeing Tong gangster between the shoulder blades. A thin, high wail ended his life. Smoke touched a finger to his bare forehead.

"Obliged," he told the archer.

Others of the young priests had fanned out through the house. The sound of breaking glass came again as a youthful Tong member made his escape. By ones and twos the volunteers began to return to this central room to report the place as empty. Smoke looked around at the havoc they had created.

"That happened too easy," Smoke told them.

Their young, happily smiling faces contradicted him. "We have no objection to that," Quo spoke for them all.

"What I'm getting at is, there are a whole lot more of them out there. They will be coming, you can be sure of that."

"Then we will not be going on to help the others?" Quo asked, uncertain.

"Not right away, Quo. We'll have our hands full any minute now," Smoke responded, as he opened the loading gate of his Peacemaker and began shucking out empty shell casings.

Louis Longmont eased his way along a dark alley in Chinatown. Close at his side came five of his fifteen volunteer priests. For all the danger they faced, these young men held uniform expressions of calm and confidence. An unusually tall, lean Chinese beside him clutched a bo stick with supple fingers. They came to a dark, recessed entrance to a cellar and the youthful martial artist tensed slightly, glided forward a step, and swung his stick.

It made a sharp *klock!* against the head of a sentry and the Tong soldier went down hard. The youth with the bo stick nodded slightly and slid on past. He raised a hand and indicated first one, then a second, ground-level doorway. The other ten young men had offered to take the place from the front. Theirs would be the risky job, Louis considered. He glanced down at the unconscious sentry as he passed the steps to the basement.

That stick, he thought. Something like a quarter-staff. Right out of the Middle Ages. Louis Longmont had been a gunfighter long enough to know that the "right" weapon did not exist. Whatever did the job when it had to be done worked. He caught up to the Chinese youth with the bo stick. Now all they had to do was wait until the rest hit the front door.

It turned out not to be a long wait. Shouts of alarm and cries of pain came from inside the Tong headquarters less than two minutes later. At first, no one showed at the rear entrance, then the door flung open and a skinny man with a waist-long pigtail rushed out. A hatchet in his left hand reflected moonlight as he raised it defensively. One of the temple students closed on him, a halberd with an elongated tip blade held ready. The hatchetman changed his weapon from the defensive to the offensive. Metal clanged as he batted the pike head with the flat of his blade. His opponent lunged, driving the shaft of his device forward in a lightning move.

No sound came when the slender blade drove into the gut of the Tong soldier. His eyes went wide and his mouth formed a pain-twisted "O." His knees went out from under him and he dragged the halberd down as he collapsed on the steps. The youthful volunteer wrenched his blade free. It made a soft sucking sound as it left the dying flesh. Two more of the Iron Fan

Tong warriors burst through the open doorway. Louis took quick aim and shot the first. He kept on running for enough steps to pitch headlong off the stoop. Already, the high, rounded front sight of the gun in the hand of Louis Longmont lined up on the second target.

His revolver gave a comfortable, familiar jolt to his hand when the hammer fell on a fresh cartridge. The Tong thug broke stride and looked down at his chest. Surprise registered a moment before he keeled over to one side and fell heavily on his right shoulder. Even then, he tried to throw his hatchet at Louis, who shot him again. The sounds of a scuffle came from inside. Although the back hallway had been darkened, Louis could make out the figures of two men. They flowed rapidly through the postures of several recognizable creatures. Now a crane, now a tiger, now a snake. With each ripple, an arm or foot would lash out and strike at the other. Louis well appreciated the skill they exhibited, yet he had no time to be an interested observer.

Two Tong members came down a wooden fire escape attached to the rear wall. One paused to hurl his hand-ax at Louis. It stuck in the siding six inches from the head of the man from New Orleans. Louis reacted instantly. His shot knocked the man from the ladder, and the scream he uttered lasted until he hit the ground. The other hatchetman flung his weapon at Louis. It struck Louis on the left shoulder with the handle. Sharp pain, quickly stifled, radiated from the point of impact.

Louis put a bullet in the thrower's head, ending his days of ruthlessness. When the sound of the shot reverberated down the alleyway, Louis found it totally silent inside the building. He entered to find the Tong's nest in the hands of his young fighters.

"We could burn this place, but it would take the whole block," Louis informed his troops. "Five of you, stay here, in case any of the rest of the Tong comes back. The others, come with me. We'll go lend a hand to Smoke."

Tai Chiu found most of the Blue Lotus Tong at home. They boiled out of the dilapidated godown they used as a headquarters like a swarm of aroused bees. Passersby looked away and scurried for safety as their hatchets flashed in the red-and-yellow light of lanterns strung from post to post. Without hesitation, Tai's pupils waded in.

One avoided a hatchet blow with a rising forearm block, then kicked the Tong member in the gut. Air whooshed out of a distorted mouth, only to be battered back inside by an open palm smash to the lips. Blood flew black in the colored illumination. Two of the hatchetmen came for Tai Chiu.

Their weapons did no harm as the old man melted away from in front of them. Crouched low, Tai lashed out with a side-kick that knocked the legs from under one of his attackers. Chiu's robe fluttered like wings as he spun on the ball of one foot and delivered another kick to the exposed chest of the second thug. The Tong hatchet swished by just an inch short of Tai Chiu's extended leg.

Without a blink, he took a crane stance and snapped extended fingers at the face of the hatchetman. Blood sprang from four fine lines along his face. He tried another swing with the hatchet, only to have his nose smashed by a backhand blow. Before he could recover, the elderly monk kicked him three times under the chin. The hatchetman dropped to the ground to twitch out his life. Tai Chiu moved on to engage a short, stout thug with a revolver in his hand.

His first attack kicked the gun from the startled gangster's grip. The Chinese thug had not even gotten off a shot. Tai knocked him senseless with a smooth routine of fist and elbow blows and well-aimed kicks. Beyond him, two of the Blue Lotus members sprinted away from the center of the melee. There would be more coming soon, he realized regretfully.

Smoke Jensen considered it better to fight in the open, so he led his volunteers out of the Celestial Hatchets Tong headquarters to take on the reinforcements who had arrived during the past five minutes. Several of them carried swords similar to the ones with which the student priests had armed themselves. One of these darted forward and made an overhand swing at a Tong thug. The sword in the hard case's hand rose swiftly to parry the swing.

The edges met with a ring. Like lightning, the young student's left hand flashed out and slammed into his opponent's face. At once, another Tong member leaped toward the volunteer. He never made it. Breaking the engagement of their blades, the supple youth made a horizontal slash with his sword and all but decapitated the Tong thug. The last hatchetman, with an oversized cutlass, raised his weapon and set himself for a blow to the back of the exposed head of the young student.

Smoke Jensen shot the Tong member between the eyes. A shout came from down the street and Smoke looked that way to see some ten railroad detectives. In their uniforms of brown suits and derby hats, they rushed toward the scene of conflict, pick handles in their hands.

ELEVEN

They were in for it now, Smoke judged. A moment later, the yard bulls crashed into the line of students. The fighting spread out, two of the enemy on each one of the students. When one of Murchison's gunhawks pulled iron, Smoke Jensen stepped in. The Colt Peacemaker bucked in Smoke's hand and spat a slug that pulverized the gunman's right shoulder.

He howled and staggered off, only to be given a kick to the head by a young Chinese. Down he went, limp and unmoving. More of Heck Grange's henchmen poured into the narrow side street in Chinatown. They went after the allies of Smoke Jensen only to be knocked down and out time after time. Three closed in on Smoke. The one in the lead, a thick-chested brute with a snarling face, drew a pocket pistol and fired hastily.

His bullet cracked past Smoke's head and the last mountain man pumped a round into the man's chest. He shook himself and came on. He cocked his pistol again and took aim at Smoke. The .45 Colt in Smoke's hand bucked and a second slug ripped into his attacker's chest. Still the man remained on his feet. Smoke shot him once again.

This time, Smoke noticed that not a drop of blood flew from the wound. Smoke raised his aim and put a round in his opponent's forehead. Quickly he swung his Peacemaker to another of the armed thugs. They traded shots. The yard bull missed. Smoke Jensen didn't.

Facing only a single enemy, Smoke leveled his .45 Colt and fired the last round in the cylinder. The thug took it in his belly, an inch above his hipbone. Quickly Smoke changed revolvers. He made it just in time. A lance of flame spurted from the Merwin and Hulbert the hard case carried. His bullet punched a hole through the body of the coat worn by Smoke Jensen and exited out the back. Too close a call.

Smoke ended the man's railroad career with a sizzling .45 slug in the heart. Smoke went forward to inspect the corpse of the man who had absorbed so many bullets. Bending low, he pulled open the shirt. Just as he had suspected: the dead man wore a fitted piece of boiler plate, its backside thickly padded with cotton quilting.

Smoke's soft lead bullets had smashed against it and spread out to the diameter of a quarter. If he ran into too many like that one, he would really be in trouble, Smoke reckoned. Another shout rose among the battling figures in the middle of the block. Smoke looked up in time to see more Tong soldiers storming down the street.

Jing Gow had run all the way from the Celestial Hatchets Tong club house to the Wu Fong theater, where most of the members were attending a recital by a famous Chinese lute player. They filled the balcony and two of the larger boxes to the side of the stage. Word went around quickly and nearly half of the audience walked out in the middle of the performance. Now, he trotted along Plum Seed Street with his Tong brothers toward the sounds of a fight.

He did not feel the cuts made by the glass from when he had jumped through the window. In the second floor leap he had also sprained an ankle, and he limped painfully. All he could think of was the huge *qua'lo* who had burst into the room during counting time for their weekly squeeze money. That one had the ferocity of a dragon. Jing had jumped through a curtained doorway and run upstairs. Now, blood dripped down his chest and belly. When they rounded the corner to face the battle scene, Jing Gow felt light-headed. How long had he been cut and not taken care of it?

A haze seemed to settle over the street. Jing swiped at his eyes to try to ward off the fuzzy vision. He found his hand covered with dried blood. The fog remained. It even grew darker. Jing saw the giant foreign devil and raised his hatchet. A howl of fury ripped from his throat.

Jing Gow threw his hatchet, only the big man dodged to one side. Then a terrible force struck Jing in the chest and he saw smoke and flame gush from the *qua'lo*'s gun. Awful pain radiated from the area around his heart and the world turned dark for Jing Gow. He did not feel a thing when he fell face-first onto the cobblestones.

It appeared to Louis Longmont that every person under the age of fifty in Chinatown was a Tong member. They kept coming from buildings and down both ends of the street near the building used by the Iron Fan Tong as a headquarters. He had run dangerously low on ammunition.

The thought occurred, why hadn't the police come?

It didn't matter, he decided, as he jammed a hard fist into the face of another Tong hatchetman to save on cartridges. He heard the crack of a shot from behind him and whirled to reply. In so doing, he nearly shot Brian Pullen. The young lawyer competently held a .44 Colt Lightning in his hand, a dead Tong member at his feet.

"I heard about this Tong war and thought I'd come lend a hand," Pullen explained.

Louis nodded to the corpse. "You got here just in time. I hope you brought enough ammunition."

"I have two boxes of cartridges. Will that be enough?"

"I doubt it. What we need is a shotgun. Something to clear the street with."

Brian Pullen looked blankly at Louis Longmont and snapped his fingers. "I never thought of that. Hang on, I'll be back." He ran through the back of the house before Louis could reply.

Twenty minutes went by in a frenzy of fighting the likes of which Louis had never seen. The young Chinese volunteers used a form of personal combat unlike anything he had heard of. Three of them went down, victims of hatchet blows, yet the rest continued to take a bloody, deadly toll on the Tong fighters. When Brian Pullen returned, he brought along two finely made, expensive Parker 10-gauge shotguns and a large net bag filled with brass cartridges.

Louis Longmont hid his surprise. "That should do the job."

He took one, loaded it, and blasted two Tong thugs off the stoop of the building with a single round. Pullen put the other Parker to good use, ending the career of a short, squat extortionist. Quickly the men reloaded and pushed out into the street. Four more loads of buckshot broke the fanatic assault of the Tong hatchetmen. Six of their companions had been killed in a matter of seconds. The two grim-faced *qua'lo* did not hesitate as they advanced. They reloaded on the move, paused, and then downed more Tong members. At first, a trickle of young gangsters faded away. Then the remaining street thugs abandoned the battle and fled out of sight.

"I think we should check the Blue Lotus Tong," Louis calmly suggested.

Wang Toy had successfully hidden from the enraged priests from the Golden Harmony temple. He had watched his Tong brothers being beaten and some of them killed by those led by the old priest, Tai Chiu. The aged one had never had the proper respect for those of the Triad Society. He should have been disposed of long ago. Although the killing of priests was frowned upon by Xiang Wai Lee, Wang Toy would have been pleased to carry out that assignment.

Now he skulked in the dusty attic of the Blue Lotus club house and worried about his own safety. When the last of his companions had run away, he had been left behind, unable to come out of hiding so long as the practitioners of *kung fu* remained around the building. They had left, after a short while, yet he remained in his undiscovered lair. In all his seventeen years he had never been so frightened. At last he goaded himself into opening the square hatch in the floor and lowered himself to the second-floor hallway.

Embarrassed and shamed by his cowardly behavior, Wang Toy slunk to the stairwell and started down. At the landing, he pulled his hatchet from his belt and held it at the ready. He would find his brothers and rally them. Wang reached the last step at the same time the front door flew open. The first person through it was a *qua'lo* with a double-barreled shotgun. That was the last thing Wang Toy saw because Louis Longmont blew his head off with a load of buckshot.

Smoke Jensen had barely finished counting the number of Tong gangsters when a hoard of more young Chinese men rounded the far corner. It took him a moment to realize that several of them wore the saffron robes of the student priests. They fell on the hatchetmen from behind and began to chop and kick them with terrible efficiency. Only the guns of the railroad detectives saved the Tong members from total destruction.

Two burly hard cases shot the same student at one time. One of them did not get to crow about it, for Smoke Jensen blasted the life out of him. His partner whirled and threw a shot in Smoke's direction. The bullet slammed into the doorjamb behind Smoke. His assailant tried for another round, only to be blasted to perdition by a slug from the .45 Colt in Smoke's hand. In the far distance, Smoke heard the shrill of police whistles. Recalling the incident at the bordello, he wondered whose side they would take.

He decided to leave when the first bluecoats arrived on the scene and began to club the students with their nightsticks. "Time to be moving on," he told Quo Chung Wu, who stood steadfastly at his side.

"You will run from these men?" Quo asked in disbelief.

"The last I heard, I was a wanted man. The police have gone over to the yard bulls. What do you think they will do when they reach us?"

Quo nodded and shouted to his companions in Cantonese. "We will go to the temple. Make these men bring the fight to us."

At once the volunteers broke off their fighting and sprinted off down the street. Smoke Jensen and Quo Chung Wu formed the rear guard. It did not take much convincing to delay pursuit. Smoke shot one of the Tong henchmen in the leg and the whole crowd hung back. Smoke saw the last of them, shouting among themselves, as he rounded the corner into a wide boulevard that led to the market square.

A sharp pang of unease nearly doubled Sally Jensen over as she sat on the edge of her bed. Smoke was in dreadful danger;

she had no idea from what or whom. She only knew, as clearly as the September harvest moon shone a silver pool on the braided rug which covered the smooth planks of the floor, that her man was close to losing his life. She had awakened only a few moments before, and the fragments of the dream that had disturbed her still clung to her.

She tried to make sense of the strange images which had tumbled through her dozing mind. Odd-looking lanterns bobbed in a breeze. Men in yellow robes wielded strange weapons. A heavy mist or fog hung over black water. There were screams and cries that echoed in her head. And Smoke was somehow mixed up with it all. She hadn't *seen* him in that kaleidoscope of weird impressions, only sensed his involvement. Hugging herself across her stomach, she rose and headed for the kitchen. A cup of coffee might help.

Sally scratched a lucifer to life and lighted the oil lamp on the table. Still troubled, she added wood to the stove and put water to boil in the pot. While she scooped coffee into the basket of the percolator, she tried again to piece together her premonition. To her annoyance, nothing meaningful came to the surface. She started when a soft knock came on the back door.

"Anything wrong, Miss Sally?" Cole Travis stood, hat in hand, a worried expression on his face.

"No," Sally replied promptly, then added, "yes. No, I don't know. That's what is so bothersome, Cole." She tried to force a smile and swiped at a stray lock of raven hair that hung over one cheek. "I'm not given to womanly vapors," she said lightly. "But I was awakened a while ago by the strongest impression that Smoke was in trouble."

Their winter foreman put on a sympathetic face. "Any idea what or where?"

Sally considered the shards of her dream. "In San Francisco, obviously. Only I can't make sense of what I remember of the dream." She abandoned the subject. "I was fixing coffee, Cole. Would you like a cup?"

Despite his silver hair, Cole Travis took on the expression of an impish boy. "Would you happen to have a piece of that pie left from supper to go with it?"

That brought the sunniness back to Sally's face. "Of course I do. Come on in. Maybe we can figure out what it is going on around Smoke."

People scattered before the retreating students. Their movement through the market square set off ripples like a stone dropped in water. In the forefront of those who pursued them came the railroad police. Indifferent to the Chinese citizens of San Francisco, they roughly shoved those who impeded them out of the way. Even so, they made little headway. When the men they sought veered toward the Golden Harmony Temple, they redoubled their efforts.

They looked on from halfway across the square as the last to arrive, Smoke Jensen and Quo Chung Wu, paused long enough to swing closed a spike-topped gate in the Moon arch that fronted the temple grounds. Snarling at this impediment, they pushed through the late-night shoppers. When they reached the closed partition, several of Murchison's henchmen grabbed on and began to yank it furiously.

A police sergeant and several of his subordinates shouldered their way to where the men struggled with the gateway. "Here, now," he bellowed. "We can't go in there. It's sacred ground. A sanctuary."

"Don't mean nothin' to us. Mr. Murchison wants this stopped, and we reckon to do just that," Heck Grange growled.

The sergeant scowled at him, unmoved by the declaration. "Not with our help. We

212

got orders, all the way down from the mayor. Treat these Chinee places with respect."

"What are you going to do?"

"What we can; surround the temple and make sure no one gets out."

Granger's voice turned nasty with contempt. "While you're doing that, we'll just open up this little box and see what's inside."

Stubborn was the sergeant's middle name. "You try it and we'll arrest you. We believe there's a wanted man in there, and he belongs to the police."

For the first time, Heck Grange regretted his idea about reporting the shootings to the police. If he killed Longmont and Jensen outright, it could get sticky. No matter, his thug's brain reasoned, they wouldn't give up without a fight. And anything could happen then. He turned a disarming smile on the lawman.

"Go on, then. I'll send some of my boys along to take up the slack."

"I appreciate that," the sergeant said stiffly. "Don't worry. We'll get them if we have to wait until morning."

"What about these Chinee fellers with the hatchets?"

Looking around him, the sergeant

shrugged. "If they want to go in there, there's nothing I can do about it," he dismissed.

At once, the young Tong members started for the walls.

Inside the temple, Tai Chiu urged his diminished force to take the hidden passageway so as to come out behind their enemies. Smoke Jensen considered it a moment.

"We should hold out here for as long as we can," he advised. "Everyone could use the rest. If we only had some surprises to slow down anyone coming in after us," he added wishfully.

Old Tai Chiu smiled enigmatically. "There are . . . certain defenses built into the temple. They are activated by levers. We can engage them as we leave."

Smoke began to look around. It took a while, though finally he began to recognize a number of clever obstacles, or what might be turned into such. A large log hung suspended from two ropes. It appeared to be intended for ringing a huge brass gong. The position of the line that propelled it had been placed in such a way that it could be used to draw the thick cleaned and polished tree limb upward to one side. In front of it, a too-regular line in the flooring indicated to Smoke the presence of a pressure pad. He smiled.

Other things came to his sight. A large candelabra hung suspended over the center of the worship area. Directly under it was another hidden trip device. He did not know that for centuries, this particular caste of warrior-monks had been harassed by the warlords in China. He did appreciate that they had become wise in the ways of secret defenses. Slits in the domed roof suggested that arrows could be fired through them, or objects dropped on unsuspecting heads. Well, now, that was fine and dandy with him. His thoughts took another line.

Where was Louis? Had he encountered trouble? One of the volunteers hurried up to interrupt his musings. "The Triads are scaling the walls," the young Chinese informed him.

"All we need," Smoke snapped. He quickly checked and reloaded his six-guns. His fingers told him he had only nine spare rounds. Well, let them come, he thought of the enemy outside. We'll welcome them in style.

None of the Blue Lotus Tong returned to their club house. Louis Longmont rounded up the volunteers who had come with him. "We will go to this Celestial Hatchets building. They are the largest Tong, *non?*"

He thought primarily of his friend Smoke Jensen. Smoke had taken on the greater number because that was the way Smoke Jensen did things. While the students had ransacked the Tong headquarters and scrawled signs on the wall in Chinese warning the gangsters that they were no longer welcome in Chinatown, Louis had stood guard outside. In the distance he had heard the shrill sound of police whistles. Like Smoke, his mind went to the visit by police to Francie's. If the law joined in, it would hamper how they dealt with those who opposed them. It wouldn't do to kill a legitimate policeman.

When the last of the young monks had finished smashing furniture and breaking glass inside, Louis called them together and made his announcement. Eagerness shined in their eyes, though most kept their faces impassive. At once, they left in a body.

Disappointment waited for Louis Longmont when his contingent of trash collectors reached the converted warehouse occupied by the Celestial Hatchets Tong.

The place had been demolished inside. A few bodies lay about, among them some Occidentals Louis figured for railroad bulls. Silence filled both floors. Not a sign of Smoke Jensen.

"If they had finished here, and heard the police come . . ." Quo Chung Wu suggested, then added, "Yes, I heard their whistles, too."

Louis understood at once. "The only safe place would be back at the temple, or on the junk." He paused only a moment. "I say the temple; it is closer."

They started that way. Along the route, Louis noted more injured, unconscious, or dead Tong thugs and railroad detectives in their brown bowler hats. No question that the night had taken a terrible toll on the Triad Society. It pleased him. At the edge of the market square, Louis halted his followers abruptly. He pointed toward the temple.

"I believe we arrived a bit too late." He noted of the swarm of police, railroad thugs, and Tong members around the walls of the temple courtyard.

"Not necessarily," Brian Pullen offered at the side of Louis Longmont. "I believe that is Sergeant O'Malley over there. In all that's happened, I forgot to tell you of

217

one piece of good news.

"Actually, it's the reason I made such an effort to find you and Mr. Jensen. I received an injunction against the California Central Railroad, enjoining them to cease and desist in any attempt to apprehend you or Mr. Jensen." Pullen patted the breast pocket of his suit coat. "I also have a writ from the court ordering the police to disregard any complaint made against the two of you. All I have to do is serve them and the odds go down dramatically."

"What says either side will obey them?" Louis asked sensibly.

"O'Malley will. Above all other things, he is an honest cop. He'll take the writ back to the station house and give it to his lieutenant. That will effectively end the police manhunt for the both of you."

"And if Murchison's minions refuse?"

"Not a chance. They will have been served right in front of O'Malley. If they keep at it, O'Malley and the boys in blue will arrest the lot and throw them in jail."

Louis called after Pullen as the young lawyer stepped off on his errand. "I wish I shared your confidence."

"Not a problem," Pullen gave back jauntily.

Matters did not go quite so smoothly as Brian Pullen had predicted. Sgt. O'Malley spluttered and fussed awhile when handed the writ. "Ye should have delivered this to the station house."

"I tried, and was told everyone was out in the field — in Chinatown, to be exact. If your lieutenant is handy, I'll be glad to give it to him."

O'Malley looked one way and the next, then murmured, "He's at that big red an' gold gate at the front of this place, don't ye know?"

"I came in another way. What do you say, O'Malley?" He turned to Heck Grange. "I have a little something for you, Chief." He continued after slapping the paper into Grange's hand. "It is a temporary restraining order stopping your railroad police from any punitive action against Misters Jensen and Longmont. They are to be left alone."

Grange went scarlet in the face. "I take my orders from Cyrus Murchison, not some goddamned judge."

Brian Pullen turned to Paddy O'Malley. "Sergeant, you know your duty. If these — hooligans violate this injunction, now or in the future, I'm sure you'll do it."

O'Malley's broad Irish face beamed. He had always figured this Grange feller a bit too smooth an operator. It would be his pleasure to raise a few lumps on that oversized skull. He also recalled that the big one with the six-gun had been careful not to fire on any of his policemen. Might be there was somethin' to what young Pullen said, not just some fancy lawyer tricks. He came to his decision.

"Ye'll be movin' yer men on now, Mr. Grange, won't ye, now?" His brogue thickened with the assertion of his authority.

Heck Grange found himself up against someone impossible to take odds with. He deflated and pulled a sour face. "Yes. But we'll get those two, you mark my words, O'Malley."

TWELVE

By that time, the first of the Tong members had scaled the top of the temple wall. They went over with a shout and others scrambled to follow. Heck Grange made curt gestures to two of his henchmen and sent them off to round up their number among the railroad police detachment. He'd see to an end of this, he thought furiously. Cyrus Murchison owned more than one judge. What one had done, another of them could undo.

He headed off to care for that at once, tossing behind him a curt command to Earl Rankin. "Get 'em out of here, Earl."

"Yes, sir, Chief," Rankin answered, somewhat relieved. Being around all these roused-up Chinamen with hatchets made him nervous. A chilling shout from inside the compound added speed to his feet.

Watching first the railroad police, then the city police, withdraw, Louis Longmont nodded in approval. That feisty lawyer had some sand. He spoke to Quo Chung Wu. "Now, we catch the men of the Tongs between us."

A shot came from inside the temple grounds and the volunteers in the marketplace started forward. Recognizing friends, no one made a move to get in their way. Louis Longmont had his shotgun and that of Brian Pullen. When he reached the young attorney, he handed one of the Parkers to him.

"Maybe we should have asked the police to stay to take charge of the Tong members," Brian asked.

"Sometimes, it is not wise to think like a lawyer. I don't think these students are in much of a mood to take prisoners," Louis told him grimly.

Consternation mingled with doubt on Brian's face. "But . . . these men have broken laws here for years. They deserve to be punished."

"*Dead* is about as punished as one can get, *mon ami*, don't you think?"

Brian paled. "I — uh — never looked at it that way before."

"Start to, or you may wind up with a hatchet between your eyes."

Unobserved, Xiang Wai Lee joined his underlings outside the cursed temple of those twice-cursed *Chau Chu* monks. His face grew thunderous as he took note of how few of the Society remained among the fighters. This could not be tolerated. His cheeks burned in sympathetic humiliation while he watched that puny lawyer take the face from both the police and their supposed allies from the railroad.

Then his expression hardened into bitter contempt. He had personally opposed the Triad Society joining forces with these foreign devils. What did they know of the honor and tradition of the Society? What, indeed, did they know of ruling by fear? A few, quick words sent new energy through his flagged-out men.

Even while the *qua'lo* argued over the meaningless bits of paper, the Tongs united and rushed the walls. A smile broke his stony expression a while as he recalled that glorious day when his Celestial Hatchets had come down through the hills and stormed that other *Chau Chu* temple. Blood had run in rivers and the riches of the frugal monks had been theirs. It had financed their journey to this strange land of foreign devils and established their power in San Francisco. Truly the Goddess of Fortune had smiled upon him that day. Just as she had done in making it his destiny to be away when these students and the two *qua'lo* had attacked.

Xiang had viewed the destruction and death only minutes before. "This must not happen," he had hissed to his second in command, Tang Hu Li. "We must find our brothers and see that they bring me the heads of these white devils."

Now, he observed that busy hands had been at work on the gate and went that way. A gunshot roared from inside and his followers ducked low. Xiang made a stately figure as he advanced without even a flinch. As he had calculated, it inspired the drove of hatchetmen. They stormed through the open gate and flowed across the lawn. Only one firearm barked in defiance.

What of the other man? Out of ammunition, or injured? Either way, it boded fortuitously for the Triad. Xiang had moved up in the Society since coming to America. Under his bloody direction, the wasteful inter-Tong warfare had been ended. Now he ruled over all three in Chinatown, and had liaison with Tongs in other cities. He had literally murdered his way to the top, with more than fifty killings to his credit. One day a network would extend from every Chinese settlement in every major city in this country. And he would rule it all. The euphoria of his recurring fantasy lifted him even now.

Then reality came crashing back as a segment of the inner face of the compound wall suddenly lost its integrity and crashed downward onto seven Tong warriors. They died, screaming horribly. Dust billowed and obscured the front of the temple. Yellow-orange flame lanced through the murk and another member shrieked and grabbed at his chest. Xiang looked anxiously around him in consternation.

A second later, two shotguns blasted from the gateway through which Xiang had walked only moments before. To his left a stout Tong hatchetman's head turned into a red pulp. Another groaned softly and sagged to the ground, his white shirt speckled with red. All Xiang could do was hurry forward into the mouth of that deadly six-gun. As he did, he broke with tradition. From his coat pocket he pulled a light-framed .38 Smith and Wesson. He had found it useful in his rise to power for the sort of killing he usually did. Right here, he had doubts of how effective it would be, though better to have it out and ready than not to have it at all.

He might have regretted that line of thought if Smoke Jensen had given him time.

★ ★ ★

Smoke saw the distinguished man with the long black queue swaying behind his head start up the steps to the temple. He also saw the small revolver in his hand and the deferential way the other Tong gangsters behaved toward him. Rage glittered in the ebony eyes, and the face held a cruel cast. This had to be the bossman of them all!

"Ho, Coolie-Boy!" Smoke taunted him. "It's me you're looking for. Face me like a man, not a dog."

Xiang Wai Lee hissed a command in Cantonese and made a harsh gesture that scattered his minions. "So, white devil, you have some courage, after all. You have a twisty mouth." His accent gave the English words an unpleasant flavor. "Are you brave enough to fight me in my own style?"

Smoke nodded at the Triad leader. "You have a gun in your hand, use it."

Insolently, Xiang thought, Smoke returned his own six-gun to its holster. It proved too much for Xiang's pride. He took another step toward Smoke Jensen and raised his gunarm. Taking careful aim, he squeezed on the trigger. Slowly the hammer started backward. Then the impossible happened.

226

With lightning speed, Smoke Jensen drew. Before Xiang's hammer reached its apex, the big Colt roared and blinding pain exploded in the chest of Xiang Wai Lee. He staggered and took a step back. His own weapon discharged. The slug gouged stone from a step above him. An unfamiliar numbness began to spread through him. Was this what his enemies had felt before they'd died?

He banished the thought with a Chinese curse and tried to raise his arm to fire again. A flash of excruciating pain exploded in his head and a balloon of blackness quickly filled it. Xiang Wai Lee went over backward and rolled head over heels to the bottom of the steps. His dreams of a Tong empire went with him.

With the death of Xiang Wai Lee, the fight went out of the Tong members. The three nearest to where their leader had been slain spread the word quickly. Then, shouting their defiance and rage, they spent their lives in an attempt to avenge their leader and recover his face. They made the terrible error of attacking Smoke Jensen all at once. He welcomed the first one with a bullet, his last, which split the Chinese thug's breastbone and riddled his heart with bone chips.

He went rubber-legged and sprawled halfway up on the steps. Then the hatchet-men discovered that their enemy had a hand-ax of his own. With his last round expended, Smoke reholstered his six-gun and pulled his tomahawk free. A well-made, perfectly balanced weapon, the 'hawk had been made by a master Dakota craftsman. The head was steel and it honed down to a keen, long-lasting edge. Genuine stone beads dangled on rawhide strips from the base of the haft.

That 'hawk had saved the life of Smoke Jensen more times than he could recall. Old Spotted Elk Runs, who'd made it, told him: "I fashioned this in the proper time of the moon, said all the proper prayers, even gave of it a bit of my blood to drink. So long as you prove worthy to own it, this warhawk will never fail you."

Knew what he was talking about, too, Smoke reckoned. It had a fine balance and sure, deep bite. A Tong assassin named Quon Khan had learned the hard way when he'd closed in on Smoke and raised his own Tong hatchet. Quon had come up against wooden handles before, but this time his studded iron haft failed to perform its usual magic.

When he swung, Smoke Jensen parried with the Sioux warhawk. The Osage orangewood of the handle was springy and incredibly tough. It bent slightly — the best war bows were made from the same wood — and held. Smoke used the moment of stalemate to punch his enemy in the chest. Air whooshed from Quon's lungs and dark spots danced before his eyes as he tried to reply with a kick.

Then Smoke make a quick disengage by bending his knees and pivoting to his left. Every knife fighter knows that save for a period of sizing up an opponent, the actual engagement lasts only seconds. So it was for Quon Khan. As the pressure of his attack eased on Smoke's 'hawk, the mountain man struck his own blow. The keen edge of the warhawk sliced through knuckles and laid bare a long portion of forearm.

Quon screamed and dropped his weapon. Instantly, Smoke struck again. White Wolf's Fang — the Dakota craftsman had insisted that Smoke give his tomahawk a name, for strong medicine, he had maintained — struck Quon and split his skull. The blade sank to the haft. It cleaved Quon's brow and split a part of his nose. Immediately, Smoke wrenched it free, with the aid of a kick, and turned to face his third opponent, while Quon sank in a welter of gore.

Bug-eyed, the skinny teen-aged thug with a bad rash of pimples froze in astonishment. No one, especially a *qua'lo,* could move so fast and strike so hard. Only two in the Triad Society had reputations for such prowess. And this foreign devil was not one of them. He felt his knees go weak and a warm wetness spread from his crotch, down both legs, as the huge *qua'lo* turned his attentions toward him. To his consternation, the white fiend smiled, then spoke.

"Do you want to live?" Dumbly the Tong brat nodded affirmatively. "Then drop that thing and get out of here."

At first he hesitated. He raised the hatchet in a menacing manner, and the big *qua'lo* took a step forward. That decided him. His Tong hatchet clanged on the stone step and he turned tail. Black, slipperlike shoes made a soft scrabble on the walkway of crushed white rock. Quon looked neither to left nor right, and certainly not behind, as he took flight. First one, then another of his comrades saw him and joined in.

Spurred on by the steady boom of the

shotguns, they cleared the temple grounds in what became the first of a concerted rush.

Apprehension began to fill Agatha Murchison when a messenger arrived from Chief Granger's railroad police. It had been at midnight, and she had awakened to the rumble of her husband's bass voice, clear down in the front hall.

"At last, by God, we've got them cornered. Get back to Grange and tell him to keep pressing. I want those two finished off tonight. Tell him I want regular reports."

Cyrus Murchison had seen the man out, then padded through the house to the two-room suite next to the kitchen that housed the cook and her husband, the butler. He roused cook and put her to preparing coffee. Agatha had managed to remain in bed for another three-quarters of an hour. A voluminous velvet robe over her nightdress, she came to where Cyrus waited further news in the breakfast room. The coffee service, her good porcelain one, sat on the table, along with three cherry tarts left over from dinner. Cyrus looked up at her entrance.

"You needn't have discomfited yourself, my dear. It is only a matter of business."

"What sort of business, Cyrus?"

"The usual," Murchison evaded, and began to demolish the tarts one after another.

"I'm worried, Cyrus," Agatha announced. "Ever since this alliance you worked up with Gaylord and Titus, you've been a changed man. It seems you never have time to rest . . . or for me."

Murchison's face crumpled and he put aside the fork, with its burden of red cherries and crust. "That's not so, my dear. I think of you always. Lord knows, there are enough reminders around my office. As you know, I have replaced that old tintype with an oil portrait of you, and there are those new-fangled glass plate photographs. And we do have many nights together." He looked miserable.

" 'Many,' " Agatha repeated. "But not like it used to be, not *most* nights. What is this about fighting in Chinatown?"

"You overheard?" Murchison asked, his face suddenly drawn and secretive.

"I could not help but hear, with all the noise you two were making. Whatever have those heathen Chinese to do with your railroad?"

That prompted a harsh, albeit evasive, reply. "Outside of the fact that a lot of them helped build it, nothing."

"Then why are your men mixing in their affairs?"

Murchison's brow furrowed and he took a moment to contain himself. "It is not their affairs. Two very dangerous men, who mean harm to the California Central, have been seen there. Grange sent some of his men after them. Somehow it got the Chinese aroused."

"I shouldn't wonder. After all, it is the only place they may live as they are accustomed." A sudden insight came to her. "Was there any shooting?"

"*Of course* there was shooting," Murchison responded testily.

Agatha replied mildly. "Then I don't blame the Chinese for being upset." For her it was the end of the subject.

In his usual manner, Cyrus also saw it that way, this time with relief. They sat in silence a while, until the knocker resounded through the hallway loudly enough to be heard in the breakfast room. Cyrus rose to answer the summons. Agatha clutched at her lace handkerchief. Worry teased her mind. She seriously believed this alliance to be a terrible mistake. It had an aura of something illegal about it. For all his standing among the elite of San

Francisco, Agatha knew that there were limits set by the power structure that could not be crossed with impunity. For a moment, a secret smile lifted the corners of her mouth.

For all the frivolous nature of the lives of society women, Agatha Marie Endicott Murchison had a fine, quick, and active mind. She had learned early to mask it under the usual vapid expressions practiced by her chums at school. Agatha Marie Endicott had been a lively, lovely young girl. She wore her long blond hair in the stylish sausage curls of her youth and had a trim figure. She had never gone through that leggy, coltish stage in her early teens. She had been lithe and graceful at her matriculation at her debutante ball at the end of May in 1860. It was there that she had met the dashing, handsome older man who would become her husband.

Cyrus Roland Murchison came from wealth. Old money had resided in his family for three generations. His great-grandfather had made the family fortune in whaling on Nantucket Island. His grandfather had added to the vast resources by pioneering a railroad in New York State that eventually put the Erie

234

Canal out of business. His father had answered the siren call of the California gold fields and moved his fledgling family — his wife, his eldest, Cyrus, and three siblings — to Sacramento.

Quincy Murchison soon found he had no eye or hand for prospecting. When subterranean mining began, he fell back on the family talent. He engineered and supervised the installation of tracks for ore cars. He expanded to trestle bridges and eventually worked for Leland Stanford on his Union Pacific Railroad. Cyrus Murchison had followed in his father's footsteps. He had attended Harvard and an advanced technical institute and had been working as an engineer for the UP for a year when he attended the cotillion where he met Agatha.

For her part, Agatha Endicott maintained a cool demeanor, though her heart pounded at each glance at her ardent suitor. Cyrus had fallen in love at first sight. When the ball ended, he asked permission to call on her. Coquettishly, she had stalled him, said she must consult her social calendar. Two days later, she'd sent her calling card around to the Murchison mansion, now located in San Francisco. On the back, she had penned a brief message.

"Friday? A carriage in the park? Eleven o'clock of the morning."

It had stunned her when he replied with a huge armload of long-stemmed roses and an attached note. *"My world will remain in dreariness until blessed Friday. Eleven will be delightful, my dear Miss Agatha. I shall bring a hamper."* It was signed: *"CM."*

He called for her in a spanking surrey. A dappled gray pranced in glittering harness. With consummate gallantry, Cyrus handed her into the carriage, mounted and took up the reins. They rode off with Agatha in a rosy glow of anticipation.

Now his angry voice brought Agatha out of the pink warmth of reflection.

"What the hell do you mean, they took on the Tongs?" The answer came in a low, indistinguishable murmur. "Did the Triad Society kill Jensen and Longmont?"

This time she heard everything clearly. "No, sir. It was the other way around. By now most of them are either dead, wounded, or runned off."

"What about your men? What did Grange do?"

"We tried. We really did. Only the cops turned on us. Some mealy-mouthed lawyer feller showed up when we had 'em trapped in some Chinee church. He had papers

236

from the court ordering us and the police to lay off this Jensen and Longmont."

Murchison exploded. "What the hell! What judge would have the grit to defy my wishes?"

"I reckon you'd have to take that up with Chief Grange, sir."

A low growl came from Cyrus. "You get back there and tell Grange I want to see him now. Not tomorrow morning, right now."

"Yes, sir. Right away, sir. An-anything else, sir?"

Agatha could hear her husband's teeth grind. "Just don't let Jensen and Longmont get away."

Cyrus Murchison returned to the breakfast room with a thunderstorm in his visage. Agatha Murchison sighed and poured more coffee.

An uneasy silence had fallen over Chinatown. Without a word, old men with wheelbarrows went about collecting the dead and wounded Tong men. The Occidentals of Murchison's railroad police waited to the last. These the elderly carted to the main entrance to Chinatown and deposited on the curb across the street. While they went about it, Smoke Jensen,

Louis Longmont, and Tai Chiu discussed their situation.

"Is it to be back to the *Whang Fai?*" Louis asked.

"I'll tell you, pard, this street fighting isn't to my liking. I'm out of my element," Smoke allowed.

Tai Chiu stared at this big warrior in astonishment. Less than thirty-five Tong members, roughly divided among all three Tongs, remained in Chinatown. Yet this fighter with his gun — aha! gunfighter — said he was out of his element. What more could he do there?

Louis Longmont appeared to have read the old monk's mind. Through a low chuckle, he spoke to Smoke Jensen. "You wanted to finish them all, is that it, *mon ami?*"

"At least break their backs. Have you ever seen a rattler with a broken back?"

"I do not believe I have," Tai Chiu responded hesitantly.

Louis shook his head in the negative. "There are not so many rattlesnakes in New Orleans. Now, water moccasins I know about. And other such vipers."

Smoke smiled. "Then I'm sure you know what I'm talking about. A rattler with a broken back gets so worked up about his body not doing what his brain tells it to that it begins to bite itself. Of course, rattlers are immune to their own venom."

Louis joined in with a chuckle. "It is the same with other venomous snakes, eh? What they do is use up all their poison striking at themselves. Then they can be safely picked up."

Smoke nodded. "I've been acquainted with those other deadly critters. To me, there's none of them worth picking up. Except for the rattler. His meat is mighty tasty, and a feller can always sell his skin and rattles to tenderfeet. Other than that, what use are they to anyone but themselves?"

Tai Chiu nodded enthusiastically. "Yes. Snake meat is quite a delicacy to my people. But this is not solving our immediate problem. What do you suggest we do now, Mr. Smoke Jensen?"

Smoke considered it a moment. "Going back to the ship — er — junk seems to me to be like giving up. Can your students and the other volunteers keep at it a while?" At Tai's nod in the affirmative, he went on, "Then I suggest you put them to cleaning up the last of the Tongs. It might be wise to send some of them through that tunnel of yours and hit the Tong hatchetmen by surprise. It can only serve to discompose them."

Tai Chiu smiled fleetingly. "And what will you be doing while we accomplish this?"

Smoke nodded to Louis and Brian. "The three of us have to go to the heart of this thing. We're going after Murchison and his co-conspirators."

THIRTEEN

Pearlescent light filtered through the fog of a pale dawn when Smoke Jensen, Louis Longmont, and Brian Pullen left Chinatown. Behind them, the house-to-house and shop-to-shop search for the remaining Tong members had already borne fruit. Kicking and screaming, several youths, still in the black trouser and white shirt uniforms of the Tongs, had been dragged from their homes. Frightened and helpless, parents stood uselessly to the side, looking on with shocked eyes.

Pitiful cries and pleas for mercy rose from frightened throats as these callow youths had their bottoms bared and slatted bamboo rods appeared in the hands of stern, muscular Chinese disciplinarians. Stroke after stroke fell on the exposed backsides of the former Tong terrorists. Smoke made a backward glance to take in all this. He stifled a smile and gave a satisfied nod.

Humiliation alone, from this ignominious form of punishment, would drive the

Tong trash from the city, he reasoned. A loud rumble in his belly reminded the last mountain man that he had not eaten since early the previous morning. Not that he had not gone longer without food; many were the times he had been compelled to fast for three or more days. Like that time when wet powder and a horse with a broken leg had compelled him to evade a party of blood-lusting Snake warriors . . .

. . . Smoke Jensen had ridden into what had appeared to be a friendly village of the Snake tribe, along the middle fork of the Salmon River. He had been welcomed, given meat and salt, and a generous portion of roasted cammus bulbs. Years before, he had learned the traditional lore of Indian customs.

"Iffin' they feed ya'. Especially if they share their precious salt with ye," Preacher had solemnly told him. "Then ye can be certain they'll never lift yer hair while ye stay in theys camp."

"Sort of . . . safe passage?" the sixteen-year-old Kirby Jensen had offered.

"Well, naw. Once you leave their lodges an' clear the ground they count as their campsite, you jist might be fair game again."

"Ain't that sort of — ah — treacherous?"

242

"Nope, Kirb. It's all in how they sees things. Once you've been tooken in, they's honor bound to treat you fair and square. Once you've left the bosom of their harth, you become jist another white man an' an enemy."

And so it had proved to be for Smoke Jensen when he'd set out alone from the Snake village. Within half an hour he became aware of pursuit. He pulled off the trail, circled back, and watched. Sure enough, here came better than a dozen Snakes, war clubs, lances, and bows clutched in hands; the men's faces were painted for war.

Once they had passed him, Smoke crossed the trail, then returned to wipe out his sign. He led his stout horse, Sunfish, deep into the thick tangle of fir and bracken north of the trail he had ridden out on. He continued northward for a day.

Often he doubled back, wiped out his sign, then moved along on a parallel track. Twice he laid dead-falls. It was late in his second day when the thunderstorm formed over the mountains and sent down torrents of water. Sunfish slipped on a clay bank and went down. A squirrel gun pop sounded when the stallion's cannon bone broke. A shrill whinny told Smoke the disaster was beyond repair. Flash-flooding threatened to take the stream he traveled along out of its banks. Yet in this unending downpour, he could not cap and fire his big Hall .70 pistol.

He considered any other means of ending the suffering of Sunfish to be unacceptable cruelty to an animal that had so unstintingly served him. The suffering of the horse tore at his heart. The tempest thrashed and whipped at the man and horse for long minutes, then swept on to the east, leaving a light drizzle behind. Quickly, Smoke wiped the nipple of his pistol, capped it, and fired a .70 caliber into the brain of his faithful companion. He dared not stay here, and he could not make any time with the saddle over his back.

Regretfully, Smoke stripped the saddlebags, which contained his scant possessions, and his bedroll from the saddle and left his valiant mount behind. Even with the storm, sharp ears would have heard the report of his mercy round. It still rained too hard for Smoke to reload, so he would have to rely on his other two pistols and the Hawken rifle he had yanked from the saddle scabbard.

No matter. He had been alone, and

afoot, with less. He trudged off along the edge of the roiling mountain stream, far enough into the torrent to wash out his footprints. The storm had hardly abated three hours later. That's when the Snakes caught up to him.

With triumphant whoops and yips, mud-smeared warriors materialized out of the mist of rain to one side and from behind. Their bowstrings softened to uselessness by the deluge, they relied on lances and warhawks. Smoke dropped one with a .70 Hall, then a second. The Hawken rifle at his shoulder, he aimed for the most elaborately festooned Snake, the man he remembered had been most outgoing in his welcome to the village. One who had been introduced as the greatest fighter of all the Snakes.

He needed to down this war leader to buy even a small bit of time. The Hawken fired and the ball sped toward its target. A pipebone chest plate exploded into fragments when the .54 caliber projectile slammed into it. It smashed through his chest wall and flattened somewhat before it ripped a jagged hole in his heart. He dropped like a fallen pine. Hoots of victory changed into howls of outrage and superstitious fear.

Grabbing up their dead leader, the Snake warriors flitted off through the trees. Quickly, Smoke sheltered the muzzle of the rifle and reloaded. His three pistols quickly followed. Rather than set off in a panicked run, he held his ground. Night-fall swept over the canyon and the Snakes had not returned. That didn't mean they wouldn't, Smoke reminded himself. The rain had ceased to fall an hour before, yet Smoke could not risk a small fire, even if he could find dry wood.

Back against a tree, the last mountain man settled in for a long, miserable night. From his saddlebags, he withdrew a strip of venison jerky and a ball of fry bread left from the Snake village. His munched thoughtfully while his eyes adjusted to the gathering darkness. He was not even aware of when he slipped into an uneasy slumber.

Morning brought back the Snakes. They slithered through a ground mist so thick that it obscured the cattails along the stream. Smoke saw them at the last mo-ment and wished wistfully for at least one cup of coffee before they hit his camp. He snapped a cap on the Hawkin and downed a bold warrior who leaped at him from a huge granite boulder. Two more burst out of the brush, warhawks raised to strike. Smoke set aside his rifle and filled both hands with the butts of pistols.

First one, then the second Hall bucked and spat flame. Big, whistling .70 caliber balls cut through the air. The first cut a swath through the gut of a howling Snake. He dropped to his knees, a hand over the seeping entry wound, eyes wide. Smoke's other round found meat in the shoulder of a thick-waisted warrior of middle age. He made a grimace and gave testimony to the canine nature of Smoke's ancestry. Smoke Jensen hastily drew his remaining pistol.

He cocked the weapon and triggered it. The hammer fell on the cap, which made its characteristic flat crack. Nothing else happened, except the Snake kept coming. Quickly Smoke drew his 'hawk and hefted it. He ran his hand through the trailing thong, so it could not be wrenched from his grasp. Then he went after the wounded warrior. Four more of them, all that remained, gathered around, anticipating a quick end for this white dog . . .

. . . It had been one hell of a fight, Smoke recalled. The wet powder in his last pistol had put him in terrible danger. The wounded man had been no problem. He quickly dispatched the Snake with a feint and an overhand blow that split the warrior's skull. That still left four more. Awed by his obvious fighting ferocity, they held back. Smoke had not been granted that luxury. With a wolf-howl, he had waded in. The nearest of the four went down with a slashed belly.

His intestines spilled on the ground as Smoke whipped past him and whirled the warhawk in a circular motion that denied his enemy an opening. He spun and lashed out with a foot. His boot sole smacked solidly into the chest of a younger warrior, hardly more than a boy, who flew backward to splash noisily in the stream. He howled in frustration as the current, still high from the recent rains, rapidly whirled him out of sight. That left him with two.

Had Smoke been a seriously religious man, he might have prayed for strength, or for victory. Instead, he offered himself up to the Great Spirit. "It's a good day to die!" he had yelled into the startled face of the Snake facing him.

And, as Smoke now recalled, it had been the Snake who had done the dying. The last one had turned tail and run. That left Smoke Jensen alone to find his way on foot out of the Yellowjacket Mountains. He had made it, or he would not be in San Francisco, on the edge of Chinatown, walking down a street toward the offices of his present enemy. Another rumble of hunger reminded him again.

"What say we take on some grub before we face down Murchison?" he suggested.

"Suits," Brian Pullen readily agreed.

Louis Longmont looked around in trepidation. "Is there anyplace . . . suitable?"

Smoke made a sour face. "Louis, you disappoint me. I'm sure we can find something. Although I doubt they'll have escargots."

Smoke Jensen finished a last cup of coffee and pushed back his chair. The ham had been fresh, juicy, and thick. Three eggs and a mound of fried potatoes, liberally laced with onions, rounded out their repast. The walk to Murchison's office on Market Street took little time.

Early employees strolled toward the Murchison offices when the four grim-faced men rounded the corner and approached the building. Quo Chung Wu had caught up to the other three at the cafe. His sincerity could not be doubted, and he had been welcomed to the party determined to crush Murchison's dark scheme. Smoke Jensen signaled a halt and they stepped back against shop fronts on the opposite side of the street.

To make their presence less conspicuous, Brian Pullen purchased a copy of the morning *Chronicle* from a newsboy with a stack under one arm. He frowned at the dime Brian gave him and turned a button nose up to the well-dressed lawyer. "Don't got any change. That's the first I sold."

"Keep the change," Brian informed him.

Brightening, the kid scuffed the toe of one clodhopper over the other. "Really? Thanks, Mister." A small, newsprint-blackened hand shoved the ten-cent piece into a pocket and he set off to hawk his papers. "Read all about it! Big battle in Chinatown!"

Brian cut his eyes to Smoke Jensen. "Looks like we made the papers."

"Not by name, I hope," Smoke returned.

Quickly, Brian scanned the front page story. While he read, a fancy carriage arrived and a portly, well-dressed gentleman stepped down and entered the building. "Who is that?" Smoke asked.

Brian looked up. "Cyrus Murchison." He went back to his perusal of the article. A flicker of relieved smile lifted Brian's lips. "Not by name, anyway. It says here that it looks like a band of dockworkers invaded Chinatown for some unknown reason and laid waste to a number or residents and store owners. Promises more details to follow."

Smoke's observation came out dry and sour. "No doubt what those 'details' will be like. Unless we can make an end of this right now."

Brian grew serious "We'll have to catch them red-handed 'fore anyone will believe us."

"Murchison has that much influence?"

"Oh, hell, Smoke, they all three do," Brian advised him.

"Then we'd best be gettin' in there and find proof of what they have in mind," the last mountain man suggested.

The determined quartet crossed the street diagonally and brushed aside several California Central employees. They ignored the startled yelps of complaint, quickly silenced when the offended parties got a look at the grim faces of the four men. Smoke Jensen shoved ahead of a prissy-looking clerk type and the others followed. They entered the lobby of the California Central building and came face-to-face with a trio of burly rock-faced railroad detectives, in their brown suits and matching derbies.

Murchison's minions took in the grim, powder-grimed faces, the belligerent postures, the number of weapons, and the scarred black leather gloves on the hands of Smoke Jensen. Without any need to consult one another, they began to sidle around the edge of the room, never taking their eyes off the four intruders. Their actions did nothing to deter Smoke and his companions. They walked purposefully toward the gate behind a railing that separated the lobby from the business portion of the first floor. Behind them, the three railroad detectives bolted out the door.

A dandified secretary looked up from his desk at their approach. His eyes went wide and he knew in the depth of his heart that these men certainly had no legitimate business here. He raised a soft, well-manicured hand in a halting gesture.

"I say, there, gentlemen — you cannot go in there." He gasped in exasperation when he saw they had no intention of obeying. "Please, fellows, let's not be hasty."

Brian turned to the sissified secretary. "We're here to serve a warrant on Cyrus Murchison."

Already wide eyes rolled in pique. "I will accept service on his behalf."

"Sorry," Brian pressed. "It has to be served in person."

"Mr. Murchison is not in at the present," the defender of the gate lied smoothly.

Smoke Jensen took a menacing step forward, the fingers of his gloved right hand flexing suggestively. "Sonny, we just saw him come in. Are you going to show us the way, or do I squeeze your adam's apple until it pops outten your mouth like a skun grape?"

Defeated and demoralized, the secretary raised a feeble arm and pointed the way. "Upstairs, third floor, at the back," he bleated.

Quo Chung Wu remained behind to keep the secretary in line, while Smoke and his companions strode quickly down the hall and started up the staircase toward Murchison's office. Behind them, they heard the dulcet voice of the secretary purring.

"Ooh, a Chinese boy. How very nice. I *love* Oriental food."

Brian Pullen made gagging signs; Smoke Jensen twisted his face with a look of disgust; Louis Longmont produced a sardonic expression. Then they stood before the door. Smoke positioned Brian and Louis to either side, their shotguns at the ready. Then he raised a foot and kicked in the heavy portal. Wood shattered around the thick latch.

Moving smoothly on oiled hinges, the thick oak panel swung noiselessly until it collided with the inside wall. Beyond, Smoke saw a large expensive desk, ranks of bookshelves, an ornate sideboard with decanters of brandy and sherry, and flag poles with the United States flag and that of the California Central Railroad. He also noted heavy curtains that billowed into the room, driven by the breeze through open windows. Of Cyrus Murchison they found no sign.

"He got away," Smoke spoke plainly.

Brian gasped. "It's three stories down."

Smoke led the way to the window. Outside, an iron fire escape clung to the brick wall. Somehow, Murchison had learned of their presence and eluded them by this handy way out. From the direction of the stairwell, Smoke heard the sounds of a fight in the lobby below. He nodded that way.

"Sounds like those hard cases came back."

In the lobby, the secretary quailed under his desk while Quo Chung Wu tore into half a dozen railroad detectives. The timid soul peeped from the legwell of the rolltop from time to time when a strange warble or animal cry came from the lips of the Chinese student. He could not believe his eyes.

Two men already lay on the floor, writhing in agony. The Chinese boy moved so quickly and unpredictably that the others were unable to get a clear shot. He whirled and pranced, then came up on one toe and lashed out a blurred kick that rocked back the head of one detective. Staggered, the man crashed into the dividing rail and draped himself over it, unconscious and bleeding from the mouth. The handsome boy, the secretary had heard him called Quo, did not hesitate to enjoy his victory.

At once he spun and ducked and blocked a blow from an ax handle. The owner of that deadly device stared stupidly while Quo kicked him three times: in the chest, the gut, and the crotch. He went to his knees with a moan. Quo moved on. At the same time, a dozen more bully boys rushed into the lobby. Their charge was checked by the bellow of a 12-gauge Parker shotgun.

Brian Pullen arrived on the scene in time

to drop two gunhands who had taken aim at Quo Chung Wu. The roar of the scattergun froze everyone in the lobby for a moment. It gave Brian time to reload. He needed it. Three hard cases turned his way slowly, as though under water. The Parker bucked in Brian's hands and a load of buckshot slashed into one before he had completed his move.

He did not make a sound as he flew backward into another railroad thug. They sprawled on the floor in a heap; the un-wounded one squirmed and kicked to free himself. Quo had not delayed. The moment he knew where the shotgun pointed, he went into action.

Instead of avoiding the new threat, he waded into the middle of it, elbow, back-fist, knee blows, and kicks rained on the stunned henchmen of Cyrus Murchison. One of the railroad policemen, accustomed to dealing with brawling hobos, leaped at Quo, only to end up hurtling through the air in his original direction bent double, his shoulder dislocated and an arm broken at the elbow. It had the affect of a bowling ball among ninepins.

Brown suits flew in all directions. Brian butt-stroked a lantern jaw of one and stepped aside to allow the unconscious man to skid into the railing. Before the railroad detectives could organize themselves, Smoke Jensen and Louis Longmont arrived on the scene.

Smoke waded right in. He grabbed the coat of a hard case by one lapel and yanked him into a hard fist to the jaw. Saliva flew and his lips twisted into an ugly pucker. Smoke popped him again and threw him aside. A yard bull grabbed Smoke by one shoulder and heaved to spin him around.

Jensen did not even budge. Instead, he shrugged the thug off and drove an elbow into the man's gut. Air hissed out and the face of the company policeman turned scarlet. Before he could recover, Smoke gave him a right-left in the face that split one cheek and mashed his lips.

Two more turned on Smoke Jensen. One had a thick chest, with bulges of muscles for arms. He stood on tree-trunk legs, with long, wide boots to hold it all up. His partner weighed in at only a bit less menace. Growling, they went for Smoke with their bare hands. First to reach him, the smaller giant tried for a bear hug.

Smoke batted one arm away and sent a sizzling left up inside the loop it formed to crash in right under the big man's ribs. He grunted and blinked . . . and kept on coming. A quick sidestep by Smoke evaded his clutching arms. Smoke popped him on the ear with a sharp right.

Again, all he did was blink. This could get tiresome right quick, Smoke reasoned. He disliked the idea of shooting an apparently unarmed man. Yet, from the corner of his eye he saw the other brute moving to find an opening. End it now, Smoke demanded of himself.

His left hand found the haft of his tomahawk and pulled it free. He dodged back a step and swung from his toes. The flat of the blade smacked into the forehead of the colossus with a soft ringing sound. His eyes crossed and he went to his knees. Smoke reached out quickly and pushed him to one side. He fell silently. Smoke looked up in time to see a fist slam into his face.

Starbursts went off in his head and he dropped his 'hawk. Bells rang and he felt himself losing control of his legs. He gulped air, rocked back, and swung in the blind. Due to the eagerness of the huge railroad detective to follow up his advantage, Smoke landed a good one. It gave Smoke time to recover his sight.

It went quickly then. He pumped lefts

and rights to the gut of the gargantuan. Liquor-tainted air boiled out over his lips. Smoke waded in. His opponent lowered his guard to protect his stomach. Smoke went for his face. The hard case recognized the need for a change of tactics and reached under his coat for a holdout gun.

Lightning fast, Smoke snatched his warhawk from the floor and swung in a circular motion. The keen edge whirred through the air and neatly severed the man's wrist. Hand and gun hit the floor. Gaping at the torrent of blood that flowed from the cut artery, the man gave a soft moan and passed out.

"Smoke, behind you," Louis Longmont warned.

Smoke whirled, his right-hand Colt appearing in his hand as he moved. A hard case with a short-barreled H&R .44 Bulldog gritted his teeth as he tightened his finger on the trigger. Fire and smoke leaped from the muzzle of Smoke's Peacemaker. His slug punched into the protruding belly behind the small revolver and its owner dropped the Bulldog to cover the hole in his gut.

"The door," Smoke yelled to his companions.

Understanding, they changed their tactics. Every move Louis, Quo, Brian and Smoke made took them closer to the tall double doors of the main entrance. By studied effort, they cut a swath through their enemy. Aching, wounded, and dead reeled in their wake. Smoke Jensen broke free first, then turned back to batter an open face and create a pathway for his friends.

He jerked two hard cases together so violently that their heads clunked together loudly and they fell as though hit with sledgehammers. It took some time for the dazed thugs to realize the purpose of their opponents. Deafened by the loud reports of shotgun and six-shooter, they reeled in confusion while the four companions fought their way clear.

Smoke and Louis barreled into the street together, followed shortly by Brian and Quo. With an angry roar, the railroad's hoodlums recognized what had happened and charged the doorway. Smoke and his Western companions laid down a blistering fire that kept the hard cases inside while the quartet backed down the street. At the corner, they rounded a building and sprinted off into the center of the city.

"Where now?" Louis asked.

"We have to find Murchison," Smoke

stated the obvious. "My bet he'll be some-where around his railroad yards. First stop is the livery to get horses. Quo, can you ride?"

A blank expression came over the young Chinese student's face. "I have never done so before. But, if I can master T'ai Chi, I can stay on top of a horse."

Smoke did not know what T'ai Chi might be, but he already had doubts about the student priest's horsemanship. Nothing for it, they had to move fast.

FOURTEEN

Not until the full extent of damage had been assessed did Cyrus Murchison realize the danger in which he found himself. With the pale pink light of dawn spreading over the hills of San Francisco, he sent urgent messages to his co-conspirators. Not a one of the judges whom he had wined and dined so lavishly, always making certain they departed with fat envelopes of large-denomination currency for their "campaign chests," would even receive Cyrus in his time of peril. Nor, he was certain, would they seriously consider overruling a decision by a colleague.

That resulted in the plain and urgent summons to Titus Hobson and Gaylord Huntley. It urged them to gather what men they had on hand and go directly to the California Central yard office. All were to bring horses. He dispatched Heck Grange on the same errand, with additional instructions to have the yard master assemble a "special" — at least six livestock cars, four chair cars, and his private coach. It was to be stocked with food and liquor and held in readiness at the yard office.

That settled, Cyrus Murchison went about his usual morning routine. He shaved, and he brushed and patted his thick shock of white hair into place. Then removed his dressing gown. His gentlemen's gentleman assisted him in donning his usual starched white shirt, pinstriped blue-gray trousers, vest, and suit coat. He put his feet in glossy black shoes and sat patiently while his manservant adjusted pearl-gray spats. He would select a suitable hat from the rack in the front hall. On his way out the door to his bedroom, he looked back at the servant.

"Oh, Henry, will you see to packing my field clothes? That's a good man. See that they are delivered to the yard office at once."

"Yes, sir. Very good, sir."

"And while you're at it, select a rifle and brace of revolvers, with ample ammunition for a long stay, and send them along also."

Henry's eyes widened, though he reserved comment. Like all of the servants, he had become aware of the turmoil in the latter half of the night. Something boded quite wrong for the master if he made such preparations so early in the morning. Henry would bide his time and see what developed.

Downstairs, Agatha had breakfast waiting for them. A fresh pot of Arabica coffee, date muffins, a favorite of Cyrus's, eggs scrambled with sausage and topped with a lemony Hollandaise sauce, ham, fried potatoes lyonnaise, and a compote of mixed fruit. In spite of his troubled thoughts, Cyrus ate wolfishly. He and Agatha chatted of inconsequences until he had had his fill. Then, pushed back with a final cup of coffee and another muffin, Cyrus invited the remarks he felt certain would come.

"We're going to be in for some sort of change, aren't we, dear?" Agatha asked.

Cyrus considered a moment revealing the full extent of the change he anticipated. "There have been setbacks, yes," he allowed. "Nothing to concern you greatly. Although I will be required to be out of town for a while. At least until certain matters are — ah — attended to."

Agatha frowned. "You mean the killing of those two men who upset your plans," she stated flatly.

"Tut-tut, my dear, that is hardly a concern of yours."

Agatha Endicott Murchison had the proverbial bull by the horns and had no intention of letting go. "Come, Cyrus. I may choose to appear as vapid and vacant as

264

my society sisters, but you know full well I am no fool. If you must leave town, this must be serious indeed. How badly can it affect our fortune?"

A rapid shift came to the expression of mild disdain on the face of Cyrus Murchison. A scowl replaced it. "I could be disgraced, humiliated, ruined," he listed harshly.

"Prison?" Agatha prompted.

"Possibly. It would remain to be seen how much could be traced directly to me."

"How much of what, Cyrus?"

Cyrus Murchison pressed himself up from his chair. "*That* I will not go into in detail with you, my dear. You are better off knowing nothing. I realize that women, even in your favored position, are still considered chattel. Even so, that does not exempt them from going to prison for not reporting prior knowledge of criminal events. I'm going east for a while. I'll not be home tonight, nor for some time to come, I fear. Keep your chin up, and always insist you know nothing of anything I may be accused of having done. Goodbye, my dearest."

They kissed as usual on the porch and Cyrus Murchison took his shiny carriage to the California Central Building on

Market Street as he would any other day. There he found himself compelled to beat a hasty retreat far sooner than anticipated. He arrived at the railroad yard office short of breath, his usually impeccable clothes in disarray.

"Get everyone aboard at once," he demanded of the yard master.

"Horses are already loaded, Mr. Murchison," that worthy responded in his defense.

"Excellent. Did you send for my bay?"

"Chief Grange arranged for that. Oh, and Mr. Hobson and Mr. Huntley are waiting in the drawing room of your car, sir."

"Good. I'll join them. Heck," he raised his voice to summon. "Get this motley collection of ne'er-do-wells aboard. Did you arrange for food?"

"I did. And whiskey, too."

Murchison scowled. "Keep a tight lid on that. All we need is a load of drunken protectors."

Any attempt to trail Cyrus Murchison through the early morning rush of people on the way to work would be useless. Smoke Jensen announced that conclusion to the others as they stood in the alleyway behind the California Central Building. He then offered an alternate approach.

"Odds are he's headed for the trainyard. We can go directly there, or try to find if his partners in this are still around. I say we do the latter."

That received quick agreement and the four hunters set out. At the offices of Hobson's mining company, they learned that he was not in and had sent word that he would not be in that day. In the dockyard office of Huntley's maritime shipping company, one of those newfangled telephones jangled on the desk of the receptionist. He looked at it aggrievedly and assured them that Mr. Huntley had telephoned early to say he would be out of town for a few days.

"They're all at the railroad," Smoke summed up. "We'd best get over there."

They rode at what speed they could through the throng of milling pedestrians — all to no avail, they soon discovered. Reluctant to make any answer, the yard master had a change of heart when Smoke Jensen used one big hand to bunch the bib of the man's striped railroad overalls and lifted him clear of the ground.

"Y-you just missed them. Mr. Murchison and his associates had a 'special' made up. They and a whole lot of rough-looking characters rolled out of here not fifteen minutes ago."

"Headed which way?" Smoke demanded.

Newfound defiance rang in the voice of the yard master. "I don't reckon I should tell you that."

Smoke gave him a shake and got his face down close to that of the other man. "I reckon you'd better, or I'll have these fellers string you up by the ankles and I'll slit your throat and let you bleed out like a sheep."

Face suddenly gone white, the yard master bleated like one of the woolly critters. "E-E-East! Th-They went east on the Main Line. Clear to Carson City, in Nevada Territory."

"Why, thank you, Mr. Yard Master," Smoke drawled. "We're obliged. When's the next train go that way?"

"N-not until tonight. The local leaves at five o'clock, to pick up freight along the run."

"Won't do. See what you can do about rustlin' us up another train to take out right now," Smoke demanded.

"B-but that's impossible!" the yard boss stammered. "Running one train right behind the other is too dangerous."

"Suppose you let me worry about danger. Are there cars and a locomotive in the yard now?"

"Well, yes, of course. But . . ."

Smoke's gray eyes turned to black ice. "But nothing. Like I said, we'll worry about any danger. Where'd we find a likely train?"

"Out — out there," came the reply from the yard master, his eyes wide with fear.

Smoke thought on it for a minute. "Quo, you an' Louis go scout out a train that'll suit us. Let me know pronto." After they left, he turned back to the hapless captive. "I see you got one of Mr. Bell's squawk boxes." He lowered the thoroughly cowed yard boss to the floor and released him. Smoke's Green River blade appeared in his hand. "I think we'll just take that along with us. That telegraph key, too. That way, if you get the urge to send word down the line and warn Mr. Murchison about us, you'll have a hard time doing it."

"But — but that's railroad property," the man sputtered.

Smoke snorted through his aquiline nose his opinion of the severity of taking railroad property. "So's that train we're taking."

Quo Chung Wu returned, excitement

lighting his face. "We found one. A locomotive, tender, baggage car, and stock car.
Louis said they were just making it up."

"What's Louis doing?" Smoke asked.

Quo broke into a grin. "He's keeping the
engineer and fireman peaceful. Also
making them back up to a chair car."

"Now, that's nice. But we can do without
the extra weight. It'll only slow us. Run tell
Louis to forget it. We'll be with you
shortly."

After Quo departed, Brian Pullen offered some advice. "Whatever we do, word
will get out fairly soon. Even tied up, when
the yard master is found, he'll spill everything."

Smoke made a tight smile. "Well, then,
we take him along. If he's not to be found,
everyone will assume he's off on some
business."

"I ain't goin'," the yard master blurted.
Smoke glowered him into silence.

Ten minutes later, they boarded the
train. The yard master cowered in one
corner of the baggage car. Quo remained
in the cab of the locomotive to, as he put
it, "keep the engineer and fireman honest."
This he did with T'ai Chi kicks and
painful pressure holds. With a nervous eye
on the young Chinese, the engineer

opened the throttle and the train steamed out of the yard.

Five miles down the track, with San Francisco dwindling in the distance, Smoke Jensen signaled for a halt. He dismounted from the baggage car and scaled a telegraph pole. He cut the three lines and descended. He would do the same several times more.

Once under way, Smoke settled down for a strategy session with Louis and Brian. "There's not a hell of a lot we can do except chase after them. At full throttle we can close the distance, given time."

"And then?" Louis prompted.

Smoke frowned, considering it. He was not an expert on trains, even though he had worked for the Denver and Rio Grande as a right-of-way scout. He visualized the exterior of the locomotive that pulled them. "There's a walkway along both sides of the boiler on our locomotive. I reckon we can use that to board the other train. When we do that, what we have to do is take on Murchison and his partners without their hard cases mixing in."

"Easier said," Brian began, to be cut off by Louis.

"Do not despair. Once in that private car

271

we can jam the doors at both ends so no one can enter. That will make our task much easier."

"What if there's a nest of them in there already?" Brian persisted.

Louis Longmont shrugged. "That is for Smoke and myself to deal with, *non?* For that matter, you do quite well with that shotgun. Quo Chung Wu is . . . Quo Chung Wu. He may eschew firearms, but the truth is, he is a weapon himself. We will do all right."

Brian Pullen sighed heavily, resigned. "I hope you are right."

Sally Jensen drove the dasher into her churn for the last time. She pushed back a stray lock of black hair, then removed the lid and beater. With a dainty finger, she wiped the blades clean, then reached into the conical wooden device and removed a large ball of pale white butter. She dropped it into a large crockery bowl and lifted the heavy churn, made up of wooden slats like a barrel.

From it, she poured a stream of buttermilk into a hinged-top jug. Setting it aside, she selected a large pinch of dried dandelion blossoms and powdered them between her palms. She dropped the yellow substance into the bowl with her butter, added salt, and began to knead it, to work out the last of the buttermilk. A pale, amber hue spread through the blob. Without warning, an enormous wave of relief washed through her bosom.

So intense was the dissolving of tension that her head sank to her chest and she uttered a violent sob of release. Smoke no longer faced such immense danger; she knew it. It made her heart sing. She wanted to break into a joyful ditty. In fact, she did begin to hum to herself.

"Oh, Susannah, don't you cry for me," the words rang in her head. She wanted to tell someone. Quickly she looked around. To her surprise and pleasure, she saw Monte Carson cantering up the lane from the far-off main gate to Sugarloaf.

Monte brought more substantial good news. "I've heard from Smoke. He telegraphed to say he was about to wind up his business in San Francisco. Should be home in a week."

"When did it come, Monte?" Sally asked eagerly.

"This mornin'. I come on out right away I seened it."

"Oh, thank you. I just know everything will be all right now."

273

Cyrus Murchison set down the brandy decanter and offered glasses to Titus Hobson and Gaylord Huntley. They had finished a sumptuous dinner at noon, in the dining room of Murchison's private car. Over coffee and rolls that morning, Murchison had explained the current situation to his partners in crime. Since then, Titus Hobson had complained about the moderate speed of the special train.

"Can't go any faster," Cyrus Murchison explained. "The *Daylight Express* is ahead of us by only half an hour. The slightest delay for them would result in a disaster when we rear-ended the other train."

Hobson frowned. "Can't word of an unexpected halt be sent to us by telegraph?"

"There's no such thing as wireless telegraphy. Won't ever be." Murchison loaded his words with scorn for the uninitiated. "One has to be attached to the wire to get a message. So we run in the blind."

"Did you send along word of our 'special'?" Gaylord Huntley asked.

"Of course I did."

"Then we could get flagged down in case of trouble, right?"

"True. But the faster we're going, the longer it takes to slow down and stop.

Relax. Enjoy your brandy. There's no one chasing us. At least, none who can go as fast as we're going now."

"What do we do now?" Hobson bleated.

Murchison frowned. He had never seen this yellow streak in the mining magnate before. What caused it? He carefully chose the words he wanted. "We go as far east as we need to. Lie low, wait and see if anything is done officially. Actually, there's nothing that can be done. Only the three of us know what we have in mind. I assure you, Jensen and Longmont have no idea where we are going. *They* are our only enemy. When we have a chance to regroup, we'll strike back at them. And believe me, the consequences for Jensen and Longmont will be dire indeed."

At the insistence of the engineer, the pirated train that bore Smoke Jensen and his allies made a water stop at a small tank-town located on the eastern downslope of the coastal range. Even though it was the gateway to the Central Valley, all the roads to be seen from the water tank were narrow and rutted. Truly, Smoke Jensen mused, the California Central could be considered the single vital artery to the area. To the south by twenty miles ran the tracks of the Union Pacific, which curved through the San Joaquin Mountains, from the first rail terminus at Sacramento to San Francisco.

No doubt the pressure of competition from the larger, more robust UP had been a factor in the decision for a power grab by Cyrus Murchison. No matter the man's reasons, he had gone far outside the law and had harmed untold innocent people in his determination to amass control over all of Central California and he had to be stopped. Smoke Jensen considered himself the right person to bring an end to Murchison's reign of bloodshed and terror.

His speculations interrupted by a hiss of steam and single hoot of the whistle, Smoke Jensen climbed back aboard the baggage car. A moment later, the train creaked and groaned and began to roll down the track. Louis had taken care of cutting the telegraph line. There would be so many breaks that it would take a week to repair them all, Smoke mused. Too bad. Catching Murchison and his partners came first. A question he had left unspoken so far came to him.

"Louis, what brought you to San Francisco in the first place?"

To Smoke's surprise, Louis flushed a

deep pink. "A certain situation had become untenable for me in New Orleans. You know I had invested extensively in certain establishments in the Vieux Carré. Restaurants, a casino. Another casino on a riverboat. In fact, I had overextended. We had a run of heavy losses. Money became tight. One individual in particular, who sought to gain control of my businesses, pressed hard.

"He became obnoxious over it. Silly as it may sound, I found myself forced into an affair of honor with him. Dueling has been outlawed since the Recent Unpleasantness. One of the gifts of Reconstruction. In spite of that, we fought . . . and I killed him." Louis paused, wiped at imaginary perspiration on his forehead. "Fortunately, I was exonerated. I later found out this man worked as an agent for Cyrus Murchison of San Francisco. Digging deeper, I found out about Murchison's grand scheme. It appeared he could not be content with Central California, he wanted to expand. So I came here to find out all I could."

"Why didn't you tell me this from the git-go?" Smoke pressed.

Louis sighed. "Because I am convinced I behaved so foolishly. Like a twenty-year-old who still believes he is immortal. What could I do, alone, against such powerful men?"

"So you contacted me."

Louis eyed Smoke levelly. "Only after I learned much of the scope of their plans. Three days later, Francie was killed. I knew I had to see it out. I loved that woman, *mon ami*. She was truly *une belle femme*. We set her up in that lavish establishment, do you remember? It was after you got her out of that tight spot in Denver."

"Only so well, my friend. And I agree. Francie was indeed the lovely lady. She — deserved much better." Smoke Jensen did not waste his time on if-onlies, yet the thought flitted briefly through his mind: *If only Francie had chosen a different life.* He turned to look out the open door.

Fields ripe for the harvest flashed past as the train gained speed. A short conference with the reluctant engineer provided him the information they would reach the town of Parkerville shortly after noon. Smoke wondered what they would meet there.

When the 'special' slowed to a stop at the depot in Parkerville, Heck Grange prevailed upon Cyrus Murchison to give the men in the chair cars an opportunity to

278

stretch their legs. With permission granted, they began to climb from the train. At once, Heck Grange spotted a familiar face.

"Ty!" he shouted above the hiss and chuff of the locomotive. "Tyrone Beal."

Beal turned, then headed his way. Before Beal could speak, Grange pushed on. "You were supposed to be back in San Fran on the *Midnight Flyer*."

"I know. Only there was some delay. Some hick-town sheriff got on our case about the fire and the dead man at that freight company. By the time he could verify our identity as railroad detectives, I missed the train." Beal nodded to the throng of hard cases. "What's going on here?"

"We could have used you in town. One hell of a fight with Longmont and his friend Jensen. Ol' Cyrus Murchison's got some wind up his tail. Seems he thinks those two are chasin' after him and he wants to fall back and regroup. You and those others might as well throw in with us for now."

"Glad to, though except for Monk Diller, the rest ain't worth a pinch of coon crap."

"Bring who you see as best, then. And

after you get them aboard, come back to Mr. Murchison's car."

In five minutes, hat in hand, Tyrone Beal stood on the observation platform of Murchison's private car. He stepped across the threshold of the rear door on invitation. Murchison sat behind a large, highly polished rosewood desk, Hobson and Huntley in wingback chairs to either side.

"Ah, Mr. Beal. I am sure Gaylord here is anxious to hear your report."

"Yes, sir. We got that farmer all right. Burned his freight office to the ground. Pounded on him hard enough to get some sense into him, too. Actually, he got a bit much of a pounding. He died."

A sardonic, cynical smile flickered on Huntley's face. "Too bad. At least that's one gnat out of our faces. You do good work, Mr. Beal."

"Thank you, sir."

"You can do some more for us. I have only this minute learned from the station master that the lines are all dead west of us. The telegrapher received only part of a message that spoke of a runaway train headed this way. It is my belief that Longmont and Jensen, and whatever ragtag band of vigilantes they could round up, are in pursuit of us. I would be obliged if you took some of Heck's men and set up a delaying action. It would mean a considerable bonus for you if you succeeded."

Ty Beal inflated his chest in sudden pride. "You can count on me, Mr. Murchison. We'll hold 'em, never you mind. Hold them long enough, anyway."

"Fine. I'm counting on you. Now I rather think we should be on our way. Pick your men, and good luck."

Forty-five minutes later, the commandeered train commanded by Smoke Jensen rolled into Parkerville. Nothing seemed untoward at first glance. Five boxcars stood coupled together on one of three sidings. On the other side, beyond the double tracks of the main line, a passenger car idled, attached to a standard caboose. Like a suckling pig, the locomotive nosed up to the water tank and took on precious liquid. The fireman hurled wood aboard the tender, aided by Quo Chung Wu and the brakeman.

Relieved to be out of their cramped quarters, if only for a little while, Smoke Jensen, Louis Longmont, and Brian Pullen walked out the kinks, stretched legs at an angle from a wooden slat bench, and breathed deeply of the country air. They had only begun to relax when a fusillade erupted from the boxcars.

FIFTEEN

Hot lead flew swift and thick. Trapped in the open, Smoke Jensen and his companions had no choice than to duck low and return fire. Smoke concentrated on the open door of a boxcar. The hardwood planking of the inner walls deflected his bullets and they ricocheted around the interior with bloody results. Yelps of pain, groans, and ouches came from the occupants.

Louis Longmont quickly duplicated Smoke Jensen's efforts. The results proved spectacular. Curses and howls came from inside the cars. Then, from the opposite sides, away from the supposedly trapped quartet of avengers, came the sound of steel wheels in roller tracks. Light shone through the opening doors. Moments later, the hard cases left by Heck Grange deserted their vantage points, which had suddenly become hot spots.

Quo Chung Wu soon became frustrated with his inability to close with the enemy enough to be effective. He turned to Brian Pullen. "How do you use one of those?" he asked, with a nod toward Brian's six-gun.

Brian gave it a moment's thought. "Best use one of these," he announced, giving a toss to his Parker and the net bag of brass cartridges. "Beginners do better with a shotgun."

Grinning, Quo hefted the weapon, shouldered it, and squeezed the trigger. Nothing happened. Brian shook his head in frustration. "You have to cock the hammer first. Then, when you've fired both barrels, open it with that lever between the barrels, take out the spent shells, and replace them with fresh."

"Oh, yes. I see. Thank you." Quo's first shot ground the shoulder of one hard case into gory hamburger. "I think I have it now," he called out cheerily.

"I suppose you do," Brian responded drily, as he watched the wounded thug stumble away.

Gunfire continued unabated from the other cars and from beyond the second siding, where the grade had been built up to keep the track level. It was from there that the charge came. Half a dozen gunmen rose up and rushed the idling train with six-guns blazing. Return fire was sporadic at best. Louis Longmont downed one hard case, then ducked low behind the steel wheels of the lead truck of one car to reload. The shotgun in the hands of Quo belched smoke and fire and another of Murchison's gang screamed his way to oblivion.

"One can apply the principles of *Chi* to shooting," Quo observed wonderingly.

That left four gunhawks. Smoke Jensen zeroed in on one and cut his legs out from under. With the enemy routed on one side, Smoke took quick stock.

"Get back on board," he commanded. He raised his voice to the engineer. "Get this thing moving!" He remained as a rear guard.

Quo seemed unhappy at having to give up on his newfound skill. He went up the ladder to the cab with agile speed, even with the shotgun in one hand.

Louis Longmont reduced the attacking force to half its original size before boarding the baggage car. The remaining trio faltered. At that moment, a burly figure stepped out of the depot, a smoking six-gun in one hand. "Which one of you is Smoke Jensen?"

Smoke answered quietly. "I am."

Eyes narrowed, Tyrone Beal took a menacing step toward the mountain man. "I want you, Jensen. I'm gonna take you down hard."

Smoke laughed. "Not likely."

"You've got a gun in your hand, Jensen. Use it."

For a moment, Smoke Jensen stared in disbelief at this cocky gunhawk. Confidence? Or was he completely loco? "If I do, you'll die, whoever you are." Slowly and deliberately, he holstered his Colt.

"M'name's Tyrone Beal. I had a good thing goin' before you showed up. Now, I'm gonna make you pay for upsettin' my apple cart."

The more mouth a man used, the less shoot he had in him, Smoke Jensen had learned long ago from Preacher. He decided to goad this lippy one further. "Road apples, if you ask me."

Beal's face clouded. "C'mon, you loud-mouthed bastid, make your play."

"You're too easy, Beal. I'd feel guilty about it. It would be like killing a kid."

Froth formed at the corners of Beal's mouth. The locomotive whistle gave a preliminary hoot and steam hissed into the driver pistons. The big drivers spun with a metallic screech. Tyrone Beal's eyes went wide and white a moment before he swung the muzzle of his six-gun up in line with the chest of Smoke Jensen. His thumb reached for the hammer.

Smoke Jensen whipped out the .45 Peacemaker and shot Tyrone Beal through the chest before the first click of Beal's sear notch sounded. Disbelief warred with agony on the face of Tyrone Beal. He made a small, tottery step toward Smoke Jensen, then abruptly sat on his rump.

"I'm kilt," he gasped. "Goddamn you . . . Smoke . . . Jensen!"

Then he died. Smoke quickly boarded the already moving train and settled down in the baggage car.

Rolling through the peaceful autumn countryside, Cyrus Murchison was almost able to forget he had been forced to flee an empire he believed to have firmly in his grasp. At least, he did until those meddling sons of mangy dogs interfered. Titus Hobson had told him that Smoke Jensen was a one-man army. Ruefully, he recalled that he had scoffed at that. He knew better now.

Louis Longmont, who was considered to be a dandy, a fop, had proved far tougher than anticipated, also. How did a New Orleans gambler get to be so accomplished a shootist? If he moved in company like Smoke Jensen's, he must be one of the best gunmen in the country.

And that little snit Pullen. Until now, Brian Pullen had been the least-feared lawyer in San Francisco. Where did he learn to fight like that? Where did he learn to shoot?

The way the three of them had gone through the Tong gangs impressed Cyrus Murchison. For all his fine education and refined manners, he actually preferred using raw brute force to accomplish his goals. As a boy, he had dominated his friends, always been the one to decide what games they played. Later, when away from home at school, Cyrus had been fiercely competitive. He would brook not the slightest error in the work of his lab or his student engineering partners.

When at home during the summer, he worked with his father on the Union Pacific and frequently used his superior intellect, fast reactions, and utter fearlessness to knock resentful gandy dancers and other underlings into line. Yet here he sat, in his private car, running away from a fight. The mere thought of it infuriated him. A burning indignation rose within his chest and he decided to change his tactics.

At their last stop, a fragmentary message had caught up to him. It told enough. The men pursuing him had not been stopped at

Parkerville. Beal had failed, and was dead in the bargain. Cyrus pounded a fist on the arm of his chair in frustration. From now on, Jensen and Longmont would have to pay for every inch of track they gained.

For the past hour, the commandeered train had been climbing a barely perceptible upgrade. The foothills of the Sierra Madre lay ahead. To keep up to the top speed safety would allow consumed far more fuel. The engineer conveyed that to Quo Chung Wu, who relayed the message via a pulley-and-rope device rigged between the baggage car and cab. Smoke Jensen replied that the train was to stop at the next station and take on all the wood it could hold.

When the train with the four avengers aboard arrived at Grass Valley, all appeared peaceful and serene. Only the engineer recognized a familiar car on the end of a train on the main line, alongside the depot. Suddenly, a switch was thrown and their stolen train rolled onto a siding and all hell broke loose.

From the three parlor cars, a torrent of lead blasted toward the three-car train. After the first stunned moment, Smoke Jensen saw that none of the rounds seemed aimed at the stock car. Relieved for the safety of the horses, he concentrated on returning fire. At once a hard case in the window of a chair car went down behind a shower of shattered glass. Up ahead, Smoke caught a quick look at the switch. A red ball atop the upright told him the switch was set against them. Fully occupied with suppressing the volume of incoming rounds, he hadn't the time to scribble a message and send it to Quo. Fortunately, the thick, heavy desks used for sorting mail successfully absorbed the bullets flying through the doorway. It became a very dangerous waiting game.

When at last the baggage car of the slowing train rolled past the lead passenger car of the other train, Smoke seized the chance to write a brief note. "*Quo, send the switchman to throw the switch and let us through,*" it read. Smoke affixed it to the signal cord on the far side of the train and ran it forward. He did not expect a reply and did not get one. Meanwhile, the thugs in the other train were trashing the coach behind the baggage car. A shout came from two of them when they spotted the switchman headed forward to change the switch.

They fired in unison and their bullets

struck the hapless man in the back. He jerked, spun, and fell in the ballast along the track. A sudden lull came in the firing and Smoke steeled himself for what he knew must come next. He alerted his companions.

Feeling quite smug, Cyrus Murchison ordered his henchmen out of the train to rush the one opposite on the siding. They ran forward eagerly, unaware of how well Smoke Jensen had instructed his three companions. With a shout, three of the hard cases rushed up to the grab-iron and ladder to the locomotive. They didn't know it at the time, but they were about to get a lesson in the etiquette of boarding a train unwelcomed.

First to reach the ladder, one thug clambered toward the cab, shouting an order for the engineer and fireman to go down the other side. For his efforts, he received a foot in the face that broke his nose and jaw. He flew off the iron rungs with a strangled cry. He hit in the gravel and cinders of the track ballast a moaning, bloodied wreck. Those with him hesitated only a second.

Six-guns crashed and bullets spanged off the metal walls and roof of the cab. Their momentary delay had given Quo time to dodge below the protecting wall of metal beside the cringing engineer. Quo looked at the terrified railroad employee with disdain. If one could not conquer fear, one could never fully know oneself. Outside, the situation quickly changed.

Covered by fire from both, one of the remaining hard cases climbed the ladder. The hand holding his six-gun came above the steel plates of the cab flooring first. Quo saw it and shifted position. When a hatless head slid up next, Quo set himself and aimed a deadly, full-thrust kick. Bushy brows followed and Quo let fly.

His training-hardened sole crashed into the exposed forehead and snapped the skull backward with such force that Quo could clearly hear the snap of vertebra. Not a sound came from the thug as he fell, twitching, to his death, his neck broken. That convinced his companion, who headed in the opposite direction. A shotgun roared from the open doorway of the baggage car and a swath of buckshot swept the fleeing hoodlum off his feet.

A rifle and six-gun took up the defense and a withering fire came from the riddled car that rapidly thinned the ranks. It slowed, then halted the advance. From their exposed position, most of the hard cases saw no advantage in rushing men barricaded behind thick counters. Several made to withdraw. A sudden ragged volley came from both sides of the track that slashed into the armed longshoremen and railroad police caught between the trains.

"What the hell is this?" Cyrus Murchison bellowed at the sight of his henchmen retreating toward the train.

Titus Hobson peered from the window, the red velvet curtain held aside in his rough hand. "It appears to me your local farmers and merchants have failed to be cowed by the thugs you sent out here, Cyrus," he replied sarcastically.

A bullet hole appeared noisily in the window out of which Gaylord Huntley gazed. He yelped and flopped on the floor. Cyrus Murchison cast a worried glance his direction.

"Are you injured, Gaylord?"

"N-No, but it was a close call. Let's get the hell out of here."

Cyrus Murchison cut his eyes to Heck Grange. "Get those men back on board."

Reluctantly, then, he reached for the signal cord after Grange left for the observation platform. Three mournful hoots came in reply from the distant locomotive and steam hissed from all the relief valves. Slowly the pistons began to shove against the walking beams. The big drivers rolled forward, spun, and regained purchase. A moment later, the creak, groan, and jolt of the cars elongating trembled through the train. Ponderously, it began to move forward.

Only then did an expression of abject relief cross the face of Gaylord Huntley. Some of the color returned to the features of Titus Hobson, who reached for the brandy decanter with trembling fingers. Cyrus Murchison covered his face with an unsteady paw and repeated the dying words of Tyrone Beal.

"Goddamn you . . . Smoke . . . Jensen!"

Agatha Murchison read with horror the bold, black headline of the afternoon *Chronicle*. Her heart fluttered in her breast.

RAILROAD POLICE AND TONGS
FIGHT IT OUT!

Was this the problem that had taken Cyrus from home and office? If his police minions had clashed with those heathen Chinese, his life must be in danger. Tears

294

stung Agatha's eyes. She did not want to read further, but she knew she must.

Late last night, elements of the California Central Railroad police clashed with members of the secret societies of Chinatown, variously called the Tongs or Triad Society. Much bloodshed resulted. More than twenty men died in the conflict, with a hundred more injured. Listed among the dead was an ominous figure known as Xiang Wai Lee, reputed Triad Society leader. When the smoke cleared, no sign could be found of the railroad police or of the sinister foreign gangsters of the Tongs.

Attempts early this morning by the *Chronicle* to contact Chief Hector Grange of the Central California Police elicited the information that the chief was not available. Likewise, attempts to reach Cyrus Murchison, President of the California Central Railroad proved fruitless. Sources in the railroad offices stated that Mr. Murchison had left the city on business and was not expected back for several days. Our Chinatown contacts responded with terse replies of "No comment." The *Chronicle*'s Chinatown reporter, Robert Gee, informed us that a sect of Buddhist priests were also attacked by the Tongs. We have often spoken out against vigilantism in our fair city, and this time is no exception. However, until we learn the motivation behind this most recent outbreak of citizen violence, we must reserve judgment.

Yet duty clearly calls for this newspaper to demand an investigation . . .

Agatha laid aside the fiery words of the editorializing journalist and swallowed to banish the tightness in her throat. Something became undeniably clear to her sharp mind: if whatever had compelled Cyrus to order his police into Chinatown had been a legitimate reason, he would have had no reason to go into hiding. Unless, of course, there had been some — some — She could not use the word "criminal." Had there been something unlawful about the association of her husband with those Chinese? Suddenly she went cold and still.

Hadn't that one in the article, that Xiang Wai Lee, been right in this very house not long ago? Slowly she lowered her head and covered her face with hands that trembled. Hadn't he?

★ ★ ★

When Murchison's train began slowly to gain momentum, Smoke Jensen climbed from the baggage car and waved his thanks to the local citizens. They cheered him and a few fired parting shots at the fleeing moguls. Smoke took his hat from his head and waved it to quiet the local vigilantes.

"If that fight didn't give you a bellyful, we could use some help. Anyone who wants to come along, put your mount on board and take a seat in that parlor car."

More cheers answered him, and men headed for their horses. Smoke went forward and swung up into the cab. His stern, powder-grimed face struck pure terror in the heart of the engineer, not a man to show yellow before anyone. But with the muzzle of Smoke Jensen's Peacemaker jammed against his head, he decided now would not be the time to show undue bravado.

"I want you to explain to my friend here how to throw that switch when that train clears it. Don't steer him wrong, or you'll answer to me."

"I won't, Mister. I surely won't." At once he began to outline the steps to activate the switch.

Quo Chung Wu listened intently, then

dismounted and ran forward. By then, Murchison's 'special' had cleared the switch. Looking down, Quo located the lever that swung the hinged tracks to give the siding access to the main line. Only minutes separated the two trains, and every second counted. Quo raised the arm into the position described and heaved on it.

Total resistance. The wrong way. Sweating, Quo reversed his stance and pushed. With a metallic creak, the steel rails swung away from the closed position and rode across the space between tracks. When the thin end of the right-hand rail mated to the inside edge of the main line track. Behind him, he heard the locomotive gather itself to rush forward.

He stood upright and gave a friendly wave. Then, fists on hips, he waited for the stolen train to come to him. More time was lost to allow horses and volunteers to board. Then Quo stepped beside to allow the locomotive to rumble past. When the grab iron came next to him, he reached out and swung aboard with all the ease of one who had had years of practice. He was surprised to see that Smoke Jensen had gone back to the bullet-riddled baggage car. Flame leaped from the open door of the firebox and Quo gave it a satisfied smile. They would catch up soon.

Speed came on the runaway as it rattled through and beyond the switch. Behind it, in the bay window section of the depot, the telegrapher frantically worked his key. The dots and dashes of Morse code sped down the line with the speed of an electric spark. Tersely, he advised stations to the east of two extras, one a stolen runaway, hurtling in their direction. Abruptly, he looked up when his sounder took on that flat buzz that came from talking to no one.

His eyes narrowed as he saw a local merchant shinny down a telegraph pole. The line sagged to the ground in both directions from the cross arm. "Thunderation, Hiram, why in hell did you do that?" he roared his frustration.

Hiram made an obscene gesture. "We're tired of takin' hind tit to the likes of Cyrus Murchison. I tell you, he's up to somethin' no good, Rupe. I seed the flash of a marshal's badge on one o' them fellers shootin' at his train. A U. S. marshal's badge."

For the first time since he had gone to work for the railroad at the age of twelve, Rupe gave serious thought to ending his career.

SIXTEEN

Gaylord Huntley looked apprehensively back along the track. Greasy sweat popped out on his forehead. "By God, they're gainin' on us."

"We still have them outgunned," Cyrus Murchison responded, with a tone of indifference he certainly did not feel.

"I don't think so anymore," Heck Grange injected. "I saw some of those local bumpkins jump on board back there."

"Well, Zach Bourchard is a trustworthy man. He'll send word along the line. Up ahead there's a siding just beyond a wide curve. When we reach it, we'll pull onto it and throw the switch against them. I don't like wrecking a locomotive, but I'll do it if it stops those damnable gunfighters."

"Sort of costly, isn't it?" Titus Hobson suggested.

Cyrus Murchison revealed his anxiety in a flash. His fist pounded the edge of his desk. "Damn the expense! These men are not dolts. That they are on the verge of ruining us right now should prove it." His

300

eyes narrowed. "We could still lose it all, gentlemen. I have an idea. I own this fine long-range hunting rifle. It has a telescope on it. You are such an excellent shot, Gaylord, what say you stop worrying and make yourself useful? See if you can pick off the engineer of that train."

Huntley pulled a droll expression. "I thought you just finished praising his loyalty?"

Impatience at such dullness flashed on Murchison's face. "I was talking about the station master at Grass Valley. Although you have to admit, I have a point about Terry O'Brian, the engineer. Otherwise, he would not be running that locomotive, would he?"

Doubt in his face, Gaylord Huntley turned away from his vigil and reached for the rifle. He pushed in the loading gate cover and checked that a round was ready to chamber. With care he raised the muzzle to the ceiling and turned back to the platform door. His shoulders, slumped in resignation, more noticeable than his words, he opened the door and walked out on the observation deck. He knelt and brought the rifle to his shoulder.

Carefully he eased the eyepiece closer and established a field. The sway of the

301

train made it difficult to settle the cross-hairs on the head and left shoulder of the engineer. Satisfied, Huntley worked the lever action and chambered a long, fat .45-70-500 Express round. Then he returned to his study of the target.

Steady . . . steady . . . lower now . . . easy . . . Damn it! The train lurched violently and destroyed his aim. Gaylord Huntley eased off the telescope and let the bright spot fade in his right eye. Try again. Lord, that loco must be a thousand yards off. He fined his sight picture, elevated the muzzle, and squeezed off.

The powerful Winchester Express slammed into his shoulder. A second later he saw the flash of a spark as the bullet whanged off the face plate of the cab a foot above the open window. A quick glimpse through the scope revealed that the engineer had not even flinched. Quickly he ejected the spent cartridge and chambered another.

His second shot screamed along the outside of the boiler and burst into a shower of lead fragments when it hit the thick iron plate of the cab face. Quickly he reloaded. The third round went two feet wide of the cab when the private car hurtled sharply to the left as the speeding train swung into a curve. Gaylord did some quick mental arithmetic. Four rounds left. He rose from his cramped pose and eased his numb legs.

When he returned to his position, he quickly expended two more bullets. They did no more good than the other three. Time to reload, he figured. He'd fire one more round first. A wild lurch of the car sent his bullet high; had he been on board the pursuing locomotive, he'd have heard the bell halfway down the boiler clang with a fractured tone.

Back in the plush interior of Murchison's private car, Huntley went to the gun cabinet and located and shoved fresh cartridges into the Winchester. He ran a nervous hand through his oily black hair and worked his foreshortened upper lip over his rodent-like teeth. Huntley knew what he needed and went directly to it.

Three fingers of brandy warmed the cold specter of defeat in his gut and spread calm through his limbs. Thus fortified, he returned to the observation platform and knelt to steady his aim. Huntley failed to notice that in his absence, someone else had entered the cab of the locomotive behind them. He also did not observe that the newcomer held a Winchester Express like his own.

Huntley took aim and took up the slack in the trigger. Then, through the circular rescale of the telescopic sight, he saw a lance of flame and a curl of smoke. A split second later, hot lead spanged against the brass cap of the platform rail and showered shards of metal into the face of Gaylord Huntley. Sharp pains radiated from the wounds and he screamed in horror as he felt a sliver pierce his exposed eye.

Reflexively he dropped the rifle and fell backward onto his butt. Beyond the rail, his tearing eyes took in another flash. Terrible pain erupted in his chest and he was flung backward against the doorjamb. Gaylord Huntley's mouth sagged and darkness swarmed over him. Beyond him in the parlor section, unaware of what had happened, Cyrus Murchison froze, half out of his chair, hands flat on the desk, eyes bugged, as he stared in confused astonishment at the body of his former associate.

Smoke Jensen lowered the Winchester Express from his shoulder when he saw the body of Gaylord Huntley sprawl backward in his death throes. One less, he thought grimly. The chase continued, though the gap had rapidly closed. Hauling more cars, the lead locomotive could not maintain its distance advantage for long. At the suggestion of the suddenly and surprisingly cooperative engineer, the whistle shrilled constantly, a tactic that Smoke Jensen thought would unnerve those they pursued. Torn snatches of answering screams came from sidetracked westbound trains as the two locomotives ran headlong through the foothills of the Sierra Nevada mountains. Train crews stared after them with eyes wide and mouths agape. Tediously, the distance shortened to half the original 1000 yards.

From there on, time was suspended as the trailing locomotive rushed toward the private car of Cyrus Murchison. Smoke judged it time to put his rough plan in motion. He left the baggage car to talk to the volunteers in the chair coach behind. The two dozen of farmers and townies who had jumped aboard Smoke's commandeered train gathered around at his summons. He eyed them with concentration.

"Now, this is going to be tricky. None of you are required to do what I'm going to ask. First off, I want to know how many among you consider yourselves sure-footed."

Nearly all hands went up. Smoke suppressed a smile and nodded. "Take a look outside and forward." By turns they went to the open windows and did so. Several recoiled from the blast of wind created by their swift passage. "See that catwalk along the boiler? How many of you surefooted ones think you can walk that while the train is moving?"

Not so many hands went up this time. Smoke considered that with himself and Louis, and six of these willing volunteers, they could carry off his plan. It didn't matter to him what happened to the rest of the train. What they needed to do was isolate the rear car containing Murchison and Hobson. Now for the tricky part.

"That's good. We need six men to come with Louis and me. What we are going to try to do is close in and ram that observation car. The idea is to derail it." Startled expressions broke out among the plain country folk facing Smoke Jensen. "Failing that, those of you who come with us are to be ready to advance along the catwalks on both sides of the locomotive and board the other train while we are in motion."

"That sounds a tall order, Mister," a farmer with sun-reddened face observed.

"Yeah," a pimply store clerk picked it up. "Why should we take such a risk for you? Besides, who are you, anyway?"

"Folks call me Smoke Jensen."

Color drained from the lippy clerk's face. "Oh, Jesus. I've heard of you. Read all about you in them Ned Buntline books."

Smoke gave him a hard, straight face. "Buntline lies. I've never shot a man in the back who hadn't turned it after I squeezed the trigger."

Eyes widened, the clerk gulped, "You've read all them dime novels?"

"A fellah needs to know what others are sayin' about him," Smoke said simply. "Now, like I say, do you think you can walk that narrow track and jump, if need be?"

Seven responded in the affirmative. "Better than I expected," Louis Longmont stated drily.

Smoke let the other shoe drop. "Remember, there are still a lot of hard cases aboard that train. If we don't isolate the rear car, the fighting will be rough."

Only one of the hands went down. "All right," Smoke announced. "I'll lead you. Louis here will give you the word when the time is right."

Terence O'Brian did not mind shattering the nerves of those they pursued. Besides, he reasoned, it gave them more of a chance by warning approaching trains onto sidings. When he heard the blathering of that crazy man he knew the boy-o had slipped a cog somewhere. Jumping from one train to another? Pure madness. When the tough-faced gilly ordered the throttle opened to full again, he said as much.

"That's a lunatic idea if I ever heard one. Why, at the speed we're goin', we could ram that train ahead of us." Smoke Jensen's reply left him thunder blasted.

"Exactly what I had in mind."

"Not with my beautiful baby, ye won't," Terry O'Brian blurted in indignation. "Ye'll derail us both!"

Smoke Jensen pulled an amused face. "The thought occurred to me. Only, I want you to just knock them off the track, not us."

Gloved hand on hip, O'Brian snapped his defiance. "Can't be done. We hit them hard enough to derail that heavy car, we go off, too."

Smoke though a moment. "You're the engineer. If you say that's the case, I'll believe you. Can you do this? Get us close enough that men can jump from the front of this locomotive to the rear car of that train?"

"Sure. Easy. If anyone is crazy enough to try makin' the leap. Thing is, I don't want to ram them."

"I understand. Only, give it a try and see what we can do."

"You're stark ravin' crazy, ye are," O'Brian offered his opinion again. Then, in exasperation, he put hand to throttle and shoved it forward.

It took a while for the big drivers to respond. With the rush of steam, they spun free of traction for a moment, then O'Brian added sand and the engine leaped forward. The gap quickly closed. At two hundred yards, four men appeared on the top of the private car. Two took up sitting positions, while one knelt and the other flattened out prone. Smoke took note of it and hefted his Express rifle.

Aiming through the forward window, opposite the engineer, Smoke squeezed off a round. One of the seated hard cases reared backward, fell to one side, and rolled off the car. The others opened fire.

"Get down!" Smoke shouted to O'Brian. "Not you," he barked at the fireman. "Keep stoking that boiler."

Bullets spanged off the metal plates of the locomotive. Smoke hunkered down and took aim again. The Winchester bucked and another thug sprang backward from his kneeling position and sprawled flat on the walkway atop Murchison's car.

A slug cracked past Smoke's left ear and he reflexively jerked his head to the side. Damn, they have some good shots over there, Smoke thought. Not the time to ease up.

He fired again. As the hammer fell, the private car swayed to the left and their locomotive jinked right. Smoke's bullet sped through empty air. He cycled a fresh cartridge into the chamber. When the careening rolling stock settled down, he drew a bead on the chubby gunhand lying on his belly.

At the bullet's impact, the fat hard case jerked upward and flopped back down, shot though the top of his head. *Not bad,* Smoke judged his performance. At the last moment, before Smoke could sight in on him, the fourth of Murchison's gunmen gave it up and ran for the safety of the car ahead. Smoke held his fire as the thug's head disappeared below the lip of the roof overhang. Time to get ready, he decided, and turned away.

When he returned to the cab, the distance had narrowed to less than a hundred feet. Gingerly, O'Brian brought his behemoth up to within twenty feet, his hand playing the throttle like an organist at a mighty pipe organ console. Smoke gave him the nod. Swallowing against the lump of fear in his throat, the engineer opened the throttle again and the big Baldwin 4-6-2 sped into the rear of the Pullman-manufactured private car.

Violent impact knocked many of the volunteers off their feet. One clung desperately to the grab-rail to keep from falling down among the spinning drivers. Smoke staggered as the two vehicles slammed together. With a terrible screech, the observation platform rail sheered off and went flying to the sides of the track.

Murchison's car jolted forcefully and the rear truck raised, then slammed back. Unasked, O'Brian eased back. The blunt nose of the locomotive withdrew from its menace over the beleaguered carriage and held steady, three yards off the shattered rear platform. Terence O'Brian looked pleadingly at Smoke Jensen. Smoke nodded to him.

"Bring it in as close as possible. We'll jump."

Cyrus Murchison could not believe what he saw through the open door at the rear of his private car. Beyond the gap between it and the chase train, men stood on both sides of the locomotive boiler, slowly advancing to the nose of the steaming monster. He had been knocked out of his chair by the collision. At first he could not figure out what these lunatics had in mind. Then the reality struck him.

They intended to jump from the speeding locomotive to his car! If they made it, it would be all over, he thought in a panic. He waved to a slowly recovering Heck Grange. "Got to get some of the men in here. Those crazy bastards are coming after us."

"How?" Heck demanded.

"They are going to jump over here, you idiot. Now, do as I say. Get a dozen, no, twenty guns in here right now."

Heck started for the front door of the car. He worked the latch handle and passed through at an uneven gait. Wobbling on unsteady legs, Grange pushed into the next car. Concerned faces looked up. He stared them down, swaying with the roll of the car, one hand on the butt of his six-gun.

"We're in for it, boys. Jensen's comin' after us. Gonna jump from train to train. The boss wants twenty of you in his car right now."

"Hell, Chief, we can't get twenty men in there. Maybe eight or ten. Even then, we'd be crammed so close it would be like shootin' fish in a stock tank."

"I know that, Miller. Best thing is to be ready on the vestibule, in case those gunhawks get through. Mr. Murchison will never know if there's twenty or five in there. Now, let's get going."

Smoke Jensen looked down at the dizzying blur of ballast and cross-ties in the space between the cowcatcher of the Baldwin loco and the rocking platform ahead. He swallowed to regain his equilibrium, flexed his knees, and prepared to spring. Behind him he heard a voice raised in sincere prayer.

". . . *Holy Mary, mother of God, pray for us sinners, now and at the hour of our death . . .*"

Well, that might be right now, the last mountain man considered. What he proposed to do, what they were about to do, could easily be considered suicidal. One or all of them could be dead within the next two minutes. The rail-like bars of the cowcatcher inched closer, closer. Another foot. Two feet. Smoke Jensen reached forward with his gloved hands. Smoke took his mind off the rush of death below and sucked in a breath.

Jump! Smoke left his insecure perch and sailed over the gap between the two trains. He seemed to pause in the middle, while the gap widened. A moment later the Baldwin surged forward and Smoke hit the platform on hands and knees. He landed solidly, thankful for the gloves he wore. A burly farmer crashed to the platform beside him. Smoke looked up to see the car interior was empty.

He came to his feet as two more men landed on the observation deck. A moment later, the door at the far end flew open. Five men poured in. Smoke filled his hand with a .45 Colt and set it to barking. Crystal shattered and tinkled down on the expensive Oriental carpets that covered the floor. The hard case in the lead jerked and spilled on his face in the narrow passage that paralleled the bedrooms. The man behind him threw a wild shot and tripped over the supine corpse.

More glass shattered, this time an etched panel between the dining room and the parlor area. Smoke sidestepped and a shotgun behind him roared. Two thugs screamed and slapped at invisible wasps that stung them with buckshot fury. More gunhands pushed through the vestibule door. By now, four of the volunteers had gained the hurtling lead train.

Louis Longmont appeared at Smoke Jensen's side. "The last two are on their way."

"Good. No chance to secure that door now. No reason, really. Murchison and Hobson got away."

"They can't go far," Louis stated the obvious.

With the arrival of the last volunteers, the volume of fire became too much for the armed ruffians. Their ranks devastated, they chose to withdraw from the hail of lead that cut them down mercilessly. Smoke Jensen's last slug slammed into the thick wooden door of the private car. A muffled howl of pain came from the other side.

"Not as sturdy as I thought," Smoke said lightly to Louis. "I say we go ahead."

Louis cocked an eyebrow. "They will be waiting for us."

Smoke grinned. "Yep. I know. That's why I brought these." From the pocket of his vest, Smoke produced half a dozen bright red packets, covered and sealed with tin foil.

"What are those?" Louis asked.

"Railroad torpedoes," Smoke explained. "I picked them up from the utility box in the cab of the other train."

Louis still did not follow. "What do you do with those?"

Smoke showed mischief in his twinkling gray eyes. "We have one of these fine gentlemen toss them through the far door, one at a time, and shoot them like clay pigeons.

"What good will that do, *mon ami?*"

"They make a hell of a bang. Enough explosive to jar the lead truck of a locomotive and be heard over the noise of the engine."

"Powerful. What gave you the idea?"

"I learned about these torpedoes when I worked for the D&RG. When a train breaks down on the main line and there is no siding, a trackwalker goes back half a mile and lays out a series of torpedoes. The number of bangs tells the engineer what is wrong and prepares him to slow and stop his train. In the construction camp we used to shoot them for sport, so I know it will work."

A sardonic smile turned down the lips of Louis Longmont. "Then, by all means, let us get to it, my friend."

Smoke turned to the volunteers. "Any of you good at Abner Doubleday's game of baseball?" Three of the Valley men nodded their heads. "One of you consider yourself a good hurler?"

"Ay bin fairly good, Mr. Yensen," a cotton-haired Swede declared with suppressed pride.

"Olie's right," one of his companions offered. "He's hell at the pitch."

Smoke smiled. "Good, then. Here, I want you to take these," he began, explaining his plan to the Swede pitcher.

Two minutes later, Smoke, Louis, and Olie crossed the gap between vestibules and got ready. Louis yanked open the door. Olie gave a slow underhand pitch that sailed one of the red torpedoes down the aisle, flat side toward the door. Smoke brought up his .45 Colt before the startled hard cases could react, and fired.

A bright flash and shattering explosion followed. Glass rang musically as windows blew out all along the car. Men screamed and clutched their ears. At Smoke's nod, Olie pitched another one. One man, blood streaming from his nose, leaped from his seat and stumbled down the passage toward the far end of the coach. A strong odor of kerosene rose from pools under the broken lamps. Smoke signaled for another.

With an expression of awe on his broad face, Olie flung another torpedo. A weakened portion of the sidewall, complete with blown-out window sash, ripped away from the side of the car. It whipped off along the rushing train. The gunhands who remained conscious could stand it no longer. Pandemonium broke out as they surged toward the next car forward.

Smoke signaled to the waiting volunteers and led the way after the fleeing enemy. He skidded to a stop and jumped to one side when a torrent of bullets ripped through the facing wall and the door. Tinted-edged glass shattered in the upper panel of the door and one clipped the shoulder of a farmer from the Central Valley.

"Ow, damn them," he complained. "Toss in some o' them bombs, Olie."

Smoke gave the nod and Olie complied. The first one went off before Smoke could fire. The startled gunhand who had shot it gaped in disbelief. Olie recovered instantly and hurled another. Smoke blasted it a third of the way down the car. Window-panes disappeared. Men groaned and cursed. Powder smoke filled the afternoon air. Sunlight filtered through the billows of dust and burnt explosive in sickly orange shafts. Another torpedo put the defenders in panic.

They raced off to find security in the next car. Smoke watched as the last man through the entry paused to throw the lock. He cut his eyes to Louis.

"We're going to have to do this the hard way," Smoke stated flatly, as he paused to reload. The vision haunted him. Someone among his volunteers would die before this was over.

SEVENTEEN

Smoke Jensen stationed three men at the vestibule door, to keep the attention of the hard cases beyond. Then he and Louis led the others to the rear of that car and out onto the narrow platform. He pointed to a set of iron rungs which led to the roof. With difficulty they climbed the ladder, fighting against the jerk and sway of the careening train.

On top of the car, Smoke went forward with the volunteers following. Clouds had formed, Smoke noticed, as he worked his way toward the car-full of gunmen. A light misty rain fell, whipped into their faces by the rush of wind. The air smelled of woodsmoke, which gushed from the tall, grinder-fitted stack. It was filled with fine, gritty cinders and inky exhaust, which quickly blackened their faces and clothing. Footing became treacherous on the damp strips of wood that formed the walkway. When they reached the gap between cars, Smoke stopped to consider the alternatives.

Climb down, cross over and climb back up, or jump. He tested his boot soles against the wood to gauge the security of the roof walk. He took a quick, appraising glance at the strained faces behind him, then he moved back toward them, took three, quick, running steps, and jumped. At the last instant, his foot slipped.

Smoke hurtled in an awkward sprawl toward the forward chair car roof. The toe of his boot caught on the trailing lip of the walkway and sent him to his hands and knees. He hung there, painfully aware that he could have cost them the element of surprise. After two, long, worrisome minutes, he inched forward. Still challenging fire to come up through the roof, he paused again. Perhaps the idea did not occur to those below that they could penetrate the thin roof of the car. Smoke pressed himself up onto his boots and motioned for the others to follow.

To his relief, they made it without undue noise. When they had gathered as best they could, Smoke explained what he had in mind. "Spread out. We're going to fire at random through the roof. May not hit anyone, but it will stir them up some. The next coach is the smoking car. My bet is that Murchison and Hobson are in there.

If we can rig the doors of the next car, jam them somehow, we can trap his gunmen there and go after the leaders with little risk."

"Sounds good," a thick-shouldered feed store owner judged.

"Then let's get to it," Smoke urged.

Smoke and Louis went forward and climbed down. Two volunteers went down the nearer ladder. Smoke used the coupler release bar to tightly jam the latch to the parlor car. To his disappointment, they could find nothing to do the same to the rear entrance to the smoking coach. Accepting the setback, they returned to the top. Seconds later, bullets punched through the roof to send showers of splinters and shards of the stamped tin ceiling down onto the unsuspecting gunhawks. Already demoralized by the exploding torpedoes, they made as one for the doors at each end. Slugs continued to snap and crack past them. More bullets smashed through the ceiling.

One man cried out in pain, shot through the top of his shoulder. His ragged breath and the pink froth on his lips told his companions the round had gone through his right lung from top to bottom. He wasn't long for this world. Another hard case uttered a groan and fell heavily to the floor. From ahead a shout of rage rang through the car when Murchison's gunsels found the latch somehow secured against them.

Shots sounded from within the car and shards of glass tinkled out onto the vestibule platform. Eager hands reached through to wrestle with the obstructing bar. After ample curses and some furious struggle, it came free. Men sprang instantly across to the smoking car. Smoke Jensen had no choice but to make the best of a failed plan. He prepared to lead the volunteers forward when a sudden jolt nearly knocked them all off their feet and over the side.

"Cut it loose! Cut it loose!" the familiar voice of Cyrus Murchison shouted from the open doorway to the smoking lounge.

Metal grated against metal, and with a lurch, the couplers opened and the front part of the train sped away from the rear portion, which began to lose forward momentum. Smoke cut his eyes behind them and saw the chase locomotive swelling rapidly in size.

"Get down and hold on!" he shouted.

Beyond Smoke, the second train plowed into the rear of the first. The force of the impact telescoped along the line of cars. The momentum drove the open couplers together, momentarily reattaching the last three cars. The men clinging to the catwalk bounced and whipped about like rag dolls in the hands of an angry child. With an explosive roar, steam exploded from the ruptured boiler of the trailing locomotive. The good and bad alike sprawled in the aisles. Men in the baggage car of the rear train slammed forward, tumbled over sorting tables and crashed into the front wall of the car. Worse was yet to come.

First, the private car of Cyrus Murchison left the rails, crumpling in on itself as it drove forward. The coach ahead teetered and began to lean to the left. It fell ponderously. Domino-like, the next chair car began to cant to one side. Only the remaining forward motion of the reconnected cars prevented total disaster. When the car under them began to waver, Smoke Jensen shouted to the men with him, "Get off of here. Jump to the right."

Unmindful of possible broken bones, the eight clinging men threw themselves away from the reeling car. The unsecured coupler twisted at the joint and separated. It let the car pitch over onto one side, to skid a distance before it came to rest at an acute angle. The eight wheels on the trucks spun as it lay in a cloud of dust. Beyond them, the train with Murchison aboard rolled serenely away. A man next to Smoke Jensen groaned.

"I think I broke my leg," he stated, his mind dulled by the sudden crisis.

"Hang on. I'll get you some help." Smoke looked beyond the billows of dirt and steam to see the occupants of the wounded locomotive leap clear to escape the explosion that would surely follow. With banshee screams, the 140 tons of iron and steel ground to a stop.

Smoke came to his boots to take stock of the disaster. He saw that the Baldwin had derailed on only one side, the lead truck of the tender dangling in empty space above the rails. Miraculously, the stock car had not jumped the track. Even more astonishing, the boiler did not explode. It hissed and belched steam, and remained intact. Gloved fists on hips, Smoke watched while Brian Pullen and the rest of the volunteers climbed shakily from the baggage car.

"What the hell happened?" Pullen asked, his tone of voice clearly conveying his disturbed condition.

Smoke's reply cut through the fog in Brian's mind. "Murchison cut the rear of the train loose. You ran into it."

Brian shook his head, as though to clear it of fog. "Well, hell's-fire, if that just don't beat all." Then he remembered the chase. "What happened to Murchison?"

"They went on. Let's get those horses out and head after them," Smoke urged. "Chances are we've lost them for now, but we can try."

Pullen took stock of the destruction all around them. "I'm not sure that's a good idea."

Cyrus Murchison, acting as conductor, signaled the engineer to slow the train when he observed the marker indicating a curve and a siding. A switchman dropped off the side and ran forward as the big 2-4-4-0 American Locomotive Works main liner slowed even more. He threw the switch and the bobtailed train rolled smoothly through the switch onto the siding.

"What are you doing?" Titus Hobson demanded.

"We do not know if the other locomotive derailed. In light of that, we cannot take the chance of remaining on this train." He turned to Heck Grange. "Off-load mounts for everyone remaining, with a spare, if possible. We'll go to Carson City by horse-back."

Titus Hobson winced as he recalled how long it had been since he had sat astride a horse. The remaining — how many? — miles to Carson City would be sheer torture. His tightly squinched features reflected his thoughts. To his outrage, Cyrus Murchison read his opinion and laughed at him.

"Think of it as a pleasant outing in the bracing mountain air, Titus. Come, we'll sleep in tents, under the stars, feast on venison and bear, clear our lungs of the city's miasma, and commune with nature."

Hobson chose primness for his reply. "I hardly think this is a time for levity, Cyrus."

"Why not?" Murchison's face darkened with suspicion. "If you cannot laugh at adversity, you're doomed. Don't you know that?"

Hobson reacted from his fear-driven anger. "My God, you're priggish when you get philosophical, Cyrus."

Heck Grange's return took away a need for Cyrus Murchison to make a reply. "The horses are coming off now. We can leave in ten minutes."

"Good," Murchison snapped testily. "We

may not have that much time."

"We're ten miles from where we cut loose those cars. With luck, them and their rolling stock are all busted up."

"You're right, Heck. Only we cannot rely on that."

Unaffected by the mindset of his boss, Heck came right back. "So? Even if they got out of that mess, it will take the better part of two hours to get here from there."

Murchison relented. "You're right, of course. See to everything, Heck. Be sure to off-load those chests from the baggage car."

Grange left to see to the task. Murchison set to work poking into the drawers and shelves of the smoking car. He retrieved two boxes of excellent hand-rolled cigars made in Havana, five bottles of brandy, tinned sardines, cheeses, and other delicacies. He stuffed all of it into a hinged-top box. The brandy he wrapped in bar towels. He looked up into the startled expression of Titus Hobson.

"No reason to deprive ourselves, is there, Titus? The amenities of life are what make us appreciate it."

"It will slow us down."

"No more than the tents and other supplies I had the forethought to put aboard.

One more pannier on the back of a pack-horse will not hinder our progress."

Titus Hobson looked at his partner with new eyes. "You anticipated this happening?"

Murchison made a deprecating gesture. "Nothing quite so drastic, old boy. But I did have grounds to suspect that all would not go smoothly. Come, we can make this small setback into a lark. How long has it been since you've been away from your wife's sharp tongue, and those cloying children?"

A wistful expression came onto Hobson's face. A man who had married late in life, he found his brood of five children, all under the age of thirteen, to be a burden he would prefer not to have to bear. And his wife had become more acid-tongued with the birth of each offspring — as though it was *his* fault she kept cropping a new brat. A tiny light began to glow in his mind. Perhaps this enforced separation would prove to be a boon.

"All right, Cyrus. I'll give you your due. This could turn out to be . . . interesting."

"Yes. But, only if we hurry. Jensen and Longmont are still back there."

Shaken, though essentially unharmed, the volunteers who had joined Smoke

Jensen and Louis Longmont went quickly about saddling horses. They prowled through the kitchen of Cyrus Murchison's ruined private car and provisioned themselves with a wide variety of expensive and exotic food. Smoke gathered them when everything had been gotten into readiness.

"This is going to be rough. Those who have been injured or wounded should head back. There's no telling how long we will be on the trail."

"How far do you intend to go, Mr. Jensen?" a grizzled older farmer asked.

"All the way to Carson City, if necessary."

The oldster shrugged. "Then I'd best go back with the rest. My rhumatiz won't let me abide with damp ground and cold nights for that long."

"Go ahead," Smoke prompted. "And no shame be on you. The rest of us will start off along the tracks, see if we can catch up to that train."

"We'll leave a few men behind, to delay them if they do come," Murchison directed.

Heck Grange disagreed. "It will only waste lives needlessly. Jensen's not dumb. He'll be lookin' for that. I reckon the place to lay an ambush is up around Piney Creek, just ahead of the upgrade into the Sierras."

Murchison considered that. He accepted that Heck Grange, with his war experiences with the Union Army had a better grasp of tactics than himself. Yet he was loath to appear to not be entirely in charge. Now was not the time for vanity, Cyrus reminded himself

"All right, let's do it that way."

They rode for two hours. Bluejays and woodpeckers flitted from tree to tree, scolding the interlopers with shrill squawks. Squirrels took up the protest in wild chatter. A bad moment developed when a fat, old, near-sighted skunk waddled out onto the trail and set the nearest horses into a panic. For men accustomed to walking or riding everywhere in wheeled vehicles, it took some doing to bring the beasts under control. At last, Heck Grange was compelled to shoot the skunk.

That caused more trouble as its scent glands voided. An almost visible miasma fogged over the trail, contaminating the clothing of one and sundry among the collection of thugs, riffraff, and hard cases. Curses turned the air blue and fifteen minutes were lost trying to gain the upper hand over wall-eyed horses and red-faced, tear-streaked men. A halt resulted to allow everyone to wash off the strident effluvium from Mr. Skunk.

Back in the saddle, Murchison's henchmen grumbled among themselves. The majority were city-bred and -raised. The skunk unsettled them. What more, and worse, might be out there? The grade steepened and even this complaining died out. At three o'clock the big party reached the banks of Piney Creek.

Cyrus Murchison had Heck Grange toll off nine men to set up an ambush in the rocks and cluster of willows that lined the stream bed. None of the hard cases liked being left behind, yet the possibility of ending their ongoing problem appealed to most. They dug in, arranging stones and making dirt parapets in front of scooped-out hollows in the creek bank. When all met the approval of Heck Grange, he reported to Murchison.

"We're ready. Might as well head out."

"You've done a fine job, Heck. This should rid us of Jensen and Longmont. I'll sleep better tonight knowing that."

The rumble of departing hoofbeats had barely faded out when the first uncertainties arose over the idea of the ambush. "I

332

hear there are bears around here, Harvey," one slightly built, long-necked thug remarked to a companion who had also been left behind at the ambush site.

"Don't think so, Caleb," the other railroad cop said around a stalk of rye grass. Unlike the skinny one, who worked as a clerk in the California Central police office, he had a barrel chest, thick, corded muscles in arms and legs, and a flat belly ridged with more brawn. "They keep to the high country up in the Snowy Mountains," he added, using a rough English translation of the Spanish, "Sierra Nevada."

When the Spanish first came to California, the mountain peaks to the east had worn a constant mantle of snow, hence the name "Sierra Nevada." In the three centuries since they had first sighted those awesome ramparts, the climate had altered enough that only the highest remained white all year. It had not done the Donner Party much good, because the snows in even the lower passes began early. The big railroad bull's assurance about bears did ease the worries of his friend. Perhaps it should not have.

Smoke Jensen kept pushing the volunteers. At his own insistence, Louis Longmont rode the drag to make certain they hadn't any stragglers. The afternoon seemed to have too few hours in it. Long red shafts of sunlight slanted through the broken overcast to warn of approaching evening. Smoke wanted to get as far along the trail as possible.

He had not had any difficulty finding signs of what direction the fleeing men had taken. Heavy-laden packhorses had left deep gouges in the soft soil of the gentle slopes, and it seemed the inexperienced riders could not keep their mounts in a single file. Within ten minutes of reaching the abandoned train, Smoke had an accurate count of the numbers they faced. It was more than he would have liked, yet far less than had started out. Now he gave consideration to the twenty-five riders and the possibility someone in charge might consider an ambush.

"We'll stop here for a while," Smoke announced, his decision made. "That map I found shows Piney Creek not far from here. The stream runs through the easiest pass leading to the high country." Smoke's eyes twinkled with suspicion. "The creek would also make a good place for an ambush."

"You are going to scout it out, I assume," Louis offered.

"That I am, my friend. You are welcome to come along."

Louis did not hesitate. "Perhaps next time."

Smoke chuckled. "I'll remember that."

"I'll see to making camp. No fires, I assume?"

"No, Louis. They are running from us. I doubt they'll turn back and attack. A cold camp won't make our friends very happy. It'll give them a chance to cook some of those fancy victuals they took from Murchison's private larder."

Five minutes later, he rode out in a circuitous route that would take him up on the blind side of Piney Creek.

Caleb Varner cut his eyes away from the distant glow of campfires to gaze pointedly at Harvey Moran. "They ain't comin', Harvey."

Harvey let his gaze wander away from the face of his companion, to stare at where the burble of water over stones located Piney Creek. "At least, not tonight, I'd wager."

Caleb looked ghastly in the sickly light of the high-altitude twilight. "That means we have to spend the night here?"

"Sure does."

"But there's bears, Harvey."

"Dang it now, Caleb, I've done told you there are no bears anywhere around here."

Caleb considered that and found a new horror. "What about timber rattlers? I hear they like to crawl right inside a feller's bedroll with him to keep warm."

Harvey did not feel like playing this game. "String a rope around your sleepin' place. Snake won't cross a rope. Thinks it's a brother."

"Really? I don't know."

"Shut up, you two," another ambusher called harshly. "Can't a man grab a snooze in peace? What with the two of you flappin' yer jaws, ain't nobody gonna get any rest tonight."

"Don't you have first watch?" Harvey challenged. "Got no business sleepin' if you do." That should hold him, Harvey thought.

Unseen by any of the neophyte woodsmen, Smoke Jensen slipped away from the camp set up by those manning the ambush. He moved soundlessly through the underbrush with a big smirk on his face. He knew what he could do now. When he reached the ancient Sequoia where he had ground anchored his horse, he reached into one saddlebag. He rummaged around for a moment and came out with what he wanted.

Simple in construction, the first item had come from a friendly Cheyenne youngster he had often taken fishing. The boy had made it himself and proudly gave it to Smoke. It consisted of a gourd on a thin oak stick. Inside were polished pebbles. When shaken just right, it sounded like the grandfather of all rattlesnakes. The second object came from Smoke's past.

Preacher had helped him make it, on a lark, one deep, frigid winter night when they had had nothing else to do. It was a boxlike affair, with a hollowed reed for a mouthpiece. Inside Preacher had fastened an assortment of gut and sinew strings of varying length and thickness. By changes of intensity in breath and a hand waved over the open end, it could be made to produce a remarkably realistic sound. With nothing to do for several hours, Smoke waited calmly beside his 'Palouse stallion.

At near on midnight, Smoke Jensen roused himself. He dusted off his trousers and set out for the camp. When he settled on a position upstream from the enemy site, he eased back against a large granite boulder and gave his thoughts to being a giant timber rattler.

"B'zzzziiiiit! B'zzzzzzziiiiit! B'zzzzziit!"

Smoke went still while the voices came to him from the darkness. "M'God, Harvey, you hear that?"

"Hush up, Caleb," came a muzzy reply. Then, head clearing, Harvey asked, "Hear what?"

"I heard a rattler. A *big* rattlesnake."

"Horse pucky. Ain't no snakes around here," Harvey grumbled, his patience with this tenderfoot near an end.

"B'zzzzziiiiit!"

"Awh . . . shit," Harvey grunted out.

Blankets rustled in the darkness. "I'm gettin' outta here, Harvey. That thing sounds big enough to eat us whole."

"Where you gonna go in the dark, Caleb?"

"I dunno. Somewhere, anywhere there ain't any rattlers."

"Git in a tree. Snakes can't climb, yu'know," Harvey said calmly, trying not to let his own worry show.

A moment later, a heavy snuffling came from downwind. Even Harvey froze at that. He counted heartbeats between it and the next time. Louder now, the snuffle had a low snarl mixed in. Another pause, then the crash of brush sounded near the edge of the campsite. The full-throated roar of an enraged bear split the silence that followed.

"Oh, Jesus! *It's a bear!*" Caleb wailed. A warm wetness spread from his groin.

"Emory, Emory, do somethin' for chrissakes!" a thoroughly shaken Harvey cried.

Emory and Harvey opened fire at the same time. The grizzly roared again and charged.

EIGHTEEN

Smoke Jensen shoved on the huge boulder and sent it thundering downhill through the underbrush. Immediately he dived behind a larger slab of granite. He made it with scant seconds to spare. Six-guns roared and a Winchester cracked in the camp below. The mammoth stone careened forward on a zigzag course and splashed turbulently into Piney Creek.

A regular battlefield of gunshots boomed off the hillsides. Muzzle flashes reflected off the undersides of pine boughs. Lead cracked and whined through the air. Shouts of fright and confusion rose in a mad babble. Unable to contain his glee over the success of his toys, Smoke Jensen grinned like a kid in a vacant candy store.

Then Emory Yates spoiled it all. "Stop it! Stop it! Quit shooting at nothing, you idiots. There ain't no bear!" Slowly the discharge of weapons ceased. Emory immediately jumped on the men he led. "Don't you ever use your heads? They could hear you all the way to Parkerville. Do you think those gunfighters we're supposed to ambush can't hear? They all deef?"

He slammed his hat on the ground in disgust. "We ain't gonna surprise nobody after that dumb-ass stunt. Shootin' at shadows and funny noises."

Before he could say more, the hairs on the back of his neck rose as the awesome growl of the bear came again. "Jeeezus! First light, we're gonna pull out of here. Can't do an ambush here anymore. Four of you keep watch through the rest of the night."

"Hell, *all of us* are gonna watch. Ain't nobody gonna sleep with that bear around," Caleb stammered.

Red-faced, Emory bellowed at Caleb, up close in the man's face. "There ain't no goddamned bear."

Chuckling softly to himself, Smoke Jensen eased from behind the chunk of granite and silently stole off into the night.

In the camp established by Cyrus Murchison, the main fire had died down to a low, rose-orange glow of pulsing coals. Murchison sat with his back propped against the bole of an aged ponderosa pine. He had a half-filled bottle of brandy in one hand and an unlighted cigar in the other.

He did not want to let go of the liquor in order to light his stogie, though he dearly wanted the consolation of the rich smoke. An uneasy Titus Hobson approached.

"Light me a strip of kindling and bring it, will you, Titus?" Murchison greeted his partner.

Hobson did as bidden, ignited the cigar, then settled down beside Murchison and reached for the bottle. "That thunder sound we heard a little while ago? I have a feeling it wasn't caused by the weather."

"Sorry to say, I agree. Either those people chasing us stumbled into the ambush and it's all over. Or . . ."

"Or they rode right over the men you left back there," Hobson completed the unwelcome thought.

Shortly after dark, the men left behind by Heck Grange to spy on the approaching avengers had ridden into camp to report a force of some twenty hot on the trail. That many could easily overwhelm the seven men at Piney Creek. That news had sent Cyrus Murchison to the bottle. Then, about two hours ago, the sounds of a brief, ferocious battle came to them, muffled by distance. Could it be that late?

Cyrus pulled his fat, gold-cased watch

from his vest pocket. Half past two o'clock. There would be no sleep this night. A sudden crash in the brush banished his gloom. Startled from his lethargy, Murchison jerked away from the tree trunk and listened intently.

More crackling of small branches and shrubs came from above the camp. Dulled by years in large cities and aboard the locomotives of two railroads, the ears of Cyrus Murchison only dimly picked out a grunting, snuffling sound. Growls followed, growing louder. Then the full-throated bellow of an enraged grizzly split the night. Cyrus Murchison did not take time to consider that nothing larger than roly-poly brown bears still lived in the Sierra Nevada. He immediately tried to scale the trunk of the overhanging ponderosa. The slick surface of the bark gave him scant help. The smooth leather soles of his boots scrabbled for purchase, propelled by a repeat of the ferocious roar. He jammed the toes of his custom-made boots into cracks and climbed about ten feet. Sweating with effort, he clung there, paralyzed by the sting from broken fingernails. From below came the fearful bleating of Titus Hobson.

"Shoot him! Kill that bear!"

His bear act had played rather well at the ambush, Smoke allowed, so he decided to try it again. In the larger camp, it created even more pandemonium. Groggy figures jumped from blanket rolls, ghostlike in their longjohns. Blindly they fired into the darkness in all directions. Some traded shots with others equally disorganized. The cooler heads among the gang of misfits lay low in an attempt not to attract a bullet. The bear bellowed a third time.

Horses began to whinny and shy at the picket line. Several reared, their squeals of terror bright in the blackness. That brought forth another fusillade. Three horses, struck by bullets, went splay-legged and sagged down loose-limbed. From his panic-driven perch, Cyrus Murchison cried out in alarm, "Stop it! Stop! You're killing the horses."

A fourth snarling whoop from the bear removed any chance of compliance. Bullets flew in a hailstorm of deadly lead. Heck Grange, smarter than any of his men, rushed to dump wood on the firepit. He kept low to avoid the whirlwind of slugs while he added more. The blaze caught slowly, then went up with a *whoosh*.

Over its roar Heck shouted to the frenzied men. "This way. Get around the fire. Bears don't like fire. And stop that damned shooting!"

When the volume of fire reduced, Smoke Jensen crept out of his hiding place and stealthily approached the picketed horses. His Green River knife flickered in the pale starlight for a moment, then slashed upward and severed the rope to which the mounts had been tethered. He loosed half a dozen, then stepped back quickly to cup his hands around his mouth. A guttural snarl ripped up past his lips.

When the panther cough reached the ears of the horses, they lost their minds. Those who had been freed dashed off pell-mell into the night. The rest reared and stomped and jerked at the picket line until they broke it and stormed off in a loose-knit herd. Reality suddenly took root in the brain of Cyrus Murchison. Enlightenment brought with it misery. He knew . . . he *knew* the cause behind it.

"God . . . damn . . . you . . . Smoke Jensen," he groaned into the rough bark of the pine he hugged.

Morning found eyelids heavy and tempers short. Few of the hard cases had managed more than an hour's sleep. Cyrus

Murchison chafed while riders went out to recover their horses. His mood did not improve when the men from the ambush straggled in reeking of defeat.

"Why aren't you lying in wait for them?" he bellowed, rising from the fire, a cup of coffee steaming in his hand.

"We got attacked," Emory Yates explained limply.

"I gathered that. We heard the shooting. Did you stop any of them?"

"It weren't men," Caleb butted in. "It was critters. A giant rattlesnake and a bear."

A cold fist closed around the heart of Cyrus Murchison. "I think you will find that your rattler and bear are named Smoke Jensen."

"Huh?" Caleb gulped.

"You have been bamboozled, my parochial friend," Cyrus grated. "So, for that matter, have we. Smoke Jensen got around you, found your camp, and engaged in a little leg-pulling. Disastrous play, if you ask me."

"What now, Mr. Murchison?" Caleb asked.

"What? Well, once we get our horses back . . ." his face flushed crimson. "Once we get our horses back, we keep going. It is a good three days to the pass. Somewhere along the way we'll lay another ambush."

"You reckon they'll follow us?" Emory inquired, hoping to get a negative answer.

"Of course they'll follow. Louis Longmont and Smoke Jensen are determined to ruin me — ruin Titus and me," he hastily amended. "Only we'll have to outsmart them. So long as I have the support of you, my loyal employees, I am confident we will prevail."

Smoke Jensen paused long enough for the volunteers to examine the ambush site. It would help make them aware of what they faced, he reasoned. It had the desired effect. When they set out again, their usual chatter dried up by seeming mutual consent. Silence held the higher they went into the foothills. When they came to the place where Murchison had camped the previous night, the impromptu posse halted again.

Everyone listened intently while Smoke interpreted the sign left behind. Then he described what he had done to cause them to create the disorganized scuffs and gouges in the dirt. That brought full, hearty laughs. Aware now that riches and power, and a lot of hired guns, did not make anyone invincible, they resumed their good-natured ragging when the column set off again.

Three hours later, they came upon the scene of last night's disaster in the main camp. Smoke's modest recounting of what transpired delighted them and bolstered their fortitude. Smoke found the trail their enemy left to be wide and clear. He called that to the attention of Louis.

"They're not making any effort to hide their tracks. Makes a feller wonder."

Louis Longmont chuckled sardonically. "Not for long, though, eh? It seems they want us to know where they are going and follow along at all good speed."

"You've not lost your trailcraft, old friend," Smoke praised. "I think I'll take Quo Wu and scout ahead. You bring the others along, only at a nice, easy pace. Try to keep no more than a mile between us."

Louis nodded knowingly. "*Très bon, mon ami.* Very good indeed. This way, if they are brazen enough to lay another ambush, the cavalry will be close at hand to ride to the rescue."

Smoke shook his head ruefully. "I can't figure what's so funny about that, but it suits what I've got in mind. Take care, now, old friend."

"I always do," Louis replied jauntily.

To his pleased satisfaction, Smoke Jensen had already found Quo Chung Wu to be nearly as skilled at silent movement as himself. It would come in handy on this little jaunt, he felt certain. On the hunch that Murchison would want to have as much space between the main body and any ambush he might set up, Smoke called a halt a quarter short of five miles.

"We'll go on foot from here on. Circle wide of the trail they left and keep off the skyline," Smoke instructed.

Quo Wu bowed his head and spoke without the least condescension. "The art of remaining unseen is ancient in our order. It is a shame that talent does not extend to our horses," he added wryly.

Smoke was ready for that one. "Among the Spirit Walkers of the Cheyenne, it is believed that they can extend their cloak of invisibility to their ponies. It might be they have something there, after all. I've had half a dozen of them pop up on me on open prairie sort of out of nowhere."

"You are possessed of this magic?" Quo Wu asked, impressed.

A modest reply seemed called for. "Somewhat. At least, enough that if there is anyone out there waitin' for us, they won't know Thunder and me are anywhere close until it's too late."

"How does it work?"

Smoke smiled at Quo. "Accordin' to the Cheyenne, all we have to do is think of ourselves and our horses as grass. Or in our case here, as trees."

Quo seemed taken aback. "That is all? We are taught to think of ourselves as birds, flying high above the gaze of our enemies."

"Seems a mite complicated, masterin' all those motions a bird has to go through to stay in the air."

Realizing that Smoke was teasing him, Quo flushed a light pink under his pale brown cheeks. "I have . . . flown twice."

Smoke did not know what to make of that. He did have to suppress a laugh. "No foolin'?"

Quo blurted his explanation through the embarrassment of having shown such unworthy pride. "Of course, my body never left the ground. Only my spirit soared."

Considering that, Smoke clapped a big hand on one muscular thigh. "That fits with what the Cheyenne say. So, you an' your horse will be birds, an' me an' Thunder will be trees. Either way, if there's anyone out there, we'll be in among them, raisin' hell, before they have an inkling."

Orville Dooling, known as "Doolie" to his fellow railroad police, thought he caught a hint of movement from the corner of one eye. He turned his head and peered in that direction. Nothing. He switched his gaze back down the wide, well-marked trail that had been left from the camp beyond Piney Creek. Once more a flicker of motion impinged on his awareness. Orville shook his head as though to rid it of such notions. An instant later he froze at the soft sound of a whispering voice.

"Say goodnight."

A shower of stars, quickly extinguished by a wave of darkness, filled Doolie Dooling's head. The accompanying pain lasted only a second. Smoke Jensen stepped over the supine gunman and removed his weapons. No sense in leaving them for the rest of this rabble. That accounted for the right flank guard, Smoke noted, as he moved back behind the arc of the ambush to pick another target.

Two hard cases lounged close to each other, backs supported by a thick bush. Smoke glided soundlessly up to them and reached his arms wide. With a swift, powerful sweep, he grasped them over their ears and banged their heads together. The rest of those involved in the ambush remained oblivious to his actions, particularly the one being throttled by Quo Chung Wu at that very moment. Faintly, Smoke's superb hearing picked out the drum of hooves on the spongy terrain beyond the rise where the ambush had been laid.

A second later, the lead element of the posse hove into view and a shot banged flatly from one of the hidden gunhands. Four more thugs opened up, one from so close to Smoke Jensen, he felt the heat of the muzzle blast. Smoke drew and fired.

His shot dissolved his seeming invisibility. It appeared that all five of the remaining hard cases saw him at once. Smoke flexed his legs and dived to one side, while hot lead smacked into trees and screamed off rocks where he had stood a moment before. From the opposite end of the arc of gunhawks, a shotgun boomed and two of Murchison's henchmen screamed in torment.

Immediately, the hidden shooters turned toward this new threat. That gave Smoke a chance to account for another thug. A street brawler born and bred, he reared up from his concealed position to take a shot at Quo Chung Wu. Smoke cocked his Peacemaker and called to him.

"Over here!"

The slow-witted lout began to swing his .44 Smith, eyes widening at the presence of someone right in among them. His surprise did not get to register on his face. A bullet from Smoke Jensen's .45 Colt reached him first. The red knob of his nose turned into a black hole, its edges splashed with scarlet. He went over backward, draped across the fallen pine trunk he had used for shelter.

Disorganized by the sudden appearance of two men in their midst, the railroad police and dockwallopers completely forgot about the eighteen armed vigilantes riding down on them. That proved a fatal error. Feeding on long-accumulated anger over their mistreatment, the farmers and merchants of the Central Valley swarmed in among their would-be assassins and wrought terrible vengeance.

In less than five minutes the battle ended. Only the unconscious among the hard cases remained alive. Those were trussed up like hogs for the slaughter and left behind, to be retrieved later. "When you come back through here, don't forget these men," Smoke advised.

Nightfall found Cyrus Murchison and his henchmen in a cold, miserable camp. Considering the events of the previous night, Heck Grange had insisted on no fires. The assortment of longshoremen, railroad police, and freelance would-be gunfighters grumbled noisily while they ate cold sardines and other preserved food from tins crudely hacked open by their knives. They had not been close enough to hear the detail of the brief, furious fight at the ambush site. It had sounded like nothing more than a loosened boulder rolling downhill.

Considering the debacle of the previous night, Cyrus Murchison put another meaning on it. Now, guided only by starlight, he made his way across the encampment to find Titus Hobson and share his revelation. He found Heck Grange seated beside Titus and poured each of them a generous dollop of brandy. He opened his mouth to speak when the chilling howl of a gray wolf broke the silence of the night.

Smoke Jensen had spent four tedious hours creeping up on the area in which he had estimated Murchison would make camp. He found them within three hundred yards of his picked spot. They could have done better to have reasoned like Smoke. Yet the chosen place appeared secure enough.

On the top of a small, domed knoll, the tired, uncertain hard cases sprawled in uneasy slumber. Unlike the previous night, someone had shown sense enough not to light fires, and to put out roving sentries, with pickets posted closer in. It would make his task harder, yet Smoke Jensen flowed through them as though truly invisible. He came up behind one less-than-observant hard case with laughable ease.

Smoke's braided rawhide lariat snaked out soundlessly and settled around the rider's shoulders, pinning his arms to his sides. A swift yank whipped him out of the saddle before he could give an alarm. His butt's contact with the solid ground drove the air from his lungs and blackness swam before his eyes, while Smoke Jensen walked the rope to the captive and klonked him solidly behind one ear.

Using pigging strings from his saddlebags, he secured the unconscious man. Then he dragged the musclebound longshoreman to a shallow ravine and unceremoniously rolled him in. Soundlessly whistling a jolly tune, Smoke recoiled his lariat and strode off into the night. Near the base of the hillock, he found a lone tree, which he scaled with ease. Poised on a sturdy limb, he waited for the passage of another guard.

Within five minutes, Smoke's patience was rewarded. Dozing in the saddle, an exhausted railroad policeman approached, his unguided mount in a self-directed amble. Smoke tensed as the animal wandered by under his branch. A moment later, he launched himself. His bootheels struck solidly between the thug's shoulder blades. Smoke did an immediate backroll off the rump of the startled, shying mount and landed on his feet.

His target did not fare so well. He ended up on his head. The bones of his neck made a nasty sound when they broke. Smoke Jensen spared only a split second for regret, then moved on.

He next surprised an adenoidal youth, far too young and green to be in the company of such reprobates as those who surrounded him. His eyes went wide and he wet his drawers when Smoke took him from behind and clamped a big, callused hand over the boy's mouth. Wisely, the youngster did not struggle. He appreciated his good sense a moment later when Smoke laid the flat of the blade of his Green River against the teenager's neck.

Smoke's urgency carried through the

whisper. "If you want to live, make up your mind to take this horse I brought for you and ride clear the hell out of here. Don't stop and don't even look back. It's that, or I slit your gullet and send you off to your Maker."

If he could have, the kid would have wet himself again. He certainly wanted to. With effort, he nodded his head up and down. "Mummmf, unnnh — hunnn."

"Does that mean you agree?" Smoke whisper-probed.

"Unnnn — hunnn."

Smoke's voice hissed like Old Man Death himself in the youth's ear. "If I let you go, you won't give the alarm?"

"Nuuh-uuuh."

Smoke eased his grip and reached behind him. "All right. Here's the reins. Walk him about a mile, then hit the saddle and ride like the hounds of hell are after you." He paused for effect, then put an ominous tone in his voice, knowing what he planned next. "You never know . . . they might be."

Panting, the boy showed his gratitude. "Thank you, thankyou-thankyou-thankyou."

Smoke looked after the young man as he led the horse off from the mound. Then the last mountain man turned and started uphill. Half way to the top, he paused. He gave the kid another five minutes, then threw back his head, cupped palms around his mouth and gave the mournful howl of a timber wolf.

NINETEEN

Hairs rose at the nape of the neck of every man in the hilltop camp. This time, Heck Grange's discipline took hold and no one fired wildly into the darkness. That did not keep them from filling their hands with any close-by weapon. Eyes showing a lot of white, they peered tensely into the stygian night. Most had barely conquered their nerves when the wolf howled again.

This time it seemed to come from closer in. Another wolf answered it from the opposite side of the camp. Fear gripped all of them, especially Cyrus Murchison. His childhood had been filled with thoroughly spuriously stories about wolves carrying off children and devouring them. Now this ingrained myth came back to haunt him.

"That can't be Jensen," he stated shakily to Titus Hobson. "He couldn't move that fast. There are *real* wolves out there."

His own unease gnawing at his vitals, Titus answered in a subdued voice. "I couldn't agree more. What are we going to do?"

"Do? We'll have to build a fire. No matter those behind us will see it now. We do it or those wolves will be in among us before we know it."

"Who is going to move and draw their attention?" Hobson queried.

"Grange, of course," Murchison courageously suggested. He raised his voice. "Heck, get a fire started."

"Already under way, Mr. Murchison," the boss gunman answered blandly. "Look for the fire glow reflected in their eyes. We'll know how many there are that way."

A tiny point of light bloomed at the top of the knoll. Kindling began to blaze, and men instinctively moved that way. The two wolves howled again.

Smoke Jensen could not believe his good fortune. A live, breathing wolf had answered his call. He raised his head again and uttered another wail, answered almost at once from the other side of the mound. *Scare the be-Jazus outta them,* he thought in the manner of Paddy Flynn, an old mountain man friend of Preacher's.

Another wolf howl, answered promptly, and then he readied the three horses he had collected from the incautious sentries. He loosened their saddles and removed bits, reins, and headstalls. He got them pointed in the general direction of the hilltop camp and stepped away into the night. A fourth ululating lupine howl sent them off in a panicked canter. Smoke listened intently for the results.

Cries of alarm and consternation came from the camp moments later, when the frightened creatures blundered in among the men and raced mindlessly past the fire. Three men opened fire. Sparks rose as one of the horses blundered into the fire pit. A man's voice rose to a shriek.

"My God, they're here, they're after us."

Smoke started to make his way back to Thunder when he caught a hint of movement off to his right. A gray-white-and-black object moved stealthily through the darkness. Smoke waited patiently. Then he saw it clearly. Even the distant firelight put a yellow-green phosphorescent glow in those big, intelligent eyes.

Smoke hunkered down, extended a hand, and uttered the low whine that conveyed friendly submission among wolves. The great, shaggy beast advanced, crouched low, and came forward at a crouch. He sniffed, his educated scent telling a lot about this two-legged being. Slowly, he closed. Another inspection by nose, then the long, wet tongue shot out and licked at the hand of Smoke Jensen.

"Good boy, good boy," Smoke whispered. "You came to help. I could send you up there among them to cap this off nicely, but I'm afraid you'd get shot. Go on, now. Go run down a couple of fit raccoons for your supper." Cautiously, Smoke reached out and patted the wolf. It might be more intelligent than a domesticated dog, Smoke reminded himself but it was still wild.

A soft whine came from the long gray muzzle and the wolf rolled over on its back, exposing its vulnerable belly. Smoke petted it and then made a shooing motion. He turned and walked away, back toward Thunder. A good night's work, he reasoned. When they found the lookouts in the morning, that would spook them even more.

When the roving patrol failed to return at the end of their four-hour stint, alarm spread through the camp again. Cyrus Murchison and Heck Grange barely managed to quell the general decision to search at once. By morning's early light, the gang managed to locate the missing sentries.

Bound and gagged, all were fully conscious and furious. "It was that god-damned Jensen, I tell you," one outraged thug growled.

"There was two wolves out here last night," Monk Diller stated positively.

"They sure as hell don't carry pieces of rope an' tie up a feller," the complaining sentry countered. "It was Smoke Jensen."

"God . . . damn . . . you . . . Smoke Jensen," Cyrus Murchison thought, though he did not give voice to his impotent curse.

Those with even a scant talent toward it cooked up a breakfast of fatback, potatoes, and skillet cornbread. One man with a passing skill as a woodsman found a clump of wild onions to add to the potatoes, and another dug a huge, fat yucca root to bake in the coals. Their bellies filled, the company of hard cases rode out, headed for the distant pass and Carson City beyond. Try as they might, none of them could find evidence of the presence of Smoke Jensen beyond the bits of rope.

Winds born over the far-off Pacific Ocean pushed thick cumulus clouds toward the coast. They grew as they progressed eastward. Many with fat black bellies climbed beyond 35,000 feet, their heads flattening out into the anvil shape of cumulonimbus. Storm clouds, thunderheads. Steadily they climbed as they raced over San Francisco and beyond to the Central Valley.

Their outriders arrived over the Sierra Nevada at ten o'clock in the morning. For the past half hour, Smoke Jensen had been marking the threatening appearance of the sky to the west. When the first dirty-gray billows whisked across the sun, he nodded in understanding and acceptance. Wise in the ways of mountains, Smoke knew for certain a tremendous thunderstorm would soon sweep over them. He made his companions aware of it.

"Storm's comin'. Better get out your rain slickers."

Tyler Estes, the barber in Grass Valley, gave him a concerned look. "A lot of us don't have anything. These are borrowed horses and such."

Smoke shrugged, indifferent to physical discomfort. "You'll just get wet, then. Or you can wrap up in your ground sheets."

"Our blankets will get wet that way," Estes protested.

A quick smile flickered on Smoke's face. "One way or the other, something is going to get wet."

Half an hour later, the first fat drops of

rain fell from the solid sea of gray-black clouds. The wind whipped up and whirled last winter's fallen leaves around the legs and heads of their horses. In a sudden plunge, the temperature fell twenty degrees. "Here it comes," Smoke warned.

Already in his bright yellow India rubber slicker, Smoke had only to button up and turn his collar. The brim of his sturdy 5X Stetson kept most of the water out of his face. With their backs to the storm, the posse continued on its way. A trickle of cold rain ran down the back of Smoke Jensen's collar. The wind gusted higher as he worked to snug it tighter. Then the core of the storm struck.

Thunder bellowed around then and bright streaks lanced to the ground and trees to one side. The air smelled heavily of ozone. Smoke curled from a lightning-shattered ponderosa. A big hickory smouldered on the opposite side. They had been bracketed by near simultaneous shafts of celestial electricity.

"B'God, it hit both sides of us," Estes gulped out the obvious.

With a seething rattle, like the rush of the tide on a pebbly beach, a curtain of white hurtled toward them from the rear. Visibility dropped to zero and a wall of ice pebbles swept across the huddled men.

"Owie! Ouch! Hey, this stuff is tearing me up," a young livery stable hand yelped when the line of hail rushed over the rear of the column.

"Let's get under the trees!" Tyler Estes shouted.

"No!" Smoke turned his mount to stare them down. "You saw what the lightning did to those trees back there, right? Picture bein' under one of them when it hit. You'd be right sure fried."

Estes shivered at the image created by the words of Smoke Jensen. He looked around for some escape, while the hail battered at them all. "What can we do, then?"

"Dismount and control your horses. Get on the downwind side of them and use them for what shelter it provides. It'll be over 'fore long."

It proved to be damned little protection. Quarter-sized ice balls pelted down to bruise skin protected by no more than a light coat or flannel shirt. Smoke had been right about the duration. Within ten minutes, the hailstorm crashed on to the northeast. It had been with them long enough to turn the ground a glittering white, to a thickness of some three inches.

"Give me snow any time," Brice Rucker

complained. "That stuff ain't hard."

Smoke favored him with a glance. "You've never seen snow on the high plains, have you? I was there one time with Preacher. We had a heavy snow, followed by an ice storm. The wind got up so that it flung the ice-coated snow at us. It was like razors, it was so sharp. Be thankful for small favors. All we come out of this with is a few bruises."

"Few," the always complaining barber repeated. "I'll be black and blue for a month."

"Too tender a hide, Tyler," Rucker teased him.

"Go kiss yer mule, Rucker," Tyler pouted.

"One bright spot," Smoke said through the rain to defuse the testy volunteers. "Think how that storm is going to play hell with those fellers ahead of us."

Wistfulness filled the voice of Tyler Estes. "Yes. They can't fare any better than us. Worse, more likely."

Louis Longmont entered the conversation. "Murchison and Hobson are soft from years of easy living. I would imagine they are completely miserable about now."

Lacking Smoke Jensen's knowledge of the outdoors, the storm caught Cyrus

Murchison and his motley crew by surprise. Instantly soaked to the skin, they had not even covered themselves with slickers before the hail had hit. Two men were driven from their saddles by now fist-sized stones of ice. Their horses ran off screaming in misery.

Turned instantly into a rabble, the men milled about in confusion. The sky turned stark white and a tremendous crash of thunder followed in the blink of an eye. The huge green top of a spectacular lone Sequoia burst into flame and the upper two thirds canted dangerously toward the trail. Then it fell with aching slowness. Fearing for their lives, the hard cases scattered.

Blazing furiously, the tree dropped across the trail to block forward progress. Its resin-rich leaves spat and hissed in the torrent of rain that fell, unable to quell the flames.

"If the wind was down, we could put up tents."

Cyrus Murchison looked blankly at Titus Hobson. Could the man have completely forgotten everything he had learned about such storms during his mining days? "What good would that do?" he demanded. "The hail would only punch holes through the canvas the minute we stretched it tight."

Titus blinked. Why had he not thought of that? He made steeples of his shoulders to hide his embarrassment. "It's a while since I've been out in anything like this."

"So I gather," his partner responded. "We might as well hold fast here until that fire goes out. No sense in taking the risk of men falling into the flames going around it." He decided to relent on his harsh outburst at Titus. "You're right, though. When the hail quits, we should set up the tents. A warm, dry camp is bound to be appreciated."

Despite the storm-induced darkness, Cyrus judged it to be no more than mid-afternoon. They would lose nearly half a day, yet it would be important to let the runoff firm up the trail. No matter how many men pursued them, they would have been caught in the open, too, he reasoned. And, it might dampen the penchant of Smoke Jensen for those childish, although dangerous, pranks. Only time would tell.

Late that night, Smoke Jensen worked quietly and alone. It had taken him a quarter of an hour to select the right tent and the most suitable sapling. He spent another fifteen minutes in attaching the end of a rope to the springy young tree. Half an hour went by while he painstakingly pulled the limber trunk downward over a pivot point made of a smooth, barkless length of ash limb. He secured it there, then took the other end of the rope and tied it off to the peak of the tent roof.

With everything in readiness, Smoke stepped back to inspect his handiwork. It pleased him. All he had to do was cut the pigging string that held the spring trap in place and nature would take care of the rest. Suddenly he stiffened at the rustle of sound from inside the tent next to the one he had rigged.

Groggy with sleep, one of the hard cases stepped through the flap and headed for the low fire in a large stone ring. He had a coffeepot in one hand. The thug must have caught sight of Smoke from the corner of one eye. He turned that way and spoke softly.

"What's up? You drainin' yer lily?"

Smoke muffled his voice, turned three-quarters away from his challenger. "Yep."

"Too much coffee, or too small a bladder, eh?"

"Unh-huh."

"I reckon I'd best be joinin' you," his

questioner suggested, as he tucked his speckled blue granite cup behind his belt and reached for his fly.

He stepped closer and Smoke tensed. The bearded thug fumbled with the buttons as he came up to Smoke. He opened his mouth to make another remark and met a fist-full of knuckles. Bright lights exploded in his head and he rocked over backward. Smoke hit him again under the hinge of his jaw and the man sighed his way into unconsciousness.

Smoke Jensen stepped quickly to where he had secured the line between the bent sapling and the tent roof. His Green River knife came out and flashed down toward the pigging string. It severed with a snap and the tree instantly swung back toward its natural position. Smoke cut loose with a panther cough and yowl while the tent tie-downs sang musically as they strained, then let go. Like the conjuring trick of a medicine show magician, the tent whisked away, skyward, exposing the sleeping men inside.

Before anyone could react, Smoke Jensen slipped away into the darkness.

Several of the volunteers gathered around Smoke Jensen the next morning at the breakfast fire. The big granite pot of coffee made its final round. They had eaten well on shaved ham and gravy over biscuits, with the ubiquitous fried potatoes and onions, and tins of peaches and cherries, courtesy of the larder in the private car of Cyrus Murchison. They laughed heartily when he recounted what he had done the night before.

"Them fellers must have filled their drawers," Brice Rucker chortled. "Those that were in them, at least. I bet more'n a few jumped right out of their longjohns."

"I didn't wait to see," Smoke answered dryly. That brought more whoops of laughter. "Saddle up, men, we've got them running scared now."

Smoke led his small force away only scant minutes after the sun broke over the distant ramparts of the Sierra Nevada. He had told them that by the next day they would be high in the mountains. Another day after that they would be able to sweep down on Murchison's gang and bring an end to it. His words received powerful support shortly before midmorning.

Four tired, harried-looking men rode toward them from up the trail. When they sighted the vigilantes, they halted and waited quietly. As Smoke Jensen and Louis Longmont came within fifty yards of them, they raised their empty hands over their heads.

"We're out of it," their self-appointed leader informed the gunfighters. "We done quit the railroad police and left Murchison to his own ends. There was sixty of us when we started. Now there's less than half." His eyes narrowed. "Which one of you is Smoke Jensen?"

"I am," Smoke told him, readying his hand to draw his .45 Colt.

A chuckle, not a challenge, came from the former railroad bull. "You sure got 'em stirred up, Mr. Jensen. Got *us* all exercised, that's for sure. Those boys up there are quaking in their boots. After what happened to that tent, we quit first thing this morning. An' there's about a dozen more ready to give it up, too."

"Good to hear, gentlemen. You're free to ride on. Only one thing," he added, a hand raised to stop them. "We'd be obliged if you left all but five rounds of ammunition with us. We're a little short as it is, and every round will be appreciated."

Their leader snickered, a gloved hand over his mustache and full lips. "And, it sort of makes certain we can't turn back and hit you in the rear, don't it?"

Smoke nodded and joined his laughter. "That possibility did occur to me. So, what do you say?" His eyes narrowed to glittering slits of gray. "Lighten your load and ride free? Or open the dance right now?"

The jovial one quickly showed both hands, open and empty. "Ain't got time to waltz, Mr. Jensen. We'll just leave some cartridges with you and be on our way."

Smoke's smile held the breezy warmth of a June day. "That's mighty thoughtful of you. I'll take you up on that and then we can ride on."

In ten minutes it was done and the volunteer posse grew richer by two hundred thirty rounds. Smoke watched the deserters from Murchison's cause from time to time until they rode out of sight. He showed a sunny mood to everyone as he picked up the pace.

Wilber Evers spoke around a hard knot of grief in his throat that night in the vigilante camp. "He was my brother. My brother, and they shot him down like a dog. One of . . . one of them took a rope to his kids and beat them. Raised welts on their backs."

Another sorrow-softened voice responded. "Yeah, I know. You hear about Ruby Benson?"

"The widow Benson?" Evers asked.

"Yep. That's the one. Only she's not so much an old widow. She's rather young. Anyway, some of these riff-raff came along from the railroad and told her to sell out the farm to Murchison. She refused. So they jumped her, had their way with her and left her a ruined woman. She — she's my sister."

"I'm sorry," Smoke Jensen added his feelings to the discussion around the supper fire. "What did you reckon to do about it?"

"She described them to me. If I find them among those with Murchison, I'm gonna hang the lot of them."

Smoke nodded. "Suits. Preacher hanged some rapists more than once. I know, because I was with him a couple of times. There's even a story going around that he one time hanged a man who messed around with children."

"Served him right, I say," the brother of Ruby Benson growled.

"What else has been done that you know of for certain?" Smoke probed.

Several voices clamored for his attention. One bull bellow overrode the others.

"They burnt my barn and shot my cows. Scared my wife so much she delivered early. We lost the baby."

"Do you know them?"

"Sort of. They had flour sacks over their heads, but two of them didn't change clothes from earlier in the day. I'd know those two anywhere. They work at the depot in Parkerville. Name of Dawkins and Lusk. I meant to go shoot them when I ran into these other fellows and joined in on this little affair."

Angry mutters went around the firepit. "I had myself primed to set my sights on one of Huntley's bullies. He tormented me an' my wife until I was forced to sell two freight wagons to Huntley's outfit. I cussed myself as a yellow-belly ever since. When I heard there was trouble in Grass Valley, I hightailed it for there right away." The grayhaired man stopped there and looked around for approval from his companions.

It came quickly. "Ain't nothin' yeller about you, Paul. Why, we was right pleased to see you join us."

Paul drew himself up and came to his boots. "Well, I thank ye, Lester. Boys, I think I've got enough jawin' for one night. I'm for my bedroll. We got a bushel of work to do tomorrow."

Smoke Jensen silently agreed and pushed away from the circle of gabbers. What he had heard angered and disturbed him. All of their atrocities considered, he doubted that Murchison and his gang would be inclined to give up easily.

TWENTY

Crouched in a jumble of rocks, Smoke Jensen cracked a satisfied smile. After hearing the accounts of those victimized on Murchison's orders, he decided to try a different approach. He did not wait as long as he had for the previous night visits to the gangster camp. He wanted the men up and moving around. Smoke had selected his spot carefully and settled in to observe.

Tensions had thickened what with so many fellows forced to rub elbows for so long, he marked first. No longer did they all crowd around a large, central fire. Seven smaller blazes lighted the night, with men grouped in twos and threes, with a solitary loner at one. Smoke settled on him for his first dirty trick of the night. That determined, he slid away into the darkness around the camp.

After he had circled the campsite, he paused to relocate his target. Then, holding a deep breath, he ghosted up on the unsuspecting thug hunkered down by the fire. With panther swiftness, Smoke whipped an arm around the brute's neck and gave a sudden yank. Unseen by the comrades of the hard case, Smoke whisked him out of sight.

Using a trick of the Cheyenne Dog Soldiers, Smoke increased the pressure of his arm until he stifled the thug into unconsciousness. Then he hefted the limp form over one shoulder and carried him away. Far away. When next the man woke up, he would find himself tied to a tree in a strange place, well out of sight of the camp he had last seen. Smoke Jensen made certain it would be on the route to be taken by Murchison and the gang the next morning. Making sure with the rope that his captive could not escape on his own, Smoke returned to wipe out all trace of his presence.

"That went so smooth, there's no reason not to try for another one," Smoke muttered to himself.

He found another one easily enough. A city dude had gone out in the trees to relieve himself. And, naturally, he plain got lost. In his wandering, he blundered into Smoke Jensen. That quick he became the next to disappear without a trace.

Unaware of the doings of Smoke Jensen, and the fact that Smoke now crouched in some rocks not thirty feet away, Cyrus Murchison and his partners discussed his decision to move on to Carson City.

"We could go back to the main line," Murchison said agreeably. "Only those miserable sons of perdition are between us and it. No, Titus, Heck, it will take longer, but to continue on horseback is the wisest choice."

Titus Hobson answered testily. "*I* say the wisest thing would have been to stay in San Francisco. You own the mayor and the city fathers. And, between us, we own nearly all the judges. The chief of police plays poker with us and gets drunk in that gentlemen's club of yours. There's no way Longmont or Jensen can show any proof of our involvement in anything illegal. *They can't bring any charges.*"

For the first time, Cyrus Murchison found it necessary to reveal his real fear. "You said it yourself, Titus. Smoke Jensen is a gunfighter. The best there is. And there's not a hair's breadth between him and Longmont. Listen to me, your life depends on it. Those two are not in the habit of bringing charges . . . *except the ones in their six-guns.*"

Hobson paled. "You mean, they'll just . . . kill us?"

"Precisely. For men like them, justice comes out of the barrel of a gun. No, we'll keep on overland. The Central's tracks have been extended into Carson City. We can get reinforcements there. Then we'll return to California and wipe out these interfering scum." Cyrus Murchison came up on his scuffed, dusty, although once highly polished, boots. Buoyed by his self-delusion, he spoke lightly. "It is time to turn in. I'm looking forward to a sound night's sleep."

"I wish you the joy of it," Titus Hobson grumbled, uncomfortable at being reminded he was the one to identify exactly what Smoke Jensen and Louis Longmont were.

A sudden shout stopped them. "Chief! Chief, there's two of us missin'."

Heck Grange came upright. "Did you see any sign of Smoke Jensen?"

"Nope. Nothin'. Just some tracks where the boys was. They've plum disappeared."

Early the next morning, Smoke Jensen changed his tactics. In the faint gray light that preceded sunrise, he led the posse of vigilantes out at a fair pace. "We're through chasing Murchison and his mob of butchers," he informed his companions.

"Today we get ahead of them and see how they enjoy an ambush." Expectant smiles answered him. "With a good early start, we can swing wide and bypass their present camp."

Everyone rode with high spirits. As the day grew brighter, Smoke increased the pace. Every hour, they dismounted and walked their horses for ten minutes. Many of those who lacked experience with saddle mounts marveled at the stamina that this provided their animals. Shortly before the noon hour, Smoke called a halt.

He gestured to where the sheer hillsides closed in on the trail. It narrowed and the grade grew much steeper. "Up there a ways is the place we'll start. Some of you see if you can locate any fallen logs. Make sure they're not bigger around than a man's body and not too dried out."

"Why don't we cut what we want?" Tyler Estes asked.

"We don't have a lot of time, Mr. Estes. The less we have to spend on this the better," Smoke informed him. "Those of you with shovels come with me. I'll show you what to do."

They worked quickly and well. Smoke supervised the building of an even dozen nasty surprises for Murchison's hirelings.

Two long, narrow pits had been dug parallel to the trail, covered with leaves and brush. At a point farther along, where the mountain's breast overhung the narrow trace, Smoke saw an ideal place for a particularly nasty trap. He set men to work weaving a large net from vines and ropes.

While they did that, Smoke himself climbed to the top of the lip and sprawled out flat. Working by feel, he drove the pointed end of an arm-thick limb into the soil. He draped a double twist of lariat over the beam it formed and lowered it to the ground. Then he returned to the busy weavers.

"When you get that done, fill it with rocks and attach these ropes at the top to keep it closed. Then stick brush in the net, to make it look like a big bush."

"Then what?" Estes asked.

"We attach the trip line." Smoke turned away to check on other progress while he let them figure that one out.

Three and a half hours later, the project neared completion. Smoke Jensen made a final, careful check, then gathered the volunteers. "Everyone pick a position up above the last trap. Make sure you have a clear field of fire. And be careful going up there. You don't want to set off one of those things on yourself."

"You can say that again," Tyler Estes blurted out. When he had taken in the scope of what Smoke had in mind, his eyes bugged and the usually timid barber had thrilled in the blood lust that heated him at the thought of all these awful things going off in the midst of that gang of thugs. He remained impressed as he worked his way up above the deadly ambush site.

"Do you expect them to fall for this?" Louis Longmont asked, a critical eye roving over the concealed traps and trip lines.

Smoke gave it some thought. "For most of it. It depends on how well those boys can shoot up there whether we break them right here." Smoke cast a glance at the sun. "Either way, we'll know soon enough."

Cyrus Murchison and his army of gun-slingers set out a leisurely two hours after sunrise. Everything went well for the first three hours. Then the two men in the lead flew from the backs of their horses, driven off by a long, supple sapling that had been bent back behind a pile of rocks along the trail. They landed hard, both breaking ribs. One of them snapped a leg.

"That damn well ties it!" Heck Grange

shouted. "We'll be forever getting to the top of the pass now. How many more of these things are out there waiting for us?"

Cyrus Murchison responded with an air of indifference. "Tell the men to go slow and we'll find out. But keep them going."

With the column on the move again, Murchison settled down to a gloomy contemplation of exactly *how many* such traps they would find. And worse, how much harm would be done.

Nervous, and made more cautious, the band of thugs continued on toward the top of the pass. No more hidden dangers had shown up by the time Murchison's henchmen stopped for their nooning. Titus Hobson had managed to convince himself that someone other than Smoke Jensen had rigged that trap. An Indian, perhaps, to catch some form of game. He shared his thought with Cyrus Murchison. Oddly, Murchison found himself agreeing. Until now he had harbored the sneaking suspicion that the two wily gunfighters had gotten ahead of them, yet he said nothing to Hobson. Half an hour further along the trail he quickly learned to regret that decision.

An agonized scream echoed along the high, enclosing walls of the gorge that led to the high pass of the Sierra Nevada. Its eerie wail jerked Cyrus Murchison out of his dark ruminations and sent a chill down his spine. Up ahead, he saw a thigh-thick log swish back and forth, after striking the lead rider. Jagged flakes of quartz protruded from the face, three of them dripped blood.

Unthinkingly, Murchison spoke his thoughts aloud. "Hideous. It's hideous. They — they're nothing but barbarians."

Heck Grange took charge. "Dismount! Walk your horses and look where you are going."

Severely shaken, his face pale, Cyrus Murchison did as the rest. He reached the spot where the man lay dead, his blood a pool around his crumpled form, when a rope twanged musically ahead and four saplings swished out to slap men and horses in the face. The hard cases shouted in alarm and jumped to the side of the trail. Fragile brush crackled and gave way under their weight. Their yells changed to screams of agony as they impaled themselves on sharpened stakes in the bottom of shallow trenches.

A voice came from one thug behind Murchison. "That does it. I'm getting out of here."

Murchison whirled. "No, wait. Stay with us. There can't be much more of this."

"*Any more* is too damn much for me, Mr. Murchison. You can send my pay to my house."

An idea struck Cyrus Murchison. "Anyone who deserts won't get paid!" he shouted.

"Who cares, at least we'll be alive," another truculent voice replied.

Four men took to their horses, turned tail, and fled without a backward look. Cyrus Murchison cursed and stomped his boot on the hard ground. Up ahead a trigger tripped and a loud roar filled the air. Hundreds of large rocks rained down on the men and horses below.

Whinnies of the frightened critters filled the air as the stones bruised and cut their hide. Dust rose in thick clouds. The rumble of bounding boulders drowned out the shrieks of pain from the injured hard cases. Those the farthest along the trail broke free only to be met with a wall of powder smoke. Bullets cracked through the air. Thugs died horribly.

Belatedly, those behind recovered and drew weapons. They surged forward, yelling to their fellow stupefied comrades over the tumult to keep moving forward.

The thrust became a rallying point, which grew into a concerted charge. Six-guns and rifles blazing, they mounted and dashed at the ambush, indifferent to any possible traps that remained.

By sheer force of numbers, they stormed through the weak center of the hidden vigilantes. In a matter of seconds the last of Murchison's shattered column thundered over a rise and out of sight. Louis Longmont came out of the rocks where he had forted up. Smoke Jensen appeared on the slope opposite him. He quickly read the question on the face of Louis.

"We go after them, of course," Smoke said duly.

"We can't keep going on," Titus Hobson raged at Cyrus Murchison. "They've been ahead of us at every turn. Look at those poor wretches we found along the trail this morning. This is suicidal."

Murchison fought to remain calm. "No, it's not. We got through them, didn't we? The thing is, we're nearly at the summit. When we get there we'll dig in and make them come to us."

"I think it's a dangerous mistake," Titus objected.

Basically a coward at heart, Titus

388

Hobson had been a schoolyard bully as a child. He used his strength and size to intimidate smaller children. Later, as a prospector, he had developed his brawn to an impressive degree. His bulging muscles, craggy face, and bushy brows made it easier to cow those who sought to oppose him. His confidence grew, and with it, his wealth. Not until this wild flight into the wilderness had he been effectively challenged.

Now it frightened him witless. He had been close enough to the unfortunate lout who took the log in the chest to have blood splatter on his shirt and face. He *knew* Smoke Jensen was too dangerous for them to provoke. Why had he let Cyrus drag him into this? Yet he knew that Murchison was also dangerous. A man all too quick to use the final solution of death to end any opposition. Titus knew he dare not let his true feelings be seen too clearly. He tried to placate Murchison before this discussion took a hazardous turn.

"All right, Cyrus. We have little choice anyway. I suggest we make an effort to block the trail further on. Anything to slow them. I gather that this gorge narrows, the farther up we go?" At Murchison's nod, he outlined an idea that had worked in the gold fields against a band of outlaws led by the notorious Mexican bandit Gilberto Oliveras. "When we reach the top, we should close off the entire pass. Fell trees and build firing stands of them. Move rocks, boulders, seal off the trail. Then we can hold off that scum until they run out of ammunition."

Murchison considered that a moment. "Good idea, Titus. Where did you come up with this?"

Hobson showed a hint of modesty. "I was at the Battle of Wheeler's Meadow."

"My Lord, I never knew that. Well, old fellow, I propose you take charge of our delaying actions and the fortifications. Is it true that there were only seventeen of you against nearly a hundred Mexican bandits?"

"Yes. But we had all the tools and we built well. They couldn't get to us. We held them until they ran out of powder and shot. Simple after that."

"I like that. I do like that. We'll do it your way, and watch Smoke Jensen dash his brains out against our stout walls."

Smoke Jensen stood with his right fist on his hip, his left hand on the slanted holster high on his left side. Fallen trees blocked the trail ahead. Louis Longmont joined him while the volunteers labored to clear the obstacles. With a shout from Brian Pullen, horses strained on ropes attached to the first trunk and it swung slowly, ponderously.

"What are you thinking, *mon ami?*"

"They are waiting for us up ahead. I'd bet my last cigar that we'll run into more of these roadblocks, and finally reach the place they're forted up."

Louis nodded. "I think you are right. And no doubt you are going out there to find them tonight. This time I'm going with you."

Smoke made a fake shocked expression. "Louis, you astonish me. Whatever brought you to this? How can you think of risking that elegant neck?"

Louis produced a look of such wounded pride, only to be spoiled by the laughter that bubbled up deep inside himself. "I know you prefer to work alone, my friend. But they have grown bold after breaking out of our nice little trap, *non?* It would be well that for tonight you had someone to watch your back."

Without a show of any reluctance, Smoke agreed. His spirit lightened when the second downed pine had been dragged clear of the narrow spot in the trail. Smoke took the lead, with Louis at his side. Brian Pullen and Quo Chung Wu brought up the rear. Already Smoke's fertile imagination labored to concoct new nastiness to inflict upon Murchison and his henchmen.

Three more blockades had to be torn down by the time Smoke Jensen called a halt for the day. He had ridden ahead and scouted out the fortifications erected by Murchison's mongrels. Murchison, or someone, had chosen well. Located at the restricted point, at the crest of the high pass, it had taken little effort to build a thick, impenetrable wall. They seemed determined to stand and fight, he reasoned. It might be he could change their minds.

Smoke would have liked to use fire. If he did, he knew, he took the risk that the whole of the forest would be wiped out. Sort of like swatting a fly with a scoop shovel, he reckoned it. That left him with the three other elements as the Indians saw their universe: air, earth, and water. By the time he had returned to discuss it with Louis, he had made up his mind which they would use.

The breeze cooperated nicely, having whipped up into a stiff blow. It would mask any sounds they might make. Thankfully, it held even after the sun had set. Clouds had built up over the late afternoon, another gift of nature, and blotted out the blanket of stars and the thin crescent of moon. Smoke and Louis set out when total darkness descended.

They left their horses three hundred yards from the barrier erected by the hard cases. When they stealthily approached, they found that, rather than looming over them, the bulwark had been built only to shoulder height. All the better, Smoke saw it. He held a whispered conference with Louis and they took position near one end.

Less than five minutes went by before a roving sentry appeared on the opposite side of the barricade. Louis Longmont waited until he went past, then rose on tiptoe to stare over the wall.

"Psssst!" Louis hissed.

Galvanized by the unexpected sound, the hard case spun in Louis's direction, his rifle headed for his shoulder. Smoke Jensen came up behind him and clamped one hand over his mouth, the other on his throat, and yanked him over the wall. Louis stepped close and rapped the man on the head with the butt of his revolver. Smoke tied him tightly and they moved along the wall to wait again.

Another lookout paced his bit of the defenses, his attention wandering between the convivial firelight behind and the thick blackness beyond the bastion. Louis popped up and hissed again when the guard looked inward. He turned abruptly and Smoke hauled him off his feet. He wound up as tightly bound as the first one, unconscious on the outside of the partition.

Smoke and Louis repeated their little ruse until every watcher had been removed from the rampart. With that accomplished, they stole off into the night. When the thugs found their friends in the morning, they might not be so sure the wall would protect them.

"Here they come!" one lookout shouted from the barricade.

Cyrus Murchison and his riff-raff had only finished cussing and stomping about the waylaid sentries of the night before and gone back to breakfast. That clever bastard, Cyrus Murchison thought of Smoke Jensen. He would be smart enough to wait for the last shift to pull that. They weren't even missed until daylight. Now, before a man could even enjoy a decent breakfast, the whole lot of that rabble is attacking. With a regretful sigh, Murchison set aside his plate and reached for the rifle resting against a boulder beside him.

"Hold your fire until they get in close," Heck Grange advised. "Pick a few of them out of the saddle and the rest will turn tail. I know these bumpkins."

It turned out he didn't know them as well as he believed. Twenty-four strong, led by Smoke Jensen and Louis Longmont, the vigilante posse rode up toward the barrier. At a hundred yards, those with rifles opened fire. Anyone shooting from a moving horse had to be blessed with a lot of luck. It turned out two of the avengers were.

One hard case made a strangled cry when a bullet tore through his throat. He went down in a welter of blood. Off to the left, a second thug made a harsh grunt when a slug angled off the top of the receiver of his rifle and popped through his right eye. Already misshapen, the hunk of lead shredded a path through his brain and blew out the back of his skull.

That ended all restraint. Rifles crackled along the wall of earth and logs. One volunteer flew from his saddle, shot through the heart. He bounced twice when he reached the ground. Another took a bullet in the shoulder and slumped forward along the neck of his mount. A third, gut-shot, made a pitiful cry and turned his horse aside.

That caused several others to falter. Singly, at first, then the whole body spun their mounts and streaked off downhill to the shelter of a cluster of trees. For the time being, the fight turned into a contest of long-range sniping. Not for long, though.

After half an hour, Smoke Jensen's Winchester Express flattened a hard case who had bent over to pour a cup of coffee across the fire pit. When several of his comrades ran to his rescue, Smoke exhorted his volunteers.

"Time to hit them again. Mount up and let's ride."

TWENTY-ONE

Whooping like wild Indians, the vigilantes charged the fortifications. Caught unprepared, clearly half of the gunmen were wolfing down biscuits and gulping fresh coffee. Three of them did not make it back to the barrier.

At one hundred yards, the posse opened up again. The exposed men died in that first fusillade. At fifty yards, the toughs who manned the wall began to return fire. At first, they had little effect. Then their jangled nerves smoothed and their bullets began to find flesh.

Two of Smoke's volunteers took slugs, one in the shoulder, the other through a thigh. His horse didn't fare well, either. The hot lead punched through its hide and into a lung. Pink froth appeared on its muzzle and lips and it faltered abruptly, then its legs folded under it and the wounded rider pitched over its head.

"Get me outta here," he wailed.

A farmer, who fancied himself a good hand at horsemanship, cut to his right and bent at the waist. Arm hooked, he snagged the injured man and yanked him up behind.

"Ow, damn it!" the victim complained ungratefully. "That hurt worse than bein' shot."

"Be glad I looked out for you, you old fool," his rescuer grumped.

Tyler Estes found shooting from horseback to be rather a pain. He had just gotten the hang of it when all the targets disappeared. "Show yourselves and fight like a man," he challenged, as he jumped his horse to within thirty yards of the wall.

A head appeared, followed by shoulders and a rifle. The gunman fired and cut the hat from the head of Estes. His eyes went wide and he let out a little bleat before he clapped the cheek plate of his rifle to his face and took aim. His horse obediently halted for him and Tyler Estes released the reins for a moment to steady the barrel of his long gun. The .44 Winchester cracked sharply and the head of the thug who had shot at him snapped backward in a shower of red spray.

"That'll learn ya," Estes chortled, then wheeled away to find another target.

Another posseman cut across in front of Smoke Jensen, causing the last mountain man to rein in sharply. That saved Smoke's life, although it did not do much for the unfortunate eager one. He died in Smoke's place, drilled through the head. The suddenness of it changed Smoke Jensen's mind. They could never outlast the number of guns they faced.

"Pull back!" he shouted over the crackle of gunfire. "Pull back to the trees."

Smoke Jensen led the way to a campsite well out of sight of the forted-up gunmen. When the last of the wounded limped in, Smoke called the posse together. His face wore a serious, concerned expression. The losses they had taken preyed on his mind. These men deserved the opportunity to clean up their own yards, he reckoned. Yet they deserved to live. This fight belonged to him and Louis alone. From here on they would carry it through that way. He told that to them in a calm, quiet voice.

Brian Pullen spoke up forcefully. "Don't think you are going to get rid of me that easily. I'm in to the end."

"These . . . honored gentlemen have . . . families . . . and property . . . to care for. It is . . . reasonable that they return to them at this time. But," Quo Chung Wu went on with a fleeting smile, "it would be . . . unmanly for a priest . . . with neither wife and child . . . nor even a home . . . of my own . . . to take the path of . . . safety. I . . . too . . . will stay . . . beside you." He bowed to Smoke.

"There's no need," Smoke started his protest. Then he correctly read the expression on Quo's face. "I am honored to have your help," he amended.

Consternation ran among the men from the Central Valley. "What about us? Ain't we got a say in this?" one complained.

Smoke Jensen shook his head. "Five of you are dead and seven wounded. You've done your share. Now is the time for you to leave the rest to those who are trained for the killing game. Believe me, what we are going to have to do you don't want on your consciences."

"You mean you're goin' to lynch them all?" Tyler Estes blurted.

"No," Smoke answered levelly. "Those who give up we'll let the law handle."

"When do you want us to leave?" a disappointed posseman asked.

"You don't have to leave. Come morning, I'm sure Murchison will believe he won a big victory and pull out. We'll be going after them. You can stay here, rest up for a day or two, and give the wounded a chance to knit some before heading to your homes."

Tyler Estes scratched the balding spot on the crown of his head, and summed up for all of them. "Well, it'll be nice to get back to the shop. I reckon little Joey Pitchel will be needin' a trim, before them red locks o' his turns into long sissy curls."

That brought an understanding laugh, yet a gloomy pall settled over the volunteers, even though they faced the happy prospect of safely returning to their homes and families. Smoke Jensen sat long into the night, thinking about it.

Emboldened by their apparent easy success, particularly when nothing happened during the night, Cyrus Murchison pushed on with his surviving henchmen. He left two men behind to report of the defeated posse. They waited in the shade of a big oak a ways behind the wall, which had been left in place. The drowsy warmth of mid-morning got to them and they soon dozed off.

They heard nothing when the four riders approached. Smoke Jensen saw them at once and halted. Signing the other three to remain silent, he eased over the wall and cautiously closed in on the sleeping men. A fly buzzed around a thick lock of hair that hung down on the forehead of one lout. It had made three more circles by the time Smoke reached the slumbering hard case. Then, as Smoke stepped up to him, it landed on his nose.

With a start and a sodden mutter, the thug took a blind swipe at the offending insect. His last conscious thought must have been that for a darned fly, it sure packed a wallop. Still clutching the cylinder of his .45 Colt, Smoke turned to the other snoozing lout and smacked him on the head also.

"We'll take their horses," he called back to the others. "Without mounts, they won't go forward. If they move fast, they can catch up to the posse before those fellers leave."

"That's cold, Smoke," Brian Pullen objected. "Leaving a man without a horse in this country can get him killed."

"Only if he's stupid. The old mountain men, like Preacher, walked the whole of the High Lonesome more than one time."

"Mr. Smoke . . . is right, Mr. Brian," Quo Chung Wu offered. "This is . . . the first time I know of . . . that one of our Order has . . . ever ridden anywhere. We walked . . . for centuries in China. It is . . . a requirement," he added with his cheeks flushed.

"I am sure that Tai Chiu will forgive you," Louis Longmont told Quo Chung Wu.

Quo blushed again. "He . . . already has . . . before we . . . left. I was . . . thinking . . . of the . . . Lord Buddha."

Smoke pulled a face. "Well, considerin' what we're headed into, now's sure the time to get religion, as Preacher would say."

Louis Longmont looked from the wall to the unconscious thugs. "Too bad you knocked out those scrudy trash. Now we have to clear the trail ourselves."

"Allergic to hard, dirty work, Louis?" Smoke jibed.

Louis wrinkled his nose. "Only when I can't get a bath. We had better proceed."

It took the four companions an hour to open a pathway through the barricade. With that accomplished, they struck out on the wide trail left by Murchison and his mob. Most of the day's travel was downhill with only a single file of peaks between them and the long, deceptive grade through a lush meadow that led to Donner Pass.

Smoke estimated they would catch up to Murchison's gang at that fateful spot where less than forty years ago, men and women stranded by an early blizzard had been forced to commit the most appalling of human failings. Starving in the snow-blocked pass, they had fallen upon the corpses of their fellows to sustain their lives. How ironic it would be if Cyrus Murchison met his end there, Smoke mused.

He would find out, Smoke promised himself, two days from now.

Shouts of disgust and outrage awakened Cyrus Murchison the next morning. He pulled on trousers and boots and fumbled with sleep-numbed fingers to button his shirt. A quick splash of frigid water removed the gumminess from his eyes. He had gone to bed feeling rather better about their enforced exile.

When the two men left behind to spy out the posse had not returned by nightfall, he preferred to assume that they had nothing to report so far. Which would indicate, he convinced himself, that Jensen and Longmont and those local malcontents had turned back. Now, this, whatever it turned out to be, riling up the men. He reached for his hat as the flap opened and Heck Grange entered, his face grim, lips drawn in a hard line.

"What is it out there that has them all stirred up?"

Words clipped and sharp-edged, Heck Grange told him. "We're not shut of Smoke Jensen yet. He was here sometime last night. He left us three of my men as a warning." Finally the enormity of what he had seen overcame his forced restraint. "Goddamnit, they were strung up by the ankles, throats slit, and bled out like sheep."

For all his cruel nature, that affected Cyrus Murchison more than anything else. His face went white, his mouth sagged, and he placed the hat on his head with a shaking hand. "That's an abomination," he gasped out.

"You haven't actually seen it as yet. Which you'll have to do soon or we'll lose men like rats off a swamped barge." Grange went on to instruct his employer. "One thing you should point out is that it looks like one of the boys got a piece of Jensen. His knife is bloody."

Murchison pursed his thick lips. "More likely, Jensen used it to do for them."

Grange studied on that a moment. "I

405

don't think so. The knife was on the ground, right below his outstretched hand, which was bloody, too."

Cyrus drew himself up. "Well, then, we'll dwell on that. Anything to keep the men together."

It proved to be too little, too late. Already, three of Huntley's remaining longshoremen had pulled stakes and left camp. By nightfall, five more would desert the cause.

Tom, Dick, and Harry Newcomb — their father obviously had a twisted sense of humor — topped the first rise outside Murchison's camp and started on the long downgrade to the valley floor. For defeated men, they showed considerable energy in the way they kept their heads up and studied their surroundings in great detail. It did them little good, though. They rode right past two men sheltered in a thicket of brush along the trail.

They swiveled their heads once more, and when they looked forward again, two men appeared on the trace in front of them, six-guns in hand. Tom, Dick, and Harry reined their horses furiously in an attempt to turn and flee back to the camp, only to find two more people blocking their way, weapons at the ready. Desperately they spun their mounts again.

"Who are you?" Tom demanded, for want of something better to say.

The hard-faced one with cold eyes answered him. "We're your worst dream come true."

Somewhat less daunted than his brothers, Dick pushed the issue. "What's your name, Mister?"

"Smoke Jensen."

Awareness dawned. "Awh, Jesus," Tom groaned.

"We're dead men for sure," Harry concluded for his brother.

"Not necessarily," the hard-faced messenger of death told him.

"We saw what you did to those fellers last night."

Fire flashed in the ruddy eyes. "One of them came after me with a knife."

The brothers saw it then, a thickness of the left shoulder of Smoke Jensen. Tom also noted a rent in the cloth of the jacket, with red-brown stains around it. It fed him a dose of false bravado.

"What about the other two?"

"They got in the way." Then Smoke read the expression on their faces. "Don't worry, they were dead when I strung them up."

Dick, worried over the condition of his hide, asked Smoke the fateful question. "You gonna do the same to us?"

"Not unless I have to," Smoke answered calmly. "I gather you have given up on Mr. Murchison's little enterprise?"

"Yessir, yes, we sure have," Harry hastened to say. "Anyway, we worked for Mr. Huntley, an' he's long gone."

"Then you are free to go. All we ask is that you limit yourselves to a single weapon each, and leave all but five rounds with us."

Shocked by this, Tom blurted, "That ain't fair."

"I think you will find that life is not fair. Do it that way or be left for the buzzards and wolves."

"God, you're a hard man, Mr. Jensen," Tom blustered.

"Enough talk," a man with a Frenchy-sounding accent told Tom, Dick, and Harry. "Do it or die."

Quickly, Tom, Dick, and Harry divested themselves of six-guns, hideout pistols, and one spare rifle, and pockets-full of ammunition. Sweating profusely they rode off down the trail.

"That's a good start," Smoke Jensen told his companions. "Though there's a lot more where they came from."

★ ★ ★

The next dawn brought a cold, sharp wind and thick-bellied clouds Smoke Jensen knew to be laden with snow. All four ate heartily and fortified themselves with plenty of coffee. Smoke gnawed on a final biscuit while Brian Pullen covered the fire pit. The first lacy white flakes danced in the air as they took to saddle and set off.

Two miles down the trail, they encountered five disgruntled former employees of the California Central Road. The exchange went much as the one with the Newcomb brothers. None of the demoralized hard cases liked the idea of travel in this country so lightly armed, yet the alternative held not the least attraction. They did provide one gem of information. Their departure had left Murchison with only twenty-three men.

"Better odds, wouldn't you say?" Smoke Jensen quipped, as the five men rode away.

Louis Longmont answered him drily. "We have them out-numbered, *mon ami.*"

"When do you propose hitting them again?" Brian Pullen asked.

Smoke made an unusual admission. "This arm smarts like the fires of hell. I'd as soon get it over with. But I think we should let them tire themselves out a bit more. It'll be time enough at Donner Pass."

They rode on in silence for an hour, the snow falling heavier by the minute. Every tree and bush wore a mantle of white. Except for the mournful wail of the wind off the sheer rock faces, their surroundings had taken on a cotton-wool quiet. Three inches accumulated almost before they knew it. Their horses' hooves creaked eerily in that underfoot. Smoke called for a halt.

"We had better gather some wood. Otherwise it will be too wet later on."

He set the example by rounding up an armful and wrapping it in his slicker. He tied the bundle behind his saddle. When they pointed the noses of their horses east again, the snow had deepened to six inches.

"I don't like this at all," Brian Pullen lamented. "It never snows in San Francisco."

Smoke spoke through a snort of laughter. "Get used to it. I reckon we'll have a lot more before this storm moves on."

City men all, except for Titus Hobson and his mine police, the snow storm caught the column of Cyrus Murchison's men by surprise. It slowed, then halted their movement. By mid-afternoon, the horses stood knee-deep in cold discomfort. Heck Grange urged his boss to have the men keep going. He reminded Murchison of the fate of the Donner party, and again suggested that they could rig some sort of plow to clear a lane, dragging it by horse-back.

"To what purpose? It will exhaust the men and animals. Have the tents set up here and we'll shelter until the storm blows over." An icy gale whipped his words away.

Folding tin stoves came from the back of one packhorse and men installed them as soon as the tents had been erected. Stove pipes poked through specially prepared openings, and before long, ribbons of blue-gray smoke rose into the air to be shattered into ragged wisps by the turning whirl of the wind. Because of their thin walls, the stoves could burn only thin twigs and small branches. Fuel went up at a rapid rate, yet the drawback held one positive side. Heat radiated quickly, warmed the men, and boiled water for coffee.

Before long, savory aromas came from each tent as pots of stew began to simmer. In his large, well-appointed shelter, Cyrus

Murchison opened a bottle of sherry and poured a glass for Titus Hobson and himself. He also cracked the lid on a blue, hinge-gate Mason jar that held neat stacks of small, white spheroids.

"Pickled quail eggs," he offered them to Hobson. "Quite tasty. Only so rich, one does not want more than a few at a time." Murchison helped himself and lifted his glass. "To better times."

"Oh, quite well put," a tired, cold, and wet Titus Hobson responded. He swallowed a sip, munched an egg, and peered at the jar. "Say, what's this in the bottom?"

"What is left of the shells. After boiling the eggs, they are put in with the shells on. The vinegar dissolves the calcium and the residue falls to the bottom."

"Clever. I suppose picking the shells off of hundreds of these little things could drive someone quite dotty."

"Tedious work at best," Murchison agreed. Then he spoke the fear that still rode them both. "After the other night, there's no question Jensen and Longmont are still on our trail. I admit I am at my wit's end to find a way to stop them."

"Short of losing all of our men, you mean?"

"Exactly, Titus. Has anything occurred to you?"

Hobson took his time answering. "Other than surrendering, I haven't much to say that is encouraging. You do realize we are in one damnable position, don't you? If those left with Jensen and Longmont come at us now, we are about equally matched in numbers. Our men are fighting for money. Those valley yokels are fighting for what they see as a cause. They won't give up. If we have to face them we badly need reinforcements."

Cyrus Murchison scowled. "That's why we have to keep going to Carson City. It's only seventy miles, once we reach Donner Pass. There are enough track layers and more yard police there to fill our needs."

Titus canted his head to indicate the tempest outside the tent. "And if we get trapped in the pass by a storm like this? Do we feed on one another like the Donner party?"

Impatience painted lines on Murchison's face. "Spare me the grotesqueries." Then he argued from a basis of reason. "This is the first storm of the year. The snow will not last past the first few hours of sun on it. There probably won't be another until we are well down on the desert."

"You have no way of knowing that. It only seems to me that your way takes a whole lot for granted."

"Titus, Titus, you disappoint me. I always believed prospectors and mine owners were classical gamblers. Given what is at stake, don't you think that risking all is in order?"

Silently, Hobson considered this, his face a morose study. "Yes, I suppose so," he admitted reluctantly. Then he downed his sherry. "I need something stronger than this. How's the brandy supply?"

"Still holding out. Courvoisier VSOP, to be exact. I'll take one, too." With snifters poured, Murchison raised his in a toast. "Confusion to the enemy."

Smoke Jensen did not stay confused for long. Another night wasted. When the day dawned clear and cold, he rolled out of the snow-dusted blankets. The stockpile of wood soon provided a small fire to warm the stiffness from fingers and toes. He let the others sleep while he gnawed on a cold biscuit and set water to boil for coffee. Louis Longmont turned out next.

"Hell of a morning, *mon ami*," he greeted Smoke.

"It'll pass. Sun's already got some heat

414

in it. Way I measure, we have two feet of snow. Soon as it begins to slag down we'll head out. Coffee's ready."

Louis accepted a cup. "Is there any cornmeal?"

"Enough, I'd say," Smoke told him.

"I'll make some Southern-style mush. It will warm us and last a while."

Smoke Jensen knew all about Southern mush. It had shreds of bacon in it, plenty of eggs, when available, and cooked to the consistency of wall plaster. Some old-timers still called it belly plaster. Smoke nodded.

"There's enough ham to fry some, if you want."

"Done. Too bad we have no eggs." Louis shrugged it off. He downed his coffee and went to work.

They left an hour later. Snow-melt trickled down summer-sun-dried water courses. Slowly the birds found new life and cause to celebrate a fresh day. Their music filled the air. As a boy, Smoke often wondered if they were telling each other about the storm that had blown away at last, sharing gossip. A foolish notion he soon abandoned in the cold light of being alone and a kid in the awesome vastness of the High Lonesome.

Now he had a scrap of that youthful fantasy return to him. Somehow it turned out to be comforting. Endless days and nights of fighting and bloodshed needed a counterpoint. For years it had been his lovely, raven-haired Sally. Out here in these strange mountains, he needed to cling to something.

"Cling to yourself, you maudlin old fool!" Preacher's voice roared at him in his head. And so he did. By one hour after noon, they came upon the site of Murchison's encampment. From the condition of the ground, he estimated the hard cases had been gone no more than three hours. There would be a little catch-up tonight.

TWENTY-TWO

Angry voices rasped around the campfires the next morning to wash away the good feelings of Cyrus Murchison on the previous evening. During the night, six more men deserted the camp. Now only seventeen gunmen remained. Cursing under his breath, Murchison stuffed himself into clothes, donned a heavy sheepskin coat, and stomped out to quell the upheaval.

"Nothing has changed, men. Nothing at all. We still outnumber them even if they all come after us."

"Yeah, and they kicked our butts right good every time before," one wag taunted.

"What's to say that the fighting and the weather haven't had a similar effect on them?" He wanted to avoid direct acknowledgment of the desertions.

No one could come up with an answer for that. Murchison seized on it to regain control. "Break camp and make ready to ride."

Muttering, some of those on the fringe of the angry assembly turned away to begin packing. Gradually, the remainder joined them, stared down by an aroused Cyrus Murchison. When the last had left, Murchison turned to his partner.

"Titus, is it going to be like this every day?"

Hobson sighed and jinked one shoulder. "Don't ask me. If they leave us alone, I don't think so. But another storm like that last one, and I won't hold out much hope."

"Bugger the weather," Murchison grumped. "If we push ourselves, we can be to the next pass before nightfall." He withheld the fateful name "Donner."

"I agree. It is critical that we make it. I'll talk to my men."

Murchison clapped him on the back. "Good. It can only help. Oh, and at noon, we won't stop to cook a meal. Have everyone bring along something they can eat in the saddle. I am going to beat Smoke Jensen at his own game."

By noon, Smoke Jensen had put his small band a good five miles beyond Murchison's overnight camp. Most of the snow had melted; only on the shady northern sides did drifts and patches still remain. In its wake it left a quagmire of slippery mud.

Smoke nodded to this. "It will slow them down more than us. Those heavy-loaded packhorses will make hard goin' of the mud."

"Shall we be visiting them tonight?" Louis asked.

"Oh, yes, I am sure we will. The ground is wet enough to use a little fire this time."

They came an hour after sundown. Smoke Jensen led the way, a flaming torch held at arm's length in his left hand. His right worked a big .45 Colt. The reins hung over the saddle horn and he steered Thunder with his knees. Louis Longmont rode to his left with another torch. Behind them came Brian Pullen and Quo Chung Wu.

Quo fired the Purdy shotgun one-handed and clung to his saddle with the other. Brian emptied one of the four revolvers he carried into one of the smaller tents as he raced past. Thugs cried in alarm and crashed through the low door flaps of other canvas lodges. Smoke reined in sharply and hurled his flambeau onto the roof of the tent that housed Cyrus Murchison. Cries of alarm came from inside as the heavy billet burned its way through. The blazing canvas illuminated the entire campsite.

Louis fired the other large tent, sheets of flame rushing up from the fringed roof overhang. This time the shouts of alarm came from outside.

"The supplies! They're burning the supplies."

"Get away. There's ammunition in there," Heck Grange shouted. "There's dynamite in there, too."

Cyrus Murchison burst clear of his doomed tent, his clothes in hasty disarray. He waved an awkward, long-barreled Smith and Wesson American in one hand and shouted for Heck Grange. Grange reached his side in a moment and the agitated railroad mogul made frantic gestures back toward the tent.

"Titus Hobson is still in there. Get some men to pull him out. A wall support hit him on the head."

"Right away, Mr. Murchison." Heck Grange sent two men into the burning tent to retrieve the unconscious form of Titus Hobson.

When they laid him on the ground, Titus Hobson swam slowly back into the real world. He coughed clear a phlegmy throat and tried to sit upright. Everything swirled around him. He caught himself with one hand before he could fall back. Fuzzily, he made out the face of Cyrus Murchison as it hovered over him.

"Are you all right, Titus?" Murchison queried.

"I think . . ." Titus Hobson began his answer, when the detonator caps in the supply tent let go.

The dynamite quickly followed from sympathetic detonation. A tremendous white flash and crushing blast followed. The ground heaved, heat waves washed over everything, and the concussion knocked Titus Hobson flat, along with nearly everyone else. A huge cloud of dust and powder smoke filled the clearing. The horrendous sound echoed off the surrounding peaks for a long time, while the stunned men tried to regain their feet.

"We should have never brought that along," Titus stated with feeling.

Quo Chung Wu found himself faced by five men made more dangerous by their desperation. He downed one with the last round in his shotgun. With no time to reload, he put the weapon aside and met their charge with fists and feet when the remaining four swarmed over him. His

421

kicks found their targets and two men fell back. The other pair came at Quo from opposite directions.

He dodged the first lout and the other thug connected with a knife in the shoulder of the one facing him. The city trash howled and Quo jumped nimbly from between them. By then the first hard cases had recovered enough to return to the fight. They circled Quo, one with a knife, the other with his clubbed, empty revolver. Quo kept pace with them . . . at least until the knife artist who had stabbed his comrade chose to try again.

Now, Quo faced enemies on three sides. He used every bit of his martial arts skill to keep them at bay. They circled, feinted, snarled, and cursed. Quo made small whistling and warbling sounds, his hands and arms describing figures in the air, weaving his spell, lulling these dull-witted *qua'lo*. It worked rather well, until the fourth gunhand joined his companions.

Quo realized at once he had to take the offensive. He spun, lashed out a foot, and kicked one thug low in the gut. The injured dolt bent double and vomited up his supper. Quo pivoted gracefully and delivered another jolt to the side of the exposed head. The hard case went down, twitched, and lay still. The other three rushed Quo at once. The young priest's fists and feet moved in blurs. Another went down, then one with a knife got in close and drove the blade into Quo's back, over a kidney.

His mouth opened in a soundless scream and the strength left his legs. Quo stumbled forward and the knife twisted clear of his back. The grinning goon who held it thrust again, the keen edge sliding between two of Quo's ribs and into a lung. A fountain of blood gushed from his pain-twisted lips. Blackness swarmed over Quo Chung Wu as he pitched forward onto his face, never to rise again.

Smoke Jensen saw Quo Chung Wu go down and a moment of sharp regret filled him. The young Chinese priest had known the dangers involved in this battle and had come along at his own wish. Any of them, all of them, could die right here in this mountain pass, where so many had perished before. His lament for Quo ended, Smoke turned to check on Brian.

Exhibiting a skill at gunfighting unusual for a young lawyer, Brian held off three men with a coolness lacking in many a more experienced shootist. Disoriented by the wavering flames and billows of smoke, the trio of rascals threw wild shots in the general direction of Brian.

He obliged them by gunning down one of their number and smoothly replacing his spent revolver with the third of his quartet. The .45 Peacemaker in Brian's hand bucked and snorted and sent another hard case off to explain himself to his Maker. The third experienced a momentary flash of brilliance. He emptied his hands and thrust them high over his head.

Brian stepped in and smacked the man behind one ear. He dropped like a stone. Taking a deep breath, Brian turned to find another enemy. Disappointment flashed on his face as two reprobates fled from the conflict, thoroughly defeated. That left only Heck Grange, Cyrus Murchison, and Titus Hobson, who had once more regained consciousness.

Forced back on their own resources, the three candidates for hell reverted to their basic savagery. Heck Grange put a bullet through the left shoulder of Brian Pullen. A second later, he found himself facing Smoke Jensen. This would be nowhere as easy. Heck cocked his .44 Frontier Colt and the hammer dropped on a spent primer.

Frantically, he let go of the weapon and

clawed for another thrust into the waist-band of his trousers. Smoke Jensen waited for him. The muzzle came free and Heck Grange saw a momentary glimmer of hope. Then Smoke Jensen filled his hand with a .45 Peacemaker and triggered a round.

Smoke's bullet hit Heck in the meaty portion of his shoulder. Rocked by the slug, the chief lawman of the railroad grimly completed his intended action. Flame leapt from the muzzle of his six-gun. A solid impact rocked Smoke Jensen and he stumbled to the left, a sharp pain in his side. Gradually that numbed as he centered his Colt on the chest of Heck Grange. Smoke eared back the hammer of his Peacemaker a fraction of a second before a chunk of firewood, hurled by Titus Hobson, crashed into the side of his head.

Stars and vivid colors exploded inside the skull of Smoke Jensen. His six-gun blasted harmlessly into the ground at the feet of Heck Grange. That gave Grange a chance to fire again. The hot slug broke skin on the side of Smoke Jensen's neck. A sheet of blood washed warmly downward. Through the throbbing in his head, Smoke tried to steady himself.

Concentrating desperately, he willed his

vision to return. Heck Grange swam erratically in the involuntary tears that filled Smoke's eyes when he could at last see. He steadied his hand and eared back the hammer. The Peacemaker roared once more. Heck Grange's knees buckled and he went down hard.

He caught himself with his free hand and cried out at the pain that lanced through his body from his wounded shoulder. Once again he tried to finish off Smoke Jensen. The six-gun in Smoke's hand spoke first.

Hot lead spat from the muzzle and caught Heck Grange in his left nostril. Grange reared backward and kept on going to land on the back of his head, which had been blown off along with his hat.

Smoke spared the hard case no more time. He felt dizzy and light-headed. Dimly he saw Louis Longmont turn toward Titus Hobson as though wading under the ocean. Hobson also moved in slow motion. He pulled a .44 Colt Lightning from his Coggshell Saddlery shoulder holster and fired almost immediately.

His bullet struck Louis Longmont in the upper right thigh. Louis went to one knee, although he continued his swing. His own six-gun bucked in his hand and the slug sped true. The eyes of Titus Hobson went wide and white when pain exploded in his chest. He tried to cycle the double-action revolver again. This time the projectile missed Longmont entirely.

Weakened by rapid blood loss, Louis Longmont fired his last bullet and missed. He sank to his side on the ground. Head still whirling, Smoke Jensen went to the side of his friend. Hobson, light-headed from his wound, came at the two of them, firing recklessly. Smoke returned the favor and his bullet tore a chunk from the heaving side of Hobson. The Colt Lightning struck an expended cartridge and a expression of shock washed Hobson's face white.

Smoke Jensen knew that he had fired his last round. When the wounded Hobson recovered himself, he snatched up another stick of firewood and advanced on Smoke. Determined to save the life of his friend, Smoke Jensen drew his war-hawk and readied himself. Hobson, though unsteady on his feet, gave him little time for that.

Titus Hobson swung the billet like an ax handle. It swished past over the head of Smoke Jensen, who had ducked. Smoke feinted with the tomahawk and the fighters separated. They appeared to be nothing more than two vicious predators quarreling over a choice bit of carrion. Smoke carefully kept himself between Hobson and Louis. Titus Hobson tried a fake on Smoke Jensen.

It failed and the war-hawk sailed by dangerously close to the face of Hobson. They backed off. Smoke risked a glance at Louis and saw the light in those gray eyes begin to dim.

"Louis, if you can hear me, cover that wound and use your belt for a tourniquet. Do it now!"

His concern for Longmont almost cost Smoke that fight that moment. Titus Hobson lunged and swung the wrist-thick stick at the side of Smoke's head. Smoke spun and parried the blow, did a quick reverse, and cleaved the length of wood in half. Hobson let out a startled yelp and jumped back.

"Damn you, Smoke Jensen. Damn you straight to hell."

Smoke laughed at Hobson. His side had become a continuous lightning strike. Quickly he changed hands with his war-hawk. The movement confused Titus Hobson and he stood blinking. That hesitation proved enough for Smoke Jensen.

Swiftly he swung the deadly 'hawk and felt the solid impact as the keen edge sank into flesh and bone near the base of the neck of Titus Hobson. Muscles and tendon severed, Hobson's head drooped to the opposite side at an odd angle.

A gurgle came from deep in his throat and his eyes rolled up. The foreshortened piece of wood fell from numb fingers and Titus Hobson spilled onto the ground, taking Smoke Jensen's tomahawk with him. Smoke took time only for two quick, deep gulps of air, then turned to Louis.

Louis Longmont sat upright now, shoulders drooped, chest heaving with the effort to breathe. His leg wore a tightly drawn belt above the wound and a square of impeccably white linen kerchief covered the bullet hole. He raised his head and cut his eyes to Smoke Jensen.

"You know, we're getting too old for this sort of thing, *mon ami*."

"Speak for yourself, Louis," Smoke panted. Then he remembered Cyrus Murchison.

Quickly as his injured body would obey, Smoke Jensen turned to his left to find Cyrus Murchison on his knees, trembling hands raised in abject surrender. His lips quivered as he spoke.

"I — I've never seen anyone fight so ferociously. D-Don't hurt me. I'm giving myself up. I'll fight the charges in court." A sardonic smile replaced the fear in the man. "And I'll win, too."

Smoke Jensen looked from him to Louis Longmont, then cut his eyes to Brian Pullen. Pullen's expression told Smoke volumes. Smoke sighed. "With his money, he likely will win." Then he returned to the matter at hand. "Let's patch one another up and take in our prisoner. There's been enough blood shed in the Donner Pass."

A day's journey to the east and those who had come out of the Donner Pass alive turned south. At the insistence of Smoke Jensen, they had brought along the bodies of Quo Chung Wu, Titus Hobson, and Heck Grange. The rest they buried as well as they could. Two more long, hard days to the south put them alongside the tracks of the California Central Railroad.

Cyrus Murchison proved entirely cooperative. He instructed Smoke Jensen in how to rig a signal that would stop the first westbound train. Half a day went by before the distant wail of a steam whistle announced the approach of the daily express run. To the relief of them all, the signal worked.

"We could be in a tight spot rather fast," a weakened Louis Longmont advised from the travois on which he rode as he and the others studied the hard faces of the crew.

"We still have a few things going for us, old friend," Smoke Jensen advised him lightly.

"Such as what?"

"We do have their boss as a prisoner," Smoke suggested.

"That is precisely what I see as the source of our problems," Louis stated drily.

Smoke showed no reaction. "Let's see what they say . . . or do first."

The engineer braced them first. "Isn't that Mr. Murchison you have trussed up like a Christmas goose?" Smoke Jensen allowed as how it was indeed. "What the hell is that all about?" the locomotive driver demanded.

This time, Louis Longmont replied. "He is under arrest."

"By whose authority?" the truculent engineer snapped.

Smoke took a step forward. "By mine. We are going to board your train and ride to San Francisco and turn him over to the police."

A defiant curl came to the thick lips of the trainman. "You will, like hell."

Smoke flashed his badge. "I think we will. I'm a deputy U. S. marshal. If I'm forced to, I'll simply commandeer the train, throw your ass in irons and run it myself."

Two burly switchmen grumbled at this, yet they made no move to interfere. That quickly decided the engineer. "All right, all right. You can board. But you'll have to ride in a chair car. Ain't got no fancy coach hooked up."

"I'm sure Mr. Murchison won't mind," Smoke quipped.

They arrived in San Francisco an hour before sundown. The huge red-orange globe rested a finger's width above the flat, glassy sea and sent long shafts of magenta over the rippling water of the bay. The first order of business was to take Cyrus Murchison to the police station. Smoke surrendered him directly to the chief of police and listed the charges.

After a sad journey to the Golden Harmony temple in Chinatown with the body of Quo Chung Wu, Smoke, Louis, and Brian headed for the bordello. Two of their hired protectors met them on the porch. A minute later, Lucy Glover dashed out to join them.

"I was afraid something had happened to you," she blurted, staring directly into the face of Brian Pullen.

It instantly became obvious to Smoke and Louis that the pair shared mutual stars in their eyes. Smoke cleared his throat. That broke the thick web of enthrallment. Reluctantly, Lucy and Brian turned their attention to the big man with a white bandage on his neck.

"Brian and I have been talking about the future of this — er — establishment. I have decided to ask you to continue in charge of the — ah — operation. Louis is going to stay in San Francisco and make arrangements to sell my latest acquisition."

Shock and worry clouded Lucy's face. "You're going to *sell?*"

Smoke chuckled softly. "Yes, and as quickly and quietly as possible."

"Don't you realize that this place can make a fortune for you?"

"Granted," Smoke declared. "And if my dear Sally ever found out about it, she would have a fit."

"But — but, what will I — I and the girls — *do* after it's sold?"

"The girls can pool their resources and

make a bid. Anything reasonable will be considered. For your own part, if I'm not mistaken, young woman, you have a career change ahead in the near future."

Lucy Clover cut her eyes from Smoke Jensen to Brian Pullen, who blushed furiously. "You're right, Smoke, if I have anything to say about it," the young lawyer said softly.

The two gunfighters chuckled indulgently. Then Smoke Jensen ended their embarrassment. "I'll just gather my things and be on my way."

Lucy was shaken. "You're leaving so soon?"

"I have to. I've been away from the Sugarloaf too long."

"But your wounds," Lucy and Brian protested together.

Smoke gave Lucy a sunny smile. "They'll heal better in the High Lonesome. Especially with Sally there to pamper me." He turned to Louis Longmont. "Louis, it's been good working with you again. After you have this out of the way, come up to the Sugarloaf for a while. The latch-string is always out."

"I appreciate that, *mon ami,* and I will give the invitation serious consideration. For now, then, I will only say *adieu.*"

"Farewell, old friend, and ride an easy saddle."

With that, Smoke Jensen was gone.